Internet of Behaviors Implementation in Organizational Contexts

Luísa Cagica Carvalho
Instituto Politécnico de Setúbal, Portugal

Clara Silveira
Polytechnic Institute of Guarda, Portugal

Leonilde Reis
Instituto Politecnico de Setubal, Portugal

Nelson Russo
Universidade Aberta, Portugal

A volume in the Advances in Web Technologies
and Engineering (AWTE) Book Series

Published in the United States of America by
IGI Global
Engineering Science Reference (an imprint of IGI Global)
701 E. Chocolate Avenue
Hershey PA, USA 17033
Tel: 717-533-8845
Fax: 717-533-8661
E-mail: cust@igi-global.com
Web site: http://www.igi-global.com

Library of Congress Cataloging-in-Publication Data

Names: Carvalho, Luísa Cagica, 1970- editor. | Silveira, Clara, 1964-
    editor. | Reis, Leonilde, 1962- editor. | Russo, Nelson, 1974- editor.
Title: Internet of behaviors implementation in organizational contexts /
    edited by Luisa Cagica Carvalho, Clara Silveira, Leonilde Reis, Nelson
    Russo.
Description: Hershey, PA : Engineering Science Reference, [2023] | Includes
    bibliographical references and index. | Summary: "This book explores and
    discusses, through innovative studies, case studies, systematic
    literature reviews, and reports. The content within this publication
    represents research encompassing the internet of behaviors, internet of
    things, big data, artificial intelligence, blockchain, smart cities,
    human-centric approach for digital technologies, ICT sustainability, and
    more. This vital reference source led by an editor with over two decades
    of experience is optimized for university professors, researchers,
    undergraduate and graduate level students, and business managers and
    professionals across several industries related to or utilizing the
    internet of things (IoT)"-- Provided by publisher.
Identifiers: LCCN 2023024200 (print) | LCCN 2023024201 (ebook) | ISBN
    9781668490396 (hardcover) | ISBN 9781668490402 (paperback) | ISBN
    9781668490419 (ebook)
Subjects: LCSH: Internet of things--Social aspects. | Internet of
    things--Economic aspects. | Human-computer interaction. | Electronic
    commerce. | Business--Data processing.
Classification: LCC TK5105.8857 .I543 2023 (print) | LCC TK5105.8857
    (ebook) | DDC 004.67/8--dc23/eng/20230729
LC record available at https://lccn.loc.gov/2023024200
LC ebook record available at https://lccn.loc.gov/2023024201

This book is published in the IGI Global book series Advances in Web Technologies and Engineering (AWTE) (ISSN: 2328-2762; eISSN: 2328-2754)

British Cataloguing in Publication Data
A Cataloguing in Publication record for this book is available from the British Library.

All work contributed to this book is new, previously-unpublished material. The views expressed in this book are those of the authors, but not necessarily of the publisher.

For electronic access to this publication, please contact: eresources@igi-global.com.

Advances in Web Technologies and Engineering (AWTE) Book Series

Ghazi I. Alkhatib
The Hashemite University, Jordan
David C. Rine
George Mason University, USA

ISSN:2328-2762
EISSN:2328-2754

MISSION

The **Advances in Web Technologies and Engineering (AWTE) Book Series** aims to provide a platform for research in the area of Information Technology (IT) concepts, tools, methodologies, and ethnography, in the contexts of global communication systems and Web engineered applications. Organizations are continuously overwhelmed by a variety of new information technologies, many are Web based. These new technologies are capitalizing on the widespread use of network and communication technologies for seamless integration of various issues in information and knowledge sharing within and among organizations. This emphasis on integrated approaches is unique to this book series and dictates cross platform and multidisciplinary strategy to research and practice.

The **Advances in Web Technologies and Engineering (AWTE) Book Series** seeks to create a stage where comprehensive publications are distributed for the objective of bettering and expanding the field of web systems, knowledge capture, and communication technologies. The series will provide researchers and practitioners with solutions for improving how technology is utilized for the purpose of a growing awareness of the importance of web applications and engineering.

COVERAGE

- Data and knowledge capture and quality issues
- Competitive/intelligent information systems
- Metrics-based performance measurement of IT-based and web-based organizations
- Integrated user profile, provisioning, and context-based processing
- Information filtering and display adaptation techniques for wireless devices
- Human factors and cultural impact of IT-based systems
- Data analytics for business and government organizations
- IT readiness and technology transfer studies
- IT education and training
- Strategies for linking business needs and IT

IGI Global is currently accepting manuscripts for publication within this series. To submit a proposal for a volume in this series, please contact our Acquisition Editors at Acquisitions@igi-global.com or visit: http://www.igi-global.com/publish/.

Titles in this Series

For a list of additional titles in this series, please visit: www.igi-global.com/book-series

Supporting Technologies and the Impact of Blockchain on Organizations and Society
Luís Ferreira (Polytechnic Institute of Cávado and Ave, Portugal) Miguel Rosado Cruz (Polytechnic Institute of Viana do Castelo, Portugal) Estrela Ferreira Cruz (Polytechnic Institute of Viana do Castelo, Portugal) Hélder Quintela (Polytechnic Institute of Cavado and Ave, Portugal) and Manuela Cruz Cunha (Polytechnic Institute of Cavado and Ave, Porugal)
Engineering Science Reference • © 2023 • 337pp • H/C (ISBN: 9781668457474) • US $270.00

Concepts, Technologies, Challenges, and the Future of Web 3
Pooja Lekhi (University Canada West, Canada) and Guneet Kaur (University of Stirling, UK & Cointelegraph USA)
Engineering Science Reference • © 2023 • 602pp • H/C (ISBN: 9781668499191) • US $360.00

Perspectives on Social Welfare Applications' Optimization and Enhanced Computer Applications
Ponnusamy Sivaram (G.H. Raisoni College of Engineering, Nagpur, India) S. Senthilkumar (University College of Engineering, BIT Campus, Anna University, Tiruchirappalli, India) Lipika Gupta (Department of Electronics and Communication Engineering, Chitkara University Institute of Engineering and Technology, Chitkara University, India) and Nelligere S. Lokesh (Department of CSE-AIML, AMC Engineering College, Bengaluru, India)
Engineering Science Reference • © 2023 • 336pp • H/C (ISBN: 9781668483060) • US $270.00

Advancements in the New World of Web 3 A Look Toward the Decentralized Future
Jane Thomason (UCL London Blockchain Centre, UK) and Elizabeth Ivwurie (British Blockchain and Frontier Technology Association, UK)
Engineering Science Reference • © 2023 • 323pp • H/C (ISBN: 9781668466582) • US $240.00

Architectural Framework for Web Development and Micro Distributed Applications
Guillermo Rodriguez (QuantiLogic, USA)
Engineering Science Reference • © 2023 • 268pp • H/C (ISBN: 9781668448496) • US $250.00

Trends, Applications, and Challenges of Chatbot Technology
Mohammad Amin Kuhail (Zayed University, UAE) Bayan Abu Shawar (Al-Ain University, UAE) and Rawad Hammad (University of East London, UK)
Engineering Science Reference • © 2023 • 373pp • H/C (ISBN: 9781668462348) • US $270.00

Strategies and Opportunities for Technology in the Metaverse World
P.C. Lai (University of Malaya, Malaysia)
Engineering Science Reference • © 2023 • 390pp • H/C (ISBN: 9781668457320) • US $270.00

701 East Chocolate Avenue, Hershey, PA 17033, USA
Tel: 717-533-8845 x100 • Fax: 717-533-8661
E-Mail: cust@igi-global.com • www.igi-global.com

Table of Contents

Section 2
Exploring the Dynamics of IoB in Education and Healthcare

Section 3
Challenges and New Avenues

Detailed Table of Contents

Section 1
The Role of IoB in Transforming Business Models

Chapter 1

Nelson Russo, Universidade Aberta, Portugal
Leonilde Reis, Instituto Politécnico de Setúbal, Portugal

The Internet of Behavior (IoB) is expanding rapidly, offering valuable insights into users' behavior, interests, and preferences. The integration of requirements for ensuring business continuity faces certain constraints. This chapter presents a set of concerns about business continuity in software and explores the certification domain for invoicing software in Portugal. The concept of developing continuity by-design software and a methodological approach for business continuity management is introduced to enhance ICT and address sustainability concerns. This approach aims to foster innovative solutions and behavior optimization. Given the specificity of the issue under study, the methodology adopted was design science research. The main results include the development of artifacts that optimize the decision process for implementing electronic invoicing issuance and archiving, integrating the concept of continuity-by-design in the creation of resilient software. These efforts encompass multiple dimensions of sustainability and innovation, considering stakeholders' behavior.

Chapter 2

Helena Caria, School of Health, Polytechnic Institute of Setúbal, Portugal

Scientific and technological developments are unquestionable, being health in general and human genetics specifically, domains where high throughputs are gorgeous. The internet is changing the behavior of patients with clinicians and health organizations. The project of human genomes ensured new approaches to estimate cause-disease relations. Genotype-phenotype correlations and screening of mutation are now available to all researchers. However, the scientific data are also available to the patients, bringing them to the floor as active partners in therapeutic processes searching with "Dr. Google" for symptoms, treatments, and cures. Hereditary deafness is not escaping from this civil movement, being a good example of the behavioral change associated with the explosion of the internet, with the commercial offers of hearing aids and cochlear implants offers to be common nowadays. In the chapter, the authors discuss the internet of behaviors in the context of biomedical sciences as human genetics, and hearing loss.

Chapter 3

José M. Soares, Instituto Politécnico da Guarda, Portugal
Miguel Brito, Instituto Politécnico da Guarda, Portugal
Celestino Gonçalves, Instituto Politécnico da Guarda, Portugal

This work presents the design and implementation of Codeflex, a web-based platform and repository of programming problems, that enables the learning and practice of competitive programming in multiple programming language paradigms. The Codeflex programming platform performs automatic evaluation of submitted solutions for a very diverse set of programming languages, in real time, considering the specificities and requirements of different programming paradigms, being prepared to analyze and detect plagiarism in tournament submissions. The use of Codeflex platform in a real context allowed the test and validation of its functionalities. In particular, several programming tournaments were organized, for Haskell and Prolog programming languages – functional and logic programming tournaments, respectively, within the scope of programming curricular units of computer science undergraduate degree. The findings suggest that Codeflex is a valuable contribution in enhancing programming skills and providing an efficient evaluation system for educational and professional settings.

Chapter 4

Nelson Russo, Universidade Aberta, Portugal

As a consequence of the evolution and digital transition, organizations depend more on ICT. The behavioral data generated through interactions with ICT is collected and analyzed by the Internet of Behaviors (IoB). In this context, cybersecurity is a critical aspect of business continuity (BC). Organizations must ensure that their ICT systems are protected from cyber-attacks to avoid disruptions to their operations. A BC Plan (BCP) that considers cybersecurity can help ensure the continuity of critical functions in the event of a cyber-attack. Raising awareness is relevant to promote safe practices and minimize the risk of successful cyberattacks and loss of behavioral data. Therefore, a solid BC Management System (BCMS) should address cybersecurity and assure that all stakeholders are aware of the subjacent risks to a business and how to avoid, mitigate, or cope with them. This chapter presents the BC components and activities of a BCP that includes cybersecurity. Following the guidelines of the activities can result in avoiding or mitigating security risks by creating a successful BCP.

Chapter 5

Catarina Delgado, Escola Superior de Educação, Instituto Politécnico de Setúbal, Portugal
Fátima Mendes, Escola Superior de Educação, Instituto Politécnico de Setúbal, Portugal
Joana Brocardo, Escola Superior de Educação, Instituto Politécnico de Setúbal, Portugal
Ana Maria Boavida, Escola Superior de Educação, Instituto Politécnico de Setúbal,
Portugal

This chapter reflects on the challenges that arise when it is intended that all students can experience an Education 5.0 and proposes a set of practical actions that may support teachers' educational practice. It analyses and discusses a study involving 18 primary teachers and their 358 students (ages 6-10), which informed specific adjustments in some educational technological games about mathematics and confirmed, or not, several of the potentialities that intentionally underlined their design. The analysis focused on some problematic aspects related to moving towards an Education 5.0, which allows the integration of digital technologies in a more meaningful way in the learning process, aiming at the development of critical and creative thinking and collaborative work. Finally, suggestions are systematized about the development of quality educational technological tools and teacher training.

Chapter 6
    Duarte Xara-Brasil, Instituto Politécnico de Setúbal, Portugal
    Carla Viana, Instituto Politécnico de Setúbal, Portugal
    Maria Inês F. S. Cruz, Faculdade de Ciências, Universidade de Lisboa, Portugal

Digital transformation is a reality in practically all business industries and has influenced the development of new marketing practices and, consequently, consumer experiences, particularly in the health sector. The aim of this research is to analyze the potential benefits that digital transformation and digital marketing may have in the customer's experiences with health service providers. This study allowed the confirmation of many of the aspects researched in previous academic works and reinforced the importance of using more technological solutions for current users, as well as the need to improve, namely in terms of service personalization, with greater speed and response, and quality of the service provided in an integrated way by the different touchpoints. Furthermore, it reinforced some important objections of users, namely related to the presumed greater difficulty of personal interaction, especially in cases of dissatisfaction and complaint, or in groups of patients with less digital training.

Section 2
Exploring the Dynamics of IoB in Education and Healthcare

Chapter 7
    Conceição Aleixo, Polytechnic Institute of Setúbal, Portugal
    Susana Silva, Polytechnic Institute of Setúbal, Portugal
    Teresa Godinho, Polytechnic Institute of Setúbal, Portugal

Higher education institutions play a crucial role in the teaching-learning process as they are primarily responsible for preparing students for their entry into the business environment. The aim of this study is to assess students' perceptions of a new teaching approach and its impact on their personal and professional development. At the level of course coordination, the findings will inform reflections on which pedagogical practices should be implemented to align with the student-focused teaching paradigm and the implementation of an Education 5.0 framework in the bachelor's degree program in accounting and finance at the Polytechnic Institute of Setúbal. The research employs a qualitative analysis approach, and the main results indicate that participants recognize the importance of Education 5.0 for their personal and professional development as certified accountants.

Chapter 8
    Mahsa Amiri, Faculty of Economics, University of Algarve, Portugal
    Célia M. Q. Ramos, ESGHT and CinTurs, University of Algarve, Portugal

Several technologies emerged and disrupted how they operate in the Tourism 4.0 environment surrounding tourism companies. One, the digitalization of processes has become a way to support survival, and second, data grows exponentially daily. In this environment, a business intelligence tool can help to improve decision-making while enabling managers to realize complex information quickly and make more efficient decisions. The benefits of BI adoption in businesses encourage scholars to study and research this topic. This study aims to understand the effects and potentialities of business intelligence systems conjugated with artificial intelligence for tourism companies. As the main findings, the potential of BI helps the tourism company to increase destination sustainability support and to create a shared decision-maker environment between the companies.

Chapter 9
Helena Cristina Roque, School of Business Administration, Polytechnic Institute of Setúbal, Portugal
Madalena Ramos, University Institute of Lisbon, Portugal

Moments of crisis exacerbate social inequalities, highlighting the paramount importance of the debate on inclusion. The promotion of social inclusion can and should be pursued and implemented at various levels. In this sense, leadership can play a fundamental role in the inclusion of individuals in organizations and, consequently, in society. Inclusion in the workplace is about creating an environment where individuals from diverse backgrounds feel valued, respected, and have equal opportunities to contribute and succeed. Leaders have the power to shape the culture, policies, and practices that promote or hinder inclusion. This chapter will review the literature on inclusion based on the responsible leadership and inclusive leadership approaches, seeking to understand how these types of leadership can contribute with effective responses to inclusion in the work context. The chapter will end with a proposal of a set of practices that may be relevant for the inclusion of individuals in organizations.

Chapter 10
Janaína Almeida Bastos, Pontifícia Universidade Católica de São Paulo, Brazil
João Pinheiro de Barros Neto, Pontifícia Universidade Católica de São Paulo, Brazil

In 2020, Brazilians were faced with the COVID-19 health crisis that caused a rupture in market and business standards, technologies, and models, directly affecting the way people relate to each other, work, and live, reshaping the social, cultural, and economic contexts. Among these changes, remote work has never been so evident in the daily life of companies and their employees. In this context, the question that guides this work is: What is the impact of working from home on people management in companies from the human resources point of view? This study is an exploratory survey carried out by means of an online questionnaire, responded to by 121 participants. The results indicate that telework can be a more humane way of working and a solution to numerous problems of modern society.

Chapter 11
Nilamadhab Mishra, VIT Bhopal University, India
Getachew Mekuria Habtemariam, Addis Ababa Science and Technology University, Ethiopia
Anubhav De, VIT Bhopal University, India

The IoE Grid Computing Framework will be used to look into high-performance computing tools for higher education institutions. The primary and secondary data from higher education organizations are used to make the model and architecture. So, using a computational IoE grid and the supported toolkits, a model of the event was made. To see how well resources and related algorithms work, they are put to the test in different situations, such as by confirming the number of resources and users with different needs. To determine the level of demand for high-performance computing tools, data were gathered from particular colleges and universities. Before the data was fed into the system, preprocessing tasks like handling missing values and choosing features were completed. The findings demonstrate that these traits and the requirement for high-performance computing resources in higher education institutions are strongly related.

Section 3
Challenges and New Avenues

Chapter 12

The Internet of Behaviors (IoB) is an emerging trend that aims to revolutionize human interactions by analyzing and influencing behavior using data from connected devices. This study explores the importance of blockchain technology in addressing the IoB challenges and enhancing the security and privacy of IoB business models. Blockchain technology provides a decentralized and transparent platform for behavioral data storage and sharing, mitigating privacy concerns. Individuals are empowered with control over their personal data through smart contracts and decentralized identifiers, enabling them to decide how their data is accessed and used within IoB systems. In this study, significant blockchain-based solutions and approaches are presented that can enhance IoB business models through examples. Exploration of blockchain potential in IoB systems will ensure new insights for further advancement and evolution of the IoB paradigm.

Chapter 13

In the evolving landscape of technological advancements, the Internet of Behavior (IoB) emerges as a pivotal concept, harnessing the power of data to understand and influence humans. IoB finds its most profound application in Society 5.0, a vision of a super-smart society where digital and physical realms harmoniously coexist. New business and economic models like the circular economy, sharing economy, smart cities, platform business model, social enterprise model, and blockchain technology will be explored. Emerging healthcare, agriculture, hospitality, and energy business models are discussed. Challenges arise as innovative organizations emerge to create a more sustainable and inclusive culture. Data privacy and security, blockchain high energy consumption, technologically unprepared workforce, and artificial intelligence bias must be addressed. This chapter aims to demonstrate emerging economies, business models, and related technologies that facilitate Society 5.0 as it evolves from human behavior insights gained from IoB.

Chapter 14

Rui Teixeira Dias, Instituto Politécnico de Setúbal, Portugal
Mariana Chambino, Instituto Politécnico de Setúbal, Portugal
Cristina Palma, Instituto Politécnico de Setúbal, Portugal
Liliana Almeida, Instituto Politécnico de Setúbal, Portugal
Paulo Alexandre, Instituto Politécnico de Setúbal, Portugal

This chapter aims to analyze the price efficiency of Bitcoin (BTC), DASH, EOS, Ethereum (ETH), LISK, Litecoin (LTC), Monero, NEO, QUANTUM, RIPPLE, STELLAR, and ZCASH in their weak form between March 1, 2018 and March 1, 2023 and determine whether they experience overreactions. The results show that cryptocurrencies exhibit positive and negative autocorrelations, which can reduce volatility and moderate price fluctuations. The results also show persistence in cryptocurrency returns, suggesting long-term trends or market patterns that individual and institutional investors can exploit. It is essential to recognize that cryptocurrencies are characterized by a high degree of complexity and instability. Investors need to monitor market trends and make the necessary adjustments to their investment strategies to anticipate market changes.

Chapter 15

Alexandra Costa, Instituto Politécnico de Setúbal, Portugal
Elis Ossmane, Instituto Politécnico de Setúbal, Portugal
Hortense Santos, Instituto Politécnico de Setúbal, Portugal
Jéssica Camargo, Instituto Politécnico de Setúbal, Portugal
Luísa Carvalho, Instituto Politécnico de Setúbal, Portugal

With the increasing focus of literature and research consolidating a positive relationship between circular business models and digital technologies, this chapter proposes a literature review on the ReSOLVE framework as a key factor to enable the development of new business models oriented towards the circular economy, in particular circular business models (CBM). For this purpose, topics such as sustainability and sustainable business models work as starting points to contextualize the urgency of rethinking alternatives to patterns of linear production and consumption in industries. In a more specific approach, the authors also seek to understand the potential of virtualization pillar under the ReSOLVE framework to implement circular economy principles in business models, as their catalysts and enablers to a sustainable industry through digitalization.

Chapter 16

Duc Huu Pham, International University-Vietnam National University Ho Chi Minh City,
Vietnam

The Internet has helped to collect and exchange information and data with its constant expansion and evolution for devices to be intertwined with each other. These advances provide invaluable information about people and issues related to their lives including behaviors, interests, and preferences which have brought about the Internet of Behaviors (IoB) in attempts to understand the data collected from users' online activities. From a behavioral psychology perspective, the IoB can address the question of how to understand the data, and how to apply that understanding to create things that benefit humans. The IoB is related to many fields of research including technology, data analytics, and behavior science in relationship with stylometry. The applications of stylometry within the IoB framework such as analyzing the writing style of social media posts, online reviews, journal articles, or literary works at tertiary educational organizations could provide insights into the personality or motivations of the author. Thus, stylometry could potentially be used to identify authorship.

    Gonçalo Santos, Instituto Politécnico da Guarda, Portugal
    Gonçalo Vicente, Instituto Politécnico da Guarda, Portugal
    Telmo Salvado, Instituto Politécnico da Guarda, Portugal
    Celestino Gonçalves, Instituto Politécnico da Guarda, Portugal
    Filipe Caetano, Instituto Politécnico da Guarda, Portugal
    Clara Silveira, Instituto Politécnico da Guarda, Portugal

Water scarcity is probably one of the most serious problems that humanity will have to face globally. For that reason, it will certainly be urgent to try to define practices and find solutions that, in a first phase, allow to mitigate the problem, but whose ultimate objective will be to overcome the situation. This chapter presents an irrigation system set on an internet of things platform, able to act in real time according to the atmospheric conditions. Through parameterized and automated systems, it is possible to stop the irrigation. Later, using sensors, the system may or may not be activated in case the levels of soil moisture and luminosity do not respond to the parameterized needs. It is an efficient and sustainable solution that is available for all agriculture irrigation systems. To test the proposed solution, unit tests were conducted, and a group of tests with all sensors connected was also considered. This system implements an alternative method for the data flow and its monitoring, including the fact that the system is aware of the user.

    Rui Manuel Teixeira Santos Teixeira Dias, Polytechnic Institute of Setubal, Portugal
    Mariana Chambino, Polytechnic Institute of Setúbal, Portugal
    Paulo Alexandre, Polytechnic Institute of Setúbal, Portugal
    Cristina Morais da Palma, Instituto Politécnico de Setúbal, Portugal
    Liliana Almeida, Polytechnic Institute of Setúbal, Portugal

This study investigates whether Bitcoin may act as a safe haven in the capital markets, including France (CAC 40), Germany (DAX 30), the US (DJI), the UK (FTSE 100), Italy (FTSE MIB), Hong Kong (HANG SENG), Spain (IBEX 35), South Korea (KOSPI), Russia (IMOEX), and Japan (NIKKEI 225), as well as in commodities such as gold (GOLD HANDY HARMAN) and petroleum (WTI), and U.S. 10-year sovereign yields, during the 2020-2022 events. The authors analyze the financial integration and movements of markets to understand how BTC behaves during periods of global economic uncertainty. During the stress period, BTC did not integrate with the analyzed markets, suggesting that BTC exhibits properties of a hedge and a safe haven. BTC has properties of a hedge and a safe haven, and investors in these markets can benefit from investing in it as a secure asset and hedge. It is affected by CAC 40, FTSE 100, HANG SENG, and NIKKEI 225 stock indexes, and investors must carefully evaluate their investment strategies and risk tolerance when including BTC in their portfolio.

Preface

The narrative unfolds in the realm of Society 5.0, a stage where digitalization and Information and Communication Technologies (ICT) emerge as pivotal forces shaping organizational dynamics. The objective is not merely technological advancement but a strategic harnessing of these tools to enhance the quality of life, address societal challenges, and align with Sustainable Development Goals (SDGs) by 2030.

This book immerses itself in the multifaceted landscape of Internet of Behaviours (IoB) implementation in organizational contexts, spanning from the Internet of Things to Smart Cities, Big Data to Social Inclusion. The exploration extends across social, economic, technical, environmental, and human dimensions, all deeply intertwined with the organizational dynamics. Through diverse methods—innovative studies, case analyses, literature reviews, and insightful reports—the text unravels complexities and spotlights key developments.

In the pursuit of global priorities outlined by SDGs, the book advocates for the integration of sustainability into organizational contexts attending to the influence of this dinamics in the orgamnizations. From tackling social issues to exploring ICT sustainability and digital transformation, the narrative becomes a guide navigating the uncharted territories of internet and ICT. The lens zooms in on emerging trends like Smart Agriculture, Education 5.0 and digitalization, and a human-centric approach to digital technologies, all viewed through the prism of organizational behavior.

An integral aspect is the discussion on the implementation of the IoB within organizational contexts. It not only examines the conceptual and theoretical frameworks but also endeavors to bridge the gap between research and practical applications.

This literary endeavor aims to be a catalyst for change in the organizational landscape. By disseminating research with practical applications, the book seeks to empower organizations and individuals, offering innovative solutions amidst the transformative wave of digitalization and ICT futher society.

This book aspires to be more than a repository of knowledge; it seeks to be a catalyst for change. By disseminating research with practical applications, it endeavors to create opportunities for innovative solutions, empowering organizations and individuals alike.

The book consists of eighteen chapters which the editors decided to organize in three sections:

Section 1 – The Role of IoB in Transforming Business Models: Focus in the digitalization of Business Models and the crucial role of the ICT in this process.

Section 2 – Exploring the Dynamics of IoB in education and Healthcare: Provide a discussion around the impact and dynamics of the IoB in the sectors of education and healthcare, where this technologies are important promotors of innovation.

Section 3 – Challenges and New Avenues: Provide a set of research around new trends and opportunities to improve research in this field.

The chapters included in the book are presented below:

Section 1: The Role of IoB in Transforming Business Models

The first chapter, "New Business Models for Society 5.0," authored by Ferebee & Lessen presents IoB as a pivotal concept, harnessing the power of data to understand and influence humans. IoB finds its most profound application in Society 5.0, a vision of a super-smart society where digital and physical realms harmoniously coexist. New business and economic models like the circular economy, sharing economy, smart cities, platform business model, social enterprise model, and blockchain technology will be explored. Emerging healthcare, agriculture, hospitality, and energy business models are discussed. Challenges arise as innovative organizations emerge to create a more sustainable and inclusive culture. Data privacy and security, blockchain high energy consumption, technologically unprepared workforce, and artificial intelligence bias must be addressed. This chapter aims to demonstrate emerging economies, business models, and related technologies that facilitate Society 5.0 as it evolves from human behavior insights gained from IoB.

The second chapter, "ReSOLVE Framework: When Circular Business Models Become Digital: Evidences From Brazil," authored by Costa et al, analyzes the increasing focus of literature and research consolidating a positive relationship between circular business models and digital technologies. This chapter proposes a literature review on the ReSOLVE framework as a key factor to enable the development of New Business Models oriented towards the Circular Economy, in particular Circular Business Models (CBM). For this purpose, topics such as sustainability and sustainable business models work as starting points to contextualize the urgency of rethinking alternatives to patterns of linear production and consumption in industries. In a more specific approach, the authors also seek to understand the potential of Virtualization pillar under the ReSOLVE framework to implement circular economy principles in business models, as their catalysts and enablers to a sustainable industry through digitalization.

The third chapter, "Moving Towards Internet of Behaviors: Transforming Business Models With Blockchain," authored by Kose, presents IoB as an emerging trend that aims to revolutionize human interactions by analyzing and influencing behavior using data from connected devices. This study explores the importance of blockchain technology in addressing the IoB challenges and enhancing the security and privacy of IoB business models. Blockchain technology provides a decentralized and transparent platform for behavioral data storage and sharing, mitigating privacy concerns. Individuals are empowered with control over their personal data through smart contracts and decentralized identifiers, enabling them to decide how their data is accessed and used within IoB systems. In this study, significant blockchain based solutions and approaches are presented that can enhance IoB business models through examples. Exploration of blockchain potential in IoB systems will ensure new insights for further advancement and evolution of IoB paradigm.

The fourth chapter, "Codeflex 2.0: Experience With Competitive Programming in Logical and Functional Paradigms," authored by Soares, Brito, & Gonçalves presents the design and implementation of Codeflex, a web-based platform and repository of programming problems, that enables the learning and practice of competitive programming in multiple programming language paradigms. The Codeflex programming platform performs automatic evaluation of submitted solutions for a very diverse set of programming languages, in real time, considering the specificities and requirements of different programming paradigms, being prepared to analyze and detect plagiarism in tournament submissions. The use of Codeflex platform in a real context allowed the test and validation of its functionalities. In particular, several programming tournaments were organized, for Haskell and Prolog programming languages - functional and logic programming tournaments, respectively, within the scope of programming curricular units of Computer Science undergraduate degree. The findings suggest that Codeflex is a valuable contribution in enhancing programming skills and providing an efficient evaluation system for educational and professional settings.

The fifth chapter, "Empowering Diversity: The Role of Leadership in Inclusion in the Organizational Context," was submitted by Roque, & Ramos. This chapter empathizes that the moments of crisis exacerbate social inequalities, highlighting the paramount importance of the debate on inclusion. The promotion of social inclusion can and should be pursued and implemented at various levels. In this sense, leadership can play a fundamental role in the inclusion of individuals in organizations and, consequently, in society. Inclusion in the workplace is about creating an environment where individuals from diverse backgrounds feel valued, respected, and have equal opportunities to contribute and succeed. Leaders have the power to shape the culture, policies and practices that promote or hinder inclusion. This chapter will review the literature on inclusion based on the responsible leadership and inclusive leadership approaches, seeking to understand how these types of leadership can contribute with effective responses to inclusion in the work context. The chapter will end with a proposal of a set of practices that may be relevant for the inclusion of individuals in organizations.

The sixth chapter, "Human Behavior in Telework: A Modality of Work Centered on the Human Being That Promotes Opportunities and Social Integration," was submitted by Bastos, & Neto. This chapter states that in 2020, Brazilians were faced with the COVID-19 health crisis that caused a rupture in market and business standards, technologies, and models, directly affecting the way people relate to each other, work, and live, reshaping the social, cultural, and economic contexts. Among these changes, remote work has never been so evident in the daily life of companies and their employees. In this context, the question that guides this work is: what is the impact of working from home on people management in companies from the human resources point of view? This study is an exploratory survey carried out by means of an online questionnaire, responded by 121 participants. The results indicate that telework can be a more humane way of working and a solution to numerous problems of modern society.

Section 2: Exploring the Dynamics of IoB in Education and Healthcare

The seventh chapter, "Digital Educational Games: A Resource to Promote Education 5.0?" authored by Delgado, Mendes, Brocardo, & Boavida reflects on the challenges that arise when it is intended that all students can experience an Education 5.0 and proposes a set of practical actions that may support teachers' educational practice. It analyses and discusses a study involving 18 primary teachers and their 358 students (ages 6-10), which informed specific adjustments in some educational technological games about mathematics and confirmed, or not, several of the potentialities that intentionally underlined their design. The analysis focused on some problematic aspects related to moving towards an Education 5.0, which allows the integration of digital technologies in a more meaningful way in the learning process, aiming at the development of critical and creative thinking and collaborative work. Finally, suggestions are systematized about the development of quality educational technological tools and teacher training.

The eight chapter, "Education 5.0 in the Context of Teaching Accounting," authored by Aleixo, Silva, & Godinho, discusses that the higher education institutions play a crucial role in the teaching-learning process as they are primarily responsible for preparing students for their entry into the business environment. The aim of this study is to assess students' perception of a new teaching approach and its impact on their personal and professional development. At the level of course coordination, the findings will inform reflections on which pedagogical practices should be implemented to align with the student-focused teaching paradigm and the implementation of an Education 5.0 framework in the bachelor's degree program in accounting and finance at the Polytechnic University of Setúbal. The research employs a qualitative analysis approach, and the main results indicate that participants recognize the importance of Education 5.0 for their personal and professional development as Certified Accountants.

The ninth chapter, "Investigation of High-Performance Computing Tools for Higher Education Institutions Using the IoE Grid Computing Framework," authored by Mishra, Habtemariam, & De discuses that the IoE Grid Computing Framework will be used to look into high-performance computing tools for higher education institutions. The primary and secondary data from higher education organizations are used to make the model and architecture. So, using a computational IoE grid and the supported toolkits, a model of the event was made. To see how well resources and related algorithms work, they are put to the test in different situations, such as by confirming the number of resources and users with different needs. To determine the level of demand for high-performance computing tools, data were gathered from particular colleges and universities. Before the data was fed into the system, preprocessing tasks like handling missing values and choosing features were completed. The findings demonstrate that these traits and the requirement for high-performance computing resources in higher education institutions are strongly related.

The tenth chapter, "Changes of Communication in Biomedical Sciences and Health: 'Dr Google' and Hearing Loss," authored by Caria argue that scientific and technological developments are unquestionable, being Health in general and Human genetics specifically, domains where highthrouputs are gorgeous. The Internet is changing the behavior of patients with clinicians and health organizations. The project of Human genomes ensured new approaches to estimate cause-disease relations. Genotype-phenotype correlations and screening of mutation are now available to all researchers. However, this scientific data are also available to the patients, bringing them to the floor as active partners in therapeutic processes searching with "Dr. Google" for symptoms, treatments, and cures. Hereditary deafness is not escaping from this civil movement, being a good example of the behavioral change associated with the explosion of the internet, with the commercial offers of hearing aids and cochlear implants offers to be common nowadays. In the present chapter, the author discuss the internet of behaviors in the context of biomedical sciences as human genetics, and Hearing Loss.

The eleventh chapter, "Digitalization and the Consumer Experience: The Case of the Health Sector in Portugal," authored by Xara-Brasil, Viana, & Cruz, considers that the digital transformation is a reality in practically all business industries and has influenced the development of new marketing practices and, consequently, consumer experiences, particularly in the health sector. The aim of this research is to analyze the potential benefits that digital transformation and digital marketing may have in the customer's experiences with health service providers. This study allowed the confirmation of many of the aspects researched in previous academic works and reinforced the importance of using more technological solutions for current users, as well as the need to improve, namely in terms of service personalization, with greater speed and response, and quality of the service provided in an integrated way by the different touchpoints. Furthermore, it reinforced some important objections of users, namely related to the presumed greater difficulty of personal interaction, especially in cases of dissatisfaction and complaint, or in groups of patients with less digital training.

Section 3: Challenges and New Avenues

The twelfth chapter, "Cybersecurity and Business Continuity: An Essential Partnership in an Era of Digital Interactions," submitted by Russo, states that as a consequence of the evolution and digital transition, organizations depend more on ICT. The behavioral data generated through interactions with ICT is collected and analyzed by the Internet of Behaviors (IoB). In this context, cybersecurity is a critical aspect of Business Continuity (BC). Organizations must ensure that their ICT systems are protected from cyber-attacks to avoid disruptions to their operations. A BC Plan (BCP) that considers cybersecurity can help ensure the continuity of critical functions in the event of a cyber-attack. Raising awareness is relevant to promote safe practices and minimize the risk of successful cyberattacks and loss of behavioral data. Therefore, a solid BC Management System (BCMS) should address cybersecurity and assure that all stakeholders are aware of the subjacent risks to a business, how to avoid, mitigate or cope with them. This chapter presents the BC components and activities of a BCP that includes cybersecurity. Following the guidelines of the activities can result in avoiding or mitigating security risks by creating a successful BCP.

The thirteenth chapter, "Effects and Potentials of Business Intelligence Tools on Tourism Companies in a Tourism 4.0 Environment," was submitted by Amiri, & Ramos. This chapter presents that the several technologies emerged and disrupted how they operate in the Tourism 4.0 environment surrounding tourism companies. One, the digitalization of processes has become a way to support survival, and second, data grows exponentially daily. In this environment, a Business Intelligence tool can help to improve decision-making while enabling managers to realize complex information quickly and make more efficient decisions. The benefits of BI adoption in businesses encourage scholars to study and research this topic. This study aims to understand the effects and potentialities of business intelligence systems conjugated with artificial intelligence for tourism companies. As the main findings, the potential of BI helps the tourism company to increase destination sustainability support and to create a shared decision-maker environment between the companies.

The fourteenth chapter, "Stylometry-Based Authorship Identification: An Approach From the Internet of Behaviors Perspective Through Contrastive Linguistic Analysis," was submitted by Pham. This chapter argues that the Internet has helped to collect and exchange information and data with its constant expansion and evolution for devices to be intertwined with each other. These advances provide invaluable information about people and issues related to their lives including behaviors, interests and preferences which have brought about the Internet of Behaviors (IoB) in attempts to understand the data collected from users' online activities. From a behavioral psychology perspective, the IoB can address the question of how to understand the data, and how to apply that understanding to create things that benefit humans. The IoB is related to many fields of research including technology, data analytics, and behavior science in relationship with stylometry. The applications of stylometry within the IoB framework such as analyzing the writing style of social media posts, online reviews, journal articles, or literary works at tertiary educational organizations could provide insights into the personality or motivations of the author. Thus, stylometry could potentially be used to identify authorship.

The fifteenth chapter, "Unveiling Bitcoin's Safe Haven and Hedging Properties Beyond Diversification," submitted by Dias et al. This chapter presents a study that investigates whether Bitcoin may act as a safe haven in the capital markets, including France (CAC 40), Germany (DAX 30), the US (DJI), the UK (FTSE 100), Italy (FTSE MIB), Hong Kong (HANG SENG), Spain (IBEX 35), South Korea (KOSPI), Russia (IMOEX), and Japan (NIKKEI 225), as well as in commodities such as gold (GOLD

HANDY HARMAN) and petroleum (WTI), and U.S. 10-year sovereign yields, during the 2020-2022 events. The authors analyze the financial integration and movements of markets to understand how BTC behaves during periods of global economic uncertainty. During the Stress period, BTC did not integrate with the analyzed markets, suggesting that BTC exhibits properties of a hedge and a safe haven. BTC has properties of a hedge and a safe haven, and investors in these markets can benefit from investing in it as a secure asset and hedge. It is affected by CAC 40, FTSE 100, HANG SENG, and NIKKEI 225 stock indexes, and investors must carefully evaluate their investment strategies and risk tolerance when including BTC in their portfolio.

The sixteenth chapter, "Behaviour Perspectives as a Contribution to Business Continuity in the ICT Context," is authored by Russo & Reis. This chapter states that the Internet of Behavior (IoB) is expanding rapidly, offering valuable insights into users' behavior, interests, and preferences. The integration of requirements for ensuring business continuity faces certain constraints. This chapter presents a set of concerns about business continuity in software and explores the certification domain for invoicing software in Portugal. The concept of developing continuity by-design software and a methodological approach for business continuity management is introduced to enhance ICT and address sustainability concerns. This approach aims to foster innovative solutions and behavior optimization. Given the specificity of the issue under study, the methodology adopted was Design Science Research. The main results include the development of artifacts that optimize the decision process for implementing electronic invoicing issuance and archiving, integrating the concept of continuity-by-design in the creation of resilient software. These efforts encompass multiple dimensions of sustainability and innovation, considering stakeholders' behavior.

The seventeenth chapter, "Sustainable and Autonomous Soil Irrigation: Agro Smart Solution," submitted by Santos et al. This chapter presents that the water scarcity is probably one of the most serious problems that humanity will have to face globally. For that reason, it will certainly be urgent to try to define practices and find solutions that, in a first phase, allow to mitigate the problem, but whose ultimate objective will be to overcome the situation. This chapter presents an irrigation system set on an Internet of Things platform, able to act in real time accordingly to the atmospheric conditions. Through parameterized and automated systems, it is possible to stop the irrigation. Later, using sensors, the system may or may not be activated in case the levels of soil moisture and luminosity do not respond to the parameterized needs. It is an efficient and sustainable solution that is available for all agriculture irrigation systems. To test the proposed solution, unit tests were conducted, and a group of tests with all sensors connected was also considered. This system implements an alternative method for the data flow and its monitoring, including the fact that the system is aware of the user.

The eighteenth chapter, "Overreaction, Underreaction, and Short-Term Efficient Reaction Evidence for Cryptocurrencies," submitted by Dias, & Chambino. This chapter aims to analyze the price efficiency of Bitcoin (BTC), DASH, EOS, Ethereum (ETH), LISK, Litecoin (LTC), Monero, NEO, QUANTUM, RIPPLE, STELLAR, and ZCASH in their weak form between March 1, 2018 and March 1, 2023, and determine whether they experience overreactions. The results show that cryptocurrencies exhibit positive and negative autocorrelations, which can reduce volatility and moderate price fluctuations. The results also show persistence in cryptocurrency returns, suggesting long-term trends or market patterns that individual and institutional investors can exploit. It is essential to recognize that cryptocurrencies are characterized by a high degree of complexity and instability. Investors need to monitor market trends and make the necessary adjustments to their investment strategies to anticipate market changes.

To conclude, we would like to thank the authors whose collaboration has made this project possible and express our hope that readers will find this publication inspiring and useful.

Luísa Cagica Carvalho
Instituto Politécnico de Setúbal, Portugal

Clara Silveira
Polytechnic Institute of Guarda, Portugal

Leonilde Reis
Instituto Politecnico de Setúbal, Portugal

Nelson Russo
Universidade Aberta, Portugal

Section 1
The Role of IoB in Transforming Business Models

Chapter 1
Behaviour Perspectives as a Contribution to Business Continuity in the ICT Context

Nelson Russo

https://orcid.org/0000-0001-9664-7148
Universidade Aberta, Portugal

Leonilde Reis

https://orcid.org/0000-0002-4398-8384
Instituto Politécnico de Setúbal, Portugal

ABSTRACT

The Internet of Behavior (IoB) is expanding rapidly, offering valuable insights into users' behavior, interests, and preferences. The integration of requirements for ensuring business continuity faces certain constraints. This chapter presents a set of concerns about business continuity in software and explores the certification domain for invoicing software in Portugal. The concept of developing continuity by-design software and a methodological approach for business continuity management is introduced to enhance ICT and address sustainability concerns. This approach aims to foster innovative solutions and behavior optimization. Given the specificity of the issue under study, the methodology adopted was design science research. The main results include the development of artifacts that optimize the decision process for implementing electronic invoicing issuance and archiving, integrating the concept of continuity-by-design in the creation of resilient software. These efforts encompass multiple dimensions of sustainability and innovation, considering stakeholders' behavior.

INTRODUCTION

The concept used here, continuity-by-design, derives from security-by-design. The development process integrating security-by-design aims to support a software producer in building and implementing a secure solution, taking into account potential security issues from the beginning of the development

DOI: 10.4018/978-1-6684-9039-6.ch001

process, in order to reduce the risks associated with vulnerabilities and existing threats (Casola et al., 2018). Continuity-by-design focuses on enhancing service availability by incorporating possible controls, measures, and compliance with Business Continuity (BC) requirements throughout the product or service lifecycle.

This chapter presents a set of concerns with a view to including business continuity and resilience measures in software in the context of covid-19, as well as characterizing the domain of certification of invoicing software in Portugal.

In this perspective, the authors aim to present a research path that aims to guide producers of Invoicing Software Programs (ISP) and organizational decision-makers in identifying the issues that enhance BC in the design and implementation of an invoicing software solution.

The research was initiated with a guide to support the design of a Business Continuity Plan (BCP) in organizations with ISP (Russo, 2019). The guide addressed the main theoretical and empirical considerations that support the design of a BCP, based on a literature review, particularly in the area of Business Continuity Management (BCM).

The literature review on BC, along with the acquired knowledge, allowed for the design of a methodological approach for the systematization of BC in organizations (Russo & Reis, 2020b). The systematization involved the definition and implementation of a set of interconnected phases necessary to optimize the planning and response to disruptions in business processes, aligned with the organizational strategy and tailored to the Information and Communication Technologies (ICT) needs of the organization.

In this context, an analysis of the problem underlying the certification of ISP was conducted (Russo & Reis, 2019a), highlighting the technical requirements integrated into Portuguese tax legislation that involve BC. Constraints in their implementation were addressed, including technical issues, interpretation of tax legislation, or the selection of standards and best practices in the ICT field. This work was updated to include considerations on electronic document archiving (Russo & Reis, 2020d).

Furthermore, it became necessary to characterize the companies and invoicing in Portugal using certified ISP, aiming to improve organizations' perception of the certification process and contribute to increasing the number of certified ISPs (Russo & Reis, 2019b).

A study was conducted to characterize electronic invoicing in Portugal (Russo & Reis, 2020c), including its utilization by organizations and the communication of invoice elements to the Tax and Customs Authority (AT). The objective was to support companies in the process of implementing an ISP certified by the AT, whether through internal development or the acquisition of an ISP.

In line with this objective of supporting ISP producers and users, a set of best practices was published, including diagrams and details of various involved requirements. Topics covered included considerations on data backup policies, ISP downtime, or program access control (Russo & Reis, 2020a).

The recent simplification of fiscal legislation has created conditions for the dematerialization of documents, allowing for the possibility of waiving the use of printed invoices and encouraging the adoption of electronic invoicing and electronic document archiving systems. In this context, electronic invoicing and archiving adoption within the scope of ISP certification, can be a driving factor for entrepreneurship, innovation, and sustainability (Russo & Reis, 2021).

Lessons can be learned by the organizations influenced by the COVID-19 pandemic and they should take into account the potential of this legislative approach (Russo & Reis, 2021). The focus on online businesses, amplified by the increased use of remote work resulting from pandemic containment measures, allows certain management, optimization, and control functions to be performed remotely. The effects are reflected in the need to optimize business processes and time spent on activities, but above all, in the technological transition that mitigates the underlying gaps in this new vision of the business and digital world. This new vision depends on the dynamism of ICT in business processes and the swift response to this goal, where there is a need to make quick and effective decisions with the necessary efficiency for the change to be appropriate.

Thus, the objective of the research is to support decision-making processes in the development of a resilient invoicing software solution, considering BC aspects in accordance with legal and fiscal requirements. It is considered that electronic invoicing and electronic archiving incorporate relevant requirements to enhance the organization's strategic ability to respond to disruptions and continue business operations at an acceptable predefined level.

Contributing to achieving these objectives is the characterization of invoicing, electronic invoicing, and electronic archiving in Portugal, as well as a set of relevant considerations for application development, aimed at supporting organizations and ISP producers in the certification of ISP by the AT.

The integration of the Design Science Research methodology, involving ISP producers and the researcher as an ISP certifier from the AT, facilitated direct contact with technological capabilities and constraints experienced by organizations, guiding relevant themes in the development of an IT solution and the design of a BCP.

The added value is considered to lie in the presentation of the correct procedures, requirements, and legislation surrounding an electronic invoicing or electronic document archiving system that enhances BC and service delivery, and expedites the development of an ISP certified by the AT.

From this perspective, there is an additional contribution to decision support in a BC perspective when acquiring or developing an ISP (Russo & Reis, 2019a, 2020d). Thus, in a simplified approach to its life cycle, the various software development phases are covered: supporting the planning of the ICT solution, defining requirements and best practices that influence its development and implementation, and providing support during the testing phase, where failure scenarios and expected results are identified. The guide for designing a BCP (Russo, 2019), addressing the specificities of an ISP certified by the AT, has a greater focus on the maintenance and evolution phases.

It is therefore considered relevant to provide organizations with ISP with a theoretical instrument to support the implementation of a BCP. The identification of areas of action and advantages in the digital transition to electronic invoicing and electronic archiving, supported by the requirements defined in legislation, is essential, allowing for support in the definition phase of "ICT Strategy" as a component of BCM, with an impact on the development of the ISP.

This chapter is organized into five sections, where the first introduces the problem, and the second presents the literature review. The adopted methodology is integrated into the third section, and the results are presented and discussed in the fourth section. The fifth and final section presents the conclusions underlying the study of the subject and interrelates the various research conducted.

LITERATURE REVIEW

The literature review on the topic of BC was relevant for the construction of the theoretical framework, which includes standards and best practices. Fiscal legislation was necessary to provide a framework for ISPs, their requirements, and their certification by the AT.

Business Continuity

BC is based on the strategic and tactical capability of an organization to plan and respond to incidents and business disruptions, with the objective of continuing business operations at an acceptable predefined level (Ramakrishnan & Viswanathan, 2011). However, economic, technological, and human uncertainties confront organizations with the possibility of crises arising, impeding their ability to operate and ultimately survive (Herbane, 2010).

According to (Arduini & Morabito, 2010), BC is a framework of disciplines, processes, and techniques that aim to provide continuous operation for essential business functions in all circumstances.

As a formal organizational activity, crisis management, in a broad sense, is characterized by the paradox that organizations plan for events they do not wish to occur but are often known possibilities (Russo, 2019). This planning may require organizations to commit to investing in resources that may never be used, and whose "value" or "return" cannot be determined with the same level of certainty as other strategic investment decisions. Business processes that have more points of contact with customers need to be addressed first (Russo & Reis, 2020a) and those who affect the behavior of the users.

In this sense, BC encompasses a mechanism for responding to emergencies and crises resulting from a disaster or disruptive event, with the establishment of plans that outline procedures to enable an organization to successfully achieve the following aspects (Al-shammari & Alsaqre, 2012): provide an immediate and adequate response to emergency situations, reduce the impact on the business, resume critical business services, ensure the continuity of business services, and restore and operate quickly after a disaster.

Business Continuity Management

Contingency planning and disaster recovery have largely been responses led by ICT to natural disasters and terrorism. However, these processes should be led by the business and cover preparation for various forms of business interruption, thus forming BCM (Tangen & Austin, 2020).

In this perspective, organizations must find solutions to ensure data integrity and mitigate service interruptions, effectively implementing BCM to avoid serious consequences and severe disruptions to their business. This way, planning for BCM prepares the organization to maintain the continuity of its services during a disaster by implementing a contingency plan, specifically a BCP (Russo, 2019).

However, in order to plan the response, it is necessary to at least understand the organization, its vital and prioritized business processes, expected recovery times, and the ICT capacity for recovery and business restoration (Russo & Reis, 2020a). Detecting an event as early as possible allows for timely notification or action on the problem, providing an appropriate response before it spreads to other services, which can lead to system inoperability and, consequently, the failure to deliver ICT services correctly.

BCM is a management process that incorporates risk management (Torabi et al., 2016) among other aspects, to identify potential intentional and unintentional threats to an organization. Its objective is to build the organization's capability to respond to these threats. Technology, people, and processes are three fundamental aspects in the BCM approach (Mansol et al., 2015), and there are benefits in implementing a BCM project (Russo & Reis, 2020b). Understanding the behavior of users, customers and business partners can enhance and improve the BC solution.

In this context, BCM goes beyond risk management, and there are several components that enable effective continuity management in a BCP. Figure 1 presents the essential components of BCM according to the methodology for designing a BCP (Russo & Reis, 2020b). Within this framework, organizations can adapt the methodology to their context, considering their requirements, size, scope, objectives, and technological capacity (Russo, 2019).

Figure 1. BCM components
Source: Russo and Reis (2020b)

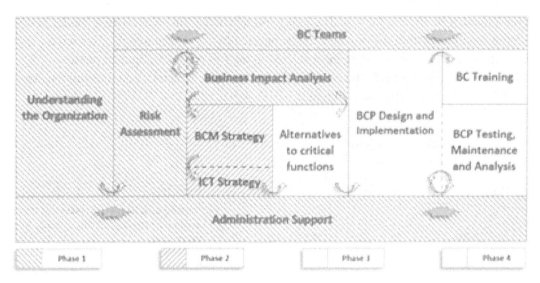

Figure 1 presents a sequence of actions and interrelation of BCM components. It represents a temporal phasing in the methodological approach for designing and maintaining a BCP, suggesting the set of components that need to be completed before moving on to the next phase.

It is worth mentioning that although ICT departments in Portugal face obstacles in implementing technological change and often operate reactively (Russo & Reis, 2019b), 74% of Portuguese organizations have implemented a digital strategy, with data security being the main function assigned to their departments. Despite some resistance to ICT practices in Portugal in 2016, about half of the applications were already hosted in the cloud (Russo & Reis, 2019b). Therefore, BC teams should be partially composed of members from the ICT department due to their extensive knowledge of the organization's business processes. Their contribution is essential for defining the ICT strategy and for identifying alternatives for critical functions, which are primarily composed of ICT solutions.

Business Continuity Plan

Organizational resilience is the ability to increase the continuity capacity of any system against disruptive incidents, whether they are internal or external variations, changes, disturbances, disruptions, or surprises (Sahebjamnia et al., 2018). Resilience encompasses effective planning for responding to situations where operations are interrupted following disruptive events, both for short-term business process relaunching (with BCP) and long-term recovery (with Disaster Recovery Plan).

A BCP is designed to prevent or mitigate risks, reduce the impact of a disaster condition, and shorten the time required to restore conditions to a normal operating state (Cerullo & Cerullo, 2004), aiming to preserve an organization's assets (Hiles, 2007).

In this context, ISO 22301:2019 defines BCP as documented procedures that guide organizations in responding, recovering, resuming, and restoring to a predefined level of operation after an interruption. It typically covers resources, services, and activities necessary to ensure the continuity of critical business functions (ISO 22301, 2019).

Several vital activities for the design of a BCP have been identified and are relevant (Russo, 2019). However, defining an ICT strategy and technological resource requirements are crucial factors for success. The development of strategies, plans, and actions to protect or determine alternative modes of operation for essential functions within the organization, supported by these technological resources, should be delineated in advance, especially to be incorporated in the software development phase.

In this context, the planning should consider the phases that characterize an interruption, addressing its entire life spectrum, as depicted in Figure 2.

Figure 2. Business interruption phases
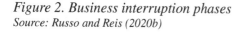
Source: Russo and Reis (2020b)

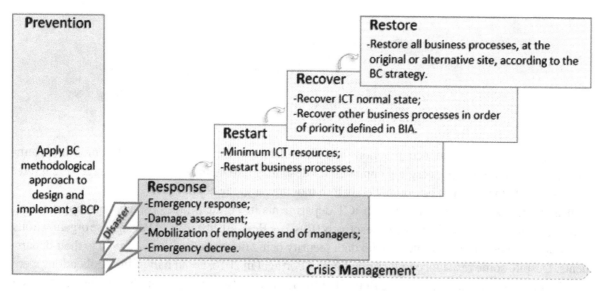

The prevention phase, as depicted in Figure 2, is considered the ideal moment to integrate BC concepts into application development. The benefits will be noticeable in the restart phase when the designed solution allows the delivery of minimal ICT services, enabling the organization to restart its business processes. It is necessary to understand the organization and its information flows (Russo & Reis, 2020a), its vital and prioritized business processes, recovery times, and the minimum capacity of ICT that enables business restart, recovery, and restoration.

The plan should be simple, clear, unambiguous, and comprehensive. Plans based on different risk scenarios, such as fire or mechanical failures, are generally not effective: it is usually not the cause of the disaster that matters, but rather the outcome (Hiles, 2011b).

Standards

With the aim of providing an underlying perspective to product engineering and development, it is listed relevant standards, models, and frameworks in the ICT field that address the topic of BC.

Information Technology Infrastructure Library

The Information Technology Infrastructure Library (ITIL) is a framework for ICT Service Management that aims to align ICT services with business needs. The guidance provided by the ITIL best practices can be adopted and adapted by all types of organizations and services (ITIL, 2019). ITIL is a framework that ensures continuity and includes practices related to service continuity management (Russo, 2019), (Russo & Reis, 2019a).

The ITIL perspective on the underlying requirements of the decision-making process (Russo & Reis, 2021) and the development and implementation of an ISPAT can be aligned with the key messages and concepts defined in ITIL (Russo & Reis, 2020a).

Control Objectives for Information and Related Technologies

The Control Objectives for Information and Related Technology (COBIT), developed by the Information Systems Audit and Control Association (ISACA), is a best-practice reference guide for implementing governance in ICT, including the technical, process, and people aspects, which should be adapted to each organization (ISACA, 2018). COBIT aligns ICT with the business, improving organizational ICT governance and management, enabling a holistic view of the entire organization (ISACA, 2018).

Russo and Reis (2020a) and Russo (2019) present the guidelines of the framework regarding continuity management, defined in the fourth process of Delivery Service and Support (DDS): "DSS4 - Managed continuity." The justification and motivation, as defined in COBIT, for investing in innovation by implementing electronic invoicing and electronic archiving functionalities, are relevant (Russo & Reis, 2020d), as well as its vision on the importance of requirements management and compliance with external requirements (Russo & Reis, 2021).

Capability Maturity Model Integration

The Capability Maturity Model Integration (CMMI) is a proven set of global best practices that helps organizations improve business performance and create and compare key capabilities that address common business challenges (CMMI Institute, 2020).

CMMI V2.0 addresses various management topics in the "Managing Business Resilience" Capability Area, which aims to anticipate and adapt to disruptions and opportunities. Russo and Reis (2020a, 2020b) and Russo (2019) present considerations on incorporating the practice areas of "Incident Resolution and Prevention," "Risk and Opportunity Management," and "Continuity" to improve organizational performance and capabilities in the field of business continuity.

In the context of ISP development, the "Engineering and Developing Products" and "Requirements Development and Management" Capability Areas are also highlighted as areas that aim to create products that meet customer expectations, based on gathered requirements aligned with their needs (Russo & Reis, 2021).

ISO 22301:2019

The ISO 22301:2019 "Security and resilience - Business continuity management systems - Requirements" is a standard for implementing a BC management system and continuously improving BC resources based on management priorities and feedback. It specifies the requirements for implementing, maintaining, and improving a management system to protect against, reduce the likelihood of occurrence, prepare for, respond to, and recover from disruptions when they arise (ISO 22301, 2019).

In this context, the ISO 22313:2020 "Security and resilience - Business continuity management systems - Guidance on the use of ISO 22301" provides guidelines and recommendations for applying the BCM System requirements stated in the ISO 22301 standard.

These standards have been revised, including the considerations mentioned in subclauses 8.4.4 "Business Continuity Plans" and 8.4.5 "Recovery," with particular relevance to BCP design (Russo, 2019) and BCM methodology (Russo & Reis, 2020b).

ISO/IEC 27031:2011

The international standard ISO/IEC 27031:2011 "Information technology - Security techniques - Guidelines for information and communication technology readiness for business continuity" describes the concepts and principles of ICT readiness for business continuity. It provides a framework of methods and processes to identify and specify all aspects (such as performance criteria, design, and implementation) to enhance an organization's ICT readiness to ensure business continuity (ISO/IEC 27031).

The guidelines from this standard have been incorporated into the design of the BCP guide (Russo, 2019) and the practical guide for business continuity in organizations with ISP (Russo & Reis, 2020a).

The guidance in this standard ensures that ICT services are resilient and appropriate and can be recovered to predetermined levels within a required timeframe agreed upon by the organization. Thus, the availability and readiness of ICT, in a broad sense, should effectively reduce the impact of incidents affecting continuity and information security in the organization, in terms of their scope, duration, and/or consequences.

An ISP seeking certification by the AT should consider the guidelines and infer the requirements presented in this standard (Russo & Reis, 2020a).

NFPA 1600 2019

The National Fire Protection Association (NFPA) standard, known as NFPA 1600, can be applicable to all types of entities. NFPA 1600 2019 is a voluntary consensus standard for emergency preparedness (NFPA, 2020).

The standard consists of 10 chapters and 13 annexes that establish a common set of criteria for all hazards in disaster, crisis, and emergency management, as well as for BC or operations programs. It follows the Plan-Do-Check-Act approach, providing the essential criteria for preparedness and resilience, including planning, implementation, execution, evaluation, and maintenance of programs for prevention, mitigation, response, continuity, and recovery (NFPA 1600, 2019).

Framework for Software Engineering

The Kernel and Language for Software Engineering Methods (Essence) is an approach for specifying scalable, extensible, and user-friendly software (Object Management Group, 2014). It defines a single-layer architecture of the method composed of practices and the Essence kernel Alphas: stakeholders, opportunity, requirements, software system, team, work, and way of working (Russo & Reis, 2021).

Figure 3 presents the "things" that a practitioner of the method should always work with, according to the area of interest.

Figure 3. Areas of interest, alphas, and what you work with
Source: Jacobson et al. (2012)

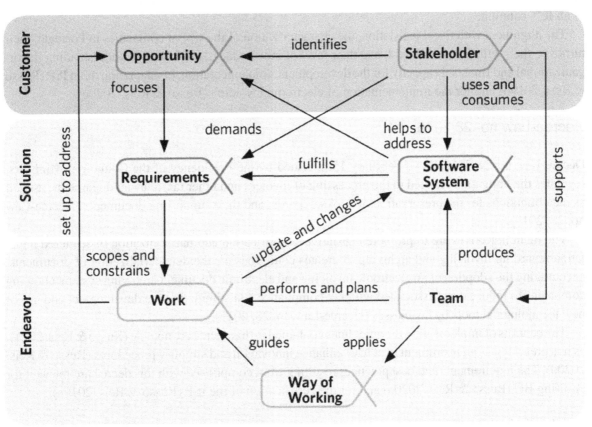

By using the presented method and according to the areas of interest of the solution and the client represented in Figure 3, the practitioner aims to perceive the demands and needs of the stakeholders to understand the requirements and ensure their satisfaction. Russo and Reis (2021) suggest that, considering the main objectives of the ISP are to meet the requirements defined in fiscal legislation, this method can help address the opportunities created by electronic invoicing and electronic archiving as a requirement for an ICT solution that integrates continuity and enables the streamlining of the ISP certification process.

The decision-making processes throughout the application development are based on the correct interpretation of the requirements. By applying the method, it is considered that the ISP can be developed rapidly, meeting the main requirements, leveraging opportunities created in terms of sustainability, embracing innovation, and streamlining business processes (Russo & Reis, 2021).

Fiscal Legislation

Portuguese fiscal legislation regulates invoicing primarily through the Value Added Tax (VAT) code. Considering the fiscal framework for invoicing and ISP certification, as well as within the scope of BC (Russo & Reis, 2020a), is relevant for designing a solution (Russo & Reis, 2019b). Different aspects, such as communication of invoices to the Tax Authority (Russo & Reis, 2020c), transportation documents, electronic invoicing, and electronic archiving (Russo & Reis, 2019a), influence the development of an ICT solution.

The alignment with fiscal legislation, the characterization of the size of companies in Portugal, their turnover, their willingness to invest, and their level of indebtedness, contribute to understanding the organizational and financial capacity for the development, implementation, or adaptation of an ISP (Russo & Reis, 2019b) and for the implementation of electronic invoicing (Russo & Reis, 2020c).

Decree-Law no. 28/2019

Decree-Law no. 28/2019, dated February 15th, issued by the Presidency of the Council of Ministers, regulates the obligations related to the processing of invoices and other tax-relevant documents, as well as the obligations for the preservation of books, records, and their supporting documents (Decree-Law no. 28, 2019).

The main objectives are to promote legislative simplification and harmonization of scattered legislation regarding invoicing and archiving. It creates conditions for the dematerialization of documents, encouraging the adoption of an electronic invoicing and electronic document archiving system, allowing companies to reduce costs associated with tax compliance and stimulating the development and use of new technological tools by businesses (Decree-Law no. 28, 2019).

The benefits of implementing the guidelines contained in this decree are notable (Russo & Reis, 2021), as it is presented as an instrument to at least enhance innovation and simplify procedures (Russo & Reis, 2020d). The requirements and best practices resulting from compliance with this decree are relevant for ensuring BC (Russo & Reis, 2020a) and for the certification of the ISP (Russo & Reis, 2019a).

Electronic Invoicing

In the Decree-Law No. 28/2019, relevant requirements related to electronic invoicing are presented, some of which are transposed from Council Directive 2010/45/EU of July 13, 2010.

In addition to printing the original and duplicate copies of the invoice on paper, Decree-Law No. 28/2019 states that invoices and other tax-relevant documents may, with the recipient's acceptance, be issued electronically. It specifies a set of requirements that must be ensured from the moment of document issuance until the end of the archiving period (Decree-Law no. 28, 2019).

The most relevant requirements in this matter are characterized (Russo & Reis, 2019b), as well as a set of advantages (Russo & Reis, 2020c), best practices (Russo & Reis, 2020a), and considerations for implementing an ISP that incorporates electronic invoicing (Russo & Reis, 2021).

The size of companies in Portugal is characterized (Russo & Reis, 2020c), along with their turnover and their willingness to invest, in order to assess their organizational and financial capacity for implementing or adapting an ISP, specifically for electronic invoicing. From this perspective, ICT departments may need to implement electronic issuance functionalities, which involve investments (Russo & Reis, 2019b) in the organization's technological capacity, human resources, and interpretation and development of associated requirements.

Electronic Archive

The tax legislation states that it is mandatory to archive and keep in good order all books, records, and related supporting documents for a period of 10 years, as well as the documentation related to the analysis, programming, and execution of computer treatments and the backup copies of data supporting invoicing and accounting software (Decree-Law no. 28, 2019).

Electronic archiving can be presented as a set of functionalities to reduce the paper document archive, minimizing, at least, the risk of destruction or deterioration of invoices issued or received (Russo, 2019; Russo & Reis, 2020c, 2020d).

The advantages, benefits, and requirements of implementing electronic archiving are identified (Russo & Reis, 2020a), including secure storage of records during the legal period, accessibility and legibility of information, location of the archive in both paper and electronic format, archive plan, scanning paper documents for electronic archiving, backup copies of electronic media, separate location for originals and backup copies, integrity, accuracy, and reliability of archiving, detection of changes, destruction or deterioration of archived records, reproduction of readable and intelligible copies of recorded data, and, of special interest to this work, the requirements that ensure data recovery in the event of an incident (Russo, 2019), (Russo & Reis, 2021).

Decree-Law no. 198/2012

In order to encourage compliance with the obligation to issue invoices, tax benefits were established for individuals (Decree-Law no. 198, 2012). In this context, Decree-Law no. 198/2012, dated August 24th, issued by the Ministry of Finance, created measures to control invoice issuance and established the EFatura service, which allows for the electronic transmission of invoice data to the tax authority (Decree-Law no. 198, 2012).

Since the issuance of an invoice is mandatory, even in cases where final consumers do not request it (AT, 2019), the resulting communication of invoice data to the tax authority has stimulated invoicing in Portugal, introducing important compliance requirements with a set of advantages for the country, sellers, and customers (Russo & Reis, 2020a).

It should be noted that this communication can be done through real-time electronic transmission integrated into a certified ISP, using a webservice provided by the tax authority, or by sending a summarized file based on a tax audit model file, exported periodically (usually monthly) by a certified ISP (Decree-Law no. 198, 2012).

Russo and Reis (2020c) present a study that characterizes the use of invoice communication to the tax authority. They present the technical requirements and a perspective regarding electronic invoice issuance in order to perceive the volume of documents that are communicated to the tax authority. They conclude on the existing potential in the development of functionalities that streamline the process of electronic invoice issuance, the potential for cost reduction, and the possibility of maintaining the entire lifecycle of a document in electronic format, from its issuance, reception, and archiving.

Invoicing Software Certification

Compliance with the provisions of Ordinance no. 363/2010, dated June 23rd, allows for obtaining the title of ISP certified by the AT (Ordinance no. 363, 2010). Certification by the tax authority is important to promote compliance with legal and technical requirements, as well as ICT best practices (Russo & Reis, 2019a).

The certification process begins with the submission of a form on the Finance Portal. The procedures, requirements, and objectives of the conformity tests preceding the issuance of the certificate are presented by Russo and Reis (2019a, 2020c, 2020d). To standardize procedures and serve as a guide for ISP implementation, some technical requirements for ISPs have been defined, including ensuring data integrity, information security, and business continuity (Order no. 8632, 2014). A set of best practices (Russo, 2019) and considerations (Russo & Reis, 2020a, 2020c) are presented to streamline the certification process, including the definition of a decision-making process (Russo & Reis, 2020c) that aims to direct the reader to the most relevant issues, supporting the discovery of the requirements inherent to certification and the inclusion of functionalities that ensure business continuity.

Order no. 8632/2014

Order no. 8632/2014, dated July 3rd, issued by the Ministry of Finance contains the necessary technical requirements for obtaining the certificate issued by the AT for an ISP. Therefore, ISPs, even if already certified, must comply with approximately 100 technical requirements (Order no. 8632, 2014), including integration of documents through duplicates that are not part of the backup copy or backup policies.

These requirements are analyzed by Russo and Reis (2020a, 2020c) and Russo (2019), where they highlight the diagrams developed with recommended procedures in case of program inoperability, as well as the templates for defining a backup policy and archive plans.

METHODOLOGY

The methodological strategy of Design Science Research (DSR) has contributed to reducing the complexity of the problem (Hevner et al., 2004) by focusing on the framework of external and internal factors within organizations across various dimensions.

By completing a preliminary research to identify and define the problem, the first phase of the DSR Process Model proposed by (Peffers et al., 2007) was successfully achieved. In this regard, the literature review has allowed for the identification of a theoretical framework for analyzing requirements and constraints in Portugal, including the characterization of companies, ICT professionals, fiscal legislation, electronic invoicing and archiving, and the ISP certification process by the AT.

The literature review on Business Continuity and its essential components in management has identified activities that contribute to the design of a BCP, where the ISP can integrate and contribute to ensuring continuity. To simplify the analysis of underlying requirements and guide the decision-making process in identifying alternatives that influence the ISP implementation within an organization, a decision-making process supported by a questionnaire was created. This complies with step 3 of the DSR.

For step 4 and 5 of the DSR, the framework was presented to invoicing software producers to assist in specifying ISP requirements based on the constraints experienced by the participants.

RESULTS AND DISCUSSION

As the main result of the research, a guide for designing a BCP is introduced, initiated with the application of a questionnaire (Russo & Reis, 2019a) presented in Figure 4. The guide is structured into specific areas of knowledge that ICT managers should address when analyzing the problem and identifying requirements for the ISP (Russo & Reis, 2021). Its application allows for the characterization of electronic invoicing issuance and archiving, enabling inferences to be made about the procedures and adoption of technology in invoicing systems (Russo & Reis, 2019b). This guide results in an improved understanding of the involved requirements and the definition of conceptual technological solutions to ensure continuity (Russo, 2019).

The questionnaire in Figure 4 consists of 21 questions, with the conclusions of the decision-making process based on multiple-choice responses.

Therefore, the proposed guide considers the organization and aligns it with a predetermined set of solutions (Russo, 2019), addressing BC at a sufficient level to comply with requirements stemming from fiscal legislation, norms, and ICT best practices.

In this regard, the technological implementation of the ISP or the party responsible for its development can provide insights into the decision-making capability regarding available functionalities (Russo, 2019). It allows inferences to be made about the implemented BC, such as the printing of original and duplicate documents or the possibility of implementing electronic issuance (Russo & Reis, 2020c).

Figure 5 illustrates the complexity and combines all decision-making processes (Russo, 2019) in a simplified view of the necessary information to collect, the inferences that can be drawn, and the legal basis supporting it. The objective of this tool is to eliminate the complexity of analyzing and understanding (almost) all the involved requirements.

The Decree-Law no. 28/2019 had a significant impact on the vision of document dematerialization and electronic issuance and archiving, considering the disadvantages and limiting factors regarding the use of paper media, especially thermal paper (Russo, 2019), (Russo & Reis, 2021).

Opting to natively issue documents electronically eliminates the need for subsequent scanning for archiving, reduces costs (Russo & Reis, 2021), and contributes to the efficiency of the organization's business processes, resulting in better control and implementation management (Russo & Reis, 2020c). In this regard, the decision-making process guides the detailed analysis of all the involved requirements, given the specificity of the technologies to be implemented within the organization.

Figure 4. Questionnaire to support the decision-making process
Source: Russo and Reis (2020d)

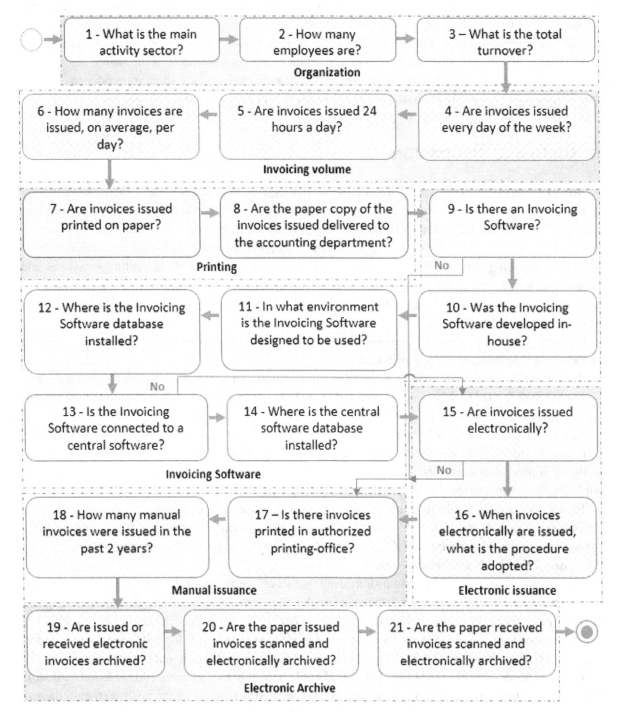

Figure 5. Decision process for the implementation of a certified ISP
Source: Russo (2019)

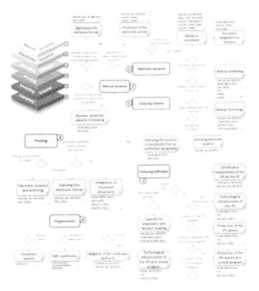

Concluding the decision-making process allows for the characterization of the initial requirements for the ISP (Russo, 2019) to be implemented and provides a foundation for defining additional requirements within the solution. As a result, the decision-maker will have a solid basis for aligning supported requirements and business processes represented in the ISP, including the method used to communicate invoice elements to the tax authority (Russo & Reis, 2020c). In this context, the strategic objectives of the BCP can be defined, regardless of the current effective implementation of ICT, to be less dependent on technological solutions and focus on what the organization wants rather than how it can be done (Russo & Reis, 2021).

Consequently, a program for the framework was developed, presented in Figure 6, which applies the questionnaire and proposes possible solutions for business continuity within the organization (Russo, 2019).

Figure 6 displays the program screen that allows you to answer the 21 questions created for the guide. The last tab allows you to view the summary of questionnaire responses and the inferred conclusions.

Hence, by considering the answers in the Organization domain (questions 1 to 3 in Figure 4), the decision maker can infer conclusions. The decision maker can get a perspective of the volume of data produced and the type of documents normally issued for the activity sector (invoices only, invoices and transport documents, budgets, etc.). Then, as depicted in the Organization sub diagram in Figure 5, other inferences are available. Based on the number of employees and the annual turnover, the program can present the Small and Medium-sized Enterprises (SME) classification, or even the mandatory use of a AT certified invoicing software.

With the SME classification and the annual turnover, the program can infer the investment capacity, supported by PORDATA data entitled *"Taxa de investimento: total e por ramo de atividade"* (Investment rate: total and by industry) (PORDATA, 2023). Therefore, considering the investment rate, the proposed solution can be leveled by the investment capacity of the organization, meaning simpler solutions to small enterprises (e.g. offsite backups to external hard drives or Network-Attached Storage (NAS)), or more elaborated solutions to medium enterprises (e.g. cloud storage, or remote backup services).

Figure 6. Decision support program
Source: Russo (2019)

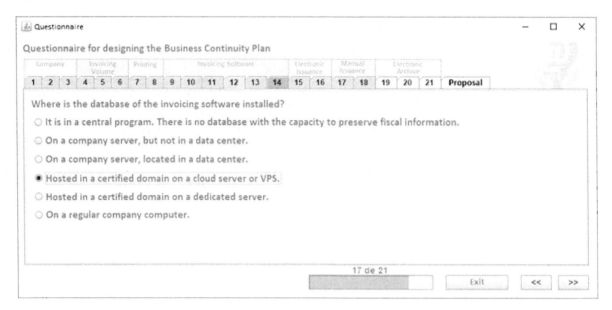

CONCLUSION

Recent legislative changes have prompted a shift in the invoice issuance and communication paradigm, highlighting the need for organizations to prepare for the challenge of innovation or technological adaptation in electronic invoicing and electronic archiving, ensuring continuity.

Given that the majority of SME are required to use an ISP certified by the AT, it was deemed relevant in the research path to contribute to the characterization of companies, departments, and ICT professionals in Portugal. Additionally, understanding the financial and technical constraints that influence the decision-making process regarding an ISP was considered crucial. The investment rate of companies represents approximately 20% of their turnover, and a portion of this investment is directed towards innovation and ICT capacity building.

In this context, fiscal legislation stipulates the formalities of financially relevant documents and the requirements that an ISP must fulfill to obtain certification from the AT. It allows for the issuance and archiving of documents electronically, as well as their electronic transmission to the AT. Understanding the correct procedures and requirements involved in the certification process of an ISP in Portugal was deemed important for companies developing an ISP. This understanding enables the incorporation of functionalities that enhance continuity into the design of the software solution. The certification of an ISP is a crucial factor that should be considered during its development and should be treated and managed as a project, particularly during the development phase.

Furthermore, the identification of constraints experienced by organizations in designing a BCP guided the literature review and the identification of questions within the context of supporting the design of a BCP guide. The literature review on the topic of business continuity considered a set of international standards and best practices. A methodology was proposed to provide organizations with a tool that systematically integrates processes and projects to streamline BCM within the organization. This methodology defines a strategy for ICT and can be followed by organizations implementing an ISP. Its mission is to encourage the adoption of concrete strategies and procedures for business continuity in organizations.

Consequently, a guide for the design of a BCP was proposed to reduce the perceived constraints faced by companies, enhancing the understanding of the BCP design process, the variables to be considered, and the legislative and regulatory aspects that guide decision-making, especially during the ISP design phase. The guide equipped organizations with a tool that allows for the consideration of technological and procedural alternatives for the systematic inclusion of business continuity within the organization.

In this perspective, the developed questionnaire supports the ICT strategy for ISP implementation by systematizing the underlying variables related to fiscal requirements, existing technological infrastructure, and implemented invoicing and archiving procedures. Through an analysis of the questionnaire responses, vulnerabilities and the need for business continuity and disaster recovery were identified.

The questionnaire supports the decision-making process, enabling companies to assess their level of knowledge regarding the involved requirements and guiding them towards essential questions when implementing an ISP. Consequently, the company can gain insights into the functionalities it intends to implement, the constraints or perspectives included for each question, and potentially recognize the level of human and financial resources required to achieve compliance for ISP certification or to acquire the most suitable solution for their company. As future work, the use of a case study is recommended to demonstrate the applicability of the proposed guide.

In conclusion, the shift in the paradigm of invoice issuance and communication has triggered the need for organizations to prepare for the challenges of innovation and technological adaptation in electronic invoicing and archiving. The COVID-19 pandemic situation has accelerated the need for digital transition, driving innovation in terms of new software products, marketing approaches, and business practices.

It is considered that the perceived constraints faced by organizations have been reduced through a better understanding of the variables they need to consider, the legislation and regulations they need to adhere to, as well as the human and technological resource requirements based on their investment capacity.

Furthermore, this work promotes continuity-by-design, encouraging the adoption of specific strategies and procedures to incorporate business continuity into the design of a resilient software program, where electronic invoicing and archiving may be relevant for organizations with an AT-certified ISP.

Thus, it contributes to the focus on the pillar of digital transformation (República Portuguesa, 2020), stimulating the digitalization of companies, consolidating scientific and technological knowledge, and transferring that knowledge to the economy.

REFERENCES

Al-shammari, M. M., & Alsaqre, F. E. (2012). IT Disaster Recovery and Business Continuity for Kuwait Oil Company (KOC). *Int. Conf. Inf. Technol. Syst. Manag. (ICITSM 2012)*, 25–31.

Arduini, F., & Morabito, V. (2010). Business continuity and the banking industry. *Communications of the ACM*, *53*(3), 121–125. doi:10.1145/1666420.1666452

AT. (2019, September 21). *Sobre o E-Fatura*. Retrieved from Portal das Finanças: https://info.portal-dasfinancas.gov.pt/pt/faturas/pages/sobre_efatura.aspx

Casola, V., Benedictis, A. D., Rak, M., & Villano, U. (2018). Security-by-design in multi-cloud applications: An optimization approach. *Information Sciences*, *454-455*, 344–362. doi:10.1016/j.ins.2018.04.081

Cerullo, V., & Cerullo, M. J. (2004). Business Continuity Planning: A Comprehensive Approach. *Journal Information Systems Management, 21*, 70-78. doi:10.1201/1078/44432.21.3.20040601/82480.11

CMMI Institute. (2020). *Introducing CMMI V2.0*. Retrieved abril 23, 2020, from CMMI Institute: https://cmmiinstitute.com/cmmi

Decree-Law no. 198. (2012, August 24). Decree-Law no. 198/2012, August 24th. Ministry of Finance.

Decree-Law no. 28. (2019, February 15). Decree-Law no. 28/2019, February 15th. Presidency of the Council of Ministers.

Herbane, B. (2010). The evolution of business continuity management: A historical review of practices and drivers. *Business History*, *52*(6), 978–1002. doi:10.1080/00076791.2010.511185

Hevner, A. R., March, S. T., Park, J., & Ram, S. (2004). Design Science in Information Systems Research. *Management Information Systems Quarterly*, *28*(1), 75–105. doi:10.2307/25148625

Hiles, A. (2007). An introduction to business continuity planning. In A. Hiles (Ed.), *The Definitive Handbook of Business Continuity Planning* (2nd ed., pp. xxiii–xxvii). John Wiley & Sons, Ltd.

Hiles, A. (2011b). Developing and implementing the written plan. In A. Hiles (Ed.), *The definitive handbook of Business Continuity Management* (3rd ed.). John Wiley & Sons, Ltd.

ISACA. (2018). *COBIT 2019 Framework - Governance and Management Objectives*. Schaumburg, IL 60173, USA: ISACA.

ISO 22301. (2019). *Societal security - Business continuity management systems - Requirements*. Switzerland: ISO.

ISO/IEC 27031. (2011). *Information technology - Security techniques - Guidelines for information and communication technology readiness for business continuity*. ISO/IEC.

ITIL. (2019). *ITIL Foundation ITIL* (4th ed.). AXELOS.

Jacobson, I., Ng, P.-W., McMahon, P. E., Spence, I., & Lidman, S. (2012). The essence of software engineering: The SEMAT kernel. *Communications of the ACM*, *55*(12), 42–49. Advance online publication. doi:10.1145/2380656.2380670

Mansol, N. H., Mohd Alwi, N. H., & Ismail, W. (2015). Managing organizational culture requirement for Business Continuity Management (BCM) implementation Using Goal-Question-Metric (GQM) approach. *2015 IEEE Conference on Open Systems (ICOS)*, 85-90. 10.1109/ICOS.2015.7377283

NFPA. (2020, April 28). *NFPA 1600® Standard on Continuity, Emergency, and Crisis Management*. Retrieved April 28, 2020, from National Fire Protection Association: https://www.nfpa.org/codes-and-standards/all-codes-and-standards/list-of-codes-and-standards/detail?code=1600

NFPA 1600. (2019). *NFPA 1600® Standard on Continuity, Emergency, and Crisis Management 2019 Edition*. National Fire Protection Association.

Object Management Group. (2014). *Kernel and Language for Software Engineering Methods (Essence), Version 1.0*. OMG. Retrieved from https://www.omg.org/spec/Essence/1.0/

Order no. 8632. (2014, July 03). Order no. 8632/2014, July 3rd. Ministry of Finance.

Ordinance no. 363. (2010, June 23). Ordinance no. 363, June 23th. Autoridade Tributária e Aduaneira.

Peffers, K., Tuunanen, T., Rothenberger, M. A., & Chatterjee, S. (2007). A Design Science Research Methodology for Information Systems Research. *Journal of Management Information Systems*, 24(3), 45–77. doi:10.2753/MIS0742-1222240302

PORDATA. (2023). *Taxa de investimento: total e por ramo de atividade*. Retrieved from PORDATA - Estatísticas sobre Portugal e Europa: https://www.pordata.pt/portugal/taxa+de+investimento+total+e +por+ramo+de+atividade-2302

Ramakrishnan, R. K., & Viswanathan, S. (2011). The importance of Business Strategy in Business Continuity Planingem. In A. Hiles (Ed.), *The definitive handbook of Business Continuity Management* (3rd ed.). John Wiley & Sons, Ltd.

República Portuguesa. (2020). *Plano de Ação para a Transição Digital de Portugal. Portugal Digital*.

Russo, N. (2019). *Guia de Apoio à Conceção de Plano de Continuidade de Negócio nas Organizações com Programas Informáticos de Faturação* [Master's thesis]. Instituto Politécnico de Setúbal.

Russo, N., & Reis, L. (2019a). Análise da Problemática Subjacente à Certificação de Programas Informáticos de Faturação. *CISTI'2019 - 14th Iberian Conference on Information Systems and Technologies*. 10.23919/CISTI.2019.8760638

Russo, N., & Reis, L. (2019b). Caracterização da Faturação em Portugal: Sob a perspetiva da certificação de programas informáticos de faturação. *Revista de Ciências da Computação [Online]*, 14, 67–84.

Russo, N., & Reis, L. (2020a). *Programas de Faturação Certificados - Guia Prático para a Continuidade de Negócio*. FCA - Editora de Informática.

Russo, N., & Reis, L. (2020b). Methodological Approach to Systematization of Business Continuity in Organizations. In L. C. Carvalho, L. Reis, A. Prata, & R. Pereira (Eds.), Handbook of Research on Multidisciplinary Approaches to Entrepreneurship, Innovation, and ICTs (pp. 200-223). IGI Global. doi:10.4018/978-1-7998-4099-2.ch010

Russo, N., & Reis, L. (2020c). Caracterização da Faturação Eletrónica em Portugal: sob a perspetiva da certificação de programas informáticos. *Revista Egitania Sciencia, 2*(27), 163-184. Retrieved from https://egitaniasciencia2.ipg.pt/index.php/egitania_sciencia/article/view/344

Russo, N., & Reis, L. (2020d, November 27). Updated analysis of business continuity issues underlying the certification of invoicing software, considering a pandemic scenario. *Advances in Science, Technology and Engineering Systems Journal, 5*(6), 845-852. https://doi.org/https://dx.doi.org/10.25046/aj0506101

Russo, N., & Reis, L. (2021). Certified Invoicing Software - Boosting Entrepreneurship, Innovation and Sustainability in the Post-COVID-19 era. In L. C. Carvalho, L. Reis, & C. Silveira (Eds.), *Handbook of Research on Entrepreneurship, Innovation, Sustainability, and ICTs in the Post-COVID-19 Era*. IGI Global. doi:10.4018/978-1-7998-6776-0.ch008

Sahebjamnia, N., Torabi, S. A., & Mansouri, S. A. (2018). Building organizational resilience in the face of multiple disruptions. *International Journal of Production Economics*, *197*, 63–83. doi:10.1016/j. ijpe.2017.12.009

Tangen, S., & Austin, D. (2020, March 13). *Business continuity - ISO 22301 when things go seriously wrong*. Retrieved from International Organization for Standardization: https://www.iso.org/news/2012/06/ Ref1602.html

Torabi, S. A., Giahi, R., & Sahebjamnia, N. (2016). An enhanced risk assessment framework for business continuity management systems. *Safety Science*, *89*, 201–218. doi:10.1016/j.ssci.2016.06.015

KEY TERMS AND DEFINITIONS

Business Continuity: Capability of an organization to continue the delivery of products and services within acceptable time frames at predefined capacity during a disruption (ISO 22301, 2019).

Business Continuity Plan: Business continuity plans are made up of documented procedures. Organizations use these procedures to respond to disruptive incidents, to guide recovery efforts, to resume prioritized activities, and to restore operations to acceptable predefined levels. Business continuity plans usually identify the services, activities, and resources needed to ensure that prioritized business activities and functions could continue whenever disruptions occur (ISO 22301, 2019).

Disaster Recovery: Is an organization's method of regaining access and functionality to its IT infrastructure, to continue the delivery of services that support business processes, after a disruptive incident.

Electronic Invoice: An invoice that has been issued and received in electronic format (Decree-Law no. 28, 2019) that must ensure the authenticity of the origin, the integrity of the content, and legibility.

Requirement: Need or expectation that is stated, generally implied or obligatory (ISO 22301, 2019). What the software system must do to address the opportunity and satisfy the stakeholders.

Risk Assessment: Overall process of risk (effect of uncertainty on objectives (ISO 22301, 2019) identification, risk analysis and risk evaluation.

Service Delivery: Is the manner in which a corporation provides users access to IT services, which include applications, data storage and other business resources.

Chapter 2
Changes of Communication in Biomedical Sciences and Health:
"Dr Google" and Hearing Loss

Helena Caria

https://orcid.org/0000-0002-2175-2303

School of Health, Polytechnic Institute of Setúbal, Portugal

ABSTRACT

Scientific and technological developments are unquestionable, being health in general and human genetics specifically, domains where high throughputs are gorgeous. The internet is changing the behavior of patients with clinicians and health organizations. The project of human genomes ensured new approaches to estimate cause-disease relations. Genotype-phenotype correlations and screening of mutation are now available to all researchers. However, the scientific data are also available to the patients, bringing them to the floor as active partners in therapeutic processes searching with "Dr. Google" for symptoms, treatments, and cures. Hereditary deafness is not escaping from this civil movement, being a good example of the behavioral change associated with the explosion of the internet, with the commercial offers of hearing aids and cochlear implants offers to be common nowadays. In the chapter, the authors discuss the internet of behaviors in the context of biomedical sciences as human genetics, and hearing loss.

INTRODUCTION

Biomedical and Health sciences are a domain of science where innovations have a direct impact on improving the wellbeing and disease management of patients, being impressive the number of scientific papers published every day in common scientific databases.

These areas have developed in parallel with other areas of a technological nature, and today there is a clear advance in terms of diagnosis associated with better equipment and better software. All these advances have contributed to the development of research and clinical support tools with high potential in supporting the improvement of health care. None of this is independent of the free online availability of scientific outputs.

DOI: 10.4018/978-1-6684-9039-6.ch002

Genetic diseases are good examples of conditions where the advances of the internet have changed the behaviour of patients who become aware of the scientific innovations regarding disease etiology, new treatments, and also the possibility to improve communication between people suffering from the same situation. Most of the persons with hearing loss present a genetic condition, thus this particular situation is a good study case for the behavioural changes associated with the internet revolution in health and biomedical sciences.

In the present paper, we also explore the relation of Portuguese hearing loss persons with the internet as a tool to learn about the genetic condition in general and deafness specifically.

Biomedical and Health Sciences and Internet

Considering the technical and scientific advances in Science in general and Biomedical Sciences in particular, is easy to understand that healthcare has also benefited from these advances mobilizing them to the relation with patients. Internet and all the digital tools increase the way researchers share innovations and mobilize them to the general public.

Scientific communications were in the hands of researchers who published their results in specialized scientific journals or presented their results at specialized congresses. These outputs were intended for colleagues, health professionals, and researchers in general. Patients and their families, as well as citizens in general, had little access to these articles and, above all, had difficulty understanding scientific jargon. This led to the Media, namely TV, and magazines general citizens assuming a role in the approximation between layperson and science (Iyengar et al., 2018). Currently, there is a notable effort on the part of researchers in the field of science communication, with many institutions having organizational structures specialized in sharing scientific results, directly contributing to decreasing the gap between scientific outputs and general citizens. Once again, none of this is independent of the online availability of scientific innovations and findings.

The Internet is a powerful information equalizer that radically transformed the way people identify and access relevant information for them and at some time brought a revolution to the spread of scientific results to all areas of society. The high point for online searches is focused on health issues, with most people already looking for information online about signs and symptoms, causes of diseases, diagnoses, and nutritional aspects (Lee, K et al., 2017), reaching 87% of the individuals between 14 and 22 years old in the USA (Ennis-O'Connor, 2018) with similar results for EU/UK citizens (Lee, K. et al., 2017).

Biomedical and Health sciences face today a huge advance in terms of diagnosis that is associated with the free availability of scientific outputs online. The rigor of scientific information continues to be guaranteed by scientific publications that currently follow an open-access policy, in the vast majority. Free access to credible information ensures greater access to innovative scientific outputs changing the way biological discoveries are shared with society and researchers, as already mentioned.

Increased access to information brings increased risks of misunderstanding or even misinformation. Misinformation has been defined as incorrect information spread, possibly, by accident (Scheufele, DA and Krause, NM, 2019; Swire-Thomson, B and Lazer, D, 2020). If incorrect information is intentionally spread is defined as disinformation and is associated with fake news.

Apart from the risks of misinformation or even disinformation, it is accepted that in general citizens rely on the information available online (Swire-Thomson, B and Lazer, D, 2020) to learn more about their health, being assumed that we are living in the age of Digital citizens.

BACKGROUND

Human Genetic: Jumping From the Lab to the Society

The approach between citizens and science innovations that the internet allows is driven by the advances in Biological Sciences, the basis for Biomedical and Health sciences, mostly due to the advances in Human genetics.

Human Genome Project: Starts the Digital Biology Era

The Human Genome Project (HGP) was a project in Biology aiming to comprehensively study all of the Human DNA, known as a genome (Gibbs, RA, 2020; www.genome.gov/human-genome.project). Starting by 1990 and completed by 2003, had a worldly presentation of the first sequence of the human genome by 2000. The HGP has accelerated the study of human biology and improved the practice of medicine by opening the door to the discovery and the molecular basis of inherited human disorders (Gibbs, RA. 2020). Molecular diagnostics, genetic screening, and even prenatal or pre-implantation diagnostic tests have become clinical realities.

Science to All: Impossible to Patent Human Genes

HGP also contributes to making science more accessible, encouraging the free distribution of research data, thus acting as a ground-breaking step for scientific research (https://www.yourgenome.org/stories/how-did-the-human-genome-project-make-science-more-accessible/). Technologists recognized that the HGP was the gateway to the new era of digital biology evidencing the jump from the earliest PC and Apple products in the 80's as the only computer in the laboratories of geneticists to the world scientific shares with internet (Gibbs, RA. 2020). The online accessibility of genetic information maintains this perspective of humanity with the impossibility regulated by legislation in different continents to patent genetic sequences or human genes. These laws are a consequence of the decision of the Supreme Court of the United States that ruled that human genes cannot be patented in the USA because DNA is a "product of nature". This decision invalidated more than 4300 human genes patented before 2013 (https://medlineplus.gov/genetics/understanding/testing/genep atents/), in what was followed by other countries. This situation has a scientific and a political dimension, meaning that currently any one of us can have free access to the complete sequence of a human gene. Directly, the free online access to knowledge about human genes contributes to the establishment of genetic diagnosis worldwide and is not countered by commercial companies (www.genome.gov/human-genome.project).

Combining the knowledge of the era post-HGP with the parallel revolution of Computer and Genetics sciences a new framework of biology was set upped (Gibbs, RA., 2020), existing several networks and data-shared centers supporting researchers and clinics that directly contributed to advances in genetic diagnosis.

The economic view of the advances in genetics and hereditary diseases, clearly illustrates the post-HGP impact, with the average cost of 3 billion dollars to sequence a whole genome by 2000, dropping to around 100-1000 dollars nowadays (Gibbs, RA., 2020).

Applications of the Genetics for the Society

Human genetics ensures knowledge about the structure and location of genes on chromosomes making it possible to study gene regulation and gene expression. The expression of genes guarantees the production of all the proteins that make up the human being. Proteins are a large family of molecules that cover all the functions of our cells and are thus responsible for our phenotype. Genes make up our genotype, with our genome being the total of our DNA.

Many of these DNA sequences are considered markers since they are common to all human beings, with small variations allowing that each individual can be identified by himself as a unique genetic profile. This highlights the genetic similarity between all people but also the importance of genetic variability in the normality of all of us.

The feasibility with which scientific information is currently shared allows different forensic medicine services to use batteries of markers to identify people through comparative analysis within a family. The identification of criminals has also become possible through the analysis of DNA obtained at crime scenes. Worldwide databases with restricted access allow sharing of this information to fight crime on a worldwide scale.

Digital Phenotyping: A New Standard

Another sign emerging in societies, in the human genetics post-HGP era, is Digital phenotyping which is rapidly growing in popularity (Jagesar, RR et al., 2014). Digital phenotyping companies are focused on recreative genetics and blow up due to the free online access to genetic outputs. Consequently, online paragons as "*Discover more about you and your family*" (https://www.Genomelink.io), or "*Find out what your DNA says about you and your family*"(https://www.23andme.com/en-int/) and "*The science behind your story*" (https://www.Ancestry.com) are commercial offers available online and intend to provide genetic information according to personal interests in knowing more about the genetic history of themselves and their relatives. Some companies, keep the DNA samples for a long time and provides updates on personal genetic susceptibility for specific diseases. The rapid development of this field accentuates the importance of the reliability and safety of online genetic information available (Jagesar, RR et al., 2014), and it's important to clearly clarify that genetic diagnosis is not a ludic activity.

Genetic Diseases

Imbalances in gene functions are associated with genetic diseases, thus, knowing genetic alterations of gene sequences is o good start to knowing the cause of so-called genetic or hereditary diseases. The group of genes is the so-called genome, thus genome research is crucial to understanding genetic diseases. Genes also are expressed through proteins, and these molecules are responsible for all the functions and characteristics of the body and, thus, are responsible for our phenotype.

The genetic diagnosis makes it possible to confirm the presence of a genetic condition and also, in many cases, to inform about prognosis and severity, as well as the association with syndromic cases, where several manifestations coexist leading to different alterations in different organs simultaneously.

Some diseases are syndromic, where the mutated genes express proteins that act in different tissues or organs simultaneously or isolated being designated non-syndromic conditions. Genetic diseases can also be monogenic when just one gene is altered or mutated to justify the condition or complex when several genes account for the final phenotype as occurs in the most common genetic forms of HL.

Ear Anatomy and Function

The ear is a bilateral sensorial organ of the human body known for its main role of hearing, which arises from the ability to transduce sound waves into a neural message (Heine, PA, 2004).

External sounds are captured by the external ear compartment and amplified by the tympanic membrane, due to its elastic properties, before being sent to the middle ear where the three auditory ossicles. These bones due to a mechanical amplification of the sound wave send it to the inner ear. The inner ear is composed by the cochlea, filled with lymph, the ideal media for propagating the sound wave to the Corti organ, the structure that occupies all the inside of the cochlea. Corti organs are specialized epithelial groups of cells with high levels of differentiation where ciliated cells, external and internal, exhibit cilia movement as a consequence of lymph movements. Cilia movements allow the circulation of potassium ion (K^+) within the Corti organ and end with chemical stimulation of the auditive nerve as well as devolution of K^+ to the lymph at *Stria vascularis* cells, a specific region of the Corti organ that allows with this recirculation of potassium, the restart of the whole hearing process. Thus, the ear has the function of switching a sound wave into a neurochemical signal that the brain integrates and understands according to each frequency and intensity of the sound.

Malfunction in any part of this symphony leads to HL, being neurosensorial Hl the type associated with the inner ear, essentially ciliated cells or auditive nerve.

Hereditary Hearing Loss

Deafness or Hearing Loss (HL) is a condition where the person is unable to have a hearing threshold of 20dB or better, in both ears (WHO, 2023). There are no geographical prevalence of HL and nearly 20% of the global population (WHO, 2023), live with some form of hearing disability. Considering lifespan, it's estimated that 34 million children and approximately 30% of people over 60 years of age have some form of HL (WHO, 2023).

Hereditary or genetic HL encodes all HL forms that can be inherited from parents and transmitted to siblings. These forms are associated with gene mutations or alterations that avoid the normal function of specific genes crucial to hearing and thus the malfunction leads to HL. There exist autosomal forms that will always be transmitted to siblings; recessive forms that will be transmitted to siblings only if both parents carry the mutation even if are not affected and also HL associated with sexual chromosomes and mtDNA.

The most common recessive gene whose mutations account for more than 50% of congenital cases is the GJB2 gene being 35delG the most common mutation in European populations (Beach, R et al., 2020).

Hereditary HL has seen great clinical advances with the introduction of neonatal auditory screening where suspected cases are confirmed with molecular diagnosis allowing early rehabilitation of newborns. Thus, rehabilitation nowadays starts before 1 year of life which brings higher efficacy rates (Purcel, PL et al., 2021)

Also, gene therapy is a promising curative approach for HL, as it can provide precise treatment to restore auditory function, which cannot be accomplished by traditional therapeutic options. As mentioned before, the cochlea is a highly complex structure composed of different cell types that possess distinct functions due to their unique gene expression patterns. Deafness genes can be divided into three major categories according to the cells of the Corti Organ where they are expressed: genes expressed in ciliated cells; genes expressed in supporting cells and those expressed in the stria vascularis and also few others expressed in other sites such as tectorial membrane and Reissner's membrane (Jeana, P., et al., 2023). Promising results are described in mouse model studies and also some clinical trials for humans have been implemented (REF) looking for a successful way to restore ciliated cells of the inner ear which would be the best way to restore age-related Hl and all neurosensorial forms of HL.

Nowadays genetic tests are made by using DNA sequencing techniques usually using rapid testing methods such as gene panels to search known gene mutations and rapidly characterize the genetic HL. These panels can include a huge number of genes, ranging from around 100 genes for non-syndromic HL to 288 non-coding variants (CeGAT-Genetic Diagnosis, 2023; Blueprint genetics, 2023), whose results are available in one month to more than 1000 different genes.

Genetic Information and Deaf Person

It's described that genetic testing provides positive psychological effects on deaf adults who learn why they are deaf (Palmer, C. et al., 2013). These effects are increased by tailored counselling strategies that promote genetic services to deaf individuals and culturally and linguistically appropriate genetic services. Although several studies have demonstrated that deaf individuals are interested in learning why they are deaf and seek genetic counselling (Palmer, C. et al., 2013) a low utilization of genetic services by deaf adults due to difficulties in understanding complex concepts of hereditary diseases.

Screening for genetic HL provides a huge amount of genetic information about known genes and mutations, and will also provide the identification of predisposing for example to age-related hearing loss and noise-induced hearing loss. Consequently, this information due to its complexity and eventual misunderstanding, requires complex counselling (Robin, N, 2004) to be effectively beneficial to citizens and must be done by an adequate geneticist.

Nowadays, with the spread of the internet where access to information become global as already discussed, the accuracy of scientific information understandable by Deaf people is an important aspect of the wellbeing of these individuals.

PURPOSE

The main goal of the present study is to analyse the change of behaviour induced by the Internet among Biomedical Sciences and Health considering as a case study People with Hearing Loss. E-health is a common approach nowadays and has increased due to the global potential of the internet. Thus, it seems to us to be relevant to analyse how free access to the information affects patients' empowerment regarding health conditions, especially considering genetic diseases and communication disabilities that are observed in hearing loss populations.

METHODOLOGY

The present paper follows an exploratory methodology with a quantitative approach.

Starting with a theoretical analysis regarding the advances of biomedical sciences and health, particularly human genetics since the end of xx century until today and the crucial role of the internet among all players, researchers, clinicians, patients, and the general population, we define a framework for

The convenience sample was selected among members of the Portuguese Association "OUVIR", who agreed to voluntarily respond to the questions. Only two inclusion criteria were defined: having some form of hearing loss and being an adult. Questions were organized in a Google form and all the responses were anonymous.

The OUVIR association defends the oral rehabilitation of people with deafness, advocating the use of prostheses and implants to ensure some type of oral communication. Being the OUVIR Association a Portuguese one, its members are only Portuguese speakers, naturally from Portugal or Brazil.

MAIN FOCUS AND RESULTS

Hearing impairment is one of the most prevalent disabilities, also because hearing deteriorates with age (van Wier, MF et al., 2021), associated with diverse etiology but currently most cases are of genetic origin (Chora, J et al., 2010). There are cases of congenital deafness associated with infections, such as rubella or measles contracted by pregnant women (Caroça, C et al., 2017). However, these cases are decreasing proportionally to the improvement in health care for populations. A small percentage of congenital cases can be associated with ototoxic antibiotics that damage the inner ear and even these situations have a genetic susceptibility to occur, as mentioned before. Major causes of genetics HL (WHO, 2022) include congenital or early onset childhood hearing loss, noise-induced HL, and age-related hearing loss (ARHL).

The impacts of HL are vast and quite harmful, presenting relevant societal costs and reduced options for employment (WHO, 2023). These impacts are associated with an important inability to communicate with others, delayed language development in children, and consequently a lower academic performance (WHO, 2023). Social isolation, loneliness, anxiety, and frustration, particularly among older people with ARHL are also relevant impacts described (Haider, H et al., 2017; Landry, EC, 2022), explaining why this form of HL is called social deafness. These symptoms are described as being more prevalent in older impaired individuals than in their peers without hearing problems (van Wier, MF et al., 2021), making this type of HL crucial in today's developed societies where around 25% of persons between the ages of 50 and 65 years have mild to severe hearing loss (van Wier, MF et al., 2021).

Scientific innovations to better treat ARHL are emerging, based on genetic and molecular mechanisms to develop potential drugs and targets to promote the regeneration of hair cells and synaptic pathways (Landry, EC et al., 2022). Meanwhile hearing aids are still the best approach for hearing rehabilitation (Hartl, RMB, 2020).

Many of the impacts of HL can be mitigated through early detection and precocious interventions including education programs and sign language instruction for children and their families. Communication with others through the Internet could replace some personal contacts and mitigate some negative outcomes (van Wier, MF et al., 2021) internet-based communication tools can improve the strategies for communication among hearing impaired persons, such as speech reading, hearing aids, and hearing assistive technology in general and can be offered by teleaudiology services (van Wier, MF et al., 2021;

Irace, LA et al., 2021). Internet access among older adults with ARHL is inconclusive regarding their normal hearing peers (Thorén, ES et al., 2013), with many data collected in a time when the internet was mostly accessed through desktop computers. Thus, was less intrusive in daily life and there are no doubts that the COVID pandemic sped up the shift to remote support (van Wier, MF et al., 2021).

Use of the Internet by Hearing Impaired People

Concerns about access to the internet by disabled people combined with concerns about misinformation in eHealth (Scheufele, DA and Krause, NM, 2019) arise from reports of insecurity and more anxiety.

Questions such as *How to select the information?*; *How to decide which site to trust?* or even *How can I be sure that the searched information applies to my case?*, are often reported by some participants in the our study.

Portuguese Spoken HL People: A Case Study

To better clarify this issue, we organized an online pilot survey with hearing-impaired adults. Our sample is composed of 24 participants, from Portugal (50%) and Brazil (50%), with more than 18 years (Table 1), 56,3% women. Most of the participants hold a bachelor's degree (62,5%), 31,3% have the secondary level and only one participant (6,2%) presents primary level education.

Table 1. Age distribution among the participants in our online survey

Age Class (Years Old, YO)	% of Participants
18-30 yo	12,5
31-45yo	31,3
46-56yo	37,5
57-64 yo	12,5
65 yo	6,3

The role of the internet for our participants is evidenced by one participant that says "*Internet it was enlightening*". Another participant indicates "*the help of technology, such as the internet, is important for me*".

When asked about the contribution of the internet to understanding their deafness, (Figure 1), our participants recognize (65%) that the internet is useful to understand their condition with 16,7% indicating that only sometimes feels to be supported by internet searches.

Regarding the advantages of online-seeking information about deafness, our participants refer that the internet "*Helps break down communication barriers*" or "*It helps a little*" and that internet is a "*Good access to information*". This feedback evidence the role of the internet as a strategic communication tool, mitigating social inclusion mentioned by one participant that indicate that to him internet is the "*Best means of communication to entertain with my hearing impaired friends and to search for information when I need it.*" Thus, the internet can also support psychosocial health by fostering social connection (van Wier, MF et al., 2021) in hearing impaired individuals.

Figure 1. Distributions in % of participant answering to the question "Did the internet help you to understand your deafness?"

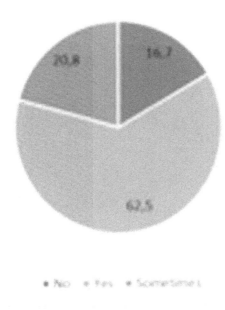

The contribution of the internet for communication between populations sharing similar conditions is also highlighted by our group of participants *"It is always useful to follow people who go through the same, and good doctors who delve into these issues, regarding research studies and real cases. I like to follow good professionals"* and *"It brings me accurate information, it helps me deal with my condition providing more peace of mind"* or *"Best means of communication to entertain with my hearing impaired friends and to search for information when I need it."*

In the context of complex chronic management, our participants valued the Internet as a useful source of health information that is similar to what is described to the general hearing population (Marcu et al., 2019).

The contribution of the internet for communication between populations sharing similar conditions is also highlighted by our group of participants *"It is always useful to follow people who go through the same, and good doctors who delve into these issues, regarding research studies and real cases. I like to follow good professionals"* and "It brings me accurate information, it helps me deal with my condition providing more peace of mind", what illustrates a change of behavior for HL patients as it is described by others (Brice, S. and Almond, H., 2023)

EHealth literacy is described as an internal barrier to online health information-seeking (Lee, K. et al., 2017), especially in domains like hereditary diseases among general citizens. For us, was important to study this effect on our group of HL citizens.

Our participants indicate (Figure 2) to search online (42%) about hereditary deafness at least some-times (29%).

Figure 2. Distributions in % of participant answering to the question "Do you search internet for information about the genetic causes of your deafness?"

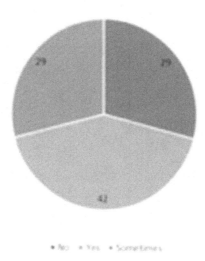

Thus, we can assume that the majority of the cases of HL in our participant's group are of genetic etiology. This justifies that the majority of our participants (54,2%) indicate to search online about genes and mutations associated with hereditary deafness (Figure 3).

Figure 3. Distributions in % of participant answering to the question "When you found out the genetic cause of your deafness, did you started search the internet about deafness genes and mutations?"

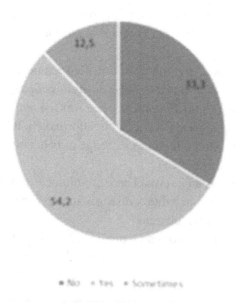

The majority of our participants (58,3%) indicate not getting confused about the genetics of deafness-information searched-online (Figure 4).

Figure 4. Distributions in % of participant answering to the question "When you search for online- information about the genetics of deafness do you get confused?"

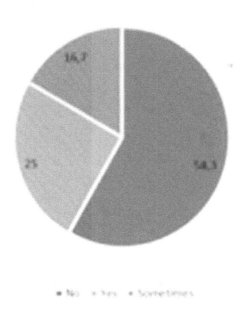

These results can be explained by the high-education level of our participants, a key element to fight eHealth illiteracy.

A large amount of inaccurate information between different online sources is a common barrier (Fiksdal, AS et al., 2014; Lee, K. et al. 2017; Ennis-O'Connor, M., 2018) to online searches, mostly due to the absence of quality filters and the volume of available information (Gibbs, RA., 2020). This can also be described as an intrinsic barrier to online health-information-seeking behavior pointing to the need to know credible and trust-prediction websites (Marcu et al., 2014; Fiksdal, AS et al., 2014; Swie-Thompson, B and Lazer, D, 2020). Supporting these findings, the majority of the participants report getting scared (41,7%), at least sometimes (12,5%), when accessing information about hereditary deafness (Figure 5).

Participants also mention the advantage of the Internet to actualized innovations and accurate scientific information in specialized websites: "*It serves as an aid because Deafness is not something so common and the Internet gives me information disseminated daily*", or "*Internet helped me clarify some contents*" and they also report that "*Accompanying specialized pages or deafness has helped a lot*".

Thus, the large majority of our participants indicated that before (42%) or after (50%) going to the ENT clinical consultation at least sometimes, respectively 33% and 29%, went online to search issues related to their health feedback (Figures 6 and 7, respectively).

Figure 5. Distributions in % of participant answering to the question "Did you already got scared when you search online information about the genetics of deafness?"

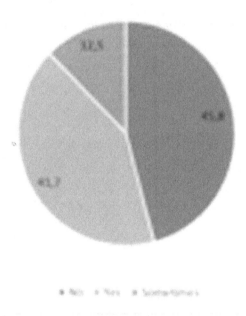

Figure 6. Distributions in % of participant answering to the question: "Before going to the ENT, do you go online to see the cause of your symptoms?"

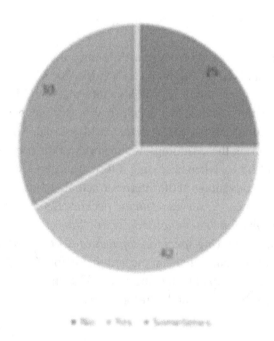

Figure 7. Distributions in % of participant answering to the question: "When you come from the ENT doctor, do you go to the internet to check the information that you got?"

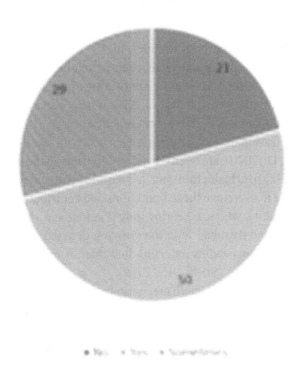

Our preliminary results are in concordance with others available (Mam et al., 2019; Masalky et al, 2014) and corroborate that hearing-impaired people valued the internet as a useful source of health information, as any other group of persons. Also, access to online- Health information and services through computer, smartphone, tablet, or smartwatch are transforming the doctor-patient relationship (Paglialonga, A et al., 2018) as we shown to occur also in our group of participants. Our participants mention the advantage of the Internet to actualized innovations and accurate scientific information in specialized websites reposting that "It serves as an aid because Deafness is not something so common and the Internet gives me information disseminated daily", or "Internet helped me clarify some contents" and also "Accompanying specialized pages or deafness has helped a lot".

One participant indicates "About deafness and other illnesses, I always consult the doctor and not Dr. Google!" or "Never went to the internet to search health issues" evidencing not navigational needs, since the survey was a Google form, but instead a choice by health professional support.

However, 93,8% of our participants report using Google as the main search tool for HL searches, which is in concordance with general online users (Fiksdal, AS et al., 2014; Lee, K. et al., 2017; Ennis-O'Connor, M., 2018; Sriram, R., 2019), validating the common expression of "Dr. Google" that reflected the role of Google for Health searches.

FUTURE RESEARCH DIRECTIONS

Challenges of Hearing Rehabilitation: From Technical Aid/ Cochlear Implant to Individualized eHealth Support

HL was neglected as a health priority for many decades, mostly due to its invisible non-life threatening nature (Swanepoel, D., 2020), and just recently has been recognized as an important global burden. Principal treatments, depending on the HL severity, are hearing aids and cochlear implants (CI), effective both to improve oral communication and also in general health and wellbeing, with oral outcome associated with social context (Chora, et al, 2012) and genetic etiology (Chora, J, et al, 2010). The limited availability of health professionals and the costs associated with these devices offered by centered service-delivery (Swanepoel, D., 2020), are been considered barriers to the worldwide spread of hearing technical aids (Hartl, RMB, 2020). eHealth tools, made possible by the Internet, are now responsible for new audiological services able to overcome these limitations and contribute to a rapid growth of eHealth services for adults and older adults who use hearing aids (Paglialonga, A et al., 2018; Swanepoel, D., 2020). Not everything is easy and trustable with the growing demand for online support what makes "Dr. Google" the focus of numerous studies reporting that there is evidence in the inability an online symptom checker to accurate diagnose (Sriram, R., 2019).

However, there are no doubts that the eHealth area promises to increase cost-efficiency, enable better access to care, and improve patient outcomes and satisfaction, with ample use of offline and Internet-based platforms (Paglialonga, A et al., 2018; Landry EC et al, 2022). The clinical uptake of mobile services is still limited compared to more mature offline and Internet-based platforms. Most of the eHealth services observed are related to the areas of education and information (42.5%) and hearing rehabilitation (40.4%), whereas 10.7% were related to screening and assessment, and 6.4% to general tele-audiology services (Paglialonga, A et al., 2018).

The growth of the global hearing implant market is supported by the growing prevalence of HL identified due to the early diagnosis and to the efforts by researchers and clinicians to enhance the hearing outcomes for patients, mostly due to aged societies as mentioned before (Hilbert, M, 2011). Furthermore, the increasing demand for CI among children and older adults across the globe is anticipated to create opportunities for the hearing market being expected to increase by us dollars 1,7 million in 2031 due to higher availability and improvements on online-technical support (Hilbert, M, 2011). Hearing Implant Market Report, 2023). Early genetic diagnosis and the introduction of medical guidelines for CI use would, definitively, boost the hearing aids market.

Researchers, technicians, and clinicians dedicated efforts to enhance the hearing outcomes of patients. Thus, the companies that have developed implantable hearing aids continue to work towards device improvement (Hartl, RMB, 2020). Further improvements in design are aimed at miniaturizing device components to allow use in more challenging otologic cases and work towards other fully implantable options.

Continuous advances in inner ear gene therapy provide new hope for treating Hereditary HL and insights into the treatment of other hereditary diseases, they can't be ignored for the future challenging of HL rehabilitation based on personal genetics treatments (Jiang, L et al., 2023).

CONCLUSION

The increase in offers, the task shifting in public health for HL and the availability of fee online information contribute directly to the growth of aggressive marketing companies (Fourie, C., 2023). The number of online retailer selling devices that are nothing more than cheap amplifiers, particularly on Facebook, (Fourie, C., 2023) associated with the increased marketing on TV and commercials outdoors points to a situation raising potential consumer protection issues especially since we are focused on impaired individuals.

These aspects reinforce the concerns of online Health misinformation, in particular regarding hearing health (Swire-Thompson, S and Laze, D, 2020).

The increase in eHealth literacy combined with the involvement of health professionals as arbitrators of credible web-navigational support (Ennis-O'Connor, M., 2018) would enable access to eHealth technologies and help patients to surpass these online tricks. (Fourie, C., 2023)

Personal digital technologies-smartphone linked, in particular, provides a powerful and ubiquitous tool for HL-telehealth support (Swanepoel, D., 2020; Irace, AL et al. 2021). Thus, eHealth solutions can therefore minimize and ever negate traditional barriers to hearing care, while enabling new models of care with greater access and affordability based on hearing tests conducted remotely in home settings (Masalki, M et al., 2014; Swanepoel, D., 2020), what also ensure credibility and security for patients. Acceptance of these new hearing health tools by healthcare professionals of conventional HL services, in UK, essentially to allow early adult diagnosis is well seen(Olson, A et al., 2022), which could have parallelism in other high-income countries.

REFERENCES

andMe organization. (2023). *Health + Ancestry Service.* https://www.23andme.com/dna-health-ancestry/

Ancestry Organization. (2023). https://www.Ancestry.com

Beach, R., Abitbol, J. M., Allman, B. L., Esseltine, J. L., Shao, Q., & Laird, D. W. (2020). GJB2 Mutations Linked to Hearing Loss Exhibit Differential Trafficking and Functional Defects as Revealed in Cochlear-Relevant Cells. *Frontiers in Cell and Developmental Biology*, 8, 215. doi:10.3389/fcell.2020.00215 PMID:32300592

Blueprint Genetics. (2023). *Comprehensive Hearing Loss and Deafness Panel.*https://blueprintgenetics. com/tests/panels/ear-nose-throat/comprehensive-hearing-loss-and-deafness-panel/

Brice, S., & Almond, H. (2023). Behavior change in chronic health: Reviewing what we know, what is happening, and what is next for Hearing Loss. *International Journal of Environmental Research and Public Health*, 20(8), 5605. doi:10.3390/ijerph20085605 PMID:37107887

Caroça, C., Vicente, V., Campelo, P., Chasqueira, M., Caria, M., Silva, S., Paixão, P., & Paço, P. (2017). Rubella in Sub-Saharan Africa and sensorineural hearing loss: A case control study. *BMC Public Health*, 17(1), 146. doi:10.118612889-017-4077-2 PMID:28143602

CeGAT-Genetic Diagnosis. (2023). *Hearing Loss: Analysis of all known genes associated with hearing loss.* https://cegat.com/diagnostics/rare-diseases/hearing-loss/

Chora, J., Matos, T., Martins, J., Alves, M., Andrade, S., Silva, L., Ribeiro, C., Antunes, M., Fialho, G., & Caria, H. (2010). DFNB1-associated deafness in Portuguese cochlear implant users: Prevalence and impact on oral outcome. *International Journal of Pediatric Otorhinolaryngology*, *74*(10), 1135–1139. doi:10.1016/j.ijporl.2010.06.014 PMID:20650534

Chora, J., Simões-Teixeira, H., Matos, T.D., Martins, J., Alves, M., Ferreia, R., Silva, L., Ribeiro, C., Fialho, G., & Caria, H. (2012). Two Portuguese Cochlear Implanted Dizygotic Twins: A Case Report. *Case Reports in Genetics*. doi:10.1155/2012/623860

Ennis-O'Connor, M. (2018). *Dr. Google Turns 20: How Has It Changed Healthcare?* https://www.linkedin.com/pulse/dr-google-turns-20-how-has-changed-healthcare-marie-ennis-o-connor

Fiksdal, A. S., Kumbamu, A., Jadha, A. S., Cocos, C., Nelsen, L. A., Pathak, J., & McCormick, J. B. (2014). Evaluating the Process of Online Health Information Searching: A Qualitative Approach to Exploring Consumer Perspectives. *Journal of Medical Internet Research*, *16*(10), e224. doi:10.2196/jmir.3341 PMID:25348028

Fourie, C. (2023). *How to identify & avoid hearing industry tricks that disempower you.* https://www.valuehearing.com.au/news/how-to-identify-and-avoid-the-hearing-industry-tricks-designed-to-disempower-you

Genomelink Organization. (2023). https://www.Genomelink.io

Gibbs, R. A. (2020). The Human Genome Project changed everything. *Nature Reviews. Genetics*, *21*(10), 575–576. doi:10.103841576-020-0275-3 PMID:32770171

Haider, H. F., Flook, M., Aparício, M., Ribeiro, D., Antunes, M., Szczepek, A. J., Hoare, D. J., Fialho, G., Paço, J. C., & Caria, H. (2017). Biomarkers of Presbycusis and Tinnitus in a Portuguese Older Population. *Frontiers in Aging Neuroscience*, *1*(9), 346. doi:10.3389/fnagi.2017.00346 PMID:29163129

Hartl, R. M. B. (2020). Implantable Hearing Aids: Where are we in 2020? *Laryngoscope Investigative Otolaryngology*, *5*(6), 1184–1191. doi:10.1002/lio2.495 PMID:33364411

Hearing Implant Market Report. (2023). *Future Market Insights.* https://www.futuremarketinsights.com/reports/hearing-implants-market

Heine, P. A. (2004). Anatomy of the ear. *The Veterinary Clinics of North America. Small Animal Practice*, *34*(2), 379–395. doi:10.1016/j.cvsm.2003.10.003 PMID:15062614

Hilbert, M. (2011). *GoOnline! Marketing in the hearing industry.* https://www.audiologypractices.org/go-online-marketing-in-the-hearing-industry

Irace, A. L., Sharma, K., Reed, N. S., & Golub, J. S. (2021). Smartphone-Based Applications to Detect Hearing Loss: A Review of Current Technology. *Journal of the American Geriatrics Society*, *69*(2), 307–316. doi:10.1111/jgs.16985 PMID:33341098

Jagesar, R. R., Vorstman, J. A., & Kas, M. J. (2014). Requirements and Operational Guidelines for Secure and Sustainable Digital Phenotyping: Design and Development Study. *Journal of Medical Internet Research*, *23*(4), e20996. doi:10.2196/20996 PMID:33825695

Jeana, P., Tai, F., Singh-Estivalet, A., Lelli, A., Scandola, C., & Megharba, S. (2023). Single-cell transcriptomic profiling of the mouse cochlea: An atlas for targeted therapies. *Proceedings of the National Academy of Sciences of the United States of America, 120*(26), e2221744120. doi:10.1073/pnas.2221744120 PMID:37339214

Jiang, L., Wang, D., He, Y., & Shu, Y. (2023). Advances in gene therapy hold promise for treating hereditary hearing loss. *Molecular Therapy, 31*(4), 934–950. doi:10.1016/j.ymthe.2023.02.001 PMID:36755494

Landry, E.C., Scholte, M., Su, P.M., Hostink, Y., Mandavia, Rovers, M.M., & Schilder, A.G.M. (2022). Early Health Economic Modeling of Novel Therapeutics in Age-related Hearing Loss. *Front Neurosci., 16*, 769983. http://doi.org/.769983 doi:10.3389/fnins.2022

Lee, K., Hoti, K., Hughes, J.D., & Emmerton, L. (2017). Dr Google Is Here to Stay but Health Care Professionals Are Still Valued: An Analysis of Health Care Consumers' Internet Navigation Support Preferences. *J Med Internet Res, 19*(6), e210:1-9

Masalki, M., Grysiński, T., & Kręcicki, T. (2014, January). Biological Calibration for Web-Based Hearing Tests: Evaluation of the Methods. *Journal of Medical Internet Research, 16*(1), e11. doi:10.2196/jmir.2798 PMID:24429353

Medline Plus organization. (2023). *Can genes be patented?* https://medlineplus.gov/genetics/understanding/testing/genepatents/

Olson, A., Maidment, D. W., & Fergunson, M. A. (2022). Consensus on connected hearing health technologies and service delivery models in the UK: A Delphi review. *International Journal of Auditing, 61*(4), 344–351. doi:10.1080/14992027.2021.1936223 PMID:34182863

Paglialonga, A., Nielsen, A. C., Ingo, E., Barr, C., & Laplante-Levesque, A. (2018). eHealth and the hearing aid adult patient journey: A state-of-the-art review. *Biomedical Engineering Online, 17*(1), 101. doi:10.118612938-018-0531-3 PMID:30064497

Palmer, C., Boudreault, P., Baldwin, E., Fox, M., Deignan, J., Kobayash, Y., Sininger, Y., Grody, W., & Sinsheimer, J. (2013). Deaf Genetic Testing and Psychological Well-Being in Deaf Adults. *Journal of Genetic Counseling, 22*(4), 492–507. doi:10.100710897-013-9573-7 PMID:23430402

Purcell, P. L., Deep, N. L., Waltzman, S. B., Roland, J. T. Jr, Cushing, S. L., Papsin, B. C., & Gordon, K. (2021). Cochlear Implantation in Infants: Why and How. *Trends in Hearing, 25*, 1–10. doi:10.1177/23312165211031751 PMID:34281434

Robin, N. (2004). Genetic testing for deafness is here, but how do we do it? *Genetics in Medicine, 6*(6), 463–464. doi:10.1097/01.GIM.0000144186.09716.CF PMID:15545740

Scheufele, D. A., & Krause, N. M. (2019). Science audience, misinformation, and fake news. *Proceedings of the National Academy of Sciences of the United States of America, 116*(16), 7662–7669. doi:10.1073/pnas.1805871115 PMID:30642953

Sriram, R. (2019). *Expert Insights: when to be cautious of Dr Google's diagnosis.* https://www.healtheuropa.com/when-to-be-cautious-of-dr-googles/93725/

Swanepoel, D. (2020). eHealth Technologies Enable more Accessible Hearing Care. *Seminars in Hearing*, *41*(2), 133–140. doi:10.1055-0040-1708510 PMID:32269417

Swire-Thompson, B., & Laze, D. (2020). Public health and online misinformation: Challenges and recommendations. *Annual Review of Public Health*, *41*(1), 433–451. doi:10.1146/annurev-publhealth-040119-094127 PMID:31874069

Thorén, E.S., Öberg, M., Wänström, G., Andersson, G., & Lunner, T. (2013). Internet Access and Use in Adults With Hearing Loss. *J Med Internet Res.*, *15*(5), e91. : doi:10.2196/jmir.2221

van Wier, M.F., Urry, E., Lissenberg-Witte, B.I., & Kramer, S.E. (2021). A Comparison of the Use of Smart Devices, Apps, and Social Media Between Adults With and Without Hearing Impairment: Cross-sectional Web-Based Study. *J Med Internet Res.*, *23*(12), e27599. doi:10.2196/27599

WHO, World Health Organization. (2023). https://www.who.int/health-topics/hearing-loss#tab=tab_1

Your Genome Organization. (2023). *How did the Human Genome Project make science more accessible?* https://www.yourgenome.org/

KEY TERMS AND DEFINITIONS

Biomedical Sciences: Are a set of natural sciences focused on Biology of the Human health and diseases that play a pivotal and essential role in health and healthcare. Ranging from more general to more specialized areas of knowledge, includes disciplines as anatomy and physiology, cell biology, biochemistry, microbiology, genetics and molecular biology, pharmacology, immunology, mathematics and statistics, and bioinformatics. Are essential to the investigation and understanding of many of the current controversies, concerns and dilemmas of modern life such as diet and health, food safety, new microbiological threats, the potential impact of various biotechnologies such as genomics, proteomics, stem cell technology and reproductive technologies on health and well-being, and associated ethical concerns. They are critical to the understanding of major biological processes, such as ageing, and health problems of international importance such as infectious diseases, cardiovascular disease, diabetes, obesity, cancer and dementia. Biomedical Sciences are the major focus of bioscience research and funding in the 21st century (*Subject Benchmark Statement UK Quality Code for Higher Education Part A: Setting and maintaining academic standards Biomedical Sciences, 2015*, https://www.rsb.org.uk/images/SBS-Biomedical-sciences-15.pdf)

Deafness: Also called hearing loss, is the condition where the individual is unable to hear some sounds. Considering the possible types, hearing loss can be Conductive, if associated with head bones from the outer and middle ear; Sensorineural if associated with the inner ear (Organ of Corti and ciliated cells) and the auditive nerve or even Mixed. Can be profound, severe, moderate or mild according to the severity. Can also be congenital if present at birth, post –lingual if present after acquision of language or even age-related if associated with older individuals.

E-Health: Refers to healthcare services supported by digital processes, communication or technology and also to healthcare practice using the internet. Also includes health applications (App) to provide information, collect data or ensure communication between patients and healthcare providers.

Hereditary Deafness: Also defined as genetic hearing loss, is a subarea of human genetics focused in genetic etiology of hearing loss situations. It studies genes, mutations and non-functional proteins responsible for some loss of hearing. Gene mutations can cause hearing loss in several ways. Genetic factors make some people more susceptible to hearing loss than others. Age-related hearing loss is accepted to have also a genetic background. Nowadays, this area is also focused in molecular genetic rehabilitation of ciliated cells in order to restore some kind of sensorineural deafness. Hereditary deafness distinguish between syndromic and non-syndromic forms, being the last ones the most common ones. Is also possible to distinguish between autossomic cases, where the mutations and genes related are in chromosomes 1 to 22; cases related to X or Y chromosome or even associated to mitochondrial genome. The genetic of the autossomic cases can be dominant or recessive, where the genes or mutations associated can be inherited just from one or by both parents, respectively.

Human Genetics: Is the area of genetics that study the inheritance as it occurs in human beings. Encompasses a set of overlapping areas as classical genetics, cytogenetics, molecular genetics, biochemical genetics, genomics, population genetics, developmental genetics, clinical genetics, and genetic counseling. This studies contribute to better understand hereditary diseases and to develop molecular diagnosis and better treatments.

Oral Rehabilitation: Is a process that encompasses a set of practices by which people with HL have optimizing abilities to present oral communication. Can include the use of auditive prosthesis or ear implants e.g. the cochlear implants. Several biomedical studies are going on combining molecular genetics and cells regeneration in order to restore ciliated cells whose damage is the major cause of sensorineural HL cases, as age-related hearing loss, due to the incapacity of Human being regenerate these cells.

Chapter 3
Codeflex 2.0:
Experience With Competitive Programming in Logical and Functional Paradigms

José M. Soares
Instituto Politécnico da Guarda, Portugal

Miguel Brito
Instituto Politécnico da Guarda, Portugal

Celestino Gonçalves
(iD) https://orcid.org/0000-0001-6144-0980
Instituto Politécnico da Guarda, Portugal

ABSTRACT

This work presents the design and implementation of Codeflex, a web-based platform and repository of programming problems, that enables the learning and practice of competitive programming in multiple programming language paradigms. The Codeflex programming platform performs automatic evaluation of submitted solutions for a very diverse set of programming languages, in real time, considering the specificities and requirements of different programming paradigms, being prepared to analyze and detect plagiarism in tournament submissions. The use of Codeflex platform in a real context allowed the test and validation of its functionalities. In particular, several programming tournaments were organized, for Haskell and Prolog programming languages – functional and logic programming tournaments, respectively, within the scope of programming curricular units of computer science undergraduate degree. The findings suggest that Codeflex is a valuable contribution in enhancing programming skills and providing an efficient evaluation system for educational and professional settings.

DOI: 10.4018/978-1-6684-9039-6.ch003

INTRODUCTION

As the demand for programming skills continues to grow in the tech industry and beyond, educators and coding enthusiasts face the challenge of finding efficient and effective ways to enhance their programming skills. At the education level, traditionally, the evaluation process has been a time-consuming and error-prone task for teachers who manually evaluate code submissions from students, making it difficult to provide timely feedback and detect instances of plagiarism (Luxton-Reilly et al., 2023). To address these issues, we present an extended version of Codeflex (Brito & Gonçalves, 2019), a web-based platform designed to provide a user-friendly, reliable, and efficient resource for competitive programming. The new implementation introduces advanced functionalities such as compilation and evaluation for Haskell and Prolog submissions, from functional and logical programming paradigms, imposing specific requirements on the compilation process. At the same time, it also provides a more manageable system to facilitate the process of inclusion of new programming languages, that might be added in the future, improves the visualization mechanisms of users submissions and adds plagiarism detection tools.

In this chapter we describe the development of the new version of Codeflex, its current features and benefits, and its potential to improve access to competitive programming resources and to facilitate the development of programming skills among students and enthusiasts.

To demonstrate the effectiveness of Codeflex, we conducted competitive programming tournaments at our school in the context of programming courses of the Computer Science undergraduate degree. The platform allowed us to compile and evaluate code submissions in real-time, providing instant feedback to students and enabling instructors to track their progress. Codeflex's plagiarism detection tools also facilitated a thorough analysis of code submissions and automatic identification of any instances of plagiarism, stating the importance of academic integrity in the competitive programming community. The successful implementation of Codeflex will contribute to the improvement of the process of code evaluation, making it easier for students to practice programming problems, benefiting their skill development, enhancing access to competitive programming resources, and provide teachers with an effective way to evaluate student performance.

The chapter is organized as follows. Next section discusses the state of the art, analyzing and comparing existing competitive programming platforms, followed by a section describing the work methodology used in the development of the programming platform. Then we expose the system design, particularly the requirements analysis and the characterization of the desired web-based programming platform and repository of programming problems. Next we will describe the developed programming platform, considering the overall architecture, the submission compilation process, prepared to accept submissions with demands and specificities of different programming paradigms, the plagiarism detection service and the tournament management module. Next section discusses and analyzes the achieved results with the platform operation in real context. Finally, we end the chapter with some conclusions that are drawn from the developed work and mention the work that is intended to be done in the future.

STATE OF THE ART

There is currently a great demand for professionals in the areas of Information Technologies, particularly in Computer Programming, for which there are greater difficulties in satisfying the needs of the market. The study and practice of algorithms, data structures and programming languages is thus essential and of prime importance for the solution of the problem and the only possible way in the construction and growth of the computers programming professional. The academic environment is one of the main ways to the introduction to the subject and where the fundamental concepts are worked and developed (Combéfis, 2022), but it is essential an increase in the number of exercises solved by the students, which is, however, far from being the ideal due to the work and complexity involved for their evaluation.

In this context, online platforms of competitive programming are of great importance as a way for learning, for practice, and for evaluation, and as such, there is a need for an application that can gather and group type problems to facilitate a greater immersion of users in solving problems using different programming languages of different programming paradigms. Its characteristics of automatic evaluation of programming problems and of competitive learning effectively improves students' motivation, performance and productivity, being, at the same time, an excellent pedagogical tool (Paiva et al., 2022). The authors of (Luxton-Reilly et al., 2023) emphasize the importance of the feedback given to students in this contexts, stressing the benefits in multiple examples and situations experienced by them. The diversity and availability of those automatic evaluation tools is considerable (Paiva et al., 2022) (Combéfis, 2022). According to (Wasik et al., 2018), and considering the main potential applications of such programming platforms, it is suitable to organize them into 6 classes: platforms for competitive programming contests, platforms for educational purposes, platforms for recruitment purposes, platforms for data-mining purposes, online compilers, and development platforms. The most representative class, quite outstanding in terms of available solutions, is the competitive programming class.

On the other hand, one of the major difficulties in using these programming environments is that they are essentially prepared and available for imperative programming languages. The so-called non-conventional or non-imperative programming languages, such as those of the logical and functional paradigms, have their own characteristics and specific requirements, always requiring a prior modification or adaptation of the programming environment provided by these pedagogical tools (Ribeiro & Guerreiro, 2008). For example, they are not usually compiled languages, being the execution of the programs obtained through an interpreter, where the programs are previously loaded. As a consequence, the existence in literature of experiences with programming languages of those paradigms are also less frequent. Still, we can mention some cases with Prolog (Ribeiro & Guerreiro, 2008) (Ribeiro et al., 2009) and with Haskell (Ribeiro & Guerreiro, 2008) (Kappelmann et al., 2022) (Strijbol et al., 2023).

Existing Competitive Programming Platforms

Analyzing existing market applications is essential to create a successful and effective platform for competitive programming. That study will help to identify the gaps and limitations in current application models and supports informed decision-making about suitable tools and technologies to incorporate into the desired solution.

To achieve this, we have analyzed the current and prevailing competitive programming platforms, chosen due to the coincidence of objectives and characteristics with the intended platform: LeetCode (LeetCode, n.d.), Codeforces (Codeforces, n.d.), HackerRank (HackerRank, n.d.), CodeWars (Codewars, n.d.), CodeChef (CodeChef, n.d.), CodinGame (CodinGame, n.d.), HackerEarth (HackerEarth, n.d.), CodeSignal (CodeSignal, n.d.) and TopCoder (Topcoder, n.d.). Table 1 summarizes the results of the study, where we highlight features related to different aspects of competition and tournament organization, recruitment, plagiarism detection, supported programming languages and relevance of platform utilization. Through this analysis, we identified each platform's strengths and weaknesses and determined which features and functionalities should be considered and implemented in our solution. This critical analysis to the existing platforms allowed us to gain a deeper understanding of the limitations and areas for improvement in the current competitive programming landscape.

The existing competitive programming platforms offer various strengths and limitations. Out of the platforms mentioned in Table 1, LeetCode and HackerRank stand out from the rest. The reason for their choice is related to the fact that they were identified as the most comprehensive and popular platforms due to their high rankings on similarweb and also because they have characteristics and objectives in common with the intended Codeflex platform. The LeetCode platform focuses primarily on interviews preparation and learning, but lacks the functionality for users to create tournaments. Yet, HackerRank is an excellent solution for competitive programming, but the functionality for creating tournaments does not allow them to be classified as private.

Table 1. Comparative analysis of competitive programming platforms

Platform Features	Codeflex	LeetCode	Codeforces	HackerRank	CodeWars	CodeChef	CodinGame	HackerEarth	CodeSignal	TopCoder
Tournaments	✓	✓	✓	✓	✓	✓	✓	✓		✓
Challenge practice	✓	✓	✓	✓	✓	✓	✓	✓		✓
Tournament simulation		✓								
Achievements				✓		✓				✓
Ranking	✓	✓	✓	✓	✓	✓	✓	✓		✓
Job search		✓		✓	✓		✓	✓	✓	✓
Networking		✓	✓	✓	✓	✓	✓	✓	✓	✓
Mock interviews		✓		✓	✓		✓	✓	✓	
Private tournaments	✓									
Plagiarism detection	✓			✓		✓		✓	✓	
Supported Programming Languages	5	14	17	>40	>55	>50	>25	>40	>70	>7
similarweb global rank [a]	--	2,411	8,135	9,356	23,245	33,989	53,253	57,745	104,641	111,579

[a]May 2023 (https://www.similarweb.com/)

In addition to the aforementioned platforms, two other categories of resources for competitive programming, equally important, can be highlighted: international programing contests and assessment tools focused mainly on education purposes. In the first case, we can mention the ACM International Collegiate Programming Contest (ICPC) (ACM/ICPC, n.d.), probably the most iconic, given its importance and relevance, but also Google's Coding Competitions (Google/CodingCompetitions, n.d.), Microsoft Imagine Cup (Microsoft/ImagineCup, n.d.) or Facebook Meta Hacker Cup (Facebook/HackerCup, n.d.). For the second category, programming platforms for education and academic purposes, we can point out Jutge.org (Petit et al., 2018), Mooshak (Leal & Silva, 2003), ArTEMis (Kappelmann et al., 2022), and TESTed (Strijbol et al., 2023), as illustrative examples with relevance, in some way, to our interest in the development of the Codeflex platform.

One of the main gaps in the existing platforms is the absence of private tournament functionality, which provides users with more flexibility in situations such as hackathons or onsite competitions and can also be used to evaluate and prepare students for programming courses. The Codeflex platform addresses this gap and enhances the user's experience by providing a competitive and flexible platform with private tournament functionality. By filling this gap, the Codeflex platform offers a valuable solution in the market of competitive programming applications.

WORK METHODOLOGY

The project was developed following the Scrum methodology, a widely adopted agile project management approach in software development (Sommerville, 2011). However, due to the solo nature of this project, the Scrum process was adapted to fit the requirements. The methodology was divided into three main stages: planning, execution, and monitoring.

The project goals and requirements were defined in the planning phase, and the product backlog was created. The backlog contained all the functionalities to be developed, including implementing plagiarism detection tools, adding Haskell and Prolog submissions evaluation, and redesigning the user interface.

During the execution phase, the product backlog was broken down into smaller tasks, which were prioritized and added to the sprint backlog. Sprints were held over two weeks, and at the end of each sprint, a review meeting was held to evaluate the progress and the completed tasks.

The monitoring phase consisted of constant feedback and monitoring to ensure the development process was on track. Meetings were held frequently with the project manager to discuss the platform's implementation and to identify any immediate issues.

Overall, the Scrum methodology provided a well-structured and inclusive approach to our programming platform development, ensuring its optimization and readiness for deployment in the intended context. All this methodology was applied using the Jira platform (Jira, n.d.).

REQUIREMENTS ANALYSIS

System requirements are a set of information about what the application is expected and allowed to do. Taking into account the importance of the requirements of a system, and after establishing their initial objectives, an analysis was carried out using the Unified Modeling Language (UML), a visual modeling language, in order to plan some of the use cases of the application.

The main objective is the design and implementation of a web-based platform and repository of programming problems, that enables the learning and practice of competitive programming in multiple paradigms. This practice consists of creating solutions to a given problem, proposed by other users, or in the context of a tournament, using code that is later validated and executed for predefined and unknown test-cases. If the code submitted by the user generates the desired solutions, the answer is considered valid. The main functionalities to consider are the following: (1) user authentication system; (2) challenges to practice without time constraints, organized by categories; (3) tournaments limited by time; (4) creation of private tournaments by the end user; (5) automatic evaluation of submitted solutions for a very diverse set of programming languages; (6) evaluation process adapted to the specificities and requirements of different programming paradigms (imperative, functional and logical paradigms) and (7) analysis and detection of plagiarism in tournament submissions.

The use cases diagram was designed to illustrate the system's functionality, and sequence diagrams were created to depict the flow of events between system components. Therefore, the use cases diagram of Figure 1 represents the information about the identified actors, programmer and contents manager, and the respective use cases of the system. It illustrates the interaction between the various types of users with the programming platform.

Figure 1. Codeflex platform use cases diagram

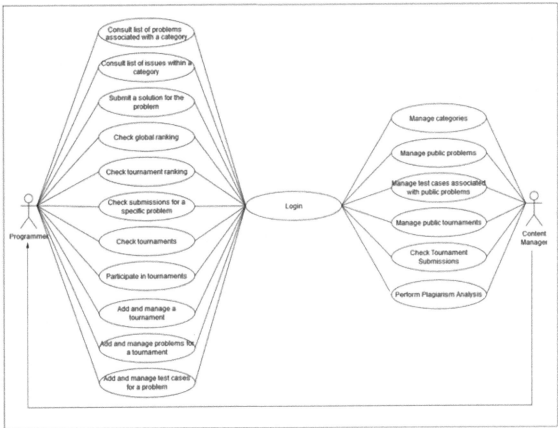

Use cases descriptions show the sequence of actions required for a user to complete a process. For illustrative purposes, the sequence diagrams for use cases "Submission of solution for one problem" and "Plagiarism Analysis" are presented next. The first, Figure 2, can be considered in two different situations: solving problems for practical learning purposes, or solving problems in the context of a competition. Figure 3 presents the sequence diagram relating to the plagiarism analysis process of submissions in a given tournament. The analysis is carried out by the contents manager, so it is not available to other users of the platform.

Figure 2. Sequence diagram: "Submission of Solution for One Problem"

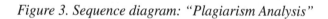

Figure 3. Sequence diagram: "Plagiarism Analysis"

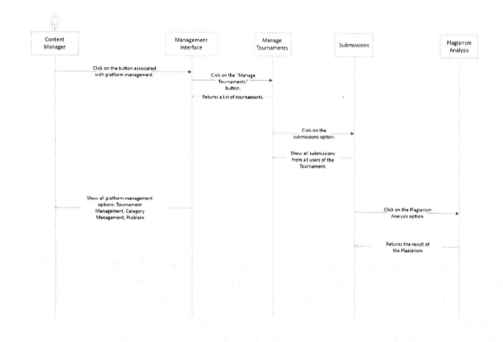

PROGRAMMING PLATFORM ARCHITECTURE

The platform's architecture is designed as a web services-based system, providing a modular and flexible approach that simplifies deployment and organization. All services are encapsulated within Docker containers (Docker, n.d.), as illustrated in Figure 4, which enhances scalability, portability, and reliability, making it easy to deploy and maintain the platform (Špaček et al., 2015).

Figure 4. Codeflex platform services in docker containers

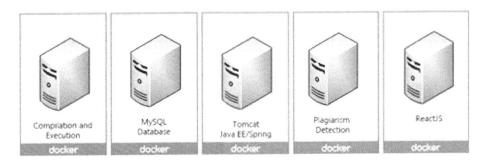

The platform consists of several components, as illustrated in Figure 5. The compiler server is responsible for compiling and executing code submissions from users. The platform's backend is built using Spring, connecting all the other services. The frontend, built using React, provides an intuitive user interface, and enables users to interact with the platform's functionality. The MySql module serves as the database management system, storing and retrieving data as needed. Additionally, the plagiarism detection system, which operates independently without affecting the platform's performance, is modular and designed to identify similarities between code submissions.

Figure 5. Codeflex platform architecture

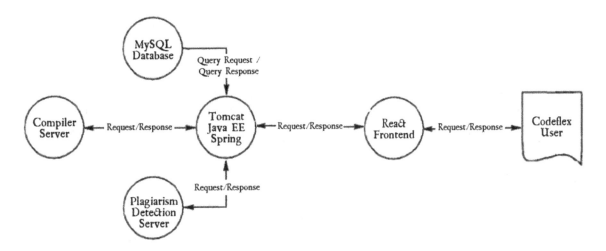

A token authentication system utilizing JavaScript Object Notation (JSON) Web Tokens (JWT) (JWT, n.d.) was implemented to ensure the platform's security. This system authorizes user access and transmission of information while maintaining the integrity and confidentiality of user data.

Overall, the system architecture design supports the project's objectives, enabling it to be modular and flexible, ensuring it is optimized and ready for deployment in the intended context.

Compilation Module

The compilation process depicted in Figure 6 shows the steps in compiling a user submission for a given programming exercise. The submission is securely transmitted to the backend via Secure Shell (SSH), a widely used protocol for secure remote access to a computer system. The backend then compiles the submission and generates a result for evaluation against the solution to the problem the user is solving.

Figure 6. Compilation process

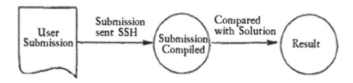

The compilation process involves specific instructions for different programming languages. For instance, next command outlines the instruction for compiling Java code using the "javac" compiler, assuming the file is in the location where the command is executed.

```
javac submission.java 2> compilerError;
```

This command compiles the file "submission.java". Any errors during the compilation process are saved in the file "compilerError". Once the file is compiled successfully, a file named "submission" is created. It can be executed using next command.

```
java submission 2> run_error.txt > runOutput.txt;
```

If an error occurs during the execution process, the output is stored in the file "run_error.txt". In contrast, successful execution is saved in the file "runOutput.txt". If no compilation errors occurs, the result stored in "runOutput.txt" is compared with the test cases to determine the final evaluation. If an error occurs, then the content of the file "run_error.txt" is sent back to the user to fix the submission.

Alternative Compilation Process

The compilation process for different programming languages can vary, with each compiler having unique parameters and methods of operation. Therefore, to support new languages on our platform, we developed drivers that could facilitate compilation while preserving the integrity of the existing processes. For instance, when importing libraries, it is often unnecessary for students to include commonly used libraries in their submissions. In such cases, we ensured that the required libraries were automatically included to simplify the compilation process. In other instances, some languages, such as Prolog, have unique features that make their code output more complex and, thus, require different evaluation methods. Our platform considers these differences, allowing for accurate and efficient compilation and evaluation of code across various programming languages.

The following example demonstrates the example of a Prolog code compilation and the need to use drivers to get the submission evaluated correctly. Let us consider the exercise represented in Figure 7:

Figure 7. Example of prolog problem

Define a predicate that, given an integer value, presents all integers from that value to 1. Examples:

```
?- problem1( 1 ).
1
true

?- problem1( 3 ).
3
2
1
true
```

A typical solution for this problem should be the code represented in Figure 8. However, the Prolog compiler does not work with this solution, as it enters interactive mode without producing an output that we can use to evaluate user submission.

To achieve the desired output, additional code must be added to the submission, which is not a default feature. While using an online Prolog compiler may work out-of-the-box, it is not the case for our situation when using a command line compiler. Therefore, to produce the desired output, the submission for this exercise should be as shown in Figure 9.

Figure 8. Solution to prolog problem

```
problem( 1 ):- write( 1 ).
problem( N ):-N>1, write( N ), nl, M is N-1, problem( M ).
```

Figure 9. Example of prolog driver

```
:-style_check( -singleton ).

%% Submission code from user

print_status( F ) :-
    ( F ) -> write( 'true' )
    ;( \+F ) -> write( 'false' ).

main :-
    print_status( problem( 3 ) ),
    halt.
```

The drivers come to solve this problem through code injection, transparently where needed. As shown in Figure 10, the platform uses the corresponding driver for the selected programming language to manage the compilation process when a submission is received. The user submission goes directly to the compiler if there is no need for additional code or libraries for the compilation process. This approach ensures that the platform is flexible and can accommodate new programming languages in the future without the need for changes to the compiler system.

Figure 10. Alternative compilation process

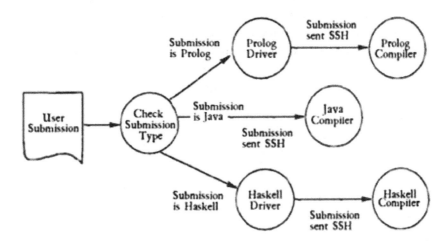

Plagiarism Detection Module

The problem of source-code plagiarism in submissions of solutions to programming problems in the academic context is a common reality that all teachers have to deal with. The problem is very complex, on the one hand because it is not just about comparing the degree of similarity of two solutions to the same problem, and on the other hand because it can be relatively easy to try to mask an original solution by changing some of its elements or components (Jiffriya et al., 2021). In the first case, students during their study, or during classes, may be confronted with the same solutions or equivalent solutions for a given problem under analysis and, on the other hand, code reuse may be a possibility or even a requirement (Albluwi, 2019). In the second case, it may not be trivial to unmask the plagiarized solution in which fraudulent mechanisms were used to hide plagiarism, such as those as simple as syntactic changes, or more elaborated as semantic changes, like the change of logical processes, the change of data structures, or even the inclusion of code that is never used, among others (Modiba et al., 2016). Thus, programming platforms must contribute to the solution of this extremely difficult problem, it is imperative.

Existing Tools for Plagiarism Detection

We started by carrying out a survey about the available plagiarism detection tools and their characteristics. The following tools were considered and analyzed: Sim (Gitchell & Tran, 1999), AC2 (Freire, 2008), MOSS (Schleimer et al., 2003), JPlag (Prechelt et al., 2002), Plaggie (Ahtiainen et al., 2006), Sherlock (Joy & Luck, 1999) and Holmes (Hage et al., 2013). Table 2 gathers and compares the obtained results.

To select the most suitable tool for plagiarism analysis, evaluating the advantages and disadvantages of the available tools is important. Out of the tools mentioned in Table 2, MOSS and Sim were selected due to their contrasting characteristics. They have different functionalities, and their suitability depends on critical criteria such as online/local availability, extensibility and performance. Therefore, it is crucial to consider the platform's specific needs before choosing one tool over the other. By carefully analyzing the features and capabilities of these tools, one can select the most appropriate option and ensure efficient and reliable plagiarism analysis. Considering online/local availability, MOSS is a third-party dependent online service, while Sim is a locally installed tool, offering higher stability. With regard to extensibility, although both platforms support several programming languages, only Sim offers extensibility, allowing the tool to accommodate additional programming languages. Finally, regarding performance, MOSS and Sim's performance depends on the submitted code's size and complexity. MOSS had longer response times than Sim for larger and more complex submissions in tests.

Table 2. Comparative analysis of plagiarism detection tools

Platform Features	Sim[a]	AC2[b]	MOSS[c]	JPlag[d]	Plaggie[e]	Sherlock[f]	Holmes
Open source	✔	✔	✗	✗	✔	✗	✔
Supported programming languages	8	9	40	12	1	3	1
Extensible to other programming languages	✔	✔	✗	✔	✗	✗	✗
Online/Local availability	local	local	online	online	local	local	local
Haskell support	✗	✗	✔	✗	✗	✗	✔
Prolog support	✗	✗	✗	✗	✗	✗	✗

[a]https://github.com/mpanczyk/sim
[b]https://github.com/manuel-freire/ac2
[c]https://theory.stanford.edu/~aiken/moss
[d]https://github.com/jplag/jplag
[e]https://www.cs.hut.fi/Software/Plaggie/
[f]https://github.com/diogocabral/sherlock

Extension of Sim Tool

After evaluating the aforementioned tools, a crucial decision was made regarding the solution for plagiarism detection. The tool should function locally to eliminate dependence on external services, which could potentially fail and compromise the platform's operation. Furthermore, the tool's extensibility was considered during the development process to ensure the platform could be updated and new programming languages could be supported. This required the tool to be expandable and adaptable to evolving platform needs.

Moreover, plagiarism detection methods fall into three main categories in the way they evaluate code, through structure, semantics, and behavior (Bejarano et al., 2015). Sim uses a structural analysis approach, calculating similarity by matching the code structure between two files (Gitchell & Tran, 1999).

Thereby, the Sim tool was chosen for plagiarism detection due to its favorable characteristics for integration with the platform, except for the lack of out-of-the-box language support for both the languages where the platform is going to be evaluated, Haskell and Prolog, but this was something fixable due to the tool being open-source and expandable.

Tokenization Process and Extending Sim for Haskell and Prolog Support

Plagiarism detection methods rely on various techniques for code analysis, and one critical step is the tokenization process. This process involves breaking down the source code into discrete units called tokens, which represent specific language elements such as keywords, identifiers, operators, and literals. Tokenization aims to simplify the code's structure and remove inessential information like white spaces and comments, before performing code comparisons.

After extending the platform to support languages like Haskell and Prolog, this adaptation process involves the creation of language-specific "dictionaries" for each supported language and recompiling the source code. These language-specific "dictionaries" explicitly specify language-specific operators, keywords, and syntax rules. For instance, in the Haskell "dictionary," the '--' notation is recognized as a comment indicator. This means that when the Sim tool tokenizes Haskell code, it understands that '--' signifies a comment, and can identify other language-specific operators and elements for accurate tokenization.

In essence, the Sim tool's adaptability to specific programming languages is made possible by the creation of language-specific "dictionaries." This flexibility allows the tool to accurately tokenize code written in various programming languages, enhancing its versatility and effectiveness in plagiarism detection across diverse coding environments.

Consider an example in a common programming language, such as C++, where a simple FOR loop like the following

```
for (i=0; i<max; i++)
```

is converted, and the final output after tokenization is represented in Figure 11.

Figure 11. FOR loop after tokenization

```
TKN_FOR TKN_LPAREN TKN_ID_I TKN_EQUALS TKN_ZERO
TKN_SEMICLN TKN_ID_I TKN_LT TKN_ID_MAX TKN_SEMICLN
TKN_ID_I TKN_PLUSPLUS TKN_RPAREN
```

This tokenization process allows the Sim tool to work with code from various programming languages as long as they can be tokenized in a similar manner. It allows the tool to be language-agnostic, meaning it can be used to compare files written in any programming language, as long as they have been tokenized.

Once the input files have been tokenized, the Sim tool uses a structural analysis approach to calculate the similarity between the two files. The tool compares the code structure of the tokens in each file rather than the files' content.

To address the lack of out-of-the-box language support for Haskell and Prolog, the Sim tool was thus extended by recompiling the code with modifications to support both languages. As a result, a bash script is required for each language, taken two files as input and returning the plagiarism analysis as the output:

```
haskell_sim file1.hs file2.hs, for Haskell, and
prolog_sim file1.pl file2.pl, for Prolog.
```

Plagiarism Detection Web Service Development

An automated plagiarism detection service was developed to interconnect the previously developed solution with the Codeflex platform to enable the detection of similar submissions and automate the process. This service was integrated into the Codeflex platform as a web service created to receive submissions through an Application Programming Interface (API), perform the analysis, and return the results to the platform. The service is also designed as a modular tool that can be used independently.

The plagiarism detection web service consists of the following steps:

- Reception of JSON submissions through the API;
- Removal of any folders from previous analyses;
- Creation of a temporary folder;
- Creation of folders for each user and subfolders for each problem;
- Decoding and storage of the submissions within the corresponding folders;
- Generation of commands for all the submissions of a problem;
- Evaluation of all submissions using the extended version of Sim;
- Delivery of the analysis report to the platform via API.

The plagiarism detection service organizes submissions by problem, creating subfolders and storing the paths of each one in an object for easy execution, as illustrated in Figure 12.

Figure 12. Auto generated script for submissions analysis

```
      }
    problem: '5',
     exec_path: ' ./tmp/RicardoAndrade/5/24.pl ./tmp/RicardoAndrade
  ./tmp/PauloTomasLda/5/29.pl ./tmp/PauloTomasLda/5/32.pl ./tmp/Paul
  ./tmp/Guilherme Alves/5/31.pl ./tmp/NobleLip/5/26.pl ./tmp/NobleLi
  ./tmp/RodrigoMartins/5/39.pl'
    },
    {
     problem: '6',
     exec_path: ' ./tmp/RicardoAndrade/6/30.pl ./tmp/NobleLip/6/37.pl'
    }
```

Subsequently, the script is executed for each problem. The result has the structure presented in Figure 13, which is sent back to the programming platform.

With the development of this web service, the Codeflex platform now has a reliable and efficient plagiarism detection system, ensuring the integrity of the evaluation process for all submissions.

Figure 13. Results of the plagiarism analysis service

```
File ./tmp/mustafa.bukh/4/7.pl: 25 tokens, 3 lines
File ./tmp/mustafa.bukh/4/14.pl: 25 tokens, 3 lines
File ./tmp/NobleLip/4/12.pl: 29 tokens, 6 lines
File ./tmp/NobleLip/4/13.pl: 29 tokens, 6 lines
File ./tmp/NobleLip/4/15.pl: 33 tokens, 7 lines
File ./tmp/Rui Condesso/4/16.pl: 27 tokens, 2 lines
File ./tmp/RodrigoMartins/4/18.pl: 27 tokens, 2 lines
File ./tmp/afonso/4/20.pl: 20 tokens, 2 lines
File ./tmp/DiogoNeto/4/33.pl: 33 tokens, 9 lines

./tmp/PauloTomasLda/4/4.pl consists for 100% of ./tmp/DiogoNeto/4/33
./tmp/Rui Condesso/4/16.pl consists for 100% of ./tmp/RodrigoMartins
./tmp/170509¼/41.pl consists for 86% of./tmp/raquelvidal99@hotmail
./tmp/NobleLip/4/15.pl consists for 76% of ./tmp/afonso/4/38.pl mate
```

Tournament Management Module

Tournament rules and ranking systems are critical components of the regulations governing competitive programming tournaments, enabling contestants, or students, to be evaluated fairly. The programming tournaments were implemented ensuring that they ran smoothly and complied with the stipulated regulations. The aim was to enhance the accuracy and reliability of the ranking system, while ensuring that the rules were applied uniformly to all participants.

A typical programming tournament consists of 4 problems, of increasing complexity, each one rated for one hundred points. To ensure that participants are evaluated fairly, problems are unlocked only when the previous one is solved, or has reached the maximum number of submissions allowed, as illustrated in Figure 14. In fact, each problem can be submitted up to a maximum of five times, allowing participants to refine their solutions before submission. However, if problem validation is unsuccessful, twenty points will be deducted from the final score for each unsuccessful submission. This process ensures that participants are challenged and incentivized to perform to the best of their capacities.

VALIDATION OF PLATFORM OPERATION IN REAL CONTEXT

This section describes the main functionalities and utilization in real context of the developed competitive programming platform. The platform was structured as a repository of problems in order to make available activities of programming practice and of competition. Some programming tournaments were setup, with two phases each, the preparation phase and the final competition, for Haskell and Prolog programming languages. The current implementation of Codeflex is available on GitHub at the following address: https://github.com/zemmsoares/codeflex2.

Figure 14. Codeflex tournament: Next problem unlocked

Programming Practice and Tournaments Setup

The first contact with the platform should be the user login or user registration, in this case with two possible profiles, programming practitioner or contents manager. Figure 15 illustrates the login interface of Codeflex platform.

Figure 15. Codeflex platform login interface

After user validation, the Codeflex dashboard is the interface that follows - Figure 16. The illustrated navigation menu is available to all users, except the management options which are intended only for the contents manager. The purpose of this interface is to capture attention and interest in using the platform. The possible activities of choice are learning, competition and organization. With learning, the user can explore a problem repository, organized by programming language, category and degree of difficulty, where he can find a suitable challenge to fit his preferences and learning needs. In the case of competition, a set of different programming tournaments are available where the user can sign up to compete with opponents, for example friends, colleagues or other users of the platform. With organization, and unlike other similar platforms, it is given to the regular user the possibility to organize private tournaments that can be shared through a private code.

Figure 16. Codeflex platform dashboard

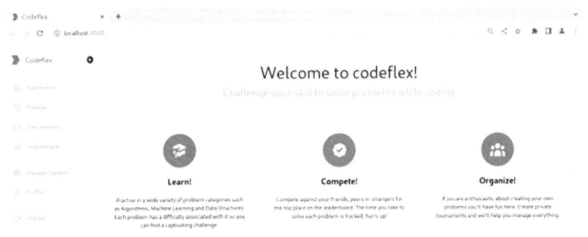

The interface to create a tournament, Figure 17, allows the configuration of a programming tournament, defining the name, description, duration and the access code that allows the tournament to be private.

To include a problem in a given tournament it is necessary to use the add problem interface, shown in Figure 18. The problem is characterized by indicating name, category, level of difficulty, description of the problem and the maximum score in points.

Figure 19 illustrates the problem interface, where the programming problem is characterized, and where the user develops and submits the respective solution. In this interface it is also possible to consult the submissions and the leaderboard of the problem.

When the code of a submission has compiler errors, Figure 20, the platform displays the respective compiler error information, aiding users in identifying and rectifying their coding mistakes before proceeding with a new submission.

Figure 17. Codeflex tournament creation interface

Figure 18. Add problem Codeflex interface

If the code compiles without errors, it is executed against an unspecified set of predefined test cases. The results are displayed to the user, offering a comprehensive overview of the submission's performance, indicating which test cases were successfully passed and which ones failed, and determining the submission total score.

In the interface of Figure 21, List of Available Tournaments, the user can register in available tournaments, as well as to view all the tournaments in which he is registered.

Figure 19. Codeflex problem interface

Figure 20. Codeflex problem submission compiler error

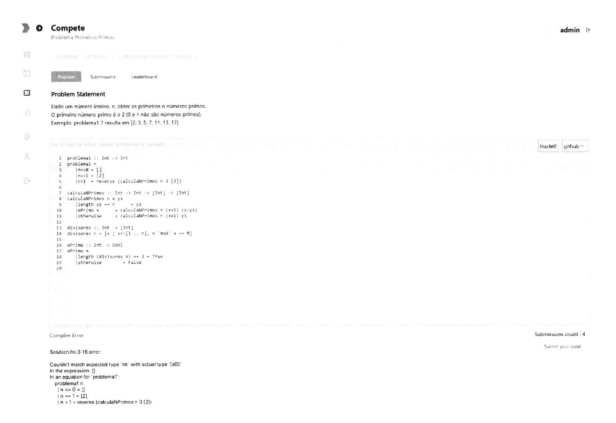

Figure 21. Codeflex available tournaments interface

The interface shown in Figure 22 visualizes all the submissions of the contestants of a given tournament. The contents manager has, thus, the possibility to view and follow the performance of participants in a given programming tournament.

The interface in Figure 23, Plagiarism Analysis Interface, presents to the contents manager the results of an analysis performed on all submissions for tournament problems, with the aim of plagiarism detection.

Figure 22. Codeflex tournament submissions interface

Figure 23. Codeflex plagiarism analysis interface

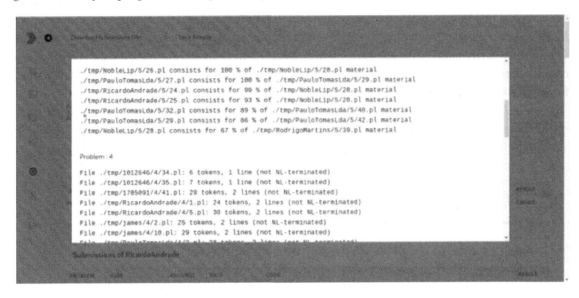

Functional Programming Tournament

In order to validate the operation of the Codeflex platform in a real context, two functional programming tournaments were organized within the scope of the Functional Programming course, taught in the third year of the Computer Science undergraduate degree at Guarda Polytechnique. The course is the first introduction of the students to the functional programming paradigm. Each tournament consists of two phases, the preparation phase and the final phase, which takes place a week after the first phase. Students enrolled in the tournament organize themselves into teams and try to solve a set of 4 problems with Haskell programming language, presented in an increasing degree of difficulty, Figure 24. For each problem, a maximum of 5 solution attempts are allowed, which will have to pass through a set of test cases, not known. The Haskell programming tournament was integrated as an assignment of the Functional Programming course and in itself accounted for 50% of the final grade in the course.

Figure 24. Problems of Haskell tournament

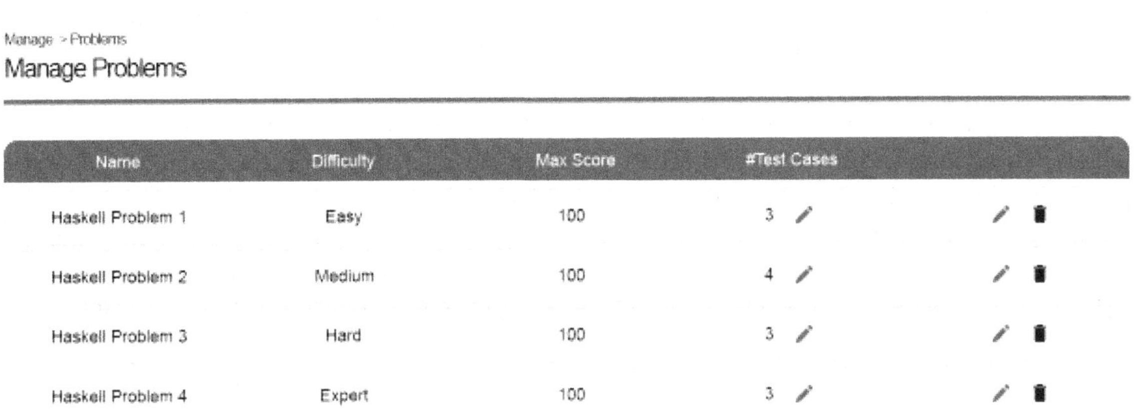

Manage > Problems
Manage Problems

Name	Difficulty	Max Score	#Test Cases			
Haskell Problem 1	Easy	100	3	✎	✎	🗑
Haskell Problem 2	Medium	100	4	✎	✎	🗑
Haskell Problem 3	Hard	100	3	✎	✎	🗑
Haskell Problem 4	Expert	100	3	✎	✎	🗑

The first Haskell tournament took place on June 6, 2022, with the competition between 4 teams of students. While this first experience went well and successfully evaluated the competing students, it also highlighted several issues, including a lack of visualization of user submissions by the tournament manager, a total crash of the platform due to an invalid character in a student submission, and no plagiarism detection of problem submissions. To address these issues, the platform underwent further development and improvements before the next tournament.

The second Haskell tournament, that took place on May 25, 2023, with the competition between 6 teams of students, worked as expected and validated the new features of the current Codeflex platform implementation, including plagiarism analysis of tournament submissions, presented in Figure 25.

Figure 25. Haskell tournament plagiarism analysis

```
codeflex2-plagiarism-1  |  ./tmp/PfJn/3/5.hs consists for 41 % of ./tmp/PauloTomas/3/7.hs material
codeflex2-plagiarism-1  |  ./tmp/luisbarros/3/3.hs consists for 41 % of ./tmp/PfJn/3/4.hs material
codeflex2-plagiarism-1  |  ./tmp/luisbarros/3/3.hs consists for 38 % of ./tmp/Satlher/3/6.hs material
codeflex2-plagiarism-1  |  ./tmp/Satlher/3/6.hs consists for 26 % of ./tmp/RicardoSousaJoao/3/10.hs material

codeflex2-plagiarism-1  |  ./tmp/PfJn/4/24.hs consists for 43 % of ./tmp/RicardoSousaJoao/4/54.hs material
codeflex2-plagiarism-1  |  ./tmp/PfJn/4/24.hs consists for 18 % of ./tmp/PauloTomas/4/33.hs material
codeflex2-plagiarism-1  |  ./tmp/luisbarros/4/18.hs consists for 28 % of ./tmp/PauloTomas/4/33.hs material

codeflex2-plagiarism-1  |  ./tmp/luisbarros/5/29.hs consists for 100 % of ./tmp/PauloTomas/5/41.hs material
```

Logical Programming Tournament

In the subsequent phase of the platform's development, a Prolog tournament was held as part of the Artificial Intelligence course, taught at Guarda Polytechnique in the first semester of the third year of the Computer Science undergraduate degree. The Artificial Intelligence course is the first introduction of the Computer Science students to the logical programming paradigm and the Prolog programming tournament was integrated as an assignment that, in itself, accounted for 10% of the final grade in the course. The tournament took place on December 14, 2022, and involved twenty-four students competing in 17 teams to solve four problems with Prolog programming language. Figure 26 presents the result of Codeflex automatic assessment of the submissions of one of the contestants, and Figure 27 the final leaderboard of the tournament.

The Prolog tournament aimed to validate the platform's potential and effectiveness in evaluating students performance and detecting plagiarism. The improvements made based on the findings from the first Haskell tournament ensured the success of this Prolog tournament.

The separate consideration of the Haskell and Prolog tournaments provides a clearer understanding of the platform's performance in different contexts. It demonstrates how Codeflex evolved and addressed the identified issues, making it a valuable tool for education and coding enthusiasts. The success of the three tournaments highlights the platform's effectiveness in evaluating performance and detecting plagiarism.

Figure 26. Assessment of submissions of one contestant of prolog tournament

Submissions of RicardoAndrade — Status: All

PROBLEM	USER	LANGUAGE	DATE	CODE	RESULT
CFinal Problema 1	RicardoAndrade	Prolog	15:27 14/12/2022	problema1(X,Y):- write(X), nl, N1 is X+1, N1 =< Y,problema1(N1,Y). problema1(Y,Y).	Correct
CFinal Problema 2	RicardoAndrade	Prolog	15:34 14/12/2022	pessoa(joana,borges,feminino,48,arquitecto). pessoa(francisco,silva,masculino,35,medico). pessoa(paula,sousa,feminino,28,medico). pessoa(martin,santos,masculino,23,quimico). pessoa(maria,sousa,feminino,24,programador). pessoa(martin,ribeiro,masculino,49,medico). pessoa(nelson,pereira,masculino,39,programador). pessoa(ana,silva,feminino,32,medico). problema2(A,B):- pessoa(A,_,_,X,Y), pessoa(B,_,_,Z,W), W==Y, Z>30, Z<50, X>30, X<50.	Incorrect
CFinal Problema 2	RicardoAndrade	Prolog	15:35 14/12/2022	pessoa(joana,borges,feminino,48,arquitecto). pessoa(francisco,silva,masculino,35,medico). pessoa(paula,sousa,feminino,28,medico). pessoa(martin,santos,masculino,23,quimico). pessoa(maria,sousa,feminino,24,programador). pessoa(martin,ribeiro,masculino,49,medico). pessoa(nelson,pereira,masculino,39,programador). pessoa(ana,silva,feminino,32,medico). problema2(A,B):- pessoa(A,H,_,X,Y), pessoa(B,J,_,Z,W), W==Y, H\=J, Z>30, Z<50, X>30, X<50.	Correct
CFinal Problema 3	RicardoAndrade	Prolog	15:50 14/12/2022	conversa([]). conversa([X,Y,Z|L]):- cao(X), cao(Y), gato(Z), conversa(L).	Incorrect
CFinal Problema 3	RicardoAndrade	Prolog	15:50 14/12/2022	cao(wouf). gato(miau). cao(wrrouf). gato(miaaauuu). cao(grr). gato(miauauau). cao(aoaouuuuuu). gato(ronron). conversa([]). conversa([X,Y,Z|L]):- cao(X), cao(Y), gato(Z), conversa(L).	Compiler Error
CFinal Problema 3	RicardoAndrade	Prolog	15:52 14/12/2022	cao(wouf). cao(wrrouf). cao(grr). cao(aoaouuuuuu). gato(miau). gato(miaaauuu). gato(miauauau). gato(ronron). conversa([]). conversa([X,Y,Z|L]):- cao(X), cao(Y), gato(Z), conversa(L).	Incorrect
CFinal Problema 3	RicardoAndrade	Prolog	15:53 14/12/2022	cao(wouf). cao(wrrouf). cao(grr). cao(aoaouuuuuu). gato(miau). gato(miaaauuu). gato(miauauau). gato(ronron). problema3([]). problema3([X,Y,Z|L]):- cao(X), cao(Y), gato(Z), conversa(L).	Incorrect
CFinal Problema 3	RicardoAndrade	Prolog	15:54 14/12/2022	cao(wouf). cao(wrrouf). cao(grr). cao(aoaouuuuuu). gato(miau). gato(miaaauuu). gato(miauauau). gato(ronron). problema3([]). problema3([X,Y,Z|L]):- cao(X), cao(Y), gato(Z), problema3(L).	Correct
CFinal Problema 4	RicardoAndrade	Prolog	16:23 14/12/2022	problema4([],[],_,_). problema4([X|L1],[Y|L2],N,[H|T]):- problema4(L1,L2,N,T), X>=N, Y>=N, X==Y.	Incorrect

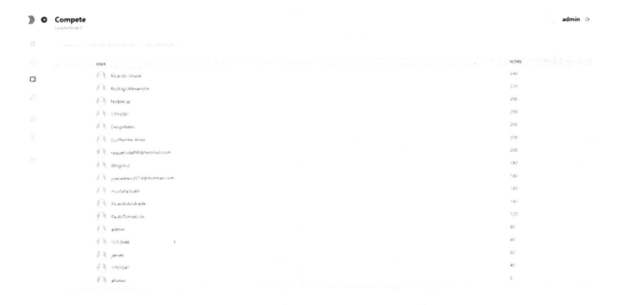

Figure 27. Leaderboard of the prolog tournament

CONCLUSIONS AND FUTURE WORK

Codeflex is a web-based competitive programming platform that enables the creation and participation of users in competitive programming tournaments through the automatic compilation and evaluation of code submissions. The programming platform has been extended and upgraded with new functionalities and updates, including improved visualization of user performance, expanded compilation capabilities, in order to support additional programming languages of different programming paradigms, and plagiarism detection features, to ensure academic integrity and to prevent from fraud.

The successful implementation and validation of Codeflex in real-world scenarios, such as the academic programming tournaments that were organized, for Haskell and Prolog programming languages, functional programming tournaments and logic programming tournaments, respectively, demonstrates its effectiveness and potential for future improvements. In fact, the Codeflex platform responded correctly to all requests, allowed the evaluation of students' performance in solving programming problems, and the results of their participation in the tournaments were used to classify them in the respective programming curricular units at Polytechnic of Guarda.

The Codeflex competitive programing platform is a valuable tool for both academic use and coding enthusiasts who wish to enhance their skills. Teachers can now evaluate students submissions more efficiently, while providing timely feedback, and coding enthusiasts can practice programming problems in a more reliable and user-friendly environment. Overall, this extended version of Codeflex represents a significant advancement in using technology to improve education and student performance evaluation while also serving the needs of the broader coding community.

As future work, and in order to achieve a more comprehensive programming platform, as a pedagogical tool that we want to be available to the various programming curricular units of the Computer Science course, we intend to continue expanding the set of available programming languages to learn and practice, as well as to enlarge and enrich the problem-type repositories, in the diverse programming languages available of the different paradigms considered.

REFERENCES

ACM/ICPC. (n.d.). *The ICPC International Collegiate Programming Contest*. Retrieved 5 29, 2023, from https://icpc.global/

Ahtiainen, A., Surakka, S., & Rahikainen, M. (2006). Plaggie: GNU-licensed Source Code Plagiarism Detection Engine for Java Exercises. *In ACM Proceedings of the 6th Baltic Sea Conference on Computing Education Research: Koli Calling*, 141-142.

Albluwi, I. (2019). Plagiarism in Programming Assessments: A Systematic Review. *ACM Transactions on Computing Education*, 20(1), 1–28. doi:10.1145/3371156

Bejarano, A. M., García, L. E., & Zurek, E. E. (2015). Detection of source code similitude in academic environments. *Computer Applications in Engineering Education*, 23(1), 13–22. doi:10.1002/cae.21571

Brito, M., & Gonçalves, C. (2019). Codeflex: A Web-based Platform for Competitive Programming. *14th Iberian Conference on Information Systems and Technologies (CISTI)*, 1-6. 10.23919/CISTI.2019.8760776

CodeChef. (n.d.). *CodeChef Platform*. Retrieved 11 21, 2022, from https://www.codechef.com/

Codeforces. (n.d.). *Codeforces Platform*. Retrieved 11 21, 2022, from https://codeforces.com/

CodeSignal. (n.d.). *CodeSignal Platform*. Retrieved 11 21, 2022, from https://codesignal.com/

Codewars. (n.d.). *Codewars Platform*. Retrieved 11 21, 2022, from https://www.codewars.com/

CodinGame. (n.d.). *CodinGame Platform*. Retrieved 11 21, 2022, from https://www.codingame.com/start

Combéfis, S. (2022). Automated Code Assessment for Education: Review, Classification and Perspectives on Techniques and Tools. *Software*, *1*(1), 3–30. doi:10.3390oftware1010002

Docker. (n.d.). *Docker: Accelerated, Containerized Application Development*. Retrieved 09 22, 2022, from https://www.docker.com/ Facebook/HackerCup

Freire, M. (2008). Visualizing Program Similarity in the AC Plagiarism Detection System. *In ACM Proceedings of the Working Conference on Advanced Visual Interfaces*, 404-407.

Gitchell, D., & Tran, N. (1999). Sim: A Utility For Detecting Similarity in Computer Programs. *SIGCSE Bulletin*, *31*(1), 266–270. doi:10.1145/384266.299783

Google/CodingCompetitions. (n.d.). *Google's Coding Competitions*. Retrieved 5 29, 2023, from https://codingcompetitions.withgoogle.com/

HackerEarth. (n.d.). *HackerEarth Platform*. Retrieved 11 21, 2022, from https://www.hackerearth.com/

HackerRank. (n.d.). *HackerRank Platform*. Retrieved 11 21, 2022, from https://www.hackerrank.com/

Hage, J., Vermeer, B., & Verburg, G. (2013). Plagiarism Detection for Haskell with Holmes. *ACM Proceedings of the 3rd Computer Science Education Research Conference on Computer Science Education Research*, 19-30.

Jiffriya, M., Jahan, M. A., & Ragel, R. (2021). Plagiarism detection tools and techniques: A comprehensive survey. *Journal of Science-FAS-SEUSL*, *2*(02), 47–64.

Jira. (n.d.). *Jira Software*. Retrieved 9 15, 2022, from https://www.atlassian.com/software/jira

Joy, M., & Luck, M. (1999). Plagiarism in Programming Assignments. *IEEE Transactions on Education*, *42*(2), 129–133. doi:10.1109/13.762946

JWT. (n.d.). *JSON Web Tokens*. Retrieved 9 15, 2022, from https://jwt.io/

Kappelmann, K., Rädle, J., & Stevens, L. (2022). Engaging, Large-Scale Functional Programming Education in Physical and Virtual Space. *Electronic Proceedings in Theoretical Computer Science*, *363*, 93–113. doi:10.4204/EPTCS.363.6

Leal, J. P., & Silva, F. (2003). Mooshak: A Web-based multi-site programming contest system. *Software, Practice & Experience*, *33*(6), 567–581. doi:10.1002pe.522

LeetCode. (n.d.). *LeetCode Programming Platform*. Retrieved 11 21, 2022, from https://leetcode.com/

Luxton-Reilly, A., Tempero, E., Arachchilage, N., Chang, A., Denny, P., Fowler, A., . . . Ye, X. (2023). Automated Assessment: Experiences From the Trenches. *ACM Proceedings of the 25th Australasian Computing Education Conference*, 1-10.

Microsoft/ImagineCup. (n.d.). *Microsoft Imagine Cup*. Retrieved 5 29, 2023, from https://imaginecup.microsoft.com/pt-pt

Modiba, P., Pieterse, V., & Haskins, B. (2016). Evaluating plagiarism detection software for introductory programming assignments. *Proceedings of the Computer Science Education Research Conference*, 37-46. 10.1145/2998551.2998558

Paiva, J. C., Leal, J. P., & Figueira, Á. (2022). Automated Assessment in Computer Science Education: A State-of-the-Art Review. *ACM Transactions on Computing Education*, *22*(3), 1–40. doi:10.1145/3513140

Petit, J., Roura, S., Carmona, J., Cortadella, J., Duch, A., Giménez, O., Mani, A., Mas, J., Rodriguez-Carbonell, E., Rubio, E., Pedro, E. S., & Venkataramani, D. (2018). Jutge.org: Characteristics and Experiences. *IEEE Transactions on Learning Technologies*, *11*(3), 321–333. doi:10.1109/TLT.2017.2723389

Prechelt, L., Malpohl, G., & Philippsen, M. (2002). Finding Plagiarisms among a Set of Programs with JPlag. *Journal of Universal Computer Science*, *8*(11), 1016–1038.

Ribeiro, P., & Guerreiro, P. (2008). Early Introduction of Competitive Programming. *Olympiads in Informatics*, *2*, 149–162.

Ribeiro, P., Simões, H., & Ferreira, M. (2009). Teaching Artificial Intelligence and Logic Programming in a Competitive Environment. *Informatics in Education*, *8*(1), 85–100. doi:10.15388/infedu.2009.06

Schleimer, S., Wilkerson, D. S., & Aiken, A. (2003). Winnowing: Local Algorithms for Document Fingerprinting. *Proceedings of ACM SIGMOD International Conference on Management of Data*, 76-85.

Sommerville, I. (2011). Software Engineering. Pearson Education Inc.

Špaček, F., Sohlich, R., & Dulík, T. (2015). Docker as Platform for Assignments Evaluation. *Procedia Engineering*, *100*, 1665–1671. doi:10.1016/j.proeng.2015.01.541

Strijbol, N., Van Petegem, C., Maertens, R., Sels, B., Scholliers, C., Dawyndt, P., & Mesuere, B. (2023). TESTed - An educational testing framework with language-agnostic test suites for programming exercises. *SoftwareX*, *22*, 1–6. doi:10.1016/j.softx.2023.101404

Topcoder. (n.d.). *Topcoder Platform*. Retrieved 11 21, 2022, from https://www.topcoder.com/

Wasik, S., Antczak, M., Badura, J., Laskowski, A., & Sternal, T. (2018). A Survey on Online Judge Systems and Their Applications. *ACM Computing Surveys*, *51*(1), 1–34. doi:10.1145/3143560

KEY TERMS AND DEFINITIONS

Automated Assessment: Automated assessment is the process of evaluating and grading programming assignments or coding tasks using computerized systems. It involves running tests and analyzing the output produced by the submitted code to determine its correctness and efficiency.

Code Submission: Code submission refers to the act of submitting source code or a programming solution for evaluation, typically in the context of programming competitions, coding challenges, or online learning platforms. The submitted code is usually assessed for correctness, efficiency, and adherence to the specified requirements.

Competitive Programming: Competitive programming is a mind sport that involves solving algorithmic problems within a specified time limit. Participants compete against each other to solve problems efficiently and produce correct solutions.

Compilation Process: The compilation process is the transformation of human-readable source code into machine-executable code. It involves several stages, including lexical analysis, syntax analysis, semantic analysis, code generation, and optimization. The result is an executable program that can be run on a computer.

Programming Paradigm: A programming paradigm refers to a specific approach or style of programming. It encompasses a set of principles, concepts, and techniques that guide the development of software. Examples of programming paradigms include procedural, object-oriented, functional, and logical programming.

Programming Platform: A programming platform, also known as a development platform, is a software environment or framework that provides tools, libraries, and resources for developing and running software applications. It often includes an Integrated Development Environment (IDE) and supports multiple paradigms and programming languages.

Programming Tournament: A programming tournament is an event or competition where programmers compete against each other to solve a series of programming challenges. Participants typically showcase their problem-solving skills and coding abilities within a given time frame.

Web Service: A web service is a software system or component that enables communication and interaction between different applications over a network, typically the Internet. It provides a standardized way for software components to exchange data and invoke functionality remotely using web protocols like HTTP.

Chapter 4
Cybersecurity and Business Continuity:
An Essential Partnership in an Era of Digital Interactions

Nelson Russo

https://orcid.org/0000-0001-9664-7148

Universidade Aberta, Portugal

ABSTRACT

As a consequence of the evolution and digital transition, organizations depend more on ICT. The behavioral data generated through interactions with ICT is collected and analyzed by the Internet of Behaviors (IoB). In this context, cybersecurity is a critical aspect of business continuity (BC). Organizations must ensure that their ICT systems are protected from cyber-attacks to avoid disruptions to their operations. A BC Plan (BCP) that considers cybersecurity can help ensure the continuity of critical functions in the event of a cyber-attack. Raising awareness is relevant to promote safe practices and minimize the risk of successful cyberattacks and loss of behavioral data. Therefore, a solid BC Management System (BCMS) should address cybersecurity and assure that all stakeholders are aware of the subjacent risks to a business and how to avoid, mitigate, or cope with them. This chapter presents the BC components and activities of a BCP that includes cybersecurity. Following the guidelines of the activities can result in avoiding or mitigating security risks by creating a successful BCP.

INTRODUCTION

Modern ICT architectures are key success factors for each and any digital transformation journey, enabling it to evolve iteratively, manage change holistically, and stimulate innovation (Rimboiu, 2020). Therefore, the practical usage of Information and Communication Technologies (ICT) as a driver of value creation, although at different levels of dependency, is nowadays unavoidable.

DOI: 10.4018/978-1-6684-9039-6.ch004

A network of physically connected objects called the Internet of Things (IoT) uses the Internet to gather and exchange data and information. Most objects process data autonomously in their equipment and preserve it until it is transferred to the cloud (Bhatti et al., 2019). The number of global IoT connections grew by 18% in 2022 to 14.3 billion active IoT endpoints. In 2023, IoT Analytics expects the global number of connected IoT devices to grow another 16% to 16.7 billion active endpoints (Sinha, 2023).

Global IoT connectivity is dominated by three key technologies: Wi-Fi, Bluetooth, and cellular IoT. Wi-Fi makes up 31% of all IoT connections and its technology is leading IoT connectivity in sectors such as smart homes, buildings, and healthcare. Bluetooth represents 27% of global IoT connections, gaining interest in the industrial sector, for example, by allowing for wireless communication between sensors/actuators and an I/O master (IoT Analytics, 2023). Cellular IoT makes up nearly 20% of global IoT connections.

The previous numbers of IoT object collecting data are a strong indicator that industrial data is being collected, but also personal or individual data. IoT devices can collect vast quantities of granular data about individuals' daily habits and activities. The data that these devices can collect include consumption rate data, location data, and health-related data, among other data types (Elvy, 2022). When utilizing and purchasing IoT products and services, people frequently have to agree to a company's privacy policy. These agreements can provide businesses permission to transfer and disclose specific data to third parties as well as utilize personally identifiable information for their purposes.

Now, data that was on the scope of the individual or related to using the IoT device is transferred, preserved, and probably processed and analyzed by business companies. Thus, it becomes part of the company's data, and the information has to be protected as data produced and owned by the company.

The Internet of Behaviors (IoB) refers to the collection and analysis of behavioral data generated by individuals through their interactions with technology, such as their internet use, social media activity, wearable device usage, and IoT device interaction. This data is used to gain insights into human behavior, as well as to drive personalized experiences and decision-making.

The use of IoT-generated data poses, or can be affected by the same risks as data natively collected by the companies. The Risk Assessment (RA) is an essential step toward the design of a solution that helps protect data (Păunescu & Argatu, 2020). Cybersecurity risks can be considered a class of risks. These risks can pose significant threats to the confidentiality, integrity, and availability of digital information and systems (Cremer et al., 2022), making cybersecurity an important aspect of risk management for organizations and individuals alike.

Cybersecurity and cyberattacks have been a focus of research in the last years (Russo et al., 2023), along with ICT strategies to provide specific planning guidelines for dealing with cybersecurity incidents (Veerasamy et al., 2019) (Pramudya & Fajar, 2019). In this context, cybersecurity fits especially within the scope of disaster recovery (Budiman et al., 2020).

Following a disruptive event or disaster, disaster recovery focuses on restoring and recovering crucial systems and data. By addressing possible threats and vulnerabilities that may appear during or after a disaster, cybersecurity plays a critical role in this process. Therefore, it is crucial to include cybersecurity measures as part of disaster recovery planning and implementation to guarantee the integrity, confidentiality, and availability of data and systems during the recovery process. To avoid or mitigate potential cyberattacks, that could hinder or threaten the successful recovery of systems and data, includes creating security controls, accomplishing vulnerability assessments, executing penetration tests, and strengthening security protocols. Organizations can improve their capacity to recover and resume crucial operations while lowering the risk of additional disruption or data breaches by including cybersecurity in disaster recovery plans.

Thus, as disaster recovery integrates into a broader concept of business continuity, cybersecurity fits within the scope of business continuity. Given the significant volume of data being gathered and the ongoing digital transformation that is driving changes across organizations, they must adapt to new technologies and processes, incorporating them into the contingency plans they might have. This underscores the importance of having a flexible Business Continuity Plan (BCP) that can adjust to these changes.

Therefore, this chapter presents the activities that should be considered for defining a BCP that includes cybersecurity, namely by addressing the Business Continuity (BC) components in the scope of a Business Continuity Management System (BCMS).

This chapter is organized into five sections. The first section introduces the problem, while the second section presents the literature review. The adopted methodology is integrated into the third section, and the results are presented and discussed in the fourth section. This section highlights the importance of each component and guides on how organizations can effectively address them. Finally, the fifth section presents the conclusions, emphasizing the growing importance of integrating cybersecurity into Business Continuity Management (BCM) processes. It emphasizes the need for organizations to prepare and respond to incidents or disruptions by following the structured BCM Model, which ensures the continuity of critical business functions while considering cybersecurity aspects.

LITERATURE REVIEW

In the development of the strategic BC guidelines, it was deemed relevant to include the best practices of ICT-related standards and the literature review on the subject of BC. The following sections present key definitions that support the results and provide a summary of the ICT-related standards utilized.

Resilience and Business Continuity

Business continuity is evolving from a focus on just recovering from disruptions to a broader focus on building resilience. This means that organizations are looking to not only recover from disruptions but also to minimize the impact of these disruptions and become more agile in their response, enhancing resilience.

In today's dynamic business landscape, organizational resilience is paramount to proactively tackle both internal and external challenges while ensuring uninterrupted operations. In this context, organizational resilience is the ability to enhance the continuity capacity of any system against disruptive incidents, whether they are internal or external variations, changes, disruptions, disturbances, or surprises (Sahebjamnia et al., 2018).

By fostering organizational resilience, businesses can prepare against the uncertainties of the ever-changing landscape. Therefore, BC is the foundation of protection against the unknown and the unpredictable, which can strike anywhere and at any time (Burtles, 2015). Resilience can be achieved by implementing actions previously prepared or by adapting normal functioning to a changing situation. Preparing the actions involves preparing a response. Therefore, the response is a reaction to an event with a prepared action plan, and recovery is a return to a normal state after an event, including limiting or eliminating potential threats (Ewertowski, 2022).

The mentioned preparation is enhanced with a defined strategy. A BC strategy usually comes together with a crisis recovery plan which involves the resumption and restoration of operation (Cook, 2015). Therefore, by defining the strategy and preparing the response, BC enhances the ability of a company to continue its operations even if some form of failure or disaster occurs (Bajgoric & Moon, 2009).

Thus, BC encompasses an organization's ability to plan and respond to disruptions and emergencies, including maintaining "business as usual" and returning to a normal state (Sterling, 2011). This includes understanding the organization's position in terms of BC and crisis management, specifically relating to staff, vendors, supply chains, and ICT operations and infrastructure (Aldianto et al., 2021). According to (Budiman et al., 2020), BC is a business objective to keep the business running smoothly. This definition is complemented by (Fani & Subriadi, 2019), which defines BC as an effort to ensure that critical business functions are available to customers, suppliers, and other entities, allowing the entity to access its functions within an organization when a risk occurs.

However, BC also establishes the necessary strategies, procedures, and critical actions to respond to and manage a crisis situation (Brás & Guerreiro, 2016). In their work, (Pramudya & Fajar, 2019) consider the overall objective of BC to be the identification, planning, implementation, and maintenance of various forms of operation if an organization faces a crisis.

The scope of BC management can be expanded by considering BC as a holistic management process that identifies potential impacts threatening an organization and provides a framework to create resilience and the capacity for an effective response that protects the interests of key stakeholders, reputation, brand, and value-creating activities (Ramakrishnan & Viswanathan, 2011).

Cybersecurity

Business continuity refers to an organization's ability to maintain its critical functions and services during and after unexpected events. This includes the preservation of data generated within the organization as well as data collected by systems or devices, such as IoT devices. Protecting this exposed data from threats is a major concern and presents a significant challenge.

Considering the evolving threat landscape, a proactive and robust cybersecurity strategy is vital to safeguard business continuity. As digital technologies become more prevalent in organizations, cybersecurity has emerged as a crucial aspect of BC. Organizations must ensure the security of their information technology systems and data to safeguard against cyber-attacks that have the potential to disrupt operations. Hence, BC plays a critical role in building an organization's cyber resiliency capabilities, thereby enabling it to counter future cyber Threats (Assibi, 2023).

In the face of constantly evolving threats, organizations must be prepared to respond swiftly and effectively to cybersecurity incidents that may impact their business continuity. Incidents are generally defined as adverse events or occurrences that disrupt normal business operations or compromise the security of information systems and data. In the context of cybersecurity, incidents typically refer to security breaches or unauthorized access to computer networks, systems, or data (Sarker et al., 2020).

Therefore, cybersecurity focuses on protecting internet-connected systems, including hardware, software, and data, from attacks, damage, or unauthorized access (Liu et al., 2022). Creating awareness on this subject involves understanding specific issues, such as cybersecurity risks, and taking proactive steps to address them.

By fostering awareness about cybersecurity risks and promoting safe practices, organizations can bolster their business continuity plans and protect against potential disruptions and data breaches. Maintaining business continuity relies on robust cybersecurity measures as cyber threats can disrupt operations, lead to data loss or theft, and damage an organization's reputation (Phillips & Tanner, 2019). A well-planned BCP combined with a strong cybersecurity program can ensure the continuity of critical functions and services in the event of a cyber-attack. Additionally, raising awareness about cybersecurity among employees is crucial to promote safe online practices and minimize the risk of successful cyberattacks.

Regardless of the specific context, immediate attention and response are required to mitigate the impact of cybersecurity incidents and minimize potential damages. Effective incident management involves timely detection, containment, investigation, and resolution of the incident, as well as implementing measures to prevent similar incidents in the future (Sarker et al., 2020).

In the pursuit of an effective security culture, organizations must prioritize incident management as a crucial component in mitigating cyber-attacks and safeguarding against potential damages. The subject of cybersecurity and mitigating cyber-attacks falls within the realm of security (Russo et al., 2023). Challenges in this area include fostering a security culture, acquiring expertise in information security and cybersecurity, and developing robust security policies (Moody et al., 2018).

The recovery of data following a security incident is a significant concern and also a challenge. A Security Management Program is proposed as a strategic guideline to reduce the probability of incident occurrence (Russo et al., 2023). This program addresses the objectives, scope, performance, and effectiveness of both the security management plan and the operational implementation of the plan (York & MacAlister, 2015).

The gathering and analysis of behavioral data introduce additional risks in terms of cybersecurity. Risk management must consider the risks, and the business impact analysis must address them. Cyber-criminals may target organizations and governments that collect and retain vast volumes of sensitive and personal data to steal or alter it for their illicit purposes. In addition, attacks that attempt to change or tamper with the results may target the algorithms that are used to analyze the data and make judgments. Strong cybersecurity measures must be implemented by organizations to safeguard data, as well as to guarantee the accountability and transparency of the algorithms being utilized, in order to handle these concerns when planning and structuring the continuity response.

In this context, an incident response plan or cybersecurity-based BCP has several advantages, such as minimizing business interruption by defining clear stages, actions, and responsibilities and raising overall company knowledge of cyber hazards that can help stop events from happening (Assibi, 2023). By proactively preparing its incident response, a company can ensure compliance with General Data Protection Regulation (GDPR) and other relevant regulations (Goldstein & Flynn, 2022).

Business Continuity Management

The collaboration between Cybersecurity and Business Continuity Management ensures a comprehensive approach to safeguarding against disruptions and protecting critical assets. According to ISO 22300:2021, which presents the vocabulary in the security and resilience field, BCM is the process of implementing and maintaining BC (ISO 22300, 2021). This process is strategic for the organization and is formalized in BCM. BCM prepares the organization to maintain the continuity of its services, business processes, or mission during a disaster by implementing a contingency plan (Syed, 2004).

However, an adequate and effective BCMS implementation is a challenging, demanding, time-consuming, and holistic process (Aronis & Stratopoulos, 2016). Hence, partial solutions to the implementation problem have been proposed with frameworks that address specific components of the BCM, to the detriment of a comprehensive framework with a holistic view of the BCM components (Winkler et al., 2010), (Järveläinen, 2013), (Torabi et al., 2014), (Torabi et al., 2016), (Soufi et al., 2019), (Gracey, 2019).

The authors Farr and Bailey (2019) explore the interrelation between various programs in the BC scope, such as operational risk management, the BCM, and other related programs, as an effective risk framework for an organization. In their research, Sahebjamnia et al. (2018) state that managers need to address the specific characteristics of the BCP and Disaster Recovery Planning (DRP) to implement effective BCM systems through both prescriptive and non-prescriptive approaches. However, regardless of the method used, some practical issues need to be addressed, such as attention to improvement and change processes or inappropriate approaches to process execution (Fernando, 2017).

With this objective and a focus on risk, Păunescu and Argatu (2020) outline the constituent elements of BCM and present the interactions between these elements aimed at ensuring the foundation for effective BCM. The planning of BC response significantly impacts the design of an effective BCP, followed by exercises, maintenance, and review of BCM, as well as its integration into the organizational culture.

Therefore, regardless of the approach used to describe BCM, a starting point for sustainability practice and BCM can be the PDCA cycle, involving planning, establishing, implementing, operating, monitoring, reviewing, maintaining, and continuously improving the effectiveness of the organization's BC processes (Urbánek et al., 2012).

Business Continuity Plan

The BCP is a crucial element within BCM, as it outlines strategies and procedures to respond to crises and disruptions while ensuring the organization's continued operations. Nevertheless, the usefulness of a BCP can be discussed (Putra & Nazief, 2018). The BCP should establish strategies, procedures, and documented critical actions to respond to a crisis situation or disruptive incident and define how the organization will proceed or recover its activities within a predetermined timeframe (Brás, 2018).

Strategies may cover organizational awareness or training on the BCP, as they are key aspects to enhance preparedness, responsiveness, and overall resilience (Burtles, 2016). Therefore, they are some of the preparatory steps for the BCP design and implementation (Păunescu, 2017). Recent research address security issues under the scope of a BCP, focusing on cybersecurity (Veerasamy et al., 2019) and the procedures for mitigating risk (Ohlhausen & McGarvey, 2018). The definition of security policies encourages a safety culture and suggests improving the preparation of ICT professionals with training and practice (Moody et al., 2018).

To develop an effective BCP that ensures the continuity of information systems, organizations must consider a methodology. There are many methodologies for designing a BCP, focused on ICT (Russo & Reis, 2020). A comprehensive BCP that ensures the continuity of information systems describes the authorities, responsibilities, procedures, and relocation strategies. The seven steps in the process to develop and maintain a comprehensive plan should include (NIST 800-34, 2010):

1. Develop the contingency planning policy;
2. Conduct the Business Impact Analysis (BIA);
3. Identify preventive controls;

4. Create contingency strategies;
5. Develop an information system contingency plan;
6. Ensure plan testing, training, and exercises;
7. Ensure plan maintenance.

In this process, it should be considered the roles, responsibilities, and necessary competencies for entity personnel and third-party service providers, solutions for various types of foreseeable disruptions, including cyber threats, and escalation thresholds (NIST 800-34, 2010). Should be taken into consideration immediate steps to protect personnel and clients and minimize damage, prioritization, and procedures for recovering functions, services, and processes and protecting critical information.

A methodology for a BCP with a focus on ICT is proposed which consists of five phases (Vasquez & Ortega, 2020):

- Understanding the organization;
- BIA;
- Risk identification;
- Preventive measures;
- Recovery strategies.

A BCP can include a cybersecurity plan, which, to be comprehensive, should focus on three key areas: prevention, resolution, and restitution (Fisher et al., 2017). To establish "cyber readiness", organizations need to address the following fundamental issues (Veerasamy et al., 2019):

- Implement a cybersecurity plan;
- Increase awareness and training in cybersecurity;
- Provide training to enhance cybersecurity expertise;
- Conduct risk assessments;
- Improve BCPs and Disaster recovery Plans;

Regarding the understanding of the organization, one of the key aspects in defining a BCP is properly identifying the company's assets and establishing which ones are critical to the business and will be considered priorities. This information should be collected before the BIA, and it is essential to have a clear understanding of the most critical processes and the sequence that should be followed when conducting a recovery within the BCP (Vasquez & Ortega, 2020).

When understanding the organization and effectively managing risk, organizations need to identify their stakeholders and understand their interests, needs, and concerns. Stakeholders refer to individuals, groups, or organizations that have an interest or impact on an issue or a decision. In the context of risk management, stakeholders can be affected by the risks posed to an organization, and they can also play a role in avoiding or mitigating those risks. This includes employees, customers, partners, shareholders, and regulatory agencies, among others.

Considering the stakeholders, businesses are becoming more interdependent with suppliers, customers, and partners (ITIL, 2019). It is important to understand these interdependencies and plan for potential disruptions to avoid cascading failures that could impact multiple organizations. In this context, to avoid risks, organizations can implement various risk management strategies (Torabi et al., 2014):

- Conducting regular risk assessments to identify potential risks and prioritize their management;
- Developing and implementing risk mitigation plans to reduce the likelihood or impact of identified risks;
- Providing training and awareness programs to educate employees and stakeholders about risk management and risk mitigation;
- Implementing strong cybersecurity measures to protect against cyber threats;
- Establishing crisis management plans and conducting regular drills to ensure readiness in the event of an emergency;
- Involvement and collaboration of stakeholders in the risk management process can also help in avoiding risks as they can provide valuable perspectives and insights.

Thus, the BCP must ensure that the organization's plans can sustain its operations in any incident. This implies that critical processes of the organization should be able to be restarted within an acceptable timeframe, as determined (Lindström, 2012).

However, the BCP is typically activated and executed simultaneously with the Disaster Recovery Plan (DRP) when necessary, restoring critical functions at alternate locations (Caballero, 2009). Thus, one of the main tasks of the ICT department's BCP, the DRP, is to ensure that incidents affecting the ICT infrastructure do not impact the availability of business processes dependent on ICT beyond an acceptable degree (Zambon et al., 2007).

Regarding the topic of predetermined timeframes, a key element in a BCP is the establishment of metrics for the Recovery Point Objective (RPO) and Recovery Time Objective (RTO) for data and applications. These metrics can be used by the ICT department when creating its DRP and configuring redundancy backups and external replication.

The RTO is crucial for selecting appropriate technologies that are best suited to meet the Maximum Tolerable Downtime (MTD) (Sambo & Bankole, 2016). The Minimum Business Continuity Objective (MBCO) is the minimum operational level for each key product that is deemed acceptable for the organization to achieve its business objectives (Torabi et al., 2014).

However, one of the key objectives of the BCP is to achieve the recovery of crucial business processes within a Maximum Tolerable Period of Disruption (MTPD) (Zambon et al., 2007). The MTPD is the time interval, following a disruption, within which the interrupted functions should be resumed (Torabi et al., 2014). The MTPD expresses the maximum acceptable downtime to ensure business continuity. The MTPD greatly depends on the organization's business objectives and, therefore, is defined within the business processes and determined by the business unit (Zambon et al., 2007).

In this context, a Business Continuity Objective (BCO) is used to define strategic and tactical goals for ensuring business continuity. The BCO should consider the minimum level of products and services that is acceptable for the organization to achieve its business objectives.

The BCP can also include plans for physical facility security, which require training in the plan, ensuring that personnel is familiar with the plan, its content/procedures, and their roles in the event of an incident, and conducting exercises at least once a year (Fisher et al., 2017).

Standards, Models, and Frameworks

This section provides an underlying perspective of the standards, models, and frameworks in the ICT field that address the topic of BC and are used to infer the results and provide discussion.

The International Organization for Standardization (ISO) has published the ISO 22301:2019, specifying requirements for implementing, maintaining, and improving a management system. It aims to protect, reduce the likelihood of occurrence, prepare, respond, and recover from disruptions when they arise (ISO 22301, 2019). ISO 22301 framework is the primary framework for BC adopted by organizations (Russo et al., 2023).

ISO 27001 provides requirements for an Information Security Management System (ISMS), as a tool for risk management, cyber-resilience, and operational excellence. Conformity with ISO/IEC 27001 means that an organization or business has put in place a system to manage risks related to the security of data owned or handled by the company and that this system respects all the best practices and principles (ISO/IEC 27001, 2023). ISO/IEC 27002: 2022 provides a reference set of generic information security controls including implementation guidance within the context of an ISMS based on ISO/IEC 27001 for implementing information security controls and for developing information security management guidelines (ISO/IEC 27002, 2022)

The Control Objectives for Information and related Technology (COBIT) provides a framework for enterprise ICT governance and management. The COBIT 2019 was explored since it provides a plan to enable companies and ICT organizations to respond to incidents and adapt quickly to outages (ISACA, 2018).

A set of best practices is provided by the Information Technology Infrastructure Library (ITIL). The ITIL 4 release provides guidance for tackling service management challenges and harnessing the potential of modern technology. It presents the Service Continuity Management Practices to guarantee the availability and performance of a service, in case of a disaster (ITIL, 2019).

NIST Special Publication 800-34 Rev. 1 provides guidelines for preparing and maintaining Information System Contingency Plans (ISCP). It assists organizations in understanding the purpose, process, and format of ISCP development through practical, real-world guidelines (NIST 800-34, 2010). The purpose of considered NIST SP 800-171 Rev. 2 publication is to provide federal agencies with recommended security requirements for protecting the confidentiality of controlled unclassified information (NIST 800-171, 2020).

The National Fire Protection Association (NFPA) 1600 standard provides fundamental criteria for preparedness and resilience through a program that addresses prevention, mitigation, response, continuity, and recovery (NFPA 1600, 2019).

The Capability Maturity Model Integration (CMMI) V2.0 is a set of best practices enabling companies to improve performance and propose planning mitigation activities to deal with significant disruptions in business operations (CMMI Institute, 2020).

These frameworks are divided into several objectives, practices, and activities. They provide a perspective on how disasters, crises, or disruptions in the provision of goods or services should be approached, guided, reduced, dealt with, or responded to.

METHODOLOGY

A two-phase approach was conducted to gather the strategic guidelines to implement or design a BCP focused on ICT and cybersecurity oriented. A protocol was followed to select and decompose a BCM Model that fits the research. The first phase is depicted in Figure 1.

Figure 1. First phase of the approach

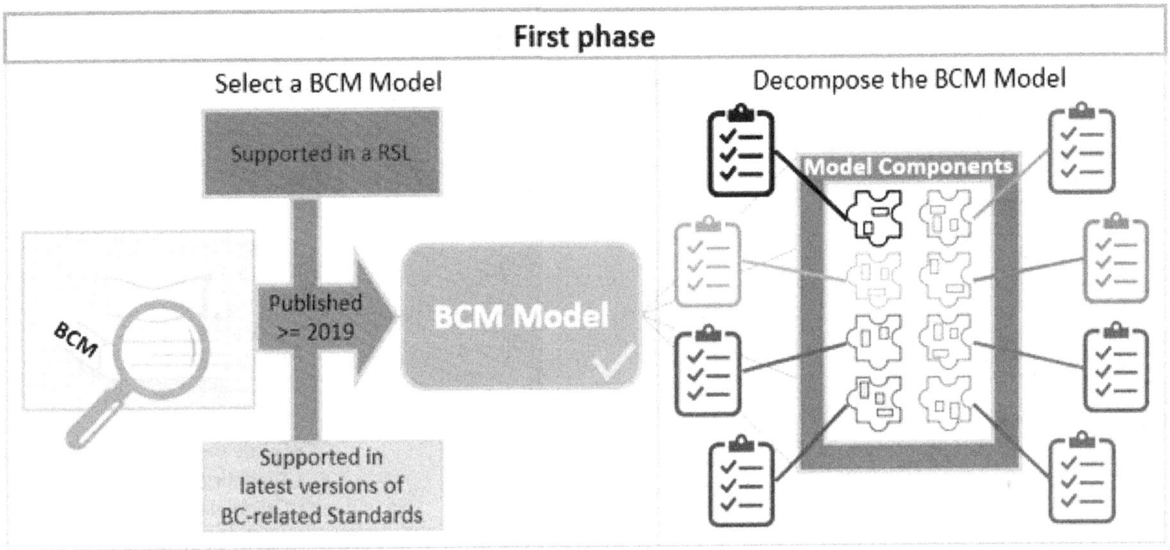

The BCM Model was required to be published after 2019, the date when the ICT-related standards were updated. The model must be supported by a systematic literature review conducted after 2019 and based on recent peer-reviewed publications. It was required that the model considers the latest versions of BC-related standards.

To select the BCM Model, the BC components must be identified and described in the model and follow the Plan-Do-Check-Act cycle. The BC component should be decomposable into assertive activities to design the guidelines in the second phase.

In the second phase of the approach, as presented in Figure 2, it is required to understand the relations between the BC components of the model.

The process included weighting the relative importance of BC components and activities conducted through the analyses of the number of quality publications that address a specific topic. This involved reading the standards to find common solutions and designations for the same issues, enhancing each guideline with the added value of each standard, and creating a compiled description of the guidelines.

Various criteria were considered during the assessment, including adaptability to different organization sizes and scalability, ensuring the capacity to grow evenly and support additional guidelines. The alignment with BC-related standards and relevant regulations was also taken into account.

The priority of activities, as either inferred or declared, along with the maturity level described in the BC Model and the description of BC activities, were all taken into consideration to outline the BC strategic guidelines. As part of this task, the objective is to define the guidelines and determine how they can be presented in accordance with the mentioned standards and literature.

Figure 2. Second phase of the approach

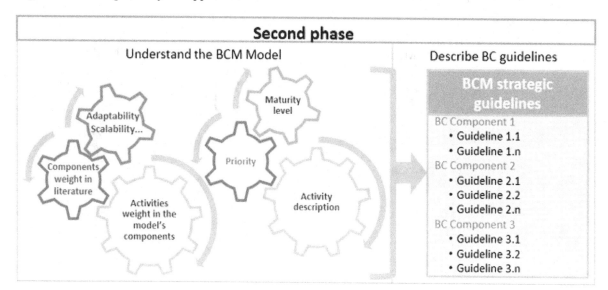

RESULTS AND DISCUSSION

As a result of the research, the following sections present the main guidelines to develop or improve a BCP that considers cybersecurity and a BC response to disruptions, whether they are incidents or disasters. It discusses the various components that a BCMS should address and their key objectives.

The BCM Model proposed by (Russo et al., 2022) is appropriate for this research since it was validated by ICT and BC professionals and by different sizes of organizations in representative business sectors. It is based on some of the most recognized international ICT-related standards and by a systematic literature review (Russo et al., 2023). The selected model is designed to help organizations prepare for and respond to incidents or disruptions that may impact business continuity.

The discussion highlights the importance of each component and guides on how organizations can effectively address them. It is important to note that the discussion presented is an overview of the BCM Model and its components. (Russo et al., 2022) present specific information on the results and discussions related to the demonstration, validation, implementation, or effectiveness of the model. The BCM Model is presented in Figure 3.

The Model defines the components that comprehend relevant areas in BCM and helps prepare the BC response to an incident or disaster interruption. According to (Russo et al., 2022), the components and their key objectives are:

- **Top Management Commitment** - describes the continuous management activities and follow-up to the BCM program. Top Management must demonstrate leadership, commitment, and support for the BCMS activities;
- **Understand the organization** - determine which factors are relevant to the organization's mission, which involve the delivery of products and/or services;

Figure 3. BCM model components
Source: Russo et al. (2022)

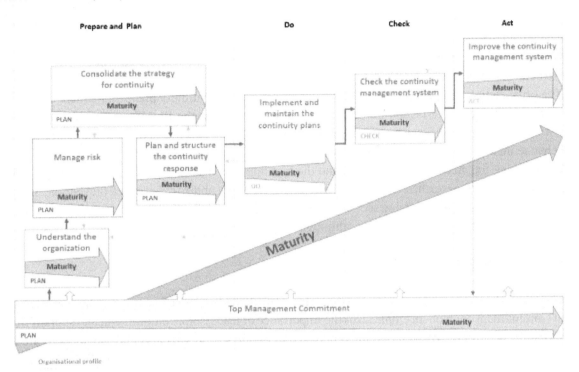

- **Manage risk** - determine risks according to the results of understanding the organization, assess the impact of risks and opportunities identified, and plan risk management according to the defined strategy;
- **Consolidate the strategy for continuity** – definition of strategies that allow the BC objectives achievement, according to requirements and available resources;
- **Plan and structure the continuity response** - develop and document the plans and the needed capacity to execute the defined strategy;
- **Implement and maintain continuity plans** - implement the assumptions, actions, solutions, and processes necessary to achieve the continuity objectives;
- **Check the continuity management system** - ensure that the organization verifies the adequacy and effectiveness of the BCMS and its requirements;
- **Improve the continuity management system** - ensure the organization determines the opportunities for improvement according to the verification performed and implements the actions necessary to achieve the continuity objectives.

In the BCM Model, each component consists of activities that need to be explored in order to accomplish the overall goals of the model components (Russo et al., 2022). To identify the context of the activities, the activities are organized into domains of action. Each domain therefore groups activities that describe, among other things, the possible actions, tasks, intentions, initiatives, projects, plans, strategies, or policies.

The starting point suggested in the Model is to understand the organization. It is essential for controlling risk and carrying out BIA because of its business operations and information flows (Russo et al., 2022). Given the peculiarities of the business, consolidating the continuity strategy, approved by top management with the help of the BC teams, includes a vision for ICT. The BCP's documentation and the establishment of the necessary circumstances for carrying out the BC response are under the planning and structuring of the continuity response.

The organization will then be ready to carry out and maintain continuity plans, implement solutions, and carry out exercises, tests, and training. It is crucial to examine the BCMS, especially concerning how it is being used. Verification, which emphasizes continuous improvement, corrective procedures, and change management, is decisive and necessary for enhancing the BCMS.

Considering the presented components and the fact that they also contribute to maintaining a valid response to incidents, nevertheless, some activities are more applicable to cyberattack prevention, mitigation, or preparedness. The following sections intend to present the main guidelines to develop or improve a BCP that considers the BC disciplines, although focused on ICT and Cybersecurity.

Top Management Commitment

Commitment to achieving objectives is a success factor in all management disciplines. The Top Management Commitment component emphasizes the importance of leadership, commitment, and support from Top Management for the BCM program, as depicted in Figure 4. The activities in these domains are the foundations of a successful implementation of BC and cybersecurity. It involves continuous management activities, follow-up, and the demonstration of support for BCMS activities.

In the leadership domain, the main focus is on defining the strategy, and objectives, and how they align and are achieved within the organization. This involves setting clear goals and directions for the business. Additionally, it includes defining and communicating policies that guide the actions and behaviors of individuals within the organization. Strong leadership in this domain ensures that the organization operates cohesively and effectively toward its strategic goals.

In the support domain, the focus is on establishing effective structures and processes to provide the necessary support for the business continuity program. This includes appointing individuals and teams and defining their roles, responsibilities, and authority to carry out their respective tasks. It also involves ensuring that compliance requirements are integrated and effectively communicated throughout the organization. The support domain further emphasizes the importance of conducting regular reviews and evaluations, supporting corrective actions, and fostering a culture of continuous improvement.

By providing adequate support, the organization enhances its ability to effectively implement and maintain its business continuity initiatives.

In the commitment domain, the emphasis is on demonstrating a strong commitment and active involvement in the management of business continuity. This includes showing dedication and support for the development and implementation of BCPs and initiatives. It also involves ensuring the availability of appropriate resources, including financial, human, and technological resources, to effectively address continuity needs.

By actively engaging in these efforts and providing the necessary resources, the organization strengthens its ability to effectively manage and respond to disruptions, ensuring the continuity of its critical business operations.

Figure 4. Top management commitment domains

Understanding the Organization

Understanding the organization is a decisive business factor. Having a deep understanding of the organization is crucial for making informed decisions, setting strategic goals, and achieving sustainable growth. This understanding influences strategic planning, resource allocation, risk management, adaptability, and overall organizational effectiveness.

Therefore, it is important to understand the defined strategy, mission, objectives, and obligations to prioritize the most important issues that condition continuity. At a lower level, it is relevant to understand the organization's structures, business functions, requirements, and responsibilities. Identification of the organizational culture and individual behavior is paramount, along with the description of the necessary skills of human resources and their training. Figure 5 shows the domains required to understand the organization.

In the Process and Technology domains, it is essential to identify various elements. This includes recognizing the services offered, the infrastructure and assets in place, as well as the technology and applications used. Furthermore, it is important to identify the products and services provided by the organization, along with their associated processes, activities, flows, and resources. Additionally, understanding the necessary information and knowledge required for effective operation is crucial, as well as identifying the technologies needed to support these processes.

Figure 5. Understanding the organization domains

Lastly, gaining insight into the needs, capabilities, relationships, and information flows of stakeholders is vital. This involves identifying both internal and external issues, along with their specific requirements and formalities. By undertaking these identification processes, organizations can develop a comprehensive understanding of their operations and create a solid foundation for effective decision-making, strategic planning, and risk management.

Manage Risk

The Manage risk component focuses on identifying and assessing risks based on the understanding of the organization. According to the domains depicted in Figure 6, the component involves evaluating the impact of risks, planning risk management strategies, and implementing risk mitigation measures aligned with the defined strategy.

Therefore, managing risk is an important BC component that should be maintained. In this context, within the governance domain, organizations must focus on developing a robust risk or opportunity management strategy. This involves creating a well-defined plan for managing risks or opportunities that may arise.

Figure 6. Manage risk domains

Effective risk or opportunity management requires implementing planned activities and ensuring on-going consultation with stakeholders to gather valuable insights. It is essential to identify any constraints, establish priorities, and consider trade-offs when managing risks. Additionally, organizations should design their products and services in a way that addresses the prioritized risks. A key aspect of successful risk management is the incorporation and demonstration of appropriate risk management culture and behaviors throughout the organization. By embracing these principles, organizations can proactively mitigate risks and seize opportunities, leading to enhanced governance and overall performance.

Within the Manage Risk domain, it is crucial to engage in a systematic approach to identify, document, evaluate, and monitor uncertainties, threats, and vulnerabilities. This includes identifying and documenting both risks and opportunities and categorizing them appropriately for better understanding and analysis. Organizations must thoroughly analyze the identified risks and opportunities, assessing their potential impacts and the likelihood of occurrence. It is essential to continually evaluate, monitor, and communicate risks, keeping stakeholders informed and involved throughout the process.

Effective risk management involves assessing and monitoring the implementation of risk mitigation strategies. In order to mitigate risks, organizations should develop and implement response plans tailored to address specific risks. Evaluating alternative courses of action is vital to ensure the most appropriate responses to risks. Regularly reviewing the risk assessment process allows for continuous improvement and adaptation to changing circumstances. By following these practices, organizations can effectively manage risks and seize opportunities while minimizing negative impacts on their operations and objectives.

In the domain of BIA, organizations undertake crucial activities to assess and understand the potential impacts of risks. Firstly, conducting a comprehensive BIA involves evaluating and estimating the likelihood, impact, and proximity of risks. This enables prioritization of risks based on their significance and understanding of the organization's exposure to risk.

Through the BIA process, various types of resources, activities, and processes required for the organization to fulfill its mission are identified. This helps in gaining a comprehensive understanding of the critical components of the organization's operations. Additionally, evaluating the BIA allows for a thorough assessment of the potential consequences of identified risks, helping organizations make informed decisions regarding risk management strategies.

Continuously monitoring the probability and severity of risk occurrences is essential to stay proactive in risk mitigation efforts. Lastly, periodic reviews of the BIA ensure its relevance and accuracy, considering any changes in the organization's context or the risk landscape.

By effectively conducting the BIA and following these steps, organizations can gain valuable insights into their operational vulnerabilities and make informed decisions to enhance resilience and mitigate potential impacts.

Consolidate the Strategy for Continuity

The Consolidate the strategy for continuity component involves defining strategies that align with the organization's business continuity objectives and available resources. It includes developing plans, capacity, and solutions necessary to execute the continuity strategy. Figure 7 presents the component domains.

In order to consolidate the strategy for continuity, several key considerations include developing a BCMS, contingency strategies, and utilizing BIA to develop strategies. Additionally, it is important to consider the development of backup policies and contingency planning policies. Implementing alternative solutions, such as manual processes, during the restoration of ICT systems, is also crucial. Furthermore, exploring solutions that minimize the unavailability of normal work locations should be taken into account.

By focusing on these aspects, organizations can enhance their ability to effectively manage and maintain business continuity in the face of disruptions.

It is important to consider the development of communication and reporting strategies in the event of an incident or disaster. Supporting these strategies and plans involves ensuring the effectiveness and availability of financial resources and investments. Additionally, prioritizing the protection and continuity of essential activities is crucial.

Organizations should also consider developing vendor strategies to appropriately manage suppliers and ensure the continuous supply of products and services. Lastly, developing strategies for employee assistance and support should be taken into account to ensure their well-being during disruptions.

By addressing these aspects, organizations can better manage and maintain business continuity while safeguarding their operations and supporting their workforce.

In technology and security domains several considerations should be made. Managing ICT assets is relevant. This includes the management of contracted ICT services, incidents, and service requests related to ICT. Organizations should also focus on managing platforms and ICT infrastructures used within the organization. When it comes to facility management, organizations should consider managing facilities, including power and communication equipment.

Figure 7. Consolidate the strategy for continuity domains

Implementing contingency solutions for information systems and ICT is important to ensure BC. Developing backup strategies that maintain the availability of critical business information is crucial. Furthermore, considering the development of information security policies and implementing security controls for establishing policies, integrity, and contingency measures for information systems and ICT is essential.

Procedural management related to security controls should be in place to protect information systems and ICT. It is vital to implement and maintain preventive, detection, and corrective measures to safeguard information systems and ICT from software vulnerabilities and malicious attacks.

By addressing these aspects, organizations can effectively manage their facilities, protect their ICT assets, and ensure the integrity and availability of critical business information.

Ensuring the effectiveness of plans is vital, keeping them up-to-date to accurately reflect system requirements, procedures, organizational structure, and policies. Monitoring and managing events that may lead to incidents or disasters should be in line with event monitoring policies. Implementing monitoring and protection measures against environmental factors is important to mitigate risks.

Developing strategies for periodic training of personnel responsible for the plans is essential to enhance their preparedness. Additionally, devising strategies for conducting exercises and tests of the plans helps validate their effectiveness and identify areas for improvement.

By focusing on these aspects, organizations can effectively manage, maintain plan readiness, monitor events, protect against environmental factors, and enhance the skills of personnel involved in the plans.

Plan and Structure the Continuity Response

The Plan and structure of the continuity response component focus on developing and documenting plans that outline the necessary actions and resources to execute the continuity strategy. It includes governance, scope, and documentation aspects, such as developing various continuity plans, defining roles and responsibilities, and establishing communication procedures.

Plan and structure the continuity response can be divided into the following domains, as presented in Figure 8: governance, scope, and documentation.

Figure 8. Plan and structure the continuity response domains

In the governance domain, it is important to utilize the defined strategy and information from the BIA to develop and continuously update plans. This involves coordinating strategies, resources, budgets, and timelines among different types of plans within the organization during the plan development and update processes. It is crucial to involve and validate the organization's plans with the identified stakeholders. By following these steps, organizations can ensure alignment between their strategic objectives, business impact analysis, and the plans in place, while also fostering engagement and validation from relevant stakeholders.

In the scope domain, the focus is on developing various continuity plans to address different aspects of the organization's operations. BCPs are designed to sustain prioritized business activities and processes, while Operation Continuity Plans aim to restore essential mission functions at alternate locations. DRPs specifically target information systems and ICT, potentially requiring relocation. Contingency plans for information systems establish procedures for system assessment and recovery.

Incident response and cybersecurity plans outline procedures for detecting, responding, and recovering from information security incidents. Communication plans document standard procedures for internal and external communication during disruptive events. Crisis management plans are developed to effectively handle matters or events with a high likelihood of severe impact. Additionally, the plans address supply chain disruption and prioritize the health and safety of personnel.

By incorporating these elements into the plans, organizations can ensure comprehensive preparedness and response in various critical areas.

In the documentation domain, it is crucial to establish a standardized structure for the documentation of plans. This includes documenting the activation, notification, and recovery phases of an incident or disaster, as well as the reconstitution and cessation processes after its conclusion. Additionally, defining and documenting the conditions, dependencies, and procedures for the recovery and restoration of processes, technology, information, services, resources, facilities, programs, and infrastructure is essential.

Each plan should clearly document the roles, responsibilities, and competencies of the designated teams responsible for plan implementation, including task lists with assigned individuals. Furthermore, the plans should outline the procedures to ensure continuous operation and delivery of products and services, along with details on managing the immediate consequences of the interruption.

By meticulously documenting these aspects, organizations can ensure clarity, consistency, and effectiveness in their preparedness and response efforts.

Implement and Maintain Continuity Plans

Implement and maintain continuity plans is traditionally where things are done. The Implement and maintain continuity plans component emphasizes the implementation and maintenance of the documented continuity plans. It involves ensuring the availability of resources, funding, and assets necessary to execute the plans. It also includes implementing preventive, detection, and corrective measures, as well as conducting regular testing, updating, and backup procedures. These component domains are depicted in Figure 9.

In the Feasibility and Documentation domains, it is essential to maintain the availability of resources, funding, assets, and information at an acceptable level to execute processes in the event of significant disruption. This includes securely storing and distributing each plan and supporting documentation to authorized stakeholders, ensuring accessibility and usability in all disruption scenarios and at the necessary time and location. Additionally, it is crucial to keep the plans up to date with new documentable information and maintain them in a state of readiness that accurately reflects the system requirements, procedures, organizational structure, and policies.

By adhering to these practices, organizations can effectively respond to disruptions and ensure the continuity of operations.

Figure 9. Implement and maintain continuity plans domains

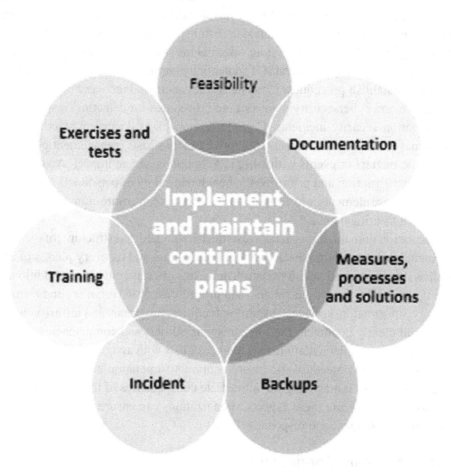

In the Measures, Processes, and Solutions and Backups domains, it is crucial to implement and maintain preventive, detection, and corrective security measures, including protection against malicious attacks on information systems and ICT. Additionally, selected BC solutions should be implemented and kept ready for activation when needed.

Processes and automation should be established to operationalize the defined boundaries, criteria, and policies outlined in the event monitoring policy. Regular testing, updating, and backup procedures for systems, applications, data, and documentation should be implemented, ensuring uninterrupted operations either on-site or off-site according to a defined schedule.

By implementing these measures, organizations can enhance their resilience and mitigate potential disruptions effectively.

In the Incident domain, it is essential to develop, maintain, and adhere to an approach for incident prevention and resolution. This approach should encompass activities such as incident logging, tracking, and communication of status updates. By establishing and following this approach, organizations can effectively manage and mitigate incidents, ensuring timely response and resolution. Keeping the incident management process updated and consistently applied allows for better incident tracking and facilitates effective communication among relevant stakeholders.

In the Training, Exercises, and Tests domains, it is crucial to implement regular awareness and training initiatives for the plans, following the planned schedule. This includes developing and maintaining up-to-date materials for continuity training. Additionally, organizations should create a competency-based training curriculum to support the stakeholders involved in plan activities.

It is also important to develop and document periodic exercises and tests to validate the plans and assess the effectiveness of their business continuity strategies and solutions over time.

By consistently conducting these exercises and tests, organizations can ensure their readiness and improve their ability to respond to disruptions effectively.

Check the Continuity Management System

Check the continuity management system component involves verifying the adequacy and effectiveness of the BCMS and its requirements. It includes monitoring and evaluating the implementation of the BCMS, conducting periodic reviews, and taking corrective actions when necessary. Under this component, there are six relevant domains presented in Figure 10.

In the Change Management domain, it is essential to regularly assess the adequacy and effectiveness of BIA, risk assessment, strategies, solutions, plans, and procedures to determine requirements and priorities, particularly when significant changes occur.

The responsible teams should review and approve continuity plans, identifying necessary changes and actions to address. Regular plan reviews should take place after scheduled exercises, incidents, activations, lessons learned, operational performance, and BCMS performance, as well as whenever a significant system change occurs. It is crucial to evaluate and document the implementation of changes resulting from preventive and corrective actions to assess their success.

By consistently evaluating and adapting to changes, organizations can ensure the continued effectiveness and relevance of their business continuity efforts.

In the Monitoring domain, it is important to employ methodologies that enable continuous monitoring, measurement, analysis, and evaluation of the performance and effectiveness of the BCMS. By implementing robust monitoring practices, organizations can assess the functionality and efficiency of their BCMS, identify areas for improvement, and ensure ongoing compliance with established standards and objectives.

Adequate documentation should be retained as evidence of the monitoring, measurement, analysis, and evaluation results, providing a record of the BCMS's performance and effectiveness over time. This documented information serves as a valuable resource for decision-making, reporting, and demonstrating regulatory compliance.

In the Compliance and Audit domains, it is important to assess compliance with applicable legal and regulatory requirements, industry best practices, and alignment with the organization's continuity policy and objectives. Regular evaluations should be conducted on policies, programs, plans, procedures, and capabilities using performance objectives reflected in the BCMS.

Figure 10. Check the continuity management system domains

Planned internal or external audits should be conducted to provide information on the compliance and effectiveness of the BCMS, as defined in the audit programs. By conducting thorough assessments and audits, organizations can ensure adherence to standards, identify areas for improvement, and maintain the effectiveness of their BC practices.

In the Suppliers domain, it is crucial to assess the BC capability of relevant partners and suppliers. Contracts and service levels should be reviewed to ensure that suppliers provide adequate support to meet system availability requirements. By evaluating the business continuity readiness of partners and suppliers and ensuring that contractual agreements align with the organization's continuity needs, organizations can mitigate risks associated with external dependencies and maintain the continuity of their operations.

In the Training, Exercises, and Tests domains, it is essential to assess the continuity training according to the established plan. The evaluation helps ensure that the training provided aligns with the objectives and requirements of the organization's BC program. Additionally, evaluating the training materials with the affected stakeholders helps gauge their effectiveness and relevance in conveying the necessary knowledge and skills. Similarly, assessing the exercises and tests conducted for each plan allows for an evaluation of the procedures, training, capabilities, and achievements attained, thereby identifying areas for improvement.

Ongoing monitoring of aptitudes and competencies, based on the results of exercises and plan tests, ensures that individuals maintain the necessary skills to effectively respond to disruptions and fulfill their roles in the continuity program.

Improve the Continuity Management System

The Improve the continuity management system component focuses on continuous improvement based on the findings from the verification process. It involves identifying opportunities for improvement, implementing necessary actions, and enhancing the BCMS to achieve the continuity objectives. As depicted in Figure 11, improving the continuity management system is organized into four domains: Change management, Corrective process, Continuous improvement, and Training, exercises, and tests.

Figure 11. Improve the continuity management system domains

In the Change Management domain, it is crucial to maintain a lifecycle management process for the BC program and change control to ensure ongoing monitoring and reporting. This involves regularly updating the plans to accurately reflect the evolving business requirements. Additionally, it is important to consider evaluating the implementation of changes resulting from preventive and corrective actions. This evaluation helps identify opportunities to enhance plan effectiveness by proposing or revising preventive or corrective measures.

By actively assessing and adapting the continuity plans, organizations can ensure they remain responsive to the changing needs of the business and continually improve their resilience.

In the Corrective Process domain, it is important to establish a documented process for preventive and corrective actions and to implement the necessary actions to achieve the desired outcomes of the business continuity program. This includes identifying and addressing any gaps or deficiencies in the program. Additionally, continuous improvement of the business continuity program is achieved through regular review and the implementation of corrective actions.

By actively identifying areas for improvement and taking appropriate corrective measures, organizations can enhance the effectiveness and maturity of their BC practices.

In the Continuous Improvement domain, organizations strive to maintain and regularly communicate the overall quality plan that promotes continuous improvement. This plan serves as a framework for driving ongoing enhancements in the BC program. To facilitate informed decision-making for improvement, accurate and well-analyzed information is crucial. This enables organizations to identify areas for enhancement and take appropriate actions. It is also important to consider the role of suppliers and contracts in the improvement effort, as they can contribute to the overall effectiveness of the BC program.

By evaluating the policies, programs, procedures, and capabilities of the program against performance objectives, organizations can continually improve their BC practices and ensure they are aligned with industry standards and best practices.

In the Training, Exercises, and Tests domain, organizations continuously review and update their training materials to reflect changes in the BCPs and incorporate feedback on training effectiveness. This ensures that training remains relevant and up to date. Additionally, the results of exercises and tests are carefully evaluated to identify areas for improvement and to enhance the organization's ability to respond to significant disruptions.

By analyzing these results, organizations can address any identified issues, refine their response strategies, and strengthen their overall resilience.

CONCLUSION

Business Continuity is a knowledge area that has been growing and gaining increased attention and awareness in recent times, mainly due to disruptive events of natural origin or cybersecurity attacks. BC goes beyond simply recovering from disruptions; it aims to build resilience by minimizing the impact of disruptions and enhancing response capabilities. With the ongoing digital transformation and increasing reliance on technology, organizations must adapt their contingency plans and embrace a flexible BCP that can adjust to evolving cyber threats and technological changes.

The integration of cybersecurity into BCM processes is of growing importance in today's digital landscape Therefore any organization that aims to be prepared to deal with the consequences of such disruptive events should preferably systematize BCM to ensure a timely response and enhance its effectiveness.

Cybersecurity plays a critical role in ensuring the continuity of critical functions and services during and after unexpected events. It involves protecting internet-connected systems, hardware, software, and data from attacks, unauthorized access, and data breaches. The gathering and analysis of behavioral data through IoT devices introduce additional cybersecurity risks that organizations must address.

This chapter relates and integrates cybersecurity into BCM processes. The challenges posed by cyber-attacks to business continuity are similar to other types of incidents or disasters since it is not so important to know the origin of the problem, but instead the impact it had, or will have on business. In the event of a cybersecurity incident, the primary focus of an organization is to contain the breach, mitigate the damage, and restore critical systems and operations. The immediate response is aimed at minimizing the impact of the attack and restoring, as quickly as possible, to normal operation. This chapter also outlines some of the steps organizations can take to ensure BC in the face of such threats, in the form of guidelines.

A well-planned BCP that includes cybersecurity measures can help organizations maintain critical operations and minimize the risk of data breaches or disruptions caused by cyberattacks. It should include strategies, procedures, and critical actions to respond to crises or disruptive incidents, as well as measures to prevent similar incidents in the future.

The BCM Model proposed by Russo et al. (2022) is part of a comprehensive framework that outlines the components and activities necessary to prepare and respond to incidents or disruptions in business operations. The model focuses on ensuring the continuity of critical business functions and aligning them with cybersecurity considerations.

The BCM Model consists of several components, each with its specific objectives and activities. Overall, the BCM Model provides a structured approach to business continuity management, encompassing various domains and activities necessary to prepare for and respond to incidents or disruptions. It emphasizes the involvement of top management, understanding the organization, managing risks, developing strategies, planning and structuring the response, implementing and maintaining plans, and continuously improving the BCMS. By following this model, organizations can enhance their resilience and ensure the continuity of critical business functions while considering cybersecurity aspects.

Therefore, the author believes that this chapter provides valuable insights into the components and activities necessary for developing a robust BCP that considers cybersecurity and BC. By following the guidelines presented, organizations can enhance their preparedness and response capabilities, ensuring the continuity of critical business operations in the face of disruptions. They can be useful for organizations looking to develop or improve their BCM processes in the face of cyber threats.

REFERENCES

Aldianto, L., Anggadwita, G., Permatasari, A., Mirzanti, I., & Williamson, I. (2021). Toward a Business Resilience Framework for Startups. *Sustainability (Basel)*, *13*(6), 3132. Advance online publication. doi:10.3390u13063132

Aronis, S., & Stratopoulos, G. (2016). Implementing business continuity management systems and sharing best practices at a European bank. *Journal of Business Continuity & Emergency Planning, 9*(3), 203–217. PMID:26897617

Assibi, A. (2023). Literature Review on Building Cyber Resilience Capabilities to Counter Future Cyber Threats: The Role of Enterprise Risk Management (ERM) and Business Continuity (BC). *OAlib, 10*(4), 1–15. doi:10.4236/oalib.1109882

Bajgoric, N. (2006). Information technologies for business continuity: An implementation framework. *Information Management & Computer Security, 14*(5), 450–466. doi:10.1108/09685220610717754

Bajgoric, N., & Moon, Y. B. (2009). Enhancing systems integration by incorporating business continuity drivers. *Industrial Management & Data Systems, 109*(1), 74–97. doi:10.1108/02635570910926609

Bhatti, F., Shah, M., Maple, C., & Islam, S. (2019). A Novel Internet of Things-Enabled Accident Detection and Reporting System for Smart City Environments. *Sensors (Basel), 19*(9), 2071. Advance online publication. doi:10.339019092071 PMID:31058879

Brás, J. (2018). Bootstrapping enterprise models with business continuity processes and DEMO.

Brás, J., & Guerreiro, S. (2016). Designing Business Continuity Processes Using DEMO: An Insurance Company Case Study. In R. Pergl, M. Molhanec, E. Babkin, & S. Fosso Wamba (Eds.), *Enterprise and Organizational Modeling and Simulation. EOMAS 2016. Lecture Notes in Business Information Processing, 272*. doi:10.1007/978-3-319-49454-8_11

Budiman, K., Arini, F., & Sugiharti, E. (2020). Disaster recovery planning with distributed replicated block device in synchronized API systems. *Journal of Physics: Conference Series, 1567*(3), 032023. Advance online publication. doi:10.1088/1742-6596/1567/3/032023

Burtles, J. (2015). The hexagon hypothesis: Six disruptive scenarios. *Journal of Business Continuity & Emergency Planning, 9*(1), 60–69. PMID:26420396

Burtles, J. (2016). *Manager's Guide to Business Continuity Exercises: Testing Your Plan*. Rothstein Publishing eBook Collection.

Caballero, A. (2009). Information Security Essentials for IT Managers: Protecting Mission-Critical Systems. In J. R. Vacca (Ed.), *Computer and Information Security Handbook* (pp. 225–252). Elsevier Inc. doi:10.1016/B978-0-12-374354-1.00014-5

Clark, P. (2010). Contingency Planning and Strategies. 2010 Information Security Curriculum Development Conference (pp. 131–140). Association for Computing Machinery. doi:10.1145/1940941.1940969

CMMI Institute. (2020). *Introducing CMMI V2.0*. https://cmmiinstitute.com/cmmi

Cook, J. (2015). A six-stage business continuity and disaster recovery planning cycle. *S.A.M. Advanced Management Journal, 80*(3), 22–33.

Cremer, F., Sheehan, B., Fortmann, M., Kia, A. N., Mullins, M., Murphy, F., & Materne, S. (2022). Cyber risk and cybersecurity: A systematic review of data availability. *The Geneva Papers on Risk and Insurance. Issues and Practice, 47*(3), 698–736. doi:10.105741288-022-00266-6 PMID:35194352

Elvy, S.-A. (2022). *Data privacy and the Internet of Things.* Retrieved from UNESCO Inclusive Policy Lab: https://en.unesco.org/inclusivepolicylab/analytics/data-privacy-and-internet-things

Ewertowski, T. (2022). A Standard-Based Concept of the Integration of the Corporate Recovery Management Systems: Coping with Adversity and Uncertainty during a Pandemic. *Sustainability (Basel), 14*(3), 1254. Advance online publication. doi:10.3390u14031254

Fani, S. V., & Subriadi, A. P. (2019). Business Continuity Plan: Examining of Multi-Usable Framework. *Procedia Computer Science, 161*, 275–282. doi:10.1016/j.procs.2019.11.124

Farr, M., & Bailey, D. (2019). Uniting business continuity management and operational risk management. *Journal of Business Continuity & Emergency Planning, 12*(4), 294–300. PMID:31200792

Fernando, M. S. (2017). IT disaster recovery system to ensure the business continuity of an organization. *2017 National Information Technology Conference (NITC)*, 46-48. 10.1109/NITC.2017.8285648

Fisher, R., Norman, M., & Klett, M. (2017). Enhancing infrastructure resilience through business continuity planning. *Journal of Business Continuity & Emergency Planning, 11*(2), 163–173. PMID:29256383

Goldstein, M., & Flynn, S. (2022). Business Continuity Management Lessons Learned from COVID-19. *Journal of Business Continuity & Emergency Planning, 15*, 360–380. PMID:35619223

Gracey, A. (2019). Building an organisational resilience maturity framework. *Journal of Business Continuity & Emergency Planning, 13*(4). PMID:32438952

Hecht, J. A. (2002). Business continuity management. *Communications of the Association for Information Systems, 8*, 444–450. doi:10.17705/1CAIS.00830

IoT Analytics. (2023). *IoT connections forecast.* IoT Analytics. Retrieved June 2023, from https://iot-analytics.com/number-connected-iot-devices/

ISACA. (2018). *COBIT 2019 Framework - Governance and Management Objectives.* ISACA.

ISO 22300. (2021). *Security and resilience - Vocabulary.* Geneva, Suiça: ISO.

ISO 22301. (2019). *Societal security - Business continuity management systems - Requirements.* Switzerland: ISO.

ISO/IEC 27001. (2023). *ISO/IEC 27001 Information security management systems Requirements.* Retrieved from ISO: https://www.iso.org/standard/27001 ISO/IEC 27002. (2022). *Information security, cybersecurity and privacy protection - Information security controls.* Switzerland: ISO.

ITIL. (2019). *ITIL Foundation ITIL* (4th ed.). AXELOS.

Järveläinen, J. (2013). IT incidents and business impacts: Validating a framework for continuity management in information systems. *International Journal of Information Management, 33*(3), 583–590. doi:10.1016/j.ijinfomgt.2013.03.001

King, D. L. (2003). Moving Towards a Business Continuity Culture. *Network Security, 1*(12). https://doi.org/https://doi.org/10.1016/S1353-4858(03)00112-0

Lindström, J. (2012). A model to explain a business contingency process. *Disaster Prevention and Management, 21*(2), 269–281. doi:10.1108/09653561211220052

Liu, X., Ahmad, S. F., Anser, M. K., Ke, J., Irshad, M., Ul-Haq, J., & Abbas, S. (2022, October 19). Cyber security threats: A never-ending challenge for e-commerce. *Frontiers in Psychology, 13*, 927398. Advance online publication. doi:10.3389/fpsyg.2022.927398 PMID:36337532

Moody, G. D., Siponen, M., & Pahnila, S. (2018). Toward a Unified Model of Information Security Policy Compliance. *Management Information Systems Quarterly, 42*(1), 285–A22. doi:10.25300/MISQ/2018/13853

NFPA 1600. (2019). *NFPA 1600® Standard on Continuity, Emergency, and Crisis Management 2019 Edition.* National Fire Protection Association.

NIST 800-171. (2020). *NIST Special Publication 800-171 Revision 2 - Protecting Controlled Unclassified Information in Nonfederal Systems and Organizations.* Gaithersburg, Maryland, USA: National Institute of Standards and Technology. doi:10.6028/NIST.SP.800-171r2

NIST 800-34. (2010). *NIST Special Publication 800-34 Rev. 1 - Contingency Planning Guide for Federal Information Systems.* Gaithersburg: National Institute of Standards and Technology.

Ohlhausen, P. E., & McGarvey, D. (2018). The use of metrics to manage enterprise security risks: Understanding, evaluation and persuasion. *Journal of Business Continuity & Emergency Planning, 12*(1), 6–16. PMID:30126523

Păunescu, C. (2017). How Prepared are Small and Medium Sized Companies for Business Continuity Management? *Quality - Access to Success, 18*(161), 43–48.

Păunescu, C., & Argatu, R. (2020). Critical functions in ensuring effective business continuity management. Evidence from Romanian companies. *Journal of Business Economics and Management, 21*(2), 497–520. Advance online publication. doi:10.3846/jbem.2020.12205

Phillips, R., & Tanner, B. (2019). Breaking down silos between business continuity and cyber security. *J Bus Contin Emer Plan, 12*(3), 224-232.

Pramudya, G., & Fajar, A. (2019). Business continuity plan using ISO 22301:2012 in IT solution company (pt. ABC). *International Journal of Mechanical Engineering and Technology, 10*(2), 865–872.

Putra, E. P., & Nazief, B. A. (2018). Analysis of Main Cause Factors and Improvement Recommendation of IT Disaster Recovery Problems: A Case Study of XYZ Organization. *AIP Conference Proceedings*, 020024. doi:10.1063/1.5042880

Ramakrishnan, R. K., & Viswanathan, S. (2011). The importance of Business Strategy in Business Continuity Planing. In A. Hiles (Ed.), *The definitive handbook of Business Continuity Management* (3rd ed.). John Wiley & Sons, Ltd.

Rimboiu, C. (2020). *Modern IT architecture to manage change, foster innovation.* Retrieved from CXOtoday Corner Office: https://www.cxotoday.com/corner-office/modern-it-architecture-to-manage-change-foster-innovation/

Roitz, J., & Jackson, E. (2006). AT&T adds business continuity to the long list of telework's advantages. *Journal of Organizational Excellence*, *25*(2), 3–12. doi:10.1002/joe.20085

Russo, N., Mamede, H. S., Reis, L., & Silveira, C. (2022). FAMMOCN - Demonstration and evaluation of a framework for the multidisciplinary assessment of organisational maturity on business continuity. *Heliyon*, *8*(9), e10566. doi:10.1016/j.heliyon.2022.e10566 PMID:36148280

Russo, N., & Reis, L. (2020). Methodological Approach to Systematization of Business Continuity in Organizations. In L. C. Carvalho, L. Reis, A. Prata, & R. Pereira (Eds.), Handbook of Research on Multidisciplinary Approaches to Entrepreneurship, Innovation, and ICTs (pp. 200-223). IGI Global. doi:10.4018/978-1-7998-4099-2.ch010

Russo, N., Reis, L., Silveira, C., & Mamede, H. S. (2023). Towards a Comprehensive Framework for the Multidisciplinary Evaluation of Organizational Maturity on Business Continuity Program Management: A Systematic Literature Review. *Information Security Journal: A Global Perspective*. doi:10.10 80/19393555.2023.2195577

Sahebjamnia, N., Torabi, S. A., & Mansouri, S. A. (2018). Building organizational resilience in the face of multiple disruptions. *International Journal of Production Economics*, *197*, 63–83. doi:10.1016/j. ijpe.2017.12.009

Sambo, F., & Bankole, F. O. (2016). A Normative Process Model for ICT Business Continuity Plan for Disaster Management in Small, Medium and Large Enterprises. *International Journal of Electrical & Computer Engineering*, 2425–2431.

Sarker, I., Kayes, A., Badsha, S., Alqahtani, H., Watters, P., & Ng, A. (2020). Cybersecurity data science: An overview from machine learning perspective. *Journal of Big Data*, *7*(1), 41. Advance online publication. doi:10.118640537-020-00318-5

Sinha, S. (2023). *State of IoT 2023: Number of connected IoT devices growing 16% to 16.7 billion globally.* IOT Analytics. Retrieved from https://iot-analytics.com/number-connected-iot-devices/

Soufi, H. R., Torabi, S. A., & Sahebjamnia, N. (2019). Developing a novel quantitative framework for business continuity planning. *International Journal of Production Research*, *57*(3), 779–800. doi:10.1 080/00207543.2018.1483586

Sterling, S. (2011). Encouraging resilience within SMEs: The Cabinet Office's proposed approach. *Journal of Business Continuity & Emergency Planning*, *5*(2), 128–139. PMID:21835751

Syed, A. (2004). *Business Continuity Planning Methodology.* Academic Press.

Torabi, S. A., Giahi, R., & Sahebjamnia, N. (2016). An enhanced risk assessment framework for business continuity management systems. *Safety Science*, *89*, 201–218. doi:10.1016/j.ssci.2016.06.015

Torabi, S. A., Soufi, H. R., & Sahebjamnia, N. (2014). A new framework for business impact analysis in business continuity management (with a case study). *Safety Science*, *68*, 309–323. doi:10.1016/j. ssci.2014.04.017

Urbánek, J. F., Raclavská, J. S. A., O., Š., & Vonlehmden, J. (2012). Organization Continuity Planning & Management and Societal Security Scenarios Economics and Management. University of Defence in Brno.

Vasquez, E. J., & Ortega, J. C. (2020). Design of a business contingency plan. Case study: Municipality of Cantón Suscal. *2020 International Conference on Intelligent Systems and Computer Vision (ISCV)*, 1-10. 10.1109/ISCV49265.2020.9204334

Veerasamy, N., Mashiane, T., & Pillay, K. (2019). Contextualising cybersecurity readiness in South Africa. *14th International Conference on Cyber Warfare and Security*, 467-475.

Winkler, U., Fritzsche, M., Gilani, W., & Marshall, A. (2010). A Model-Driven Framework for Process-centric Business Continuity Management. *2010 Seventh International Conference on the Quality of Information and Communications Technology*, 248-252. 10.1109/QUATIC.2010.46

York, T. W., & MacAlister, D. (2015). Program Documentation and Performance Measures. In Hospital and Healthcare Security (Sixth Edition) (pp. 289-313). Elsevier. doi:10.1016/B978-0-12-420048-7.00012-X

Zambon, E., Bolzoni, D., Etalle, S., & Salvato, M. (2007). A Model Supporting Business Continuity Auditing and Planning in Information Systems. *Second International Conference on Internet Monitoring and Protection (ICIMP 2007)*. 10.1109/ICIMP.2007.4

KEY TERMS AND DEFINITIONS

Business Continuity: Capability of an organization to continue the delivery of products and services within acceptable time frames at predefined capacity during a disruption (ISO 22301, 2019).

Business Continuity Plan: Business continuity plans consist of documented procedures. Organizations use these procedures to respond to disruptive incidents, guide recovery efforts, resume prioritized activities, and restore operations to acceptable predefined levels. Business continuity plans usually identify the services, activities, and resources needed to ensure that prioritized business activities and functions could continue whenever disruptions occur (ISO 22301, 2019).

Business Impact Analysis: The process of analyzing the impact (the outcome of a disruption affecting objectives) over time of a disruption on the organization. The outcome of BIA is a statement and justification of BC requirements (ISO 22301, 2019).

Cybersecurity: Refers to the protection of internet-connected systems, including hardware, software, and data, from attack, damage, or unauthorized access.

Disaster Recovery: Is an organization's method of regaining access and functionality to its IT infrastructure, to continue the delivery of services that support business processes after a disruptive incident.

Incident: An event that can be, or lead to a disruption, loss, emergency, or crisis (ISO 22301, 2019).

Resilience: Resilience is the capacity of a person, group, or system to withstand stress and emerge stronger from it. It is the ability to adjust, recover, and flourish in the face of difficulties, adjustments, or trying circumstances. Building and maintaining a solid foundation that permits efficient coping mechanisms, problem-solving abilities, and the capacity to recover and rebuild following setbacks are all components of resilience. It includes psychological, emotional, and physical components as well as the capacity to take lessons from past mistakes and adapt them to new circumstances. Resilience enables people and institutions to overcome challenges and grow stronger as a result.

Risk Assessment: Overall process of risk (effect of uncertainty on objectives (ISO 22301, 2019) identification, risk analysis, and risk evaluation.

Chapter 5
Digital Educational Games:
A Resource to Promote Education 5.0?

Catarina Delgado

https://orcid.org/0000-0001-8146-1236

Escola Superior de Educação, Instituto Politécnico de Setúbal, Portugal

Fátima Mendes

https://orcid.org/0000-0002-7112-9034

Escola Superior de Educação, Instituto Politécnico de Setúbal, Portugal

Joana Brocardo

Escola Superior de Educação, Instituto Politécnico de Setúbal, Portugal

Ana Maria Boavida

Escola Superior de Educação, Instituto Politécnico de Setúbal, Portugal

ABSTRACT

This chapter reflects on the challenges that arise when it is intended that all students can experience an Education 5.0 and proposes a set of practical actions that may support teachers' educational practice. It analyses and discusses a study involving 18 primary teachers and their 358 students (ages 6-10), which informed specific adjustments in some educational technological games about mathematics and confirmed, or not, several of the potentialities that intentionally underlined their design. The analysis focused on some problematic aspects related to moving towards an Education 5.0, which allows the integration of digital technologies in a more meaningful way in the learning process, aiming at the development of critical and creative thinking and collaborative work. Finally, suggestions are systematized about the development of quality educational technological tools and teacher training.

DOI: 10.4018/978-1-6684-9039-6.ch005

INTRODUCTION

The term "Education 5.0" is not yet widely recognized, and there is no consensus on what it exactly means. However, it generally refers to the integration of new technologies to create a more personalized and inclusive learning experience, valuing, in addition to skills related with use of information and communication technologies (ICT), skills such as critical thinking, creativity, and collaboration. In this sense, "Education 5.0 refers to the purpose of competence-based education, based on the four pillars of education: learning to live together, learning to know, learning to do, and learning to be" (Possato et al., 2022, p. 24).

In Education 5.0, the teaching and learning process involves creating a more dynamic, flexible, and student-centered learning environment that prepares learners for the challenges of the 21st century. To overcome those challenges European Union (EU) proposed an action plan for digital education that reflects EU educational policy and sets out a common vision about the actions to promote high-quality inclusive and accessible digital education in Europe (European Commission, 2018). This plan aims to support the adaptation of the education and training systems of Member States to the digital age. Among other aspects, it emphasizes the need to guarantee the development of student's digital skills.

In Portugal, a recommendation of the National Council of Education points out that to achieve this goal it is important to invest in teacher training, equipping them with the knowledge to develop their relationship with digital in curricular and pedagogical terms (Cravinho et al., 2022). This recommendation highlights that to move in this direction it is important to "assess how digital tools, pedagogical strategies, and educational environments considered innovative and on-going actually affect education and, specifically student achievement and students' relationship with knowledge" (p. 7). The attention to these aspects is essential to ensure that the kind of skills that are being developed for students are not limited to technological mastering, and that investment is made in the development of foundational skills, such as computational thinking, critical thinking, problem solving, creativity, cooperation, etc. (Cravinho et al., 2022).

These fundamental skills are also highlighted in the Students' Profile at the End of Compulsory Schooling (Martins et al., 2017), a document that, in the Portuguese context, aims to support the development of a curriculum for the 21st century, identifying ten areas of competence, including technical knowledge and technologies and which involve, in an integrated way, knowledge, skills and attitudes. Thus, technologies and digital resources should be used in the classroom context to prepare future citizens for the multiple challenges they will face in a world that is unpredictable and subject to accelerated changes.

It is critical to integrate digital resources in the classroom because they promote greater student engagement and motivation, personalized learning, independent learning, and the development of digital literacy (Chan, 2019). Referring to these types of resources, Gros (2006) highlights digital games as an increasingly promising resource in the teaching context, if emphasis is placed on the connection between experiences, context, and learning. This author warns that one of the reasons that usually justify the use of digital games is related to the motivation of the student's participation. However, "possibly what is most important about digital games is the combination of motivation, engagement, adaptivity, simulation, collaboration and data collection" (Gros, 2006, p. 17).

This chapter reflects on the challenges of enabling all students to experience Education 5.0 and proposes a set of practical actions that can support teachers' educational practice. It analyses and discusses a study on the design and validation of digital educational resources in the area of mathematics. It also aims to identify aspects associated with Education 5.0, which allows digital technologies to be integrated more meaningfully into the learning process, with a view to developing critical and creative thinking and collaborative work. The chapter ends with some suggestions on the development of quality educational technology tools and teacher training to promote the appropriate use of digital resources in the classroom.

DIGITAL GAMES TO LEARN MATHEMATICS

Two years ago, the Portuguese General Directorate of Education proposed to a group of researchers to transform a set of existing didactic materials into interactive games that could be used not only by teachers in their classes, but also played autonomously by children and/or with their parents outside school.

Mathematical materials had been designed with certain educational intentions among which was the importance of learning mathematics with understanding and of valuing the capacities of problem-solving, mathematical reasoning and mathematical communication, which are fundamental in contemporary society. It is in this context that Digital Mathematics Education Resources (DER-MAT) emerged with the general aim to support the learning of mathematics in core topics of the curriculum for children aged 6 to 10. These resources, 10 freely accessible educational games available on the Internet (https://redge.dge.mec.pt/ilha/periscopio/topic-list/4dqbEL90 nyHFjP3FhGCz), were designed to maintain the aforementioned intentions and its design integrated important research recommendations.

Guideline 1. Games are learning tools that integrates the results of research carried out on mathematical topics as Number Sense, Geometry, Statistics and Measurement

The games should integrate the advancement of knowledge about the learning of the various mathematical topics included in the first years of schooling. This orientation includes two articulated strands: on the one hand, each game should reflect an educational intentionality that the literature highlights as central to the learning of the various topics of the primary curriculum and, on the other, the possibility of addressing misconceptions. More specifically, it has been considered, for example, that developing mental calculation involves articulating the knowledge of simple numerical facts with the use of numerical relationships that allow to quickly and accurately determine the value of a wide variety of numerical expressions (Threlfall, 2009) or that the development of spatial reasoning should emphasis on visualization and spatial orientation and that Orienting, Building and Operating with Shapes and Figures are essential aspects that must be developed from the early years of schooling (Gifford et al., 2022). Each game also included the possibility of addressing misconceptions identified in the literature, such as the tendency to confuse the number that represents the frequency of the most frequent data with the mode of a distribution (data with the highest value (Martins & Ponte, 2011) or the different views of a solid (Battista, & Clements, 1996).

Guideline 2. Articulate learning and 'having fun'

As highlighted in the literature (Pan et al., 2021) the interrelationship between games and learning is not linear. In fact, games can be very attractive but do not contribute to the intended learning or have a lot of educational value but do not arouse any interest in learners. Therefore, games could not just be fun, and their design should ensure a balance between fun and learning (Sera & Wheeler, 2017).

Interactivity and 'having fun' are strongly associated in digital games research (Cheung & Ng, 2021). In the design of the games, it was essential what we can call 'pedagogical interactivity', that in addition to allowing the child to have immediate feedback on their options/choices throughout the game facilitates learning from the mistakes they make. Therefore, the feedback for the students' actions included several possibilities of attempts and, in some cases, help via information that related what was being asked with aspects that potentially he had already worked on during the game. The player, in case of continuing to make mistakes, loses lives, but always has access to the correct answer.

For the design of the games, it was also essential to keep in mind that the mechanics of the game and its aesthetics should arouse interest in the activity of playing (Cheung & Ng, 2021). Therefore, all games were based on the possibility to choose the mathematics subject and the realization of a path with challenges for the child to overcome.

For instance, suppose a pupil chooses the game The Fisherman because he wants to improve his arithmetic knowledge or because his teacher challenges him to explore this game. When he opens the game, he must start by choosing the arithmetic operation he wants to operate with: addition, subtraction, multiplication, or division (Figure. 1).

Figure 1. Image showing the arithmetic operations in Game 1: The Fisherman
Source: Printout of one of the screens in Game 1

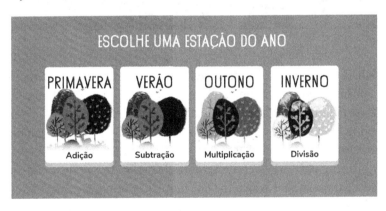

Figure 2. Image showing the numerical universes available in Game 1: The Fisherman
Source: Printout of one of the screens in Game 1

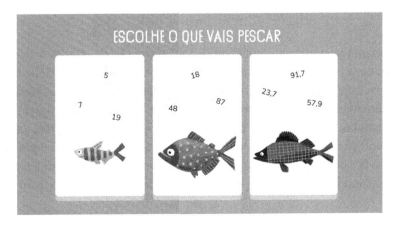

Next, the student must choose the numerical universe with which he wants to perform the calculations (Figure. 2). In this case, he can select numbers up to 20, numbers up to 100 or, even, non-integer rational numbers.

Finally, the pupil starts playing following a path with several stops. Each stop represents an arithmetic challenge that the pupil must solve. From one stop to the next one, the level of difficulty increases (Figure. 3).

Figure 3. Image showing the path to be taken in Game 1: The Fisherman, regarding one of the selected arithmetic operations
Source: Printout of one of the screens in Game 1

Each proposed path, in addition to being designed based on 'pedagogical interactivity', underlies the general philosophy, concretized for each topic, of progressing from what each one knows to advance in the knowledge associated with the mathematical concepts involved.

The score obtained in each game, associated with the number of lives that can be preserved and the time used to play are also important elements that accentuate the 'fun' character of these resources. Also, the possibility of being able to select the level of difficulty favors the child's interest in playing, as they can freely choose the route for which they have sufficient mathematical knowledge or in which they feel more confident. Although the range of options is more limited for children at the beginning of schooling (6/7 years old), they too can play several of the options of many of the proposed games. Similarly, many of the games are suitable for learning with 10/12 years.

Guideline 3. Personalized and independent learning

Finally, an important recommendation that guided the design of the games was that each game can offer challenges that each person can customize by choosing the one that best suits his knowledge. Everyone has control over the game and can live an independent and autonomous learning experience as recommended in international literature (Cheung & Ng, 2021). Therefore, it is important to be able to start playing each game without needing many instructions and giving the feeling that each one can choose freely what to play with and at what level and difficulty. For example, in the field of Arithmetic, in the same game, there are possibilities to choose the numerical universe (whole numbers up to 100, greater than 100 or decimals) and the operations to be used. In the field of Geometry, there are possibilities to use figures with 2 or 3 dimensions, simple constructions of cubes or more complex ones, with one or several colors. In the topic of Data organization, there are possibilities to use or not data represented by mathematical objects (geometric shapes, numbers, food, or animals) and to choose the data representation he wishes to use. When following the path, the truck driver must take to transport each of those goods, there are several stops. What enables progress on the path is the correct organization of data into a certain type of graphical representation. To support the organization of data we designed 'help options'. For example, in the Venn diagram it is possible to visualize another representation of the same data, with the Carroll diagram. From a didactic point of view, this option promotes the establishment of relationships between these different types of representations. In addition, the possibility of children being able to "carry non-mathematical objects", specifically food and animals, allows the mobilization of knowledge from the curriculum area of Environmental Studies and favors the integration of knowledge.

Although the study conducted by Hanson et al. (2010) focused on college students, its conclusions can also have some significant meaning for younger students that also tend to use tablet devices and mobile phones (if only those of the parents). As these authors underline the high usage of those mobile devices may indicate that is important to have the possibility to play outside the classroom, using other devices than computers. Therefore, we emphasize that the fact that all the mathematical games developed can be used on the computers, cell phone or tablets, enhances both the autonomy of the student, that can choose when and where to play, and favors the existence of more learning opportunities.

Guideline 4. Integrating examples of teacher's actions via 10 teaching guides

As several authors argue, digital game-based learning is an important educational pathway to improve education in the classrooms of the future (Bertram, 2020). Several studies show that this option can allow diversifying teaching, increasing students' interest and motivation, and providing positive and effective learning experiences (Bertram, 2020; Cheung & Ng, 2021; Dabbous, 2022). However, learning is a complex issue and the effectiveness of games in this process cannot be considered unquestionable (Bertram, 2020) and, above all, independent of the teacher's action.

Reinforcing the indications of several researchers Brocardo et al. (2022) and Mendes et al. (2022) focusing on mathematical reasoning, recognize that teachers face several difficulties when organizing and delivering teaching activities that aim to work on and consolidate non-routine skills and that they need to understand what mathematical reasoning consists of, how to adapt and explore tasks and how to conduct collective discussions with their students to promote mathematical reasoning. These recommendations are equally valid in situations that involve complex tasks or innovative didactic resources that still are not integrated in common teacher practice, as is the case with interactive games.

The didactic guide that we developed for each game, freely available in Portuguese General Directorate of Education site (https://redge.dge.mec.pt/sie/node/6) was developed with the purpose to help teachers to integrate the exploration of the games into their teaching activity. It includes the educational purpose of the game, its integration into the official curriculum and the overall organization of the game, detailing the specific objectives of each path proposed in the game. It also includes examples of questions that teachers can pose to children, either in writing or orally.

METHODOLOGY

This study followed an action-research methodology in which prototypes of the various games were trialed and validated by primary school students and teachers. This methodological option is linked to the DER project's objective of designing and producing interactive digital educational resources.

The Process of Building the Games

In the first phase, the team was set the challenge of transforming a set of didactic materials, previously made on 'paper', into DER, to be used by primary school teachers in their classrooms. The paper resources had been constructed with a certain intent, bearing in mind the idea of learning math with understanding, and seeking to promote the development of essential mathematical skills such as problem solving.

In the process of transforming these didactic materials into DER, the math's team assumed that these resources would be designed as an interactive game for 1st cycle students. They also decided to maintain both the perspective on the teaching and learning of math and the learning content that had underpinned the construction of the initial materials. She also considered that the games to be produced should have the following characteristics:

- favors children's involvement, i.e., be interactive and sufficiently challenging, but suited to the players' abilities, i.e., the players should feel competent to play and overcome the game's challenges;
- have different levels of difficulty to allow learning to progress at an appropriate pace;
- encourage a positive relationship with math, as it was hoped that the children would enjoy playing, experiencing feelings of pleasure and satisfaction;
- allow children to feel in control of the game, giving them a sense of independence, mastery, autonomy, power and freedom;
- allowing them to start playing without the need for extensive instructions.

The work carried out went far beyond adapting materials that had already been made, as the construction of RED involved new logic and new ways of looking at mathematical content. Proposals for scripts for ten math games were subsequently drawn up and sent to the iNOVA Media Lab team. Each of the proposals gave rise to a game that was developed in collaboration with the team.

The Game Validation Process

The validation of the DER-MAT Games involved 358 elementary school students, from first to fourth grade, and their eighteen female teachers. Sixty-nine students were interviewed, and all teachers participated in a final evaluation session focused on their experience of using these resources.

The validation of these games was not as initially conceived. In fact, these teaching resources were tested in a pandemic context, marked by phases of distance learning and unexpected interruptions of teaching (when some teachers contracted Covid-19). We had three distant working meetings (via Zoom) with the teachers and visited each classroom once.

As initially planned, all teachers had complete freedom to explore the games with their students when they considered it appropriate and to adapt the didactic guidance provided. Also as planned, before each teacher started exploring a particular game with their pupils, they were asked to answer a pre-test that focused on the contents of each game. After the students had explored the game, the teacher administered a post-test. Pos-tests were applied five weeks, approximately, after pre-tests.

The items included in the pre-test and post-test were the same since, given the age of the children, the distance of more than one month between their application, the conditions in which this application took place and the type of items considered, it was not considered plausible that they would memorize the correct answers for each item.The tests were constructed collaboratively by the researchers and the teachers. Each of the teachers worked with one of the researchers, focusing on the particular game she would explore with her students, selecting the questions to be included in the test and deciding on how to collect the results obtained. Each test included a set of questions, with diverse levels of complexity, which aimed to illustrate the different types of situations that the children would face while playing the game.

The variability of situations imposed by the pandemic context made it impossible to standardize the testing of the games. Teachers tended to ask pupils to explore the games at home and dedicated no more than one working session to exploring the games in the classroom. However, the interactions that we had with the teachers helped us to improve the initial version of the games, improving both their didactical quality and eliminating bugs.

THE GAMES

There are ten games, each of which has been given a name referring to a profession: Game 1 - The Fisherman, Game 2- The Farmer, Game 3 - The Truck Driver, Game 4 - The Climber, Game 5 - The Builder, Game 6 - The Archaeologist, Game 7 - The Architect, Game 8 - The Drone Driver, Game 9 - The Grocer and Game 10 - The Analyst.

The focus of each game is diverse and covers almost all the major mathematical themes included in the above-mentioned curriculum. Four of the games focus on the theme *Numbers* and, more specifically, on mental calculation (*The Fisherman*), to locate numbers on the number line (The *Farmer game*), addition and subtraction (*The Mountain Climber*), and multiplication and division (*The Builder*). There are also four games focused on *Geometry and Measurement*: classification of shapes (The Archaeologist game), identification of a two-dimensional representation of a three-dimensional object and vice-versa (The *Architect game*), spatial orientation (*The Drone Driver*), and measuring various quantities using several measurement processes and also non-standard and standard units (*The Grocer*). Finally, two of the games are related to the theme *Data* including both processes of organizing data (*The Truck Driver*) and of representing data using several types of graphs (*The Analyst*). This distribution of the games across the mathematical themes is consistent with the weight that these themes have in the mathematics curricula.

As mentioned before, all games consist in following a path with several stops that represent different mathematical challenges that student must overcame and integrate and articulate the main characteristics of Education 5.0, consisting in a challenge that 1) integrates a general philosophy of progression, developed from what each one knows and proposing a path to construct new knowledge; (2) questions and contexts that research has identified as favoring the emergence and problematization of misconceptions about important mathematical ideas and concepts.

For example, in *The Fisherman* game that focus mental calculus, one of the challenges proposed to the player is to indicate a product that he knows and use it to determine the result of other related products. If the player would choose 0.1x63 and correctly indicate the result of this multiplication, he or she would then have to successively calculate 0.2x63, 0.4x 63, 0.1x126 and 0.1x126, structuring/consolidating the relations of doubling and multiplication by one tenth.

A characteristic on which the entire construction of the games was founded is interactivity, with immediate feedback that integrates suggestions to correct the answer or that corrects it. All the games are based on constant interaction between the player and the proposed challenges, and each answer is associated with a sound and/or a color that allows him to perceive the correctness of the move. If the player continues to make a mistake, he loses lives, but always has access to the correct answer and can, in some cases, consult examples that support self-correction.

The score obtained in each game, associated with the number of lives the player can preserve and the time used to play, are important elements that accentuate the ludic character of these resources. Also, the possibility of being able to select the difficulty level favors a child's interest in playing, since he can choose the route for which he has sufficient mathematical knowledge or in which he feels more confident. Although the games are primarily designed to support mathematics learning for children of certain ages/years of schooling, they offer opportunities to explore various mathematical topics for children along their schooling, as they present increasing levels of complexity.

Overall, the resources offer challenges that everyone can customize by choosing the one that best suits their knowledge. Everyone has control over the game and can live an independent and autonomous learning experience.

POTENTIALITIES OF THE GAMES

Data collected allow us to discuss aspects related with the potential and limitations of the 10 games for learning mathematics, focusing on aspects of Education 5.0 that the participants, students and teachers, explain when referring to the experience they had with these games.

A first potentiality of the games concerns the progression in learning mathematics that can be analyzed in table 1, with the data related to the first five games, and in table 2 with the results related to the last five games. Although without identifying a major increase, the percentage of correct answers from pre-test to post-test always increased.

The fact that there was always an increase indicates that games are a tool that supports pupils' learning, but not, as we knew in advance, a 'magic solution'. Above all, it indicates that games should be explored over an extended period. Indeed, as mentioned in connection with the presentation of the games, they have several parts and each one can be explored at different stages of the learning of mathematics. A more substantial benefit to learning can only be expected in a context where games are exploited with some regularity, whenever they relate to the topics which are being worked on.

Table 1. Percentage of correct answers in the tests: Games 1, 2, 3, 4, and 5

Game	Percentage									
	Pre-Test					Post-Test				
Game	G1	G2	G3	G4	G5	G1	G2	G3	G4	G5
Average	54	81	78	89	69	69	89	91	91	77

Source: Own elaboration

Table 2. Percentage of correct answers in the tests: Games 6, 7, 8, 9, and 10

	Percentage									
	Pre-Test					Post-Test				
Game	G6	G7	G8	G9	G10	G6	G7	G8	G9	G10
Average	54	83	65	56	84	61	92	78	67	91

Source: Own elaboration

Largely due to the pandemic context, the ten games were freely explored by the students and analyzed in class only during a collective discussion session with the teacher. The necessary reflection around the core aspects of each game, where the overall emphasis is on developing higher-order knowledge, was very limited and the teacher's role as a mediator of learning was very weak. A teacher's role is central to pupils' learning and indispensable in helping pupils to progress in the development of knowledge, especially, as was the case, when it goes well beyond the use of routine techniques.

It should be noted that the teachers unanimously appreciated very positively the potential of the game that their students explored and recognized that an articulation can be made between its exploration and the contents to be taught. As one teacher said: "There are certain points that we can address, based on the game and taking into account the relationships between the numbers". However, the majority recognized that this articulation was not achieved.

Another data that deserves some reflection regarding the potential of the games for learning mathematics, concerns the information collected in the final evaluation session with the teachers that indicated the tendency of pupils with more difficulties to improve their results from the pre-test to the post-test. In a context of autonomous exploitation of the games, pupils who have more difficulty in mathematics tend to reduce their experience with the games. In contrast, their peers that like mathematics tend to prolong their experience of playing.

These data suggest that the ten games enhance students' learning, but so that it can be more meaningful, it is important that the teacher can assume his central role as facilitator of learning, fundamental for all students, especially for those with more difficulties in mathematics.

A second potentiality of the games concerns their simplicity in understanding how to deal with the objects that are on the screens, how to choose the various alternatives, how it is possible to continue to play the game and identify the mathematical aspects that it focused on. In fact, in the interviews conducted with the students, we found that they all manage to understand the screens of the game, how they could advance from one screen to another and how they could get more points. It also concluded that all pupils were able to identify the focus of each game.

The following transcripts illustrate the aspects mentioned above:

S: You choose the volume first, then the difficulty level and then a sort of grocery store image appears... it's like as the grocery store was walking until to the little yellow balls. Then you press Play and the first stage starts. The buttons of a keyboard appear, but only with numbers. There's a delete key ... and I think there's another one I can't remember. Then you have the right key, the one that you must press. A picture appears on the other side and the objective is to answer the question by measuring the measure of that figure. (Grade 4)

S: I would say you have to choose the house or the building and that each one had several difficulty levels. When you clicked on the levels you had questions about the solids. . . . The game is very fun and appeals to our imagination because we must assemble the pieces. (Grade 3)

Finally, a third potentiality concerns the enthusiasm for playing. Interviewed students unanimously associated the experience of playing games with the word's *enthusiasm, joy, learning, easy* and *different*, highlighting the playful aspect of each game. In the following transcripts we illustrate the reference to some of these aspects:

S: I think it's fun even for adults because I played with my mom and she also got some things wrong, but she learned. (Level 4).

E: So. imagine you came home today and told her (his mother) you had been playing. What would you tell her?

S: That I really enjoyed the game, that it had a lot of questions, some more difficult than others. I also concluded that at the end of the game the questions get harder. (Level 3)

This aspect is also highlighted by the teachers who unanimously mentioned the interest that each game aroused in the students. Recognizing that this interest was not always the same for everyone, they nevertheless highlight the willingness that many students showed to explore the game at home or in the final moments of the working day.

The collected data confirmed that digital games offer activities and challenges that everyone can customize and that support learning progress. However, their effective integration into teacher practices is still tenuous. There is a long way to go to take advantage of the potential of these tools. In particular, it is important to rethink the use of more appropriate methodologies for the development of students' learning. At the same time, the integration of playfulness, of the enthusiasm generated by games, of the flexibility for everyone to follow their own way, tends to be underutilized in the classroom, which seems to limit learning progression.

REANALYZING THE GUIDELINES USED FOR EDUCATIONAL GAME DESIGN

These data and their discussion confirm the pertinence of the four guidelines we followed to materialize the design of DER-MAT resources (https://redge.dge.mec.pt/ilha/periscopio/topic-list/4dqbEL90 nyHFjP3FhGCz). However, they lead us to explicitly discuss the implications of how we implemented Guideline 1 (*Games are learning tools that integrate the results of research carried out on mathematical topics Number Sense, Geometry, Statistics, and Measurement*) Guideline 3 (*Personalized and independent learning should involve*) and Guideline 4 (*Integrate examples of teacher's actions via 10 teaching guides*).

Guideline 1 was concretized with the support of a cooperative work involving a team of six mathematics educators, including the authors of this chapter, all with extensive experience in the initial and continuous training of teachers and with research focused on student learning in different mathematical topics. It also involved a team from iNova Media Lab, including three researchers specialized in the use of teaching technologies and two multimedia content producers. The work was carried out in close collaboration between the two teams: the initial scripts conceived by the team of mathematics educators were presented to the iNova Media Lab team, who, after analyzing them, proposed technological implementations. This collaboration involved many revisions and adjustments from both sides, with each team working to ensure the necessary scientific rigor and effective integration of the first three recommendations. On several occasions, either one or the other team tested initial versions of the games with students to assess the real integration of guidelines 1, 2, and 3. The team of mathematics educators ensured that each game script included the curricular recommendations highlighted by research to consolidate a mathematical education for the 21st century. In fact, the development of reasoning, critical thinking, and flexibility when analyzing how to play and taking advantage of what each student knows, was essential. The iNova Media Lab team analyzed the feasibility of the script devised by the mathematics educators in terms of a high-quality multimedia product. Each of these teams explicitly stated the necessary adjustments to be made, reviewing successive versions of the developed multimedia products. It was a time-consuming effort that involved many hours of joint work from both teams. The final products, the 10 games now available online, reflect this collaborative work developed by highly qualified individuals and, also, the limitations imposed by the choice of enabling playing the game on any mobile device, that posed successive restrictions on the objects to include on each game screen.

This experience supports recommendation 1:

Multimedia products designed for Education 5.0 require the involvement of specialized teams with up-to-date and consistent scientific knowledge on how to promote learning aiming at the development of high order thinking skills such as reasoning and critical thinking.

Although the collected data clearly indicates children's interest and enthusiasm in playing the games, the best students seemed to use them autonomously more often. In fact, students with more difficulties naturally tend not to take the initiative to engage in extra activities that focus on topics they do not usually like. Thus, somehow, their learning process is limited to the use of few interesting resources.

We concluded that implementing Guideline 3 (*Promote personalized and independent learning*) for all students poses some challenges, even when, as was the case with produced games, it is possible to choose different levels of difficulty.

Therefore, we propose recommendation 2:

Alongside individual exploration and collective discussion with the whole class, it seems sensible to suggest creating alternative work where small groups of students focus on analyzing what is needed to improve their game score. This objective can help students with more difficulties to feel involved and enthusiastic about mastering the mathematical knowledge necessary to progress while.

In close connection with what we stated above and with the limited integration of games in teaching practice, it seems reasonable to rethink the adopted design in implementing Guideline 4 (*Integrate examples of teacher's actions via 10 teaching guides*). Thus, in addition to the already contemplated components - the educational purpose of the game, its integration into the official curriculum, overall organization of the game, and examples of questions that teachers can pose to the children, either in writing or orally - we think it is relevant to propose, at least, a detailed lesson plan focused on developing the analysis of the more complex aspects involved in each game and suggesting specific paths to integrate students with more difficulties.

The above reflection supports recommendation 3:

Allied to the use of quality digital educational resources, it is important to provide materials that support the teacher's practice, aiming to work with students with different levels of knowledge and providing concrete ways of working in the classroom.

CONCLUDING REMARKS: PROBLEMATIC ASPECTS TO MOVE TOWARDS EDUCATION 5.0

This chapter analyzes and discusses a study, which informed specific adjustments in some educational technological games and confirmed, or not, several of the potentialities that intentionally underlined their design. Analyzed data contextualizes a discussion on some problematic aspects related to moving towards Education 5.0, which allows the integration of digital technologies in a more meaningful way in the learning process, aiming at the development of critical and creative thinking and collaborative work. Those problematic aspects are related to the development of quality educational technological tools and teacher training.

Development of Quality Educational Technological Tools

The type and quality of technological tools that can and should be used in education are of central importance. "Designing personalised technology is a process that requires, apart from technical competence, extensive subject domain and cognitive modelling expertise, and therefore typically requires the input from varied experts "(Vanbecelaere & Benton, 2021, p. 1793). In fact, if we want to develop high order thinking skills (problem-solving, metacognition, reasoning, etc.), we cannot rely solely on educational tools that mainly appeal to repetition, mastery of routine techniques, or memorization. In the case of students' mathematical education, this is a particularly critical aspect since most available online technological resources tend to reproduce a general philosophy of knowledge transmission and repetitive practice (Bertram, 2020; Moreira et al., 2020).

While admitting that it will be possible to produce educational technological resources following a different organization from what we adopted, we believe that three essential conditions must be guaranteed in their design. The first concerns the need for qualified designers. This means that the subject matter involved (in our case, mathematics) must reflect the knowledge of educational researchers. Indeed, while emphasizing that experienced teachers can make valuable contributions, their knowledge is predominantly practical (Johnson, 1984) and therefore naturally less specialized in designing new 'objects.' They also do not master the results of educational research or have a deep understanding of the directions of change and innovation that should guide teaching. The same applies to the field of multimedia content production.

The second condition relates to the necessary interaction of designers (disciplinary and multimedia content producers) that must accompany the entire product construction process. It is from the analysis of products under development that it is possible to progress, ensuring the required quality and rigor. During the production process new possibilities can emerge to enrich what was initially thought, but they must be critically analyzed considering the educational objectives sought.

Finally, the third condition relates to the testing of the produced materials in real schools, involving several teachers and their students. It is not enough to ask some students or some teachers to individually analyze the developing multimedia product. Although these few experiments can provide valuable contributions to improve the materials being developed, it is important to analyze how they are explored in the real educational context, i.e., in the classroom.

Teacher Training

Teacher training emerges as a central priority on the path to Education 5.0, as the strategic integration of digital technologies for the development of 21st-century competencies in students (Figueiredo, 2017) is not an easy task and requires high-quality and continuous teacher training.

The data discussed earlier add arguments to those indicated by various authors about the centrality of the teacher's role in student learning, on the one hand, and the slow integration of new or unfamiliar resources into their practice on the other (Ball et al., 2008). Although the pandemic context, with unexpected interruptions and various limitations, is an argument that justifies the limited attention given to the analysis and discussion of each game with the students, it could also be argued in the opposite direction. The games were new resources that could be used even without face-to-face classes. However, their real integration into the work with the students was much more reduced than expected.

The exploration of the games in the classroom completely shifted away from the transmission of knowledge and brought to the forefront some of the central functions of the teacher in the path towards Education 5.0: i) mediator and facilitator of learning, ii) promoter of collaboration considering the individual needs and rhythms of each student, iii) development of critical thinking, and iv) monitoring and evaluation of students, not requiring a fifth equally fundamental function, creativity, as the exploration of these games did not appeal to it.

The educational written materials also play an important role, as in our work, in explaining curricular connections, the organization and mechanics of each game, and the evaluation of the learning outcomes. They can also include, as we suggested after the experimentation, lesson plans that simulate possibilities aiming to develop the role of mediator and facilitator of learning, promoter of collaboration considering the individual needs and rhythms of each student, and development of critical thinking. However, these materials will always be insufficient as they do not rely on the analysis and necessary evolution of each teacher's practice and hardly cover all the dimensions included in Technological Pedagogical Content Knowledge (TPCK) as characterized by authors like Chai et al. (2013). Following this analysis and the finding that produced materials were rarely or not used at all in Primary classrooms, the Portuguese Ministry of Education has been implementing continuous training actions for elementary school teachers, with the aim of promoting reflection and analysis of the relevance of using DER-MAT in the classroom context (https://redge.dge.mec.pt/site/noticias/formacao-professores-do-1o-ciclo-do-ensino-basico-nut-centro).

The complexity of developing TPCK requires high-quality initial and continuous training focused on the analysis of practices and reflection on one's own practice. In other words, it requires teacher training programs that do not rely, solely, on the transmission of knowledge and that include the analysis of practice and collaboration between both teachers and trainer/researcher trainees.

Considering our experience and literature commendations, we highlight two training modalities. The first one consists in following the design of an in-service teacher education program described by Serrazina (2013) including (i) thematic sessions focused on addressing topics that would ensure a significant clarification and deepening of mathematical and didactic knowledge (Pedagogical Content Knowledge - PCK) and, as it is now relevant, TPCK, (ii) reflection sessions on the practice carried out by each teacher and (iii) classroom monitoring/supervision sessions by the trainer. We emphasize that this last aspect is very important because it is, as reported by Serrazina (2013), the main driver of change in teacher practices.

The second modality we propose consists in conducting Lesson Studies, a practice-based, collaborative, and research lesson-oriented professional development model that is considered a powerful approach to improve teaching (Hang & Huang, 2017). Lesson studies involve: i) identification of the topics to be addressed; ii) planning the work to be done with students in the classroom; iii) conducting the investigative lesson, and iv) reflecting on the lesson (Mendes et al., 2021). Lesson studies, as a formative process, contributes to the development of the teacher's pedagogical content knowledge, aiming to favor an exploratory approach to teaching (Mendes et al., 2021). This modality, that values the identification of learning objectives and the planning of detailed lessons, can be very important to support teacher's professional knowledge development. In particular, it can help to adopt different working modalities in the classroom and support collective discussions focused on the mathematics involved in the games, integrating students with lower achievement and simultaneously focusing the development of competences for the 21st century.

ACKNOWLEDGMENT

This research was co-funded by POCH, Portugal 2020 and the European Social Fund, through the Digital Educational Resources (DER) Project (POCH-04-5267-FSE-000124) developed by the Direção Geral da Educação (DGE) in partnership with the Universidade Nova de Lisboa – iNOVA Media Lab, Faculdade de Letras da Universidade de Lisboa, Instituto Politécnico de Setúbal and Universidade de Aveiro.

REFERENCES

Ball, D. L., Thames, M. H., & Phelps, G. (2008). Content knowledge for teaching: What makes it special? *Journal of Teacher Education*, *59*(5), 389–407. doi:10.1177/0022487108324554

Battista, M. T., & Clements, D. H. (1996). Students' understanding of three-dimensional rectangular arrays of cubes. *Journal for Research in Mathematics Education*, *27*(3), 258–292. doi:10.2307/749365

Bertram, L. (2020). Digital Learning Games for Mathematics and Computer Science Education: The Need for Preregistered RCTs, Standardized Methodology, and Advanced Technology. *Frontiers in Psychology*, *11*, 1–10. doi:10.3389/fpsyg.2020.02127

Brocardo, J., Delgado, C., Mendes, F., & Ponte, J. P. (2022). Ações do professor e desenvolvimento do raciocínio matemático durante a discussão coletiva de uma tarefa. *Educación Matemática*, *34*(2), 101–133. doi:10.24844/EM3402.04

Chai, C.-S., Koh, J. H.-L., & Tsai, C.-C. (2013). A Review of Technological Pedagogical Content Knowledge. *Journal of Educational Technology & Society*, *16*(2), 31–51. https://www.jstor.org/stable/jeductechsoci.16.2.31

Chan, J. (2019). Importance of Educational Technology on Learning. *Merit Research Journal of Education and Review, 7*(6), 65–67. doi:10.5281/zenodo.3255008

Cheung, S. Y., & Ng, K. Y. (2021). Application of the Educational Game to Enhance Student Learning. *Frontiers in Education, 6*, 1–10. doi:10.3389/feduc.2021.623793

Cravinho, J., Tribolet, J., Capucha, L., Silva, S., & Veiga, P. (2022). *O digital na educação*. Conselho Nacional da Educação. https://www.cnedu.pt/content/edicoes/estudos_e_relatorios/O_Digital_na_Educacao_2022.docx.pdf

Dabbous, M., Kawtharani, A., Fahs, I., Hallal, Z., Shouman, D., Akel, M., Rahal, M., & Sakr, F. (2022). The Role of Game-Based Learning in Experiential Education: Tool Validation, Motivation Assessment, and Outcomes Evaluation among a Sample of Pharmacy Students. *Education Sciences, 12*(7), 1-13. doi:10.3390/educsci12070434

European Commission. (2018). *Digital Education Action Plan*. European Commission. https://education.ec.europa.eu/focus-topics/digital-education/action-plan

Figueiredo, A. D. (2017). Que competências para as novas gerações? In *O Futuro ao nosso alcance: Homenagem a Roberto Carneiro* (pp. 325–333). Universidade Católica Portuguesa.

Gifford, S., Gripton, C., Williams, H., Lancaster, A., Bates, K. E., Williams, A. Y. Gilligan-Lee, K., Borthwick, A., & Farran, E. K. (2022). *Spatial Reasoning in early childhood*. Research Gate. https://doi.org/ doi:10.31234/osf.io/jnwpu

Gros, B. (2006). Digital games in Education: The Design of Games-Based Learning Environments. *Journal of Research on Technology in Education, 40*(1), 23–38. doi:10.1080/15391523.2007.10782494

HanX.HuangR. (2017). Promover o ensino da matemática e o desenvolvimento profissional do professor através do estudo de aula paralelo. *Quadrante, 26*(2), 5–18. doi:10.48489/quadrante.22953

Hanson, T. L., Drumheller, K., Mallard, J., McKee, C., & Schlegel, P. (2010). Cell phones, text messaging, and Facebook: Competing time demands of today's college students. *College Teaching, 59*(1), 23–30. doi:10.1080/87567555.2010.489078

Johnson, M., & Elbaz, F. (1984). Teacher Thinking: A Study of Practical Knowledge. *Curriculum Inquiry, 14*(4), 465–468. doi:10.2307/3202267

Martins, G. O., Gomes, C. S., Brocardo, J. L., Pedroso, J. V., Acosta Carrillo, J. L., Ucha, L. M., Encarnação, M., Horta, M. J., Calçada, M. T., Nery, R. V., & Rodrigues, S. V. (2017). *O perfil dos alunos à saída da escolaridade obrigatória*. Ministério da Educação. Direção Geral de Educação. http://dge.mec.pt/sites/default/files/Curriculo/Projeto_Autonomia_e_Flexibilidade/perfil_dos_alunos.pdf

Martins, M. E. & Ponte, J. P. (2011). *Organização e tratamento de dados*. ME – DGIDC.

Mendes, F., Delgado, C., & Brocardo, J. (2021). Estudo de aula: Uma experiência na formação inicial de professores de primeiro ciclo. In *Livro de Atas do 7º Congresso nacional de práticas pedagógicas no ensino superior* (pp. 162-167). Universidade de Aveiro. 10.48528/yhzq-cp97

Mendes, F., Delgado, C., & Brocardo, J. (2022). Challenges faced by Preservice Teachers in Planning and Exploring Tasks that Promote Mathematical Reasoning. *Acta Scientiae, 24*(4), 147–182. doi:10.17648/acta.scientiae.7123

MoreiraA.HenriquesS.BarrosD.GoulãoF.CaeiroD. (2020). *Educação digital em rede: princípios para o design pedagógico em tempos de pandemia.* Universidade Aberta. doi:10.34627/rfg0-ps07

Pan, L., Tlili, A., Li, J., Jiang, F., Shi, G., Yu, H., & Yang, J. (2021). How to Implement Game-Based Learning in a Smart Classroom? A Model Based on a Systematic Literature Review and Delphi Method. *Frontiers in Psychology, 12,* 1-13. doi:10.3389/fpsyg.2021.749837

Possato, A. B., Zamoner, Z., Monteiro, P. O., & Querido de Oliveira Chamon, E. M. (2022). O uso de games: Uma prática discutida como inovadora na educação 5.0. *Interação - Revista de Ensino. Pesquisa e Extensão, 24*(3), 23–41. doi:10.33836/interacao.v24i3.722

Sera, L., & Wheeler, E. (2017). Game on: The Gamification of the Pharmacy Classroom. *Currents in Pharmacy Teaching & Learning, 9*(1), 155–159. doi:10.1016/j.cptl.2016.08.046

Serrazina, M. (2013). O Programa de Formação Contínua em Matemática para Professores do 1.º ciclo e a melhoria do ensino da Matemática. *Da Investigação às Práticas, 3*(2), 75–97. https://ojs.eselx.ipl.pt/index.php/invep/article/view/34/34

Threlfall, J. (2009). Strategies and flexibility in mental calculation. *ZDM: The International Journal on Mathematics Education, 41*(5), 541-555. https://link.springer.com/article/10.1007/s11858-009-0195-3

Vanbecelaere, S., & Benton, L. (2021). Technology mediated personalized learning for younger learners: Concepts, design, methods, and practice. *British Journal of Educational Technology, 52*(5), 1793–1797. doi:10.1111/bjet.13150

KEY TERMS AND DEFINITIONS

Critical Thinking: Is the process of actively and skillfully analyzing, evaluating, and synthesizing information to form well-reasoned judgments and make informed decisions.

Digital Mathematics Games: Are interactive and engaging software applications designed to help students learn and practice various mathematical concepts in a fun and enjoyable way. These games often combine educational content with elements of play, competition, and rewards to keep students motivated and interested in learning math.

Education 5.0: Refers to a potential evolution or advancement in the field of education beyond the previous concepts like Education 1.0 (traditional teacher-centric), Education 2.0 (technology integration), Education 3.0 (personalized and self-directed learning), and Education 4.0 (industry-focused and skill-based learning). "Education 5.0" is not yet a widely accepted concept.

Educational Game Design: Is the process of creating interactive and engaging games with a specific focus on facilitating learning and educational outcomes.

Educational Technology Tools: Are digital resources and applications designed to enhance teaching and learning experience in various educational settings.

Flexibility: Refers to the ability to adapt, adjust, or change easily and willingly in response to new or changing circumstances.

Lesson Study: Is a collaborative professional development approach used in education to improve teaching practices and student learning outcomes. It originated in Japan but has been adapted in various countries worldwide. Lesson Study involves a group of teachers working together to design, observe, and analyze a specific lesson.

Pedagogical Content Knowledge (PCK): Is a framework in the field of education that describes the specialized knowledge and understanding that teachers possess about how to effectively teach a particular subject or content to students.

Reasoning: Is the cognitive process of thinking logically and systematically to make sense of information, draw conclusions, and solve problems.

Technological Pedagogical Content Knowledge (TPCK): Is a framework in the field of education that describes the knowledge and understanding required by teachers to effectively integrate technology into their teaching practices. TPCK emphasizes the integration of technology to support and enhance the teaching and learning of specific content.

Chapter 6
Digitalization and the Consumer Experience:
The Case of the Health Sector in Portugal

Duarte Xara-Brasil
iD https://orcid.org/0000-0002-0918-0373
Instituto Politécnico de Setúbal, Portugal

Carla Viana
iD https://orcid.org/0009-0002-6618-8184
Instituto Politécnico de Setúbal, Portugal

Maria Inês F. S. Cruz
Faculdade de Ciências, Universidade de Lisboa, Portugal

ABSTRACT

Digital transformation is a reality in practically all business industries and has influenced the development of new marketing practices and, consequently, consumer experiences, particularly in the health sector. The aim of this research is to analyze the potential benefits that digital transformation and digital marketing may have in the customer's experiences with health service providers. This study allowed the confirmation of many of the aspects researched in previous academic works and reinforced the importance of using more technological solutions for current users, as well as the need to improve, namely in terms of service personalization, with greater speed and response, and quality of the service provided in an integrated way by the different touchpoints. Furthermore, it reinforced some important objections of users, namely related to the presumed greater difficulty of personal interaction, especially in cases of dissatisfaction and complaint, or in groups of patients with less digital training.

DOI: 10.4018/978-1-6684-9039-6.ch006

INTRODUCTION

Digital transformation is an evolutionary process, that aims to improve an entity by triggering significant changes to its properties through combinations of information, computing, communication, and connectivity technologies (Vial, 2019). According to Ziółkowska (2021), Digital transformation is about the improvement of an organization and processes using the potential technology between platforms and functions to radically improve the quality of customer outcomes. This process of innovation is focused on customer preferences, needs, and expectations as a strategic driver to create value for customers - providing more suitable solutions to the market – and to the organization, in different functional areas, such as finance, production, and marketing, among others.

The goal of this research is to analyze the impact that digital transformation, and the actions of digital marketing have in the experience of the healthcare consumers in Portugal, so that we can identify vectors capable of improving this experience to the users. With this aim, this document will provide a review of the most updated literature focused on digital transformation in the healthcare sector, together with qualitative research centered in a group of Portuguese users of health mobile apps.

THEORETICAL BACKGROUND

Digital transformation has been revolutionizing the interactions between organizations and their stakeholders: customers, employees, shareholders, and others. For organizations, the use of digital transformation can be seen as an important opportunity for improvement. It implies the rethinking of their business model, in search of greater efficiency gains, differentiation in the face of competition, customer satisfaction and loyalty, and diversification of touchpoints. There is a need to respond to increasingly higher consumer expectations and to create a mechanism to respond to competitors' practices.

Recently, there have been at least three phenomena that greatly influence interactions with customers and the way they relate to digital platforms and consumption: technological advances/digital transformation, such as artificial intelligence (AI), and machine; the COVID-19 pandemic period; and the implications of the War in Ukraine:

- Technological advances, particularly Artificial Intelligence technology is one of the foremost original innovations that has transformed numerous sectors (Tater et al., 2022). A neural network machine learning model, called GPT-3, was trained using internet data to produce any kind of text (Tater et al., 2022); Tools like ChatGPT can analyze large datasets to identify trends and patterns, consumer behaviors and changes in market demand (Alshater, 2023).
- COVID-19 pandemic times changed lifestyles due to severe mobility restrictions and that has dramatically changed the market's position and size of the digital, leading to the need for a company's fast innovation and agility, as a means to improve customer experience (Lewnes, 2021).
- The war in Ukraine represents an unprecedented situation in recent decades, with numerous consequences regarding the increasing energy prices, cruelty, mass emigration, higher electricity bills, and the moral support for Ukraine (Palmié et al., 2023). Customer Behavior is unpredictable but shows higher emotional connections with reliable suppliers in their search for stability and value, which may include relevant business opportunities related to digital marketing tools (Zlatova, 2022).

The concept of digital transformation is present in all industries and involves the integration of technology and digital marketing in the cultural and customer interaction processes of the business (Hoffman et al., 2022; He et al., 2023; Radnan & Christin, 2023; Tariq, 2023). Digital transformation is a central component of the marketing performance of organizations, aiming to reach, engage and win consumers through increasing the use of digital actions and means (Akgün & Arslan, 2022; Kraus et al., 2022).

Digital consumers have been developing growing expectations related to the services that organizations provide them, requesting a growing level of innovation in the solutions made available through digital platforms, such as mobile digital solutions, home banking apps, streaming platforms, and internet retailing (Vial, 2019). On the other hand, companies use digital marketing, new technologies, and digital interaction platforms to achieve marketing goals related to sales, profits, loyalty, and engagement, among others.

Many organizations are adjusting the way they work due to the digital expectations of their customers, which have increased significantly in recent years. During the pandemic years of COVID-19, the world witnessed a 70% increase in smartphone usage (Shahid et al.., 2022). According to the Global Mobile Consumer Trends Report (GWI, 2023), adults spend more than 6 hours online daily via mobile phone, PC, laptop, or tablet, and online behaviors have also changed substantially. Although the Google search bar is still the starting point for about 25% of consumers, artificial intelligence is no longer a trend but a reality and artificial intelligence services like ChatGPT have become a major player. According to Hu (2023), ChatGPT is estimated to have reached 100 million monthly active users by January 2023, just three months after its launch. In comparison with other sites, Instagram took more than 2 years to reach those subscribers, and TikTok took 9 months.

In Portugal, the data are close to the global ones (Kemp, 2023), and of the 10.26 million inhabitants, 85.1% have Internet access and 78.5% are active users on social networks, spending an average of 7 hours 37 minutes on the internet, where 95.4% of the time is occupied by their smartphones. Though it is not clear what role digital technologies will play in the future and the exact impact of these three phenomena, or others, that may arise in the meantime. In fact, contrary to expectations, in 2022 and 2023, large and small technology companies have been making massive redundancies, because of market growth far below industry expectations (Trueman, 2023).

Smartphones are becoming increasingly more relevant in consumers' purchases and information search processes with organizations, highlighting retail apps, food ordering apps and Internet of Things processes, social networks, and mobile banking (Shahid et al., 2022). For example, in mobile banking apps, there has been a very significant increase in downloads of mobile banking applications and the number of daily active users, reflecting the benefits of these innovations for both account holders and banks. Users save their time and money in addition to benefiting from greater comfort and ease, while for banks, it helps save on the costs involved in maintaining physical space and human resources (Shahid et al., 2022).

DIGITAL TRANSFORMATION IN THE HEALTHCARE SECTOR

The healthcare sector is also undergoing a digital transformation, driven by rapid technological advances, and changes in patients (consumer) behavior and experiences (Aggar et al., 2020; Akgün & Arslan, 2022).

Increasing digital transformation enables more efficient diagnoses, personalized treatment plans, and more optimized communication with patients (Sangaiah et al., 2023). Advances related to artificial intelligence, Internet of Things, and data mining have been revolutionizing the performance of the healthcare sector on how it acts and manages the relationship with the patient (Chaudhary & Alam, 2022; Sangaiah et al., 2023).

Artificial intelligence is a central component of the digital transformation in healthcare, with applications ranging from technical support, and diagnosis, to the prescription of treatments that are increasingly personalized to each individual's situation. The algorithms that support artificial intelligence can analyze large amounts of data and identify patterns and trends, boosting the speed, improvement, and accuracy of diagnosis and treatment (Sangaiah et al., 2023).

Online patient records have transformed the way data is managed, stored, and shared, leading to a more efficient, coordinated, and patient-centric process, while providing companies with real-time customer data (Verhoef & Bijmolt, 2019; Chaudhary & Alam, 2022).

The personalization of services provided by artificial intelligence allows companies operating in the healthcare sector to adapt segmented communication, predict patient behaviors, and create relevant and appealing content; but it also helps them optimize resources, increase efficiency in customer and patient relations, focus on more complex tasks and value-added activities, and achieve better financial results (Aggar et al., 2020; Kopalle et al., 2022).

However, digital transformation in the healthcare sector also presents some challenges and concerns, namely issues related to privacy and security in the use of patient data (Sujan et al., 2019; Aggar et al., 2020; Mohammed-Nasir et al., 2023). For the digital transformation within the healthcare sector to be successful, it is necessary to empower the teams that have access to and work with these patient data to ensure ethics and transparency in the experience, in the relationship between the company operating in the healthcare sector and the customer or patient (Bani et al.,2020; Nurgalieva & Doherty, 2023; Tariq, 2023). Also, the limitations of technological infrastructures can be a hindrance to a successful implementation of digital transformation from the point of view of marketing. It is necessary to invest in hardware and software adapted to the activity, in addition to the need to overcome some cultural barriers, resistance to change of the teams, and limitations of the technological system itself, which being unsuitable, can become a challenging obstacle to the success of the company in the relationship with customers (Hartmann et al., 2023; Tariq, 2023).

The patient experience is a major concern for companies because patients are now better informed, have more access to information and there is more competition in the market. In this context, the use of technology to improve this experience has been one of the main objectives of healthcare companies (Tariq, 2023). Sangaiah et al. (2023) corroborates that digital transformation has the potential to significantly improve their experience, allowing companies to deliver more efficient, personalized, and affordable services.

Consumers, with an increasing desire for the use of digital media in different aspects of their lives, also expect healthcare providers to be more accessible and closer to their needs and desires (Sujan et al., 2019; Aggar et al., 2020; Hartmann et al., 2023). These changes in consumer behavior allow for the deepening use of digital marketing through the application of integrated strategies in companies operating in the healthcare sector and seeking to strengthen their competitive position (Akgün & Arslan, 2022, Verhoef & Bijmolt, 2019).

Understanding the digital transformation in patients experiences in the healthcare sector will bring clues to identify the potential of its use for businesses and patients (Mergel et al., 2019).

Digital Transformation and the Marketing Management of Organizations

Digital transformation has a major impact on the marketing management of organizations, namely in the interaction and delivery of healthcare services to patients, as well as their engagement and the management of their data (Sujan et al., 2019; Aggar et al., 2020). Techniques such as search engine optimization, social media management, email marketing, and content marketing are increasingly used to attract and retain customers more and more effectively (Drake et al., 2022; Shaikh, Vayani & Akram, 2022; Gangl & Krychtiuk, 2023). This reality stems from the potential of technology applied to digital transformation (Drake et al., 2022; Hoffman et al., 2022; Shaikh et al., 2022; Hartmann et al., 2023; Radnan & Christin, 2023).

Digital marketing is a core component of digital transformation in the healthcare sector, enabling greater reach of companies' operations and increased patientes engagement, improving service levels, and reducing errors and dissatisfaction (Akgün & Arslan, 2022). It encompasses several components, including search engine optimization, social media management, email marketing, and content marketing, which are used to attract and retain customers more effectively (Gangl & Krychtiuk, 2023; Sangaiah et al., 2023; Radnan & Christin, 2023). Management of these components may lead to greater personalization of their services and of the communication directed to patients, much faster and aligned with their real needs and desires, achieving higher levels of satisfaction, retention, and loyalty, increasing brand awareness, prestige, and recognition in the market (Verhoef & Bijmolt, 2019).

Digital marketing focuses on communicating and promoting products and services while enabling a growing number of consumers to find and select their sources of information for health-related services (Akgün & Arslan, 2022). Through digital media, consumers have the possibility o inform themselves and choose the company that best meets their wants and needs (Hartmann et al., 2023). That is why a performance focused on search engine optimization, social networks, content marketing, and e-mail marketing, is essential for the communication of companies operating in this sector (Gangl & Krychtiuk, 2023):

- Search engine optimizations can attract more users and generate more traffic, and new leads, and being able to increase engagement with users, converting leads into customers, enabling the relationship between the two to grow (Hartmann et al., 2023; Tariq, 2023). These processes aim to place a website in the first results of search engines, making it easier to navigate, and allowing them to find relevant information and purchase healthcare products and services in real-time (Akgün & Arslan, 2022).
- Digital social networks allow the health sector to have a direct relationship with patients, providing useful moments to build trust, share information and promote a sense of community (Gangl & Krychtiuk, 2023; Sangaiah et al., 2023; Radnan & Christin, 2023). Platforms such as Facebook, Instagram, and LinkedIn allow the healthcare sector and especially the companies operating in it to share updates, promote events and answer questions from patients in real time (Akgün & Arslan, 2022).
- Content marketing involves creating and sharing relevant and consistent content to attract, retain and engage a particular audience (Chen, 2023; Barbosa et al., 2023). In healthcare, this can include educational articles on the company website, social media post placement, videos, and info-

graphics covering various healthcare topics from preventative care to treatment options (Gangl & Krychtiuk, 2023). These contents should be excellent, well-written, and credible, to strategically position the company's brand in the target segment it intends to reach (Barbosa, Saura & Zekan (2023).

- Email marketing allows segmenting through the company's database, demographic information, and subscriber preferences, adapting more relevant and engaging messages to this audience (Chaudhary & Alam, 2022; Ligaraba et al., 2023). In the healthcare sector, it is also used for companies to communicate directly with potential customers or current patients, providing them with, for example, personalized information, service and product updates, consultations, and health tips (Hartmann et al., 2023; Tariq, 2023).

Customers are interacting with companies through multiple touchpoints and companies should pursue an omnichannel approach, focusing on both digital and physical channels while envisioning the optimization of the customer journey (Weber, & Chatzopoulos, 2019). In fact, digital technology can change the customer's journey from a regular customer experience into a digital journey where touchpoints are supported by digital means.

The Digital Apps

The increasing sophistication of competition and consumers' expectations regarding the whole process of interaction with organizations, before, during, and after the process, implies the need for a systematic adjustment of the points of contact with consumers around the search for a long-term relationship (Scherpen et al., 2018). With the increase in the use of smartphones and other mobile platforms - even more so in recent years, in the context of the pandemic – mobile devices have become even more relevant for consumers' purchases and information search processes with organizations (Shahid et al., 2022).

Mobile applications in the health sector allow patients to develop several interactions with healthcare providers, such as information searches, booking appointments, examinations, and treatments, as well as tracking and monitoring their health status, which enables them to develop a more active role in the management of their well-being (Radnan & Christin, 2023). For organizations, these digital applications also allow them to collect data on the behavior and preferences of their patients that lead them to a better understanding of the market to make more adjusted decisions and leading also to the development of more targeted, predictive, and effective actions (Chaudhary & Alam, 2022).

The management of the shopping experience and consequently the need for monitoring and evaluation of the consumer experience were topics identified as being among the most important research areas by the Marketing Science Institute (MSI, 2020). According to Journée & Weber (2014), customer experience is a personal and subjective response that customers have on direct or indirect contact with an organization, at several levels. In this context, companies must consistently provide positive and distinctive experiences to increase loyalty and customer advocacy through emotional, physical, sensorial, rational, and relational perceptions, that may lead to a profitable, durable, and affective relationship with potential financial and immaterial impacts.

Online and offline channels provide different experiences (Xu, Park& Lee, 2022). According to Prasad & Aryasri, (2009), consumer behavior in relation to online shopping is highly influenced by convenience, the pleasure of shopping, and the webshop environment, whereas, on the contrary, the greater difficulty of searching, lack of customization of the offer, outdated websites and unavailability of products/services, may be reasons for dissatisfaction and distrust. In addition, the absence of social contact in the online shopping environment may have a negative influence on consumers who typically need sales assistance or social contact during shopping (Prasad and Aryasri, 2009). Thus, enhancing perceived social presence in the online shopping environment increases consumers' trust and encourages purchasing (Hassanein and Head, 2007). According to Hofacker (2001, as cited in Prasad and Aryasri, 2009) trust in Internet shopping is based on the perceived size and reputation of its physical store network, the perceived privacy and quantum of risk, and the perceptions of convenience.

In e-commerce, trust is a critical variable, that represents the customer sense of reliability towards the service or product provider (Camp, 2010). In this context, Ling et al. (2010) state that e-retailers must provide honest and trustworthy information to potential web shoppers at all times to increase the level of online trust. Overall, shopping convenience is defined as time and effort saving in shopping and includes five dimensions that should be taken into consideration in digital marketing strategies and actions managers: access, search, evaluation, transaction, and possession/post-purchase convenience (Jiang, 2013).

Mobile is one of the components of online marketing, which includes the integration of portable equipment - including smartphones, tablets, and laptops - that can be used while the user is on the move (in motion), allowing the user to perform various activities and make purchasing decisions on the spur of the moment (Shankar et al., 2016). These devices bring potential functional benefits for consumers, including speed of access, permanent availability to buy and obtain information, and the reduction of geographical constraints related to geographical access to information, products, and services.

Smartphones are one of the most relevant mobile components in many consumers' purchase journeys, allowing them to extend the scope of their interactions to channels that are accessible anytime, anywhere (Shankar et al., 2016). In addition to these important functional benefits, smartphones provide emotional benefits, given their portability, their personal nature and sense of privacy, and tactile gratification, notably in times of stress, when compared to other components such as laptops (Melumad, & Pham, 2020). According to Shankar et al. (2016), there are other reasons why consumers find mobile search and discovery attractive: mobile devices provide a sense of immediacy, offering a perception of having everything accessible, literally, at their fingertips. Marketers who facilitate a sense of discovery and serendipity during the pre-purchase process will likely benefit from increased user engagement.

When focusing on mobile applications, there are specificities in their influence on consumer behavior (e.g. Kushlev & Leitao, 2020). For example, Melumad and Pham (2020) suggested that smartphones are more private and portable and are a channel in which more active interaction with consumers occurs (e.g., haptic feedback). These unique features of smartphones may reduce the psychological distance between the channel and consumers and bring more attention to feasibility aspects in comparison to the traditional online channel. Moreover, additional technological improvements in the online channel, like the incorporation of virtual reality, may decrease psychological distance and shift consumers' attentional focus toward the feasibility aspects of the online channel (Huang, T. & Liao, 2017; Keng et al., 2011)

Mobile marketing has a wide range of impacts on the shopper's behavior during all the stages of a shopper's path-to-purchase and beyond and the key drivers vary across the different stages in the shopping cycle engaged (Shankar et al., 2016). Mobile marketing apps with the greatest chance of success are those that balance functional needs with hedonic and social affiliation needs (Shankar et al., 2016). For example, the development of mobile communities of users with similar interests leads to the huge potential for using mobile apps to create deeper and more meaningful relationships because it provides instantaneous feedback to the community, with the posting of pictures, uploading videos, and writing comments via forums such as Yelp and YouTube. Mobile communication is most effective when shoppers, consumers, and users are most engaged (Shankar et al., 2016).

Despite its potential, there are challenges to be overcome when integrating sophisticated digital marketing strategies in the health sector, related to ethical, privacy, and data protection issues, in order to ensure that the information provided by the patient to the company is not used for purposes other than those related only to his or her health (Bani et al., 2020; Kopalle, et al., 2022; Mohammed-Nasir et al., 2023; Nurgalieva & Doherty, 2023). On the other hand, not all consumers are able to use the tools that digital transformation provides them, either because they have insufficient digital literacy or simply because they do not have access to the necessary technology (Kopalle, et al., 2022), and these can cause disparities in the quality of patient service (Radnan & Christin, 2023). Therefore, Sujan et al. (2019), Aggar et al. (2020), and Drake et al., (2022), stress the importance of organizations to adapt to these different consumer profiles and experiences, taking advantage of the opportunities that digital transformation and, consequently, digital marketing offers them. Verhoef & Bijmolt (2019), Akgün & Arslan (2022), and He et al. (2023) corroborate the same opinion, that marketing becomes a source of competitive advantage for organizations that adopt digital transformation applied to their customers' consumption experience.

CASE STUDY

Given the importance that digital technologies may have in the relationship between healthcare providers and their patients, it is important to analyze the innovation potential of these digital tools in the health sector. In line with the literature which states that digital transformation is an ongoing process that has been changing the interactions between organizations and their stakeholders and that the innovation process is focused on customer preferences, needs, and expectations, a qualitative methodology was used, in this case, a focus group.

The current work is based on the analyses of digital marketing practices by healthcare providers at the health services in Portugal and it takes a deeper look at how consumers experience the use of these online platforms. The aim is to identify the impact (and power) of digital tansformation in the Portuguese healthcare consumer's daily life, and to identify vectors and ways in which this experience can be improved.

Qualitative methodologies have proven to be appropriate in cases where there is a need to identify or understand new or complex topics (Powell & Single, 1996), and the focus group technique is one of the most widely used research methodologies in the social sciences for the purpose of collecting qualitative information in a group meeting environment to answer certain research questions. Focus groups consist of an informal discussion among individuals selected for the discussion of specific topics indicated by the researchers and their interest, based on their personal experience, on the topic being researched (Beck et al., 1986). The use of focus group methodology has become widespread (Voinov et al., 2016; Palermo and Hernandez, 2020). According to Wilkinson (1998), the number of participants per group is around 6 to 8 people and rarely exceeds a limit of 12 players.

Based on the objectives of this study, a script was developed for the focus groups to understand the experience of using digital technologies in the health sector - by consumers - and how they perceive the use of digital technology in the future. To this end, the present authors sought to include participants with a professional and academic background in digital marketing, not necessarily in the health sector, who could bring insights that would help to envision the role that digital transformation and mobile apps may have in the development of this business and in the engagement of users.

Two focus groups were operationalized and moderated by the organizers of this study with the participation of 13 people of Portuguese nationality from different geographical (Lisbon, Porto, Aveiro, Leiria, and Luanda) and professional backgrounds (marketers, managers, designers, engeniers, students, among others), and age groups (19 to 55 years old). The focus groups were conducted through the ZOOM platform between April and May 2023.

There was a third focus group conducted where ten subjects were expected. However, due to the absence of six of the elements, and though the results corroborate the other two groups and the literature, this group was not considered for the discussion for not contemplating the prerequisites of a minimum of six participants (Wilkinson, 1998).

FINDINGS AND DISCUSSION

The focus groups were all recorded with the express consent of the participants and the information collected was systematized into three main vectors: (1) user experience; (2) users' fears, and (3) users' expectations, which will be detailed below.

User Experience in Using Digital Technologies in the Relationship With Health Service Providers

All participants in the focus groups assumed to have some experience in using digital media in their interaction with health providers, although they expressed different levels of expertise.

The experience of autonomous digital use can be very simple - providing medications prescribed electronically by the physician - or include different touchpoints in isolation or complementarily that allow access to various services and functionalities:

- One of the younger participants reported using the chat (WhatsApp) for scheduling appointments with the doctor "I like the ease and proximity to the services I am looking for; WhatsApp and Messenger are synonymous with effectiveness. It's close, practical, I can deal with matters more quickly, and the visual record remains, and I like it."
- The website is often the first form of digital interaction with the healthcare provider. It does not require the installation of an app and "It looks better". Some of the participants mention using these two touchpoints simultaneously, such as "I start with the website and only install the app if it is differentiating. Otherwise, I uninstall it".
- Apps are used by patients with a more frequent connection with the provider. Among the most mentioned uses, the following stand out: "Appointment booking; check-in; waiting time at the permanent care services".

The advantages that are obtained from the use of these tools are very clear for the different users: simplicity and convenience - "you just grab your phone and choose", "it's super easy" and "it makes the experience of going to the doctor much easier"; the proximity - "I also receive it in SMS and email" and "I like the follow-up, which keeps us in the loop"; in this way, in cases where these interactions are successful, the users tend to repeat and deepen them, which can increase loyalty and word of mouth.

Users' Fears Regarding Health-Related Digital Technologies

Some reasons for dissatisfaction were expressed, related to the less personalized contact, the greater rigidity of the processes, the outdatedness of the contents, and the problems of operation and access that sometimes exist: "The apps and the sites do not always work". Many of the focus group participants share the opinion that digital technologies are seen by companies as a way to generate efficiency, reducing costs and personal interactions: "Many companies, when investing in technology, try to increase digital interactions and minimize personal contact". When problems/complaints occur, digital processes are usually more rigid: "It is easier for companies to communicate in an impersonal and digital way".

There are several reasons for dissatisfaction related to the performance of health service providers, related to the intermittent functioning of these platforms "Apps and websites don't always work"; "Right now the brand XYZ provider's website is down" or their outdatedness and lack of immediate response "They don't give immediate feedback, sometimes we have to wait for a confirmation". Another aspect frequently mentioned was the different levels of service enjoyed at the different touchpoints. The expectations generated through the apps or the website often do not materialize at the touchpoints, where there are sometimes delays and queues. Information is not fluid, and interactions are inadequate. In the focus groups it was mentioned that "There is often a gap between what is desired and what is real" and that "if there is a gap between the digital and the real, there starts to be a greater distance".

Patients often feel that healthcare providers invest in digital applications with the aim of reducing physical interactions and making personalized access to services more difficult. In this way, providers can save resources on customer service, for example through "virtual assistants with a limited problem-solving capacity"; or by "making it more difficult for customers to file complaints" given the difficulty in accessing human interactions and the rigidity of the responses obtained. One of the participants referred that, after being discharged from the hospital, he needed to talk to a nurse, which became impossible as the telephone call was answered by an "automatic answering service that only informed about the usual contact hours".

Regarding emotional involvement, there is a greater emotional connection related to the installation of apps than to the use of websites, which have a mainly functional use. On the other hand, patients, especially younger ones, have higher expectations regarding timely interactions, such as the ability to respond to requests for appointments, appointment reminders, shorter delays in medical procedures, etc.

Most participants in the focus groups assumed that they had little interest in using apps to find out about other health-related topics and that it could even be a cause of dissatisfaction if they were flooded with information and messages that were not required or outside their area of interest.

Expectations of the Users of Digital Technologies in the Relationship With Health Service Providers

There are great expectations related to the reinforcement of the role of digital technologies in improving experiences in health services.

Firstly, as has been mentioned several times, "The use of digital technologies should be focused mainly on the benefit to the user", which means that these apps should be seen mainly as a tool for interaction and patient satisfaction, not focusing almost exclusively on productivity gains and reduction of human care, in its various components.

The improvement of the patient experience can be achieved in several ways, all of them centered on the establishment of close relationships: "Proximity is very important, creates ways to accompany and show genuine concern", for example with "more agility, greater punctuality, ease of access to exams and analyses"; "receive alerts for delays in appointments and exams". There is also a great focus on the "need to share tests and test results outside the service providers' platforms" and eventually made available in hospital networks, always in a context of respect for privacy and confidentiality and with the patient's authorization.

Interactions should be deepened through the use of artificial intelligence and human interactions, in order to achieve a "higher level of immediate responses; greater ability to monitor processes in an integrated manner, generate proximity and satisfaction". This proximity can be achieved with a chat or sound/image platform, through which the patient can, at all times, know what the point of the situation is, clarify doubts, and follow the processes" through a patient relationship management service.

The relationship with the service provider, made through physical and digital channels, should be an integrated process: "there must be greater convergence between the apps and the physical user experience" and not represent different or even divergent levels of service and response. This means they should be complementary, which will allow efficiency gains for the provider and better care and enlightenment for the patient.

There are numerous fears that the use of apps, virtual assistants, and online medical acts imply a more impersonal relationship and difficulties in solving problems or complaints, given the predictable reduction of personal interactions. In this sense, a great effort should be made to measure patient satisfaction and to create fair mechanisms to solve complaints and bad relationship experiences.

The use of artificial intelligence may bring great improvements in interactions with patients, whether in terms of preventive medicine, be it in the articulation of the different components of the interaction process and management of medical acts, or in the provision of relevant content for the profile and expectations of each patient.

The health sector is a highly regulated area in terms of data confidentiality and ethical relationships that must always be safeguarded in interaction ns with patients.

CONCLUSION AND MANAGERIAL CONTRIBUTION

Digital transformation in digital marketing is a reality. The healthcare sector has been looking for new ways, with technology applied to marketing, to improve patient experience through the adoption of technologies, which enable greater personalization in customer service and the quality of customer outcomes. Digital marketing plays a critical role in patient experience and healthcare communication through search engine optimization, social media, content marketing, and email marketing. However, it is important to follow privacy and ethical regulations to ensure that marketing actions are beneficial to both parties.

This empirical study corroborated the theoretical framework, regarding the increasing use of digital tools by patients, namely through the complementary use of websites and apps.

Despite the significant adherence to, and satisfaction with the resources available on the websites and apps, there is no evidence of the impact of digital marketing actions on patients' perceptions, particularly in terms of adherence to social networks, content marketing, or email marketing. Since it is not clear the impact these mentioned digital marketing tools have on users, it opens up an area for further investigation. In fact, health care providers may be more conservative of their behaviors regarding regulations and codes of ethics and data protection of their users or it may be that healthcare providers lack accumulated experience and competences on these technologies.

Also, the frequent technical failures, outdated content, and lack of immediate answers, as well as the perception that investments in digital transformation are mainly made for the benefit of health service providers - not focused on patients' expectations and the improvement of their experience - is seen as a sign of distrust by individuals who want to maintain a personal relationship with other non-virtual touchpoints, namely for the treatment of more complex issues and complaints/ dissatisfactions.

It may be important for these companies to make a more segmented use of digital tools, taking advantage of their specificities, namely in terms of accessibility, portability, and type of use, as well as paying attention to market segments that need alternative forms of interaction, given their insufficient digital literacy.

The greater personalization of the relationship is seen as very relevant by users, for instance through digital patient assistants, made with human and technological means, namely artificial intelligence. This will be an important mechanism for improving the service provided and for strengthening satisfaction and emotional closeness between the parties.

This work provides a valuable/relevant theoretical contribution for it shows the importance that digital transformation has, through the utilization of digital tools by the users. The current study emphasizes the potentials and the specificities and also the difficulties and threats of digital.

LIMITATIONS

This academic research can be seen as a first stage of a more comprehensive research work that seeks to study the role of digital technologies in the health sector, namely related to the use of apps and websites and the construction of a relationship of proximity and excellence in service delivery and experience.

This is a qualitative and generic study, carried out in a specific geographical context and includes exclusively users with significant digital literacy. We identified some limitations that may be overcome in future studies, namely related to the impact of this approach to not so digital user classes; the need to develop quantitative studies, and to anticipate the role that artificial intelligence will have in the coming times, which may have a significantly transformative impact.

REFERENCES

Aggar, C., Grace, S., Smith, S. (2020). Exploring healthcare professionals' understanding and experiences of artificial intelligence technology use in the delivery of healthcare: An integrative review. *Health Informatics Journal, 26*(2), 1225-1236. doi:10.1177/1460458219874641

Akgün, Ö., & Arslan, N. (2022). Marketing Mentality of the Modern Age. *Digital Marketing. Conference: The 5th International Academic Conference on Management and Economics*. https://www.doi.org/10.33422/5th.conferenceme.2022.07.25

Alshater, M. (2023). Exploring the Role of Artificial Intelligence in Enhancing Academic Performance: A Case Study of ChatGPT. SSRN *Electronic Journal.* doi:10.2139/ssrn.4312358

Bani, W., Al, I., & Ibrahim, A. (2020). Privacy, confidentiality, security, and patient safety concerns about electronic health records. *International Nursing Review, 67*, 218–230. doi:10.1111/inr.12585

Barbosa, B., Saura, R., & Zekan, B. (2023). Defining content marketing and its influence on online user behavior: a data-driven prescriptive analytics method. *Annals of Operations Research.* doi:10.1007/s10479-023-05261-1

Beck, L., Trombetta, W., & Share, S. (1986). Using focus group sessions before decisions are made. *North Carolina Medical Journal, 47*(2), 73–74.

Camp, L. J. (2001). Trust and risk in Internet Commerce. MIT Press.

Chaudhary, K., & Alam, M. (Eds.). (2022). *Big Data Analytics: Digital Marketing and Decision-Making* (1st ed.). Auerbach Publications. doi:10.1201/9781003307761

Chen, Y. (2023). Comparing content marketing strategies of digital brands using machine learning. *Humanities and Social Sciences Communications, 10*(57). doi:10.1057/s41599-023-01544-x

Drake, L., Sassoon, I., Balatsoukas, P., Porat, T., Ashworth, M., Wright, E., Curcin, V., Chapman, M., Kokciyan, N., Modgil, S., Sklar, E., & Parsons, S. (2022). The relationship of socio-demographic factors and patient attitudes to connected health technologies: *A survey of stroke survivors. Health Informatics Journal, 28*(2). Advance online publication. doi:10.1177/14604582221102373

Gangl, C., & Krychtiuk, K. (2023). *Digital health - high tech or high touch? Wiener Medizinische Wochenschrift.* doi:10.100710354-022-00991-6

GWI. (2023). *Global Mobile Consumer Trends Report.* https://www.gwi.com/

Hartmann, K., Heitmann, M., & Siebert, C. (2023). More than a Feeling: Accuracy and Application of Sentiment Analysis. *International Journal of Research in Marketing, 40*(1), 75-87. doi:10.1016/j.ijresmar.2022.05.005

Hassanein, K., & Head, M. (2007). Manipulating perceived social presence through the web interface and its impact on attitude towards online shopping. *International Journal of Human-Computer Studies, 65*(8), 689–708. doi:10.1016/j.ijhcs.2006.11.018

He, Z., Huang, H., Choi, H., & Bilgihan, A. (2023). Building organizational resilience with digital transformation. *Journal of Service Management, 34*(1), 147–171. doi:10.1108/JOSM-06-2021-0216

Hoffman, L., Moreau, P., Stremersch, S., & Wedel, M. (2022). The Rise of New Technologies in Marketing: A Framework and Outlook. *Journal of Marketing, 86*(1), 1–6. doi:10.1177/00222429211061636

Hu, K. (2023). *ChatGPT sets record for fastest-growing user base - analyst note.* Reuters. https://www.reuters.com/technology/chatgpt-sets-record-fastest-growing-user-base-analyst-note-2023-02-01/

Huang, T., & Liao, S.-L. (2017). Creating e-shopping multisensory flow experience through augmented-reality interactive technology. *Internet Research, 27*(2), 449–475. doi:10.1108/IntR-11-2015-0321

Jiang, L., Yang, Z., & Jun, M. (2013). Measuring consumer perceptions of online shopping convenience. *Journal of Service Management, 24*(2), 191–214. doi:10.1108/09564231311323962

Journée, R. J., & Weber, M. E. (2014). A bonded experience:"value creation as the creation of an experience, within a business relationship". *Proceedings of the 7th World Conference on Mass Customization, Personalization, and Co-Creation (MCPC 2014).* 10.1007/978-3-319-04271-8_1

Kemp, S. (2023), Digital 2023 April Global Statshot Report. *Data Reportal.*

Keng, C., Ting, H., & Chen, Y. T. (2011). Effects of virtual-experience combinations on consumer- related sense of virtual community. *Internet Research, 4*(21), 408–434. doi:10.1108/10662241111158308

Kopalle, K., Gangwar, M., Kaplan, A., Ramachandran, D., Reinartz, W., & Rindfleisch, A. (2022). Examining artificial intelligence (AI) technologies in marketing via a global lens: Current trends and future research opportunities. *International Journal of Research in Marketing, 39*(2), 522–540. doi:10.1016/j.ijresmar.2021.11.002

Kraus, S., Durst, S., Ferreira, S., Veiga, P., Kailer, N., & Weinmann, A. (2022). Digital transformation in business and management research: An overview of the current status quo. *International Journal of Information Management, 63*, 1–18. doi:10.1016/j.ijinfomgt.2021.102466

Kushlev, K., & Leitao, M. R. (2020). The effects of smartphones on well-being: Theoretical integration and research agenda. *Current Opinion in Psychology, 36*, 77–82. doi:10.1016/j.copsyc.2020.05.001

Lewnes, A. (2021). Commentary: The Future of Marketing Is Agile. *Journal of Marketing, 85*(1), 64–67. doi:10.1177/0022242920972022

Ligaraba, N., Chuchu, T., & Nyagadza, B. (2023). Opt-in e-mail marketing influence on consumer behaviour: A Stimuli–Organism–Response (S–O– R) theory perspective. *Cogent Business & Management, 10*(1), 2184244. doi:10.1080/23311975.2023.2184244

Ling, K. C., Chai, L. T., & Piew, T. H. (2010). The effects of shopping orientations, online trust and prior online purchase experience toward customers' online purchase intention. *International Business Research, 3*(3), 63. doi:10.5539/ibr.v3n3p63

Melumad, S., & Pham, M. T. (2020). The smartphone as a pacifying technology. *The Journal of Consumer Research, 47*(2), 237–255. doi:10.1093/jcr/ucaa005

Mergel, I., Edelmann, N. & Haug, N. (2019). Defining digital transformation: Results from expert interviews. *Government Information Quarterly, 36.* doi:10.1016/j.giq.2019.06.002

Mohammed-Nasir, R., Oshikoya, K. A., & Oreagba, I. A. (2023). Digital Innovation in Healthcare Entrepreneurship. In Medical Entrepreneurship. Springer. doi:10.1007/978-981-19-6696-5_22

MSI. (2022). *Research Priorities 2020-2022.* Marketing Science Institute. https://www.msi.org/wp-content/uploads/2021/07/MSI-2020-22-Research-Priorities-final.pdf-WO

Nurgalieva, L., & Doherty, G. (2023). Privacy and security in digital therapeutics. Digital Therapeutics for Mental Health and Addiction. The State of the Science and Vision for the Future, 189-204. doi:10.1016/B978-0-323-90045-4.00002-2

Palermo, V., & Hernandez, Y. (2020). Group discussions on how to implement a participatory process in climate adaptation planning: A case study in Malaysia. *Ecological Economics, 177*. doi:10.1016/j.ecolecon.2020.106791

Palmié, M., Parida, V., Mader, A., & Wincent, J. (2023). Clarifying the scaling concept: A review, definition, and measure of scaling performance and an elaborate agenda for future research. *Journal of Business Research, 158*. https://doi.org/ doi:10.1016/j.jbusres.2022.113630

Powell, R., & Single, H. (1996). Focus Groups. *International Journal for Quality in Health Care, 8*(5), 499–504. doi:10.1093/intqhc/8.5.499

Prasad, C. J., & Aryasri, A. R. (2009). Determinants of shopper behaviour in e-tailing: An empirical analysis. *Paradigm, 13*(1), 73–83. doi:10.1177/0971890720090110

Radnan, Y. & Christin, V. (2023). The Effect of Self-Service Technology Service Quality on Customer Loyalty and Behavioral Intention. *KINERJA: Journal of Business and Economics, 27*(1), 107-128. doi:10.24002/kinerja.v27i1.6642

Sangaiah, K., Rezaeil S., & Javadpour, A. (2023). Explainable AI in big data intelligence of community detection for digitalization e-healthcare services. *Applied Soft Computing, 136*. doi:10.1016/j.asoc.2023.110119

Scherpen, F., Draghici, A., & Niemann, J. (2018). Customer experience management to leverage customer loyalty in the automotive industry. *Procedia: Social and Behavioral Sciences, 238*, 374–380. doi:10.1016/j.sbspro.2018.04.014

Shahid, S., Islam, J., Malik, S., & Hasan, U. (2022). Examining consumer experience in using m-banking apps: A study of its antecedents and outcomes. *Journal of Retailing and Consumer Services, 65*, 102870. Advance online publication. doi:10.1016/j.jretconser.2021.102870

Shaikh, M., Vayani, H., Akram, S., & Qamar, N. (2022). Open-source electronic health record systems: A systematic review of most recent advances. *Health Informatics Journal, 28*(2). Advance online publication. doi:10.1177/14604582221099828

Shankar, V., Kleijnen, M., Ramanathan, S., Rizley, R., Holland, S., & Morrissey, S. (2016). Mobile shopper marketing: Key issues, current insights, and future research avenues. *Journal of Interactive Marketing, 34*(1), 37–48. doi:10.1016/j.intmar.2016.03.002

Sujan, M., Scott, P., & Cresswell, K. (2019). Digital health and patient safety: Technology is not a magic wand. *Health Informatics Journal, 26*(4), 2295–2299. doi:10.1177/1460458219876183

Tariq, M. U. (2023). Healthcare Innovation & Entrepreneurship, Digital Health Entrepreneurship. In L. Raimi & I. A. Oreagba (Eds.), *Medical Entrepreneurship*. Springer. doi:10.1007/978-981-19-6696-5_16

Tater, U., & Jain, A. T. (2022). Artificial Intelligence must be a Revolutionary Technique of Marketing in. *Indian Journal of Business Administration, 15*(1), 39–45.

Trueman, C. (2023). Em foco. *Computerworld*. https://www.computerworld.com.pt/2023/01/24/despedimentos-nas-tecnologicas-em-2023-uma-linha-do-tempo/

Verhoef, C. & Bijmolt, T. (2019). Marketing perspectives on digital business models: A framework and overview of the special issue. *International Journal of Research in Marketing*, *36*(3), 341-349. doi:10.1016/j.ijresmar.2019.08.001

Vial, G. (2019). Understanding digital transformation: A review and a research agenda. *The Journal of Strategic Information Systems*, *28*(2), 118–144. doi:10.1016/j.jsis.2019.01.003

Voinov, A., Kolagani, N., McCall, M., Glynn, P., Kragt, M., Ostermann, F., Pierce, S., & Ramu, P. (2016). Modelling with stakeholders – Next generation. *Environmental Modelling & Software*, *77*, 196-220. doi:10.1016/j.envsoft.2015.11.016

Weber, M., & Chatzopoulos, C. (2019). Digital customer experience: The risk of ignoring the non-digital experience. *International Journal of Industrial Engineering and Management*, *10*(3), 201. doi:10.24867/IJIEM-2019-3-240

Wilkinson, S. (1998). Focus groups in feminist research: Power, interaction, and the co-construction of meaning. *Women's Studies International Forum, 21*(1), 111-125.

Xu, C., Park, J., & Lee, J. C. (2022). The effect of shopping channel (online vs offline) on consumer decision process and firm's marketing strategy. *Internet Research*, *32*(3), 971–978. doi:10.1108/INTR-11-2020-0660

Ziółkowska, M. J. (2021). Digital transformation and marketing activities in small and medium-sized enterprises. *Sustainability (Basel)*, *13*(5), 1–16. doi:10.3390u13052512

Zlatova, I. (2022). Digital marketing changes during the Russian war in Ukraine 2022. *Marketing and Digital Technologies*, *6*(3), 15–24. doi:10.15276/mdt.6.3.2022.2

KEY TERMS AND DEFINITIONS

Apps or Mobile Application: Is a software specific application developed to run mainly on smartphones and tablets, used to shopping, gathering information and other interactions.

Artificial Intelligence: Refers to the simulation of human intelligence by software-coded heuristics.

Customer Journey: Represents the entire experience that a customer has with an organization, including all customer interactions across all channels, devices, and touchpoints throughout every stage of the customer lifecycle.

Data Protection: Process of safeguarding personal information from other entities to avoid activities as collecting, storing, retrieving, consulting, disclosing, or sharing with someone else. Companies also need to protect their data of safeguarding important information from corruption, compromise, or loss.

Digital Marketing: Strategy and tactics that are implemented by an organization or a brand to align with set objectives and goals to attract a specific type, or types, of customer using a combination of marketing techniques.

Digital Transformation: Process of adoption of digital technology by an organization to digitize, services and interactions, innovating, gaining efficiency and increasing customer experience.

Touchpoint: A touchpoint is any time a potential customer or customer meets your brand–before, during, or after they purchase something from a company.

Section 2
Exploring the Dynamics of IoB in Education and Healthcare

Chapter 7
Education 5.0 in the Context of Teaching Accounting

Conceição Aleixo
Polytechnic Institute of Setúbal, Portugal

Susana Silva
Polytechnic Institute of Setúbal, Portugal

Teresa Godinho
(iD) https://orcid.org/0000-0002-1996-6417
Polytechnic Institute of Setúbal, Portugal

ABSTRACT

Higher education institutions play a crucial role in the teaching-learning process as they are primarily responsible for preparing students for their entry into the business environment. The aim of this study is to assess students' perceptions of a new teaching approach and its impact on their personal and professional development. At the level of course coordination, the findings will inform reflections on which pedagogical practices should be implemented to align with the student-focused teaching paradigm and the implementation of an Education 5.0 framework in the bachelor's degree program in accounting and finance at the Polytechnic Institute of Setúbal. The research employs a qualitative analysis approach, and the main results indicate that participants recognize the importance of Education 5.0 for their personal and professional development as certified accountants.

1. INTRODUCTION

In recent years we have been witnessing the digital transformation and the growing presence of new technologies in our daily lives, with artificial intelligence being increasingly present.

The progress of digital technology and automation compels the development of new proficiencies and skills for accounting professionals. Higher education institutions are responsible for preparing undergraduates for their future careers and they play a significant role in their learning process.

DOI: 10.4018/978-1-6684-9039-6.ch007

Thus, accounting education in higher education needs to be addressed in a different way, and according to Pincus et al. (2017), lecturers should understand the need for this change. The so-called Education 5.0 seeks to meet this need with a new approach to student-focused teaching, aiming to stimulate self-learning, group learning, and the use of technology and innovation. It provides the development of digital, social, emotional, and cognitive skills, as well as a greater capacity for argumentation, discussion, collaborative work, problem-solving, and a critical mindset. This approach makes students active participants in the entire teaching-learning process, building agents of a more creative and modern society. Utilizing technology in a strategic, optimized, and collaborative way (Fonseca, 2021), as a value-added and enhancer of more effective education (Loesberg & Dervojeda, 2021), is the current reality in which students assume the role of co-authors in their own learning.

2. LITERATURE REVIEW

The development of human society has had different stages, as shown in Figure 1. The concept of a creative society began to be discussed after the emergence of digital transformation. Society 5.0 aims to create a human-centred society that is capable of dealing with constant social changes. In this sense, multidisciplinary research and collaborative work become fundamental (Kabakuş et al., 2023).

Hence, it is reasonable to conclude with the assertion that Education 5.0 should play a crucial function in all higher education institutions, regardless of whether they are public or private.

Figure 1. Development of human society
Source: Adapted from Nakanishi and Kitano (2018)

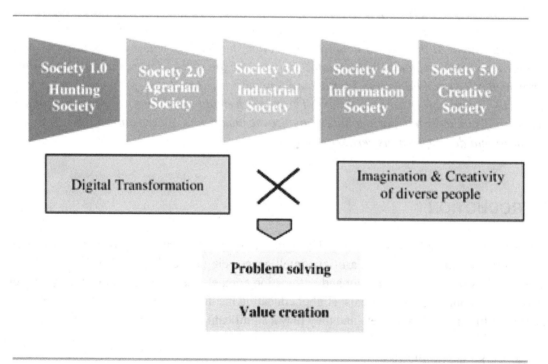

Higher education institutions have a privileged responsibility in knowledge dissemination and, therefore, should not only prepare professionals for their respective fields but also strive to meet knowledge society expectations (Vale et al., 2014).

Indeed, according to Akturk et al. (2023), "Universities . . . should be at the forefront of this development process" as leading information and technology systems, "in line with the goal of a society that absorbs information and uses technology efficiently" (p. 581).

Education 5.0, designed for the near future, fosters the development of essential skills, including creativity, critical thinking, generating new ideas, virtual collaboration, risk-taking, courage, and resilience (Bastos et al., 2019). Education 5.0 is distinguished by several competencies that set it apart from the traditional educational model, as illustrated in Figure 2.

Figure 2. Education 5.0
Source: Own elaboration.

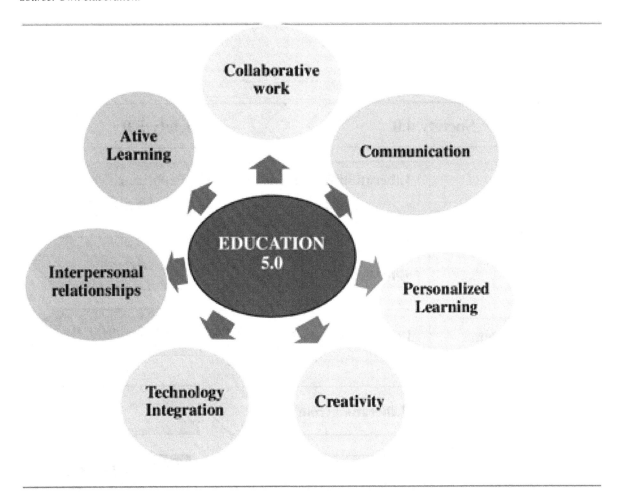

The substantial digital evolution of the last few years, where emerging technologies have assumed vital roles within our society. The COVID-19 pandemic has imposed several adaptations on educational institutions, forcing them to introduce technology and digital tools for online classes and distance learning. This new approach has brought about various changes in the teaching and learning process, particularly the need for lecturers and students to adapt to this new reality by developing specific skills to overcome challenges, almost in a daily basis. It has, thus, become imperative to combine technological and digital resources with human and socio-emotional abilities. The COVID-19 pandemic has caused a global crisis that dictated a transformation in worldview, values, consequently posing new challenges in education (Melnychenko et al., 2021).

Society's evolution has occurred in multiple stages, each with its distinct focus and approach. The 4.0 society, characterized by an information society emphasizing technologies, digitization, and artificial intelligence, where individuals are interconnected through devices and digital networks, has now transitioned to a new 5.0 society, which is briefly outlined in Figure 3.

Figure 3. From Society 4.0 to Society 5.0
Source: Nakanishi and Kitano (2018)

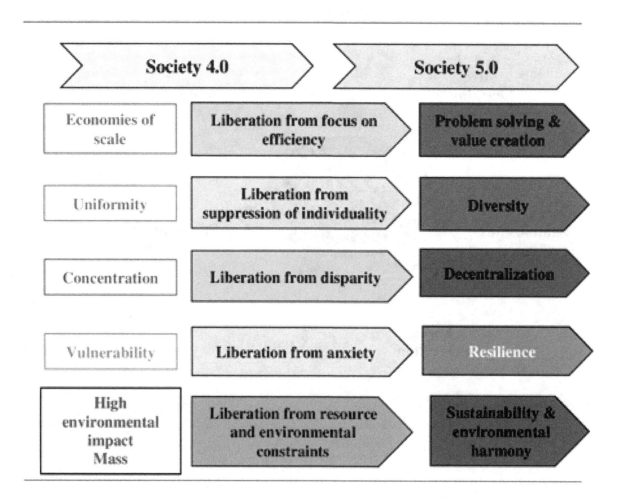

The core principles of Society 5.0 align with the idea that technology should be used to enhance human well-being and address social challenges. It emphasizes the development of skills such as empathy, creativity, and collaboration in conjunction with technological advancements and human values. Hence, Society 5.0 is a concept that envisions a society where technology and human society are integrated to create a better quality of life for individuals.

According to Vieira et al. (2023), "in recent years, there have been structural changes in education due to the new technologies of Society 5.0", which "facilitated remote access to education for many people. Technology continues to change industry, society, and thus education, but this alone is not enough to advance the expected improvement of humanity and achieve the much-needed human-centred sustainable society. In education, it is necessary to develop new learning and skills" (p. 3).

The new Society 5.0, centred on the human being and harnessing technologies to benefit people, as at its service, is a society that considers and enhances skills such as imagination, creativity, decision-making, value creation, problem-solving, skill diversity, resilience, and sustainability in an environment of well-being (Rodríguez-Abitia et al., 2022).

According to Bastos et al. (2019) "the student 5.0 as we call it, is the student that has a certain level of proficiency in core competences versus digital competences and human competences" (p. 74).

Vieira et al. (2023) argue that schools must address new challenges by undertaking new responsibilities. According to these authors, merely incorporating new information and communication technologies into the teaching and learning processes falls short.

Education systems "must respond to the pressing need for change by defining relevant learning objectives and content, introducing pedagogies that empower students, and encouraging institutions to include sustainability principles in their management structures" (Tavares et al., 2023, p. 2).

In the context of globalization, it becomes relevant for higher education institutions to be able to provide highly qualified human resources with internationally recognized competencies (Melnychenko et al., 2021).

Education has the power to change people and society. To pave the way for a society 5.0 and achieve the education 5.0's mission, Higher Education Institutions must pay attention, anticipate and prepare methodologies for success, not forgetting that well-being is an essential part of the individual. And this, an urgent call to action, is the key to achieving what is to come.

To achieve Education 5.0 and Society 5.0, Higher Education Institutions must develop effective methodologies while prioritizing individual well-being (Pinheiro & Santos, 2023).

Bastos et al. (2019) conducted a study on the inclusion of digital soft skills training in higher education. The study was conducted in various curricular units of different higher education courses in Portugal and aimed to explore the utilization of digital technologies by higher education institutions for academic purposes. The authors administered a questionnaire to a sample of 132 students from diverse fields of study, including medicine, nursing, engineering, management, arts, and literature. Obtained results indicate that higher education institutions use digital platforms to support the teaching process by providing texts, exercises, and simulated practice to solve real situations. The students mentioned that the availability of resources and simulators in higher education institutions appears to be more effective in the short term.

Technology and business evolution is creating a gap between accountants' expectations and traditional curriculum. Universities are not adequately equipping students with the necessary skills and competencies for the modern accounting profession. To address this issue, there is a growing emphasis on integrating technology-related topics into accounting curricula, to meet expected significant transformations in the accounting profession (Azevedo et al., 2023).

3. METHODOLOGY

3.1 Case Study

A case study is a research methodology that emphasizes a detailed and in-depth examination of a well-defined entity, known as the "case," within its natural context. As such, it represents a specific investigation. According to Yin (2017), a case study enables the researcher to understand the "how?" and "why?" of specific current events, which are often beyond their control. It focuses on contemporary phenomena and their real-life contexts.

One of the significant advantages of conducting a case study is that the researcher has the flexibility to change data collection methods and formulate new research questions at any point during the study. Bogdan and Biklen (1994, p. 89) state that a "case study consists of a comprehensive observation of a context, or an individual, from a single source of documents or a specific event".

According to Yin (2017), there are two types of case studies: the simple case study, which focuses on one project, and the multiple case study, which focuses on several projects. In this research work, a simple case study was conducted, focusing solely on the assessment of students in the 1st, 2nd, and 3rd years, as well as the coordinator of the bachelor's degree in accounting and finance at the Business School of the Polytechnic University of Setúbal. The study aimed to explore the meaning and significance of Education 5.0. According to Patton (1985, p. 1), "qualitative research represents an effort to comprehend a situation in its uniqueness, within a specific context, and the interactions it encompasses". According to Maulana et al. (2022), in a society undergoing constant change, qualitative approaches play an increasingly significant role in the understanding of accounting as both a social construction and a social practice.

3.2 Data Collection Method

3.2.1 Focus Group

Focus Group was one of the methods used for data collection. A Focus Group is a type of interview conducted in a group setting, to analyse and receive feedback from the participants involved in the study. According to the literature, it has defined characteristics regarding the size of the group and its composition, as well as procedures related to the way it is conducted.

According to Morgan (1997), the Focus Group is a qualitative technique that aims to facilitate and guide the discussion among a group of people, inspired by non-directive interviews. The Focus Group privileges the observation and recording of participants' experiences and reactions, which would not be possible to capture by other methods, such as individual interviews or questionnaires. According to Silva et al. (2014), the Focus Group has different levels of application and reflection, and it has been adopted in research studies across various areas, including education. For the authors, there are five phases underlying the implementation of a Focus Group process, which are briefly described in Figure 4.

According to Silva et al. (2014), the Focus Group is designed to gather information, typically of a qualitative nature, with the aim of enhancing people's understanding of a specific topic. The authors emphasize the significance of all phases in the process, with particular emphasis on moderation as the most prominent phase.

The group of participants comprising the Focus Group should share some common characteristic related to the topic being discussed (Krueger & Casey, 2009).

Figure 4. Phases underlying the implementation process of a focus group
Source: Adapted from Silva et al. (2014).

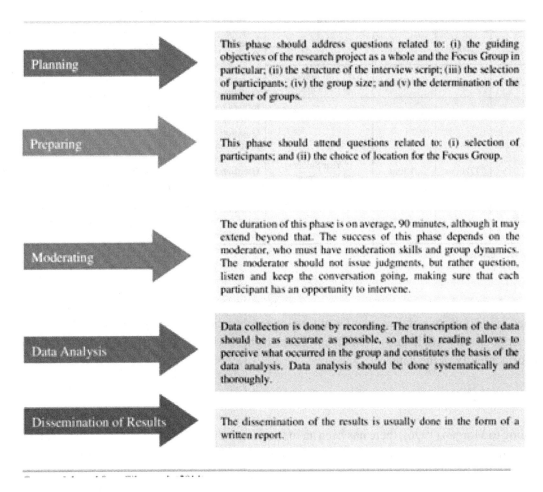

The use of a Focus Group allows for the collection of various opinions and points of view on a specific topic (Kellmereit, 2015). This technique enables the interviewer to observe the interaction among participants, who may express a collective opinion or split into subgroups with opposing ideas. Thus, the Focus Group provides a more genuine and comprehensive environment than the interview, as participants consider other´s opinions to formulate their own.

The interaction in a group interview, with participants sharing ideas and dealing with divergences, is more authentic than the dual interaction between interviewer and interviewee found in individual interviews or even is simply responding to a questionnaire (Carreira et al., 2021).

To achieve the purpose of this research work, three Focus Group were conducted, corresponding to students in the 1st, 2nd, and 3rd years of the bachelor's degree in accounting and finance at the Business School of the Polytechnic University of Setúbal. The implementation of the Focus Group adhered to the five phases mentioned above.

Table 1 presents the characteristics of the three Focus Group, including the date, time, duration, participant characterization, number of participants, and the questions asked. All Focus Groups were conducted online, using the Microsoft Teams platform.

Table 1. Characterization of the focus group

Date	Hour	Duration	Target Audience/N.º Participants	Asked Questions
27.06.2023	21h00m	1h30m	3rd Year Students (4 Participants)	**Question 1:** What you understand by Education 5.0? **Question 2:** Do you consider that throughout your academic journey, structures/skills based on Education 5.0 have been introduced?
28.06.2023	13h00m	1h30m	2nd Year Students (4 Participants)	**Question 3:** Do you believe that teaching-learning process focused on Education 5.0 will contribute to a better professional performance?
28.06.2023	17h00m	1h30m	1st Year Students (4 Participants)	**Question 4:** Do you consider that the teaching-learning process focused on Education 5.0 allows the development of the soft skills necessary for the job market? **Question 5:** Do you believe that these soft skills will contribute to better professional performance in terms of technical and human aspects (peer relationships)? **Question 6:** Could the teaching-learning process based on Education 5.0 be an opportunity for change and repositioning of the certified accountant career?

Source: Own elaboration.

All students in the 1st, 2nd and 3rd years were contacted to find out their intention to participate, being informed of the objective of the Focus Group, estimated duration and identification of the moderator and co-moderators. All participants were guaranteed the right to withdraw from the investigation, anonymity and confidentiality of the data.

3.2.2 Interview

According to Morgan (1996), there has been an increase in the use of the Focus Group in research, preferably in combination with other methods of data collection. Thus, in addition to the three Focus Group, we also conducted an interview with the coordinator of the bachelor's degree in accounting and finance of the Polytechnic University of Setúbal. The choice of the interview as a method of data collection is due to its versatility. Unlike questionnaire surveys, where answers are limited to predefined categories, interviews allow interviewees to express themselves more openly, spontaneously, and directly.

According to Bell (1997), there are three types of interviews: (i) structured; (ii) semi-structured; and (iii) unstructured. In this research work, a semi-structured interview was conducted, due to the fact that it has a high degree of freedom in the exploration of the issues and in the order in which the themes can be approached. The interview had a previously prepared script, was held on June 29, 2023, at 5:30 p.m., and lasted 60 minutes. For the sake of reliability, the questions posed to the coordinator of the bachelor's degree in accounting and finance of the Polytechnic University of Setúbal were the same as those posed to the students who participated in the Focus Group.

4. DATA ANALYSIS

The initial Focus Group took place with the third-year students enrolled in the Bachelor's degree program in Accounting and Finance at the Polytechnic University of Setúbal. The participants were then presented with the questions above.

It's important to consider that this first group of students initiated their higher educational journey in 2020 within unique circumstances. Due to the prevailing conditions at the time, they were in classes wearing masks and following strict safety protocols. They attended the Business School of the Polytechnic University of Setúbal in person only every two weeks, specifically for practical lectures, with theoretical lessons being conducted remotely through online platforms.

Due to Pandemic restrictions, what also sets this group apart is the absence of traditional student customs and initiation rituals that are deeply ingrained in the Portuguese higher education system. In the fall semester of 2020, it was impossible to have customary activities, such as students' traditions and initiation rituals observed at the beginning of every school year. These rituals, not intended to be hazing in nature, traditionally serve as a means to facilitate social integration and foster a sense of belonging among students. They provide opportunities for new students to interact, form connections, and become part of a cohesive group within the academic community.

Moreover, in Portugal, the beginning of 2021 brought a second lockdown for a period of two months, in which remote learning and limited face-to-face interaction were a reality.

All the 3rd year students mentioned that they were not aware of what Education 5.0 entailed before the session. However, upon learning that it represents a more personalized teaching-learning process that incorporates emergent technologies, the development of soft skills, and personal socioemotional growth, they all became enthusiastic. One student highlighted artificial intelligence, suggesting it as a catalyst for automation, enabling both individual and community progress, aligned with the statement made by Tavares et al. (2023).

None of the 3rd year participants believed that structures or skills based on Education 5.0 were introduced during their academic journey as bachelor's degree students in accounting and finance at the Polytechnic University of Setúbal.

Recognizing that the national pandemic context limited the lecturers' capability to make significant changes, they mentioned that socialization within the academic community was achieved through the formation of smaller groups of students rather than one large cohesive group.

This group of students acknowledged that stepping out of their comfort zone during a particular 3rd year lecture, was a significant turning point that strengthened the larger group. They also agreed that effective collaboration can be achieved when students work with peers whom they are not familiar with or are randomly assigned by the lecturers.

The group agreed that, to foster a collaborative spirit in education, particularly during the first semester, it is important to organize activities that are productive, contribute to the curriculum, or have some merit, even if the process is not entirely pleasant. This way, those involved are more likely to engage in sharing ideas, knowledge, and supporting one another. The group also suggested that, within the classroom context, lecturers could introduce a new technology or activity that offers entirely new knowledge to a working group of four or five students. The rationale behind this approach is that when individuals are in a vulnerable state and heavily reliant on one another, it fosters the development of empathy.

If the working group strategy were to be repeatedly used, both moderators and students agreed that each group should choose a different speaker for each class, to ensure that all students have equal opportunities and to make them aware of their capabilities, thus improving self-confidence and self-esteem.

The evaluation process was also talked about, having the students stated that:

- working groups formed for this purpose should have a maximum of three or four members;
- anonymous peer evaluation could give insights into socioemotional growth;
- formative evaluation could be considered, in order to fulfill the purposes of Education 5.0.

About formative evaluation, one suggestion was to conduct short analyses suitable for one class period, where all the students interact and provide feedback to one another in the end.

All 3rd year students, when responding to question number three, shared the belief that an educational approach centred around Education 5.0 would enhance their professional performance. They further agreed that in the present day, accountants have additional roles such as being analysts and consultants who need to interact with clients and possess effective communication skills. Consequently, software knowledge and communication abilities are deemed crucial in this context.

When questioned about the impact of soft skills on professional performance, both in technical and human aspects such as peer relationships, all the students shared the view that technical knowledge is no longer the primary requirement at an entry level. Instead, they believe that what truly differentiates individuals and leads to their success is the possession of strong soft skills. This opinion is supported by Tavares et al. (2023), who stated "accounting education should focus on building strong and effective relationships" (p. 3).

Finally, in relation to the teaching-learning process based on Education 5.0, the students agreed that it presents an opportunity to bring about change and reposition the certified accountant career. They expressed unanimity in stating that assuming roles as analysts or consultants in various fields of knowledge increases the likelihood of being socially respected and becoming agents of change, as identified by Azevedo et al. (2023), which preview that "time-consuming and repetitive work will be automated, and the future accountant and auditor will perform more valuable work while transforming into more finance and business consultant roles with more specific expertise" (p. 3).

The second Focus Group was held with the students of the 2nd year of the bachelor's degree in accounting and finance of the Polytechnic University of Setúbal. The participants were also asked the aforementioned questions.

This group also had constraints in their first year as Higher Education students, in 2021, as wearing masks in class was mandatory in Portuguese public buildings until April 2022 and all theoretical lectures in were online in Polytechnic University of Setúbal's Business School until June 2022.

Nevertheless, regular students' traditions and initiation rituals took place at the beginning of their first school year and safety protocols were way less strict than in 2020.

As was the case in the first Focus Group, the participants were not familiar with the Education 5.0 approach and concepts before the session. However, they all showed great interest and excitement about the potential for change and the opportunity to be part of this transformative process.

Answering the second question, some of the students considered that an extracurricular lecture Financial Accounting Complements was an example of structures based on Education 5.0 introduction.

The Pilot Project for Financial Accounting Complements (FAC) started in 2019/2020, created to optimize academic success in the curricular units of financial accounting and financial reporting. The project aims to address the difficulties students face in acquiring the necessary skills in this scientific area, as reflected in first-year retention rates. It provides continuous support to students in the field of financial accounting throughout their academic journey.

It aims to strengthen students' knowledge base in accounting by employing various teaching methodologies, offering students a dedicated space for guided study and close examination of topics covered in the curricular units of Financial Accounting I and Financial Accounting II, intending to improve their performance, not only in these units but also in other accounting and financial-related subjects.

FAC operates within the classroom setting, spanning 15 weeks of classes. Daytime sessions consist of two hours per week, while evening sessions have 1 hour per week dedicated to practical groups. The classes focus on guided study and the resolution of theoretical and practical exercises that complement the topics covered in Financial Accounting lectures.

During the 2020/2021 and 2021/2022 school years, it operated online with synchronous classes. In the second semester of 2022/2023, lessons took place in computer rooms, and accounting software was introduced. This allowed first-year students to explore it for the first time, as previously, the use of accounting software was reserved for the third year. The participants mentioned that individualized sessions allowed them to better consolidate concepts.

However, despite FAC, in general, the students believe that the lectures are heavily focused on theory. They strongly believe that technologies should be an integral part of their education since the very first beginning, rather than an additional component. This belief corroborates what Azevedo et al. (2023) stated, quoting Kruskopf et al. (2020). They also express their concern that an excessive emphasis on theory can lead to a loss of motivation and the feeling that the knowledge gained in class does not align with their future professional requirements.

Students also mentioned that some additional components are not as used by the students as it could be, because email communication fails, it makes students a bit disconnected. On the other hand, if a professor personally approaches a student and informs them about an upcoming webinar or any other event, it is easier for them to attend.

This group of students also expressed their concerns about the social disruption caused by the COVID-19 period and online lectures. They too, suggested promoting more interaction between students and lecturers through dynamic classes and working groups as a way to fulfil the goals of Education 5.0.

As the previous participants, they mentioned the evaluation process and agreed that:

- working groups formed for this purpose should have a maximum of three or four members;
- anonymous peer evaluation could give insights into socioemotional growth;
- formative evaluation fulfills the purposes of Education 5.0;
- regular oral presentation and discussion is important to improve soft skills.

These students believe that Education 5.0 should involve greater interaction between lecturers and students, as it would help in understanding their doubts and knowledge gaps, especially considering that students are sometimes hesitant to ask questions for fear of appearing foolish. They suggest that if there was more proximity in this regard, such as teachers going to students' desks and identifying errors in exercise solutions, it would foster a stronger bond and make students feel more at ease in admitting when they don't understand, cannot complete a task, or have difficulty grasping a concept fully.

All second-year students expressed their belief that adopting an educational approach centered around Education 5.0 would significantly improve their professional performance, in response to question number three.

They also unanimously considered that the teaching-learning process focused on Education 5.0 allows the development of the soft skills necessary for the job market.

As for question number five, 2nd year students stated that the soft skills advocated in Education 5.0 would contribute, in the context of the job market, far beyond improved technical professional performance. They believe that these skills would also have a significant impact on humanization, particularly in terms of interpersonal relationships among peers, where they perceive excessive competition and a lack of compassion.

About the sixth question, which relates Education 5.0 with an opportunity for change and repositioning of the certified accountant career, the 2nd year students trust that it will be crucial since they perceive that accounting is currently seen as a lesser activity by those in the field of economics or finance, who seemingly believe that accountants are those who couldn't achieve more. The participants expressed their disagreement with this narrow view, as they agree that every vocation matters, every profession has its importance and role in society, and all are significant. However, they acknowledge that repositioning accountants might contribute to increasing social distinction and dissociating accounting from the connotation of mere document classification and filing.

Regarding first-year students, one of them was under the impression that Education 5.0 focuses primarily on utilizing technology to foster relationships among people and promote cultural and religious interactions.

Like the 2nd year students, when asked the second question, some of the 1st year students referred to Financial Accounting Complements as an example of educational structures based on the introduction of Education 5.0. The participants highlighted that they have begun utilizing tools like Excel, thereby embracing a more digital approach to accounting. They have also mentioned the introduction to specific software such as "Primavera," which significantly contributed to skill development, since proficiency with digital tools holds relevance in practical scenarios. Extending this practice to the actual Financial Accounting classes would be highly beneficial, they said, again supporting Azevedo et al. (2023).

This group of students mentioned that even the simple use of PowerPoint allows for better comprehension during classes. They also highlighted the efforts to apply theoretical knowledge to real-life situations, such as providing data from actual companies to calculate ratios and indicators within the context of Financial Analysis.

In response to the second question, the group stated that the Education 5.0 model enhances professional performance by addressing the transition from the academic environment to the practical world. They believe that the knowledge gained in academia should also be applicable and useful beyond the academic setting.

As the previous participants, they mentioned the evaluation process and agreed that:

- working groups formed for this purpose should have a maximum of four members;
- anonymous peer evaluation could give insights into socioemotional growth;
- formative evaluation fulfills the purposes of Education 5.0;

In response to question number three, all first-year students expressed their conviction that embracing an educational approach focused on Education 5.0 would greatly enhance their professional performance.

The participants unanimously answered that an instructional approach centered around Education 5.0 enables the cultivation of essential soft skills required in the job market.

In response to question number five, first-year students asserted that the advocated soft skills in Education 5.0 would contribute significantly. They firmly believe that fostering harmonious group relationships ultimately leads to enhanced human actions.

Finally, regarding the potential of an Education 5.0-based teaching-learning process as an opportunity for change and repositioning of the certified accountant career, the first-year participants echoed the sentiments of their colleagues.

They highlighted that a significant portion of accounting processes, particularly accounting entries, are already automated. They emphasized that the crucial aspect of being an accountant today is not solely focused on technical expertise, but also on the ability to provide reports, offer advice to clients, and establish meaningful client relationships to provide professional support.

They expressed that it would be intriguing if accountants were equipped with interpersonal skills to effectively interact with others, as it appears to be increasingly vital in the evolving accounting profession. Constantly engaging with people is a fundamental requirement in this field. They believe that this perspective holds substantial validity, as education should transcend the confines of traditional boundaries.

In response to the first question, the bachelor's degree Coordinator explained that Education 5.0 is seen as an advancement from Education 4.0, which focused on integrating technologies like artificial intelligence and machine learning into education. He further emphasized that Education 5.0 now places a greater emphasis on people, collaborative work, interaction, and communication skills, which have received relatively less attention.

Regarding the second question, the coordinator expressed his belief in the existence of room for improvement in introducing the competencies underlying Education 5.0 during the academic journey of Accounting and Finance students. While collaborative work skills are currently fostered through group assignments and communication skills are developed through presentations, he suggested the incorporation of other elements such as workshops. He also mentioned the importance of training students in these aspects, using the example of the Ethics course, where practical cases could be presented to encourage questions and stimulate debate instead of solely focusing on statutes. The coordinator highlighted the current trend of utilizing technological advancements to handle repetitive tasks while prioritizing client relationships.

When asked about the potential contribution of a learning approach focused on Education 5.0 to better professional performance among students, the coordinator responded without hesitation, expressing their complete certainty that it would indeed have a positive impact.

Similarly, the Coordinator firmly believes that a learning approach centred around Education 5.0 would facilitate the development of soft skills, stating that these skills hold relevance and pose a challenge to be met.

Addressing the fifth question, the coordinator affirmed that soft skills do contribute to better peer relationships and expressed his belief in the essential nature of these skills. Taking his own professional experience into account, he considers that, while technical proficiency is important, possessing additional competencies is necessary for advancing hierarchically within a company. He often advises students about that reality.

Lastly, in response to the sixth question, the coordinator acknowledged the potential of this learning approach, such as Education 5.0, to bring about change and repositioning in the certified accounting profession. He emphasized that the profession is currently undergoing significant changes, with future accountants differing from today's professionals just as today's accountants differ from those of ten years ago. The Coordinator put emphasis on the increasing importance of competencies related to communication, consultancy, rationalisation, and guidance. He trusts that embracing Education 5.0 would contribute to the development of better individuals and professionals in the field of accounting.

5. CONCLUSION

The participants from different years of the bachelor's degree program in accounting and finance at the Polytechnic University of Setúbal recognize the potential benefits of Education 5.0. They show enthusiasm and interest in the personalized teaching-learning process that incorporates emergent technologies, the development of soft skills, and personal socioemotional growth.

The students who contributed to our research believe that Education 5.0 can contribute to their professional performance by preparing them for roles as analysts and consultants, which requires effective communication skills and software knowledge. They also emphasized the importance of soft skills in the job market and the positive impact on human aspects such as peer relationships.

These students see Education 5.0 as an opportunity to bring change and reposition the certified accountant career, emphasizing the need to enhance social respect and dissociate accounting from narrow connotations.

We may say that students express a desire for more interactive and dynamic classes, closer interaction with lecturers, and the integration of technology throughout their educational journey.

In line with the students' perspectives, the bachelor's degree Coordinator recognizes that Education 5.0 is an advancement from Education 4.0, focusing on integrating technologies and placing a greater emphasis on people, collaboration, interaction, and communication skills.

He acknowledged the need for improvement in introducing these competencies to Accounting and Finance students, suggesting workshops and practical cases to enhance learning. The Coordinator expressed certainty that Education 5.0 would positively impact professional performance and facilitate the development of relevant soft skills. He underlined the importance of soft skills in peer relationships and advancing within a company.

Such as the students, the coordinator recognizes Education 5.0 as an opportunity for change and repositioning within the accounting profession. The coordinator emphasizes the evolving competencies required and highlights the potential benefits of embracing this approach.

6. FUTURE RESEARCH

By conducting research, a deeper understanding of the effectiveness, challenges, and opportunities associated with Education 5.0 in accounting education can be gained, leading to further improvements and enhancements in preparing accounting and finance graduates for the evolving demands of the profession.

Based on the information provided, we found some suggestions for future research:

Comparative analysis: Compare the outcomes of accounting education programs that incorporate Education 5.0 with those that do not. This research could explore the differences in skill development and employability among graduates.

Stakeholder perspectives: Investigate the perspectives of employers and accounting professionals on the relevance and effectiveness of Education 5.0. This research could provide insights and identify any gaps.

Student perspectives across disciplines: Expand the Focus Group research to include more students. This research could support a broader understanding of the impact of Education 5.0 across various academic disciplines and explore the transferability of its principles and approaches.

Pedagogical strategies and best practices: Identify effective pedagogical strategies and best practices for implementing Education 5.0 in accounting education. This research could develop innovative teaching methods, assessment approaches, and the use of technology to enhance student engagement and personal development.

REFERENCES

Akturk, C., Talan, T., & Cerasi, C. C. (2022, September 26-28). *Education 4.0 and University 4.0 from Society 5.0 Perspective* [Paper presentation]. *12th International Conference on Advanced Computer Information Technologies (ACIT)*, Ružomberok, Slovakia. 10.1109/ACIT54803.2022.9913099

Azevedo, G., Tavares, M. C., Bastos, M. A., Vale, J., & Bandeira, A. M. (2023, June 20-23). *Universities in Era 5.0: the future accountant* [Paper presentation]. 18th Iberian Conference on Information Systems and Technologies (CISTI), Aveiro, Portugal. https://doi.org/ STI58278.2023.1021196310.23919/CI

Bastos, S., Oliveira, H., Silva, M. M., & Azevedo, L. (2019, November 7-8). Soft Digital Skills in Higher Education Curricula: HEI's 5.0. In R. Ørngreen, M. Buhl, & B. Meyer (Eds.), *Proceedings of the 18th European Conference on e-Learning: ECEL 2019, Copenhagen* (pp. 70-77). Academic Conferences and Publishing International. https://www.academic-conferenc es.org/conferences/ecel/ecel-future-and-past/

Bell, J. (1997). *Como realizar um projecto de investigação*. Gradiva.

Bogdan, R., & Biklen, S. (1994). *Investigação qualitativa em educação. Uma introdução à teoria e aos métodos*. Porto Editora.

Carreira, F., Aleixo, C., & Rebocho, S. (2021, October 14-15). *O Desenvolvimento de Competências em Auditoria: O Reconhecimento pelos Estudantes da ESCE/IPS* [Paper presentation]. XVIII Congresso Internacional de Contabilidade e Auditoria, Lisboa, Portugal. http://xviiicica.occ. pt/pt/dtrab/trabalhos/congressoxviii_cica/trabalhoscc.php

Kabakuş, A. K., Özköse, H., & Ayaz, A. (2023). Society 5.0 research: performance analysis and science mapping. *Gümüşhane Üniversitesi Sosyal Bilimler Dergisi, 14*(1), 311-328. https://derg ipark.org.tr/en/pub/gumus/issue/75752/1202690

Kellmereit, B. (2015). Focus Groups. *International Journal of Sales, Retailing & Marketing, 4*(9), 42-52. https://www.circleinternational.co.uk/journals/ijsrm/current-past-issues-ijsrm/

Krueger, R. A., & Casey, M. A. (2009). *Focus groups: A pratical guide for applied research* (4th ed.). Sage.

Maulana, B. H., Rohman, A., & Prabowo, T. (2022). Doing qualitative research of phenomenology in accounting. *Academy of Accounting and Financial Studies Journal, 26*(1S), 1-7. https://www.abacademies.org/articles/doing-qualitative-research-of-phenomenology-in-a ccounting-13120.html

Morgan, D. L. (1996a). Focus group. *Annual Review of Sociology, 22*(1), 129–152. doi:10.1146/annurev. soc.22.1.129

Morgan, D. L. (1997b). *Focus group as qualitative research* (2nd ed.). Sage., doi:10.4135/9781412984287

Nakanishi, H., & Kitano, H. (2018). *Society 5.0 Co-Creating the Future. Policy Proposals Industrial Technology*. Keidanren (Japan Business Federation). https://www.keidanren.or.jp/ en/policy/2018/095_booklet.pdf

Patton, M. Q. (1985). Quality in Qualitative Research: Methodological Principles and Recent Development. Invited address to Division J of the American Educational Research Association, Chicago.

Pinheiro, M. M., & Santos, C. A. (2023, June 20-23). *The power of education to change society: Methodologies, academic success and well-being at Higher Education* [Paper presentation]. *18th Iberian Conference on Information Systems and Technologies (CISTI)*, Aveiro, Portugal. 10.23919/CISTI58278.2023.10211665

Rodríguez-Abitia, G., Sánchez-Guerrero, M. L., Martínez-Pérez, S., & Aguas-García, N. (2022). Competencies of Information Technology Professionals in Society 5.0. *IEEE Revista Iberoamericana de Tecnologias del Aprendizaje, 17*(4), 343-350. https://doi.org/. 2022.3217136 doi:10.1109/RITA

Silva, I. S., Veloso, A. L., & Keating, J. B. (2014). Focus group: Considerações teóricas e metodológicas. *Revista Lusófona de Educação, 26*(26), 175–190. https://www.researchgate.net /publication/265215548_Focus_group_Consideracoes_teoricas_e_metodologicas

Tavares, M. C., Azevedo, G., Vale, J., & Bandeira, A. M. (2023, June 20-23). *The Accountant in the New Era: Renewing the profession for Society 5.0* [Paper presentation]. *18th Iberian Conference on Information Systems and Technologies (CISTI)*, Aveiro, Portugal. 10.23919/CISTI58278.2023.10211382

Vale, H. C. P., Costa, E. M. C., & Mercado, L. P. L. (2014, June 9-13). *Aprendizagem baseada em problemas: uma estratégia de ensino aprendizagem no curso de Biblioteconomia e Pedagogia* [Paper presentation]. XV Encuentro Internacional Virtual Educa, Lima, Peru. https://recursos.educoas.org/publicaciones/aprendizagem-baseada-em-problemas-uma-estrat-g ia-de-ensino-aprendizagem-no-curso-de

Vieira, R., Monteiro, P., Azevedo, G., & Oliveira, J. (2023, June 20-23). *Society 5.0 and Education 5.0: A Critical Reflection* [Paper presentation]. 18th Iberian Conference on Information Systems and Technologies (CISTI), Aveiro, Portugal. https://doi.org/ TI58278.2023.1021138610.23919/CIS

Yin, R. K. (2017). *Case Study Research and Applications Design and Methods* (6th ed.). Sage.

KEY TERMS AND DEFINITIONS

Accounting: It's a recording system that helps organizations to keep economic and financial movements coherent, making it easier to make effective management decisions. It involves not only recording, but also summarizing, and reporting financial transactions to help managers to keep on track assets, liabilities, costs, and earnings.

Active Methodology: Is a learner-centric approach focused on student engagement, critical thinking, and technology assimilation, in order to achieve dynamic and effective learning experiences. We may describe active methodology in the context of Education 5.0 as using Hands-On and Experiential Learning, Critical Thinking and Problem-Solving, Active Participation, Continuous Assessment and Feedback, Creativity and Innovation, Inclusive and Diverse Learning Environments.

Collaborative Work: Promotes a learning environment where students actively engage with their peers, leveraging technology, and developing a variety of necessary skills for nowadays workforce. It fosters not only academic growth but also social and interpersonal skills development, fundamental for improving success in an increasingly interconnected and friendly world. We may describe active methodology in the context of Education 5.0 as using interdependence and cooperation, diverse perspectives, team projects and activities, communication skills, project management, peer learning, conflict resolution, as well as global collaboration and preparation for the workplace.

Communication Technologies: Refer to the use of various digital tools and platforms that facilitate communication, collaboration, and information sharing in the field of education. Education 5.0 represents an advanced stage of education that leverages technology to enhance the learning experience and prepare individuals for the challenges of the digital age. Communication technologies in Education 5.0 cover a extensive assortment of digital tools and platforms, including but not limited to online learning platforms, video conferencing tools, social media, messaging apps, collaborative tools, email, blogs and wikis, discussion forums and online communities, as well as virtual reality (VR) and augmented reality (AR).

Education 5.0: Is a modern educational paradigm that integrates advanced technology, personalized learning, and the development of critical skills, emphasizing individual empowerment, creativity, and adaptability to prepare learners for the challenges of the digital age. It stands for a transformative approach to learning that harnesses the power of information, innovation, and communication technologies to cultivate not only traditional knowledge but also critical soft skills. It places a strong emphasis on active, student-centred methodologies, where learners engage with a wealth of digital information to bring creativity up, solving problems, and promote adaptability. In this collaborative environment, students are invited to work together using communication technologies, sharpening their teamwork and interpersonal abilities as they prepare for a future where the ability to innovate is paramount to evolve.

Information: Can be defined, in the context of Education 5.0, as data, facts, knowledge, and content that is relevant, accurate, and meaningful for learning and problem-solving. It is not just about the accumulation of data but also about its transformation into valuable knowledge and insights. It includes various forms of contents that both educators as learners may use to acquire, process, and apply knowledge in innovative and personalized ways. Information in Education 5.0 is typically accessed and distributed through digital technologies, enabling more flexible and tailored learning experiences.

Innovation: In the context of Education 5.0, refers to the creative and forward-thinking adoption of new and emerging technologies, pedagogical methods, and educational approaches to enhance the learning experience. It involves design and implementation of novel solutions that improve educational outcomes, promote personalized learning, and prepare students with the skills and competencies needed for the rapidly changing demands of the digital age.

Soft Skills: Are essential interpersonal and cognitive abilities, such as communication, teamwork, adaptability, critical thinking, and empathy, which play a crucial role in Education 5.0. In this educational paradigm, soft skills are emphasized as vital competencies for students to develop alongside traditional knowledge. Education 5.0 recognizes that nurturing these skills prepares learners to thrive in a complex, digitally driven world, where effective communication, collaboration, problem-solving, and emotional intelligence are key to success, innovation, and lifelong learning.

Chapter 8
Effects and Potentials of Business Intelligence Tools on Tourism Companies in a Tourism 4.0 Environment

Mahsa Amiri
https://orcid.org/0009-0007-3867-5299
Faculty of Economics, University of Algarve, Portugal

Célia M. Q. Ramos
https://orcid.org/0000-0002-3413-4897
ESGHT and CinTurs, University of Algarve, Portugal

ABSTRACT

Several technologies emerged and disrupted how they operate in the Tourism 4.0 environment surrounding tourism companies. One, the digitalization of processes has become a way to support survival, and second, data grows exponentially daily. In this environment, a business intelligence tool can help to improve decision-making while enabling managers to realize complex information quickly and make more efficient decisions. The benefits of BI adoption in businesses encourage scholars to study and research this topic. This study aims to understand the effects and potentialities of business intelligence systems conjugated with artificial intelligence for tourism companies. As the main findings, the potential of BI helps the tourism company to increase destination sustainability support and to create a shared decision-maker environment between the companies.

INTRODUCTION

The ability of firms to convert data into valuable information is increasingly important as a competitive and success aspect. Prior to the data aging and becoming unusable, the vast volume of recorded data must be quickly transformed into information (Hočevar & Jaklič, 2010).

DOI: 10.4018/978-1-6684-9039-6.ch008

The majority of client requests, including those for services related to tourism, are now made online via websites or applications thanks to daily technological advancements. As a result, there would be a vast amount of customer-related data, which might be used to store information about customer behavior and perception (Fuchs et al., 2015).

Businesses can increase their performance by using this data to their advantage. The marketplace is a place where businesses compete, and by drawing on user experiences, they can improve their competitive edge. According to Rostami (2014), in recent years, market competitiveness has become a matter of survival or bankruptcy as well as profit and loss.

The data collected through online gates needs to be analyzed and translated into useful information because it is not informative. According to Fuchs et al. (2015), business intelligence (BI) tries to process and analyze this data in order to make it valuable for the clients.

According to Bustamante et al. (2020), who conducted this study, business intelligence may be thought of as the process of extracting and evaluating data to enhance decision-making. Business intelligence (BI) is a concept that encompasses several interconnected processes, including information gathering and organization, data analysis and control, report generation, and managerial activity support.

Users of business intelligence can easily comprehend complex information and, as a result, make quicker and more effective decisions. The implementation of BI science's techniques, technologies, systems, methodologies, and applications within organizational systems enables them to gain recognition for their efforts, improve their ability to make decisions, and boost their revenues (Vajirakachorn & Chongwatpol, 2017).

The end outcome would be decreased costs and higher revenue for the businesses. According to this strategy, BI deployment can benefit any company or organization, regardless of its size, focus of business, or position in both domestic and foreign markets. The outcomes (Vajirakachorn & Chongwatpol, 2017), which lead to operational work optimization, improved customer and supplier relationships, increased profit, more supportive decisions, and competitive advantages in the market (Bustamante et al., 2020), include unprecedented insight into consumer sentiment, client demands, and the identification of new business prospects.

For tourism companies and destinations, the collaboration of BI platforms produces an intriguing analytic outcome (Bustamante et al., 2020). However, utilizing the new technology calls for the development of mathematics, training in IT (Information Technology) systems, and reengineering the management of an organization's culture, all of which could result in additional costs for businesses (Alcabnani et al., 2019) and also increase their competitiveness (Nyanga et al., 2020; Lv et al., 2022).

The advantages of BI adoption in tourism businesses motivate researchers to learn about and do research on this subject. The purpose of this study is to comprehend the business intelligence process and how it would help businesses develop and operate more the tourism business more effectively. The main questions are mentioned to help establish the direction of the investigation, and it is intended that the study will provide appropriate responses to each of these questions.

1)   What are the effects of BI in tourism companies?
2)   What are the BI potentials in Tourism companies?

The present chapter is subdivided into three sections, without considering the present introduction and the conclusions. The first section presents the background of this research, where will be presented the concepts and technologies associated with Industry 4.0 and Tourism 4.0. The second section presents the focus of the chapter about BI potentials and possibilities, will be presented the components of a BI system and the integration of AI in a BI system and potentialities to support tourism sustainability. The third section presents the discussion and future research directions and respond to the research questions.

BACKGROUND

Industry 4.0 and Tourism 4.0

The concept of Industry 4.0 is the fourth revolution in the industry, defined as using a combination of internet technologies in order to have digitalized, automated, and smart factories (Lasi et al., 2014; Lopez et al., 2019).

The term Industry 4.0 was first introduced by the German government for a high-tech recommended implementation in 2011 (Korže, 2019), and soon it was used by the Federal Ministry of Education and Research (Lasi et al., 2014).

Researchers consider various components for Industry 4.0. According to Pereira and Romero (2017), Industry 4.0 is like an umbrella concept for the recent industrial pattern, which includes a set of technological developments such as Cyber-Physical Systems (CPS), IoT (Internet of Things), IoS (Internet of Service), robotics, big data, Cloud manufacturing and AR (Augmented Reality).

As Salkin et al. (2018) explain, Industry 4.0 includes eight foundational technologies, which are robotics, artificial intelligence and big data analytics, simulation, embedded systems, communication networks like industrial internet, cloud computing, additive manufacturing, and visualisation advances. This package needs support from basic technologies like cyber security and sensors.

Also, Romero et al. (2021) explain, Industry 4.0 is mainly the interconnection between technology, machine learning, and predictive analytics, which should be connected to BI systems for making better decisions.

There would be a large amount of data generated from Industry 4.0 technologies which need to be used in decision-making. Therefore, BI must be adopted to receive data from industry 4.0 technologies (Bordeleau et al., 2018).

Industry 4.0 has influenced most industries, including the tourism industry. Industry 4.0 in the tourism and hospitality sectors aims to digitalize and personalize services by closely engaging customers (Zeqiri et al., 2020). Technologies associated with Industry 4.0 are leading to the development of business models and systems in tourism companies under the term Tourism 4.0 (Ramos & Brito, 2020).

According to a study by Korže (2019), the term tourism 4.0 has been used in Portugal for the first time. Back in that time, the concept of this term was related to start-ups and facilitating innovations in tourism. The author explains that nine European countries (Portugal, Finland, Italy, Spain, Turkey, and Slovenia) and Asia (Thailand, Bali, Malaysia) are implementing the term tourism 4.0 inside the industry under different concepts.

However, the study illustrates that the new paradigm of the term Tourism 4.0, as a creation of personalised travel experiences based on big data processing, is coming from a project called "Tourism 4.0" started by Arctur a Slovenian team in 2018 (Korže, 2019, p. 35).

Korže (2019), indicates that Tourism 4.0 is a trend of processing big data collected from tourists to recommend personal experiences. The new trend is based on high-tech computers and technologies, including AI, IoT, big data analysis, cloud computing, VR (Virtual Reality), and AR (Korže, 2019).

Peceny et al. (2019), also explains tourism 4.0 after the Slovenian project and believes that the new project makes it possible to shift from a tourist-centered focus to a focus by setting up a collaborative ecosystem which includes local inhabitants, government, authority, and tourist service suppliers. This ecosystem combines physical and digital worlds, personnel, infrastructure, and technology to enhance the experiences and expectations of the tourist. It also develops tailored products and services. In fact, the collaboration system collects tourists' history and knowledge and transfers it into digital space. The result would be a dynamic system among all tourism stakeholders which is available and accessible for everyone at any time.

Important technology elements in this system are named IoT, High-performance computing systems including AI, VR and AR for improving overall experiences, and research part for innovation methodologies, understanding all stakeholders who are involved, and applications that can be used in this system.

Big data, as an essential element of Tourism 4.0, enables businesses to have real-time information based on actual tourists' actions (Korže, 2019).

The physical world meets the digital one through cyber-physical systems, which create a global network for businesses (Pencarelli, 2020).

IoT, another essential feature of Tourism 4.0, by making a network and collecting data helps in measuring and monitoring human activities such as water and energy consumption in tourism accommodation (Peceny et al., 2019). It adopts devices equipped with sensors to connect the internet to physical reality. In the context of IoT, everything should be able to communicate and be identifiable with the physical environment (Pencarelli, 2020).

As Korže (2019) says, robots and Chatbots, while performing tasks, collect all kinds of data from a client. Chatbots or electronic agents are online assistants that offer low-price travel products and personalise the clients' services based on their preferences (Pencarelli, 2020).

Virtual reality helps visitors to choose their destination, and augmented reality advances the tourist experience by providing extra historical or adventurous information (Pencarelli, 2020).

For a more effective system, not only tourist service suppliers and government but also local communities need to take part in future developments (Peceny et al., 2019). As the study indicates, the main stakeholders in the proposed ecosystem are as follows:

- Local tourism product and service suppliers which require direct access to target clients.
- Tourists who will be encouraged to take part in the program to benefit from tailored offers and recommendations.
- Local inhabitants who not only benefit from the economic aspect but also receive better control and quality of living while hosting tourists.
- Government to provide unified data and policy regulation against disruptions and to ease innovations.

The proposed ecosystem is illustrated in Figure 1.

Adopting such systems under the concept of Tourism 4.0 brings enormous advantages not only for tourists, suppliers, and government but also for local society.

Using this model assets tourists to be connected to a real-time information source which makes recommendations based on their profile and preferences, for instance, what places to visit or which activities to participate in (Peceny et al., 2019). Capabilities of Tourism 4.0 enhance the tourist's experiences which is a development in the behavior and loyalty patterns of the users (Stankov & Gretzel, 2020).

Figure 1. The proposed ecosystem with stakeholders
Source: Adopted from Peceny et al. (2019, p. 5).

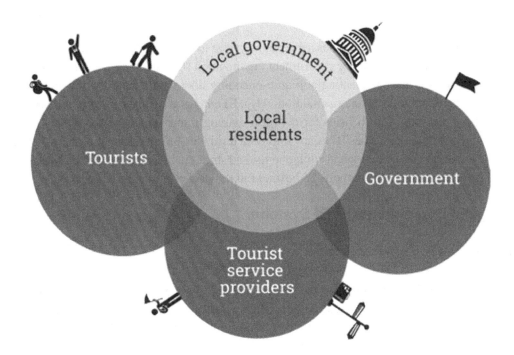

Furthermore, the model reduces negative behaviour and encourages a positive attitude regarding sustainability (Peceny et al., 2019). In the mentioned system, the number of received travelers and the accessibility of all of them are being considered. This fact not only helps in sustainability issues (production and consumption) but also in environmental preservation (Ramos & Brito, 2020). Destinations can preserve and develop cultural heritages and reduce resource consumption through this program (Peceny et al., 2019) for instance, VR technology reduces unnecessary travel (Zeqiri et al., 2020). Using Tourism 4.0 is considered a solution for sustainability achievements since its technologies are environmentally friendly. Hotels in tourism 4.0, are adopting smart links, lighting, temperature and ventilation devices, showers, and laundries which reduce the waste of energy and water. Furthermore, implementing Tourism 4.0 technologies in restaurants and hotel kitchens would allow efficient use of food (Zeqiri et al., 2020).

Also, the new paradigm brings advantages in the marketing area. Marketing advances through the program help to solve the issue of inefficiency in tourist facilities such as hotels during a year (Peceny et al., 2019). Furthermore, it gives the opportunity for smaller destinations to compete equally with the larger ones (Peceny et al., 2019).

According to Ramos and Brito (2020), this system makes improvements in three parts which are product and services, applications with tourist interactions, and real-time business intelligence and analytics, including communication between different partners.

Through such an important project, an effective business intelligence system would be required to process the data which will be shared among all stakeholders, where data can to be analyzed to create useful information that helps make strategic decisions (Peceny et al., 2019).

MAIN FOCUS OF THE CHAPTER

Business Intelligence

A business intelligence system can be described as a system to disseminate information to the various sections of any industrial, scientific, or government organization (Lund, 1958). This intelligence system uses data processing for auto-abstracting and auto-encoding documents and also for creating interest profiles for any "action points" in an organization. Also, BI can be defined as an "umbrella term" which includes systems, methods, and theories for decision-making improvements (Negash & Gray, 2008). Similarly, Muntean (2018) describes BI as an "umbrella term" for Information systems, which includes integrating several types of technological components, and strategies used by businesses to extract useful information from big data which support the business in the decision-making process.

Technological Components of BI Systems

Visualization

Visualization is defined as demonstrating the results in a visual form which can be tables, bars, charts, maps, etc. (Abellera & Bulusu, 2018). The authors explain the importance of images and indicate that the human brain comprehends images and shapes better than numbers and words, which helps viewers to pay more attention. As a result, viewers can communicate better with that information, and apprehend more.

Business intelligence also uses visualization techniques to create dashboards which accelerate the process of understanding big data and reveal key insights even for non-specialists (Hlaváč & Štefanovič, 2020).

The positive effects of visualization have made it into one of the significant trends in business intelligence, once 90% of the information is transmitted into the human brain is in visual form (Boldosova & Luoto, 2020; Calzon, 2022). Recently, visualization techniques have been combined with Machine Learning (ML), to illustrate not only present information of a business but also future visions (Hlaváč & Štefanovič, 2020), and they will continue to evolve.

ETL (Extract, Transform, and Load)

As the volume of produced data increases daily, having traditional data warehouses as data storage in a business intelligence system has caused problems such as space complexity, cost raising, and speed issues (Inamdar & Gursoy, 2019). Cloud services can be a solution to these difficulties.

Cloud benefits such as an integrated environment, adaptability, streamlined processes, advanced mobility, and high performance (Abellera & Bulusu, 2018) make this service popular among BI users. Recently, most businesses have been performing in cloud environments (Norris, 2020).

The new trend is not only a solution for complex businesses with large amounts of data, but also a beneficial approach for small and medium-sized enterprises (Horakova & Skalska, 2013; Al-Aqrabi et al., 2015). Instead of investing plenty of money in IT structures, companies may purchase online technology and pay based on their requirements. Moreover, they can upgrade the service whenever it is needed.

Software as a service (SaaS), infrastructure as a service (IaaS), and platform as a service (PaaS) are different strategies for providing cloud services on the Internet (Chen et al., 2012). Google and

Microsoft are two important examples of cloud computing providers. Google app provides a platform for hosting applications with Java and Python program language, while the Microsoft cloud platform, called Azure, introduces SQL (Structured Query Language) and cloud services such as SQL Azure or SharePoint (Chen et al., 2012).

In the study by Inamdar and Gursoy (2019), three types of Clouds are explained. These are public cloud, private cloud, and hybrid cloud. A public type of cloud could be offered free of charge since there is no privacy guarantee for users. On the other hand, a private cloud is highly secure with exceptional performance and stability, and its costs are based on different plans that users choose. The last type, the hybrid cloud, integrates private and public clouds. This feature allows users to protect high-value data in private resources and keep more frequent data in public. Consequently, the cost would be reduced in this type of cloud.

Also, it is expected that the number of enterprises which operate with cloud services will increase in the next years. Furthermore, the functionality of the cloud service, such as speed, would be developed. Hybrid cloud, as a popular service among enterprises, will continue to grow over the next decade (Norris, 2020). Furthermore, the serverless cloud is a recent trend which promises a pay-as-you-go model to companies. This option able organisations to pay only for services that are used (Höpken & Fuchs, 2022; Taylor, 2022).

Mobile-BI

Despite not being exactly a component, it is a possibility and a trend for the future - mobile business intelligence (M-BI) is the technology of applying BI features such as analyzing, decision-making, and management support on smartphones or tablets (Weichbroth et al., 2022). According to Fang et al. (2018), M-BI is an ability to access BI-related data, such as dashboards, through mobile devices.

The idea of transferring BI systems on mobile has become popular for over ten years since smartphones entered the market (Weichbroth et al., 2022). Stuff and customers can have worldwide access to crucial data, final reports, and results through phone devices. Companies are turning to M-BI to develop operations and competitive purposes (Fang et al., 2018).

Integration of AI in BI

A Brief Explanation of AI

According to Lai and Hung (2018), Artificial Intelligence (AI) is defined as a science which is capable of simulation of human actions, senses, and intelligence with the purpose of problem-solving like a human. As the study demonstrates, the key elements of AI contain reasoning, planning, learning, communication, and perceiving ability (Lai & Hung, 2018). In another study by Zohuri and Moghadam (2020) AI is explained as the ability of a computer to think and learn in the same manner as humans do.

AI includes machine learning (ML) techniques which apply algorithms to learn and become smarter. In a study by Bulchand-Gidumal (2020), machine learning is explained as a set of algorithms for repeating a process and learning through feedback each time, also considered by Knani et al. (2022). Also, deep learning (DL) is a specific type of machine learning, and both are considered parts of AI (Bulchand-Gidumal, 2020, p. 8). Similarly, Zohuri and Moghadam (2020), consider ML and DL as the sub-sets of AI.

How AI Can Improve BI Functionality

Machine learning can be adopted by BI systems for enhancement in analysis (Abellera & Bulusu, 2018). Norris (2020) believes that AI is becoming a crucial component of BI which improves the function of BI systems.

Norris (2020) considers more advantages of the adoption of AI in BI which are: turning normal users into experts, enhancement in data exploration, automated data preparation, learning from user interactions for better forecasting, and competitive advantages. Some of these benefits and their functionality in BI is explained in the following.

Data Preparation

One of the big impacts of AI on analytics could be data preparation (Abellera & Bulusu, 2018). For a successful interpretation, data need to be structured and searchable (Norris, 2020). Therefore, preparing data is one of the significant phases in analysing. With the help of machine learning algorithms, the patterns between data, even unstructured ones, would be detected automatically (Abellera & Bulusu, 2018). AI in BI is a big time-saver that reduces the data preparation process length from hours or days to minutes (Norris, 2020).

Normal Users as Data Specialists

Applying AI in BI tools enables users to discover insights, understand, and act independently of the IT section without needing to be specialized or expert (Norris, 2020).

Gaining Knowledge From End-User

AI in BI studies the interactions of the users to learn better what users want in their analysis (Norris, 2020). This feature can personalize results for the specific user and recommend dashboards for a better perception of data (Norris, 2020) and predictive analytics.

Rising in Predictive Analytics

Predictive analytics is one of the important aspects of business intelligence. Target data for this kind of analytic is current and past information of the business which would be analyzed and studied to predict the future, foresee the risks, and make recommendations (Hlaváč & Štefanovič, 2020).

By applying algorithms to data, predictive analytics finds patterns and trends to forecast the future (Negash & Gray, 2008). This ability is even more significant among tourism industries where products are perishable, which means the benefit of products would be lost forever if they are not sold. Predictive analytics helps tourism industries to manage prices in a way that can optimize the sale rate. For instance, airlines use this feature to realize how many tickets they must sell on each flight and at what prices (Calzon, 2022). This also could benefit the hospitality industry, where hotels can manage prices to have maximum occupancy while making revenue (Calzon, 2022). Companies may also benefit from this feature while considering a new product or service (Boldosova & Luoto, 2020). They can study the behavior of customers and predict how would be the reaction to the new elements and if they are going to be successful in the market (Lim et al., 2013).

Use of AI in Tourism

Tourism and hospitality are related to AI in many aspects. Tourists need information about their future destination, transport, accommodation, and other services, and the way that they are assisted in this regard influences their satisfaction (Bulchand-Gidumal, 2020; Blanco-Moreno et al., 2023). Similarly, tourism and hospitality organizations require technology to attract customers and purchase their services in the market in a way that customers prefer (Bulchand-Gidumal, 2020; Kong et al., 2023).

AI can support both groups by matching tourists to the right services and products. Various features of AI, such as forecasting systems, face recognition systems, language translation applications, digital assistance, robots etc., are helping tourists and organizations to decide and experience more efficiently (Bulchand-Gidumal, 2020).

Tourism destinations and industries are implementing AI technologies to compete in the market, attract customers, and increase the level of satisfaction. For instance, in the hospitality industry, hotels, under the name of "intelligent hotels", are upgrading systems and infrastructures based on artificial intelligence to compete in the market (Lai & Hung, 2018).

Adopting AI in travel and tourism industries reduces labor costs since AI systems and robots can work 24/7 also, an AI system such as a chatbot has the ability to handle more than one customer at the same time, which is not possible for human workers (Ivanov & Webster, 2017). As the authors claim, AI systems bring not only financial benefits but also other non-financial advantages such as higher service quality, the ability to perform in more different languages, and saving employee's time.

AI Systems

In a study by Bulchand-Gidumal (2020, p. 11), AI systems are divided into four categories which are forecasting systems, personalization and recommending systems, language translation applications and conversational systems. Some of the popular AI systems currently being used are explained in the following.

Ambient AI

Ambient intelligence is adjusting external elements related to human senses, such as temperature, light, music, etc. Adopting the right setting in the environment based on the tourist's desire, make a huge difference in perceptions and experiences.

A hotel can apply this feature in the room conditions to guests' preferences (Bulchand-Gidumal, 2020, p. 7). Marriot and Hilton are examining the effects of guest-controlled equipment for ambient adjustment (Buhalis et al., 2019).

There are also tourist attractions (like galleries and museums) which adopt ambient AI to make visitors' experiences more sensible. Furthermore, it can be used in public places like concerts, events, and airports (Bulchand-Gidumal, 2020, p. 9).

Facial Recognition

According to Samala et al. (2020), facial recognition is an application from AI for recognizing faces and comparing them with the face in the document.

This feature is not only used for realizing a specific person, but also for counting the number of people in an environment and even to observe and record the sentiments of the passengers (Bulchand-Gidumal, 2020, p. 9).

Facial recognition can be used in the check-in process on arrival (Bulchand-Gidumal, 2020), which can be at the hotel entrance or airline check-ins.

Virtual Reality and Augmented Reality

According to Guttentag (2010), VR is defined as adopting computer 3-D features to create a virtual environment which simulates human senses. In another study by Buhalis et al. (2019), VR is defined as a series of technologies related to sensory perception, such as vision, voice, and touch, which engages the user with an artificial environment.

As Guttentag (2010) explains, VR is beneficial in different areas of tourism: planning and management, marketing, entertainment, education, accessibility, and heritage preservation. Tourism and hospitality industries use VR to offer customers remote experiences and pre-arrival overviews (Buhalis et al., 2019). Sarkady et al. (2021) say this technology creates virtual holidays (a simulation of real-time experiences) when there are restrictions for traveling (like COVID-19, a dangerous destination, or political reasons). As the authors claim, VR makes more tourist locations accessible and develops tourist experiences in the sites and attractions (Sarkady et al., 2021). The hospitality industry uses VR to create virtual room tours of a hotel (Samala et al., 2020), and customers can visit the room, hotel environment, and facilities before making a reservation.

Time travelling, an ever dream of humans, becomes real with VR features (Buhalis et al., 2019). Museums and heritage sites, nowadays, trying to create a full 3-D model of historical places also antique objects to offer visitors a virtual reality experience. This advantage also helps to preserve heritage sites by reducing the number of real tours (Geisler, 2018).

Virtual tours can target travelers with disabilities who cannot travel easily. Through virtual booking tours, the airplane is simulated, which allows customers to walk through the plane and choose a seat (Samala et al., 2020).

As Guttentag (2010) indicates, augmented reality (AR) is a type of VR that enhances the real-world experience by adding computer-generated images into the scenes. AR collects the user's current environment information (through camera and GPS) and provides a layer of information for the user on a portable screen such as smartphone, tablets, and glasses (Buhalis et al., 2019). As Yung and Khoo-Lattimore (2019) explain, in VR, the user is fully engaged with the virtual environment, while in AR, most parts of what users see are still the real world.

AR enriches the quality of on-trip experiences and increases the value of complex services (Buhalis et al., 2019). For instance, museums, galleries, and events apply AR to offer contributors extra information and deeper experiences (Buhalis et al., 2019). The Hub Hotel from Premier Inn, a British resort, is an example of places that adopted AR in the business. AR features are implemented on the room walls, when guests view the walls through smartphones or tablets, they can get extra information (Revfine, 2021).

Chatbots

Chatbot is considered as a software which holds a conversation between computer and customers through texts or audio (Samala et al., 2020). Calvaresi et al. (2021) define a chatbot as a language-based computer program which is able to maintain a conversation with humans.

According to Buhalis et al. (2019), implementing chatbots inside organizations may reduce labor costs since they can answer routine questions in any language. Chatbots are accessible 24/7 and every day of the year (Samala et al., 2020). This ability encourages the tourism sector, to use chatbots as online sellers that can purchase products and services anytime. Another significant objective of chatbots is collecting data which is a precious capability in a data-driven era (Calvaresi et al., 2021).

Airlines use chatbots to offer trips to customers and sell tickets. For instance, Air France (KLM) uses chatbots via Facebook channels to sell products and services and also inform customers about times and schedules (Geisler, 2018). In the hospitality sector, Booking.com provide a chatbot for supporting bookings in the English language, which is handling 30% of customers' requirements in less than five minutes (Calvaresi et al., 2021).

Robots

According to Bulchand-Gidumal (2020) a robot is a physical machine which can act and make decisions based on artificial intelligence and sensing the environment capabilities (Jabeen et al., 2022). As Samala et al. (2020) say, robots are a type of AI technology which utilize features of IoT to operate activities. Yang et al. (2020) call robots human-like AI and categorise them into four types which are industrial, service, professional, and personal robots.

Recently, having a robot reception has been a trend in the hospitality industry (Samala et al., 2020). Customers can check into their rooms quickly without human interference (Yang et al., 2020). Henn-na Hotel in Japan was the first hotel that replaces the staff with robots (Rajesh, 2017). As further examples, the Alexa robot has become popular in some of the branches of Marriot hotels (Samala et al., 2020), and Connie is a robot in Hilton hotel which answers guest's questions and provides guidance on nearby attractions and events (Yang et al., 2020).

Robots are also being adopted in other hospitality sections. They are used for burger-turning and cocktail-making in bars and restaurants (Buhalis et al., 2019). Tipsy Robot is a bar in Las Vegas which started the business by employing two robots as bartenders who provide drinks in only 60 to 90 seconds (Yang et al., 2020). Also, Pepper is a robot hired in one of the branches of Pizza Hut in Japan, which talks to customers and takes orders (Yang et al., 2020).

BI to Support Tourism Sustainability

The tourism and hospitality industry plays a big part in world resource consumption. Besides water and energy consumption, habitat and heritage destruction, food and overall waste are also considered current challenges by tourism industries (Pan et al., 2018). Tourism sectors such as accommodation, transportation, and travel contribute to greenhouse gas emissions (GHG) production (Pan et al., 2018).

Sustainable tourism decreases the negative impacts of social, environmental, and economic tourism activities (Pan et al., 2018).

Green buildings are a solution towards sustainable tourism (Pan et al., 2018). As Pan et al. (2018) indicate, buildings, as a big consumers of energy, represent a high capacity for saving energy. Adopting recent technologies in hotel infrastructures, such as sensors and electric devices, enables business owners to create dashboards related to energy consumption and electric performances, which result in energy consumption reduction (Cardoso et al., 2021).

Heritage monuments preservation is a significant issue in tourism sustainability. The growing VR technology offers virtual tours from a distance which reduce trips and assist in cultural site preservation (Guttentag, 2010), especially those not in good condition regarding erosion impacts.

BI dashboards enabled with artificial intelligence with the help of predictive analytics discover patterns of food consumption based on past and present data and foresee the future model of food consumption. This information enables managers to plan for upcoming events and reduce the amount of wasted food. For instance, Easy Jet (an English airline), adopted systems including AI to predict requests for food and beverages on flights which not only decreased the cost (Geisler, 2018) but also improved the waste management aspect.

DISCUSSION AND FUTURE RESEARCH DIRECTIONS

Effects of BI on Tourism Companies

Better Customer Satisfaction

As described before, better customer satisfaction is an effect of BI on companies (Hočevar & Jaklič, 2010). Besides other benefits, the application makes it possible to analyze the peak times of consumption 24/7. As a result, there is the possibility to optimize the time-deployment of the waiters and kitchen staff according to the predicted amount of consumption. This would lead to a reduction of order waiting time for the clients to a minimum time. Faster services would increase customer satisfaction levels.

Positive Impacts on Profitability

Another effect of BI implementation on companies is a positive impact on profitability (Yiu et al., 2021). In the described example, another possibility of the application is registering all significant activities done by staff. Therefore, there can be a control system for the performance of all employees and their share of the total turnover. This allows to lay off staff with bad performances or to motivate beneficial employees with motivation plans such as a bonus system.

Predicting the peak time and reduction in waiting time for guests, which was described before, also makes the possibility to serve a larger number of guests, which increases the profitability.

Data collected by the application assists in reliable planning for the consumption and purchasing of foods and drinks. On the one hand, this can reduce the waste caused by unnecessary foods, for example, by reducing the ordering perishable foods. On the other hand, through a targeted bulk purchase plan for required goods, a better purchasing price can be achieved, which contributes to profitability enhancement.

Time Saving

Wixom and Watson (2010) state, timesaving is an advantage of implementing BI since it reduces the interactions between people. Within the Hostel application example, the software could be connected directly to the supplier and client applications. Therefore, requests would be delivered only through the application and there would be no need for extra phone calls or in-person actions. As explained, saving time can result in higher customer satisfaction at the same time.

Increasement in the Company's Functionality

BI provides precise information (Madyatmadja et al., 2021), which increase businesses' functionality in making decisions and planning (Hočevar & Jaklič, 2010). In the concept of Hostel application, the BI system provides useful information regarding suppliers and products. Managers can be informed about more qualified suppliers which cover a higher number of orders. Also, they would receive a review of the most ordered product and the products which bring more profits to the business.

The results not only assist the business in the current decision-making but also support the plans and predictions. For instance, if the Hostel decides to provide storage for the products to accelerate the delivery procedure, through the BI system the manager can predict what are the favorite requested products by guests and pre-order them.

Effects of BI on Travel Agencies

In the second example case, the described effects of BI on companies would be mentioned undertaking into account the specific conditions for travel agencies.

Recently, customers mostly prefer to customize their trips directly on the Internet. Benefits gained from BI can assist travel agencies to raise positive points and compete in the market to interest more customers.

Decisions Effectiveness

As Rouhani et al. (2016) mention, improving decision-making is a further effect of BI on companies.

For travel agencies, purchasing the allotments of hotel rooms and flight seats is a significant part of their business. The main challenge for such an allotment purchaser is to predict the optimal number of hotel rooms and/or flight seats for every season. Also, it is important to foresee at what price the rooms or seats can be sold to the end customer. The entrepreneurial risk here is whether the chosen allotment is appropriate for the later given situation in the market. By making a wrong decision, the company may purchase too many product allotments which can lead to a significant loss if there are not enough customers to consume those products. On the other hand, when a small allotment meets a higher demand, the company would not be able to gain the potential profit of the season.

The information obtained from the BI system can play a crucial role in this matter. Analyzing the history of the clients and the company's experiences, give a better view of investing opportunities (for example, on which destinations or at what time of the year). Furthermore, analytic trends of a BI system able travel agencies to balance the prices of the products in a way that makes the optimal benefit for the business.

Improve Awareness of Potential and New Chances

Notifying organizations about their business potential and new chances can be an effect brought by BI (Madyatmadja et al., 2021).

A study of the customers' behavior results in a better understanding of their actual and future desire. BI analytics enable travel agents to predict trends and changes of customer demands and find new travel destinations or any other tourism offers.

This effect of BI can be especially advantageous in the pot-corona time to understand whether the client's behavior has been influenced by the pandemic rules. The same thing can be applied to the impact of climate change or the current global political conflicts on customer decisions for traveling. For instance, BI dashboards can visualize if the regular clients book their trips earlier, whether they choose travel destinations with different climate if they try to avoid long distances or the influence of the above-mentioned factors on the budget.

Sales Optimization

The study by Turktarhan *et al.* (2021) confirms that BI can have notable effects on the user's sale optimization.

BI services, provide a rich analytical report for the marketing department, to customise targeting advertisements based on customer preferences. By studying the previous booking time, BI can propose the optimal time to start advertising. For example, whether the clients prefer to purchase products in the last-minute offers, prefer early bookings, or how long the time between booking and the beginning of the journey is generally.

In the same way, BI can control if the selling of the allotments is happening according to the plan, or it is necessary to add extra marketing support by targeting interested groups.

In addition, marketing measures, by observing the market continuously, may lead the business to recently opened markets caused by customer behavior changes. This can be considered a competitive advantage for tour operators since they can enter the new market early and receive a bigger market share.

BI Potentials in Tourism Companies

AI-Enabled BI in Tourism

As mentioned before, AI can be adopted as a powerful component in BI systems. AI-enabled BI creates competitive opportunities for any industry, especially Tourism and Hospitality.

One of the greatest advantages AI-enabled BI can bring is an enhancement in task automation. Chatbots are an example of AI-powered technologies which can be beneficial in data collecting (Calvaresi et al., 2021). In the following section, an effort is made to illustrate this power among tourism companies.

Notification and Recommendation

Creating an accurate notification network inside a BI system is one of the crucial tasks in tourism and hospitality companies. Alarms notify users regarding principal assignments such as delays, cancellations, deadlines, and clients' special requirements. Through the adoption of AI in a BI system, alarms and notifications can be set automatically.

Recommending influential suggestions inside a BI system is another benefit of AI algorithms. AI, by considering all existing possibilities, assists users in noticing patterns that maybe cannot be extracted with human eyes. This recommendation greatly supports CEOs and managers to receive a broad view of the situation before deciding.

Applications and Software

Automation in BI applications is also possible through AI adoption. AI algorithms can be written for operating repetitive tasks. For instance, there could be programs to order required products from related suppliers automatically, when the product number is lower than a certain amount. In this way, there would be time-saving advantages for both the business and staff.

In addition, AI facilities are enhancing the quality of software used in BI systems. Recently, some software has adopted machine learning languages to automate some stages of the ETL process, such as creating pipelines and making relations. Therefore, there should be some human factors that control the process. Even in this situation, AI optimize the consumed time by changing the process of creating to the process of controlling.

One of the capabilities of AI within Power BI is text analytics. Through Power BI, it is possible to analyse numbers but when you need to analyze the content of texts, AI will help detect language, extract keywords, or score sentiments. For example, when you have a column including comments and opinions, the AI algorithm can calculate the score sentiment, which can help to identify the positive or negative comments are mostly about.

BI and Sustainability in Tourism

Responsible consumption and production (of water, energy, and food) are one of the 17 goals of the United Nations towards the 2030 sustainable development program (United Nations, 2022), for example, there are advantages of using BI in energy consumption in terms of sustainability management.

Energy Consumption

Incorrect consumption of energy and natural resources is one of the significant issues regarding a sustainable future. Buildings are considered major consumers of energy (Pan et al., 2018). In the tourism and hospitality industries, there are various types of buildings, such as travel agencies, airline offices, airports, and hotels.

The accommodation sector in the tourism industry consumes a considerable part of the energy, water, and other resources (Băltescu, 2018). Consequently, green behavior, such as constructing green buildings, is a great hotel strategy.

The World Green Building Council (2022) defines green building as a building whose design, construction, or operation not only can reduce or eliminate negative impacts, but also can generate positive impacts on our climate and natural environment. One of the solutions towards turning a building into green is an efficient use of energy, water, and other resources.

Reports and dashboards created by BI in hotels, provide valuable information regarding water and energy consumption (like electricity and gas). This information can assist the manager in deciding productively regarding the water and energy usage plans. For instance, by observing lighting patterns in different hotel locations and guest presence patterns in those locations, it can be decided whether it is necessary to lighten up places continuously. Also, studying the energy usage pattern for ventilation equipment, lead to finding the optimal way forward utilizing them. In addition, the laundry department can also operate appropriately with the help of BI reports. For example, based on loads of the laundry machines, it can be understood that it is possible to limit the laundry days to certain days of the week and not every day, which results in water and electricity usage reduction.

Business Intelligence 4.0 (BI 4.0)

The idea of connecting data and creating an accessible environment by several members can be applied specifically to BI systems. Regarding this concept, there are huge companies which use this kind of connection only inside the same company and between different branches or departments. The method runs with a centralized dataset which is enabled with data row security rules. Therefore, accessed data for each level of the members would be different. Also, reports and dashboards are being shared easily through the related software.

Connecting BI cross-industries can be interpreted in two levels.

First, industries can share BI in the concept of results. The final result of a firm, which comes from analyzing its own data, can be accessible to other companies. For instance, an airline company can share the result of the age analysis of passengers to a certain destination with the other stakeholders of that destination. Therefore, all the members of an ecosystem can benefit from the other party's results.

The second level of connecting BI can be decision sharing. The same as companies can share their BI results, they can let others know their final decision on a certain topic. When tourism firms become aware of other companies' decisions, they can decide more efficiently for themselves, and for the whole ecosystem. Suppose an airline company has decided to introduce a new destination in its flight routes. When other stakeholders, like restaurants, accommodations, bars, etc., realize this decision, they can also plan for investing in that new destination. The sharing process can be more detailed in the specific chain. For example, when there are too many decisions regarding an Italian restaurant's investment in the destination, the other Italian restaurants know it would not be beneficial to have the same type of restaurant in that area. On the other hand, other types of restaurants, such as Chinese ones, can consider this opportunity.

In conclusion, connecting BI systems is an effective idea for the tourism and hospitality sectors. In this research, the new concept of connecting BI is called BI 4.0 since the procedure is related to Industry 4.0 and Tourism 4.0.

CONCLUSION

One of the potentials of BI systems is adopting AI technologies and using their power to enhance the competitiveness of tourism companies. One of these advantages can be automation that AI technologies offer in BI tasks such as collecting data, notification and recommendation programs, applications, and software. Increasing sustainability in energy consumption is another potential of adopting BI in the tourism and hospitality sectors. Analyzing data through BI provides dashboards which help managers to reduce the consumption of energy not only inside the buildings but also in the process of delivering products and services.

Finally, the great potential of BI in the future of the tourism sector can be connected to BI under the term of BI 4.0. connecting the BI systems cross-industries in a connected ecosystem can share not only the results of data analyzing of each firm but also the final decision of that firm on related subjects. This idea brings various benefits for all members of the ecosystem, such as centralized data, efficient decisions in greater aspects, saving time and money due to the finer decisions, reduction of similar analyses by different firms, more effective products and services, and higher customer satisfaction.

Furthermore, the idea of connecting BI is a new concept which still requires more research and study to become practical. One of the challenges of this topic would be data security and data governance issues in the ecosystem. User trust would be another important issue for running this project. There are also substantial challenges regarding the process. Standardization among companies, data centralization, new solution adoption, and user control are some challenges, which can be considered as future work.

ACKNOWLEDGMENT

This paper is financed by National Funds provided by FCT- Foundation for Science and Technology through project UIDB/04020/2020.

REFERENCES

Abellera, R., & Bulusu, L. (2018). *Oracle business intelligence with machine learning*. Artificial Intelligence Techniques in OBIEE for Actionable BI. doi:10.1007/978-1-4842-3255-2

Al-Aqrabi, H., Liu, L., Hill, R., & Antonopoulos, N. (2015). Cloud BI: Future of business intelligence in the Cloud. *Journal of Computer and System Sciences*, *81*(1), 85–96. doi:10.1016/j.jcss.2014.06.013

Alcabnani, S., Oubezza, M., & Elkafi, J. (2019). An approach for the implementation of semantic Big Data Analytics in the Social Business Intelligence process on distributed environments (Cloud computing). *Proceedings of the 4th International Conference on Big Data and Internet of Things*, 1-6. 10.1145/3372938.3373003

Băltescu, A. C. (2018). The green buildings: Sustainable development actions in the accommodation sector. *Annual Economic Series*, *3*, 130–135.

Blanco-Moreno, S., González-Fernández, A. M., & Muñoz-Gallego, P. A. (2023). Big data in tourism marketing: past research and future opportunities. *Spanish Journal of Marketing-ESIC*. doi:10.1108/SJME-06-2022-0134

Boldosova, V., & Luoto, S. (2020). Storytelling, business analytics and big data interpretation: Literature review and theoretical propositions. *Management Research Review*, *43*(2), 204–222. doi:10.1108/MRR-03-2019-0106

Bordeleau, F. E., Mosconi, E., & Santa-Eulalia, L. A. (2018) Business Intelligence in Industry 4.0: State of the art and research opportunities. In *Proceedings of the 51st Hawaii International Conference on System Sciences* (pp. 3944-3953). ICISS 10.24251/HICSS.2018.495

Buhalis, D., Harwood, T., Bogicevic, V., Viglia, G., Beldona, S., & Hofacker, C. (2019). Technological disruptions in services: Lessons from tourism and hospitality. *Journal of Service Management, 20*(4), 484–506. doi:10.1108/JOSM-12-2018-0398

Bulchand-Gidumal, J. (2020). Impact of artificial intelligence in travel, tourism, and hospitality. In *Handbook of e-Tourism* (pp. 1–20). Springer International Publishing. doi:10.1007/978-3-030-05324-6_110-1

Bustamante, A., Sebastia, L., & Onaindia, E. (2020). BITOUR: A Business Intelligence Platform for Tourism Analysis. *ISPRS International Journal of Geo-Information, 9*(11), 671. doi:10.3390/ijgi9110671

Calvaresi, D., Ibrahim, A., Calbimonte, J. P., Schegg, R., Fragniere, E., & Schumacher, M. (2021). The evolution of chatbots in tourism: A systematic literature review. *Information and Communication Technologies in Tourism, 2021*, 3–16. doi:10.1007/978-3-030-65785-7_1

Calzon, B. (2022). *13 Essential Data Visualization Techniques, Concepts & Methods To Improve Your Business – Fast.* Retrieved from: https://www.datapine.com/blog/data-visualization-techniques-concepts-and-methods/

Cardoso, P. J., Monteiro, J., Cabrita, C., Semião, J., Cruz, D. M., Pinto, N., Ramos, C. M., Oliveira, L. M., & Rodrigues, J. M. (2021). Monitoring, Predicting, and Optimizing Energy Consumptions: A Goal Toward Global Sustainability. In *Research Anthology on Clean Energy Management and Solutions* (pp. 20–47). IGI Global. doi:10.4018/978-1-7998-9152-9.ch002

Chen, H., Chiang, R. H., & Storey, V. C. (2012). Business intelligence and analytics: From big data to big impact. *Management Information Systems Quarterly, 36*(4), 1165–1188. doi:10.2307/41703503

Fang, L. Y., Azmi, N. F. M., Yahya, Y., Sarkan, H., Sjarif, N. N. A., & Chuprat, S. (2018). Mobile business intelligence acceptance model for organisational decision making. *Bulletin of Electrical Engineering and Informatics, 7*(4), 650–656. doi:10.11591/eei.v7i4.1356

Fuchs, M., Höpken, W., & Lexhagen, M. (2015). Applying business intelligence for knowledge generation in tourism destinations–A case study from Sweden. In *Tourism and leisure* (pp. 161–174). Springer Gabler. doi:10.1007/978-3-658-06660-4_11

Geisler, R. (2018). *Artificial intelligence in the travel and tourism industry adoption and impact* [Unpublished Master Thesis]. Nova School of Business and Economics.

Guttentag, D. A. (2010). Virtual reality: Applications and implications for tourism. *Tourism Management, 31*(5), 637–651. doi:10.1016/j.tourman.2009.07.003

Hlaváč, J., & Štefanovič, J. (2020). *Machine learning and business intelligence or from descriptive analytics to predictive analytics. In 2020 Cybernetics and Informatics (KandI).* IEEE.

Hočevar, B., & Jaklič, J. (2010). Assessing benefits of business intelligence systems–a case study. *Management, 15*(1), 87–119.

Höpken, W., & Fuchs, M. (2022). Business Intelligence in Tourism. In *Handbook of e-Tourism* (pp. 497–527). Springer International Publishing. doi:10.1007/978-3-030-48652-5_3

Horakova, M., & Skalska, H. (2013). Business Intelligence and Implementation in a Small Enterprise. *Journal of Systems Integration*, *4*(2), 50–61.

InamdarS.R.GursoyK.(2019).*Cloud hosted business-data driven BI platforms*.doi:10.7282/t3-f5vq-4938

Ivanov, S., & Webster, C. (2017). Adoption of robots, artificial intelligence and service automation by travel, tourism and hospitality companies – a cost-benefit analysis. *International Scientific Conference "Contemporary tourism – traditions and innovations"*.

Jabeen, F., Al Zaidi, S., & Al Dhaheri, M. H. (2022). Automation and artificial intelligence in hospitality and tourism. *Tourism Review*, *77*(4), 1043–1061. doi:10.1108/TR-09-2019-0360

Knani, M., Echchakoui, S., & Ladhari, R. (2022). Artificial intelligence in tourism and hospitality: Bibliometric analysis and research agenda. *International Journal of Hospitality Management*, *107*, 103317. doi:10.1016/j.ijhm.2022.103317

Kong, H., Wang, K., Qiu, X., Cheung, C., & Bu, N. (2023). 30 years of artificial intelligence (AI) research relating to the hospitality and tourism industry. *International Journal of Contemporary Hospitality Management*, *35*(6), 2157–2177. doi:10.1108/IJCHM-03-2022-0354

Korže, S.Z. (2019). From Industry 4.0 to Tourism 4.0. *Innovative Issues and Approaches in Social Sciences*, *12*(3), 29-52.

Lai, W. C., & Hung, W. H. (2018). A framework of cloud and AI based intelligent hotel. *Proceedings of the International Conference on Electronic Business (ICEB)*, 36-43.

Lapa, J., Bernardino, J., & Figueiredo, A. (2014). A comparative analysis of open source business intelligence platforms. *Proceedings of the International Conference on Information Systems and Design of Communication*, 86-92. 10.1145/2618168.2618182

Lasi, H., Fettke, P., Kemper, H. G., Feld, T., & Hoffmann, M. (2014). Industry 4.0. *Business & Information Systems Engineering*, *6*(4), 239–242. doi:10.100712599-014-0334-4

Lennerholt, C., van Laere, J., & Söderström, E. (2018). Implementation challenges of self service business intelligence: A literature review. *51st Hawaii International Conference on System Sciences*, 5055-5063. 10.24251/HICSS.2018.631

Lim, E. P., Chen, H., & Chen, G. (2013). Business intelligence and analytics: Research directions. *ACM Transactions on Management Information Systems*, *3*(4), 1–10. doi:10.1145/2407740.2407741

Lopez, C. P., Segura, M., & Santórum, M. (2019). Data analytics and BI framework based on collective intelligence and the Industry 4.0. *Proceedings of the 2019 2nd International Conference on Information Science and Systems*, 93-98. 10.1145/3322645.3322667

Lv, H., Shi, S., & Gursoy, D. (2022). A look back and a leap forward: A review and synthesis of big data and artificial intelligence literature in hospitality and tourism. *Journal of Hospitality Marketing & Management*, *31*(2), 145–175. doi:10.1080/19368623.2021.1937434

Madyatmadja, E. D., Adiba, C. N. A., Sembiring, D. J. M., Pristinella, D., & Putra, A. M. (2021). The Positive Impact of Implementation Business Intelligence and Big Data in Hospitality and Tourism Sector. *International Journal of Emerging Technology and Advanced Engineering, 11*(6), 59–71. doi:10.46338/ijetae0621_07

Muntean, M. (2018). Business intelligence issues for sustainability projects. *Sustainability (Basel), 10*(2), 335. doi:10.3390u10020335

Negash, S., & Gray, P. (2008). Business intelligence. In *Handbook on decision support systems 2* (pp. 175–193). Springer. doi:10.1007/978-3-540-48716-6_9

Norris, M. (2020). *The Value of AI-powered Business Intelligence*. O'Reilly Media, Incorporated.

Nyanga, C., Pansiri, J., & Chatibura, D. (2020). Enhancing competitiveness in the tourism industry through the use of business intelligence: A literature review. *Journal of Tourism Futures, 6*(2), 139–151. doi:10.1108/JTF-11-2018-0069

Pan, S. Y., Gao, M., Kim, H., Shah, K. J., Pei, S. L., & Chiang, P. C. (2018). Advances and challenges in sustainable tourism toward a green economy. *The Science of the Total Environment, 635*, 452–469. doi:10.1016/j.scitotenv.2018.04.134 PMID:29677671

Peceny, U. S., Urbančič, J., Mokorel, S., Kuralt, V., & Ilijaš, T. (2019). Tourism 4.0: Challenges in marketing a paradigm shift. Consumer Behavior and Marketing, 39-59.

Pencarelli, T. (2020). The digital revolution in the travel and tourism industry. *Information Technology & Tourism, 22*(3), 455–476. doi:10.100740558-019-00160-3

Pereira, A. C., & Romero, F. (2017). A review of the meanings and the implications of the Industry 4.0 concept. *Procedia Manufacturing, 13*, 1206–1214. doi:10.1016/j.promfg.2017.09.032

Rajesh, T. (2017). What is Artificial Intelligence? *Learning outcomes of classroom research*, 28-36.

Ramos, C. M., & Brito, I. S. (2020). The Effects of Industry 4.0 in Tourism and Hospitality and Future Trends in Portugal. In *The Emerald Handbook of ICT in Tourism and Hospitality* (pp. 367–378). Emerald Publishing Limited. doi:10.1108/978-1-83982-688-720201023

Revfine. (2021) *How Augmented Reality is Revolutionising the Travel Industry*. Retrieved from: https://www.revfine.com/augmented-reality-travel-industry/

Romero, C. A., Ortiz, J. H., Khalaf, O. I., & Ríos Prado, A. (2021). Business intelligence: Business evolution after industry 4.0. *Sustainability (Basel), 13*(18), 10026. doi:10.3390u131810026

Rostami, N. A. (2014). Integration of Business Intelligence and Knowledge Management–A literature review. *Journal of Intelligence Studies in Business, 4*(2), 30–40. doi:10.37380/jisib.v4i2.95

Rouhani, S., Ashrafi, A., Ravasan, A. Z., & Afshari, S. (2016). The impact model of business intelligence on decision support and organizational benefits. *Journal of Enterprise Information Management, 29*(1), 19–50. doi:10.1108/JEIM-12-2014-0126

Salkin, C., Oner, M., Ustundag, A., & Cevikcan, E. (2018). A conceptual framework for Industry 4.0. In *Industry 4.0: Managing the digital transformation* (pp. 3–23). Springer. doi:10.1007/978-3-319-57870-5_1

Samala, N., Katkam, B.S., Bellamkonda, R.S. & Rodriguez, R.V. (2020). Impact of AI and robotics in the tourism sector: a critical insight. *Journal of Tourism Futures, 8*(1), 73-87.

Sarkady, D., Neuburger, L., & Egger, R. (2021). Virtual reality as a travel substitution tool during COVID-19. In *Information and communication technologies in tourism 2021 (pp. 452-463)*. Springer. doi:10.1007/978-3-030-65785-7_44

Schuff, D., Corral, K., St Louis, R. D., & Schymik, G. (2018). Enabling self-service BI: A methodology and a case study for a model management warehouse. *Information Systems Frontiers, 20*(2), 275–288. doi:10.100710796-016-9722-2

Stankov, U., & Gretzel, U. (2020). Tourism 4.0 technologies and tourist experiences: A human-centered design perspective. *Information Technology & Tourism, 22*(3), 477–488. doi:10.100740558-020-00186-y

Taylor, M., Reilly, D., & Wren, C. (2020). Internet of things support for marketing activities. *Journal of Strategic Marketing, 28*(2), 149–160. doi:10.1080/0965254X.2018.1493523

Taylor, T. (2022). *Top 6 Cloud Computing Trends for 2022*. Retrieved from https://techgenix.com/top-6-cloud-computing-trends-for-2022/

Turktarhan, G., Gopalan, R. & Ozkul, E. (2021). *Big Data and Business Intelligence in Hospitality and Tourism*. University of South Florida M3 Center Publishing.

United Nation. (2022). *Goal 12: Ensure sustainable consumption and production patterns*. United Nation. Retrieved from: https://www.un.org/sustainabledevelopment/sustainable-consumption-production/

Vajirakachorn, T., & Chongwatpol, J. (2017). Application of business intelligence in the tourism industry: A case study of a local food festival in Thailand. *Tourism Management Perspectives, 23*, 75–86. doi:10.1016/j.tmp.2017.05.003

Weichbroth, P., Kowal, J., & Kalinowski, M. (2022). Toward a unified model of mobile Business Intelligence (m-BI) acceptance and use. In *Proceedings of the 55th Hawaii International Conference on System Sciences* (pp. 304-313). HICSS. 10.24251/HICSS.2022.036

Wixom, B., & Watson, H. (2010). The BI-based organization. *International Journal of Business Intelligence Research, 1*(1), 13–28. doi:10.4018/jbir.2010071702

World Green Building Council. (2022). *What is green building?* Retrieved from: https://www.worldgbc.org/what-green-building

Yang, L., Henthorne, T.L. & George, B. (2020). Artificial intelligence and robotics technology in the hospitality industry: Current applications and future trends. *Digital Transformation in Business and Society*, 211-228.

Yiu, L. D., Yeung, A. C., & Cheng, T. E. (2021). The impact of business intelligence systems on profitability and risks of firms. *International Journal of Production Research, 59*(13), 3951–3974. doi:10.1080/00207543.2020.1756506

Yung, R., & Khoo-Lattimore, C. (2019). New realities: A systematic literature review on virtual reality and augmented reality in tourism research. *Current Issues in Tourism*, *22*(17), 2056–2081. doi:10.108 0/13683500.2017.1417359

Zeqiri, A., Dahmani, M., & Youssef, A. B. (2020). Digitalization of the tourism industry: What are the impacts of the new wave of technologies. *Balkan Economic Review*, *2*, 63–82.

Zohuri, B., & Moghaddam, M. (2020). From Business Intelligence to Artificial Intelligence. *Journal of Material Sciences & Manufacturing Research*, *1*(1), 1–10.

KEY TERMS AND DEFINITIONS

Artificial Intelligence: Is the simulation of human intelligence processes, especially by computer systems. It presents many business potentialities, such as sales forecasting, customer segmentation, fraud detection, and quality control.

Business Intelligence: This results from information systems that combine data with analytical tools to provide information relevant to decision-making while seeking to improve the quality and availability of this information to decision-makers.

Decision-Making: The process of making choices. After detecting a problem involves gathering information and assessing alternative resolutions, the chosen alternative is implemented, which will be identified as the chosen decision.

Sustainability: It considers three dimensions: environmental, social and economic, interlinked to meet the needs of the present without compromising those of future generations and where the technology can support the three dimensions.

Tourism 4.0: Ecosystem that considers the technological pillars of Industry 4.0, which aims to unlock the innovative potential of tourist regions, boosting the emergence of smart tourism regions while adding value to the tourism experience.

Tourism Experience: This is a set of activities in which individuals engage on their personal terms, such as pleasant and memorable places, allowing each tourist to build his or her own travel experiences so that these satisfy a wide range of personal needs, from pleasure to a search for meaning.

Tourism Industry: One of the largest industries in the world. It emerged to satisfy the human need to travel to and see different places as part of the service sector, including hospitality (e.g., accommodation, restaurants), transportation (e.g., airlines, car rental), travel facilitation and information (e.g., tour operators, tourist information centres), and attractions and entertainment (e.g., heritage sites and traditional and cultural events).

Chapter 9
Empowering Diversity:
The Role of Leadership in Inclusion in the Organizational Context

Helena Cristina Roque

School of Business Administration, Polytechnic Institute of Setúbal, Portugal

Madalena Ramos

University Institute of Lisbon, Portugal

ABSTRACT

Moments of crisis exacerbate social inequalities, highlighting the paramount importance of the debate on inclusion. The promotion of social inclusion can and should be pursued and implemented at various levels. In this sense, leadership can play a fundamental role in the inclusion of individuals in organizations and, consequently, in society. Inclusion in the workplace is about creating an environment where individuals from diverse backgrounds feel valued, respected, and have equal opportunities to contribute and succeed. Leaders have the power to shape the culture, policies, and practices that promote or hinder inclusion. This chapter will review the literature on inclusion based on the responsible leadership and inclusive leadership approaches, seeking to understand how these types of leadership can contribute with effective responses to inclusion in the work context. The chapter will end with a proposal of a set of practices that may be relevant for the inclusion of individuals in organizations.

INTRODUCTION

In recent decades, the world has also faced problems related to the movement of people, for which globalization and wars are partly responsible. The result is the displacement of large numbers of individuals from their home territories, whether as immigrants (legal and illegal), temporary workers or refugees. Thus, societies and organizations are increasingly heterogeneous (Kuknor & Bhattacharya, 2020).

Given this scenario, it is not difficult to conclude that we are facing a complex reality with multiple challenges, namely in terms of the integration/inclusion of newcomers to host societies. And for this social inclusion, the integration in the workplace is a fundamental dimension, in which leadership can

DOI: 10.4018/978-1-6684-9039-6.ch009

play an important role. Among the various approaches to leadership, we argue that the inclusive leadership and the responsible leadership approaches can contribute decisively to the integration of individuals in the work context and, consequently, to their social integration.

First defined in 2006, inclusive leadership is understood as "words and deeds by a leader or leaders that indicate an invitation and appreciation for others' contributions" (Nembhard & Edmondson, 2006, p.927). Several authors have reflected on inclusive leadership and presented new definitions, making it difficult to find common ground among the various conceptualizations, as each one of them focuses on and values different aspects of leadership (Randel et al., 2016), ranging from the contributions of workers to the organization (Nembhard & Edmondson, 2006), to the availability, openness and accessibility of leaders (Carmeli et al., 2010), or to the leader's behaviours as promoters of the workers' sense of belonging, namely through the promotion of shared decision-making (Randel et al., 2018).

Responsible leadership has also been the subject of research by several authors, who have proposed different definitions, from which two main perspectives stand out. The first perspective views leadership as an ethical phenomenon, while the second is associated with the notion of responsibility in leaders' actions (Roque & Ramos, 2019; Roque & Ramos, 2021). According to the first perspective, leadership can be seen as "a values-based and through ethical principles driven relationship between leaders and stakeholders who are connected through a shared sense of meaning and purpose through which they raise one another to higher levels of motivation and commitment for achieving sustainable values creation and social change" (Pless, 2007, p.438). For the second perspective, leadership can be viewed as "the consideration of the consequences of one's actions for all stakeholders, as well as the exertion of influence by enabling the involvement of affected stakeholders and by engaging in an active stakeholder dialogue" (Voegtlin et al., 2012, p.59).

What kind of leadership promotes the creation of more inclusive environments? The answer to this question will be anchored on two theoretical approaches: inclusive leadership and responsible leadership. Therefore, this chapter begins with a review of the literature on inclusion and diversity in the workplace, inclusive leadership, and responsible leadership, in academic databases, such as Social Sciences Citation Index, Emerging Sources Citation Index and SCImago. The objective was not to carry out a systematic review of the literature, but to find the most relevant articles to understand the role of leadership in successful inclusion in an organizational context. Subsequently, we seek to demonstrate how these two approaches can contribute to building a set of effective practices (in the sense of requirements or premises that must be put into practice) to incorporate the diversity and achieve the goal of inclusion/integration in the work context.

BACKGROUND

Inclusion

Globalization has fostered not only the circulation of information but also the movement of people. Societies are becoming increasingly diverse, and diversity is part of all societies, as well as organizations. According to Henriques and Carvalho (2022) diversity refers to several dimensions such as age, gender, sexual orientation, marital status, social class, cultural, religious or political beliefs, ethnic diversity, and education. Thus, both societies in general and organizations in particular are faced with an enormous challenge, that of inclusion, that is, to be able to fit within themselves the existing diversity.

VUCA is a term that describes the challenging and dynamic conditions that organizations face in the contemporary world (Bennett and Lemoigne, 2014; Taskan et al. 2022). The VUCA environment requires organizations to be agile, adaptable, innovative, and resilient to survive and thrive in the competitive landscape. However, many organizations struggle to cope with the VUCA environment due to various factors, such as rigid structures, outdated processes, siloed functions, hierarchical cultures, risk-aversion, and lack of collaboration. These factors hinder the organization's ability to respond quickly and effectively to the changing conditions, to anticipate and seize opportunities, to solve problems creatively, and to learn from failures. Therefore, organizations need to transform their strategies, structures, systems, and cultures to become more VUCA-ready and VUCA-capable. Some of the possible ways to achieve this are: developing a clear vision and purpose, fostering a learning and growth mindset, empowering teams and individuals, leveraging technology and data, cultivating a culture of innovation and experimentation, but also promoting diversity and inclusion.

In everyday language, inclusion usually refers to integration within the family, wider groups or even society. In literature, the concept of social inclusion is not consensual (Bulguer, 2018). Sometimes the concept of social inclusion arises in opposition to the concept of social exclusion, suggesting that the two concepts are interdependent and closely related (Peters et al., 2014). An example of this is the definition presented by Krishna and Kummitha (2017) when they state that: "Social inclusion requires opportunities and resources that are necessary to ensure the participation of those who have been excluded in economic, social, political, and cultural life. It should then be able to provide them with a standard of living and well-being which is considered normal in the society in which they live. Furthermore, such provisions ensure that their voices are respected in any decision-making which affects their lives. Thus, it is claimed that social inclusion is a systematic process that rescues a person or community from the risks or uncertainty of exclusion" (p.13). For other authors (e.g., Silver, 2010), the two concepts represent different ideas, with inclusion associated with the dimension of "social membership" and the exclusion with that of "social problems." Bulger goes in this direction when he defines social inclusion as "the process and manifestation of recognizing what it means for everyone to be realized as a part of the whole" (2018, p.16).

Although there is no consensus in the literature on the definition of social inclusion, it is widely agreed upon that it gravitates around three dimensions: i) participation; ii) sense of belonging and, in iii) citizenship (Clifford et al., 2015; Cordier et al., 2017). According to Cordier et al. (2017), participation is associated with involvement in social spaces and activities, such as the labor market, the sense of belonging underlies the current and potential participation in the social community and organizations and citizenship is related to the rights and obligations of people as members of society.

In 1958, Schutz considered inclusion as a basic human need that people experience in their interpersonal relationships. According to the author, people, in their communication with others, demonstrate the need to be included.

However, the concept of inclusion has also reached organizations, and in an organizational context, inclusion is seen as a key element to ensure a sustainable competitive advantage (Shah et al., 2022), as well as for the health and well-being of workers (Korkmaz et al., 2022), and can encompass various dimensions such as workers participation in organizations (Roberson and Perry, 2022).

In this sense, Mor-Barack and Cherin (1998) define inclusion as the extent to which workers have access to information and resources, are involved in teamwork, and can participate in decision-making processes. Mathieu et al. (2017) argue that as work has strongly become team-based, team diversity can be a key and differentiating element. However, to fully leverage the diversity of a diverse team, leaders need to have inclusive behaviours by involving all members of their team (Robertson and Perry, 2021). At this point we consider it relevant to distinguish the concept of inclusion from the concept of diversity. Diversity can be understood as a set of attributes present in workforce that affect the way people think, feel and behave in their work, while inclusion focuses on policies, practices and the work climate and culture, reflecting the work experience of workers with the characteristics mentioned above (Garg and Sangwan, 2021; Henriques and Carvalho, 2022)

Pelled et al. (1999) defined inclusion as "the extent to which a worker is accepted and treated as an insider by others in a work system" (p. 1014). Nishii (2013) seeks to identify organizational practices that can facilitate the inclusion of workers in organizations. In general, inclusion in an organizational context impels that all workers have the possibility to contribute to the defined goals without sacrificing any part of their identity (Ferdman, 2014). Some authors have focused on equity and inclusion in organizations for minority groups (e.g., Warren and Waren, 2023; Santos et al., 2022), asserting that black people and workers from other ethnic backgrounds have been ignored by leadership, leaving them without any support in their careers and facing additional obstacles. Roberts and Roberts (2019) go even further and claim that leadership has never truly embraced the idea of inclusion.

Regardless of the definition of inclusion, for it to become a reality in organizations leaders must desire and promote it. Leaders apply the guiding principles of organizations, serving as role models and influencing other team members with their own behaviour. Therefore, they play a fundamental role in realizing inclusion. As stated by Santos et al. (2022), leaders have the power to create inclusion and they are in a strategic position to put it into practice. At the organizational level, leaders are therefore a crucial element in fostering more inclusive environments (Ferdman, 2014; Shanker et al., 2017), where everyone can express their opinions and participate in decision-making.

The creation of an inclusive environment may not be an easy task, as more and more different generations coexist in the same workplace, with different perspectives on what they consider, for example, quality in the workplace. Gen Z (born roughly between the mid-1990s and early 2010s), the last generation to arrive in the labor market, can play an important role in inclusion, taking into account some their main characteristics such as valuing honesty in the leaders' actions, valuing face-to-face communication with their superiors, the desire that their ideas are heard and the appreciation of social responsibility (Benítez-Márquez et al, 2022). Interpersonal relationships in the workplace and specifically mutual help in teams is essential for this generation (Barhate and Dirani, 2022).

In this way, we believe that this generation, with characteristics very different from the previous ones, can be a valuable help for leaders in creating a more inclusive environment, as they can themselves constitute a driving force for the incorporation of diversity in organizations.

To answer the research question (what type of leadership promotes the creation of more inclusive environments?), the following points will address the two theoretical approaches that, in our view, can play an important role - inclusive leadership and responsible leadership.

Inclusive Leadership

The concept of inclusive leadership was first introduced in 2006 by Nembhard and Edmondson. The authors defined inclusive leadership as "words and deeds by a leader or leaders that indicate an invitation and appreciation for others' contributions" (Nembhard & Edmondson, 2006, p. 927). The focus, as highlighted by Korkmaz et al. (2022), lies on the recognition of the contributions of subordinates. According to Nembhard and Edmondson (2006), subordinates develop a sense of psychological safety when they feel that leaders appreciate their contributions. Kulknor and Bhattacharya (2020) also advocate that recognizing subordinates' contributions contributes to their psychological safety, as it provides them with the opportunity to express their viewpoints on the issues at hand.

Based on the idea of psychological safety, Carmeli et al. (2010)[1] argue that leaders should demonstrate openness, accessibility, and availability in their interactions with subordinates. This contributes to the creation of a context in which subordinates feel psychologically safe to express their ideas. In other words, leaders exhibit inclusive behaviours by encouraging their subordinates to share their opinions and by demonstrating openness, accessibility, and availability.

Hollander (2012) suggests that inclusive leadership creates a situation in which both leaders and subordinates benefit, establishing a mutually beneficial relationship. However, this relationship depends on respect, recognition, responsiveness, and accountability in both directions (Hollander et al., 2008), with organizational inclusion heavily reliant on the leader's behaviours (Kuknor & Bhattacharya, 2020).

Shore et al. (2011) defined inclusion as "the degree to which an employee perceives that he or she is an esteemed member of the workgroup through experiencing treatment that satisfies his or her needs for belongingness and uniqueness" (p. 1265). This definition closely relates to the theory of optimal distinctiveness (Brewer, 2012). According to this theory, people need to be similar but also different from others. The former increases the likelihood of being accepted into a group, while the latter pertains to the recognition of being distinct and unique.

Shore and Chung (2021) further expanded on the concept of inclusion, presenting a 2x2 framework where belongingness and uniqueness are present to identify various workgroup experiences. The identified dimensions are: inclusion, assimilation, differentiation, and exclusion. Inclusion consists of high levels of both belongingness and uniqueness. Assimilation entails a high level of belongingness but a low level of uniqueness. Differentiation involves a low level of belongingness but a high level of uniqueness, while exclusion encompasses low levels of both belongingness and uniqueness.

According to Randel et al. (2018), leadership should focus on supporting group members by ensuring justice and equity and promoting shared decision-making opportunities while consistently encouraging contributions from all members. The authors state that "leaders' efforts are specifically focused on enhancing members' perceptions of the desire for, and value of, their uniqueness as a group member" (Randel et al., 2018, p. 192). In other words, the focus is on the subordinates' experience within the team and on valuing the uniqueness of each team member. To achieve this, leaders should provide support to team members, ensure fairness and equity, promote shared decision-making, encourage the contribution of all members, and assist team members in sharing their contributions (Randel et al., 2018). These behaviours aim to make team members feel supported and, as a result, comfortable to participate even when they hold different perspectives. Inclusive leadership encourages contributions by soliciting diverse perspectives, thereby fostering an environment that embraces diversity (Winters, 2013).

Similarly, other authors (Choi et al., 2015; Javed et al., 2018; Liu et al., 2016) argue that inclusive leaders treat their subordinates with respect, recognition, and tolerance, paying attention to their opinions. Consequently, subordinates feel more committed to their leaders and are more likely to exhibit innovative behaviours at work (Walumbwa et al., 2011).

According to You et al. (2021), inclusive leadership differs from other leadership approaches by being more humanistic, as it is based on three characteristics: i) leaders have a high level of tolerance and support for subordinates; ii) leaders invest time in training subordinates and celebrate their achievements; iii) leaders exhibit behaviours of transparency and fairness towards subordinates (Bakari et al., 2019).

These conceptualizations of leadership go beyond traditional approaches by focusing not only on the characteristics and abilities leaders should possess, but also on the attention leaders should pay to subordinates' needs and perceptions (Katsaros, 2022).

Studies conducted thus far draw attention to the impact and role of inclusive leadership in various dimensions. Yonas et al. (2021) reveal that inclusive leadership develops subordinates' trust in leadership integrity and reinforces citizenship behaviours. Bau et al. (2021) argue for a positive association between inclusive leadership and work commitment. Li (2022) emphasizes the importance of this type of leadership in promoting innovative work behaviours and productivity. This study also reveals that workers' psychological safety and identification with leaders are crucial in mediating relationships within the organization. Yasin et al. (2022) conclude that inclusive leadership has a positive impact on organizational commitment.

In summary, inclusive leadership has various conceptualizations, ranging from recognizing subordinates' contributions to the openness, accessibility, and availability that leaders should demonstrate in their interactions with subordinates, through the need for belongingness and uniqueness, and the encouragement of subordinates' participation in decision-making processes (Korkmaz et al., 2022).

However, is inclusive leadership alone sufficient to address the challenges posed by current societies? Can other leadership approaches, such as responsible leadership, also contribute to addressing these challenges?

Responsible Leadership

The curiosity surrounding the approach of responsible leadership has been increasing as the need for transparency in various societal contexts becomes a pressing reality (Khanam & Tarab, 2022).

Talking about responsible leadership impels us to, in a first step, analyze what is meant by responsibility. According to Waldman and Galvin (2008), responsibility is intrinsically related to the need to act considering the concerns and needs of others while simultaneously taking responsibility for one's own actions. The others can be viewed from two perspectives: the economic perspective and the stakeholder perspective.

The economic perspective is based on three principles. The first considers that the leader's responsibility begins and ends with internal stakeholders. The second asserts that responsible leadership should be strategic and calculative. The third suggests that rewards and monitoring systems should function to ensure that leaders are effectively defining their responsibilities towards internal stakeholders (Waldman & Galvin, 2008).

On the other hand, the stakeholder perspective posits that the responsibility of leaders should consider all stakeholders, whether internal or external, and decisions should respect both (Waldman & Galvin, 2008).

The stakeholder perspective also distinguishes between primary stakeholders and secondary stakeholders. The former includes customers, investors, employees, and shareholders, while the latter encompasses NGOs, local communities, and social groups. Responsible leaders should collaborate and cooperate with all stakeholders, whether primary or secondary, establishing relationships of trust.

Just as with inclusive leadership, responsible leadership can have multiple definitions[2], but it is possible to distinguish two main perspectives. The first perspective sees leadership primarily as an ethical phenomenon (Maria & Lozano, 2010; Doh & Stumpf, 2005; Pless, 2007; Pless & Maak, 2011), and responsible leadership is defined as "a values-based and through ethical principles driven relationship between leaders and stakeholders who are connected through a shared sense of meaning and purpose through which they raise one another to higher levels of motivation and commitment for achieving sustainable values creation and social change" (Pless, 2007, p.438). In this view, leaders are responsible for building sustainable relationships with all stakeholders, achieving common goals that benefit the majority (Maak, 2007).

According to the second perspective, responsible leadership can be seen as "the consideration of the consequences of one's actions for all stakeholders, as well as the exertion of influence by enabling the involvement of the affected stakeholders and by engaging in an active stakeholder dialogue. Therein responsible leaders strive to weigh and balance the interests of the forwarded claims" (Voegtlin et al., 2012, p.59). This definition of responsible leadership is thus linked to the consequences of leaders' actions which are crucial as they can improve people's lives, whether within or outside the organization (Marques et al., 2018).

Based on the behaviours of leaders', Waldman and Galvin (2008) distinguish two possible views regarding responsible leadership: the limited economic view and the extended stakeholder view. The limited economic view considers that leaders' decisions should only consider the maximisation of value for stakeholders. The extended stakeholder view, on the other hand, suggests that leaders' decisions should be more comprehensive, distinguishing between two levels of responsible behaviour: avoiding harm (proscriptive morality) and doing good (prescriptive morality). Avoiding harm refers to decisions that prevent negative consequences for stakeholders and society, while doing good encompasses contributing to a better society. The leaders' responses to the dual responsibility of preventing or minimizing harm and maximizing good demonstrate the ethical component of responsible leadership (Longest, 2017).

In their connection with stakeholders, Maak and Pless (2011) argue that responsible leadership should develop a relationship of trust with all parties involved. This relationship is built on the sharing of the business vision and common goals. According to the authors, to meet these requirements, it is necessary to consider five premises: i) consider both internal and external stakeholders; ii) define objectives in both an organizational and a social context; iii) embrace inclusion, collaboration, and cooperation with all stakeholders; iv) consider the impact of decisions on all stakeholders; and v) embrace change to achieve higher social objectives.

Regarding leaders, Liechti (2014) suggests that they should consider five dimensions in their actions: i) integration and consideration of stakeholders' interests; ii) knowledge and understanding of the ethical dilemmas inherent to all involved parties; iii) self-awareness and reflection throughout the process; iv) knowing the functioning of the system and anticipate the consequences of decisions; and v) understanding the dynamics of the change process.

According to Han et al. (2019), by making decisions that consider the interests of all stakeholders, both internal and external to the organization, responsible leadership can positively contribute to the development of organizational citizenship behaviours. A study conducted by Zhao and Zhou (2019) also demonstrates that responsible leadership is a fundamental antecedent to developing organizational citizenship behaviours. In addition to these findings, several studies reveal the role of responsible leadership in various dimensions of the lives of workers and organizations. Responsible leadership can promote employees' organizational commitment (Haque et al., 2018) and have a positive impact on workers' well-being and organizational sustainability (Haque, 2021). The results of a study by Alfasar et al. (2019) indicate that responsible leadership is a positive predictor of environmental vision and performance.

As Tan (2023) states, it is possible to identify three approaches to responsible leadership: initial approach, relational approach and holistic approach. In the initial approach, the focus is narrower and focuses mainly on shareholders. In the relational approach, the focus is on developing trust relationships with internal and external clients. And in the holistic approach, there is a concern with the exercise of social responsibility in partnership with both internal and external clients.

Relevant Leadership Practices to Promote Inclusion in an Organizational Context

In recent decades, societies have faced a series of scenarios with economic, financial, and social implications. Globalization, on one hand, has increased the circulation of information and, on the other hand, facilitated the movement of people from their countries of origin to other territories in search of new opportunities. In addition to globalization-driven migration, there are now displacements associated with poverty, wars, and climate change. Consequently, societies are now much more heterogeneous than in the past, composed of individuals with diverse backgrounds in terms of territorial origin, religion, beliefs, sexual orientations, among others. Therefore, the challenges that arise are varied, and the inclusion of diversity, an essential element in societies in general and organizations in particular, is an urgent challenge.

For full realization of inclusion, the role of leaders is crucial. In the workplace, leaders can make a difference and contribute to ensuring that all individuals feel integrated and included. The characteristics associated with inclusive leadership make it relevant in this context, as it advocates for the opportunity for all workers to participate and be heard in decision-making, with leaders recognizing the contributions of their subordinates (Korkmaz et al., 2022). In this context, leaders value the uniqueness of each team member and encourage the contributions of all.

A recent study conducted by Katsaros (2022) with participants from multinational pharmaceutical companies based in the United States revealed a positive relationship between inclusive leadership and participation, mediated by workplace belonging. The study reinforces the idea that inclusive leadership can be a key element in ensuring that all team members to feel comfortable and sufficiently recognised to participate in decision-making.

Another study, conducted by Chang et al. (2022), with 40 teams from 20 organizations located in Shanghai, revealed that inclusive leadership has a positive impact on workers' proactive behaviour. The openness and accessibility of leaders increase workers' sense of belonging and contribute to their self-efficacy. This study also revealed that inclusive leadership affects workers' trust. Lastly, the same study revealed that the climate of justice moderates the relationship between inclusive leadership and workers' proactive behaviour and the relationship between inclusive leadership and workers' trust.

Bannay et al. (2020) conducted a study with 150 individuals from the technology sector in Iraq that demonstrated that inclusive leadership and commitment were related to organizational innovation behaviours, with commitment playing a mediating role between inclusive leadership and organizational innovation behaviours. The results also showed that inclusive leadership behaviours such as openness, accessibility, and availability motivated workers to engage in organizational innovation behaviours.

In a research involving various banking and legal organizations in several cities in China, Qi et al. (2019) found that inclusive leadership was positively related to innovation behaviours, and the perception of organizational support mediated the relationship between inclusive leadership and workers' innovation behaviours. When workers perceive that leaders accept and include their ideas, they feel more valued and increase their innovation behaviours.

Based on these results, it is possible to conclude that inclusive leadership can play an important role in organizational inclusion, organizational commitment, as well as organizational citizenship behaviours. Organizational commitment is the psychological bond that connects workers to organizations and besides contributing to a reduction in turnover intentions, it is an important element in organizational performance.

Mousa and Puhakka (2019), in a study involving professionals working in four public hospitals in Egypt, demonstrated a positive association between responsible leadership and organizational inclusion, as well as between organizational inclusion and organizational commitment.

Another study, conducted by Voegtlin et al. (2019), revealed that when leaders exhibit responsible behaviours, they can achieve positive outcomes, particularly in contexts characterized by uncertainty and doubt, such as the one we are currently experiencing.

Some studies have also revealed a relationship between responsible leadership and citizenship behaviour towards the environment. This is the case of the research conducted by Han et al. (2019), involving professionals from various sectors, which concluded that responsible leadership is positively associated with organizational citizenship behaviour for the environment. They also found that responsible leadership has positive effects on autonomous and external environmental motivation. This study further revealed that autonomous and external environmental motivation play a mediating role in the relationship between responsible leadership and organizational citizenship behaviour for the environment. Similarly, another study by Alfasar et al. (2019) indicated that responsible leadership is a positive predictor of environmental vision and performance.

In 2020, a study involving workers in the banking sector in Pakistan (Yasin et al. 2020,) found a positive association between responsible leadership and ethical climate, and a negative association between ethical climate and turnover intention. The results also revealed the mediating role of ethical climate between responsible leadership and turnover intention. The authors concluded that an ethical climate is crucial for the sustainability of organizations, considering that unethical behaviours have a negative impact on organizational performance.

Drawing from the theoretical approaches of inclusive leadership and responsible leadership, Roque and Ramos (2021) propose a set of premises or assumptions on what good leadership practices should be. These premises are based on principles of inclusive leadership and responsible leadership that must be considered in moments of great unpredictability and which, from our perspective, could also be valuable for dealing with diversity and promoting inclusion in the organizational context. In this regard, leaders should act to: i) foster an environment of openness, accessibility, and availability in their interactions with subordinates; ii) promote shared decision-making opportunities by encouraging contributions from all subordinates; iii) strengthen trust relationships with all stakeholders based on inclusion, collaboration, cooperation, and communication; iv) consider the impact of decision-making on all stakeholders; v) value the ethical dimension in decision-making.

The first premise provides that the actions of the leaders should foster an environment of openness, accessibility and availability in interaction with subordinates. As mentioned by Nembhard and Edmondson (2006), it is important for subordinates to develop a sense of psychological safety. For this to happen, leaders must promote an environment of openness, accessibility, and availability in their interactions with subordinates (Carmeli et al., 2010). This is the only way to think of decision-making in which everyone feels comfortable to contribute, regardless of whether their perspective is identical to that of others. This brings us to the second premise.

The second premise suggests that leaders' actions should promote shared decision-making opportunities, encouraging contributions from all subordinates. After fostering an environment of psychological safety, it becomes easier for each subordinate to feel comfortable expressing their opinions and contributing to decision-making. Recognizing the contributions made by subordinates also helps reinforce the desired environment (Kulkarni and Bhattacharya, 2020).

The third premise states that the actions of the leaders should strengthen relationships of trust with all stakeholders based on inclusion, collaboration, cooperation, and communication. By encouraging the participation and involvement of all stakeholders, a collaborative effort is fostered in which collective concern becomes the primary focus.

The fourth premise emphasizes that leaders' actions should consider the impact of decision-making on all stakeholders. As we know, stakeholders, whether primary or secondary, are always affected by leaders' decisions. Therefore, it is important for leaders' decision-making to meet a dual requirement: avoiding harm (prescriptive morality) and doing good (prescriptive morality) (Stahl and Luque, 2014). This dual requirement contributes to the next premise.

The fifth and final premise considers the value of ethical dimension in decision-making. The credibility and integrity of leaders are crucial (Fernandez and Shaw, 2020). However, this requires that both avoiding harm and doing good are evident in the decision-making carried out by leaders. The leader must set the tone.

In summary, we reinforce the idea that inclusion is crucial for embracing the diversity that exists in societies in general and organizations in particular. When we talk about organizations, we cannot forget that they are part of a society, a community, and the interactions between an organization and its context are also factors to consider. Inclusiveness in the workplace is a concept that refers to creating a work environment where every employee feels respected, valued, and included, regardless of their identity, background, or differences. Inclusive workplaces celebrate diversity and promote fairness and equity for all employees.

Therefore, in addition to internal stakeholders, external stakeholders must not be overlooked. In this sense, we argue that the proposal of good leadership practices by Roque and Ramos (2021) is an effective tool available to organizations to facilitate the inclusion of their employees.

The implementation of inclusion can be facilitated with the presence of Generation Z in the workplace, since many of the assumptions present in the proposal by Roque and Ramos (2021) are closely linked to the values defended by this generation of young workers. Gen Z is the most diverse and digitally savvy generation in history, and they have high expectations for social and environmental responsibility from employers. Gen Z also values individual expression, collaboration, flexibility, authenticity, and dialogue. Gen Z is not afraid to challenge the status quo and demand change for a better future. They are not afraid of the authenticity, which leads to freedom of expression, and the right to be different. Therefore, the presence of these workers can help the leaders to achieve an environment conducive to inclusion in the workplace, since they themselves are spokespersons for the right to diversity, freedom of expression and, by extension, inclusion.

CONCLUSION

Diversity exists in both societies and organizations, making inclusion indispensable. Thus, in both general societies and specific organizations, leadership should foster inclusion.

The thesis we defend is that inclusive leadership and responsible leadership are approaches to consider for achieving the inclusion of workers in organizations in an increasingly global and diverse world.

Leadership plays a key role in promoting inclusion in an organizational context through a series of key approaches and starting with setting the tone. Leaders should have a clear vision and commitment to inclusion, highlighting its importance within the organization. By openly communicating and modelling inclusive behaviour, leaders act like role-models and create an environment that encourages others to follow suit.

Furthermore, leaders are responsible for creating inclusive policies and practices within the organization. They must review and revise existing policies, procedures, and practices to eliminate any biases or barriers that may impede inclusion. This may involve implementing flexible work arrangements, promoting work-life balance, and ensuring that employees from diverse backgrounds have equal access to resources and development opportunities. It may also involve providing training. By investing in training programmes that promote empathy, cultural competence and openness to diversity, leaders help build a more inclusive and understanding workforce that appreciates and respects differences.

An inclusive environment thrives on collaboration and participation, and leaders should encourage collaboration and seek input from diverse perspectives, creating platforms for employees to share their ideas, opinions and concerns. By ensuring that everyone's voice is heard and valued, leaders foster an inclusive environment in which diverse perspectives are recognised and appreciated.

Equally important for creating an inclusive culture is recognising diversity. Leaders should actively celebrate and recognize the diverse contributions and achievements of individuals and teams within the Organization. By showcasing and appreciating diverse talents, leaders reinforce the message that everyone's contributions are valued and respected, further promoting inclusivity.

Finally, leaders must hold themselves and others accountable for promoting an inclusive environment. By making inclusivity an integral part of the Organization's structure and expectations, leaders ensure that efforts toward inclusion are sustained and effective.

In summary, the fundamental principles of inclusive leadership and responsible leadership play a key role in promoting inclusion in an organizational context. Through setting the tone, cultivating diversity, creating inclusive policies, providing education, encouraging collaboration, addressing bias, celebrating diversity, and holding people accountable, leaders foster an inclusive culture that benefits both the organization and its employees. By prioritizing inclusion, leaders create an environment where individuals from diverse backgrounds can thrive and contribute their unique perspectives, ultimately leading to organizational success.

Given these principles, the proposal put forward by Roque and Ramos (2021) for good leadership practices in unpredictable contexts may be valuable in achieving the goal of including employee diversity in organizations.

It would be important for future studies to investigate whether in organizations where inclusive leadership principles and shared leadership are implemented, they effectively reinforce inclusion, as well as whether this reinforcement is consistent across all sectors of activity or whether there are differences. It would also be important to understand if inclusive leadership and shared leadership have the same impact in culturally distinct countries.

REFERENCES

Bakari, H., Hunjra, A. L., Jaros, S., & Khoso, I. (2019). Moderating role of cynicism about Organizational change between authentic leadership and commitment to change in Pakistani publica sector hospitals. *Leadership in Health Services*, *32*(3), 387–404. doi:10.1108/LHS-01-2018-0006 PMID:31298084

Bannay, D. F., Hadi, M. J., & Amanah, A. A. (2020). The impact of inclusive leadership behaviours on innovative workplace behavoir with emphasis on the mediating role of work engagement. *Problems and Perspectives in Management*, *18*(3), 479–491. doi:10.21511/ppm.18(3).2020.39

Barhate, B., & Dirani, K. M. (2022). Career aspirations of generation Z: A systematic literature review. *European Journal of Training and Development*, *46*(1/2), 139–157. doi:10.1108/EJTD-07-2020-0124

Bau, P., Xiao, Z., Bao, G., & Norderhaven, N. (2021). Inclusive leadership and employee work engagement: A moderated mediation model. *Baltic Journal of Management*, *17*(1), 124–139. doi:10.1108/BJM-06-2021-0219

Benítez-Márquez, M. D., Sánchez-Teba, E. M., Bermudez-González, G., & Núñez-Rydman, E. S. (2022). Generation Z Within the Workforce and in the Workplace: A Bibliometric Analysis. *Frontiers in Psychology*, *12*, 736820. doi:10.3389/fpsyg.2021.736820 PMID:35178005

Bennett, N., & Lemoine, G. J. (2014). What VUCA Really Means for You. *Harvard Business Review*, *92*(1/2).

Brewer, M. B. (2012). Optimal distinctiveness theory: Its history and development. In P. A. M. VanLange, A. W. Kruglanski, & E. T. Higgins (Eds.), *Handbook of theories of social psychology* (pp. 81–98). Sage Publications.

Carmeli, A., Reiter-Palmon, R., & Ziv, E. (2010). Inclusive leadership and employee involvement in creative tasks in workplace. The mediating role of psychological safety. *Creativity Research Journal*, *22*(3), 250–260. doi:10.1080/10400419.2010.504654

Chang, P. C., Ma, G., & Lin, Y. Y. (2022). Inclusive leadership and employee proactive behavior: A cross-level moderated mediation model. *Psychology Research and Behavior Management*, *15*, 1797–1809. doi:10.2147/PRBM.S363434 PMID:35860206

Choi, S. B., Tran, T. B. H., & Park, B. I. (2015). Inclusive leadership and work engagement: Mediating roles of affective Organizational commitment and creativity. *Social Behavior and Personality*, *43*(6), 931–943. doi:10.2224bp.2015.43.6.931

Cordier, R., Milbourn, B., Martin, R., Buchanan, A., Chung, D., & Speyer, R. (2017). A systematic review evaluating the psychometric properties of measure social inclusion. *PLoS One*, *12*(6), e0179109. doi:10.1371/journal.pone.0179109 PMID:28598984

Doh, L., & Stumpf, S. (2005). *Handbook of responsible leadership and governance in global business*. Edward Elgar. doi:10.4337/9781845425562

Ferdman, B. M. (2014). The practice of inclusion in diverse Organizations: Toward a systemic and inclusive framewor. In B. M. Ferdman & B. Deane (Eds.), *Diversity at work: The practice of inclusion* (pp. 3–54). Jossey-Bass.

Fernandez, A. A., & Shaw, G. P. (2020). Academic Leadership in a time of crisis: The Coronavirus and Covid 19. *Journal of Leadership Studies*, *14*(18), 1–7. doi:10.1002/jls.21684

Garg, S., & Sangwan, S. (2021). Literature Review on Diversity and Inclusion at Workplace, 2012-2017. *Vision (Basel)*, *15*(1), 1–22. PMID:35076617

Han, Z., Wang, Q., & Yan, X. (2019). How responsible leadership predicts Organizational citizenship behavior for the environment in China. *Leadership and Organization Development Journal*, *40*(3), 305–318. doi:10.1108/LODJ-07-2018-0256

Haque, A. (2021). The COVID-19 pandemic and the role of responsible leadership in health care: Thinking beyond employee well-being and Organizational sustainability. *Leadership in Health Services*, *34*(1), 52–68. doi:10.1108/LHS-09-2020-0071 PMID:33818971

Haque, A., Fernando, M., & Caputi, P. (2018). Responsible leadership, affective commitment and intention to quit: An individual level analysis. *Leadership and Organization Development Journal*, *40*(1), 45–64. doi:10.1108/LODJ-12-2017-0397

Hollander, E. (2012). *Inclusive leadership: The essential leader follower relationship*. Routledge. doi:10.4324/9780203809914

Hollander, E., & Park, B. B. (2008). Inclusive leadership and leader-follower relations: concepts, research and applications. The Member Connector, International Leadership Association, 5, 4-7.

Javed, B., Abdullah, I., Zaffar, M. A., Haque, A., & Rubab, U. (2018). Inclusive leadership and innovative work behavior: The role of psychological empowerment. *Journal of Management & Organization*, *25*(4), 554–571. doi:10.1017/jmo.2018.50

Jerónimo, H.M., Henriques, P.L., & Carvalho, S.I. (2022). Being inclusive boots impact of diversity practices on employee engagement. *Management Research: Journal of Iberoamerican Academy of Management*, *20*(29), 129-147.

Kahn, W. A. (1990). Psychological conditions of personal engagement and disengagement at work. *Academy of Management Journal*, *33*(4), 692–724. doi:10.2307/256287

Katsaros, K. (2022). Exploring the inclusive leadership and employee change participation relationship: The role of workplace belongingness and meaning-making. *Baltic Journal of Management*, *17*(2), 158–173. doi:10.1108/BJM-03-2021-0104

Khanam, Z., & Tarab, S. (2022). A moderated-mediation model of the relationship between responsible leadership, citizenship behavior and patient satisfaction. *IIM Ranchi Journal of Management Studies*, *2*(1), 114-134.

Korkmaz, A. V., Van Engen, M. L., Knappert, L., & Schalk, R. (2022). About and beyond leading uniqueness and belongingness: A systematic review of inclusive leadership research. *Human Resource Management Review*, *32*(4), 1–20. doi:10.1016/j.hrmr.2022.100894

Krishna, R., & Kummitha, R. (2017). *Social Entrepreneurship and Social Inclusion: Processes, practices and prospects*. Palgrave Macmillan.

Kuknor, S. C., & Bhattacharya, S. (2020). Inclusive leadership: New age leadership to foster Organizational inclusion. *European Journal of Training and Development*, 46(9), 771–797. doi:10.1108/EJTD-07-2019-0132

Li, X. (2022). Inclusive leadership and employee outcomes: A meta-analytic of multiple theories. *Proceedings - Academy of Management*, 1(1), 1–19. doi:10.5465/AMBPP.2022.33

Liu, Y., Zhu, W., & Zhao, S. M. (2016). Research on the influence of inclusive leadership on the relations of employment relationship and employees´ active behavior. *Management Representative*, 10(1), 1482–1489.

Longest, B. (2017). Responsible leader behavior in health sectors. *Leadership in Health Services*, 30(1), 8–15. doi:10.1108/LHS-05-2016-0020 PMID:28128048

Maak, T. (2007). Responsible leadership, stakeholder engagement and the emergence of social capital. *Journal of Business Ethics*, 74(4), 329–343. doi:10.100710551-007-9510-5

Maria, J. F., & Lozano, J. M. (2010). Responsible leaders for inclusive globalization: Cases of Nicaragua and the Democratic Republic of Congo. *Journal of Business Ethics*, 93(S1), 93–111. doi:10.100710551-010-0628-5

Márquez-Benitez, M. D., Sánchez-Teba, E. M., Bermúdez-González, G., & Nunez-Rydman, M. S. (2022). Generation Z within the Workforce and in the Workplace: A bibliometric Analysis. *Organizational Psychology*, (12), 1–12.

Mathieu, J. E., Hollenbeck, J. R., van Knippenberg, D., & Ilgen, D. R. (2017). A century of work teams in the journal of applied psychology. *The Journal of Applied Psychology*, 61(3), 349–374. doi:10.1037/apl0000128 PMID:28150984

Mousa, M. (2019). Organizational inclusion and academics' psychological contract. Can responsible leadership mediate the relationship? *Equality, Diversity and Inclusion*, 39(2), 126–144. doi:10.1108/EDI-01-2019-0014

Mousa, M., & Puhakka, V. (2019). Inspiring Organizational commitment Responsible leadership and Organizational inclusion in the Egyptian health care sector. *Journal of Management Development*, 38(3), 208–224. doi:10.1108/JMD-11-2018-0338

Nembhard, I. M., & Edmondson, A. C. (2006). Making it safe: The effects of leader inclusiveness and professional status on psychological safety and improvement efforts in health care teams. *Journal of Organizational Behavior*, 27(7), 941–966. doi:10.1002/job.413

Nishii, L. H. (2013). The benefits of climate for inclusion for gender-diverse groups. *Academy of Management Journal*, 56(6), 1754–1774. doi:10.5465/amj.2009.0823

Pelled, L. H., Ledford, G. E. Jr, & Mohrman, S. A. (1999). Demographic dissimilarity and workplace inclusion. *Journal of Management Studies*, 36(7), 1013–1031. doi:10.1111/1467-6486.00168

Peters, M. A., & Besley, T. C. (2014). Social exclusion/inclusion. Foucault's analytics of exclusion, the political ecology of social inclusion and the legitimation of inclusive education. *Open Review of Educational Research, 1*(1), 99–115. doi:10.1080/23265507.2014.972439

Pless, N. M. (2007). Understanding responsible leadership: Role identity and motivational drivers. *Journal of Business Ethics, 74*(4), 437–456. doi:10.100710551-007-9518-x

Pless, N. M., & Maak, T. (2012). Responsible leadership: Pathways to the future. *Journal of Business Ethics, 98*(S1), 3–13. doi:10.100710551-011-1114-4

Qi, L., Liu, B., Wei, X., & Hu, Y. (2019). Impact of inclusive leadership on employee innovative behavior: Perceived Organizational support as a mediator. *PLoS One, 14*(2), e0212091. doi:10.1371/journal.pone.0212091 PMID:30817753

Randel, A. E., Dean, M. A., Ehrhart, K. H., Chung, B., & Shore, L. (2016). Leader inclusiveness, psychological diversity climate, and helping behaviours. *Journal of Managerial Psychology, 31*(1), 216–234. doi:10.1108/JMP-04-2013-0123

Randel, A. E., Galvin, B. M., Shore, L. M., Ehrhart, K. H., Chung, B. G., Dean, M. A., & Kedharnath, U. (2018). Inclusive leadership: Realizing positive outcomes through belongingness and being valued for uniqueness. *Human Resource Management Review, 28*(2), 190–203. doi:10.1016/j.hrmr.2017.07.002

Roberson, Q., & Perry, J. L. (2022). Inclusive Leadership in Thought and Action: A Thematic Analysis. *Group & Organization Management, 47*(4), 755–778. doi:10.1177/10596011211013161

Roberts, L.M., & Roberts, A.J. (2019). *Toward a racially just workplace*. Academic Press.

Roque, H. C., & Ramos, M. (2019). Responsible leadership and expatriation: The influence of national culture. In N. Teixeira, T. Costa, I. Lisboa (Eds.), Handbook of Research on Entrepreneurship, Innovation and Internationalization (pp. 586-610). IGI Global.

Roque, H. C., & Ramos, M. (2021). Good leadership practices in contexts of unpredictability. In T. Costa, I. Lisboa, N. Teixeira (Eds), Handbook of Research on Reinvinting Economies and Organizations Following a Global Heath Crisis (pp.363-385). IGI Global. doi:10.4018/978-1-7998-6926-9.ch020

Santos, M., Luna, M., Reyes, D. L., Traylor, A., Lacerenza, C. N., & Salas, E. (2022). How to be an inclusive leader for gender diverse teams. *Organizational Dynamics, 51*(4), 1–6. doi:10.1016/j.orgdyn.2022.100914

Schutz, W. (1958). *Firo: A three-dimensional theory of interpersonal behavior*. Rinehart.

Shah, H. J., Ou, J. P., Attiq, S., Umer, M., & Wong, W. K. (2022). Does inclusive leadership improve the sustainability of employee relations? Test of justice theory and employee perceived insider status. *Sustainability (Basel), 14*(21), 1–19. doi:10.3390u142114257

Shanker, R., Bhanugopan, R., Van der Heijden, B. I., & Farrell, M. (2017). Organizational climate for innovation and Organizational performance: The mediating effect of innovative work behavior. *Journal of Vocational Behavior, 100*, 67–77. doi:10.1016/j.jvb.2017.02.004

Shore, L., & Chung, B. G. (2021). Inclusive leadership: How leaders sustain or discourage work group inclusion. *Group & Organization Management*, *0*(0), 1–32.

Shore, L. M., Randel, A. E., Chung, B. G., Dean, M. A., Ehrhart, K. H., & Singh, G. (2011). Inclusion and diversity in work groups: A review and model for future research. *Journal of Management*, *37*(4), 1262–1289. doi:10.1177/0149206310385943

Silver, H. (2010). Understanding social inclusion and its meaning for Australia. *The Australian Journal of Social Issues*, *45*(2), 183–211. doi:10.1002/j.1839-4655.2010.tb00174.x

Stahl, G. K., & Luque, S. (2014). Antecedents of responsible leader behavior: A research synthesis, conceptual framework and agenda for future research. *The Academy of Management Perspectives*, *28*(3), 235–254. doi:10.5465/amp.2013.0126

Tan, K. L. (2023). Responsible leadership – A brief Review of Literature. *Journal of Responsible Tourism Management*, *3*(1), 44–55.

Taskan, B., Junça-Silva, A., & Caetano, A. (2022). Clarifying the conceptual map of VUCA: A systematic review. *The International Journal of Organizational Analysis*, *30*(7), 196–217. doi:10.1108/IJOA-02-2022-3136

Voegtlin, C., Frish, C., Walther, A., & Schwab, P. (2019). Theoretical Development and Empirical Examination of a Three- Roles Model of Responsible Leadership. *Journal of Business Ethics*.

Voegtlin, C., Patzer, M., & Scheer, A. G. (2012). Responsible Leadership in Global Business: A New Approach to Leadership and its Multi-level Outcomes. *Journal of Business Ethics*, *105*(1), 1–16. doi:10.100710551-011-0952-4

Waldman, D. A., & Galvin, B. M. (2008). Alternative perspectives of responsible leadership. *Organizational Dynamics*, *37*(4), 327–341. doi:10.1016/j.orgdyn.2008.07.001

Walumbwa, F. O., Cropanzano, R., & Goldman, B. M. (2011). How leader–member exchange influences effective work behaviours: Social exchange and internal–external efficacy perspectives. *Personnel Psychology*, *64*(3), 739–770. doi:10.1111/j.1744-6570.2011.01224.x

Warren, M. A., & Warren, M. T. (2023). The EThIC Model of Virtue-Based Allyship Development: A New Approach to Equity and Inclusion in Organizations. *Journal of Business Ethics*, *182*(3), 783–803. doi:10.100710551-021-05002-z PMID:34840369

Winters, M. F. (2013). From Diversity to Inclusion: An Inclusion Equation. In B.M. Ferdman & B.R. Deane (Eds.), Diversity at work: The practice of inclusion (pp. 205-228). John Wiley & Sons.

Yasin, R., Jan, G., Huseynova, A., & Atif, M. (2022). Inclusive leadership and turnover intention: The role of follower-leader goal congruence and Organizational commitment. *Management Decision*, *61*(3), 589–609. doi:10.1108/MD-07-2021-0925

Yasin, R., Namoco, S. O., Jauhar, J., Abdul Rahin, N. F., & Zia, N. U. (2020). Responsible leadership an obstacle for turnover intention. *Social Responsibility Journal*, *17*(8), 1175–1192. doi:10.1108/SRJ-03-2020-0092

Yonas, A., Wang, D., Javed, B., & Zaffar, M. A. (2021). Moving beyond the mechanistic structures: The role of inclusive leadership in developing change-orientation Organizational citizenship behaviour. *Canadian Journal of Administrative Sciences*, *38*(1), 42–52. doi:10.1002/cjas.1586

You, J., Kim, S., Kim, K., Cho, A., & Chang, W. (2021). Conceptualizing meaningful work and its implications for HRD. *European Journal of Training and Development*, *45*(1), 36–52. doi:10.1108/EJTD-01-2020-0005

Zhao, H., & Zhou, Q. (2019). Exploring the Impact of Responsible Leadership on Organizational Citizenship Behavior for the Environment: A Leadership Identity Perspective. *Sustainability (Basel)*, *11*(4), 994–1013. doi:10.3390u11040944

KEY TERMS AND DEFINITIONS

Inclusion: practice of including all stakeholders in organizational contexts

Inclusive Leadership: the capacity to manage and lead a heterogeneous group of people efficiently, while respecting their uniqueness in an empathetic, bias-free way.

Responsible Leadership: refers to leaders who are deemed to properly and justly meet role, normative, ethical, and moral obligations they have with respect to defined stakeholders, and are willing to be held accountable for the consequences of their actions and behaviors.

Workplace Diversity: the term used for the workplace composed of employees with varying characteristics, such as different sex, gender, race, ethnicity, sexual orientation, etc.

Generation Z: refers to the generation that was born between 1997-2012, following millennials. This generation has been raised on the internet and social media, with some of the oldest finishing college by 2020 and entering the workforce.

Social Inclusion: social inclusion is a process that ensures citizens have the opportunities and resources necessary to participate fully in economic, social and cultural life and to enjoy a standard of living and well-being that is considered normal in the society in which they live.

Diversity: state of being diverse; variety.

ENDNOTES

[1]   Psychological safety means that "people are comfortable being themselves" (Edmondson, 1999, p. 354) and "feel able to show and employ one's self without fear of negative consequences to selfimage, status, or career" (Kahn, 1990, p. 708).

[2]   For more details we suggest consulting Roque & Ramos, 2019.

Chapter 10
Human Behavior in Telework:
A Modality of Work Centered on the Human Being That Promotes Opportunities and Social Integration

Janaína Almeida Bastos
Pontifícia Universidade Católica de São Paulo, Brazil

João Pinheiro de Barros Neto
 https://orcid.org/0000-0002-5680-6658
Pontifícia Universidade Católica de São Paulo, Brazil

ABSTRACT

In 2020, Brazilians were faced with the COVID-19 health crisis that caused a rupture in market and business standards, technologies, and models, directly affecting the way people relate to each other, work, and live, reshaping the social, cultural, and economic contexts. Among these changes, remote work has never been so evident in the daily life of companies and their employees. In this context, the question that guides this work is: What is the impact of working from home on people management in companies from the human resources point of view? This study is an exploratory survey carried out by means of an online questionnaire, responded to by 121 participants. The results indicate that telework can be a more humane way of working and a solution to numerous problems of modern society.

INTRODUCTION

About three years ago, the world was faced with a health crisis that caused a rupture with market and business standards, technologies, and models, directly affecting the way people related, worked, and lived. It also redesigned the social, cultural, and economic contexts. It was the perfect example of the VUCA World, i.e., Volatile, Uncertain, Complex, and Ambiguous, that requires every human being to have broader knowledge and apply new concepts and frameworks to deal with unpredictable and rapidly changing situations. VUCA forces organizations to move from linear thought patterns to a problem-solving

DOI: 10.4018/978-1-6684-9039-6.ch010

approach based on synthetic and simultaneous thinking, exploring, and developing new concepts for a new way of organizational and people management (Mack et al., 2016). Among these changes, remote work has never been so evident in the daily life of companies and their employees, the imperative need for social isolation increased, literally overnight, the number of people working from home.

Due to this change, several issues related to people management arose, amongst them stress, communication, standardization, lack of recognition, self-discipline, time management, personal-professional boundaries. Knowing more about remote work development and challenges is imperative to improve this new way of working that has become a worldwide trend.

In light of the above, the question that guided this work was: what is the impact of teleworking on people management in companies, from a Human Resources point of view? The general objective is to identify the challenges of the relationship between employees and teleworking to identify the positive and negative impacts for organizations and people management. The specific objectives are to identify the challenges of teleworking for employees, to verify how technologies influence the management and execution of the work, to understand employees' behavior in the new work environment, and to know the opinion of telecommuters about remote work.

Therefore, this study makes relevant contributions in relation to existing studies because each employee has unique experiences and different perceptions about remote work. Consequently, exploring the diversity of employees' experiences in relation to the home office, considering factors such as adapting to new ways of working, reconciling personal and professional life, psychological and physical well-being, productivity and social interaction, allows for a deeper understanding of the benefits and challenges faced by employees in relation to remote work and the behaviors adopted. Furthermore, it helps to complement visions centered on the perspective of organizations and management, which neglect the employees' voice and perceptions. By considering the employees' point of view, this research provides a more complete and holistic understanding of the impacts of teleworking on people management.

BACKGROUND

Remote Work

Working from home and telecommuting in locations outside the company using technological means have become the main alternatives for many professionals and companies around the world. The pandemic and social isolation were responsible for the large-scale adoption of these work modalities.

Home-based work, one of the types of work, is any intellectual work performed at a person´s house using technology (computers, tablets, smartphones, and Internet, either broadband, fixed and/or mobile telephony) that allows receiving and transmitting information, text files, image or sound related to the work activity (Sociedade Brasileira de Teletrabalho e Teleatividades, 2020, p. 7).

"Home office" is a term borrowed from English used in Brazil to describe work done at home. Remote work means partially or fully performing professional activities outside the company. In hybrid jobs, the employee, entrepreneur, or freelancer performs part of the tasks within the company premises and another part remotely. Therefore, remote work takes place in someone's private home with the supply of necessary tools to execute job-related activities by the employer, who is responsible for ensuring these tools. Home-based work is the possibility of doing on-site job activities at home with the use of technological resources – and the employer controls the working hours. Teleworking is an activity performed remotely, provided for in a contract, through technological resources, without control of working hours and regulated by the Labor Code - CLT (Oliveira & Tchakerian, 2020).

Home-Based Work, Remote Work, and Teleworking in Brazil

It is usual to think of teleworking as work done from any location other than the office. In fact, that idea is not wrong at all, but it is certainly incomplete. Therefore, it is important to understand the differences between home-based work, teleworking, among others.

In Brazil, teleworking must be included in the individual employment contract, which must also include the activities that will be performed by the employee. The employee working on-site can change to telecommuting as long as there is a mutual agreement with the employer and a contractual amendment is registered. The opposite situation is also possible. If the company requires on-site work, it must guarantee to its employees the minimum transition period of 15 days. The law also states that responsibility to provide the necessary equipment for telecommuting must be foreseen in the employment contract. The only specific provision is that, if provided by the employer, such loaned equipment cannot be considered employee compensation. If there is a control of the working schedule, the right to additional wages could be recognized. Otherwise, where control difficulties are identified, there is no right to the payment of overtime and nighttime additional in the telework regime (Serralvo & Manus, 2022).

The rights are, in general, the same as those of a normal worker. Although work is done remotely, there are no major differences in worker protection. Therefore, it is assured the right to a signed contract, vacations, 13th month pay, Severance Pay Fund (FGTS) deposits, among others. The Brazilian Labor Code (CLT) makes no distinction between work performed from home, at the workplace, or remotely, as long as there are conditions for employment relationship. Since there is no specific indication about meal and food allowances in remote work, the criteria for the payment of the benefit may be defined in a collective agreement or convention, or in the professional contract. Regarding the transportation allowance is that it may be suspended if the employee starts working from home, since the benefit has an indemnity nature and aims to pay for the commuting between the workplace and the employee's residence, according to Law 7,418/1985 (Pacheco & Deste, 2021). The differences between working from home and teleworking in Brazil are summarized in Table 1.

Table 1. Working from home and telecommuting features

Working From Home or Remote Work	Teleworking
Control of working hours	There is no control of working hours.
Paid overtime.	No payment for overtime.
Not regulated by specific law.	Regulated by law (Law 13,467/2017).
No need to change the employment contract.	It is necessary to change the employment contract.
The company is responsible for ensuring the same infrastructure as in the on-site modality.	The employees are responsible for the necessary infrastructure.
The employees usually go to the company a few times a week (hybrid work).	Employees go to the company only when called or on a schedule.

Source: elaborated based on Brasil (2011, 2012, 2017 and 2020), Janary (2022), Pacheco and Deste (2021), Pereira (2022), Rocha and Amador (2018), Serralvo and Manus (2022), Stürmer and Fincato (2020)

Thus, unlike teleworking, working from home is not recognized by law, since home-based work is not understood as a different work regime, but rather as conventional work being performed at home. That is, home-based work is working outside the company on a one-time, not permanent, basis. Therefore, the laws in Brazil have been adapted to include this type of work in the existing consolidations and consequently to ensure the employees their due rights, with the necessary tools to supervise them.

Home-Based Work Background

The first recorded practice of a remote work activity dates to 1857, in the United States (USA), using the telegraph, a system of message transmission, which used electricity to send coded messages through wires. "John Edgar Thompson, of Penn Railroad, began using his private telegraphy system to control the work and equipment at remote construction sites of the railroad", thus originating the concept of remote management, or telework (Silva, 2009, p. 86).

Since sending and receiving messages could happen at any time, working from home could be not only a possibility, but a necessity. However, only during the 1970s the term telework was coined and used to denote work performed outside the employer's premises. This happened when there was a worldwide oil crisis, an increase of traffic problems in the big cities, and also, an increase in women participation in the labor market. In the 1980s and 1990s, when the Internet and personal computers became popular, workers and organizations began to experiment with telecommuting. Later, the invention of laptops combined with the increased supply of WI-FI networks in public places, such as coffee shops, favored its growth around the world (Rocha & Amador, 2018).

In Brazil, the history of telework is related to entrepreneurial initiatives developed by many companies, institutions, and professionals since the late twentieth century. Remote work emerged in the 1970s, aiming to ease traffic problems associated with the oil crisis (Takano, 2020).

Maciel and Lando (2021, p. 64) ponder that the most evident change "was the growth of telework, a modality in which tasks are performed outside the employer's premises using technological resource," making it possible to maintain the performance of most professional activities remotely.

When the pandemic hit Brazil in March 2020, several employees had to adopt the remote work model. Despite being a forced change, without planning, and in many cases even without the proper structure, the experience served as a great laboratory for an incipient work configuration, since many companies allowed eventual remote work, especially those in the technology sector. In May 2020, 8.7 million Brazilians were working remotely (Amorim, 2020).

Remote work helped to preserve the employment of a significant portion of the world's population. At the same time, it offered protection against the new coronavirus by reducing social contact and, consequently, contagion and attenuating the curve of infected people in order to avoid the collapse of the health system at the beginning of the pandemic.

Remote Work for Employees

Remote work deviates from the traditional and rigid structures of a fixed and delimited workplace, allowing more geographical freedom to employees, who can, for example, work from home or even use the popular coworking spaces, which satisfactorily accommodate self-employed professionals or entire companies. Despite the autonomy offered by remote work, in some cases the lack of a fixed schedule may have its downsides, because only the most disciplined people correctly follow the working hours, as if they were punching a clock. When somebody works from home, every hour can potentially become an hour of work.

Marton and Carbinatto (2020) report that employees who work from home tend to communicate less, even digitally; The authors present a study according to which, in a group of engineers, those working in the office sent four times more work e-mails than the staff working remotely. In this case, they concluded that the productivity of those working on-site was one third higher than those working remotely.

Therefore, these are aspects that must be analyzed by companies in order to identify the reasons that lead to these situations. Otherwise, instead of helping companies and employees, this work model can produce negative results if not closely monitored. Also, many remote workers (more than half in some studies) claim to have extended their work hours during the pandemic (Tecchio, 2021). This may explain the increase in productivity that many companies perceived when adopted the remote work model.

In short, new challenges have arisen for workers, such as the need for rapid learning of new technologies, the establishment of new forms of interaction, communication between teams, a feeling of more work and more goals. Teleworkers had to reconcile work and domestic life. For many, public and private life have never been so intertwined. Families started to perform work, school, domestic and leisure activities in the same environment. Thus, as shown in Table 2, there are advantages and disadvantages to adopting remote work.

Some companies offer more flexible remote work routines. In this case, remote work allows employees to adapt their daily routines and perform tasks that previously could not be done at the workplace. In conclusion, remote work offers several advantages to companies and employees when well managed by both parties, including a diversity workplace.

Table 2. Advantages and disadvantages of remote work

Advantages	Disadvantages
Productivity increase. Resource saving for the company, which does not need to pay for the structure. It encourages employee autonomy and sense of responsibility. More flexibility. More options to organize free time. In the case of a person with physical disabilities, it lessens commuting difficulty. Opportunity to manage time and choose the best way to accomplish tasks. Family quality of life. Reduced costs with food, clothing, and travel.	Difficulty in focusing when the environment is not favorable. Difficulty in balancing work and personal life. Greater difficulty in demonstrating work accidents. More distance from colleagues who could answer questions and exchange experiences. Need for greater organization and self-discipline. Reduced career opportunities. Risk of work overload. Feeling of social isolation. Biased view against teleworking.

Source: based on Andrade (2020), Marton and Carbinatto (2020), and Silva (2021.

METHODS

This survey was conducted by means of an online electronic questionnaire, provided in a link. The form was created in Google Forms©, which is a Google application that allows the creation, provision and sharing of forms on the Internet. The survey link was sent to people in several social networking groups such as WhatsApp, e-mail, Teams, and others. The time for answers was between October 08, 2022, to October 22, 2022.

The sampling technique called snowball sampling was used to select the respondents. Creswell (2012, p. 2012) defines snowball sampling as a type of purposive sampling that happens when the researcher asks the participant to recommend someone else to be sampled. Snowball sampling, therefore, is a type of non-probability sampling in which researchers use their own judgment to choose initial participants, who in turn recruit other participants - hence the analogy, since the sample size will grow like a snowball rolling down a mountain. The technique is very efficient when used in social networks or with participants from hard-to-contact populations because it allows to draw valid conclusions and make estimates about the social network that exists in the group sampled. The main advantages of this method are being simple, fast, and inexpensive. On the other hand, it is not possible to determine sampling error or generalize about the populations sampled (Baltar & Brunet, 2012).

The survey sample consisted of 121 participants, whose responses were screened to ensure that all respondents were working in private companies that adopted remote work at the onset of the COVID-19 pandemic, that is, in March 2020.

The questionnaire consisted of twenty-three questions, of which twenty were multiple choice and 3 were open questions with short answers. In addition, the questionnaire began with an Informed Consent Form (ICF), whose basic elements are "1) the subjects are aware that they are participating in research, 2) they are aware if they run any foreseeable risk, 3) they have the freedom to consent, or not, to participate, and 4) they are aware that the researcher is committed to keeping their identity confidential" (La Taille, 2008, p. 276).

Because this is a survey that is, a public opinion poll with unidentified participants, the present study was neither registered nor evaluated by the University's Research Ethics Committee, according to Article 1, sole paragraph, item I, of Resolution No. 510/2016 of the Brazilian National Health Council (2016).

The data collected was treated, tabulated, and analyzed with Microsoft Excel©, which allows the elaboration of tables and graphs, as well as the extraction of descriptive statistics. And the open answers were analyzed with a word cloud application that helps analyze the answers by showing trending topics, i.e., which themes received more attention from the respondents. Word clouds have been widely used as tools (Prais & Rosa, 2017; Vasconcellos-Silva & Araújo-Jorge, 2019; Vilela et al., 2018; Vilela et al., 2020) to support content analysis (Bardin, 2015).

WordArt.com was used in its free version (https://wordart.com/) with the following settings to produce the cloud: common terms from Portuguese were removed. This enables a "clean representation" highlighting only those word classes that carry relevant senses and meanings, i.e., of greater importance within a text.

Quantitative Research

The first section of the questionnaire consisted of five questions and had the objective of profiling the 121 respondents. The first question classified the respondents into age groups. A balanced distribution among the 109 respondents can be seen in Table 3 – 81% of the participants were from 18 to 40 years old, 12% from 41 to 50 years old, and only 7% above 50 years old. This showed a strong presence of young people and adults in the labor market and/or remote work. On the other hand, inquiries about the respondents' gender, show a majority of females in relation to males.

Regarding the gender of the respondents, no one failed to inform (there was the option "I prefer not to answer"), so there were 39 (32.23%) male respondents and 82 (67.76%) female respondents. The marital status is shown in Table 4.

Table 3. Age group

Age	18 to 25	26 to 30	31 to 40	41 to 50	+ 51
Number	33	33	33	14	8
Percentage	27,27%	27,27%	27,27%	11,57%	6,61%

Source: questionnaires (2022)

Table 4. Marital status

Marital Status	Single	Married or Civil/Stable Union	Divorced
Number	62	56	3
Percentage	51,23%	46,28%	2,47%

Source: questionnaires (2022)

Regarding the number of children, 80 participants (66.11%) have no children, while 23 (19.00%) have only one child and 18 (14.87%) have more than one child. To finish the profiling section of the questionnaire, the participants were asked to inform in which region of the city of Sao Paulo they live (Table 3). This information is relevant because Sao Paulo a city with a very large area, and living in certain regions, such as the East Side, implies a long and time-consuming daily commute to work.

Table 5. Region of origin

Region	East	South	West	Downtown	North
Number	40	32	27	14	8
Percentage	33,05%	26,44%	22,31%	11,57%	6,61%

Source: questionnaires (2022)

Regarding the employment status of the respondents at the beginning of the COVID-19 pandemic in Brazil (March/2020), the data shown in Table 6 was collected, showing a substantial portion of workers in private companies.

The next question filtered the participants in relation to those who worked remotely, given the national decree of pandemic state and the need for social isolation that led companies to adopt the teleworking to carry on with their activities. According to the survey data, 108 people (89.25%) reported that their company had adopted remote work, which far outnumbers the 13 respondents (10.75%) whose organizations had not.

Table 7 shows the average amount of hours the participants worked from home. Among the 119 participants who answered the question, only one had a workload of less than 4 hours a day. This information shows how diverse the remote environment can be.

The participants were asked whether they were provided with adequate tools to perform their tasks remotely. This is an important question because it allows us to analyze whether, given the unexpected implementation of remote work, companies were concerned about meeting their employees' needs, since it was a time of change for both parties. As Table 8 shows, 78.63% said yes, that there was this kind of support from the hiring company; 12.82% said they had privately provided the tools to perform their tasks. Finally, 8.55% informed that they neither received support from the company nor provided it. Satisfactorily, the number of people in this survey who did not get support with the tools to perform their jobs remotely was low when compared to the total number of respondents.

Table 6. Number of people employed in private companies

Job	Number	Percentage
Private company with a signed contract	90	75,63%
Private company as a freelancer	1	0,84%
Self-employed	7	5,88%
Searching for employment	8	6,72%
Student	6	5,04%
Private company intern	4	3,36%
Public service	1	0,84%
Mixed economy company	1	0,84%
Retired	1	0,84%
Total	119	100,00%

Source: questionnaires (2022)

Table 7. Remote work participants workload

Hours	Up to 4	Up to 6	Up to 8	+ 8	Total
Number	1	42	57	19	119
Percentage	0,84%	35,29%	47,9%	15,97%	100%

Source: questionnaires (2022)

This last percentage must be carefully considered because people without the necessary support to perform their activities in a non-traditional environment can have a negative impact in their performance and harm the company by increasing the error rate or not reaching the results. Therefore, this is an issue to organizations be concerned about before proposing a change in the work modality.

Remote work requires comfort and high-quality electronic equipment. Computers that run the necessary applications with ease and good speed Wi-Fi are essential for the employee to achieve top-quality work. And by the new regulation, the employer must provide equipment for the employee to perform the activities remotely.

When it comes to freelancers, they should be concerned in the same way, because this factor can influence the achievement of results in the employment activity.

Regarding working overtime during the pandemic, Table 9 shows that 35.54% of the respondents reported working after hours on a frequent basis, thus generating overtime. On the other hand, 29.75% reported working overtime only in cases of extreme necessity, while 19.83% and 14.88% did not work

Table 8. Availability of adequate resources for remote work

Availability of Adequate Resources	Yes, Tools Provided by the Company	Yes, I Provided the Resources Myself	No, I Lacked Support	Total
Number	92	15	10	117
Percentage	78,63%	12,82%	8,55%	100%

Source: questionnaires (2022)

overtime, either on their own initiative or due to company regulations, respectively. Only a minority of companies go so far as to prohibit overtime, perhaps because of cost containment or out of concern for the mental health of employees.

Table 9. Overtime

Overtime	Frequently	Extreme Necessity	No, Because I Controlled Myself	No, Because the Company Prohibited Overtime	Total
Number	43	36	24	18	121
Percentage	35,54%	29,75%	19,38%	14,88%	100%

Source: questionnaires (2022)

Regarding whether or not people have adequate space to perform their work activities at home, considering the implementation of remote work, all 121 respondents gave their opinion, and 81 (66.94%) said they have adequate space in their homes to work remotely. The fact that 40 respondents answered negatively (33.06%) may indicate that homes are not built to be workplaces, so now that the pandemic and the urgency of remote work is over, it is important that companies plan to evaluate, not only in terms of space, but also ergonomics, the physical conditions of homes to receive a comfortable office that allows the efficient performance of work.

As for the conciliation between professional and personal life during the pandemic, we notice a certain division in the participants' opinions, as shown in Table 10; 34.71% reported having felt very relaxed about managing professional and personal life; 33.06% reported feeling some difficulty in this conciliation; 22.31% of the respondents reported that it was easy; and for 9.92% it was very difficult. This last data must be carefully analyzed because, as verified throughout this research, remote work during the pandemic was implemented without previous planning by companies, so employees were not aware of this work possibility, which meant something new for both parties. And the consequences of social isolation, i.e., the whole family in the same environment, as well as managing personal and professional life in one place may have been complicated for some people.

There are two lines of perception regarding remote work: one of autonomy, in which employees enjoy more freedom to perform their daily tasks, a situation in which they are open to decision making and responsibilities; and, on the other hand, loneliness, since the contact with colleagues and leaders depends mostly on digital channels. This aspect can create a greater distancing if the team does not take actions to make the contact closer – for example, instead of a regular call, organizing a videocall in which the team can see each other and make the remote relationship a little closer. It is important to encourage actions such as turning cameras on at these moments, as well as creating groups to share ideas and doubts, among other mechanisms.

Table 10. Balance between personal and professional life

Difficulty	Very Difficult	Difficult	Easy	Very Easy	Total
Number	12	40	27	42	121
Percentage	9,92%	33,06%	22,31%	34,71%	100%

Source: questionnaires (2022)

Furthermore, that the second highest percentage (17,94%) of remote work difficulties is "connection/technological failure," as shown in Table 11. Here we can highlight the fact that many employees have been taken by surprise with the implementation of remote work and do not have the support, especially technological, at their homes to carry on with their activities.

For instance, regarding Internet connection, a simple home network may not be enough, depending on the person's tasks and the systems they need to access. Besides, during social isolation the whole family was at home (considering a person who lives with others), sharing bandwidth, so the is a certain impact in this.

Apart from these issues, two others that stand out in a tie (37%) and are worth commenting on are "difficulty in separating family and professional life" and "more interruptions/distractions". Both can be related to a change of environment in which the employee takes work home and needs self-control and self-discipline to do the activities assertively and in the best way, and the relationship with personal life not to be negatively impacted.

Table 11. Difficulties in remote work

Difficulty	Number of Mentions	Percentage
Lack of contact with co-workers	58	26,01%
Connection/technology failures	40	17,94%
More interruptions/distractions	37	16,59%
Difficulty in separating family and professional life	37	16,59%
Increased workload	29	13,00%
Increased demands/goals	18	8,07%
Less customer flow	1	0,45%
Creation of a new sector from scratch	1	0,45%
Need for support due to lack of access	1	0,45%
Lack of adequate working space	1	0,45%
Total	223	100,00%

Source: questionnaires (2022)

Regarding Table 12, which shows benefits, both "avoid commuting" and "flexibility" were mentioned by 93% of the participants of this research. This shows how the factor time is well rated by employees, because commuting involves time to go and come, traffic jams, usually crowed public transportation, and unforeseen events. On the other hand, there is the flexibility of schedules that can be adjusted in a simpler way; and finally, the option to work from anywhere. These are a few points that can justify this greater presence in the remote work facilities category.

One of the great advantages of remote work is the possibility to decide the time one wants to work. There are people more productive and focused during the quiet hours of the night, for example, and may choose to work at that time. Also, professionals who have other responsibilities, such as taking their children to school, can fit their work schedule into their routine.

Another option highly valued by the respondents (67%) was "more interaction with family". Remote work allows more time, for example, for breakfast, family lunches and taking the children to school, which are seen as important advantages of working from home. Being able to interact more with family members promotes well-being and quality of life. Without the need to commute to work, there is more time to experience these moments.

We also see in detail which advantages and benefits of remote work are most appreciated by the respondents, who could choose more than one option. Remarkably "increased quality of life" was mentioned only once; it is common sense that working from home and quality of life are two positively related concepts, however this was not show in this research. In general, it is understood that each benefit obtained by working from home generates, even if indirectly, a positive impact on the quality of life. For example, less commuting time should imply a higher quality of life, which is not true, because quality of life will depend a lot on what one does with the time saved by not going to the workplace and not simply on having more idle time.

Table 12. Benefits of working from home

Benefit/Advantage	Number of Mentions	Percentage
More flexibility	93	21,18%
Avoid commuting	93	21,18%
Less concern with appearance	71	16,17%
More interaction with the family	67	15,26%
Productivity increase	63	14,35%
Independence in daily activities	51	11,62%
Increased quality of life	1	0,23%
Total	439	100,00%

Source: questionnaires (2022)

Aiming to identify more precisely if people felt that remote work had changed their interpersonal relationships for the better or worse, teleworkers were asked how they perceived this change. There were 109 answers. The survey showed that 48.62% (53) of the respondents reported having felt no change in interpersonal relationships, and 37.61% (41) reported having felt a positive change, leaving only 13.76%

(15) who felt a negative change. One explanation for this is that remote work generates the need for clearer communication, and to achieve this, often the need for more contacts between everyone on the team.

Teleworking revolutionized the traditional way of working because, even though several companies and institutions already operated remotely before the pandemic, social isolation generated by the coronavirus accelerated the transition to this type of work. Those who worked remotely during the pandemic were asked about the work model adopted after the pandemic ended, and Table 13 shows the answers.

Table 13. Modality of work adopted post-pandemic

Model	Totally Remote	Hybrid	Fully On-Site	Total
Number	21	70	18	109
Percentage	19,27%	64,22%	16,51%	100%

Source: questionnaires (2022)

According to the respondents, 64.22% of the companies have adopted the hybrid work model, that is, they have mixed remote and on-site shifts, in which the professionals alternate between days of activity working from home and in the office. On the other hand, 16.51% were back on-site, and 19.27% work totally remote.

After the publication of Recommendation No. 036, of May 11th, 2020 (National Health Council, 2020), which advocated more restrictive social distancing (lockdown) in Brazil, in cities with accelerated occurrences of COVID-19 cases and hospital bed occupancy rates at critical levels, some companies needed to adopt quick strategies to continue their business, given the preventive social isolation in the face of the pandemic. From then on, the companies' people management departments, based on this Recommendation, the labor legislation, and employees' contracts, were able to formally implement a new work modality, that is, by registering the change in the labor contracts. Considering this scenario, we tried to identify if companies carried out updates in their employees' contracts regarding remote work.

Table 14 shows that 51.38% of the respondents reported having no changes in their work contract, that is, everything in their contract remained valid, even when they started working from home. Also, 38.53% informed that they had received consent and formalization terms regarding the changes in the work modality, which were included in their contracts. And 10% informed that changes had occurred in the company's regulations, but without formalization (for instance, they no longer received some benefit, but this fact was not formalized).

Table 14. Formalization of remote work adoption in employment contracts

Alterations in the Contract	An Additive Term Was Signed	No Changes to the Contract	There Was No Formalization of the Changes	Total
Number	42	56	11	109
Percentage	38,53%	51,38%	10,09%	100%

Source: questionnaires (2022)

Table 15 shows how difficult people found it to demonstrate their performance, skills, and results in the remote model. In the results, it is evident that this was not a factor of concern among people. Of 109 respondents, 55 people reported that on a scale of 1 to 5 they had no difficulty demonstrating their performance to leaders. In other words, even with the change in the work modality to remote work, there was no impact on the relationship between the employee and the leader.

This is important because, even though remote work allows people to work outside the company with numerous adaptations and adjustments to the new home environment, performance was not negatively impacted, because people, in general, did not experience difficulties with the new model in terms of applying their skills to work.

Table 15. Degree of difficulty to perform remote work

Difficulty	Very Difficult	Difficult	Moderate	Easy	Very Easy	Total
Number	2	14	23	15	55	109
Percentage	1,83%	12,84%	21,10%	13,76%	50,46%	100%

Source: questionnaires (2022)

In order to assess the respondent's perception regarding the result of the adoption of remote work, that is, the effectiveness of this work modality during the pandemic, participants were asked how effective teleworking was. Table 16 shows the perception of respondents. In general, there was a high level of acceptance of the effectiveness of remote work.

Table 16. Degree of effectiveness (remote work achievement)

Effectiveness	Not Effective	Barely Effective	Moderate	Effective	Very Effective	Total
Number	0	1	3	15	90	109
Percentage	0,00%	0,92%	2,75%	13,76%	82,57%	100%

Source: questionnaires (2022)

The last question of this stage of the survey involved identifying the impact of remote work in relation to the company's people management practices, analyzing it from the employee's point of view. As expected, most people had a positive perception, as shown in Table 17.

Table 17. What is the impact of remote work on people management practices

Effectiveness	Very Negative	Negative	Neutral	Positive	Very Positive	Total
Number	2	5	27	30	45	109
Percentage	1,830%	4,59%	24,77%	27,52%	41,28%	100%

Source: questionnaires (2022)

As shown above there is a strong presence of respondents (75/68.8%) on the side of the positive scale that denotes remote work as a model that has mostly brought positive impacts on both relationships and the execution of the work itself.

Qualitative Research

The questionnaire applied in this research also included three questions with open answers that allowed people to answer freely with words or short phrases, so that it was also possible to capture more subjective aspects. These open questions were intended to map out, along with the respondents, comments, reports, and stances on the subject to find possible aspects not identified by the objective questions.

The first question was "Did you feel a change in the pace and quality of work, why?" From the 109 answers obtained, the majority said "No". In general, people did not feel any impact concerning the dynamics and quality of work, comparing the implementation of teleworking to the traditional work model. In order to help visualize the answers to this question, a word cloud was created, in which it is possible to see the most prevalent terms.

In the cloud, the most frequent words are focus, quality of life, connection and Internet, productivity, demands and goals, time, and transportation, among others. All these factors were identified by the respondents as relevant when analyzing the change of rhythm and quality of work with the implementation of teleworking. There were also negative feelings reported in the study, highlighting anxiety, doubts, challenges, excessive demands, and exhaustion.

Although working from home offers several advantages, such as flexibility and a better quality of life, this work model also presents several challenges, as seen in the theoretical framework and reinforced in the answers to the questionnaire of this research.

The second open question of the research questionnaire is "in relation to the previous question: for what reason?" (the question is "have you felt a change in your relationship with the team and the leader?" This open question was not mandatory to complete the form, therefore, there were only 60 valid answers.

The responses indicate that staying motivated when working from home is one of the great challenges of remote management. Regarding this question, most of the answers were long sentences, difficult to interpret in just words. However, some of the most significant and representative perceptions that stand out are motivation, autonomy, interaction, participation, contact, relaxation, tranquility, safety, communication, objectivity, approach, interactivity, empathy, connection, proximity.

These words express some of the team's needs, since that the lack of motivation at work directly impacts daily productivity, the sense of belonging and purpose, and can increase the feeling of individuality at work – which makes collaboration process even more difficult among team members and with other areas. Therefore, it is of utmost importance that employees have the intention and attention to change interpersonal relationships.

Technology is the main tool that assists people in remote work. Every day, technologies that facilitate teleworking are developed and improved, even for those who did not foresee this movement for their business before the pandemic. Now these technologies have has become a subject of attention and improvement in most companies. Approaching this subject, to assess the respondents' opinion regarding technology, the third question was: "for you, how has technology changed the relationship between leader and employee? Has it become easier or more difficult?".

Through the word cloud, the term most mentioned by the respondents was "facilitated" reinforcing how important technology has been in supporting the transition and adaptation of the remote work model.

However, we also noticed a strong presence of "made it difficult" probably because dealing with technology always involves technical problems and lack of knowledge about some tools, situations that drive people to go after learning more about the applications, although these are nowadays very intuitive and friendly. Regarding the relationships, there were several comments about the lack of communication, the increased distance between colleagues, and the difficulty in moments of doubt, among others, as shown in Table XX below.

Table 18. Types of comments

Positive	Negative
Fast communication	Hindered people management
Agility	Lack of feedback
Proximity	More tasks
Productivity	Absences at meetings
Facility	Dry relationships
Close Leadership	Distancing
Flexibility	Slow systems
Freedom	Social matter
Rapid exchange	Lack of clarity
Informal contact	Lack of tools
Reduced micromanagement	Worsened communication

Source: questionnaires (2022)

Therefore, we perceive a variable that depends on the company, area, leaders, and colleagues, and on the people who are willing or not to adapt to change and seek the necessary knowledge for remote work implementation and effectiveness, i.e., support and availability of resources provided by the company are essential in adapting to telecommuting.

SOLUTIONS AND RECOMMENDATIONS

The pandemic is over and new technologies, like ChatGPT, are still emerging; and, while they facilitate human work, they also replace it. Meanwhile, several companies or rather several managers, still want their teams to return to on-site work. However, as the results show, few workers would be willing to give up the flexibility and the benefits obtained through teleworking. This disagreement is a complex subject to solve, but surviving the pandemic was more difficult.

Aksoy et al. (2022) research results on remote work in twenty-seven countries, including Brazil, indicate that teleworking is consolidated. Both employees and companies have expressed the desire to work from home permanently, at least some days of the week, in a hybrid way. The employees recognized significant improvements in productivity and well-being, which are probably associated with the reduced need to commute to the workplace, as was also found in our research. Given that, workers would even be willing to accept a 5% reduction of their salary, on average, in exchange for working two or three days from home, which suggests that teleworking can help reduce wage increases, positively affecting the effort of several countries to hold back inflation.

Barrero et al. (2022) corroborate this. Their research also found that 38% of the companies in the survey have expanded remote work opportunities in the last 12 months in order to ease salary pressures. The authors report that this practice was even more significant in large companies and in specific activities, such as education, healthcare, financial and information service.

On the other hand, Coneglian (2020) draws attention to what she calls the telework paradox: because it is a type of work mediated by technology, at the same time that it brings people closer by shortening distances, it can also distance them, generating serious implications for their subjective processes and mental health. The author warns that teleworking directly affects the way teleworkers are perceived and recognized by other people and by the company where they are employed. However, she is not at all pessimistic about the future of telework and proposes insights on new formats of organization, management, and remote work policies, which are able to provide greater visibility and space for the elaboration of meaning of work, and more sustainable and humane conditions for the achievement of bio-psychosocial health of teleworkers who face the challenges of the current telework model.

It is necessary to go further on the debate about the importance of respecting fundamental rights and human dignity in labor relations, especially the rights to limit the workday, to disconnect from work to leisure time, and to health. Remote work, if implemented with respect for life and relationships of every person, has the potential to be an essential tool for maintaining the physical, mental, and social integrity of human beings (Parmegiane, 2021). Otherwise, it can seriously damage the worker's health and integrity because it is essential to guarantee the balance between worktime and the free time to develop full citizenship.

Organizations that rely on teleworkers can build a powerful competitive advantage in terms of people management, improving organizational resilience while making a real contribution in addressing important environmental, diversity, mobility, urban planning, and social issues (O'Duinn, 2021).

New information and communication technologies have transformed everyday life, but especially the way we work in the 21st century, and in the last four decades telecommuting has evolved further as technological developments have improved our ability to work remotely. Today, there are huge global variations of telework, several effects and conditions of telecommuting that have been proven to positively impact the worker and the organization performances. It is safe to say that the traditional intellectual conception that telework is performed only at home is part of the past, as "anywhere office" is a reality - such is the variety of work environments. Since technology allows to employees virtually infinite work mobility, while revealing that ambiguity about the effects of telework in today's society, it also tends to present more advantages than disadvantages (Messenger, 2019).

Mello and Dal Colletto (2019, pp. 247-248) state that telework has grown remarkably in Brazil and this is mainly due to the popularization of information technology, pressures for cost reduction and increased productivity in companies. The authors add that the global crisis of people's transportation and air pollution in large urban centers also contribute to the decisions of governments and companies to embrace remote work. However, they highlight that some resistance contributes to reduce the growth of telework. This includes managers conservativeness, aversion to administrative risk, lack of new parameters for tasks and productivity, limited knowledge of new emerging technologies and telecommunications, and a belief that one works outside the home and that home is the place for domestic chores.

FUTURE RESEARCH DIRECTIONS

It is not possible to generalize on the results obtained in this study, since it is exploratory, with a non-probability sample; however, this does not invalidate the findings. In fact, it even suggests the realization of new studies with statistically defined samples, and opens possibilities for new research, among which is possible to investigate remote work as a way to provide accessibility for all people. To this end, new research is still needed on all the necessary adaptations for the execution of remote work, in order to include professionals with restrictions, disabilities, and special needs to perform their work activities at home with much more comfort and convenience.

The standard digital environment has numerous barriers for people with disabilities, but accessibility, if it is a real concern of the hiring companies, can very well include these people. Accessibility means that every person, regardless of their physical or mental condition, has equal access to resources, without the need of external help. Digital accessibility, in turn, is a more specific term that refers specifically to digital content and offerings, such as cell phone apps, files, Internet, intranet, programs, systems, and software, which need to be operational, easy to understand and use by those with any kind of motor, neurological, visual, or sensory impairments (Lima et al., 2018).

For example, in a video conference the automatic generation of subtitles will allow deaf or hearing-impaired people to actively participate in the meeting. Also, if blind or low-vision people have a video calling platform that is compatible with screen readers (software that converts text into audio) will receive the visual information conveyed by slides or other visual aids during meetings.

Although digital accessibility is a right guaranteed in Brazil by the laws 10,098 (Brasil, 2000) and 13,146 (Brasil, 2015), less than 1% of Brazilian websites pass accessibility tests (Valente, 2020), that is, the online work of these people is an even greater challenge if companies do not provide the necessary help. Such data shows that there is a great urgency to demand the enforcement of laws and to make organizational leaders aware of the obligation to promote the workplace inclusion of people with disabilities; after all, technology has already evolved enough to meet the needs of this group of people.

The difficulties of people with disabilities in relation to work start even before they leave home, because for 70% of this people who looked for a job were unemployed (Albuquerque, 2022), and 44% of professionals with disabilities do not even go to job interviews because of locomotion difficulties, such as inappropriate sidewalks (63%), lack of accessible infrastructure, such as ramps and smart lights (26%), and inefficient or non-adapted transportation (22%). Approximately forty-five million Brazilians (24% of the population) have some form of disability, and of this total, about 400,000 are employed, that is, only 1% of people with disabilities in the country (Catho, 2022).

Given this scenario, for the millions of people with disabilities teleworking represents more autonomy, the possibility to work and at the same time avoiding transportation obstacles. In addition, these people can have more comfort in their homes since they usually already have the necessary resources.

Organizations can contribute significantly to increase the inclusion of people with disabilities in the labor market by providing accessibility solutions (digital, instrumental, or architectural), such as communication channels compatible with screen readers, equipment, and adaptation devices for using the mouse, browser, keyboard etc. In a world that is constantly and increasingly rapidly changing and where remote work is becoming the norm, even with some setbacks, prioritizing digital accessibility is a condition for breaking down existing barriers and ensuring the inclusion of people with disabilities.

CONCLUSION

Unexpected events like the coronavirus crisis provoke or accelerate intense transformations, whether in one's personal or professional life, or in society as a whole. Among the changes generated by the pandemic, the widespread adoption of remote work on a large scale has put the spotlight on the day-to-day life of companies and work in offices, after all the need for social isolation has paradoxically opened up work relationships by putting people working from home.

As the results show, teleworking, which started as a corporate solution to work and maintain social isolation during the pandemic, allowed people to work from anywhere by simply having Internet access and a portable device. It has become a potential solution to much more diverse and complex problems. The pandemic accelerated trends that were already considered inevitable in society, making telecommuting a reality that changed the nature of work. The traditional concept of work performed predominantly on-site has been replaced by work done at the employee's home, in shared spaces, or anywhere else.

Therefore, companies and people must understand the needs of this new way of working so that the organization's activities and the employees' well-being are guaranteed in the same way or better than in the traditional work model. People management must pay heed to and follow up with employees so as not to lose or undermine valuable professionals.

The need for remote work or telecommuting is emerging for some professions with both positive and negative aspects. For those who can effectively control their work schedule, taking advantage of the disconnection from work, enjoying family life, physical activities practice, reading, and leisure, among other human needs, the experience seems to be positive. Therefore, it is clear that teleworking is a broad concept and has both benefits and difficulties, and that current and future professionals must be open and prepared to adapt to this new model; just as people management should develop to meet and monitor their employees in the best possible way to ensure the best results and well-being of employees.

Throughout this paper we sought to expose points of view and facts about telecommuting in Brazil, in which, based on the theoretical framework and analysis of a questionnaire conducted with people who have had or have experience working remotely, it was possible to better understand this kind of work, as well as to verify the validity of our initial hypotheses.

We can, then, answer that the impact of remote work from the human resources point of view has been positive and evolutionary, in which companies and employees have been seeking to develop and grow this work model even more, to benefit both parties.

Furthermore, in the context of the internet of behavior (IoB), this study enriches the current literature on the IoB by analyzing employees' preferences and motivations related to remote work and what are its main perceived benefits, as well as the obstacles and concerns that may arise. This analysis helps create people management strategies to meet the needs and expectations of employees in the remote work environment in order to positively impact employee productivity and performance. Additionally, it provides a more comprehensive understanding of the behavioral and psychological aspects involved in the adoption of remote work, favoring the advancement of the field by offering valuable insights into the interactions between individuals and technology in the context of the home office from the perspective of employees.

Considering the results achieved it is possible to expand the analysis regarding the impact of teleworking on people's personal and professional lives and on society in general by helping to equate several problems of modern life in an effective and inexpensive way such as traffic congestion, queues for public, mobility crisis.

REFERENCES

Aksoy, C. G., Barrero, J. M., Bloom, N., Davis, S. J., Dolls, M., & Zarate, P. (2022, September). *Working from home around the world.* Working Paper 2022-124. Chicago, IL: Becker Friedman Institute at the University of Chicago.

Albuquerque, D. (2022, Oct. 23). A dura realidade de pessoas com deficiência em busca de emprego: de acordo com dados do IBGE, a cada dez pessoas nessas condições que buscavam emprego, sete estavam fora do mercado de trabalho. *Correio Braziliense.*

Allied. (n.d.). *The History of Telecommuting.* Allied. https://www.alliedtelecom.net/the-history-of-telecommuting/

Amorim, D. (2020). *8,073 milhões de pessoas estavam em trabalho remoto em setembro, diz IBGE.* Uol: https://economia.uol.com.br/noticias/estadao-conteudo/2020/10/23/8073-milhoes-de-pessoas-estavam-em-trabalho-remoto-em-setembro-diz-ibge.htm

Amorim, D. (2022). Brasil tem 20,4 mi de trabalhadores que poderiam trabalhar remotamente, diz Ipea. *CNN Brasil.* https://www.cnnbrasil.com.br/business/brasil-tem-204-mi-de-trabalhadores-que-poderiam-trabalhar-remotamente-diz-ipea/

Andrade, G. (2020). *As vantagens do home office: o que dizem estudos e pesquisas.* Digilândia. https://digilandia.io/home-office/vantagens-do-home-office/#Impactos_sociais_e_ambientais

Baltar, F., & Brunet, I. (2012). Social research 2.0: Virtual snowball sampling method using Facebook. *Internet Research*, *22*(1), 57–74. doi:10.1108/10662241211199960

Bardin, L. (2015). Análise de conteúdo. Lisboa, PT: Edições 70.

Barrero, J. M., Bloom, N., Davis, S. J., Meyer, B. H., & Mihaylov, E. (2022). *The shift to remote work lessens wage-growth pressures.* Working Paper 30197. Cambridge: National Bureau of Economic Research.

Brasil. Presidência da República. (2000). *Law No 10,098, of December 19, 2000*: establishes general standards and basic criteria for promoting the accessibility of people with disabilities or reduced mobility and makes other provisions. Brasília, DF.

Brasil. Presidência da República. (2011). *Law No. 12,551, of December 15, 2011.* Alters article 6 of the Consolidation of Labor Laws (CLT), approved by Decree-Law No. 5452, of May 1, 1943, to equate the legal effects of subordination exercised by telematic and computerized means to that exercised by personal and direct means. Diário Oficial da União, Brasília, DF.

Brasil. Presidência da República. (2015). *Law No. 13,146 of July 6, 2015*: establishes the Brazilian Inclusion Law for Persons with Disabilities (Estatuto da Pessoa com Deficiência). Brasília, DF.

Brasil. Presidência da República. (2017). *Law No. 13,467, of July 13, 2017.* It changes the Consolidation of Labor Laws (CLT), in order to adapt the legislation to the new labor relations Brasília, DF.

Brasil. Presidência da República. (2020). *Provisional Measure No. 927, of March 22, 2020.* Amends the Law and disposes about labor measures to face the state of public calamity. Brasília, DF.

Brasil. Superior Labor Court. (2012). *Provisional Measure No. 1499, of February 01, 2012*. Regulates telework in the scope of the Superior Labor Court and makes other provisions. Diário da Justiça do Trabalho, Brasília, DF, no. 912, Feb. 3, 2012.

Catho. (2022, Sept. 23). Home Office ajuda na inclusão de profissionais com deficiência. *Carreira & Sucesso (online)*. São Paulo, SP: Catho. https://www.catho.com.br/carreira-sucesso/carreira/home-office-ajuda-na-inclusao-de-profissionais-com-deficiencia/

Coneglian, T. N. M. (2020). *Teletrabalho Home office: identidade, subjetividade e saúde mental dos tabalhadores*. CRV. doi:10.24824/978655578154.0

Conselho Nacional de Saúde – CNS. (2020). Recomendation No 036/2020: It recommends implementing more restrictive social distancing measures (lockdown) in municipalities with accelerated occurrence of new cases of COVID-19 and with service occupancy rates reaching critical levels. Ministry of Health, Brasília, DF.

Creswell, J. W. (2012). *Educational research: Planning, conducting, and evaluating quantitative and qualitative research* (4th ed.). Pearson.

da Rocha, C. T. M., & Amador, F. S. (2018, March). O teletrabalho: Conceituação e questões para análise. *Cadernos EBAPE.BR*, *16*(1), 1–11. doi:10.1590/1679-395154516

da Silva, D. (2021). *Home office: vantagens e desvantagens para as empresas e colaboradores*. https://www.zendesk.com.br/blog/home-office-vantagens-e-desvantagens/

da Silva, R. R. (2009, January-June). Home-office: Um surgimento bem-sucedido da profissão pósfordista, uma alternativa positiva para os centros urbanos. *Revista Brasileira de Gestão Urbana, Curitiba, PR*, *1*(1), 1–11.

de La Taille, Y. (2008). Ética em pesquisa com seres humanos: dignidade e liberdade. In *Ética nas pesquisas em ciências humanas e sociais na saúde*. Aderaldo & Rothschild.

de Oliveira, A., & Tchakerian, G. (2022). *Home office e teletrabalho*. Juspodivm.

Firmino, J. (2021). *Gestão no trabalho remoto: os principais desafios e as melhores práticas*. https://blog.runrun.it/gestao-no-trabalho-remoto/#:~:text=Resultados%3A%20os%20principais%20desafios%20no%20home%20office&text=Apontada%20por%2047%25%20dos%20gestores,est%C3%A3o%20sendo%20realizadas%20pelos%20colaboradores

Gonçalves, A. G. (2020). *Home office trouxe novos desafios para gestores*. https://cfa.org.br/home-office-trouxe-novos-desafios-para-gestores/

Janary, J. (2022). *Medida provisória regulamenta teletrabalho e muda regras do auxílio-alimentação*. https://www.camara.leg.br/noticias/861554-medida-provisoria-regulamenta-teletrabalho-e-muda-regras-do-auxilio-alimentacao/

Jankavski, A. (2021). Brasileiros querem manter home office, mas temem excesso de trabalho, diz estudo. *CNN Brasil*. https://www.cnnbrasil.com.br/business/maioria-aprova-o-home-office-mas-ha-preocupacao-com-excesso-de-trabalho/

Lima, A. C. O., Leal, E. O. L., & Gandra, S. R. (2018). *Usabilidade e acessibilidade na concepção de novos sistemas inclusivos*. Appris.

Lima Filho, J. S. F., de, & Brasil, A. L. da S. (2019, January 26). O conceito legal de teletrabalho e suas repercussões nos direitos do empregado. *Juris Unitoledo*, *1*(4), 111–126.

Maciel, Á. dos S., & Lando, G. A. (2021, April). Desafios e perspectivas do mundo do trabalho pós-pandemia no Brasil: Uma análise da flexibilização trabalhista e os paradoxos do home office/anywhere office. *Revista Espaço Acadêmico*, *20*(0), 63–74.

Mack, O., Khare, A., Krämer, A., & Burgartz, T. (2016). *Managing in a VUCA World*. Springer International Publishing AG Switzerland. doi:10.1007/978-3-319-16889-0

Maia, A. C. B. (2020). *Questionário e entrevista na pesquisa qualitativa: elaboração, aplicação e análise de conteúdo*. Pedro e João.

Marton, F., & Carbinatto, B. (2022, Aug.). *E se trabalhássemos para sempre em regime de home office?* https://super.abril.com.br/ciencia/e-se-trabalhassemos-para-sempre-em-regime-de-home-office

Mello, Á., & Dal Colleto, A. (2019). Telework and its effects in Brazil. In J. C. Messenger (Ed.), *Telework in the 21st Century: An evolutionary perspective* (pp. 211–254). Edward Elgar Publishing. doi:10.4337/9781789903751.00012

Mesquita, A. (2021). *Liderança no home office: quais os desafios?* https://www.oitchau.com.br/blog/desafios-de-lideranca-no-home-office/

Messenger, J. C. (2019). *Telework in the 21st Century: an evolutionary perspective*. Edward Elgar Publishing. doi:10.4337/9781789903751

Mohsin, M. (2021). *7 estatísticas sobre home office para o ano de 2021*. https://www.oberlo.com.br/blog/estatisticas-home-office

O'Duinn, J. (2021). *Distributed teams: the art and practice of working together while physically apart*. Release Mechanix, LLC.

Pacheco, F. L., & Deste, J. A. (2021). *O teletrabalho na legislação brasileira e sua multidisciplinaridade: aspectos teóricos e práticos*. Mizuno.

Parker, C., Scott, S., & Geddes, A. (2019). Snowball Sampling. In P. Atkinson, S. Delamont, A. Cernat, J. W. Sakshaug, & R. A. Williams (Eds.), *SAGE Research Methods Foundations*.

Parmegiane, D. (2021). *Dado existencial: Análise da jornada excessiva de trabalho e o teletrabalho sob a ótica da dignidade da pessoa humana*. CRV.

Pereira, A. N. (2022). *Teletrabalho: um recorte exploratório de conceitos e de práticas normativas e jurisprudenciais celetistas e no TRT 2ª Região*. Leme: Mizuno.

Pereira, A. S., Shitsuka, D. M., Parreira, F. J., & Shitsuka, R. (2018). *Metodologia da pesquisa científica*. Santa Maria, RS: Universidade Federal de Santa Maria – UFSM; Núcleo de Tecnologia Educacional – NTE.

Prais, J. L. de S., & Rosa, V. F. da. (2017). Nuvem de palavras e mapa conceitual: estratégias e recursos tecnológicos na prática pedagógica. *Nuances: Estudos sobre Educação, 28*(1), 201-219.

Secretaria de Comunicação Social – SCS. (2020). Teletrabalho: O trabalho de onde você estiver – Material Educativo. Brasília, DF: Tribunal Superior do Trabalho (Superior Labor Court) – TST.

Serralvo, L. L. S., & Manus, P. P. T. (2022). Teletrabalho e a responsabilidade civil do empregador: implicações para o home office. São Paulo, SP: LTr.

Sociedade Brasileira de Teletrabalho e Teleatividades – SOBRATT. (2020). *Orientação para implantação e prática do Teletrabalho e home office.*

Stürmer, G., & Fincato, D. (2020). *Teletrabalho em tempos de calamidade por Covid19: impacto das medidas trabalhistas de urgência.* Jus Podvm.

Sutto, G. (2022). *85% das empresas do país adotaram o trabalho remoto na pandemia, mostra pesquisa.* https://www.infomoney.com.br/minhas-financas/85-das-empresas-do-pais-adotaram-o-trabalho-remoto-na-pandemia-mostra-pesquisa/

Tecchio, M. (2021). Home office veio para ficar, mas não da forma que funciona hoje. *CNN Brasil Business.* https://www.cnnbrasil.com.br/business/home-office-veio-para-ficar-mas-nao-da-forma-que-funciona-hoje/

Valente, J. (2020). *Menos de 1% dos sites passam em teste de acessibilidade: estudo avaliou dificuldades de acesso para pessoas com deficiência. Agência Brasil.* Empresa Brasil de Comunicação.

Vasconcellos-Silva, P., & Araújo-Jorge, T. (2019). Análise de conteúdo por meio de nuvem de palavras de postagens em comunidades virtuais: novas perspectivas e resultados preliminares. In: *Anais 8º Congresso Ibero-Americano em Investigação Qualitativa: Investigação Qualitativa na Saúde.* Lisboa: Escola Superior de Enfermagem de Lisboa.

Vilela, R. B., Ribeiro, A., & Batista, N. A. (2018). Os desafios do mestrado profissional em ensino na saúde: Uso da nuvem de palavras no apoio à pesquisa qualitativa. *CIAIQ, 2,* 652–659.

Vilela, R. B., Ribeiro, A., & Batista, N. A. (2020). Nuvem de palavras como ferramenta de análise de conteúdo. *Millenium,* (11), 29–36.

Zavanella, F., & Pinto, L. O. C. (2021). *22 Anos da SOBRATT – A Evolução do Teletrabalho: tomo I: aspectos jurídicos.* Lacier Editora.

ADDITIONAL READING

Brunsmeier, S., Diewald, M., & Reimann, M. (2023). From Computer-Assisted Work to the Digital Twins of Humans: Risks and Opportunities for Social Integration in the Workplace. In I. Gräßler, G. W. Maier, E. Steffen, & D. Roesmann (Eds.), *The Digital Twin of Humans.* Springer. doi:10.1007/978-3-031-26104-6_10

Giauque, D., Renard, K., Cornu, F., & Emery, Y. (2022). Engagement, Exhaustion, and Perceived Performance of Public Employees Before and During the COVID-19 Crisis. *Public Personnel Management*, *51*(3), 263–290. doi:10.1177/00910260211073154 PMID:36093284

Golden, T. D., Veiga, J. F., & Dino, R. N. (2008). The impact of professional isolation on teleworker job performance and turnover intentions: Does time spent teleworking, interacting face-to-face, or having access to communication-enhancing technology matter? *The Journal of Applied Psychology*, *93*(6), 1412–1421. doi:10.1037/a0012722 PMID:19025257

Park, S., & Cho, Y. J. (2020). Does telework status affect the behavior and perception of supervisors? Examining task behavior and perception in the telework context. *International Journal of Human Resource Management*, *33*(7), 1326–1351. doi:10.1080/09585192.2020.1777183

Renard, K. (2023). Perceptions of Work–Life Balance and Coworker Support Promote Teleworker Well-Being: Survey of the Swiss Public Sector During COVID-19. *Revue internationale de psychosociologie et de gestion des comportements organisationnels*, *29*, 75-99. https://doi.org/ doi:10.54695/rips2.077.0075

Urien, B. (2023). Teleworkability, Preferences for Telework, and Well-Being: A Systematic Review. *Sustainability*, *15*(13), 10631. doi:10.3390/su151310631

Valencia, A. S. (2023). Teleworking, Home Office, Digital Platforms and Super-Exploitation of Labor. In *Global Labour in the Fourth Industrial Revolution*. Brill. doi:10.1163/9789004532717_007

KEY TERMS AND DEFINITIONS

Accessibility in Terms of Labor: Refers to creating an inclusive and accessible work environment that allows for full participation and equal opportunities for all individuals, regardless of their abilities or limitations. It is the process of removing physical, technological, and social barriers that may hinder the active participation and professional achievement of individuals with disabilities or special needs. Workplace accessibility encompasses several dimensions: physical, technological, communicational, attitudinal (promoting an inclusive culture in the workplace that values diversity and respects individual differences), cognitive (adapting the work environment to meet the needs of individuals with cognitive disabilities, such as learning difficulties or autism spectrum disorders) etc.

ChatGPT: An artificial intelligence - AI language model, developed by OpenAI, based on the GPT (Generative Pre-trained Transformer) architecture, specifically GPT-3.5. It is designed to generate human-like text responses given a prompt or a conversational context. It has been trained on a vast amount of diverse text data from the internet and is capable of understanding and generating coherent and contextually relevant responses.

Consolidation of Labor Laws (CLT): Is a set of norms and regulations that establish the rights and duties of workers and employers in Brazil. It was created in 1943 by Decree-Law No. 5,452, during the government of Getúlio Vargas, and has been the main labor legislation in the country since then. The CLT's main objective is to regulate labor relations, promoting social justice, protecting workers, and ensuring harmony in the relationships between employees and employers. It covers various areas such as employment contracts, working hours, vacations, wages, benefits, occupational safety and health, and other aspects related to employment. The CLT is an important milestone in Brazilian labor legislation and has been subject to discussions and updates over the years to adapt to changes in the labor market. Furthermore, it is important to note that the CLT may undergo changes and complements through complementary laws, provisional measures, collective bargaining agreements, and judicial decisions.

Diversity Workplace: Refers to the presence of a variety of characteristics, experiences, backgrounds, abilities, and perspectives among employees within an organization. These characteristics may include, but are not limited to, ethnicity, gender, age, sexual orientation, ethnic origin, religion, disability, socioeconomic status, and education. To effectively value and promote diversity, it is necessary to foster an inclusive organizational culture, provide training and awareness programs, and adopt policies and practices that encourage diversity and prevent discrimination. Embracing diversity allows organizations to reap the benefits of a dynamic and inclusive workforce, providing a more enriching and equitable environment for all.

Fundo de Garantia por Tempo de Serviço (FGTS): Severance Pay Fund, is a benefit provided to workers in Brazil. It is a social and economic fund managed by Caixa Econômica Federal – CEF (https:// www.caixa.gov.br), aimed at protecting labor rights and promoting financial stability for workers. The FGTS is a monthly deposit equivalent to 8% of the employee's salary, made by the employer into an individual account held by the worker at CEF. The deposited amount is not deducted from the worker's salary and is the employer's obligation. The FGTS is a right guaranteed by Brazilian labor legislation, aiming to protect workers' interests and provide financial security during times of need. The funds deposited in the FGTS are adjusted for inflation and may also earn interest over time, according to the government's established policies.

Productivity: The measure of efficiency and production capacity in relation to the resources used. It is related to the quantity of results achieved in relation to the time, effort, resources, and inputs employed in an activity or process. In a business context, productivity is often evaluated in terms of the production of goods or services per unit of time or per worker. It is important to note that productivity is not just about doing more in less time but also about seeking efficiency, quality, and innovation.

Promoting Labor Accessibility: Not only fulfills legal obligations of equality and inclusion but also contributes to a more diverse, creative, and productive work environment. By creating an accessible environment, organizations provide equal opportunities to their employees and help maximize the potential of all individuals, regardless of their abilities or limitations.

Quality of Life: The overall perception of well-being, satisfaction, and fulfillment that an individual experiences in different areas of their life. It is a comprehensive concept that encompasses both objective and subjective aspects and includes various domains such as physical and mental health, interpersonal relationships, emotional well-being, job satisfaction, work-life balance, access to resources and opportunities, among others. Quality of life can be influenced by various factors, including socioeconomic conditions, physical environment, health status, personal relationships, sense of purpose and meaning in life, autonomy, security, access to services and basic resources, among other elements.

Telework: In Brazil, telework refers to a work modality in which employees carry out their activities remotely, outside the physical premises of the company. In this arrangement, the employee performs their tasks in a location of their choice, such as their residence, using technological resources to communicate and execute their duties. Telework in Brazil is regulated by Law No. 13,467/2017, known as the Labor Reform. This legislation introduced amendments to the Consolidation of Labor Laws (CLT) to encompass telework, establishing specific guidelines for this form of work. According to the law, for telework to be valid, there must be a formal agreement between the employer and the employee, usually through an individual employment contract or an addendum to an existing contract.

Workplace Inclusion: Refers to a work environment where all individuals are valued, respected, and have equal opportunities, regardless of their characteristics, backgrounds, abilities, gender identities, sexual orientations, religious beliefs, or any other dimension of diversity. It is the process of creating a workplace that embraces and values diversity, promoting full participation and engagement of all employees. Workplace inclusion is an ongoing process that requires leadership commitment, employee awareness and training, and an organizational culture that promotes diversity and inclusion as core values. By creating an inclusive work environment, organizations are able to harness the full potential of their employees, promoting innovation, productivity, and job satisfaction.

Chapter 11
Investigation of High–Performance Computing Tools for Higher Education Institutions Using the IoE Grid Computing Framework

Nilamadhab Mishra
https://orcid.org/0000-0002-1330-4869
VIT Bhopal University, India

Getachew Mekuria Habtemariam
Addis Ababa Science and Technology University, Ethiopia

Anubhav De
https://orcid.org/0009-0002-7768-4212
VIT Bhopal University, India

ABSTRACT

The IoE Grid Computing Framework will be used to look into high-performance computing tools for higher education institutions. The primary and secondary data from higher education organizations are used to make the model and architecture. So, using a computational IoE grid and the supported toolkits, a model of the event was made. To see how well resources and related algorithms work, they are put to the test in different situations, such as by confirming the number of resources and users with different needs. To determine the level of demand for high-performance computing tools, data were gathered from particular colleges and universities. Before the data was fed into the system, preprocessing tasks like handling missing values and choosing features were completed. The findings demonstrate that these traits and the requirement for high-performance computing resources in higher education institutions are strongly related.

DOI: 10.4018/978-1-6684-9039-6.ch011

1. INTRODUCTION

Distributed resources have become a platform for the next generation of computing that is used to solve big problems in IoE grid computing. Although speeds and capacities are increasing, resource-intensive applications are becoming more important. To enable academics and users to access remote data, communication, computational, and storage resources, the framework and algorithm have been developed using the Computational GridSim Toolkit and Globus. The funding of parallel computing by the Department of Advanced Research Products Agency (DARPA) in the 1980s and 1990s resulted in computer architectures with multiple CPUs, multiple memory stores, and methods for dividing and allocating problems (Mishra, N. et al., 2015, 2019). The emergence of broadband internet access and the explosion of low-cost desktop computers in recent years have given rise to the idea of widely dispersed multi-processor computers. In a way, every computer that is connected to the internet is one node in an incredibly large computing machine. The goal of computational IoE grid computing is to make the best use of this machine for both financially and socially advantageous applications.

The computational stress on the CPU reveals that only 1% of what can be done by a typical computer is being used, leaving it idle 90% of the time. This means that there is a huge opportunity to use this power for other purposes (Ferreira, L. et al., 2003). Originally designed for globally distributed computing, computational IoE grid technologies are now being used in centralized computing facilities to produce high-performance resources that can be rented to businesses that only occasionally need such power. Computational IoE grid computing has the potential to reduce computation time on complex issues from a period of months to hours. This offers a major business opportunity if there are enough customers who need such a capability. Eleven computers were used to demonstrate the operation of computational IoE grid computing in 1995 at an IEEE/ACM computing conference in San Diego. Following that meeting, several organizations, including Ian Foster, Argonne National Labs, and DARPA, expressed interest in developing standards for connecting computers to a computational IoE grid (Al-Turjman, F., & Abujubbeh, M., 2019).

Computational IoE grid computing connects computers that are scattered over a wide geographic area, allowing their computing power to be shared. Just as the World Wide Web enables access to information, computer Computational grids enable access to computing resources. These resources include data storage capacity, processing power, sensors, visualization tools, and communications (Rubab, S. et al., 2015). Therefore, Computational grids can combine the resources of thousands of different computers to create massively powerful computing resources, accessible from a personal computer and used for multiple applications, in science, research, business, and beyond (Yousif, A. et al., 2022). Universities Computational grid, in particular, can be a powerful vehicle to realize the full research potential of universities, facilitating the sharing of distributed resources while respecting the distinct administrative priorities of individual resource centers, and building inter-disciplinary collaboration where it might not otherwise have occurred. Universities' Computational IoE grid provides a means for resource owners to trade their unused cycles for access to significantly more computing power when needed for short periods. In addition, the availability of a university Computational IoE grid can bring about organizational and cultural change, with participants more willing to invest in common infrastructure (networks, computing center floor space, and institutional storage) if it is felt that such infrastructure will be available for broad benefit and impact.

This research will bring together insight into university Computational grid-building efforts at a variety of higher institutions in various stages of their university Computational grid. The researcher wishes to share their experience (both good and bad) and perspectives gained while building their university Computational grids to help other institutions make informed decisions as they contemplate the uses of Computational IoE grid technology. The researcher also believes that the research community in higher education institutions at large can benefit from encouraging, participating in, and supporting this type of collaboration. Information technology among universities or other enterprises is intended to support users and applications as they are engaged in some aspect of the organization's business. In a typical higher education research institution, "business" includes research and teaching in addition to a myriad of administrative and organizational tasks. When deploying a University Computational grid, although researchers are most often the earliest users, it is important to plan for a wide range of eventual users and uses some - of which cannot be predicted - and architect both the processes and the technology to provide flexibility, efficiency, and capability for expansion (Zhou, Z. et al., 2019).

Perhaps the easiest way to discover and classify user groups that can benefit immediately from the use of a university Computational IoE grid is to describe the nature of the demands of the applications they use, rather than the disciplines in which they would be found. Typical applications poised to benefit from a University Computational IoE grid likely meet one or more of the following criteria (Brooks, T., 2022):

- Large, distributed group collaborations, predominantly externally focused
- Applications requiring significant computing cycles (i.e., lots of CPU time and bandwidth)
- Applications that have significant data handling requirements (e.g., access to or transfer of large or distributed data sets)
- Visualization-intensive applications

While applications meeting the above criteria can be found in a multitude of disciplines, high-performance computing users working in applied sciences and mathematics are frequently the most regular university Computational IoE grid users. Innovative users ready to apply Computational IoE grid technologies to their work may be found in all disciplines, including those not historically thought of as compute-intensive, such as the social sciences and the arts. This can be attributed, in part, to the increasing size and use of application databases and the increasing need to manipulate and visualize this data within a variety of disciplines.

A university Computational IoE grid is a Computational IoE grid with the following features.

- Leverages centralized university authentication and authorization.
- It allows heterogeneous resources, for example, different hardware and operating systems.
- It allows heterogeneous users with varying needs.
- Facilitates the sharing of computing resources, for example, sharing between departments within the university and/or sharing among universities.
- It provides the capability of integrating and coordinating distributed capabilities to solve a single problem or serve a single inquiry.

In Ethiopia, different initiatives are working as part of a national capacity-building program that includes SchoolNet, and WoredaNet which aims to provide connectivity and specialized applications for schools. The Education and Research Network (EthERNet) was launched in 2001 to build and deliver highly interconnected and high-performance networks for universities and other Educational and Research Institutions in Ethiopia. More specifically, EthERNet aimed to build and deliver high-performance networking that connected these higher institutions and similar institutions in the world, and by doing this to enable them to share educational resources and collaborate both within Ethiopia and globally. Since its establishment, EthERNet has provided services like a data center, video conferences, e-library, and technical support. Even though EthERNet is providing different services to Education and research, it still needs integration of other services, and service delivery based on the new model of computing, which is Computational grid-based computing, for a better service delivery strategy and strategic utilization of computing resources.

Computational IoE grid computing is a model of distributed computing that uses geographically and administratively disparate resources that are found on the network. These resources may include processing power, storage capacity, network bandwidth, specific data, and other hardware such as input and output devices. In Computational IoE grid computing, individual users can access computers and data transparently, without having to consider location, operating system, account administration, and other details.

Moreover, the details are abstracted, and the resources are virtualized. Computational IoE grid computing seeks to achieve the secure, controlled, and flexible sharing of resources (for example, multiple computers, software, and data) among various dynamically created virtual universities, which are generally set up for collaborative problem-solving and access to Computational IoE grid resources are limited to those who are part of the research. The creation of an application that can benefit from Computational IoE grid computing (faster execution speed, linking of geographically separated resources, and interoperation of software) typically requires the installation of complex supporting software and in-depth knowledge of how this complex supporting software works.

Most notably, a Computational IoE grid among universities builds a shared computational resource out of institutions existing investment in computer resources. It can be built in several different ways: combining and sharing individual computer systems and community clusters, combining and sharing homogeneous, distributed owned collections of machines, or combining and sharing individual clusters with middleware among those universities willing to use Computational IoE grid technology.

In universities, there are hundreds even thousands of computers and other resources that are idle in their computing cycle. Additionally, most universities use microcomputers as a server that can't able to manage and share all workstations and clients' computing resources. Furthermore, all universities were not implementing Computational IoE grid computing for resource sharing, but there is a need for much more computing cycles and storage to support research and training (Yang, G. et al., 2004).

Most empirically, universities experiences, some degree of inefficiency in the utilization of their computing resources such as CPU usage, storage, bandwidth, and hardware and software resources. One reason is: - as far as our knowledge, there are no researchers tried to solve problems in this area of Computational IoE grid computing in the proper utilization of computing resources when they are idle. The second reason is that service is very complex and customized in the building resource. Hence, this study will aim to assess and model a Computational IoE grid computing framework that collaborates and share computing resources, storage, and communication within Universities.

To this end, this research will intend to get answers to the following research questions.

- How the Computational IoE grid can evolve to meet jobs requirement by obtaining the required resources or sending jobs to another Computational IoE grid to execute?
- How can a job be submitted to the appropriate resource?
- To what extent does the model optimize resource usage?

The general objective of the study is to assess and model a Computational IoE grid computing framework as a solution to provide high-performance computing resources to research, training, and complex national outbreak problems by collaboration in real or near real-time within higher education institutions.

This study will attempt to investigate and achieve the following specific objectives.

- To review related literature about computational IoE grid computing in the higher education institution
- To create awareness of the employee and universities to voluntarily share their computing resources and be Computational IoE grid members
- To facilitate collaboration between universities through the provision of direct access to computers, software, storage, and bandwidth.
- To provide access to resources (remote resources) that cannot be accessed locally
- To coordinate the sharing of distributed and heterogeneous computing resources belonging to different universities.
- To assess and model a framework for utilizing unused and dispersed computational power and bandwidth as well as unused storage capacity.

The scope of the study model covers assessing and designing a Computational IoE grid computing framework as a solution to provide high-performance computing tasks that are used in research, training, national outbreaks for complex problems, and real-time collaboration within higher education institutions.

The model results in the sharing of computational resources, storage, and communication sensors by considering the relevant attributes, and primary and secondary data that are extracted from historical records available from universities. This is because the real dataset is available in real educational institutions. The study assesses constructs and frameworks based on the Globus and Computational gridSim Toolkit, including distributed computing, so that the researchers and users can use remote resources such as data, communication, computational, and storage resources.

2. RESOURCE NEEDS REVIEWS FOR COMPUTATIONAL IoE GRID

This study will follow empirical research to achieve its objective and articulate the research question by gathering the information and then studying and observing this information. For this purpose, a series of empirical research-based experiments are conducted. Empirical Research is data-based, which often comes up with conclusions that can be verified through experiments or observation. It is important to first collect the facts and their sources, and actively take steps to stimulate the production of desired information. In this study, both primary and secondary data will be collected. Primary data will be collected from selected higher education institutions, while secondary data will be collected from different works of literature written on Computational IoE grid computing. The modeling phase is to analyze and study the phenomena expressed in the research question. Thus, the model has been built to understand and analyze the phenomena. This model includes the computational assessment and the Computational IoE grid design based on Globus and Computational gridSim Toolkit. The framework will have been built so that the researchers and users can use remote resources such as data, communication, computational, and storage resources. Moreover, the novel technique with its algorithm has been established to handle and cope with the job allocation issues involved and communication. The developed framework is tested and then evaluated to ensure that the system provides an acceptable and accurate share of resources. To this end, a group discussion will be organized with stakeholders and experts in Computational IoE grid computing for a higher education institution.

Creating or having huge computational resources is a daunting task in the current circumstance; however, having a big processor, bandwidth, and storage is essential for universities to solve emergence and complex outbreak problems by collaborating. In today's world, it is necessary to make conscious efforts to build a high computational model. Hence, the primary beneficiaries of this study are national research institutions and Higher education institutions, the Ministry of Education, and the country in general. The study also has great significance for government institutions such as research, emergence or outbreak, and training institutions as they can collaborate to solve complex problems. However, it is used highly by researchers at higher education institutions who lack high computational resources.

In the face of stagnant or decreasing budgets, unfunded mandates, and growing demands for services, colleges, and universities are coming under increased pressure to deliver additional computational power for research and teaching to better position their institutions to attract the most productive faculty and the "best and brightest" students (Mishra, L. et al., 2020). As evidence of this trend, the 2005 EDUCAUSE survey of the top-ten issues confronting information technology managers today lists funding as the most pressing IT issue. The common institutional approach to purchasing more computers to satisfy increased demand has yielded mixed results. Although computers represent the largest class of equipment purchased in higher education, most computers remain underutilized, processing only approximately 5% of the time (Gebre, E. et al., 2015). Furthermore, these existing computers already have associated investments in place to handle the space, electricity, environmental control, and systems support costs, which represent the major costs of ownership. Being able to leverage this existing investment would demonstrate responsible stewardship of scarce funding resources. To do so, a growing number of institutions are turning to computational grids and Computational IoE grid computing. The word Computational IoE grid in Computational IoE grid computing comes from an analogy to electrical power in a Computational IoE grid with electrical power, there is a very simple interface (i.e., a wall socket) through which one connects by simply inserting a plug.

Knowledge regarding the ultimate source of the electricity or the specific transmission routes from the source to the socket is unnecessary for the proper use of electricity. Following this analogy, they provide the following definition: Computational IoE grid computing is a model of distributed computing that uses geographically and administratively disparate resources. In Computational IoE grid computing, individual users can access computers and data transparently, without having to consider location, operating system, account administration, and other details. In Computational IoE grid computing, the details are abstracted, and the resources are virtualized (Dutt, A. et al., 2017). Like other technologies, Computational IoE grid computing has sometimes been oversold, leading to disappointments and frustrations. The study's approach to Computational IoE grid computing is driven by pragmatism: the researcher sees computational IoE grid computing as the most practical means to satisfy computing needs and to make the best use of existing resources. From this perspective, the promise of Computational IoE grid computing is comprehensive but not overreaching: Computational IoE grid computing can meet the needs of many users and is achievable with current technologies (Desai, S. et al., 2019).

Both the Social and Commercial models of Computational IoE grid computing systems as described above follow a similar computational distribution scheme. The major difference is that in the social model, Computational IoE grid computers are distributed throughout homes and businesses around the world. These computers are volunteered to work on socially important problems and there is no financial exchange between the project sponsors and the computer owners. So far, a social model has not been used for a commercial project. In the commercial model, computing resources usually reside within one or more central computing centers controlled and managed by the company selling the service. Vendors must control these resources to achieve a quality of service (QoS) level that meets their contract with the client. It is also essential to maintain the security of the data and the software provided by the client (Jamshidi, M. et al., 2023).

3. PROSPECT COMPUTATIONAL IOE GRID COMPUTING FRAME

The specific steps for completing a Computational grid-computing job are illustrated and described in Figure 1.

Figure 1. Our proposed computational IoE grid computing frame

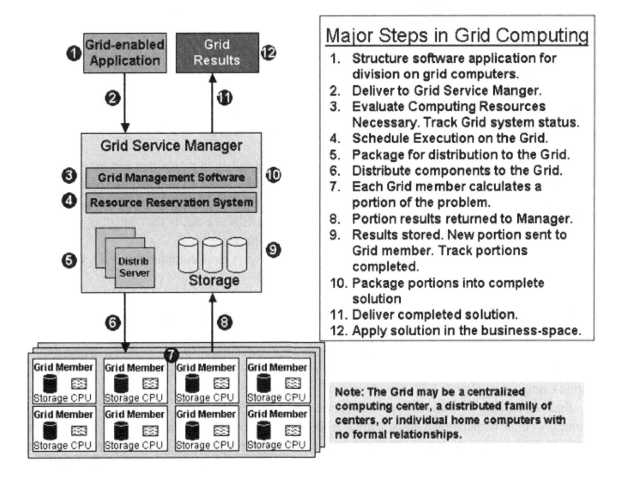

The Computational IoE grid may be a centralized computing center, a distributed family of centers, or individual home computers with no formal relationship. In Algorithm-1, we highlight only the major steps that are required for the computational and operational perspectives of IoE grid computing.

Algorithms-1: Computational Ioe Grid Computing

Major Steps
1. Structure of software application for division on-Computational IoE grid computers
2. Deliver to the Computational IoE grid service manager
3. Evaluate computing resources and Necessarily track Computational IoE grid system status
4. Schedule execution on the Computational grid
5. Package for distribution of the Computational grid
6. Distribute components to the Computational grid
7. Each Computational IoE grid member calculates the position of the problem
8. The portion result returned to the manager
9. Results stored: New portion sent to Computational IoE grid member; Track portions completed
10. Package portions into a complete solution
11. Deliver completed solution
12. Apply solutions in the business space

For several reasons, higher education is a perfect match for Computational IoE grid computing. Colleges and universities have the means, the motive, and the opportunity to realize the promise.

- Means: Higher education institutions have large concentrations of computing resources, ranging from desktops to high-end clusters, high-speed networking, access to regional and national-level networks (e.g., Internet2), and quite often, expertise with parallel and distributed computing.
- Motive: Research and education activities result in many diverse needs for computing resources that often exceed those available to individuals in the community.
- Opportunity: Higher education institutions are in many ways large communities, each with a history of sharing and an esprit corps.

3.1. Conceptual Framework of Computational IoE Grid Computing

The essence of computational IoE grid computing thinking originates from three types in a distributed system: Data Computational grid, Computational grid, scavenging Computational grid, and communication Computational grid. With the advancement of information communication technology (ICT), these three computing views have come together in the paradigm (Foster, I., & Kesselman, C., 2022). In context to the Computational grids, it aims at merging and sharing computational resources. There can be several ways in which computational resources can be merged. Any job or application can be remotely executed using Computational grids. A job can be logically partitioned and partitioned modules can be run parallel on computational grids. Lastly, there can be scenarios where a single job is required to run more than once to achieve the desired results, Computational grids can be used to execute such applications parallel on multiple Computational IoE grid nodes.

The bioinformatics Computational IoE grid integrates heterogeneous large-scale computing and storage facilities within the Computational IoE grid to provide bioinformatics supercomputing services for bioinformatics researchers through the Web interface, which is very user-friendly.

Furthermore, the Computational IoE grid can be seen as a framework for "flexible, secure, coordinated resource sharing among dynamic collections of individuals, institutions, and resources." It allows researchers in different administrative domains to use multiple resources for problem-solving and provides an infrastructure for developing larger and more complex applications potentially faster than with existing systems. China Computational IoE grid project (Li, Y. et al., 2018), founded by the Ministry of Education of China, is an attempt to achieve its goals by exploring the various resources on existing and well-developed internet infrastructure, CERNET (China Education and Research Network). In 2002, the China Ministry of Education (MOE) launched the largest Computational IoE grid computing project in China, called the China Computational IoE grid project, aiming to provide a nationwide Computational IoE grid computing platform and services for research and education purposes among 100 key universities in China. The underlying infrastructure for the China Computational IoE grid project is the CERNET, which began to run in 1994, covering 800 more universities, colleges, and institutes in China. Currently, it is the second-largest nationwide network in China. The China Computational IoE grid project is a long-term project with three different stages. The first stage period is from 2002 to 2005, covering 12 top universities in China. The focus for the first stage of the China Computational IoE grid project is on the platform and applications of the computation Computational IoE grid (e-science). These applications are varied in all scientific disciplines, from life science to computational physics. The second stage of the China Computational IoE grid project is from 2005 to 2007, covering 20 to 30 key universities in China. The focus will extend from computational IoE grid applications to information service Computational grids (e-info), including applications for distance learning Computational grids and digital Olympic Computational grids. The third stage is from 2007 to 2010, extending the coverage of the China Computational IoE grid project to all 100 key universities. The focus of the third stage of Computational IoE grid application is even more diverse; including instrument sharing (e-instrument). China Computational IoE Grid Supporting Platform (CGSP), integrates all kinds of resources in education and research environments, makes the heterogeneous and dynamic nature of resources transparent to the users, and provides reliable, secure, convenient, and transparent Computational IoE grid service for scientific computing and engineering research (Slama, S. B. et al., 2021).

Means: of the approximately 40,000 individual computers on campus, roughly 28,000 are in clusters, research laboratories, or classrooms or on the desktops of faculty and staff; the remaining 12,000 or so are in residences. These computers span several hardware configurations and capabilities. The campus has a mix of copper, fiber, and wireless networking. It is well-connected to regional, national, and international networks.

Motive: The need for computing continually increases in both intensity and breadth throughout academic institutions. More research and education are adopting computer-intensive methods such as stochastic simulation, Bayesian statistics, and Markov-chain Monte Carlo sampling to estimate an increasing number of parameters in ever larger and more complex models and data sets. The need for computing has already spread well beyond the traditionally computing-intensive areas mentioned previously into chemistry (e.g., structure and interaction modeling), life sciences (e.g., biophysics, conservation biology, landscape ecology, neurobiology, population genetics, systematics), social sciences (e.g., combinatorial optimization problems, modeling), and many other areas.

Opportunity: Numerous opportunities for better sharing of computing resources exist among the institutional groups traditionally associated with both computing resources and computing needs (e.g., computer science, physical sciences, engineering), as well as among those groups not traditionally associated with high-throughput computing needs.

The University of Maryland is now working toward utilizing campus Computational IoE grid expertise from the research community and creating a production resource that can be used routinely by students, faculty, and staff. The challenges will lie in training support staff, ensuring availability, integrating into the campus security model, and authenticating and training users. The benefit will be a potentially larger Computational IoE grid system that could utilize a significant fraction of the campus machines. According to the work (Haworth, T. J. et al., 2018), the Ox Computational grid is a result of a project undertaken by the Oxford University e-Research Centre, which began as a response to the increasing demand for high computation and storage capacity and the institution's desire to maintain its leading position in research and academics. Ox Computational grid offers a variety of computation and data storage resources to the users around the university thus providing them with the ability to perform compute-intensive tasks over the high throughput network. It also provides users with a single sign-on facility that enables them to sign in and access multiple resources without repeatedly providing their credentials. The idea is that computing resources within the university are underutilized and continue to lose their value every day and so by using the fraction of time in which they would normally be idle, high throughput computing would be achieved while maintaining the costs very low since no new computers would need to be acquired (O. Lodygensky et al., 2003). The Oxford Computational IoE grid is comprised of thousands of computers from departments and colleges and will continue to grow as more departments and colleges join the Computational grid. It allows users from around the university to prepare their long-running tasks and uses its resource management system to run the tasks on any machine from a department, college, or the supercomputing facilities offered by the OSC (Oxford Supercomputing Centre) or the National Computational IoE Grid Service (NGS) (Ang, A. et al., 2018).

The main problem of this research work is that it can only address computing resource problems for their university context by collaborating with mini and mainframe computers and a mere significant number of microcomputers. However, here in Ethiopia, most microcomputers are available. In addition, in Ethiopia, there are no independent institutions that facilitate complex problems such as national outbreaks and research and training. Hence, Universities can serve as a host for computational resources. Moreover, they further recommend modeling from the perspective of one country's universities.

This study followed empirical research to achieve its objective and articulated the research question by gathering the information and then studying and observing this information. To assess the need for computing resources, a series of empirical research-based experiments are conducted. Empirical Research is data-based, which often comes up with conclusions that can be verified through experiments or observation. It is important to first collect the facts and their sources, and actively take steps to stimulate the production of desired information.

In the Data gathering and analysis study, both primary and secondary data are collected. A survey of primary data is collected from purposively selected higher education, while secondary data will be collected from different works of literature written on Computational IoE grid computing. However, the researchers have conducted a pilot survey to understand the problem at a high level. The modeling phase is to analyze and study the phenomena expressed in the research question. Thus, the model has been built to understand and analyze the phenomena. This model includes the computational model and the Computational IoE grid design based on Globus and Computational gridSim Toolkit. In this phase, the framework has been built so that the researchers and users can use remote resources such as data, communication, computational, and storage resources.

Currently, high computing resources have been required, for instance, researchers in all universities can collaborate to find a solution for a problem that needs high computing resources and knowledge. Hence, a single computer cannot execute such kinds of tasks; we should design and implement a Computational IoE grid computing framework that can help the researchers to execute the task in the Computational grid. That is, the idle remote computers can execute and return the result. In the Computational gridSim toolkit, it is possible to create Processing Elements (PEs) with different speeds (measured in either MIPS or SPEC-like ratings) (Fahmideh, M. et al., 2022).

Then, one or more PEs can be put together to create a machine. Similarly, one or more machines can be put together to create a Computational IoE grid resource. Thus, the resulting Computational IoE grid resource can be a single processor, shared memory.

multiprocessors (SMP), or a distributed memory cluster of computers. These Computational IoE grid resources can simulate time - or space-shared scheduling depending on the allocation policy.

A single PE or SMP-type Computational IoE grid resource is typically managed by time-shared operating systems that use a round-robin scheduling policy for multitasking. The distributed memory multiprocessing systems (such as clusters) are managed by queuing systems, called space-shared schedulers, that executes a Computational IoE grid let by running it on a dedicated PE when allocated. The space-shared systems use resource allocation policies such as first-come-first-served (FCFS), backfilling, shortest-job-first served (SJFS), and so on. It should also be noted that resource allocation within high-end SMPs could also be performed using the space-shared schedulers (Yousif, A. et al., 2022). Multitasking and multiprocessing systems allow concurrently running tasks to share the system resources such as processors, memory, storage, I/O, and network by scheduling their use for very short time intervals. A detailed simulation of scheduling tasks in the systems would be complex and time-consuming. Hence, in Computational gridSim, we theoretical these physical entities and simulate their behavior using the process-oriented, discrete event "interrupt" with time an interval as large as the time required for the completion of the smallest remaining-time job. The Computational gridSim resources can send, receive, or schedule events to simulate the execution of jobs. It schedules self-events for simulating resource allocation depending on the scheduling policy and the number of jobs in queue or execution. The Computational gridSim resource simulator uses internal events to simulate the execution and allocation of PEs share with the Computational IoE grid let jobs. When jobs arrive, time-shared systems start their execution immediately and share resources among all jobs.

A complete algorithm for the simulation of time-share scheduling and execution is shown in Algorithm 1. If a newly arrived event happens to be an internal event whose tag number is the same as the most recently scheduled event, then it is recognized as a job completion event as stated in Algorithm-2.

ALGORITHM-2: Time-Shared Computational IoE grid Resource Event Handler ()

1. Wait for an event
2. If the external and Computational IoE grid lets arrival event, then:

```
 BEGIN /* a new job has arrived */
a. Allocate PE Share for Computational IoE grid lets Processed so far
b. Add arrived Computational IoE grid let to Execution _Set
```

```
c. Forecast completion time of all Computational IoE grid lets in Execution_Set
d. Schedule an event to be delivered at the smallest completion time
END
```

3.   If an event is internal and its tag value is the same as the recently scheduled internal event tag,

```
BEGIN /* a job finish event */
a. Allocate PE Share of all Computational IoE grid lets processed so far
b. Update the finished Computational IoE grid lets PE and Wall clock time pa-
rameters and send it back to the broker
 c. Remove the finished Computational girdle from the Execution_Set and add it
to Finished_Set
d. Forecast completion time of all Computational IoE grid lets in Execution_Set
e. Schedule an event to be delivered at the smallest completion time
END
```

4.   Repeat the above steps until the end of the simulation event is received

Depending on the number of Computational IoE grid lets in execution and the number of PEs in a resource, Computational gridSim allocates an appropriate amount of PE share to all Computational IoE grid lets for the event duration using the algorithm shown in Figure 8. It should be noted that the Computational IoE grid lets sharing the same PE would get an equal amount of PE share. The completed Computational IoE grid let is sent back to its originator (broker or user) and removed from the execution set. Computational gridSim schedules a new internal event to be delivered at the forecasted earliest completion time of the remaining Computational gridless. The major steps and computational process are depicted in Algorithm-3.

ALGORITHM-3: PE_Share_Allocation (Duration)

1.   Identify the total MI per PE for the duration and the number of PE that process one extra Computational gridlet

```
TotalMIperPE = MIPSRatingOfOnePE () *Duration
MinNoOfComputational gridletsPerPE = NoOfComputational gridletsInExec / NoOf-
PEs
NoOfPEsRunningOneExtraComputational gridlet = NoOfComputational gridletsInExec
% NoOfPEs
```

2.   Identify the maximum and minimum MI share that the Computational gridlet gets in the Duration

```
If(NoOfComputational gridletsInExec <= NoOfPEs), then:
MaxSharePerComputational gridlet = MinSharePerComputational gridlet = TotalMI-
perPE
MaxShareNoOfComputational gridlets = NoOfComputational gridletsInExec
```

```
Else /* NoOfComputational gridletsInExec > NoOfPEs */
MaxSharePerComputational gridlet = TotalMIperPE/ MinNoOfComputational gridlet-
sPerPE
MinSharePerComputational gridlet = TotalMIperPE/(MinNoOfComputational gridlet-
sPerPE+1)
MaxShareNoOfComputational gridlets = (NoOfPEs - NoOfPEsRunningOneExtraComputa-
tional gridlet) *
MinNoOfComputational gridletsPerPE
```

There are four tires in the architecture (Figure 2). The first tire is the campus Computational IoE grid center with high-performance computers and supercomputers. The second tire is the department tire, which includes the departments' supercomputers, PCs Clusters, instruments, and so on. These devices belong to different departments and institutions and are administered by different domains. The third tire is referred to as the servers belonging to different research groups. And the fourth tire is the user group.

There exists an agent in the second and third-tier. Its function is job scheduling, enhanced security checking, and so on. We call them the "department agent and research group agent".

Figure 2. The architecture of the campus IoE computational grid

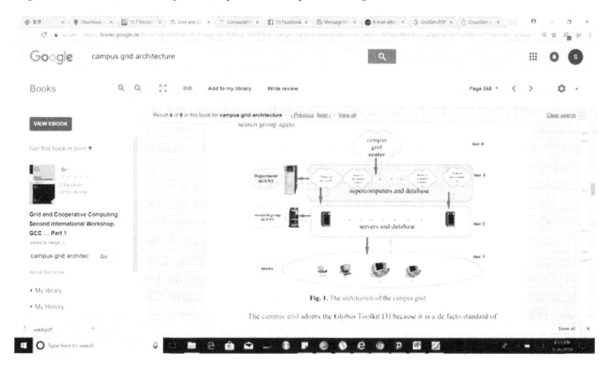

The above campus Computational IoE grid adopts and modifies the Globus Tool kit because it is a defector standard of Computational IoE grid computing. The Globus Toolkit focuses on areas of resource sharing management, data management, and security and information services. The performance of various scheduling disciplines for shared resources depends on the characteristics of workstation availabilities such as time of the day, day of the week, and schedule of the primary user. We use the trace of the utilization pattern of existing workstations in all sample universities to show the performance of the A Prototype Campus Virtual Super Computing Center (CVSCC) (Siddiqui, F. et al., 2012).

The core focus of our measurement and analysis was to address the following three questions:

- What are the characteristics of desktop CPU availability in all sample university settings?
- How do these characteristics affect the performance of Desktop Computational grids?
- Based on these characteristics, can we construct a model of High-Performance Computing that can satisfy the needs and requirements of the desktop Computational grids?

Using the previously described method, we collected 11 data sets from all purposively selected sample universities' enterprise Networks. The first one is Host availability. In a desktop Computational grid, hosts are volatile and the characterization of host volatility and reachability is essential to determine the aggregate computing power which can be harvested to CVSCC at any given time. Using traces that record only host availability for modeling desktop Computational grids is problematic because it is hard to relate uptimes to CPU cycles usable by a desktop Computational IoE grid application. Thus, traces that indicate only uptime are of dubious use for performance modeling of desktop Computational grids or driving simulations. To overcome these challenges, measuring CPU availability characterization is essential; measuring and characterizing this temporal structure is key for quantifying the performance or utility of desktop Computational grids. The second method of the studies measured the percentage of available CPU in all sample university's networks for CVSCC or desktop Computational IoE grid and analyzes temporal structures of this CPU availability for the desktop Computational grid. The data set from this method contains traces of host load or CPU utilization on groups of randomly selected workstations. These results are collected from the Operating System (OS) running on the user workstations. Several factors can affect an application's running time on a desktop Computational grid, which includes not only host availability but also CPU load and user activity. Measuring only the available CPU cycles from the host may not produce a good performance model as the result may already be affected by Operating System characteristics as seen in several instances (Lee, J. H. et al., 2022).

To minimize this gap from information collected directly on the desktop host about CPU Cycle availability, we performed the third type of measurement of CPU availability, of CPU availability perceived by an application running on CVSCC, which uses its resource management policies (e.g. task suspension for five minutes in case of keyboard/mouse activity). This method used to characterize the temporal structure of the CPU and analyze its impact on desktop Computational IoE grid applications would be the result of this method. The worker daemon recruitment policy determined the host's participation in the CVSCC. If the CPU availability is within the policy range; the host joins the CVSCC pool and is ready for utilization by the desktop Computational grid. Host availability can be used generally to determine the capacity of the desktop Computational IoE grid if all available desktop computers join CVSCC (Mohammadian, H. D., 2022). Host availability is a binary value that indicates whether a host is reachable for the desktop Computational IoE grid even if their CPU availability is not taken into consideration. The reason the host availability data set is collected is that it is usable for the desktop Computational IoE grid because the measurement method took into account the primary factors affecting CPU availability. Desktop and laptop computers attached to the data center of all selected sample universities' enterprise networks participated in this measurement.

We observed the total number of hosts available over time to determine at which times during the week and each day machines are most volatile. This can be useful for determining periods of interest when testing various scheduling heuristics. For example, it is observed that a daytime cycle of volatility begins in general during weekdays and business hours. During business hours, the machine availability range over time is relatively high and fluctuates with a large variance. During non-business hours and weekends, the variance range becomes relatively low with availability lower but more stable during business hours, the variance in the number of alive machines over time is relatively high, and during non-business hours, the number becomes relatively stable. In the case of Office Computer trace, the number of machines usually increases during business hours, whereas in the student Computer Lab trace, the number of machines can increase or decrease in a very small range. The number of Computers alive in the daytime is higher in number than at night. This difference in trends can be explained culturally (Sengupta, S., 2022). The maximum value of the CPU load traced is nearly 10%. As the traced data indicated, there is a trend of similar CPU load during working hours. The variance is small between traced records. During lunch and early in the morning CPU utilization is getting lower. Higher CPU load traced from 5 pm to 12 pm and then continually decrease through the rest of the night. The total mean value of the CPU load for this platform is close to 4%. The successful completion of a task is directly related to the size of availability intervals, i.e., intervals between two consecutive periods of unavailability. Here we show the distributions of various types of availability intervals for each platform, which characterize its volatility (Hajder, P., & Rauch, Ł., 2021).

4. DATA ANALYSIS AND EXPERIMENTATION

To design a Computational IoE grid framework and algorithms, analysis and interpretation of the data collected from the sampled respondents gathered from purposively selected first, second, and third-generation universities are conducted. The primary and secondary data which were obtained through a questionnaire, interview, pilot survey, and document analysis were presented, analyzed, and interpreted following the basic questions that were formulated in the study.

In the study, the researchers described the results of a comprehensive survey that was conducted in 11 different universities of the country to assess Scalable High-Performance Computing (HPC) requirements and satisfaction with existing services as well as solicit requirements for new and improved resource infrastructure provision within the existing available IT equipment and delivery methods aimed at high-performance scalable computing.

The survey was made between May to August 2017. Also, after the survey, data collection was made between October and February 2018. In the pilot survey, there were 22 fully completed surveys and 18 partially completed surveys returned. Only those respondents who submitted fully completed surveys were taken into consideration for this study.

In this section, we introduced the results of the Business Requirement Analysis for the HPC needs assessment survey. In the presentation of the results, the study has made use of the reporting features provided by the Statistical R computer programing survey tool. For each question in the survey, we visually presented the raw data collected and provide an explanatory paragraph analyzing the results and identifying significant trends where possible.

As described earlier in this report, one of the main aims of this survey was to determine the HPC infrastructure needs of higher institution researchers and academics, so the prevalence of responses from those with significant levels of needs is a pleasing result, and suggests that the target audience was appropriate.

Figure 3 determined the respondent's internet, CPU, and HPC memory need concerning their professional status (e.g. Diploma, master researcher, Ph.D. researcher, and Bachelor level workers). As it is illustrated in Figure 1, there was a reasonable balance in responses from diploma and master, doctoral, and bachelor level HPC memory needs that is all of them need an approximately equal percentage of memory resources to accomplish their task in comparison to the internet and CPU need. On the other hand, Bachelor researchers are the least users of the internet than Diploma users. However, like doctoral-level researchers, Masters level researchers highly depend on the internet hence, internet resource sharing becomes an issue and about 80% of master-level researcher wants to use the HPC internet from the Computational grid. As can be seen from Figure 1, HPC CPU's need is more or less similar at all levels of research.

Figure 3. Characteristics of resource and education level

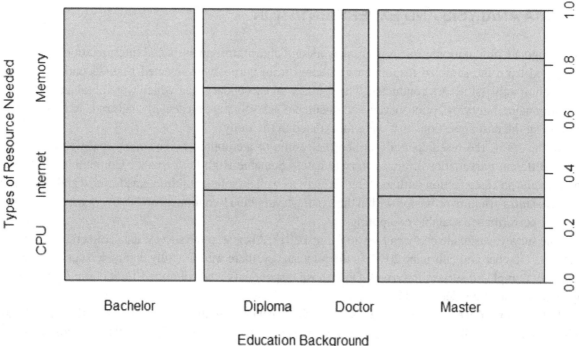

The second research question was included to determine those who participated in respondents in the survey. As it is illustrated in Figure 4, approximately equal ratios (50%) of bachelor's and diplomas have participated in the survey. Moreover, a large number of master-level researchers participated as compared to the least number of doctoral-level researcher respondents are participated in the survey.

In the study, for simplicity, the respondents are discretized into a suitable range of professionals. For instance, all respondents below diploma levels are categorized (discretized into diploma education level). Similarly, all researchers above the master's level of education are discretized into doctoral researchers and so on.

Figure 4. Candidates' education distributions

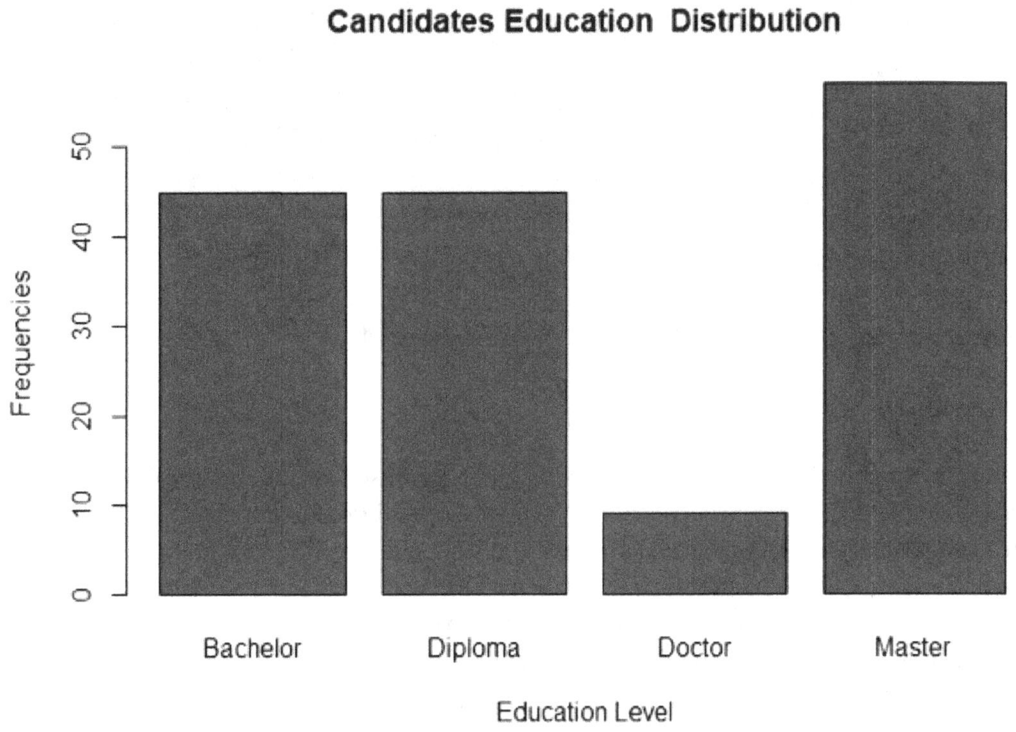

Candidates Education Distribution

In all respondents, when we compare the need for high-performance computing resources between the internet, memory, and processor, as can be seen in Figures 5-6, internet HPC is more highly needed than other resources. However, both CPU and memory resources are needed almost equally by all respondents.

In this study, we tried to include the Assistant level (diploma and bachelor degree of researchers and workers), junior level (assistant lecturer and lecturers), and senior level (Assistant professor and above the level of researchers and workers) at the university. As can be seen in Figure 6, the highest level of respondents is assistant level at about 85%, whereas the lowest level of respondents is junior level at approximately 25%. The senior-level respondents are almost 40% of participation.

Figure 5. Computing resource distribution.

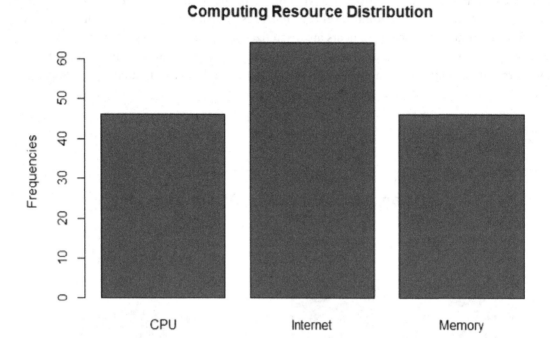

In this study, to analyze the HPC needs Regression analysis is used to find trends in data. As can be seen in Table 1. Predictors (Constant) is Resource_Type_Share and Predictors (Constant) is Resource_Type_Share. The result shows that the standard error is 0.923. Whereas, the sign F change is 0.43.

Analysis of Variance (ANOVA) (Table 2) is a statistical method used to test differences between two or more means. It may seem odd that the technique is called "Analysis of Variance" rather than "Analysis of Means." As can be seen in the figure, it is appropriate because inferences about means are made by analyzing variance. The result shows that the mean square is 0.533 and 0.851 respectively.

The difference between the observed value of the dependent variable (y) and the predicted value (ŷ) is called the residual (e). Each data point has one residual. Both the sum and the mean of the residuals are equal to zero. The summary is listed in Table 3.

A histogram is the most commonly used graph to show frequency distributions. The regression analysis of the histogram is seen in the figure. A frequency distribution shows how often each different value in a set of data occurs. As is seen in Figure 7, it looks symmetric normal distribution of respondents based on educational background.

A P-P plot compares the empirical cumulative distribution function of a variable with a specified theoretical cumulative distribution function F (). ... Like Q-Q plots and probability plots, P-P plots can be used to determine how well a theoretical distribution models a data distribution of all respondents. As is seen in Figure 8, the distribution is linear.

Figure 6. Distribution within candidates' experience

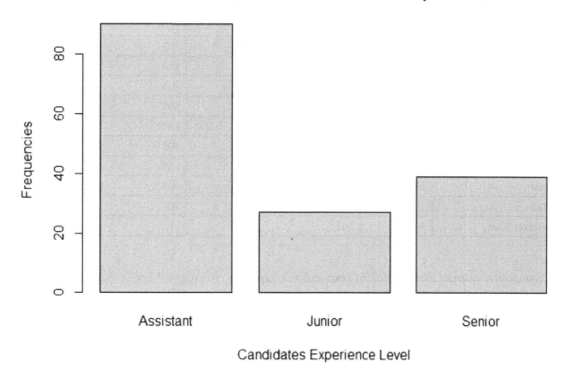

Table 1. Predictors: (Constant), Resource_Type_Share

Model Summary									
					Change Statistics				
Model	R	R Square	Adjusted R Square	Std. error in the Estimate	R Square Change	F Change	df1	df2	Sig. F Change
1	.064[a]	.004	-.002	.923	.004	.626	1	154	.430

Table 2. ANOVAb

	Model	Sum of Squares	df	Mean Square	F	Sig.
1	Regression	.533	1	.533	.626	.430[a]
	Residual	131.076	154	.851		
	Total	131.609	155			

a. Predictors: (Constant), Resource_Type_Share ;
b. Dependent Variable: EDU_BG

Table 3. Dependent Variable: EDU_BG]

Residuals Statistics					
	Minimum	Maximum	Mean	Std. Deviation	N
Predicted Value	2.11	2.26	2.19	.059	156
Std. Predicted Value	-1.298	1.298	.000	1.000	156
Standard Error of Predicted Value	.074	.121	.102	.023	156
Adjusted Predicted Value	2.09	2.28	2.19	.060	156
Residual	-1.262	1.814	.000	.920	156
Std. Residual	-1.368	1.966	.000	.997	156
Stud. Residual	-1.380	1.973	.000	1.002	156
Deleted Residual	-1.284	1.826	-.001	.930	156
Stud. Deleted Residual	-1.384	1.992	.000	1.005	156
Mahal. Distance	.000	1.685	.994	.831	156
Cook's Distance	.000	.017	.006	.005	156
Centered Leverage Value	.000	.011	.006	.005	156

Figure 7. Symmetric normal distribution of respondents based on educational background

Histogram

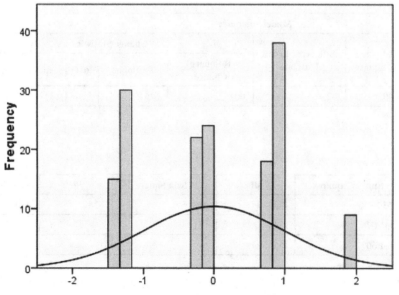

Dependent Variable: EDU_BG

Mean =-2.08E-17
Std. Dev. =0.997
N =156

Figure 8. Normal P-P plot

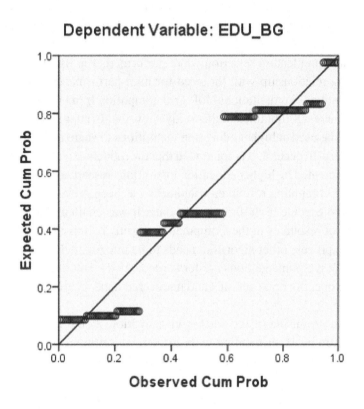

5. CONCLUSION AND RECOMMENDATIONS

Collaborative working, for example in research, to share high-performance computing resources issue is given less emphasis throughout higher education institutions. In Ethiopia, although the government gives more emphasis to the higher education research sector, collaborative working and sharing high-performance computing resources are not getting sufficient attention. The major challenge for high-performance resource sharing and collaborative working in the country is the lack of technical skills and resources. In Ethiopia, due to the lack of high-performance computing resources and collaborative working, many problems such as outbreaks and high dimensional data science which may lead to the country to serious problems have not yet been implemented. Lacks of knowledge among higher education researchers and communities, the allocation of budgets for higher education, and the lack of awareness about computational IoE grid computing are the challenges that become an obstacle to addressing the problem. We assessed the need for computational IoE grid computing in higher education institutions for high-dimensional data research to share memory, CPU, and bandwidth. We also design high-level algorithms of time and resource-sharing algorithms. Moreover, we assess and visualized the result using the statistical R programming language toolkit, and for resource framework modeling and scheduling simulation, we used Computational gridSim. It supports different application models that can be mapped to resources for execution by developing simulated application schedulers. The management of resources and scheduling of applications in such large-scale distributed systems is a complex undertaking. To prove the effectiveness of resources and associated algorithms, their performance needs to be evaluated under different scenarios such as verifying the number of resources and users with different requirements. To assess the need for high-performance computational resources data collected from purposively 11 selected higher education institutions were taken. Before feeding the data, data preprocessing activities such as handling missing values, and feature selection, were performed. The findings noticeably show that the attributes have a strong relationship with the need for high-performance computational resources for higher education institutions. Computational IoE grid computing framework and high-level algorithms have been designed. The results obtained in this study show that Computational IoE grid computing is a technology that should be used at higher education institutions to share and collaborate work with other researchers in the country. In general, it is concluded that the models experimented with within this study show that awareness is created by higher education institutions researchers, and communities. Thus, the applicability of sharing computing resources voluntarily has been proven as a useful approach for supporting researchers who execute high-dimensional data. It was challenging to integrate the algorithm that gives the security of resources in the Computational grid. To substantially support students in the field of study selection process other algorithm needs to be integrated. Hence, based on the findings of this study, the following recommendations are forwarded. As a result, the following recommendations are given based on the opening opportunities and uncovered areas by this study.

- Although this is a promising result, further investigation should be done to increase the performance of the system by experimenting with different algorithms.
- For future work, researchers would develop and improve this system by developing algorithms for the security of Computational IoE grid resources.
- The researcher recommended for future works include and share all the available resources to the Computational IoE grid and being Computational IoE grid members.
- Further study should be done on the integration of all higher education institutions and collaborative working by sharing computational resources

REFERENCES

Al-Turjman, F., & Abujubbeh, M. (2019). IoT-enabled smart grid via SM: An overview. *Future Generation Computer Systems*, *96*, 579–590. doi:10.1016/j.future.2019.02.012

Ang, A., Chen, B., Goetzmann, W. N., & Phalippou, L. (2018). Estimating private equity returns from limited partner cash flows. *The Journal of Finance*, *73*(4), 1751–1783. doi:10.1111/jofi.12688

Brooks, T. (2022). *Authentication Devices in Fog-Mobile Edge Computing Environments Through a Wireless Grid Resource Sharing Protocol*. arXiv preprint arXiv:2207.03346.

Desai, S., Alhadad, R., Chilamkurti, N., & Mahmood, A. (2019). A survey of privacy preserving schemes in IoE enabled smart grid advanced metering infrastructure. *Cluster Computing*, *22*(1), 43–69. doi:10.100710586-018-2820-9

Dutt, A., Ismail, M. A., & Herawan, T. (2017). A systematic review on educational data mining. *IEEE Access : Practical Innovations, Open Solutions*, *5*, 15991–16005. doi:10.1109/ACCESS.2017.2654247

Fahmideh, M., Yan, J., Shen, J., Ahmad, A., Mougouei, D., & Shrestha, A. (2022). *Knowledge Management for Cloud Computing Field*. arXiv preprint arXiv:2202.07875.

Foster, I., & Kesselman, C. (2022). *The history of the grid*. arXiv preprint arXiv:2204.04312.

Gebre, E., Saroyan, A., & Aulls, M. W. (2015). Conceptions of Effective Teaching and Perceived Use of Computer Technologies in Active Learning Classrooms. *International Journal on Teaching and Learning in Higher Education*, *27*(2), 204–220.

Hajder, P., & Rauch, Ł. (2021). Moving Multiscale Modelling to the Edge: Benchmarking and Load Optimization for Cellular Automata on Low Power Microcomputers. *Processes (Basel, Switzerland)*, *9*(12), 2225. doi:10.3390/pr9122225

Haworth, T. J., Clarke, C. J., Rahman, W., Winter, A. J., & Facchini, S. (2018). The FRIED grid of mass-loss rates for externally irradiated protoplanetary discs. *Monthly Notices of the Royal Astronomical Society*, *481*(1), 452–466. doi:10.1093/mnrasty2323

Jamshidi, M., Yahya, S. I., Nouri, L., Hashemi-Dezaki, H., Rezaei, A., & Chaudhary, M. A. (2023). A Super-Efficient GSM Triplexer for 5G-Enabled IoT in Sustainable Smart Grid Edge Computing and the Metaverse. *Sensors (Basel)*, *23*(7), 3775. doi:10.339023073775 PMID:37050835

Lee, J. H., Yang, G., Kim, C. H., Mahajan, R. L., Lee, S. Y., & Park, S. J. (2022). Flexible solid-state hybrid supercapacitors for the internet of everything (IoE). *Energy & Environmental Science*, *15*(6), 2233–2258. doi:10.1039/D1EE03567C

Li, Y., Guo, Y., & Chen, S. (2018, September). A survey on the Development and Challenges of the Internet of Things (IoT) in China. In *2018 International Symposium in Sensing and Instrumentation in IoT Era (ISSI)* (pp. 1-5). IEEE. 10.1109/ISSI.2018.8538281

Lodygensky, O., Fedak, G., Néri, V., Cordier, A., & Cappello, F. (2003). Monte Carlo computation on a global computing platform. Proceedings of Computing in High Energy and Nuclear Physics (CHEP2003).

Mishra, L., Gupta, T., & Shree, A. (2020). Online teaching-learning in higher education during lockdown period of COVID-19 pandemic. *International Journal of Educational Research Open*, *1*, 100012. doi:10.1016/j.ijedro.2020.100012 PMID:35059663

Mishra, N. (2019). Data Science and Knowledge Analytic Contexts on IoE Data for E-BI Application Case. In Edge Computing and Computational Intelligence Paradigms for the IoT (pp. 100-126). IGI Global. doi:10.4018/978-1-5225-8555-8.ch007

Mishra, N., Lin, C. C., & Chang, H. T. (2015). A cognitive adopted framework for IoT big-data management and knowledge discovery prospective. *International Journal of Distributed Sensor Networks*, *11*, 718390–718391. doi:10.1155/2015/718390

Mohammadian, H. D. (2022). Mapping the Future SMEs' HR Competencies via IoE Technologies and 7PS Model Through the Fifth Wave Theory. In *Management and Information Technology in the Digital Era* (Vol. 29, pp. 141–171). Emerald Publishing Limited. doi:10.1108/S1877-636120220000029010

Rubab, S., Hassan, M. F., Mahmood, A. K., & Shah, N. M. (2015). Grid Computing in Light of Resource Management Systems. *RE:view*.

Sengupta, S. (2022). IoE: An Innovative Technology for Future Enhancement. In *Computer Vision and Internet of Things* (pp. 19–28). Chapman and Hall/CRC. doi:10.1201/9781003244165-3

Siddiqui, F., Zeadally, S., Alcaraz, C., & Galvao, S. (2012, July). Smart grid privacy: Issues and solutions. In *2012 21st International Conference on Computer Communications and Networks (ICCCN)* (pp. 1-5). IEEE.

Slama, S. B., Choubani, F., Benavente-Peces, C., & Abdelkarim, A. (Eds.). (2021). Innovative and Intelligent_Technology-Based Services for Smart Environments-Smart Sensing and Artificial Intelligence. In *Proceedings of the 2nd International Conference on Smart Innovation, Ergonomics and Applied Human Factors (SEAHF'20)*. CRC Press.

Yang, G., Jin, H., Li, M., Xiao, N., Li, W., Wu, Z., Wu, Y., & Tang, F. (2004). Grid computing in China. *Journal of Grid Computing*, 2(2), 193–206. doi:10.100710723-004-4201-2

Yousif, A., Alqhtani, S. M., Bashir, M. B., Ali, A., Hamza, R., Hassan, A., & Tawfeeg, T. M. (2022). Greedy firefly algorithm for optimizing job scheduling in iot grid computing. *Sensors, 22*(3), 850.

Yousif, A., Alqhtani, S. M., Bashir, M. B., Ali, A., Hamza, R., Hassan, A., & Tawfeeg, T. M. (2022). Greedy Firefly Algorithm for Optimizing Job Scheduling in IoT Grid Computing. *Sensors (Basel), 22*(3), 850. doi:10.339022030850 PMID:35161596

Zhou, Z., Liao, H., Gu, B., Mumtaz, S., & Rodriguez, J. (2019). Resource sharing and task offloading in IoT fog computing: A contract-learning approach. *IEEE Transactions on Emerging Topics in Computational Intelligence*, 4(3), 227–240. doi:10.1109/TETCI.2019.2902869

KEY TERMS AND DEFINITIONS

Computational Grid Resource Scheduling and Sharing: The process of modular Grid Computing involves the disaggregation of a system's available computing resources. GPUs, networking, storage, and memory are just examples of the available resources. After that, the requisite computer resources and assets are integrated by IT teams, and the resulting combination is then shared to support particular services or applications.

Computational IoE Grid Computing: A Distributed analytical Platform With Multiple Uses That Is Built on Edge Computing and Computational Intelligence and Is Applied to Smart Grids.

Computational IoE Grid Resources, and Collaboration, Model, and Design: The structure of a GRID, which may be used in the processes of engineering optimization and design search. Our system will offer seamless access to an intelligent knowledge library, a variety of cutting-edge optimization and search tools, industrial-grade analytical programs, as well as distributed computing and data resources.

We lay a key emphasis on the open standards technologies that have to be leveraged for the system to be effectively executed, and we present some specific instances of how these technologies are now being put to use in real-world settings.

Computing Tools for Higher Education Institutions: College and university campuses are dynamic and complicated ecosystems of learning and discovery that cross both the borders of individual disciplines and the boundaries of the campuses themselves. Investigate the several ways in which Google for Education might be able to help you manage the complication of the issue while also maintaining everyone's connectivity and productivity.

Data Standardization: Data standardization is the process of developing standards and converting data from various sources into a uniform format that complies with the standards to enhance the model's overall effectiveness in making predictions.

High-Performance Computing: The ability to quickly assess data and carry out complex calculations without error by the collection of disparate resources that will become feasible thanks to the implementation of these Grids.

Internet of Everything (IoE): Consisting of a wide variety of appliances, devices, and other items that are all linked to the internet on a worldwide scale.

Universities Computational Grid: University Computational Grids are a type of Grid that is currently being built by a huge number of research groups situated in universities, research institutes, and businesses all over the world. These research groups are located in a variety of countries. The objective of resolving large-scale data-intensive problems in the disciplines of research, engineering, and business will be made possible by the aggregation of distributed resources that will be made possible by these Grids.

Section 3
Challenges and New Avenues

Chapter 12
Moving Towards Internet of Behaviors:
Transforming Business Models With Blockchain

Busra Ozdenizci Kose

https://orcid.org/0000-0002-8414-5252

Gebze Technical University, Turkey

ABSTRACT

The Internet of Behaviors (IoB) is an emerging trend that aims to revolutionize human interactions by analyzing and influencing behavior using data from connected devices. This study explores the importance of blockchain technology in addressing the IoB challenges and enhancing the security and privacy of IoB business models. Blockchain technology provides a decentralized and transparent platform for behavioral data storage and sharing, mitigating privacy concerns. Individuals are empowered with control over their personal data through smart contracts and decentralized identifiers, enabling them to decide how their data is accessed and used within IoB systems. In this study, significant blockchain-based solutions and approaches are presented that can enhance IoB business models through examples. Exploration of blockchain potential in IoB systems will ensure new insights for further advancement and evolution of the IoB paradigm.

INTRODUCTION

The Internet of Things (IoT) refers to a group of physical objects connected to each other that gather and share information over the Internet. These objects can include a wide range of items such as smart appliances, wearable technology, sensors, vehicles, and much more. They are equipped with unique identifiers and can transfer data over a network without requiring human-to-human or human-to-computer interaction (Atzori et al., 2010; Li et al., 2015; Whitmore et al., 2015; Al-Fuqaha et al., 2015). IoT devices can collect and exchange data, providing insights that can be used for a variety of purposes, such as improving efficiency, reducing costs, and enhancing user experiences.

DOI: 10.4018/978-1-6684-9039-6.ch012

The use of Artificial Intelligence (AI) technologies with IoT has become increasingly popular and has been widely adopted in various areas of our lives. This integration allows for self-controlled physical objects to collect and share information over the Internet, forming an intricate network of data stored in the cloud. The collection and analysis of this information started to provide valuable insights into customer behavior, preferences, and expectations (Javaid et al., 2021; Mezair et al., 2022).

The application of AI and IoT is diverse, including but not limited to smart homes, smart energy management, surveillance cameras, healthcare, and connected vehicles. (Mezair et al., 2022). As a result of the widespread adoption of AI with IoT in modern society and their continuous evolution, the Internet of Behaviors (IoB) paradigm has emerged inevitably which analyzes the collected valuable data, in other words behavioral patterns and deduce people's needs, interests, and preferences.

As a growing trend over the world, the IoB paradigm combines science, data processing, and the psychology of behavior (Javaid et. al., 2021). IoB aims to revolutionize the way we interact with the world around us by using valuable data from connected devices to monitor, analyze, and influence human behavior. As Gartner indicates 'Internet of Behavior collects the digital dust of people's lives from a variety of sources, and public or private organizations can use this information to influence behavior' (Gartner, 2020). IoB paradigm attempts to understand the data collected from users' online activity from a behavioral psychology perspective. The concept is based on the idea that every digital interaction of a person with their devices generates data that can be analyzed in order to create a "behavioral profile". Afterwards, this behavioral data can be used to predict and influence the future behavior of a person. It seeks to address how to understand the data and apply this understanding to create valuable services or market new products, all from a human psychology perspective (Stary, 2020; Sun et al., 2022; Zhao et al., 2023).

Sensors and other similar devices that can collect data about an individual's behavior are essential tools for the creation of behavioral profile. These devices can include wearables, smartphones, smart home devices, fitness trackers, cameras, and more. However, to move towards the IoB, an integrated use of several technologies is necessary, such as big data and robust data analytics, artificial intelligence and machine learning algorithms, natural language processing (NLP), cloud computing, blockchain, augmented reality (AR), virtual reality (VR), and even 5G for faster and more reliable connectivity, which enables real-time data processing and analysis.

IoB paradigm has enormous potential to transform business models. Simply, a business model can be defined as a structured strategy that delineates how a company generates value, delivers it to customers, and captures revenue. It includes the key components and approaches employed to sustain the business's operations. IoB paradigm uses data analysis and behavioral insights to develop new products and services, optimize existing ones, and improve customer experiences in business models (Sun et al., 2022; Afor et al., 2022). For example, in the healthcare sector, IoB can be used to track an individual's health behavior, including diet, exercise, sleep patterns, and medication adherence, to provide personalized health recommendations, monitor chronic conditions, and improve patient outcomes. In the retail industry, IoB can help businesses analyze customer interactions with digital products and services to understand their preferences, needs, and buying behavior, enabling them to create personalized marketing campaigns, recommend relevant products, and enhance customer loyalty. IoB can also be used to monitor customer feedback on social media and other online platforms, allowing companies to respond quickly to customer complaints and improve their brand reputation.

While the IoB has the potential to revolutionize the way we interact with the world around us, it is essential to develop appropriate regulations and safeguards to ensure that the IoB business model is ethical and respects people's rights and privacy. As the IoB relies on collecting and analyzing vast amounts of personal data from individuals, it raises concerns about potential privacy violations and risks associated with the misuse of personal information. Without proper regulations and safeguards in place, there is a risk that this data could be misused, leading to negative consequences for individuals, such as identity theft or unauthorized use of personal information. At this point, Blockchain technology should be seen as a significant enabler of IoB business models as it can provide a decentralized and transparent ledger for data storage, sharing, and decision-making in IoB applications.

This chapter sheds light on the IoB paradigm and explore the value of blockchain technology in the development of IoB business models. Blockchain, as a burgeoning trend, holds the potential to address key IoB concerns while opening doors to new use cases and applications that can empower IoB business models. The study defines five significant solutions that blockchain offers to improve IoB implementations, providing detailed insights into each solution's potential impact and benefits. The study seeks to contribute to the existing body of knowledge on IoB and blockchain by providing valuable insights, recommendations, and a deeper understanding of their synergy in the context of business models.

To accomplish this study's objectives, a bibliographic research method has been employed, involving a systematic examination of existing IoB studies and applications to draw conclusions about the contributions of blockchain technology. Bibliographic research, also known as bibliographic analysis, is a research approach that involves the review and evaluation of preexisting literature and source materials related to a specific subject or topic. Within context of the study, this method encompasses the comprehensive collection and evaluation of information found in published materials, including peer reviewed articles, research papers, conference proceedings, and relevant documents about IoB paradigm.

In the light of all this information, the chapter first outlines a brief information about Internet of Behaviors with the emerging IoB pyramid. Later, the dimensions of IoB including technology, business and challenges, ethical and privacy implications are discussed. The potential of blockchain as a decentralized ledger technology in IoB models is investigated through examples. Finally, this chapter examines the question of how blockchain technology is creating value for IoB ecosystem in terms of particularly security and privacy, and also explores it can be integrated with IoB business models. As the research landscape concerning IoB and its implementations continues to evolve, this study will provide valuable insights for the development of IoB business models, benefiting various stakeholders, including businesses and policymakers.

TOWARDS INTERNET OF BEHAVIOR

Gartner describes IoB as an extension of the IoT that connects data from multiple sources to understand behavior patterns and preferences. Gartner predicts that by 2025, over half of the world's population will be subject to at least one IoB program, whether it be commercial or government-related (Gartner, 2020). According to another report by Precedence Research (2021), 'the global internet of behaviors (IoB) market size was valued at USD 391.5 billion in 2021 and is expected to surpass around USD 2,143.57 billion by 2030, poised to grow at a compound annual growth rate (CAGR) of 20.79% from 2022 to 2030'. In addition, the report highlights that by 2025, it is projected that over 40% of the global population may potentially be enrolled in at least one IoB program and this enrollment would involve digital tracking of individuals with the purpose of influencing human behavior.

The major factors driving market growth owing to the increasing adoption of IoT devices, the increasing developments in machine learning abilities globally, the rising demand for advanced customer experience management tools as key drivers of growth in the IoB market, and the growing trend of data-driven decision-making (Precedence Research, 2021; Research Nester, 2023).

The pyramid of DIKW (data, information, knowledge, wisdom) has gained widespread recognition as a framework that guides the process from data collection to optimizing their utilization. From the perspective of DIKW pyramid, it can be observed that IoT systems generally interact with the lower layers of data and information, leaving a significant gap between the information layer and the wisdom layer. As illustrated in Figure 1, IoT is responsible for converting data into information, whereas the IoB has a potential to take our knowledge to the level of practical wisdom (Javaid et. al., 2021; Sun et al., 2022).

As a growing market, IoB should be seen as a way to leverage technology to understand people's behavior and preferences, and use this information to create personalized and tailored experiences for individuals. By analyzing data from wearable devices or social media platforms, companies can gain insights into people's health behaviors or shopping habits and use this information to create targeted marketing campaigns or personalized health recommendations.

IoB and Society 5.0

IoB is closely related to the Society 5.0 concept originated in Japan, which envisions a future society characterized by the integration of advanced technologies such as AI, IoT, big data, and robotics, with the goal of improving the quality of life for its citizens. By understanding Society 5.0, we can better appreciate the role of technology in addressing complex social issues, which can help us frame our approach to IoB.

Figure 1. Context of IoB

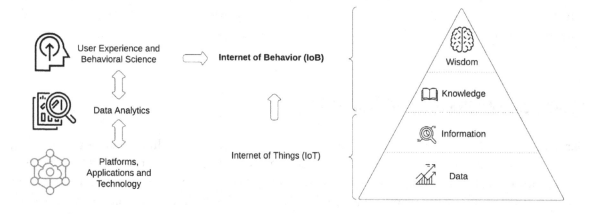

Society 5.0 builds upon previous societal stages, such as hunter-gatherer societies (Society 1.0), agricultural societies (Society 2.0), industrial societies (Society 3.0), and information societies (Society 4.0). Society 5.0 aims to create a human-centric society that solves various social problems using of

technology (Fukuyama, 2018; Shiroishi et al., 2018; Narvaez et al., 2021). For instance, cities can use IoT sensors to monitor air and water quality, traffic patterns, and other factors that affect the health and well-being of their residents. AI algorithms can then analyze this data in real-time to identify trends and patterns, which can inform decisions about city planning, resource allocation, and emergency response. As a broader concept for the next stage of human civilization, Society 5.0 aims to develop a highly advanced, interconnected and sustainable society, where technology is used to enhance human well-being.

On the other side, IoB paradigm can be used to create more efficient systems for transportation, healthcare, and other public services, as well as to create more personalized services for individuals. IoB business models can help organizations and governments gain insights into how people behave in different contexts and use that information to make more informed decisions (Bzai et al., 2022; Sun et al., 2022; Zhao et al., 2023). For example, by analyzing data from smart homes, governments can predict and prevent accidents before they occur, thereby improving public safety. Similarly, by analyzing data from healthcare wearables, doctors can diagnose and treat diseases more accurately, leading to better health outcomes for patients. By collecting and analyzing data on human behavior, IoB can provide valuable insights for creating solutions that align with Society 5.0's goals of enhancing well-being and creating a sustainable society. In this context, Society 5.0 and IoB should be seen as two complementary concepts that hold great potential for transforming society by making it more connected, efficient, and data-driven.

IoB Architecture and Technologies

There are various generic models and workflows for the architecture of the IoB (Sun et al., 2022; Elayan et al., 2022; Zhao et al., 2023). As illustrated in Figure 2, a generic IoB system comprises five components that work together to enable the collection, analysis, and use of data to influence user behavior.

(1) Behavioral Data Sensing: At the core of the IoB architecture lies the first layer, which comprises the diverse data sources that generate behavioral data. These sources include wearable devices, smartphones, social media platforms, and IoT sensors, among others. By leveraging existing IoT infrastructures, this layer collects raw data from users, such as signals, text, images, voice, and video, and uses pattern recognition or AI algorithms to perceive and recognize human behaviors. The behavioral data collected through this layer, which captures people's actions, preferences, and attitudes, is then used to build behavior models and generate insights that can inform personalized experiences and targeted interventions.

(2) Behavioral Data Computing: The second layer of the IoB architecture involves the processing of behavioral data, which entails collecting and analyzing data using various techniques such as data mining, machine learning, and natural language processing. This layer encompasses the concept of behavior computing, which refers to all computational operations involved in modeling, analyzing, understanding, and predicting human behaviors, behavioral interactions, and relationships, behavioral patterns, behavior generation, and decomposition. The aim is to extract meaningful insights from the data and turn them into actionable recommendations. The study by Zhao et al. (2023) proposes four forms of behavior computing which are intention inference, behavior derivation, behavior programming, and behavior-chain optimization.

(3) Behavioral Insights Derivation: The third layer of the IoB architecture is responsible for making informed decisions based on the results of behavioral data computing and pertains to the insights that are derived from the processed data. These insights are invaluable in understanding customer

behavior, enhancing customer experiences, catalyzing behavioral change, and providing intelligent services to users by invoking IoT devices. It can influences users' behaviors by leveraging the insights generated from the data, thereby facilitating personalized experiences and interventions.

(4) Behavioral Interventions Generation: The fourth layer of the IoB architecture encompasses the different interventions that can be employed to influence people's behavior, based on the insights derived from the data. These interventions may comprise personalized recommendations, targeted advertising, incentive programs, and more. This layer is focused on the desired outcomes of the IoB initiatives. These outcomes could be varied, such as improved health outcomes or more streamlined business operations.

In order to run the IoB architecture, several technologies work together to collect, analyze, and interpret the behavioral data. Some of the key technologies involved in IoB business models are presented as follows (Javaid et. al., 2021; Sun et al., 2022; Elayan et al., 2022; Zhao et al., 2023):

(a) Internet of Things (IoT): IoT technologies play a crucial role in IoB by establishing internet connectivity for physical devices and sensors. These devices encompass a range of items like wearables, smart home appliances, and environmental sensors, which actively gather real-time behavioral data from individuals. Wearable devices, such as smartwatches, fitness trackers, and health monitors, play a vital role in IoB technologies. These devices consistently acquire data regarding an individual's activities, sleep patterns, heart rate, and other physiological and behavioral factors; and facilitate the collection of detailed and personalized behavioral data. As primary data sources, IoT devices form the foundation of IoB applications.

Figure 2. A generic model for IoB architecture
Sources: Sun et al. (2022), Zhao et al. (2023)

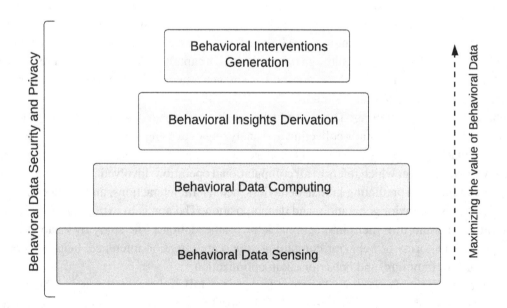

(b) Sensor Networks: Sensor networks are implemented in diverse settings, including residences, urban areas, and workplaces, with the purpose of gathering behavioral data. These networks comprise interconnected sensors that detect and measure different facets of individuals' behavior, such as motion, proximity, temperature, sound, or light. By offering data rich in contextual information, sensor networks facilitate the comprehension of behavioral patterns.

(c) Artificial Intelligence (AI): AI encompasses the utilization of machine learning algorithms to analyze data, generate forecasts and make predictions. In the context of IoB, AI is employed to analyze human behavior and anticipate future actions based on historical data. AI technologies, including machine learning, natural language processing, and computer vision, facilitate the analysis and interpretation of substantial amounts of behavioral data. By identifying patterns, correlations, and anomalies within the data, AI algorithms provide insights into individuals' behavior and preferences. AI helps in the customization of experiences and facilitates data-informed decision-making.

(d) Big Data Analytics: Big data analytics encompasses the utilization of sophisticated algorithms and tools to examine extensive datasets. In the context of IoB, big data analytics is employed to handle and analyze the massive volume of data gathered by IoT devices. These technologies process and analyze large and complex datasets, including behavioral data, with the objective of extracting valuable insights. By merging behavioral data with other contextual information like demographics or environmental factors, analytics platforms can identify behavioral trends, segment populations, and construct predictive models.

(e) Augmented Reality (AR) and Virtual Reality (VR): AR technology superimposes digital information onto the physical world, while VR technology creates a fully immersive digital environment. In IoB, AR can be leveraged to deliver personalized information to users based on their behavior, whereas VR can be utilized to simulate real-world scenarios and assess the consequences of specific behaviors. AR and VR technologies enrich the IoB experience by generating immersive environments that impact individuals' behavior. By overlaying digital information onto the physical world or providing virtual simulations, AR and VR have the capacity to shape behaviors and foster engagement across diverse domains, including training, entertainment, and marketing.

(f) Cloud Computing: Cloud computing entails the utilization of remote servers to store and process data. In the context of IoB, cloud computing is employed to store and process the substantial volumes of data generated by IoT devices. The infrastructure of cloud computing provides scalable storage and computational resources necessary for the processing and storage of extensive behavioral data. Cloud platforms facilitate efficient data management, real-time analytics, and seamless integration of diverse IoB technologies.

(g) Data Security and Privacy Technologies: As IoB involves the collection of sensitive personal data, technologies related to data privacy and security are crucial. Strong encryption, authentication, authorization, access control mechanisms, and blockchain-based solutions are used to ensure secure data transmission and storage, and protect the privacy of individuals' data.

IoB Implementations and Business Models

According to Prakash (2021), an IoB implementation requires three key elements for success: (1) a robust platform and advanced tools capable of creating efficient sensors and applications, (2) precise data and analytics to extract vital insights from the monitoring and data, and (3) a superior user experience to encourage the initial adoption and usage of the tool or application. Today, successful IoB apps, such as

Fitbit and Garmin Vivosmart, have applied these principles and gained popularity through user adoption, usage, and behavior influence (Prakash, 2021).

IoB allows for the observation of user interaction patterns and contact points. This information is then used to create a unified and coherent interface that meets the user's needs while making navigation effortless, intuitive, and valuable (Javaid et. al., 2021). Additionally, IoB enables multi-channel personalization, centralized messaging, the transmission of personalized alerts, social media integration, and the maintenance of an integrated design (Javaid et. al., 2021). The data collected is analyzed to gain insight into user behavior and can also be used to encourage desired behavior through consumer notifications.

IoB has significant implications for business models across various industries. It can transforms traditional business models by enabling a deeper understanding of customer behavior, personalization of experiences, and data-driven decision-making. It empowers organizations to create innovative solutions, enhance customer satisfaction, and drive business growth in a rapidly evolving digital landscape. Companies can examine previous performance and forecast the future using the IoB concept. Companies can also organize their development, marketing, sales and many other operations using data obtained through the IoT.

According to the existing studies, some potential implementations that can be built around IoB technology are presented hereunder:

(a) Customer insights and personalized marketing: IoB enables businesses to collect and analyze customer behavior data to deliver personalized marketing messages, tailoring their efforts and offers to specific customer segments for increased engagement and conversion rates. Additionally, companies can leverage IoB technology to analyze customer behavior and preferences, improving their products and services by identifying trends and patterns through the analysis of customer reviews, social media posts, and other relevant data sources. For example, IoB allows insurance companies to create personalized insurance plans by analyzing customer behavior and risk factors. This integration of IoB empowers businesses to optimize their marketing strategies and enhance their offerings based on a deeper understanding of customer behavior and preferences.

(b) Personalized healthcare: IoB can be used to analyze data from wearable devices, medical records, and other sources to create personalized healthcare plans for individuals. This could include remote patient monitoring, chronic disease management, precision medicine, health and wellness tracking, telehealth services, fitness tracking, physiology analysis and so on (Javaid et al., 2022). IoB facilitates personalized interventions, proactive healthcare approaches, and patient engagement. It can also support behavioral analytics for population health insights, care coordination, and clinical trials. As a good example, Fitbit collects data from its wearable devices and uses it to offer personalized fitness programs to its customers.

(c) Retail analytics: The integration of IoB technology in the retail industry offers retailers the ability to analyze customer behavior both in-store and online, leading to personalized shopping experiences. By leveraging data from various sources, retailers can acquire valuable insights into customer preferences and habits, allowing them to deliver targeted promotions, personalized product recommendations, and customized store layouts. This data-centric approach enhances the overall shopping experience, fostering higher levels of customer satisfaction, loyalty and ultimately drives sales and revenue for retailers.

(d) Smart education and personalized learning: By utilizing IoB, educational institutions can track students' learning behaviors, learning preferences and gain valuable insights into their individual progress and engagement. This data-driven approach enables the provision of personalized feedback and recommendations, tailored to each student's specific needs and learning style (Embarak, 2022). By analyzing patterns and behaviors, IoB can identify areas where students may be struggling or excelling, allowing educators to intervene with targeted support and resources.

(e) Predictive maintenance: IoB has the potential to enable predictive maintenance, where businesses can anticipate maintenance requirements and prevent equipment failures. By monitoring the behavioral patterns of machines and devices, organizations can proactively identify potential issues, allowing them to implement preventive maintenance measures and minimize downtime and expenses. Through the analysis of machine behavior, including equipment usage patterns and sensor data, IoB empowers businesses to predict maintenance needs and take timely actions to ensure optimal performance and reduce operational disruptions.

(f) Sustainable smart cities: IoB has significant applications in creating smart cities by analyzing behavior patterns and utilizing data-driven insights. By monitoring and analyzing traffic patterns, waste disposal practices, and energy consumption, IoB can contribute to improving transportation systems, reducing congestion, optimizing waste management, and enhancing energy efficiency. This includes leveraging data on traffic patterns and driver behavior to develop more efficient transportation systems (Elayan et al., 2022), reducing energy consumption by identifying areas for improvement such as inefficient appliances or heating systems, and promoting sustainability by monitoring energy usage.

(g) Security and surveillance: IoB can be effectively employed to analyze patterns of behavior in public spaces and enhance security measures. By leveraging sensors, surveillance cameras, and data analytics, IoB can detect and track suspicious behavior, allowing for early intervention and threat prevention. It can also assist in identifying lost or stolen items by analyzing movement patterns and unusual behaviors. Furthermore, IoB can help identify potential safety hazards by monitoring environmental conditions and gathering real-time data on crowd density and movement.

(h) Smart organizational context: IoB has significant implications for various organizational contexts. It enables the monitoring of employee behavior, productivity, and job satisfaction, leading to personalized recommendations for improving the work experience and enhancing organizational performance. IoB also plays a crucial role in workplace safety by collecting data on environmental conditions and employee behavior to identify potential hazards. Furthermore, IoB contributes to supply chain optimization by tracking inventory levels, analyzing shipment data, and identifying inefficiencies. It aids in fraud prevention by monitoring financial transactions and detecting anomalies that could indicate potential fraud or security breaches. Overall, IoB provides valuable insights that organizations can leverage to enhance employee engagement, safety, supply chain efficiency, fraud prevention, and customer satisfaction.

(i) Smart tourism: When it comes to smart tourism, IoB can play a significant role in enhancing the overall tourist experience (Kwok, 2023). By leveraging data from various sources and employing technologies like sensors, data analytics, and machine learning, IoB can provide personalized recommendations, real-time insights, location-based services, safety and security measures, seamless travel experiences, and feedback analysis. For instance, smart airports can use IoB technologies to track baggage, provide personalized flight updates, and offer location-based services within the airport premises. IoB systems can provide real-time insights into the current sentiment, preferences, and behavior patterns of tourists. Collected behavioral data can be utilized to provide personalized recommendations for tourist attractions, accommodations, restaurants, and activities based on a person's preferences and past behaviors.

(j) High-tech smart agriculture: IoB offers transformative opportunities for smart agriculture as well. By utilizing behavioral data and advanced technologies, farmers can implement precision farming techniques, monitor livestock health, enhance supply chain management, monitor environmental conditions, and automate agricultural processes. These applications lead to optimized resource usage, improved crop yields, enhanced animal welfare, traceability in the supply chain, reduced environmental impact, and increased efficiency and profitability in the agricultural sector. IoB enables data-driven decision-making, automation, and sustainability, paving the way for a more productive and resilient agricultural industry.

Overall, from business model perspective, an implementation of IoB can be categorized into different approaches. These include data monetization, personalization and customization, behavioral analytics and insights, proactive intervention and support, behavior modification and gamification, and optimization of operations and processes. Each approach leverages IoB technology to gather and analyze behavioral data, empowering businesses to monetize data, deliver personalized experiences, acquire insights, intervene proactively, alter behaviors, and optimize operations. It is crucial to recognize that an IoB implementation may integrate multiple categories. The specific implementation of IoB in a business model will vary depending on factors such as the industry, target audience, and organizational objectives.

CHALLENGES OF INTERNET OF BEHAVIORS

IoB represents a promising concept with the potential to enhance various aspects of people's lives, including healthcare, education, and transportation. However, it also gives rise to ethical and privacy concerns that must be effectively addressed (Rahaman, 2022). Gartner acknowledges the importance of data privacy and security in IoB technologies, as they involve the collection and analysis of personal data. To tackle these concerns, organizations should establish robust policies and procedures for data handling, governance, and consent.

As the shift towards IoB unfolds, it becomes crucial to carefully consider the potential ethical and privacy implications. Based on a comprehensive examination of existing research, challenges within the domain of the IoB can be categorized into five distinct headings:

(1) Privacy Protection: One of the main concerns with IoB is the potential invasion of privacy. Safeguarding individuals' personal information and respecting their privacy rights throughout the IoB ecosystem is crucial. This involves establishing strong data protection measures to control personal information and mitigate the risk of data misuse.

(2) Data Security: The collection and analysis of large amounts of personal data in IoB systems make them potential targets for cybercriminals. Implementing robust security measures is essential to protect IoB data from unauthorized access, or misuse.

(3) Consent and Transparency: Obtaining informed consent from individuals and ensuring transparency regarding data usage is vital. Clear and transparent mechanisms should be in place to inform individuals about how their data will be collected, stored, and utilized within IoB systems.

(4) Ethical Use of Data: Ethical considerations arise in the use of IoB data to influence behavior. Establishing ethical guidelines is necessary to ensure that IoB business models respect individual autonomy, avoid unintended consequences, and prevent discriminatory actions.

(5) Technical ang Interoperability Issues: The implementation of IoB requires significant technical infrastructure and skilled workforce. Overcoming technical challenges, such as developing advanced algorithms and analytics tools, and addressing the scarcity of technical expertise in some areas, is crucial. Also, in order to maximize the effectiveness of IoB systems, interoperability is essential. Developing standardized protocols and interfaces that enable seamless data exchange between different systems is necessary for IoB to integrate with a wide range of devices and platforms.

Addressing these challenges requires collaboration among individuals, businesses, and policymakers. Establishing clear regulations, guidelines, and ethical standards for data collection, storage, and usage in relation to human behavior is essential. By doing so, IoB technologies can be deployed in a manner that respects privacy, builds trust, and maximizes their potential benefits for individuals and society as a whole.

BLOCKCHAIN FOR INTERNET OF BEHAVIORS

The introduction of blockchain technology in 2008 revolutionized the world of digital currencies with the emergence of Bitcoin as a prominent example. Blockchain is a distributed ledger technology (DLT) that allows data to be stored in a secure and decentralized manner. This decentralized ledger technology operates on a peer-to-peer (P2P) network where every node holds a current copy of the ledger, which ensures that the system is not vulnerable to a single point of failure (Fernández-Caramés & Fraga-Lamas, 2018; Zheng et al., 2018; Wang et al., 2019). It has been adapted for use in a wide range of industries and applications.

Blockchain which constitutes the infrastructure of cryptocurrencies in 2009, has started to clearly demonstrate that it is an effective technology in restructuring economic, political, legal and social activities in many sectors in a short time. The development of blockchain technology is described in three main phases (Swan, 2015). Blockchain 1.0 is the use of blockchain technology in digital money transfer and payment systems applications to provide the infrastructure of cryptocurrencies. Bitcoin, Litecoin Dogecoin, Ripple, NXT cryptocurrencies can be given as examples. The main purpose is to decentralize money and payments. Blockchain 2.0, on the other hand, focuses on the use of blockchain infrastructure for many other types of assets—beyond cryptocurrencies—for a more general decentralization of markets. Blockchain 2.0 is the use of blockchain technology in financial and market applications to enable smart contracts in stocks, bonds, futures, loans, mortgages, title deeds and so on. Blockchain 3.0, on the other hand, is the use of blockchain technology in government, health, science, education, culture, arts – beyond money, finance and market applications.

Blockchain is a distributed and shared ledger technology among end-to-end connected users by distributing the centralization structure in trust systems based on a single center (Fernández-Caramés & Fraga-Lamas, 2018; Zheng et al., 2018; Wang et al., 2019). Unlike systems based on a single authority or center, which is a major problem today, blockchain operates with a decentralized and distributed network architecture. In this distributed environment, an automated consensus provides trust and transparency. It enables distrustful and dissimilar parties to record all kinds of assets without a central authority, to store immutable data and to exchange assets securely.

The blockchain network stores data in blocks that are chronologically linked together as shown in Figure 3. Every block in the chain includes a cryptographic hash of the preceding block, which guarantees the chain's integrity and prevents any tampering with previous transactions. To verify and record transactions, a group of participants called nodes use a consensus mechanism. Today, various consensus protocols are used in blockchain systems. Nakamoto introduced the Proof of Work (PoW) protocol as the first consensus protocol, which is based on solving complex puzzles. In addition to PoW, other consensus protocols such as Proof of Stake (PoS), Practical Byzantine Fault Tolerance (PBFT), Delegated Proof of Stake (DPoS), Proof of Bandwidth (PoB), Proof of Elapsed Time (PoET), and Proof of Authority (PoA) are also utilized (Fernández-Caramés & Fraga-Lamas, 2018; Zheng et al., 2018).

In the blockchain system, many users can request transactions (transfer money, transfer data ownership, update a common data, etc.) over nodes. When a node performs a transaction request (for example, a money transfer transaction request in Figure 4), it prepares its content with digital signature and similar cryptographic components and then publishes it on the blockchain network. The created record is propagated to the blockchain network via other nodes. The newly created record is kept in a pool along with other records created by different nodes. In order for the records to be included in the blockchain network, it is made into a timestamped candidate block by private nodes – also called miner nodes. A consensus protocol works between the nodes so that the generated candidate block can be added to the distributed registry, that is, to the chain. The consensus protocol is a puzzle, and if agreement is reached on the solution of the puzzle, the candidate block is approved. Then, this new block is added to the chain by all nodes as the new chain link of the registry (Fernández-Caramés & Fraga-Lamas, 2018).

Blockchain technology's decentralized nature eliminates the need for a central authority or intermediary to manage transactions or data. Instead, all participants in the blockchain network can access the same information, and transactions are validated and recorded using a consensus mechanism. The decentralized nature of blockchain technology provides significant benefits, including high levels of security and transparency (Zheng et al., 2018). Since the data is distributed across multiple nodes, there are no single points of failure or vulnerabilities that can be exploited by malicious actors. Furthermore, cryptographic hashing and consensus mechanisms prevent any data alterations without the network's majority agreement. Blockchain has the potential to revolutionize industries such as finance, supply chain management, healthcare, and real estate.

In the context of IoB, blockchain technology plays a crucial role, offering enhanced security and privacy features for IoB business models. As a decentralized ledger, blockchain can effectively store and manage the vast volumes of data generated by IoB devices. By utilizing blockchain, data stored on the ledger becomes immutable, meaning it cannot be altered or tampered with easily, thus providing an additional layer of security.

In IoB business models, blockchain technology can be leveraged in various ways. Based on the collected data and review analysis on IoB paradigm and its challenges, we have made some deductions, and defined five main categories of blockchain-based technological solutions that can enhance IoB implementations. These significant solutions of blockchain are described hereunder.

Figure 3. Blockchain architecture
Sources: Fernández-Caramés and Fraga-Lamas (2018), Zheng et al. (2018)

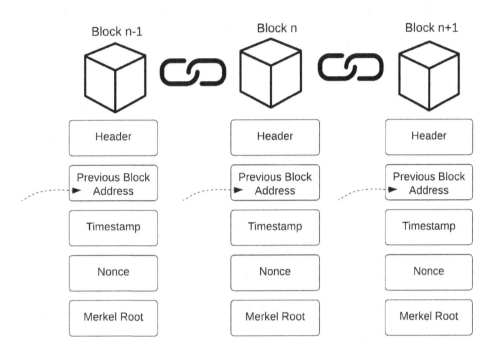

Figure 4. How blockchain works

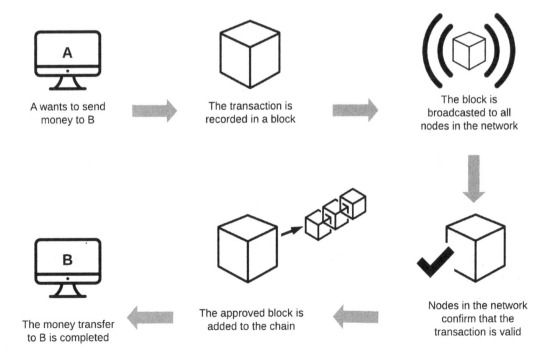

Security, Integrity, and Privacy of Behavioral Data

Behavioral data security and privacy are crucial concerns in IoB business models. To tackle these challenges, blockchain technology provides a secure and decentralized platform for data storage and sharing. Blockchain ensures that personal and behavioral data are stored in a decentralized and encrypted manner. Individuals have greater control over their data, and their privacy is protected through cryptographic algorithms such as hash functions, zero-knowledge proofs, public-key cryptography (e.g., RSA, ECC).

With its decentralized nature, blockchain ensures that data is not controlled by a single entity, making it more resistant to cyber threats. Especially, the utilization of robust public and private key encryption empowers individuals to retain control over their personal data and determine who can access it. This proactive measure addresses potential concerns regarding the misuse of personal data within IoB systems.

By capitalizing on blockchain's features such as decentralization, immutability, and transparency, data security can be significantly enhanced in IoB applications. This approach can safeguard sensitive personal information, facilitate secure data sharing between entities, and grant individuals autonomy over their data. Blockchain network can securely store and manage individual behavior data, allowing users to maintain ownership and control while authorizing access to trusted parties.

An example of how blockchain technology can enhance data security and privacy in an IoB based healthcare business model can be considered. In an IoB healthcare system, various devices and sensors collect real-time data on patients' behaviors, such as physical activity, sleep patterns, and vital signs. This data is valuable for monitoring patients' health, providing personalized treatments, and conducting research. However, ensuring the security and privacy of this sensitive health data is crucial. At this point, implementing blockchain technology can lead to significant enhancements in data security and privacy. Some of the significant benefits are defined as follows:

(1) Strong Data Encryption: When the behavioral data is collected, it can be encrypted using strong encryption algorithms like AES (Advanced Encryption Standard). This ensures that the data remains secure and only authorized individuals or entities with the correct decryption key can access it.

(2) Decentralized Data Storage: Instead of storing the data in a centralized database vulnerable to attacks, the encrypted data can be stored in a decentralized manner on the blockchain. Each block in the blockchain contains a timestamped and encrypted set of data. The decentralized nature of blockchain ensures that data is not controlled by a single entity, reducing the risk of unauthorized access and data breaches.

(3) Consensus Mechanism: Blockchain utilizes a consensus mechanism to validate and verify the integrity of data. For instance, in a permissioned blockchain network, trusted parties, such as healthcare providers, can participate in the consensus process to validate the data and ensure its accuracy. This adds an additional layer of security and trust to the system.

(4) Access Control and Privacy: Blockchain allows for granular access control, where patients can maintain ownership and control over their behavioral data. They can grant access to specific healthcare providers or researchers through the use of cryptographic keys. The use of public and private key pairs enables individuals to selectively share their data while preserving their privacy.

(5)   Immutable Audit Trail: Every transaction recorded on the blockchain is immutable, auditable and transparent. This means that any changes or alterations to the data can be easily detected, providing an audit trail of who accessed, modified, or shared the data. This feature increases transparency and accountability, ensuring the integrity of the data and building trust among stakeholders. The transparency enables stakeholders to verify the origin, authenticity, and integrity of data, fostering trust among participants.

By implementing blockchain technology in an IoB based healthcare business model, data security and privacy can be strengthened. Patients have control over their data, healthcare providers can access accurate and reliable information, and researchers can securely conduct studies while complying with privacy regulations. This approach fosters trust, enhances data protection, and promotes the responsible use of personal health information in the context of IoB.

Integration of blockchain technology into other IoB applications strengthens data security, fosters trust among stakeholders, and mitigates concerns related to privacy, data integrity, and unauthorized access. However, it is important to acknowledge that blockchain is not a universal remedy and its implementation should be tailored to the specific requirements and considerations of each IoB application.

Smart Contracts for Data Ownership, Consent, and Monetization

Smart contracts are self-executing agreements that automatically execute predefined actions when specific conditions are met. By leveraging blockchain technology, smart contracts can enhance the security, transparency, and automation of data-driven interactions, providing numerous benefits in IoB systems. For instance, a smart contract can be used to incentivize positive behavior, where a person is rewarded for healthy habits such as exercising or eating well. The smart contract can be programmed to automatically transfer the reward when the behavior is confirmed (Figure 5).

Moreover, smart contracts can be used for consent management. They enable individuals to define and enforce data usage agreements. Smart contracts can be programmed to require explicit consent from users before their data is collected, shared, or utilized. This gives individuals greater agency over their personal information and allows them to specify the terms and conditions under which their data can be accessed. For example, when users sign up for the wearable device, they are presented with a smart contract that outlines the types of data collected, how it will be used, and the consent requirements. Users can review, approve, and digitally sign the smart contract, giving explicit consent for data collection and usage.

An example where a health insurance company utilizes blockchain-based smart contracts in an IoB scenario is considered hereunder. As known, a health insurance company aims to provide personalized insurance plans that consider individuals' lifestyle choices and health data. The significant enhancements that can be provided by blockchain are explained as follows:

(a)   Data Collection: Individuals willingly choose to share their health-related data, such as fitness tracker information, diet logs, and biometric measurements, with the insurance company.

(b)   Smart Contract Creation: The insurance company creates a smart contract on a blockchain platform, outlining the terms and conditions of the insurance plan. The contract establishes predefined rules based on specific behaviors, such as regular exercise, healthy eating habits, and regular medical check-ups.

(c) Data Validation and Rewards: The smart contract automatically collects and verifies the behavioral data from trusted sources, such as fitness tracker APIs or medical records. If the predefined conditions are met, such as achieving exercise goals or maintaining a healthy BMI, the smart contract triggers the release of rewards or discounts on insurance premiums.

(d) Immutable Record: All interactions and transactions associated with the smart contract, including data updates and reward distribution, are recorded on the blockchain. This ensures a transparent and auditable history of the individual's behavior and the corresponding insurance-related actions.

By leveraging blockchain-based smart contracts in this example, the health insurance company can incentivize and motivate individuals towards healthier lifestyles. Simultaneously, individuals gain more control over their data and receive personalized insurance benefits based on their behaviors.

Figure 5. How smart contract works
Source: Analytics Vidhya (2022)

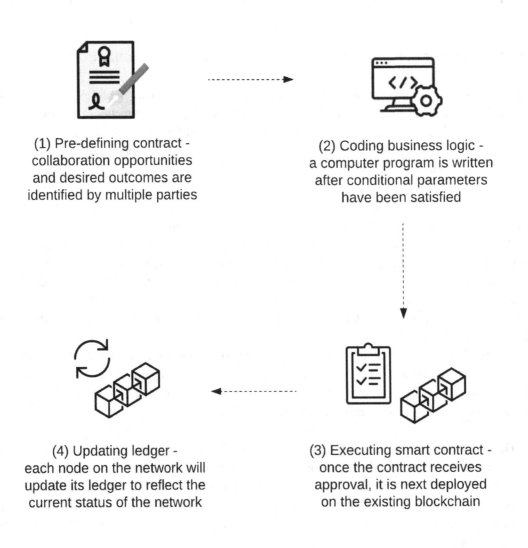

(1) Pre-defining contract - collaboration opportunities and desired outcomes are identified by multiple parties

(2) Coding business logic - a computer program is written after conditional parameters have been satisfied

(4) Updating ledger - each node on the network will update its ledger to reflect the current status of the network

(3) Executing smart contract - once the contract receives approval, it is next deployed on the existing blockchain

Moreover blockchain facilitates fair and transparent compensation models through smart contracts, allowing individuals to monetize their behavioral data while maintaining control over its usage. Blockchain introduces the potential for Behavioral Data Monetization models within the IoB ecosystem. By utilizing blockchain, individuals can have more direct control over their data and participate in data marketplaces, where they can choose to sell or license their data to interested parties while maintaining privacy and control.

Decentralized Decision-Making Platform for Behavioral Data

Decentralized decision-making in an IoB business model involves making decisions based on behavioral data in a collaborative and distributed manner, as opposed to relying on a central authority or entity.

In a traditional centralized decision-making model, a single organization or entity holds the authority to analyze behavioral data and make decisions based on it. This centralized entity has control over the entire decision-making process, from data collection to analysis and subsequent actions or interventions.

However, in a decentralized decision-making system facilitated by blockchain technology, the decision-making process is distributed across multiple nodes within a blockchain network. These nodes can represent individuals, organizations, or even devices participating in the network.

As an example, a decentralized IoB based marketplace for personalized advertising is discussed hereunder. The platform connects advertisers with consumers based on their behavioral data and preferences, without relying on a central authority. The significant enhancements that can be provided by blockchain are explained as follows:

(a) Data Collection: The marketplace collects behavioral data from consumers, such as their browsing history, social media activity, and purchase behavior. This data is securely stored on a blockchain, ensuring transparency and data integrity. Each consumer has a unique profile that contains their behavioral data, preferences, and interests. These profiles are stored on the blockchain and are accessible to all participants in the network. Also, the marketplace consists of decentralized nodes, which can be advertisers, consumers, or even AI algorithms. These nodes interact with the blockchain and contribute to the decision-making process.

(b) Distributed Decision-Making: When an advertiser wants to target a specific audience segment, the decision-making process is distributed among the network's nodes. The nodes analyze the available consumer profiles and behavioral data to determine the most relevant audience for the advertiser's campaign.

(c) Consensus Mechanism: To reach a decision, the nodes within the network collaborate and engage in consensus mechanisms. Consensus mechanisms ensure that decisions are made collectively and agree upon by a majority of participating nodes. These mechanisms, such as PoS or PoW, ensure the integrity and accuracy of the decision-making process. The nodes collaborate to reach a consensus on the target audience for the advertising campaign. They consider factors such as consumer preferences, behavior, demographics, and previous campaign performance.

(d) Smart Contracts: Smart contracts are used to automate the execution of advertising campaigns. Once a consensus is reached on the target audience, the smart contract triggers the delivery of personalized ads to the selected consumers, ensuring privacy and control over data sharing.

Through decentralized decision-making in this IoB based advertising marketplace, advertisers can reach their target audience more effectively, while consumers receive ads that align with their preferences and interests. The distributed nature of the decision-making process promotes transparency, fairness, and privacy, fostering trust between advertisers and consumers in the marketplace.

Once a decision is reached, the decentralized decision-making system can trigger actions or interventions based on the analyzed behavioral data. Ad performance data and consumer feedback are collected and stored on the blockchain, allowing advertisers and consumers to provide input and improve future decision-making processes. The outcomes and feedback from these actions can also be recorded on the blockchain, contributing to the continuous learning and improvement of the decision-making process.

Organizations can harness the collective intelligence and expertise of multiple nodes. This approach promotes transparency, accountability, and fairness in decision-making, while empowering individuals and fostering trust in the system.

Blockchain-Based Self-Sovereign Identity

Self-Sovereign Identity (SSI) is an approach to digital identity that emphasizes individuals' control over their personal information and the ability to manage and share it securely (Tobin & Reed, 2016; Mühle et al., 2018; Ferdous et al., 2019). It is a decentralized approach to identity management that allows individuals to manage their personal data, control how it is shared, and maintain privacy and security. It aims to address the limitations of traditional identity systems, where personal data is often stored and controlled by centralized authorities or service providers.

As illustrated in Figure 6, in an SSI system, individuals have a digital identity that is stored on their personal devices, such as a smartphone or computer, in the form of decentralized identifiers (DIDs). These DIDs are unique identifiers that are associated with cryptographic keys, allowing individuals to authenticate and verify their identity. In an SSI system, individuals have ownership of their identity data and can selectively disclose it to others as needed. This is achieved through the use of decentralized and distributed technologies such as blockchain and DLT. SSI leverages the concept of verifiable credentials, which are tamper-evident digital records issued by trusted sources and cryptographically signed. These credentials can be securely stored in a digital wallet controlled by the individual.

With SSI, individuals can authenticate themselves and assert their identity without revealing unnecessary personal information. They can also independently verify the authenticity of received credentials without relying on a centralized authority. This approach enhances privacy, minimizes the risk of identity theft, and allows for greater user control over personal data.

SSI has numerous potential applications, including identity verification, access control, digital signatures, and secure online transactions. It is considered a promising solution for building a more secure, privacy-preserving, and user-centric digital identity ecosystem.

Several blockchain projects and protocols like Sovrin, uPort, and Hyperledger Indy have emerged to facilitate the implementation of blockchain-based SSI. These initiatives prioritize the creation of open-source frameworks, protocols, and tools that enable the development and deployment of decentralized and interoperable SSI solutions.

As a decentralized identity model, SSI can be a powerful tool in IoB business models as well for users to manage and protect their personal data and privacy. Blockchain enables individuals to have greater ownership and control over their behavioral data. Through blockchain-based identity solutions, users can manage their digital identities and selectively share their data with trusted entities.

With SSI, users can establish and verify their identity with different IoB systems and devices without having to disclose their personal information to third-party providers or relying on centralized identity services. The blockchain network can store and verify the user's credentials. It is possible to provide a secure and transparent platform for managing digital identities and transactions.

As mentioned, the use of personal data in IoB systems raises concerns about privacy and security. SSI can help address these concerns by giving individuals greater control over their personal data. With SSI, individuals can create and manage their own digital identity, which can be used to authenticate themselves and control access to their personal data. This would allow individuals to maintain greater control over their personal data, while still allowing them to benefit from the services provided by IoB systems.

An IoB scenario in the healthcare industry can be considered. The system that collects data from wearable devices, such as fitness trackers, smartwatches, and health monitors, to monitor an individual's health and behavior in real-time. The IoB system tracks various metrics like heart rate, sleep patterns, physical activity, and nutrition. Incorporating SSI into this IoB system would enable individuals to have greater control over their personal health data. With SSI, individuals can create and manage their own digital identities, which can be used to authenticate themselves when accessing the IoB system. Using their SSI, individuals can selectively share specific health data with healthcare providers or other authorized entities, ensuring that they retain control over their personal information. For example, when visiting a doctor, individuals can present their SSI credentials to authenticate themselves and grant access to the relevant health data required for the consultation. This allows for personalized and efficient care without compromising privacy.

Figure 6. Self-sovereign identity
Source: DomiLabs (2021)

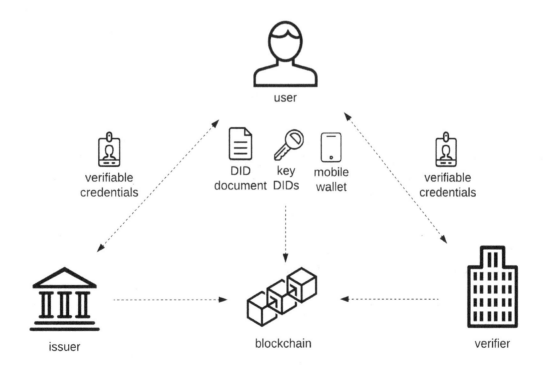

The SSI based approach ensures that individuals have control over the disclosure and sharing of their health data, protecting their privacy and maintaining the security of sensitive information. It also provides a trusted and verifiable way to authenticate and authorize access to personal health data within the IoB system. By combining IoB and SSI, individuals can benefit from personalized healthcare insights and services while having the peace of mind that their personal health data is under their control. This example highlights how SSI can enhance privacy, security, and user control within an IoB system.

Secure and Privacy-Preserving Analytics on Behavioral Data

Privacy-preserving analytics refers to the practice of analyzing data while protecting the privacy of individuals whose data is being used. In the context of the IoB, which involves collecting and analyzing data on individuals' behaviors, privacy-preserving analytics becomes even more crucial. Several techniques can be employed to ensure privacy in IoB models such as anonymization, differential privacy, homomorphic encryption, secure multi-party computation, federated learning, data minimization.

Blockchain technology can play a significant role in leveraging privacy-preserving analytics in IoB business models. It ensures data integrity and immutability, provides a decentralized and trustless environment, empowers individuals with data ownership and consent, enables secure and controlled data sharing, enhances transparency and auditability, facilitates consent management and compliance, and allows for new models of data monetization.

Blockchain can integrate with privacy-preserving techniques, such as zero-knowledge proofs or secure multi-party computation, to further enhance privacy in IoB analytics. By combining these techniques with blockchain, sensitive data can remain encrypted and private while still enabling secure computations and analytics.

By leveraging these capabilities, blockchain enhances the security, privacy, and trustworthiness of IoB analytics while giving individuals more control over their data. However, it's important to consider the trade-offs, such as scalability and computational requirements, as blockchain technology may introduce additional overhead in terms of processing power and storage.

CHALLENGES OF BLOCKCHAIN IMPLEMENTATION

The implementation of blockchain technology in IoB business models presents several challenges, including scalability, energy consumption, interoperability, regulatory uncertainty, security and vulnerabilities, costs and complexity, legal and ethical issues and so on (Zheng et al., 2018; Meva, 2018; Reyna et al., 2018; Khan et al., 2021; Belchior et al., 2021). Some of these challenges are discussed hereunder:

(1) Scalability: As blockchain networks expand, scalability poses a challenge, potentially causing difficulties in processing a large number of transactions promptly. These scalability concerns can result in delays in transaction processing and elevated operational expenses.
(2) Energy consumption: This is a notable issue, especially with blockchain networks that rely on PoW, such as Bitcoin. These networks consume substantial amounts of energy, prompting apprehensions regarding their environmental footprint.

(3)   Interoperability: Blockchain networks frequently employ distinct protocols and standards, which can create obstacles to their seamless collaboration. Interoperability challenges impede the smooth exchange of data and assets among these blockchain platforms.

(4)   Regulatory uncertainty: The regulatory landscape for blockchain and cryptocurrencies exhibits significant variations from one geographic region to another. Navigating these diverse regulations can be intricate and has the potential to influence the adoption and utilization of blockchain technology.

(5)   Costs and Complexity: Implementing and maintaining blockchain networks can be costly and complex, especially for businesses unfamiliar with the technology. There are expenses associated with infrastructure, development, and ongoing maintenance. Also, storing large volumes of data on a blockchain can be impractical due to storage constraints and cost considerations.

(6)   Privacy and Security: Despite its reputation for security, blockchain is not immune to certain risks. Smart contract vulnerabilities, 51% attacks, and privacy concerns must be addressed to enhance security.

(7)   Legal and Ethical Issues: Blockchain is used for various purposes, some of which may have legal and ethical implications, such as supply chain tracking and digital identity. Ensuring compliance with laws and ethical standards is an ongoing challenge.

CONCLUSION

The market for the IoB is expanding, encompassing the collection and analysis of data from diverse sources such as social media, mobile devices, wearables, and other internet-connected devices. Anticipated to witness substantial growth in the upcoming years, the IoB market is driven by advancements in data analytics and machine learning technologies, as well as the rising consumer inclination towards personalized and data-driven experiences.

Various industries, including healthcare, retail, transportation, and manufacturing, are expected to be significantly impacted by the IoB market. In healthcare, for instance, IoB technologies can remotely monitor patient health and behavior, facilitating the delivery of more personalized and efficient care by healthcare providers. In retail, IoB technologies can analyze customer behavior and preferences, enabling retailers to execute targeted and effective marketing campaigns.

However it also raises concerns regarding ethics and privacy. As a decentralized ledger technology, blockchain has a significant importance for the IoB as it addresses the ethical and privacy challenges associated with data collection and usage. By utilizing blockchain in IoB, it enables individuals to have control over their personal data, ensuring privacy and consent. The decentralized and transparent nature of blockchain enhances trust among users, as data transactions can be verified and audited. The immutability of blockchain ensures the integrity of data, preventing unauthorized tampering or manipulation.

Furthermore, the blockchain-based system can help the company demonstrate compliance with privacy regulations such as GDPR (General Data Protection Regulation) in all world. The immutable nature of the blockchain ensures that data transactions cannot be altered, providing an auditable trail of consent, data usage, and user interactions. This transparency and accountability help the company meet regulatory requirements and support audits. By leveraging blockchain, IoB can be implemented in an ethical and privacy-centric manner, empowering individuals and safeguarding their sensitive information.

REFERENCES

Afor, M. E., & Sahana, S. (2022, November). The internet of behaviour (IoB) and its significant impact on digital marketing. In *2022 International Conference on Computing, Communication, and Intelligent Systems (ICCCIS)* (pp. 7-12). IEEE. 10.1109/ICCCIS56430.2022.10037598

Al-Fuqaha, A., Guizani, M., Mohammadi, M., Aledhari, M., & Ayyash, M. (2015). Internet of things: A survey on enabling technologies, protocols, and applications. *IEEE Communications Surveys and Tutorials*, *17*(4), 2347–2376. doi:10.1109/COMST.2015.2444095

Analytics Vidhya. (2022). *What are Smart Contracts in Blockchain?* https://www.analyticsvidhya.com/blog/2022/11/what-are-smart-contracts-in-blockchain/

Atzori, L., Iera, A., & Morabito, G. (2010). The internet of things: A survey. *Computer Networks*, *54*(15), 2787–2805. doi:10.1016/j.comnet.2010.05.010

Belchior, R., Vasconcelos, A., Guerreiro, S., & Correia, M. (2021). A survey on blockchain interoperability: Past, present, and future trends. *ACM Computing Surveys*, *54*(8), 1–41. doi:10.1145/3471140

Bzai, J., Alam, F., Dhafer, A., Bojović, M., Altowaijri, S. M., Niazi, I. K., & Mehmood, R. (2022). Machine learning-enabled internet of things (IoT): Data, applications, and industry perspective. *Electronics (Basel)*, *11*(17), 2676. doi:10.3390/electronics11172676

DomiLabs. (2021). *A beginner's guide to self-sovereign identity.* https://domilabs.io/beginners-guide-ssi/

Elayan, H., Aloqaily, M., Karray, F., & Guizani, M. (2022). Internet of behavior (IoB) and explainable AI systems for influencing IoT behavior. *IEEE Network*, *37*(1), 62–68. doi:10.1109/MNET.009.2100500

Embarak, O. H. (2022). Internet of behaviour (IoB)-based AI models for personalized smart education systems. *Procedia Computer Science*, *203*, 103–110. doi:10.1016/j.procs.2022.07.015

Ferdous, M. S., Chowdhury, F., & Alassafi, M. O. (2019). In search of self-sovereign identity leveraging blockchain technology. *IEEE Access : Practical Innovations, Open Solutions*, *7*, 103059–103079. doi:10.1109/ACCESS.2019.2931173

Fernández-Caramés, T. M., & Fraga-Lamas, P. (2018). A review on the use of blockchain for the internet of things. *IEEE Access : Practical Innovations, Open Solutions*, *6*, 32979–33001. doi:10.1109/ACCESS.2018.2842685

Fukuyama, M. (2018). Society 5.0: Aiming for a new human-centered society. *Japan Spotlight*, *27*(5), 47–50.

Gartner. (2020). *Gartner Identifies the Top Strategic Technology Trends for 2021.* https://www.gartner.com/smarterwithgartner/gartner-top-strategic-technology-trends-for-2021

Javaid, M., Haleem, A., Singh, R. P., Khan, S., & Suman, R. (2022). An extensive study on Internet of behavior (IoB) enabled healthcare-systems: Features, facilitators, and challenges. BenchCouncil Transactions on Benchmarks. *Standards and Evaluations*, *2*(4), 100085.

Javaid, M., Haleem, A., Singh, R. P., Rab, S., & Suman, R. (2021). Internet of Behaviours (IoB) and its role in customer services. *Sensors International*, 2, 100122. doi:10.1016/j.sintl.2021.100122

Khan, D., Jung, L. T., & Hashmani, M. A. (2021). Systematic literature review of challenges in blockchain scalability. *Applied Sciences (Basel, Switzerland)*, *11*(20), 9372. doi:10.3390/app11209372

Kwok, A. O. (2023). The next frontier of the internet of behaviors: data-driven nudging in smart tourism. *Journal of Tourism Futures*, 1-7.

Li, S., Xu, L. D., & Zhao, S. (2015). The internet of things: A survey. *Information Systems Frontiers*, *17*(2), 243–259. doi:10.100710796-014-9492-7

Meva, D. (2018). Issues and challenges with blockchain: A survey. *International Journal on Computer Science and Engineering*, *6*(12), 488–491.

Mezair, T., Djenouri, Y., Belhadi, A., Srivastava, G., & Lin, J. C. W. (2022). Towards an advanced deep learning for the internet of behaviors: Application to connected vehicles. *ACM Transactions on Sensor Networks*, *19*(2), 1–18. doi:10.1145/3526192

Mühle, A., Grüner, A., Gayvoronskaya, T., & Meinel, C. (2018). A survey on essential components of a self-sovereign identity. *Computer Science Review*, *30*, 80–86. doi:10.1016/j.cosrev.2018.10.002

Narvaez Rojas, C., Alomia Peñafiel, G. A., Loaiza Buitrago, D. F., & Tavera Romero, C. A. (2021). Society 5.0: A japanese concept for a super intelligent society. *Sustainability (Basel)*, *13*(12), 6567. doi:10.3390u13126567

Prakash, V. (2021). *Holistic Digital Synergies Imperative for the Internet of Behavior (IoB)*. https://dzone.com/articles/holistic-digital-synergies-imperative-for-internet

Precedence Research. (2021). *Internet of Behaviors (IoB) Market Size, Growth, Report 2030*. https://www.precedenceresearch.com/internet-of-behaviors-market

Rahaman, T. (2022). Smart things are getting smarter: An introduction to the internet of behavior. *Medical Reference Services Quarterly*, *41*(1), 110–116. doi:10.1080/02763869.2022.2021046 PMID:35225739

Research Nester. (2023). *Internet of Behaviors (IoB) Market*. https://www.researchnester.com/reports/internet-of-behaviors-iob-market/3983

Reyna, A., Martín, C., Chen, J., Soler, E., & Díaz, M. (2018). On blockchain and its integration with IoT. Challenges and opportunities. *Future Generation Computer Systems*, *88*, 173–190. doi:10.1016/j.future.2018.05.046

Shiroishi, Y., Uchiyama, K., & Suzuki, N. (2018). Society 5.0: For human security and well-being. *Computer*, *51*(7), 91–95. doi:10.1109/MC.2018.3011041

Stary, C. (2020, December). The internet-of-behavior as organizational transformation space with choreographic intelligence. In *12th International Conference on Digital Workplace–Nucleus of Transformation*, Bremen, Germany (pp. 113-132). Springer International Publishing. 10.1007/978-3-030-64351-5_8

Sun, J., Gan, W., Chao, H. C., Philip, S. Y., & Ding, W. (2023). Internet of behaviors: A survey. *IEEE Internet of Things Journal*, *10*(13), 11117–11134. doi:10.1109/JIOT.2023.3247594

Swan, M. (2015). *Blockchain: Blueprint for a new economy*. O'Reilly Media, Inc.

Tobin, A., & Reed, D. (2016). The inevitable rise of self-sovereign identity. *The Sovrin Foundation*, *29*, 18.

Wang, L., Shen, X., Li, J., Shao, J., & Yang, Y. (2019). Cryptographic primitives in blockchains. *Journal of Network and Computer Applications*, *127*, 43–58. doi:10.1016/j.jnca.2018.11.003

Whitmore, A., Agarwal, A., & Da Xu, L. (2015). The internet of things—A survey of topics and trends. *Information Systems Frontiers*, *17*(2), 261–274. doi:10.100710796-014-9489-2

Zhao, Q., Li, G., Cai, J., Zhou, M., & Feng, L. (2023). A tutorial on internet of behaviors: Concept, architecture, technology, applications, and challenges. *IEEE Communications Surveys and Tutorials*, *25*(2), 1227–1260. doi:10.1109/COMST.2023.3246993

Zheng, Z., Xie, S., Dai, H. N., Chen, X., & Wang, H. (2018). Blockchain challenges and opportunities: A survey. *International Journal of Web and Grid Services*, *14*(4), 352–375. doi:10.1504/IJWGS.2018.095647

KEY TERMS AND DEFINITIONS

Behavioral Analytics: The process of studying and interpreting patterns, trends, and insights from the behaviors and interactions of individuals or groups, often utilizing data analysis techniques.

Behavioral Data: The data that is collected by observing and analyzing the actions, interactions, and behaviors of individuals or groups, generally gathered through digital tools, to gain insights into their preferences and decision-making patterns.

Blockchain: A decentralized digital ledger technology that records and securely stores transactions across a network of computers.

Business Model: A blueprint or approach that delineates how a company creates income and maintains its viability by leveraging its offerings, services and operational activities.

Internet of Behavior: A concept referring to the collection and analysis of data from various digital sources and devices to gain insights into and influence human behavior, preferences and decision-making patterns.

Internet of Things: A technological concept that encompasses a network of physical objects, devices and sensors interconnected through the internet, enabling them to gather, exchange, and utilize data.

Privacy: The status or situation where one's personal information, activities, or confidential matters are shielded from unauthorized intrusion, surveillance, or disclosure.

Security: The state or quality of being protected from harm, danger, unauthorized access, or threats to ensure the safety, confidentiality, integrity and availability of assets, information, or individuals.

Society 5.0: A societal framework that merges digital technology and data-driven solutions to enhance the well-being and quality of life for society.

Chapter 13
New Business Models for Society 5.0

Susan Shepherd Ferebee
https://orcid.org/0000-0002-3616-634X
Purdue University Global, USA

Nicholas Lessen
Purdue University Global, USA

ABSTRACT

In the evolving landscape of technological advancements, the Internet of Behavior (IoB) emerges as a pivotal concept, harnessing the power of data to understand and influence humans. IoB finds its most profound application in Society 5.0, a vision of a super-smart society where digital and physical realms harmoniously coexist. New business and economic models like the circular economy, sharing economy, smart cities, platform business model, social enterprise model, and blockchain technology will be explored. Emerging healthcare, agriculture, hospitality, and energy business models are discussed. Challenges arise as innovative organizations emerge to create a more sustainable and inclusive culture. Data privacy and security, blockchain high energy consumption, technologically unprepared workforce, and artificial intelligence bias must be addressed. This chapter aims to demonstrate emerging economies, business models, and related technologies that facilitate Society 5.0 as it evolves from human behavior insights gained from IoB.

INTRODUCTION

In the ever-evolving landscape of technological advancements, the Internet of Behavior (IoB) emerges as a pivotal concept, harnessing the power of data to understand and influence human behavior (Mezair et al., 2022). This intricate web of interconnected actions and reactions finds its most profound application in Society 5.0, a vision of a super-smart society where digital and physical realms harmoniously coexist (Cabinet Office Government of Japan, 2016). As we transition from an information-centric society to one that is human-centric, the business models of the past are undergoing a seismic shift. New business

DOI: 10.4018/978-1-6684-9039-6.ch013

paradigms for Society 5.0 are not just about profit maximization; they are about creating value for all stakeholders, ensuring inclusivity, sustainability, and a better quality of life. These models leverage the insights from IoB, integrating them with advanced technologies like artificial intelligence (AI) and the Internet of Things (IoT) to forge a future where businesses are not just entities for economic transactions but pillars supporting the broader societal vision (Albino et al., 2020). This data-driven approach allows a symbiotic relationship between IoB, Society 5.0, and the innovative business models they inspire for delivering tailored products and services that cater to individual needs and preferences (Dilmegani, 2023). This chapter aims to demonstrate emerging economies, business models, and related technologies that facilitate Society 5.0 as it evolves from human behavior insights gained from IoB.

BACKGROUND

Internet of Behaviors

A psychology professor named Gote Nyman was the first to introduce IoB, stating that useful information could be gained if IoT devices with known IP addresses were linked to human behavior patterns over time. According to Nyman, behavior shows whether a person will cooperate and have a proclivity to act, so analyzing behaviors is paramount to understanding how to influence people (Elayan et al., 2022).

IoB combines IoT and AI-enhanced IoT, now referred to as Artificial Intelligence of Things (AIoT), to analyze people's behavior patterns so their interests, preferences, and wants can be deduced. IoB uses sensors to collect people's data and perform behavioral science analysis on that data (Mezair et al., 2022). According to Javaid et al. (2022), in IoB, the data is gathered and analyzed to persuade people's behavior. During COVID-19, for example, systems were developed to recognize facemask use so that human behavior regarding mask use could be analyzed and applied to public policy and interventions. Financial fraud detection is another use. Knowing a credit card holder's behavior makes it easy to detect unexpected fraudulent activity. Waste management can be improved with the use of smart receptacles that record and monitor types of waste and amounts for individuals, families, and businesses. Human behavior regarding transportation habits can be observed through mass transit ticket systems, surveillance cameras, and mobile apps. Knowing these habits, informed decisions are made to optimize public transportation, making it more attractive to users and potentially improving the environment.

Elayan et al. (2022) predict that within the year 2023, 40% of the world population will be monitored with IoT devices for the purpose of influencing their behavior. The assumption is that the desired behavior changes are positive for individuals and society. Elayan et al. (2022) introduced a concept of explainable AI (XAI) to aid user's understanding of how an IoB and AI model are working to change behaviors positively. They examined a use case of reducing electricity use and related costs for the benefit of individual citizens, power companies, and society. This combined use of IoB and XAI illustrates the goals of Society 5.0 in blending business and social goals.

Data security and privacy issues emerge and are amplified as data collected and analyzed are used to influence behavior. Ethical issues of inappropriate influence arise if businesses or politicians use deceptive practices based on IoB data. Customers benefit from targeted marketing that speaks to their needs, but the customer has to be willing to give up a level of privacy to achieve the benefit (Javaid et al., 2022). Future questions are what regulations will emerge, what will human beings prioritize, and how ethical and legal behavior will be evaluated in the legal system.

Society 5.0

Environmental degradation, health issues, economic inequality, and social injustice, among others, challenge today's society. To tackle these problems, Society 5.0 has emerged as a promising framework that aims to create sustainable and inclusive communities using advanced technologies. Over the years, society has moved from Society 1.0, the hunter/gatherer society, to Society 2.0, which was agriculturally based. Society 3.0 was the industrial society, and Society 4.0 merged the physical and digital worlds, becoming the information society. Society 5.0 represents a rapid societal advancement that combines the world's physical, digital, and biological elements. Society 5.0 seeks to converge artificial intelligence (AI), robotics, biotechnology, big data analytics, and IoB to examine and improve healthcare, climate change, transportation, and aging (Cabinet Office Government of Japan, 2016). Society 5.0 supports combining economic growth with societal problem-solving, enhancing social justice, environmental sustainability, and individual lives (Albino et al., 2020). While prior societies were limited by human capability, Society 5.0 relies on artificial intelligence combined with IoB to exceed human capability, adding new value and potential to industry and society.

Society 5.0 blends cyber and physical space. AI analyzes IoT and IoB data gathered in physical and cyberspace; the results are integrated back to modify and improve the physical space. Ideally, humans are freed from routine tasks, improving their quality of life. A challenge of Society 5.0 is the large amount of personal information that must be collected and shared across all systems, demanding that sufficient security measures be implemented. Trust is a driving force for the success of Society 5.0. Inadequate or inaccurate information input will lead to insufficient results (Kasinathan et al., 2022).

SOCIETY 5.0 ECONOMIES AND BUSINESS MODELS

Circular Economy

The economic basis will also need to shift as society shifts to greater use of IoB and Society 5.0. A circular economy is regenerative in that, as an economic system, it seeks to reduce waste and promote resource reuse and recycling (Geissdoerfer et al., 2020; Stahel, 2016). Geissdoerfer et al. (2020) suggested that achieving a circular economy requires redesigning products, services, supply-chains, and considerable business process changes. Also imperative is a focus on sustainability. Geissdoerfer et al. (2020) identified four business models that support a circular economy: cycling, extending, intensifying, and dematerializing. Cycling and extending refer to designing for endurance, reuse, recycling, and remanufacturing so that products and their components continually circulate in the economy. Intensifying is a concept like Uber, where using a service/app replaces owning a product. Watching streaming movies instead of owning the movie is also intensifying (Mattos, 2019). Dematerializing is a process of providing a service or product using reduced materials and energy (Geissdoerfer et al., 2020). Tiny homes are an example of dematerialization, as is replacing a paper letter in a paper envelope compared to an email. Shifting from working in an office building to remote work is another example.

Sharing Economy

The following attributes characterize the sharing economy: a) facilitated by internet-connected platforms, b) improved use of underused assets, c) reduced costs for search and transaction, and d) creation of easy solutions to complex coordination problems by connecting strangers so users and providers can interact (Cheng et al., 2020). Examples of strangers connecting to perform transactions include ride-share services, hospitality services, and healthcare in developed and developing nations. Uber, for example, uses a private driver's underused automobile asset by providing ride service to others. This differs from a person renting a car from a car rental organization. The Uber transaction is peer-to-peer, removing the intermediary organization. Most significant about the sharing economy is its ability to match, in real-time, large-scale supply and demand of tangible assets, services, and information in a peer-to-peer network (Cheng et al., 2020).

Blockchain

Societies and economies are based on interaction and transactions between individuals and organizations (LibreTextsBoundless, 2023). An emerging technology that has captivated the collective imagination and offers possibilities for far-reaching advances in Society 5.0 is blockchain. The distributed and decentralized nature of blockchain to conduct business makes it a natural fit to link technology and services such as ridesharing to individuals in Society 5.0. Blockchain is known for being a trusted peer-to-peer architecture that does not require a third party and has a distributed ledger technology (DLT) that can constantly track transactions in the form of blocks (Guo et al., 2022). Blockchain transactions are performed transparently and include an immutable ledger system to support integrity and accountability. Smart contracts, which offer a business rules-type function that enables transactions to occur based on agreements, work in conjunction with blockchain and allow for transactions in real-time, on-demand, or at a later set date. What this makes possible for individuals in Society 5.0 is the ability to conduct highly secure transactions in real-time conveniently. For society, the economy can operate with greater transparency and higher levels of cooperation.

Blockchain does face security challenges and attack vulnerabilities. Social engineering attacks are a key threat to the blockchain. Users can share their blockchain wallet passcode, and similar efforts are made to facilitate this as in any other system (Basu et al., 2023).

Researchers are fascinated with the utility of blockchain and its potential to advance the transportation system; however, until the issue of high energy consumption by blockchain is addressed, widespread use is unlikely. The Bitcoin blockchain energy use is comparable to Thailand's power use (Meijer, 2022). The hype around blockchain technology prompted numerous studies to explore its ability to impact this industry. Next, we will examine examples of how the combination of blockchain's distributed nature and smart contracts' ability to facilitate real-time transactions can enhance individuals and society.

Ridesharing Model

A particular notable study conducted by Tyagi et al. (2023) proposed an innovative vision that included the incorporation of blockchain and smart contracts as components of an intelligent transportation system supported by autonomous electric vehicles. In this visionary approach, autonomous vehicles receive guidance from dynamic digital traffic signals to provide safe transportation to citizens. Further, the system streamlines the entire transaction process by leveraging the blockchain's smart contracts capability to automate payments based on routes and traffic patterns. Another study implemented a similar design but included an additional feature that securely shared location and awareness data between vehicles, resulting in map crowdsourcing (Jiang et al., 2023). Combining these approaches has positive implications for transportation in Society 5.0. Implementing a system like this supports the circular economy model's concept of dematerialization as many citizens may be encouraged by its conveniences to shift away from automobile ownership, which can lead to the eventual reduction of total human-operated vehicles on the road. Another advantage is that increased numbers of autonomous vehicles capable of sharing real-time traffic information can potentially lead to less traffic congestion. Moreover, with features such as traffic awareness available to most vehicles on the road, more accurate predictions of trip times are also possible. Ultimately, by leveraging blockchain's distributed ledger technology and automation from smart contracts, commuters in Society 5.0 will travel with greater safety, make informed decisions about their travel, and experience unnecessary delays.

Package Delivery Model

In Society 5.0, individuals can reap the benefits of leveraging decentralized ride-sharing models for ride-sharing and package delivery systems. With its focus on goods and parcels, this type of ridesharing has few operational differences from picking up human cargo. Dynamic ride sharing is similarly incorporated, meaning that potential drivers are matched with pickups at any time. Recently, researchers demonstrated that the potential for such a system could exist using a proposed framework that included blockchain, a GPS, and custom terminals integrated into vehicles to provide secure data exchanges (Zhang et al., 2022). The study showed that increased profitability is possible by reducing the number of trips needed through potential consolidation, again achieving dematerialization in a circular economy. Nonetheless, it became evident that leveraging this technology to serve as an intermediary brought several benefits, including significantly increased security and significant cost savings for ride-sharing applications in Society 5.0.

Examining the best practices from successful platform models and leveraging emerging technologies is essential to accomplish a broader and more inclusive vision of smart transportation. In recent years, many studies have focused on analyzing the operational strategies used by the major service providers operating in the ride-sharing industry today, mainly seeking methods to reduce the prevalent costs and complexities.

Blockchain for Improved Payment Security

Through thoroughly examining ride-sharing operational models, it is identified that reliance on third-party intermediary services increases the frequency of inconsistencies in how privacy data is managed and protected. Combining these challenges with higher operating costs has prompted researchers to look at blockchain as a potential solution to manage and track payments securely. When combined with the power of smart contracts, blockchain could efficiently utilize algorithms to match riders with drivers while providing consistent data privacy protection. One approach to delivering secure location data and protecting privacy is to incorporate a spatial cloaking technique that initially obfuscates the locations of drivers and commuters. Then, with the use of public key encryption, routes between parties can be securely shared (Vazquez & Landa-Silva, 2021).

In other studies, more advanced encryption techniques were proposed to match riders and drivers while protecting privacy data efficiently. For example, researchers recommended homomorphic encryption, which does not require decryption to perform computations but still provides data protection, and proxy re-encryption, which allows two parties to share encrypted without exchanging their private keys. (Zhang et al., 2022). Additionally, researchers evaluated secure multi-party computation (SMPC). This cryptographic obfuscation technique can distribute trust among multiple parties without granting a single party complete access to the data in the transaction (Suegami, 2022). These sophisticated and innovative encryption methods enhance privacy while enabling ride-sharing platforms to consistently protect sensitive data during every transaction in the process. Therefore, blockchain, smart contracts, and advanced encryption with cryptographic obfuscation techniques can lead individuals in Society 5.0 to secure and privacy-protected ride-sharing experiences.

Platform Business Model

The platform business model (PBM)), combined with blockchain, smart contracts, and blockchain's improved security and privacy, form the foundation of organizations like Airbnb and Uber. This model focuses on peer-to-peer exchange, decentralized value creation, and co-creation to facilitate sharing knowledge, opportunities, and resources (Hong et al., 2019). Decentralized models allow for collaboration between private and public resources across business sectors. For example, a smart transportation system could link Uber cars, private taxis, and autonomous vehicles to enable shared intelligence on ridership and traffic patterns and offer fair rates. Similarly, a decentralized lodging booking service that links all hotels and Airbnb can reduce the complexity of multiple tracking systems. At the same time, increased visibility on room availability and occupancy rates offers citizens more competitive rates, while bookings are tracked by blockchain and funded through smart contracts. This business model leads to collaboration and increased innovation in Society 5.0.

According to Micuchova (2022), PBM is highly disruptive and can quickly dominate a market. A prime example of this is how Uber and Lyft disrupted and quickly dominated the traditional taxicab businesses. Micuchova (2022) addresses the following question: How do PBMs develop, deliver, and acquire value within the business model? PBMs are a "technology-driven business model based on platforms that create value and provide an institutional and regulatory framework enabling interactions between previously unmatched demand-side and supply-side participants" (Micuchova, 2022, p 2). The primary characteristics of PBMS are related to their capability to gather, analyze, and monetize digital data (Micuchova, 2022). Gawer (2014) stated value is created by facilitating connections and lowering transaction costs. The PBM connects multiple users and customers to interact while lowering the transaction cost (Gawer, 2014).

The digital economy and digitization are central to the PBMs (Parker & Alstyne, 2014), and digital platforms are key factors in the global economy (Gawer, 2014). In the PBM, value creation does not originate from services and products, and the PBM fully uses digital technologies which form the basis for value creation in the PBM (Parker & Alstyne, 2014). A good example that puts this into perspective is looking at some of the PBM businesses as an example. UBER and LYFT do not own vehicles. Airbnb does not own homes. Social media sites like Twitter, Instagram, and Facebook do not own or create content. These organizations have in common that all of them digitalize human activities that are magnified by network effects, and the digitalized human activities create value (Micuchova, 2022). According to Gawer (2014), there is a high variance between PBM firms with regard to their perimeter choices.

For example, UBER is asset-free or asset-light, operating without car ownership or driver employees. Google, on the other hand, is asset-heavy in terms of asset ownership and employees. Also contributing to value creation in the PBM is digital data. Digital data can be used simultaneously, duplicated, and re-processed endlessly by multiple organizations. Digital data, with its characteristics of velocity, volume, variety, veracity, and value and the intensifying network effects, can quickly generate economies of massive scope and scale (Visconti et al., 2017).

PBM organizations also select digital interfaces that determine how open or closed their connectivity will be. The scope is another consideration. For example, some PBM organizations like Uber Eats began by only connecting customers to restaurants. This expanded to allow customers to connect with other stores (e.g., liquor, grocery, and pharmacies) to add items to the original grocery order. The scope of a firm can increase quickly within the PBM model and allows the organization to utilize synergies across markets, providing an even more reduced transactional cost for the consumer (Gawer, 2014). Gawer holistically describes the digital platform organizations based on three boundaries: a) scope (what is owned, who is employed, what actions occur), b) digital interfaces (the degree to which the platform and customers/users exchange data) and c) customer and user composition (who has access to the platform).

Social Enterprise Model

Dorado et al. (2019) provided insights into the social enterprise business model, which creates innovative solutions for addressing societal challenges in Society 5.0. The social enterprise is a business model designed to contribute to achieving social goals and contributing to the larger good, and it is a cause-driven model (Velez, 2021). The social enterprise business model focuses on creating a social and environmental impact while remaining financially sustainable (Dorado et al., 2019). Society 5.0 uses social enterprise business models to create innovative solutions for addressing societal challenges like poverty, inequality, and climate change.

According to Burkett (2016), a social enterprise has four characteristics:

- Perform trade to fulfill a mission.
- Gain a substantial amount of their income from trade.
- Have a cultural, social, environmental, or economic mission that is aligned to community benefit.
- Reinvest their profit to fulfill their social mission.

Burkett (2016) describes the social enterprise as one that balances "a social (or environmental, cultural or economic) mission WITH an intention to trade and manage a business" (p. 6) and suggests that this requires a blending of skills which is greater than the sum of each set of skills alone.

Social enterprises achieve their mission by organizing in three separate ways:

- Employ marginalized people.
- Offer products and services that directly meet a social need.
- Generate income specifically for social or charity uses (Burkett, 2016).

As with any business, there are key elements that go into the business model, which include 1) core partnerships, 2) value proposition, 3) core activities, 4) customer segments, 5) customer relationships, 6) key resources, 7) communication channels, 8) revenue channels, and 9) cost structure (Burkett, 2016).

What differentiates the social enterprise is the two factors, social impact, and commerce, which exist for each element. An example would be a social enterprise restaurant focusing on helping underserved populations. Under the element of core partnerships is a commercial factor that includes distributors and marketers and a social impact factor that includes hiring people with disabilities and developing social partners who work with underserved populations. In terms of the organization's customer segments, commercial customers would include walk-by customers, regulars, and local business customers, while social impact customer segments might include ethical social-minded customers, disabled customers, and nonprofit organizations that the restaurant might cater to. In terms of revenue generation, this social enterprise restaurant, under its commercial factor, would have retail and catering sales, and under its social impact factor, would have fundraising and donations.

Warby Parker is an example of a social enterprise. It creates sustainable eyewear solutions while donating some of its profits to provide glasses to those in need. Tom's shoe company is similar in that for each pair of shoes sold, a pair goes to people in developing nations. Another organization is Mitscoots, which helps homeless people receive clean socks and obtain a job. For every item a person purchases from their store, the organization gives an equal quality item to someone in need.

Smart City Model

Smart cities combine information communication technology and physical devices connected with the Internet of Things (IoT) to control city operations and provide services to the city's citizens. In a smart city, government officials directly communicate with citizens, the infrastructure, monitoring, and forecasting tools to enhance rapid, effective decision-making (Kasinathan et al., 2022). "The foundation of a smart city is multidimensional spatiotemporal feature engineering" (Lu, 2022, p. 1). The city should comprehensively gather all available information, analyze, and develop thorough data collections to effectively predict social and economic scenarios and lead to data and science-driven decisions. As in all Society 5.0 systems, security and privacy are paramount considerations (Lu, 2022).

In a smart city system, transportation and travel are significant considerations as they leverage technology to facilitate interconnectedness between individuals, their modes of transportation, and their destinations in safer and more convenient ways. In Society 5.0, the vision of travel extends far beyond its traditional purpose of simply traveling from point A to point B. Travel will involve the integration of multiple advanced technologies and inclusive approaches. This concept of a smart transportation system encompasses many elements. One essential component, smart vehicles, involves the integration of advanced features such as internet connectivity, vehicle-to-vehicle communication, and intelligent user interfaces such as voice recognition. Another component, smart traffic systems can examine existing traffic patterns for the purposes of mitigating congestion through methods such as providing recommendations to drivers to optimize their routes or adjusting signals. A smart transportation system, through integrating smart vehicles and smart traffic systems, offers a sustainable, efficient, and user-centric transportation experience for all individuals within the smart city framework (Jan et al., 2019).

Smart Transportation Model

Over the past few years, researchers have been actively engaged in proposing innovative designs to make smart transportation a reality. These designs involve the integration of various emerging technologies. One such strategy presented by Jan et al. (2019) introduced a comprehensive smart transportation system that harnessed the power of big data systems. The proposed design involved collecting and processing transportation data from a vast integration of sensors and sensor processing units installed on smart vehicles, traffic lights, and other tactical locations throughout cities. The design included several features, such as smart parking, which aimed to facilitate a safer, time-efficient, guided parking experience; additionally, the design incorporated smart traffic lights capable of adjusting operations based on traffic patterns. Tahir et al. (2023) proposed algorithms to support smart traffic systems to manage traffic flow efficiently. The design features a comprehensive classification system capable of categorizing vehicles into distinct categories based on multiple attributes. The algorithm is programmed to capture and recognize details such as size, type, and role. Examples of roles include law enforcement, emergency services, standard passenger, and commercial. With these abilities, the system can account for the diverse range of vehicles found on roads and highways.

Critical components required to enable effective law enforcement in a smart transportation system include cameras to address various aspects of traffic surveillance, including automated license plate recognition and the ability to identify and track suspects (Baran et al., 2016). Law enforcement greatly benefits from the surveillance capabilities of smart cameras, as they offer reliable footage of accident scenes to include intricate details, such as information about the vehicles involved in such incidents and images of the people involved. It can result in less reliance on human witnesses during investigations. Later studies confirmed the importance of combining traffic awareness with the ongoing utilization of smart cameras as closed-circuit television devices (CCTV) in smart cities (Dewi & Putra, 2021). The integration offered additional contributions to improve law enforcement operations by emphasizing the ability to effectively capture traffic violations and providing an automated process of issuing fines.

Hospitality Model

Another compelling opportunity to enhance individuals and businesses in Society 5.0 is with the travel booking experience in the hospitality industry. In the digital age we currently live in, prospective travelers look to the internet for guidance on their travel plans from online travel agencies (OTAs). Researchers have recognized the impact that online reviews have on the reputations of lodgings, prompting them to examine the potential effects of electronic word-of-mouth (eWoM) delivery. A study by Nam et al. (2020) provided greater context into the eWoM reviews written online by other travelers and confirmed that they could dramatically impact the reputations of lodgings. Researchers noted that the reviews have a remarkable ability to reach broad audiences, and this greatly influences decision-making. The study also found that prospective travelers regarded online reviews as a form of social proof, which fostered individual perceptions of trust and credibility. Positive reviews contributed to perceptions of popularity and desirability for lodgings, and conversely, negative reviews lowered purchase intentions for potential customers (Sharma et al., 2023). The studies highlight the pivotal role that eWoM plays in helping travelers assess the value of hospitality services, but it also highlights its significant influence on the reputations of lodgings.

However, the widespread reliance on online reviews raises important questions regarding the reliability and authenticity of the data provided in the reviews. The abundance of eWoM content delivered by multiple platforms from sources, including those that are sponsored and unsponsored, can lead to the trustworthiness of the reviews. Nowadays, travelers interested in reviewing eWoM content will find that it can appear on various online platforms, including online review websites, social media platforms, online discussion boards, blogs, and vlogs. This disparate form of content delivery makes it challenging for lodgings to be fully aware of how their patrons viewed prior experiences and to respond. Further, the impact of eWoM has been so significant that over the years, the authenticity of reviews has been a focus of many studies.

Information needs to be accurate; otherwise, travelers may encounter disappointments, such as fake listings and missing accommodations, such as free breakfast, air-conditioning, and desirable window views (Lappas et al., 2016). Researchers have unanimously concluded that the authors of fake reviews commonly include travelers, non-travelers, and hoteliers alike and proposed diverse strategies to detect them (Banerjee, 2022; Sandifer et al., 2017).

No widely adopted standard for detecting fake eWoM exists to date. It is worth noting that while these problems exist, reputable online hotel booking platforms continuously work to address these issues and provide improved user experiences. As a user, it is advisable to carefully read the terms and conditions, verify the details of the hotel, review user feedback, and contact customer support if needed to mitigate any potential problems.

The hospitality model could use a similar model proposed to enhance the transportation industry using blockchain and smart contracts. Imagine a decentralized lodging booking service that seamlessly links all hotels and accommodations, including those provided by services such as Airbnb. This integrated system can reduce the complexity of multiple tracking systems and, at the same time, increase visibility on room availability and occupancy rates. Moreover, with reduced complexities and data interconnected, individuals will benefit from more competitive rates. Through leveraging blockchain technology with the smart contracts feature, transparency, and accountability are significantly increased with the added feature of travel bookings being tracked by blockchain and funded through smart contracts. This model can also alleviate the need for travelers to visit multiple websites to book travel by providing them with a central mobile application or companion website. The result also benefits hotels by removing the need to maintain their booking processes. Their websites can forward traffic to the centralized system, similar to how the PayPal service operates with payment transactions. The model can also potentially standardize booking travel fees and eliminate hidden costs that sometimes occur on travel websites.

Another use case to consider a model with blockchain is to provide a more consistent, dependable, and centralized customer feedback system for the hospitality industry. In a recent study, researchers implemented a system that included blockchain integrated with a software application and successfully captured customer feedback from customers of a prominent library in Sweden (Ballandies et al., 2022). The study aimed to help the Swiss library analyze the copious quantities of feedback information they receive regularly, simplify it and identify the most relevant feedback. Researchers also experienced success when evaluating a blockchain-based customer feedback system for customers of green electricity services in Luxembourg (Utz et al., 2023). The researchers went a step further by including the use of digital loyalty tokens to support traditional loyalty programs offered by vendors. Since businesses are removed from managing the transaction and travel costs become more consistent, support for loyalty programs becomes an important feature to retain customers, as it can be a strategy to offer discounts. Since these system types depend on actual transactions that are attributable to a specific consumer, they can help mitigate fake reviews. As more studies like these continue to appear, we will get closer to a consistent and viable way to leverage blockchain across many industries and improve experiences for the individual and society. Additionally, by solving the problem of the need for more reliability of online reviews by leveraging technologies like blockchain, the hospitality industry can make it possible for travelers in Society 5.0 to confidently review and select travel accommodations based on authentic and trustworthy feedback.

The business cases discussed in this chapter provide compelling evidence of the immense potential for blockchain technology, smart contracts, advanced encryption techniques, and big data to enhance multiple industries. The efficient use of these technologies fosters the ability to enable real-time connectivity, greater trust, and accountability, potentially improving individuals' lives significantly. This technology can transform multiple sectors and drive Society 5.0 to a more integrated and equitable future by facilitating greater transparency, security controls, and efficiencies.

Agriculture Model

As part of the Society 5.0 initiative in Japan and also as a part of the Sustainable Development Goals formulated by the United Nations, the goal has been to create a data-driven agricultural model. NARO (The National Agricultural and Food Research Organization) conducts research on food and agriculture and was formed in 1893. In 2018, the Research Center for Agricultural Information Technology was created. NARO staff are being trained in artificial intelligence. One research outcome has been putting unmanned robot farm workers to perform tillage, planting, and harvesting. Another is the creation of a water control system for rice paddy fields (Nagasaki, 2019).

The primary mission of NARO is to synthesize physical and virtual space to innovate the food industry and create a data-driven AI-enhanced food value chain. The cyber element includes big data, AI, and a data collaboration platform. The physical space includes agricultural cultivation and harvesting, animal breeding, processing, shipping, storage, sales, and exports. Precision agriculture is part of the initiative with micro-dosing of water and nutrients to crops. Harvest ordering informed by big data and AI also contributes to the smart farming model (Nagasaki, 2019).

Colorado State University (CSU), in 2023, launched an AI Institute for Climate-Land Interactions, Mitigation, Adaptation, Tradeoffs, and Economy (AI-CLIMATE) to study taking in and storing carbon for agricultural and forestry purposes. So, while contributing to agriculture, carbon sinks are also created to improve carbon emissions. Farmers can gain economically by being compensated for the carbon dioxide their farm captures. This same project is creating digital twins of farms, ranches, and forests. The AI-guided twin encompasses all factors influencing the farm, ranch, or forest, including weather, management decisions, outcomes of the decisions related to crop yields, financials, and GHG emissions. Simulations can be performed in the twin environment to predict future needs and outcomes of interventions. This model being developed by CSU demonstrates how IoB (analyzing management decisions), AI, and big data come together to realize Society 5.0 goals of combining economic growth with societal problem-solving (DeLoss, 2023).

Healthcare Model

In 2018, Keidanren, Japan's Business Federation) noted hyper aging and a life expectancy of one hundred years as presenting key challenges to their country. Goals for healthcare in Society 5.0 included a) longer times of good health combined with overall increased longevity, b) minimized disease and disease severity, c) lifestyle consideration and course of life care, including long-term monitoring for patients with certain diseases, and d) treat healthcare as a growth industry. Trends in Society 5.0 technology that impact healthcare are biotechnology, including spatial and time-based observations of bodily functions over time. The digital person is another factor. The ability to digitize human biometrics and body functions provides large data sources to enhance diagnosis and treatment through AI.

In Society 5.0, curative care becomes care and prevention care, standardized treatment becomes personalized treatment, and physician-led healthcare becomes patient inclusion healthcare (Keidanren, 2018). In terms of technology, Society 5.0 healthcare will include data from wearable devices, genomic test results, and digital data gathered over a lifetime. Medical blockchains, IDs linked to personal medical data, and the expansion of electronic personal health records are also a part of improving healthcare (Keidanren, 2018).

The expansion of healthcare services takes two paths, as proposed by Keidanren (2018). First is integrating all health services (dietary biometrics, remote monitors, physical and mental health care, and personalized health care plans). Second is advanced medicine in the form of personalization, regenerative medication, digital therapies, automated nursing care (robotics), and genetic editing.

The holistic view of healthcare expands to champion collaboration between medical personnel and other industries. Strengthening community healthcare is another goal. Continuous learning for healthcare professionals and physicians is supported as is improved integration and collaboration between government centers, ministries, agencies, and healthcare professionals in developing health policies (Keidanren, 2018).

Personal health data is a critical privacy and security consideration as innovative technologies emerge to support healthcare in Society 5.0. The ability to share healthcare data across different health service providers is critical to improved results. Blockchain has positively impacted this ability. With blockchain, a singular record with a unique history can be created and validated across all computers in the blockchain. Records in the blockchain are immutable and accurate, ensuring accurate decisions are made based on the medical data in the record (Srivastava et al., 2022). According to Srivastava et al. (2022), blockchain provided a solution for healthcare records that reduced energy consumption and lowered costs. Blockchain proved valuable in tracking vaccine production and quality checking during COVID-19. Primary benefits of blockchain in healthcare include a) drug tracing from manufacturer to retailer and all other movements, b) non-changeable medical audits that do not rely on a third party, c) relevant medical information can be accessed without revealing patient identity, d) authenticity of medical documents is proven through blockchain technology, e) reduces time and effort in retrieving patient data from previous providers, and f) easy and accurate transfer of medical records (Srivastava et al., 2022). Basu et al. (2023) stated that national blockchain solutions provide optimal record-keeping for medical providers and patients.

In healthcare, blockchain implementation faces challenges, including government regulations and privacy, adoption drivers, technical, and organizational. There needs to be more government regulation built into blockchain technology as it is decentralized by design. Ownership and access provision of records needs to be clarified. Blockchain is an emerging technology that has yet to be fully tested. It is still being determined what the ultimate storage limits might be when using blockchain. Blockchain is not built on a standard. From an organizational perspective, leaders need to trust the blockchain, and interoperability challenges exist with organizational systems. In terms of patients and other stakeholders, adoption is only sometimes accepted. Blockchain is, by nature, unknown, and a knowledge gap must be overcome (Attaran, 2022).

Energy Sector Business Models

Decentralization, digitalization, and intelligent control are trends in the energy sector that have led to new business models. These include peer-to-peer electricity exchange, vehicle-to-grid, and virtual power plants. Digitalization increased the distributed nature of electricity generator systems, leading to new business models.

Peer-to-peer electricity exchange. The energy sector strives for decentralization, digitization, democratization, decreased consumption, and decarbonization. However, another result is intermittent production and difficulty matching demands. Local generation of electricity helps to resolve these issues. A digital platform model can be used through peer-to-peer energy and carbon exchange systems. The peer-to-peer system uses direct exchange between prosumers and consumers who trade energy without the electricity supplier as an intermediate player (Siuta-Tokarska et al., 2022). Instead, a third-party digital platform (using blockchain) allows prosumers and consumers to interact directly and becomes a platform similar to Uber or Airbnb.

Virtual Power Plants. Virtual power plants (VPP) is a system designed to combine several energy sources to provide an overall reliable energy supply. The VPP can bring together renewable and non-renewable energy sources, distributable loads, and various storage devices and participate in the energy trading market. A VPP purchases spare electrical capacity from energy organizations and manages plant production based on real-time demand (Siuta-Tokarska et al., 2022).

Vehicle to Grid. Electric vehicles have provided a new concept of vehicle-to-grid technology where an electric vehicle connected to the grid performs an exchange with the grid, providing unused electricity when the car is not in operation but providing electricity to the car when needed (Siuta-Tokarska et al., 2022).

Managing electricity through two-way electricity exchange is a new model for creating a new energy grid. New energy sector business models must rely on value-added energy exchange capabilities. This demands a sophisticated data exchange and storage system and algorithms to effectively control the distributed system. Digital transformation in the energy sector changes the industry's structure and introduces new possibilities for improving the stability and efficiency of energy delivery, integrating different energy sources, and reducing costs.

SOCIETY 5.0 CHALLENGES

Similar challenges exist across many of the Society 5.0 technologies and business models. Central to these challenges are personal privacy and security. An additional issue is accurate input data to ensure effective prediction results. Blockchain can often offer a valuable solution to improve security issues and protect data against change; however, with blockchain comes high energy consumption to maintain a real-time ledger and verify cryptographic signatures (Golosova & Romanovs, 2018). This high energy use is counter to Society 5.0 goals.

IoT often operates in insecure environments and is susceptible to physical damage (Tyagi et al., 2023). Another challenge in Society 5.0 is that where Society 4.0 is only connected to computers, in Society 5.0, all devices that individuals interact with connect and interact with each other. Multiple networks can be connected simultaneously. Internet connections and sharing are automatic (Tyagi et al., 2023).

Another challenge to the implementation of Society 5.0 is a workforce that needs to be highly skilled in the 5.0 technologies like blockchain, robotics, nanotechnology, and cybersecurity (Trehan et al., 2022). The operators need not only technical skills but also understand how to manipulate processes based on data and results received by the system. The World Manufacturing Forum identified ten critical skills needed for manufacturing 5.0. These skills demand a combination of creative thinking, adaptability, and technical and digitization skills (Mourtzis et al., 2022). Trehan et al. (2022) also highlighted the importance of combined government policy with effective and functional infrastructure. Finally, there is yet to be empirical evidence to support the financial benefit of Society 5.0 technologies and business models (Trehan et al., 2022).

Some of these challenges are easier to visualize when looking at a specific industry, such as ride sharing. Often, a strong dependence on a third-party intermediary that assumes the responsibility for facilitating secure, accurate, and reliable interactions between the driver and the rider or the vacation booker and the owner leads to security issues (Gupta & Shanbhag, 2021). Some aspects of these services are relatively easy, such as keeping track of vehicles and validating the credibility of drivers. Other services pose more critical concerns, such as securely collecting payment information, trip history, and pickup and drop-off location, as they present privacy risks. Since the intermediary assumes the responsibility for managing pricing and payments, it becomes imperative that they ensure adequate protection for the sensitive information collected from the transactions.

Studies have examined the collection processes of intermediaries and discovered that intermediaries are inconsistent with their operations when collecting and sharing privacy attributes and with their ability to control the exposure of privacy data (Hesselmann et al., 2021). Additionally, at this time, there needs to be a current regulation that compels intermediaries to do so. The findings are alarming since examples of privacy risk items commonly collected by intermediaries include riders' and drivers' names, phone numbers, and email addresses. It is essential to safeguard privacy information for ride-sharing users as a failure to do so potentially exposes them to several serious risks based on the attribute data collected during the procedure. Inconsistent data collection also suggests inconsistent data protection practices, and any data the intermediaries do not adequately protect is at risk for data breaches and identity theft. Also, since the intermediaries own the data they collect, there currently needs to be a regulation to stop them from selling that information to other companies for advertising purposes without the individual's consent.

Another challenge with the ride-sharing model, for example, revolves around how intermediaries calculate fares. Popular ride-sharing services such as Uber and Lyft employ a dynamic pricing model that adjusts commuter fares according to multiple factors such as traffic patterns, estimated trip duration, available drivers, and the number of riders requesting a pickup. Based on this model, trip prices can surge when there are not enough drivers compared to the number of ride requests. As it stands today, with drivers split between multiple service providers, the pool of available drivers in the area and the amount of rider demand are limited by those registered by the Uber app and, for example, their competition, Lyft. If consolidation of services were to occur, imagine the potential for prices to improve simply by unifying the two largest ride-sharing providers under a decentralized system. With this integration and a reimagining of the intermediary's role incorporating automation and emerging technology where possible, ridesharing becomes a safe, dependable, and secure service for commuters in Society 5.0 becomes possible.

According to Mourtzis et al. (2022), three core elements must be examined as the movement from Society 4.0 to 5.0 develops: a) human-centric action, b) sustainability, and c) the feedback loop from physical input to digital analysis back to physical output. Personal privacy and data security must be protected as part of human-centric actions.

ETHICAL ISSUES

Even though Society 5.0 is based on improving social justice, inclusion, and individual well-being, ethical issues exist. Data security and privacy are key issues with emerging business models and blockchain technologies (Tyagi et al., 2023). Because the use of AI will play a pivotal role in analyzing data, with the results being used to allegedly improve the physical world. However, algorithmic discrimination and bias are issues that must be evaluated for and resolved to ensure equality and equity (Mittelstadt et al., 2016). The current digital divide must be eliminated the more that Society 5.0 relies on technology to improve business, social outcomes, and personal lives. Additionally, as advanced technologies replace human jobs, governments must be prepared for how current workers will transition and ensure that new employment models are developed that offer employees higher-level, more creative tasks (Cabinet Office, Government of Japan, 2016). As AI becomes an autonomous system that can make decisions, how to manage these systems to ensure human oversight and correct ethical programming will be critical (Mittelstadt et al., 2016). Mittelstadt et al. (2016) stated, "Gaps between the design and operation of algorithms and our understanding of their ethical implications can have severe consequences affecting individuals as well as groups and whole societies (Abstract)."

SOLUTIONS AND RECOMMENDATIONS

Data privacy and security are critical issues as IoB, IoT, big data, and AI are used to develop Society 5.0. Blockchain, shown to provide the level of security and privacy needed, is not sustainable with the current energy consumption required. However, new algorithms are being developed that are more energy efficient. Most blockchain networks use proof-of-work (PoW) algorithms. A popular replacement algorithm is proof-of-stake (PoS). This algorithm does not rely on complex puzzle solving but rather on choosing validators based on the amount of cryptocurrency held. Cardano and Binance cryptocurrencies use this algorithm. Transitioning to PoS validation is not simple as noted by Ethereum's developer, Vatalik Buterin, who stated that moving to PoS required seven years in the planning and testing phase (Putzhammer, 2023). Data protection regulation needs to improve with more countries adopting regulations similar to the General Data Protection Regulation (GDPR) in the European Union.

The workforce must skill up. Education and training in AI, blockchain, cybersecurity, and robotics are essential. Additionally, collaboration and cooperation between government, industry, and educational institutions are needed to create the necessary career paths and opportunities. Industry needs to inform the curriculum so that it aligns with real-world requirements.

Removing bias in AI algorithms is crucial when IoB is used to inform decisions and policies. Routine algorithm audits are needed to continuously identify and remove bias. Society 5.0 aims to be an inclusive society. Biased algorithms and digital divide will erode inclusiveness if not continually monitored and improved.

Society 5.0 demands three core elements in any industry:

- Sustainability - all technology solutions must align with long-term sustainability.
- Feedback Loops – all systems provide feedback for analysis and continued improvement.
- Human Centric – technologies, systems, and processes prioritize human well-being.

Addressing these challenges and implementing solutions will foster Society 5.0 concepts and move the world closer to an inclusive, sustainable, and human-centric future where technology positively supports humanity.

FUTURE RESEARCH DIRECTIONS

Future research directions should address the challenges and potential solutions put forward in this chapter. An ethical framework to guide data use in Society 5.0 is required as a foundation for all technology design and implementation. A comparative analysis of existing frameworks or a grounded theory approach are options. Continued experimental exploration of energy-efficient blockchain algorithms is needed to facilitate what is a known data privacy and security solution. Employee skill-gap analysis applied to future curriculum and job category development is an essential research focus since Society 5.0 cannot be realized without an adept and relevant workforce.

CONCLUSION

Society 5.0 is human-centric, supporting simultaneously economic growth and societal problem-solving, improved social justice, environmental sustainability, and improved individual quality of life. The new society combines physical, digital, and biological elements, using IoB, IoT, and AI to gather and analyze data, provide results, and improve environments and individuals' lifestyles, health, and well-being. As Society 5.0 continues to emerge and develop, a circular economic model also emerges to replace the existing linear model. The circular economy supports prolonging the life of physical and virtual assets through recycling, reuse, redistribution, intensification, and dematerialization. The economy must change from a use and discard concept to a use and reuse and use and repurpose concept.

New business models have emerged organically from the focus of Society 5.0 and the values of the circular economy. The social enterprise is replacing the profit-only focus of current corporate America, shifting the focus to a business model with combined economic gain and social goals that contribute to the larger good. This chapter explored business models for the rideshare, hospitality and energy industries. New healthcare models also grew organically to focus on all individuals' improved health and lifestyle, made possible through advanced technologies and advanced medical health record sharing. Agricultural models are developing to not only automate and provide high-efficiency farms but also to use farms and forests as carbon sinks to improve the environment. Blockchain technology is underlying the new business models, which offer the ability to conveniently conduct highly secure transactions in real-time; however, without energy-efficient algorithms, blockchain is not currently sustainable. As the new philosophy and technology of Society 5,0 develop, smart cities will further advance sustainability and advanced lifestyles.

Challenges related to data privacy and security, as Society 5.0 grows, must be addressed. This challenge is present in both emerging business models and blockchain technology. Additionally, a workforce must be more appropriately prepared and trained to manage the innovative technologies and systems underlying Society 5.0. Ethical issues around AI algorithms, including bias and lack of human oversight for autonomous AI must be taken seriously and mitigated early.

Despite existing challenges, by examining the transformative power of new economic and business models and innovative technologies, we can better understand how they can shape the future of innovation, reshape industries, and create a more sustainable and inclusive society. Exploring new possibilities and opportunities will provide valuable insights for businesses, policymakers, and stakeholders seeking to navigate and thrive in the rapidly evolving landscape of Society 5.0, where technology and human-centered values intersect to create a more prosperous and harmonious society for all.

REFERENCES

Albino, V., Berardi, U., & Dangelico, R. M. (2020). Smart cities: Definitions, dimensions, performance, and initiatives. *Journal of Urban Technology*, *27*(1), 3–43. doi:10.1080/10630732.2014.942092

Attaran, M. (2022). Blockchain technology in healthcare: Challenges and opportunities. *International Journal of Healthcare Management*, *15*(1), 70–83. doi:10.1080/20479700.2020.1843887

Banerjee, S. (2022). Exaggeration in fake vs. authentic online reviews for luxury and budget hotels. *International Journal of Information Management*, *62*, 102416. doi:10.1016/j.ijinfomgt.2021.102416

Baran, R., Rusc, T., & Fornalski, P. (2016). A smart camera for the surveillance of vehicles in intelligent transportation systems. *Multimedia Tools and Applications*, *75*(17), 10471–10493. doi:10.100711042-015-3151-y

Burkett, I. (2016). *Using the business model canvas for social enterprise design*. Knode. https://cscuk.fcdo.gov.uk/wp-content/uploads/2016/07/BMC-for-Social-Enterprise.pdf

Cabinet Office Government of Japan. (2016). *Society 5.0*. Government of Japan. https://www8.cao.go.jp/cstp/english/society5_0/index.html

Cheng, H., Jung, K., Parra-Lancourt, M., & Powell, R. (2020). Does the sharing economy share or concentrate? *Frontier Technology Quarterly*. https://www.un.org/development/desa/dpad/wp-content/uploads/sites/45/publication/FTQ_Feb2020.pdf

DeLoss, J. (2023). *Colorado State University partners in $20M AI Institute focusing on climate-smart agriculture and forestry*. Colorado State University. https://source.colostate.edu/colorado-state-university-partners-in-20m-ai-institute-focusing-on-climate-smart-agriculture-and-forestry/

Dewi, N. K., & Putra, A. S. (2021, March). Law enforcement in smart transportation systems on highways. *International Conference on Education of Suryakancana (IConnects Proceedings)*.

Dilmegani, C. (2023). *Internet of Behaviors (IoB): Its nature and importance in 2023*. AI Multiple. https://research.aimultiple.com/internet-of-behaviors/

Dorado, S., Haigh, N., & Tashman, P. (2019). Advancing the understanding of social entrepreneurship: An empirical examination of the organizational processes of hybrid organizations. *Nonprofit and Voluntary Sector Quarterly*, *48*(3), 591–615.

ElayanH.AloqailyM.KarrayF.GuizaniM. (2022). *Internet of Behavior (IoB) and Explainable AI systems for influencing IoT behavior*. IEEE. arXiv:2109.07239v2 [cs.DC].

Gawer, A. (2014). Bridging differing perspectives on technological platforms: Toward an integrative framework. *Research Policy, 43*(7), 1239-1249. doi:10.1016/j.respol.2014.03.006

Geissdoerfer, M., & Pieroni, M., Pigosso, D., & Soufani, K. (2020). Circular business models: A review. *Journal of Cleaner Production*, 277.

Golosova, J., & Romanovs, A. (2018). The advantages and disadvantages of the blockchain technology. *2018 IEEE 6th Workshop on Advances in Information, Electronic and Electrical Engineering (AIEEE)*, 1-6. 10.1109/AIEEE.2018.8592253

Guo, X., Zhang, G., & Zhang, Y. (2022). A Comprehensive Review of Blockchain Technology-Enabled Smart Manufacturing: A Framework, Challenges and Future Research Directions. *Sensors (Basel), 23*(1), 155. doi:10.339023010155 PMID:36616753

Gupta, R., & Shanbhag, S. (2021). A Survey of Peer-to-Peer Ride Sharing Services using blockchain. *International Journal of Engineering Research & Technology (Ahmedabad), 10*(8), 349–353.

Hesselmann, C., Gertheiss, J., & Müller, J. P. (2021). *Ride Sharing & Data Privacy: An Analysis of the State of Practice.* arXiv preprint arXiv:2110.09188.

Hong, P., Jung, J., & Kim, H. (2019). A review of business model innovation research and trends. *Journal of Innovation Management, 7*(3), 1–20.

Jan, B., Farman, H., Khan, M., Talha, M., & Din, I. U. (2019). Designing a smart transportation system: An internet of things and big data approach. *IEEE Wireless Communications, 26*(4), 73–79. doi:10.1109/MWC.2019.1800512

Javaid, M., Haleem, A., Singh, R., Khan, S., & Suman, R. (2022). An extensive study on Internet of Behavior (IoB) enabled healthcare systems: Features, facilitators, and challenges. *BenchCouncil Transactions on Benchmarks. Standards and Evaluations, 2*, 1–10.

Jiang, S., Cao, J., Wu, H., Chen, K., & Liu, X. (2023). Privacy-preserving and efficient data sharing for blockchain-based intelligent transportation systems. *Information Sciences, 635*, 72–85. doi:10.1016/j.ins.2023.03.121

Kasinathan, P., Pugazhendhi, R., Elavarasan, R., Ramachandaramurthy, V., Ramanathan, V., Subramanian, S., Kumar, S., Nandhagopal, K., Raghavan, R., Rangasamy, S., Devendiran, R., & Alsharif, M. (2022). Realization of Sustainable Development Goals with Disruptive Technologies by Integrating Industry 5.0, Society 5.0, Smart Cities and Villages. *Sustainability (Basel), 14*(22), 15285. doi:10.3390u142215258

Keidanren. (2018). *Healthcare in Society 5.0.* Keidranen. https://www.keidanren.or.jp/en/policy/2018/021_overview.pdf

Lappas, T., Sabnis, G., & Valkanas, G. (2016). The impact of fake reviews on online visibility: A vulnerability assessment of the hotel industry. *Information Systems Research, 27*(4), 940-961.

Li, Q., Wu, H., & Dong, C. (2023). A Privacy-Preserving Ride Matching Scheme for Ride Sharing Services in a Hot Spot Area. *Electronics (Basel), 12*(4), 915.

LibreTextsBoundless. (2023). *Interaction of Individuals, Firms, and Societies*. UCDavis Libre Texts. https://socialsci.libretexts.org/Bookshelves/Economics/Economics_(Boundless)/1%3A_Principles_of_Economics/1.3%3A_Interaction_of_Individuals_Firms_and_Societies

Lu, J. (2022). Building a smart city planning system integrating multidimensional spatiotemporal features. *Scientific Programming, 2022*, 1–9. doi:10.1155/2022/2772665

Mattos, M. (2019). *How a circular economy narrows, slows, intensifies, and closes supply chain loops*. MIT Supply Chain. https://medium.com/mitsupplychain/how-a-circular-economy-narrows-slows-intensifies-and-closes-supply-chain-loops-d85d9bab869

Meijer, E. (2022). *Blockchain and our planet: Why such high energy use?* PRe´. https://pre-sustainability.com/articles/blockchain-and-our-planet-why-such-high-energy-use/

Mezair, T., Djenouri, Y., Bjelhadi, A., Srivastava, G., & Lin, J. (2022). Towards an advanced deep learning for the Internet of Behaviors: Application to connected vehicles. *ACM Transactions on Sensor Networks, 19*(2). *Article, 30*, 1–18.

Micuchova, M. (2022). Data value chain in platform business models. *Scientific Papers of the University of Pardubice, Series D, 30*(3), 16–19.

Mittelstadt, B., Allo, P., Taddeo, M., Wachter, S., & Floridi, L. (2016). The ethics of algorithms: Mapping the debate. *Big Data & Society, 3*(2). Advance online publication. doi:10.1177/2053951716679679

Mourtzis, D., Angelopoulos, J., & Panopoulos, N. (2022). A Literature Review of the Challenges and Opportunities of the Transition from Industry 4.0 to Society 5.0. *Energies, 15*(17), 6276. https://doi-org.libauth.purdueglobal.edu/10.3390/en15176276

Nagasaki, Y. (2019). *Realization of Society 5.0 by utilizing precision agriculture into smart agriculture in NARO, Japan*. FFTC Agricultural Policy Platform. https://ap.fftc.org.tw/article/1414

Nam, K., Baker, J., Ahmad, N., & Goo, J. (2020). Determinants of writing positive and negative electronic word-of-mouth: Empirical evidence for two types of expectation confirmation. *Decision Support Systems, 129*, 113168. doi:10.1016/j.dss.2019.113168

Parker, G., & Alstyne, W. V. M. (2014). *Platform Strategy*. The Palgrave Encyclopedia of Strategic Management. doi:10.2139srn.2439323

Putzhammer, M. (2023). *Most energy efficient cryptocurrencies 2023*. Trality. https://www.trality.com/blog/most-energy-efficient-cryptocurrencies

Sandifer, A. V., Wilson, C., & Olmsted, A. (2017, December). Detection of fake online hotel reviews. In *2017 12th International Conference for Internet Technology and Secured Transactions (ICITST)* (pp. 501-502). IEEE. 10.23919/ICITST.2017.8356460

Sharma, A., Sharma, P., Manalo, J. V. I., & Anh, D. N. (2023). Customers online Reviews and Its impact on Purchase Intention in Hospitality Industry: A Quantitative Investigation. *Journal of Informatics Education and Research, 3*(1).

Siuta-Tokarska, B., Kruk, S., Krzeminski, P., & Zmija, K. (2022). Digitalisation of enterprises in the energy sector: Drivers-business models-prospective directions of changes. *Energies*, *15*(8962), 8962. Advance online publication. doi:10.3390/en15238962

Srivastava, S., Pant, M., Jauhar, S., & Nagar, A. (2022, December 2). (2022). Analyzing the prospects of blockchain in healthcare industry. *Computational and Mathematical Methods in Medicine*, *2022*, 1–24. Advance online publication. doi:10.1155/2022/3727389 PMID:36506597

Stahel, W. (2016). The circular economy. *Nature*, *531*(7595), 435–438. doi:10.1038/531435a PMID:27008952

Suegami, S. (2022). Smart Contracts Obfuscation from Blockchain-based One-time Program. *Cryptology ePrint Archive*.

Tahir, W., Wagan, R. A., & Naeem, B. (2023). Smart Traffic Handling Algorithm Using Aggregated Channel Feature. In *Intelligent Sustainable Systems: Selected Papers of WorldS4 2022* (Vol. 1, pp. 635–643). Springer Nature Singapore. doi:10.1007/978-981-19-7660-5_57

Trehan, R., Machhan, R., Singh, P., & Sangwan, K. (2022). Industry 4.0 and Society 5.0: Drives and challenges. *The IUP Journal of Information Technology*, *18*(1), 40–59.

Tyagi, A. K., Dananjayan, S., Agarwal, D., & Thariq Ahmed, H. F. (2023). Blockchain—Internet of Things Applications: Opportunities and Challenges for Industry 4.0 and Society 5.0. *Sensors, 23*(2), 947. https://doi-org.libauth.purdueglobal.edu/10.3390/s23020947

Vazquez, E., & Landa-Silva, D. (2021). Towards Blockchain-based Ride-sharing Systems. In ICORES (pp. 446-452). Academic Press.

Velez, H. (2021). *What is a social enterprise*? The good trade. https://www.thegoodtrade.com/features/what-is-a-social-enterprise/

ViscontiR.LaroccaA.MarconiM. (2017). Big data-Driven Value Chains and Digital Platforms: from Value Co-Creation to Monetization. *Big Data Analytics: Tools and Technology for Effective Planning*, 355-371. doi:10.2139/ssrn.2903799

Zhang, X., Liu, J., Li, Y., Cui, Q., Tao, X., Liu, R. P., & Li, W. (2022). *Vehicle-oriented ridesharing package delivery in blockchain system*. Digital Communicatio. doi:10.1016/j.dcan.2022.12.008

KEY TERMS AND DEFINITIONS

Blockchain: Blockchain is a trusted peer-to-peer technology architecture using a distributed ledger technology (DLT) that can constantly track transactions in the form of blocks added to a transaction chain. No third part is required. Blockchain transactions are transparent and immutable.

Circular Economy: Unlike our current use-and-discard economic philosophy, a circular economy focuses on recycling, repurposing, and light asset ownership.

Internet of Behaviors: The Internet of Behaviors (IoB) extends the Internet of Things (IoT) to focus on how collected data can be analyzed to understand, influence, and predict human behavior. IoB has the potential to use data to alter people's decisions or actions.

Internet of Things: The Internet of Things (IoT) is a concept of connecting any device to the Internet, creating a vast network of connected things, and providing people-people, people-things, and things-things connections.

Platform Business Model: A business model that facilitates interaction between many participants (buyer-seller, social connections, collaborative connections, renter-owner). A platform business aims to provide a structure and rules for at-scale interactions that release network effects. Connection creation creates the value of a platform business rather than products and services.

Ride Share: A service that provides short-notice, one-way transportation through the use of an app.

Sharing Economy: At the foundation of a sharing economy are peer-to-peer (P2P) actions that acquire, share access to, or provide goods and services. A community-centric online platform is often used to facilitate connections.

Smart City: A smart city employs technological processes and sensors to collect data, analyze data, and use the results of the analysis to manage city resources, services, and assets efficiently.

Smart Transportation: Smart transportation uses technology to achieve safer travel across transport networks. Technologies used include traffic enforcement cameras, auto-generated emergency response service calls, digital speed control signs, and interfaces between transport systems.

Social Enterprise Business Model: The social enterprise model is a business that serves two purposes simultaneously: to generate measurable social value and create revenue.

Society 5.0: Society 5.0 refers to an ultra-intelligent society proposed by the Japanese government. Society 5.0 is based on a high convergence of cyber and physical space, reaching beyond human limitations and using artificial intelligence (AI) and robotics to analyze and improve environments, personal health, and industry achievement.

Chapter 14

Overreaction, Underreaction, and Short–Term Efficient Reaction Evidence for Cryptocurrencies

Rui Teixeira Dias
https://orcid.org/0000-0002-6138-3098
Instituto Politécnico de Setúbal, Portugal

Cristina Palma
https://orcid.org/0000-0002-7899-0134
Instituto Politécnico de Setúbal, Portugal

Mariana Chambino
https://orcid.org/0000-0002-9444-3333
Instituto Politécnico de Setúbal, Portugal

Liliana Almeida
https://orcid.org/0009-0002-8907-6804
Instituto Politécnico de Setúbal, Portugal

Paulo Alexandre
https://orcid.org/0000-0003-1781-7036
Instituto Politécnico de Setúbal, Portugal

ABSTRACT

This chapter aims to analyze the price efficiency of Bitcoin (BTC), DASH, EOS, Ethereum (ETH), LISK, Litecoin (LTC), Monero, NEO, QUANTUM, RIPPLE, STELLAR, and ZCASH in their weak form between March 1, 2018 and March 1, 2023 and determine whether they experience overreactions. The results show that cryptocurrencies exhibit positive and negative autocorrelations, which can reduce volatility and moderate price fluctuations. The results also show persistence in cryptocurrency returns, suggesting long-term trends or market patterns that individual and institutional investors can exploit. It is essential to recognize that cryptocurrencies are characterized by a high degree of complexity and instability. Investors need to monitor market trends and make the necessary adjustments to their investment strategies to anticipate market changes.

DOI: 10.4018/978-1-6684-9039-6.ch014

INTRODUCTION

The efficiency of markets is a fundamental concept in financial theory, whereby financial asset prices serve as appropriate signals for the purchase of resources. The market efficiency hypothesis is part of the concept that an investor cannot earn an extraordinary risk-adjusted return. Nevertheless, certain empirical investigations have demonstrated a contrary outcome, whereby an investor could potentially achieve a return that surpasses the market average (Fama, 1965a, 1970).

According to the efficient market hypothesis, stock prices incorporate all the relevant information that is available, thereby posing a challenge for investors to obtain abnormal profits by predicting future returns. Notwithstanding, several academic studies have contested this notion since the mid-1980s. Bondt and Thaler (1985) conducted a study which demonstrated that investing in stocks that have previously performed poorly (early extreme losers) and shorting those that have performed exceptionally well can result in abnormal long-term returns. (Initial extreme winners). According to the authors, the observed returns that are in opposition to the expected trend are attributed to the tendency of investors to overreact to information, leading to an excess of both positive and negative feelings in the market.

The occurrence of exaggerated reaction is a financial market anomaly that has been extensively researched. A significant alteration in price that partially reverts is commonly characterized as such (Chen and Zhu, 2005). This phenomenon can be elucidated by the psychological tendencies exhibited by investors (Achleitner et al., 2012; Chopra et al., 1992; De Bondt and Thaler, 2012), where this concept is frequently denoted as the "overreaction hypothesis" within the literature (Bondt and Thaler, 1985; De Bondt and Thaler, 1985) which has been overly studied and documented for the stock markets (Campbell et al., 1997; Lo and MacKinlay, 1988). Chopra et al. (1992) demonstrated in their complementary research that abnormal returns can still be achieved through the implementation of an opposing strategy, even after accounting for variables such as size, beta, and past returns.

Excessive fluctuations in cryptocurrency prices can be seen as a remarkable example of exaggerated reaction that has persisted for six months and deserved considerable attention from investors, regulators, policy makers and the media (Urquhart, 2018). According to the authors Amini et al. (2013), exaggerated reactions can also occur in shorter periods lasting a few minutes on various asset classes, resulting in the observation of a recurrent price pattern in financial markets with a gain followed by a collapse (or vice versa). This emphasizes the significance of doing a thorough investigation into the occurrence of exaggerated reactions to cryptocurrency prices.

Although conventional literature focuses on stock markets, this study intends to investigate empirical evidence and assess the behavior of digital currencies, a new class of assets that has piqued the interest of investors and gained importance in financial circles in recent years. As such, our research evaluates the prevalence of excessive reactions in the digital currency markets Bitcoin (BTC), DASH, EOS, Ethereum (ETH), LISK, Litecoin (LTC), MONERO, NEO, QUANTUM, RIPPLE, STELLAR, and ZCASH, as well as whether these reactions create efficiency imbalances.

This chapter adds to the current literature by modeling excessive price reaction as a price change based on 16-day lags, without the need to select any specific threshold parameter (such as a price change that exceeds 10% within a day or is two standard deviations over average). Previous work, on the other hand, was based on statistical modeling of exaggerated reactions, which includes the selection of one or more arbitrary parameters. Because the selection of such factors is such an important component of the study, the results may be biased when using this approach. Thus, our study extends to the empirical literature by assessing the scope of over-reaction behavior across various digital currencies, as well as their efficiency, in its weak form.

It's important to understand that the digital age has ushered in an era of extraordinary connectivity characterized by rapid access to news, financial analyses, and real-time market data. The emergence of social media platforms, cryptocurrency forums, and specialized news websites has fundamentally altered the manner in which information is disseminated in the digital currency ecosystem. This change has considerably enhanced the ability of market participants to respond swiftly and effectively to developing events and emerging trends, as a result of the seamless sharing of information on internet-based platforms. Consequently, the connection between internet news and the behaviors of cryptocurrency investors is of the uttermost importance. Rapid information dissemination, adaptable market sentiments, and escalating market volatility interact dynamically to create a relationship that requires both market participants and regulatory agencies to analyze it carefully. The increasing impact of internet news on cryptocurrency investments underscores the imperative need to enact policies that will enhance investor education, promote informed decision-making, and ensure market stability in this rapidly changing financial environment.The chapter is structured into five sections. Section 2 provides an overview of the literature on exaggerated reactions by investors to an effective market hypothesis in international markets. Section 3 describes the methodology and data used in the study. Section 4 presents the results of the analysis. Finally, section 5 presents the final conclusions.

BACKGROUND

In the context of the heightened volatility and ambiguity of cryptocurrency markets, it is a well observed phenomenon for investors to exhibit either an exaggerated or overreactive response to news and events. Overreaction in financial markets occurs when investors respond excessively to new information, leading to a disproportionate deviation of asset prices from their underlying intrinsic values. This phenomenon is especially common in markets that exhibit high levels of volatility and uncertainty, such as the markets for digital currencies. In contrast, underreaction occurs when investors fail to alter prices promptly in response to new information. In such situations, market participants may initially underestimate the significance of the information, leading to a progressive price adjustment over time. This behavior can also contribute to temporary market inefficiencies, as prices do not immediately reflect the complete impact of newly released information. Also, the phenomenon of a "price reversal" is a commonly observed pattern in financial markets. Over time, exaggerated reactions have the potential to result in a substantial alteration in the price of assets, with the possibility of enduring effects. Exaggerated reactions may result in market inefficiencies that can be referred to as "market inefficiencies" by experienced investors who possess the ability to discern mispricing and attain abnormal returns. Initially, investors in these markets may exhibit overreaction, resulting in rapid and exaggerated price oscillations, followed by underreaction as they progressively assimilate and incorporate the new information into their valuation frameworks. Over time, these amplified responses may culminate in significant price adjustments, which may have lasting effects. These market inefficiencies may be exploited by discerning mispriced assets and capitalizing on transient price disparities. In conclusion, the relationship between overreaction, underreaction, and efficient short-term response highlights the complex dynamics that regulate how investors interpret and react to new information in financial markets. This dynamic interplay bears implications for short-term price volatility and offers prospects for astute investors to leverage market anomalies stemming from these responses. As a result, studying the excessive fluctuations in cryptocurrency prices is critical for gaining insight into this dynamic market and making informed investment decisions, particularly in light of significant events that have influenced the formation and fluctuations of digital asset prices. The main goal of this manuscript is to examine the efficiency of various digital coin prices in their weak form and determine whether they experienced exaggerated reactions in light of the 2020 and 2022 events.

Related Studies on Exaggerated Reactions

In recent decades, it has been observed that financial markets on Wall Street exhibit a tendency towards exaggerated reactions, a phenomenon widely acknowledged in mainstream sense. Both anecdotal evidence and empirical studies corroborate the phenomenon of irrational exuberance. For example, Shiller (2022) survey findings pertaining to the 1987 stock market crash indicate that investors were primarily responding to the behavior of their peers, rather than the negative economic news that was being disseminated in the market. In previous research, Bondt and Thaler (1985), Chopra et al. (1992) argued that the average reversal in stock prices is evidenced by exaggerated reactions. Bondt and Thaler (1985) show that stocks that were extreme losers in an initial period of 3 to 5 years obtained excessive returns in subsequent years. Later, De Bondt and Thaler (2012) showed that these excessive returns could not easily be attributed to changes in risk, tax effects, or small business anomaly, arguing that excess return to losers can be explained by vicious expectations of future returns.

The authors Chopra et al. (1992), Wt Leung and Li (1998) conducted a study to investigate whether investors exhibit an overreaction or an exaggerated reaction to new information in the market. According to Chopra et al. (1992), there was an exaggerated reaction effect that had economic significance, even after adjustment to size and beta. According to the findings, portfolios constructed based on the previous five-year returns indicate that the previous extreme losers outperform the previous extreme winners by a margin of 5% to 10% annually over the subsequent five-year period. Although they find a pronounced seasonality in January, evidence suggests that the effect of an exaggerated reaction is distinct from the sales effect of tax loss. Interestingly, the overreaction effect is substantially stronger for smaller companies than for larger companies. Wt Leung and Li (1998) conducted a study to investigate the potential for excessive reaction in the Hong Kong stock market. The study utilized monthly return data for all ordinary stocks listed on the Hong Kong Stock Exchange between January 1980 and December 1995. The authors highlight that previous loser outperformed previous winners by up to 68.59% in the subsequent five-year test period. This finding can be interpreted as the investor's tendency to react super optimistically to positive and pessimistic information, causing stock prices to temporarily move away from intrinsic values and subsequently reverse again. The findings are in alignment with the research conducted by Bondt and Thaler (1985) pertaining to the market of the United States.

Later, Chen and Zhu (2005) conducted a study on the Chinese stock market's behavior subsequent to exceptional price fluctuations on a singular trading day. The authors utilized daily data from the Shanghai Composite Index spanning from July 2, 1997, to January 7, 2005, for this investigation. The study revealed that Chinese stock market investors exhibit a tendency to react unfavorably to positive news and overemphasize negative news. The finding aligns with the uncertain information hypothesis, positing that investors exhibit a tendency towards excessive caution in situations where information is ambiguous or unclear. The observed behavioral pattern among investors results in an increase in stock prices upon the release of unfavorable news, while a decrease is witnessed when favorable news is announced. This phenomenon is more likely to be observed in markets characterized by a general lack of accurate and reliable information. In complementarity, Antweiler and Frank (2011) suggest that when the news becomes public, the information is fully reflected in prices in one or two days (the efficient market hypothesis). Based on this assumption, researchers examined a set of 245.429 corporate news stories from the Wall Street Journal from 1973 to 2001. Using methods of computational linguistics, they sorted the stories according to the topic and, for each topic, identified a sufficient number of events. The authors emphasize that, on average, there exists a reversal or exaggerated reaction, whereby abnormal pre-event and post-event returns exhibit an inverse signal. Additionally, the findings demonstrate that the returns exhibit statistical significance and are observable in the days subsequent to their publication. Almudhaf (2017) has observed that in several markets, there are instances of exaggerated reactions in the price-dividend ratio, indicating the possible manifestation of irrational exuberance. The research additionally reveals compelling indications of several speculative bubbles in Botswana, Egypt, Ghana, Kenya, Nigeria, and Tunisia.

Borgards and Czudaj (2020) conducted a study to examine the frequency of exaggerated reactions on the value of twelve digital currencies in relation to the US stock market. The authors used a dynamic modeling approach in order to examine and evaluate exaggerated reactions to different intraday price levels. The research provides compelling evidence in favor of the overreaction hypothesis, suggesting that the cryptocurrency market exhibits a significant prevalence of excessive price reactions across all frequencies. Remarkably, the outcome exhibits a similarity in the occurrence of disproportionate price reactions in the stock market, notwithstanding the fundamental distinctions between the two markets. While Malkina and Ovchinnikov (2020), conducted a study on the distinctive characteristics of the cryptocurrency market, which were influenced by the notion of implicit volatility. Their research also delved into the market's asymmetric response to news. In terms of results, the authors find various forms of asymmetric responses exhibited by the cryptocurrency market towards news pertaining to the dynamics of fluctuations (rise or fall) with respect to the amplitude of such fluctuations (high or low volatility). During periods of inflation and market overheating, investors intentionally disregarded negative information, leading to a reversal of the asymmetry in the cryptocurrency market (the leverage effect employed). Conversely, amidst the decrease in prices, market participants demonstrated an exaggerated reaction to negative developments. Moreover, the asymmetrical response to the information witnessed in the phase of reduced market volatility ceased to exist as the amplitude of the volatility of the digital currency's return increased.

The study conducted by Chkioua (2021) examines the heightened volatility of stock prices observed on the Tunisian stock exchange during the period spanning from 2000 to 2017. This investigation employs information pertaining to the daily prices and transaction volumes of 22 corporations that are publicly traded on the Tunisian financial market, spanning the period of 2016 to 2017. The findings of the research suggest that the Tunisian stock market exhibited significant levels of volatility throughout the period under examination. The contention put forth by the author is that the surplus volatility observed in the market could have potentially engendered an unwarranted sense of assurance among domestic investors, thereby inducing them to engage in speculative conduct. In recent times, Diaconaşu et al. (2022), Schaub (2022) and Wen et al. (2022) conducted research to examine whether investors respond to one another's behaviors or to information that emerges in the digital currency market. Diaconaşu et al. (2022) conducted an analysis of the maturity of the Bitcoin market and examined the response of investors to unexpected favorable and unfavorable information. The study used abnormal returns and methodologies of unusual trading volumes. The research findings suggest that the Bitcoin market demonstrates a tendency towards maturation as investors' conduct becomes consistent with the uncertain information hypothesis regarding favorable and unfavorable occurrences. Nevertheless, the segmentation of the analyzed period into smaller intervals reveals that investors exhibit a moderate level of endorsement towards the notion of market efficiency with regards to positive occurrences in subsequent subperiods. Moreover, the research findings indicate that the efficacy of Bitcoin experienced a surge during the pandemic era. In Schaub's (2022) study, an analysis was conducted on the three most prominent cryptocurrencies, namely Bitcoin, Ethereum, and Tether. The study found that these cryptocurrencies exhibit an overreaction to feedback events that deviate from the norm, whether positive or negative in nature. The findings of the study indicate that Bitcoin and Ethereum exhibit an exaggerated response to such occurrences, whereas Tether demonstrates a noteworthy reversal of worth following atypical positive events. The revaluation patterns of the three cryptocurrencies following atypical positive events exhibits mixed evidence. The study conducted by Wen et al. (2022) poses findings that suggest the presence of predictability in intraday return within the cryptocurrency market. The predictability is observed to encompass both intraday dynamics and reversal. This research employs high-frequency price data pertaining to Bitcoin and draws the inference that the prognostic patterns of intraday return undergo alterations in the context of unexpected increases, FOMC ad releases, levels of liquidity, and the emergence of COVID-19. Other highly traded cryptocurrencies, including Ethereum, Litecoin, and Ripple, exhibit signs of intraday timing. The findings of the study suggest the utilization of intraday predictors in timing strategy results in a higher economic value compared to the implementation of reference strategies. The theory of late-informed investor is posited as an explanation for the observed evidence of intraday timing.

Examining whether investors respond to one another's conduct or to the information that enters the digital currency market is essential for comprehending the dynamics of the cryptocurrency market. According to behavioral financial research, the rationality of investors can be compromised, and their decision-making can be influenced by the actions of other market participants. The phenomenon of herd behavior can result in the formation of bubbles or crashes in asset prices. Furthermore, the market for digital currency is renowned for its elevated volatility and absence of regulatory oversight, underscoring the significance of scrutinizing the influence of information on investor conduct. Comprehending these dynamics has the potential to enhance investment decision-making and facilitate the creation of more effective regulatory frameworks for the cryptocurrency market.

Related Studies on Efficiency, in Its Weak Form

The author Gibson (1889) proposed the notion of market efficiency, positing that publicly traded stocks attain their best value as they incorporate full information. Based on this idea Bachelier (1900), a French mathematician, postulated that asset prices exhibit random and unpredictable fluctuations, thereby suggesting their lack of dependence on previous fluctuations. The random walk hypothesis (RW) emerged as a consequential contribution to the advancement of the market efficiency hypothesis, following from the mentioned development. The random walk hypothesis was strengthened by subsequent researchers, including Cowles (1933), Cowles (1944) and Working (1949), who showed that past prices could not be used by investors to predict future returns. Hence, it would be unrealistic to anticipate exceptional returns in a market that appears to be "flawless".

Apart from the previous studies, the academic community has extensively examined the efficient market hypothesis (EMH), which was scrutinized by scholars such as Fama (1965), who formulated the three forms of market efficiency, namely weak, semi-strong, and strong. The concept of weak efficiency posits that the current price of an asset incorporates all historical prices, whereas semi-strong efficiency contends that the current price of an asset reflects all publicly available information. The concept of strong efficiency posits that the current price of an asset incorporates all available information, whether it is publicly or privately held. Notwithstanding the ongoing debate surrounding HME, it continues to hold significant relevance in the fields of finance and economics. The matter at hand bears significance for the conduct of investors and the optimal distribution of resources in financial markets. Furthermore, the notion of market efficiency has been expanded beyond the conventional financial markets to encompass alternative markets, such as the digital currency market.

The Empirical literature of finance extensively deliberates on the Efficient Market Hypothesis (EMH). Prior research on the stock market, using predetermined deadlines and fluctuations in pricing, yielded inconclusive outcomes regarding the predictability of short-term returns. Brandi (2018) suggests a new methodology to tackle this matter, which involves utilizing drawdowns and drawups as motivators to explore the existence of short-term abnormal returns. The aforementioned measures exhibit sufficient flexibility to account for subordinate processes that are time-dependent in nature, which may result in either exaggerated reactions or underreactions in the market. The findings indicate that the majority of estimates provide support for HME. Moreover, the findings offer more robust support for the underreactions hypothesis compared to the excessive reaction's hypothesis, as return continuations were more prevalent than inversions.

The authors Gulec and Aktas (2019) conducted an empirical investigation to evaluate the potential trajectory of the cryptocurrency market through an analysis of its price dynamics and market efficiency. The researchers conducted an analysis of the market efficiency framework, considering the long memory and heteroscedasticity characteristics. They employed asymmetric GARCH models to examine the correlation between market depth and volatility structure for a total of 8 digital currencies. The findings of their study indicated that the cryptocurrencies that were tested exhibited long-term memory characteristics. Furthermore, as the volume of the market grew, the efficiency of the market also increased. The researchers arrived at the conclusion that the efficiency of the market exhibits an upward trend with the increase in market depth across all the cryptocurrencies that were examined. In addition, Tran and Leirvik (2020) have shown that the degree of market efficiency among the primary digital currencies fluctuates considerably over time. Recent research has confirmed that digital currency markets were inefficient prior to the year 2017. During the period spanning from 2017 to 2019, there was an observed increase in efficiency within cryptocurrency markets, a finding that appears to be at odds with other more recent research outcomes. The attribution of the phenomenon was ascribed to the use of a more extensive sample size in comparison to prior research endeavors, as well as the implementation of a resilient gauge of efficacy. The researchers discovered that Litecoin exhibited the highest level of efficiency among the digital currencies analyzed, whereas Ripple demonstrated the lowest level of efficiency, according to the mean values.

In recent studies, Zebende et al. (2022), Dias et al. (2022), Dias et al. (2023) have investigated the efficiency of financial markets by analyzing the adherence of returns to the random walk hypothesis (RW) and the presence of autocorrelation over time. Zebende et al. (2022) conducted a study to assess the market efficiency, in its weak form, using intraday data from the G20 capital markets. The analysis was divided into two distinct time periods, namely Period I (less than five days) and Period II (more than ten days). The study conducted revealed that amidst the COVID-19 pandemic, the efficiency of stock exchanges is observed to be limited to time scales of less than five days, as determined by the DFA method. However, for time scales exceeding ten days, the stock markets exhibit a tendency towards inefficiency. The utilization of the DCCA method in cross-correlation analysis has yielded distinct patterns for the open/

closed indexes of each individual stock exchange index. Dias et al. (2022) conducted an evaluation of the weak form of the efficient market hypothesis in capital markets across various countries, including Botswana, Egypt, Kenya, Morocco, Nigeria, South Africa, Japan, the United Kingdom, and the United States. The study was conducted over a period spanning from 2 September 2019 to 2 September 2020. The RW hypothesis was rejected across all the examined markets, as the returns exhibited temporal autocorrelation. No discernible distinctions were observed between the mature and emerging markets. Dias et al. (2023) investigated the efficiency, in its weak form, of the stock markets in Austria (ATX), Poland (WIG), Czech Republic (PX Prague), Hungary (BUX), Croatia (CROBEX), Serbia (BELEX 15), Romania (BET), and Slovenia (SBI TOP) during the period of 16 February 2018 to 15 February 2023. The study aimed to investigate whether the occurrences in 2020 and 2022 had a significant impact on the endurance of stock markets in Central Europe. The findings of the study revealed a statistically significant rise in persistence amidst the initial outbreak of COVID-19 and the incursion by Russian forces in 2022. Nonetheless, the investigation also revealed that the majority of stock exchanges already exhibit long memories, thereby partially validating the research question. The findings of the research have the potential to provide significant insights for investors and policymakers.

The efficiency of cryptocurrency markets has been analyzed in recent studies carried out by Souza and Carvalho (2023), Yi et al. (2023), Karaömer and Acaravci (2023). According to the research conducted by Souza and Carvalho (2023), Bitcoin and Ethereum exhibit efficiency in their weak form. Yi et al. (2023) employed a quantum harmonic oscillator as a means of demonstrating that the Bitcoin (BTC) market exhibits indications of partial efficiency. According to the Adaptive Market Hypothesis, Karaömer and Acaravci (2023) discovered that the efficiency of the cryptocurrency market fluctuates over time and is typically associated with positive or negative news/events. The mentioned studies underscore the necessity of adopting a multivariate methodology and implementing vigilant oversight of market efficiency by policymakers in order to regulate the occurrence of price distortion. In summary, the purpose of this investigation is to provide investors in the cryptocurrency markets with pertinent information, particularly in light of the exceedingly unstable and unpredictable nature of these markets. Due to the novelty and emergence of cryptocurrencies as an asset class, investors may lack the requisite knowledge and expertise to make well-informed investment choices. Furthermore, the cryptocurrency markets are susceptible to exaggerated reactions, manipulative behavior, and speculative strategies, thereby exacerbating the intricacies of investment determinations. The implementation of diversification as an investment strategy is crucial, as it aids in mitigating risk by distributing investments across various assets or asset classes. Considering the inherent instability of cryptocurrency markets, the practice of diversification may prove advantageous for investors who aim to optimize their returns while simultaneously mitigating risk. In general, a research endeavor that furnishes insights into the cryptocurrency markets and the prospective advantages of diversification can serve as a valuable repository of knowledge for both individual and institutional investors who aspire to invest in these complex markets.

METHODOLOGY

Data

The present study examines the price indexes for different cryptocurrencies, including Bitcoin (BTC), DASH, EOS, Ethereum (ETH), LISK, Litecoin (LTC), Monero, NEO, QUANTUM, RIPPLE, STELLAR, and ZCASH, over a five-year period from March 1, 2018, to March 1, 2023. To enhance the robustness of the results, the sample was partitioned into two distinct subperiods: a Tranquil period spanning from 1 March 2018 to 31 December 2019, and a Stress period from January 1, 2020, to March 1, 2023, which includes events of considerable complexity for the global economy, including the COVID-19 pandemic, the oil price war among OPEP members, and, as of 2022, the Russian incursion into Ukraine. The quotations are daily and obtained from the *Thomson Reuters Platform*.

Methodology

The study will undergo several phases of development. The sample was characterized using descriptive statistics, and the normal distribution was assessed using the Jarque and Bera (1980) test. In order to evaluate the stationarity of the time series, we will employ panel unit root tests developed by Levin, Lin, and Chu (2002) and Im et al. (2003). To confirm the validity of our findings, we will also utilize the Dickey and Fuller (1981) and Phillips and Perron (1988) tests, with Fisher Chi-square transformation. In order to address the first research question regarding whether cryptocurrency price series exhibit signs of exaggerated reactions, we will conduct an evaluation using the non-parametric test developed by Wright (2000), encompassing the Position Test (Rankings) and the Signal Test for heteroscedastic series. The application of these methods produces more accurate estimations in instances where the sample size is small, and exhibits a greater statistical power compared to traditional variance ratio tests when serial correlation is present (Vats and Kamaiah, 2011).

The statistics used to determine the rank and signs of the Wright (2000) test are based on certain assumptions, including:

If we assume y_t as the return of a time series with a sample dimension of t, then it is necessary to:

$$Y_t = X_t - X_{t-1} \tag{1}$$

If we assume that $r(r_t)$ represents the rank of Y_t within a set of t observations, then $r(y_t)$ can be expressed as a numerical value ranging from 1 to t, inclusive:

$$r'_{1t} = \frac{\left(r(r_t) - \frac{T+1}{2} \right)}{\sqrt{\frac{(T-1)(T+1)}{2}}} \tag{2}$$

$$r'_{2t} = \Phi^{-1}\left(\frac{r(r_t)}{T+1} \right) \tag{3}$$

Where Φ is the cumulative reverse standardized normal distribution and Φ^{-1} its reverse.

The transformation r_{1t}' is a linear standardization of the rankings, with sample mean of 0 and variance 1. On the other hand, r_{2t}' has sample mean of 0 and an approximate variance of 1. The statistical data pertaining to the ranking test has been acquired in the following manner for the q lags under consideration:

$$R_1(q) = \left(\frac{\frac{1}{Tq} \sum_{t=q+1}^{T} \left(r_{1t}' + r_{1t-1}' + \ldots + r_{1t-q}' \right)^2}{\frac{1}{T} \sum_{t=q+1}^{T} \left(r_{1t}' \right)^2} \right) \times \left(\frac{2(2q-1)(q-1)}{3qT} \right)^{-\frac{1}{2}} \tag{4}$$

$$R_2(q) = \left(\frac{\frac{1}{Tq} \sum_{t=q+1}^{T} \left(r_{2t}' + r_{2t-1}' + \ldots + r_{2t-q}' \right)^2}{\frac{1}{T} \sum_{t=q+1}^{T} \left(r_{2t}' \right)^2} \right) \times \left(\frac{2(2q-1)(q-1)}{3qT} \right)^{-\frac{1}{2}} \tag{5}$$

The statistical test for variance ratio that is based on S_1 signals is formally defined as follows:

$$S_1(q) = \left(\frac{\frac{1}{Tq} \sum_{t=q+1}^{T} \left(S_t + S_{t-1} + \ldots + S_{t-q} \right)^2}{\frac{1}{T} \sum_{t=q+1}^{T} \left(S_t \right)^2} \right) \times \left(\frac{2(2q-1)(q-1)}{3qT} \right)^{-\frac{1}{2}} \tag{6}$$

in which,

$$S_t = 2u(r_t, 0) \tag{7}$$

That is, a series i.i.d. with average 0 and variance 1 and,

$$\upsilon(x_t, p) = \begin{cases} 0.5 & se\ x_t > p \\ -0.5 & se\ x_t \leq p \end{cases} \tag{8}$$

The ratio of variances can be expressed as the ratio of the variance of q periods and the variance of a single period, with a value of 1. When the value of $VR(q)=1$, the series exhibits a random walk process. In cases where the null hypothesis is rejected, but the value of $VR(q)>1$, the time series data suggests the presence of a positive correlation. Conversely, if the value of $VR(q)<1$, the time series data indicates a negative correlation. To ascertain the validity of the results and address the second research question pertaining to the efficiency, in its weak form, of cryptocurrency markets, the Detrended Fluctuation Analysis methodology will be employed. (DFA). The DFA technique is a method of analysis that investigates time dependency in non-stationary datasets. By postulating the non-stationarity of time series, this methodology circumvents spurious outcomes that may arise when investigating the interrelationships among data series in the long-term. The interpretation presented by Detrended Fluctuation Analysis is as follows: $0<\alpha<0.5$, the series can be classified as anti-persistent. When $\alpha=0.5$, the series exhibits a random walk. For values of $0.5<\alpha<1$, the series can be classified as persistent. The purpose of this methodology is to analyze the correlation between the values xk a_nd xk+t_{at} distinct time intervals, as elucidated in the works of Zebende et al. (2022), Guedes et al. (2022) and Dias et al. (2023), which provide further insight into this econophysical model.

RESULTS

In Figure 1, we can see the evolution, in levels, of the 12 cryptocurrencies under study, namely Bitcoin (BTC), DASH, EOS, Ethereum (ETH), LISK, Litecoin (LTC), MONERO, NEO, QUANTUM, RIPPLE, STELLAR and ZCASH, between March 1, 2018, and March 1, 2023. The sample was partitioned into two distinct sub-periods: a Tranquil period of low volatility, spanning from March 1, 2018, to December 31, 2019; and a period of Stress for international financial markets, ranging from January 1, 2020, to March 1, 2023. The latter period encompassed exogenous events of considerable complexity for the global economy, including the COVID-19 pandemic, the oil price war among OPEP members, and the Russian invasion of Ukraine in 2022. The initial months of 2020 were marked by the convergence of the COVID-19 pandemic's first wave and the oil price war between Russia and Saudi Arabia. The observed behavior of the studied cryptocurrencies indicates a higher level of volatility during the second and third quarters of 2021, which is indicative of significant structural breaks. As of 2022, the Russian invasion of Ukraine has had a notable impact on the economy, leading to uncertainty regarding inflation. This has resulted in observable fluctuations in the time series of the cryptocurrencies being studied, indicating potential structural breaks. However, these fluctuations are comparatively less significant when considering the global COVID-19 pandemic. The aforementioned authors, namely Pardal, P., Dias, R., Teixeira, N. and Horta (2022), Dias, Pardal, et al. (2022),Teixeira et al. (2022), have proposed the same evidence for global financial markets.

Figure 1. Evolution, in levels, of the cryptocurrencies under analysis, from March 1, 2018, to March 1, 2023
Source: Own elaboration.

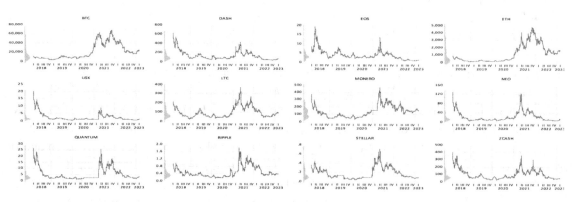

The graphical representation depicted in figure 2 illustrates the evolution, in returns, of the 12 cryptocurrencies that are under study. Through graphical interpretation, it can be observed that the average return exhibits a degree of dispersion throughout the entire sample period, though with values in close proximity to zero. During the Stress subperiod, there was a notable increase in the dispersion of average returns among cryptocurrencies. Notably, LISK and QUANTUM exhibited a more pronounced volatility, particularly in the initial months of 2021. Dias, Pereira, et al. (2022), Teixeira, Dias, and Pardal (2022), Horta et al. (2022), Horta, Dias, Revez, and Alexandre (2022) have demonstrated a significant dispersion from the average in the financial markets following the events of 2020 and 2022.

Figure 2. Evolution, in returns, of the cryptocurrencies under analysis, from March 1, 2018, to March 1, 2023
Source: Own elaboration.

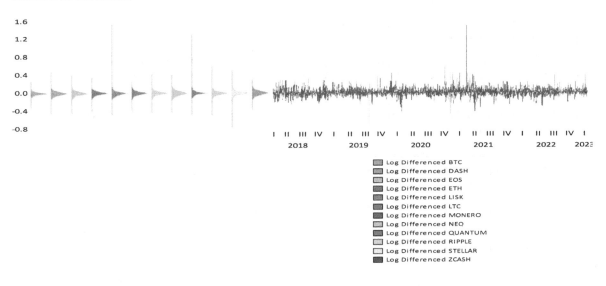

Table 1 presents a comprehensive overview of the main descriptive statistics, measured in returns, for the 12 cryptocurrencies examined in this study. Additionally, the table highlights the results of the Jarque and Bera (1980) adherence test conducted throughout the entire sample period. In relation to mean returns, our analysis reveals that solely two cryptocurrencies exhibit positive averages. Specifically, BTC (0.000571) displays the most substantial daily averages, trailed by ETH (0.000467). The remaining digital currencies exhibit negative average daily returns, with the most conspicuous instance being observed in the LISK cryptocurrency (-0.002177). The MONERO digital currency also displays a negative average return, though to a less significant extent. (-0.000562). In relation to the standard deviation, our analysis indicates that the LISK (0.075517) cryptocurrency exhibits the highest degree of dispersion, followed by QUANTUM (0.073484), EOS (0.066729), NEO (.066035), ZCASH (0.065196), DASH (.064197), RIPPLE (0.062772), STELLAR (-0.061881), LTC (0.058194), ETH (0.056324), MONERO (0.055398) and finally BTC (0.042613), which displays the least significant and therefore, the lowest standard deviation. To assess the normality of the distribution, we computed the measures of skewness and kurtosis and observed that the cryptocurrencies under investigation exhibit distinct values of 0 and

3, respectively. Furthermore, to validate the aforementioned evidence regarding the conformity of daily returns in the time series to a normal distribution with regards to their asymmetry and kurtosis values, the Jarque and Bera (1980) adherence test was conducted. The results indicate a rejection of the null hypothesis at a 1% level of significance, thus corroborating the previous evidence that the data under consideration deviate from a standard normal distribution.

In order to validate the assumption of stationarity in the time series pertaining to a range of cryptocurrencies, including Bitcoin (BTC), DASH, EOS, Ethereum (ETH), LISK, Litecoin (LTC), MONERO, NEO, QUANTUM, RIPPLE, STELLAR, and ZCASH, we will employ a summary table of unit root tests on panel data. Specifically, we will use the Levin, Lin, and Chu (2002) and Im et al. (2003) tests, and to validate the results, we will employ the Dickey and Fuller (1981) and Phillips and Perron (1988) tests with Fisher Chi-square transformation. To achieve stationarity, the first differences of the time series underwent to a logarithmic transformation. This was done to align the time series and attain the characteristics of white noise, which include a mean of 0 and constant variance. The results of this transformation validated the assumption of stationarity, as evidenced by the rejection of H_0 at a significance level of 1%, as shown in table 2.

To answer the first research question, the Wright (2000) non-parametric test was used in this investigation. The test encompasses the Ranking and Signal variance tests and was conducted over the period spanning from March 1, 2018, to March 1, 2023. The proposed methodology involves the use of two distinct tests, particularly a ranking test for homoscedastic series and a signal test for heteroscedastic series, for lags of 2 and 16 days. The digital currencies BTC, ETH, LISK, NEO, QUANTUM, and STELLAR exhibit positive serial autocorrelation in both the Rankings and Signals tests. This suggests that the fluctuations in cryptocurrency prices are not entirely stochastic and are impacted by past price trends. This evidence suggests that investors may be exhibiting exaggerated reactions to information that comes to the market. Under such circumstances, favorable news or information pertaining to a specific cryptocurrency has the potential to trigger an increase in its value as investors express a heightened sense of optimism regarding its future prospects. As a result, it is reasonable to anticipate a subsequent surge in purchases, which may further fuel additional price hikes. The results of the analysis indicate that the DASH, EOS, and LTC currencies exhibit balance in the Ranking test, but display negative serial autocorrelation in the Signal test. Conversely, the MONERO and RIPPLE cryptocurrencies reveal negative autocorrelation in The Ranking Test but exhibit positive autocorrelation in the Signal Test. The ZCASH currency, on the other hand, demonstrates both positive and negative autocorrelation in both the homoscedastic and heteroscedastic tests. The fluctuations in cryptocurrency prices are practically determined by the impact of prior favorable and unfavorable price fluctuations. In the present context, investors may exhibit distinct reactions to both positive and negative news or information related to a specific cryptocurrency. The dissemination of favorable information could potentially result in an increase in value, as stakeholders exhibit heightened levels of confidence regarding the future outlook of digital currency. Nonetheless, the extent of the escalation in price could be comparatively lesser in the presence of positive serial autocorrelation. In a similar vein, adverse news can potentially result in a transaction as investors adopt a more negative outlook towards the future prospects of cryptocurrency. To conclude, it can be inferred that the presence of positive and negative serial autocorrelation in cryptocurrencies may result in reduced volatility and relatively restrained price fluctuations. Reducing the probability of being influenced by exaggerated reactions to news or information could help investors in making more informed investment choices.

Table 1. Summary table of descriptive statistics, in returns, in respect of the cryptocurrencies under analysis, from March 1, 2018, to March 1, 2023

	BTC	DASH	EOS	ETH	LISK	LTC	MONERO	NEO	QUANTUM	RIPPLE	STELLAR	ZCASH
Mean	0.000571	-0.001657	-0.001529	0.000467	-0.002177	-0.000624	-0.000562	-0.001811	-0.001604	-0.000684	-0.001049	-0.001714
Std. Dev.	0.042613	0.064197	0.066729	0.056324	0.075517	0.058194	0.055398	0.066035	0.073484	0.062772	0.061881	0.065196
Skewness	-0.474092	-0.002465	-0.146585	-0.359280	5.579036	-0.536404	-0.504036	-0.202070	3.630120	0.674267	-0.801490	-0.314126
Kurtosis	7.963501	9.467086	8.249220	7.468006	121.0497	7.605415	10.21548	7.828584	73.43264	15.81223	24.18074	6.004688
Jarque-Bera	1388.487	2274.138	1502.939	1113.568	764525.1	1215.867	2886.192	1276.646	272607.3	9024.711	24533.64	512.3676
Probability	0.000000	0.000000	0.000000	0.000000	0.000000	0.000000	0.000000	0.000000	0.000000	0.000000	0.000000	0.000000
Observations	1305	1305	1305	1305	1305	1305	1305	1305	1305	1305	1305	1305

Source: Own elaboration.

Table 2. Summary table of panel unit root tests, in returns, concerning the cryptocurrencies under analysis, from March 1, 2018, to March 1, 2023.

Group Unit Root Test: Summary				
Method	Statistic	Prob.**	Cross-sections	Obs
Null: Unit root (assumes common unit root process)				
Levin, Lin & Chu t*	-101.661	0.0000	12	15608
Null: Unit root (assumes individual unit root process)				
Im, Pesaran and Shin W-stat	-91.7055	0.0000	12	15608
ADF - Fisher Chi-square	1653.61	0.0000	12	15608
PP - Fisher Chi-square	1107.54	0.0000	12	15636

Source: Own elaboration. Note: ** Probabilities for Fisher tests are computed using an asymptotic Chi- square distribution. All other tests assume asymptotic normality.

Table 3 presents the results of the Detrended Fluctuation Analysis (DFA) exponents that were applied to analyze the time series of various cryptocurrencies, including Bitcoin (BTC), DASH, EOS, Ethereum (ETH), LISK, Litecoin (LTC), MONERO, NEO, QUANTUM, RIPPLE, STELLAR, and ZCASH. The analysis was conducted over a period spanning from March 1, 2018, to March 1, 2023. To enhance the reliability of the findings, the sample was partitioned into two discrete sub-periods, specifically, Tranquil and Stress, which encompassed episodes of heightened complexity for the global economy, such as the COVID-19 pandemic, the oil price conflict among OPEP members, and, more recently in 2022, the Russian incursion into Ukraine.

In the Tranquil subperiod, within the period from March 1, 2018, to December 31, 2019, we conducted an analysis to determine the presence of long memories among different cryptocurrencies, including ETH, EOS, NEO, RIPPLE, DASH, STELLAR, LISK, ZCASH, BTC, QUANTUM, and MONERO. Our findings indicate that these cryptocurrencies exhibit long memories, with correlation coefficients ranging from 0.54 to 0.62. However, LTC appears to demonstrate some degree of balance, and as such, the random walk hypothesis cannot be rejected. During the Stress subperiod, spanning from January 1, 2020, to March 1, 2023, it is evident that all cryptocurrencies exhibit significant signs of (in)efficiency, with the exception of EOS (0.50) digital currency, which indicates a degree of stability during the occurrences of 2020 and 2022. This observation suggests that the random walk hypothesis cannot be rejected. The main findings of the persistence in returns exhibited by cryptocurrency markets indicate the possibility of long-term trends or patterns in the market that could be leveraged by both individual and institutional investors. Specifically, if cryptocurrency returns display autocorrelation in their residues, it can be inferred that past returns hold predictive value for future returns. Consequently, technical analysis techniques such as trend tracking, or momentum trading could lead to profitable results. It is noteworthy that the persistence in returns does not necessarily imply the predictability of the market or the assurance of profits. The cryptocurrency market is subject to numerous variables that can impact the valuation of digital assets, and the volatility of this market can pose challenges for traders seeking to achieve sustained profitability. Consequently, it is advisable for investors to exercise prudence and meticulously evaluate their risk appetite prior to investing in cryptocurrency markets. The aforementioned results are consistent with the evidence presented by Dias et al. (2020), Vasco et al. (2021) and Dias et al. (2021), demonstrating a sustained pattern in returns in global markets.

Figure 3a. The rank and signal variance ratio tests from Write (2000), of the cryptocurrencies under analysis, from March 1, 2018 to March 1, 2023

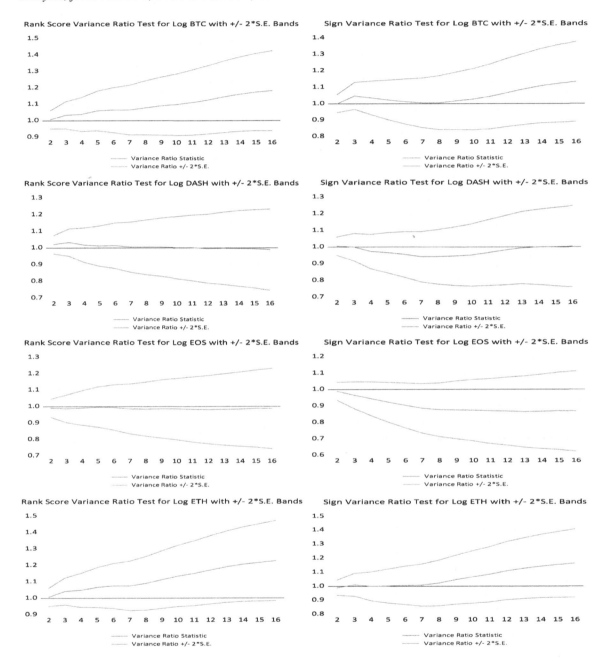

Figure 3b.

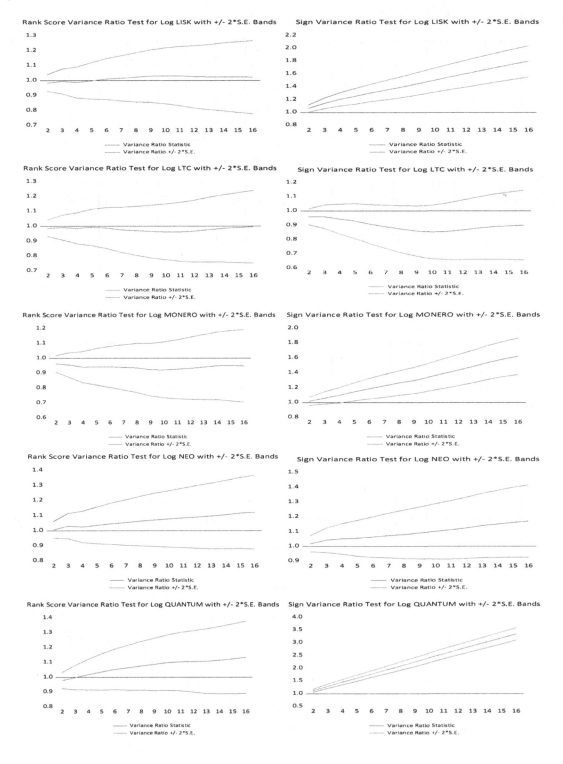

Figure 3c.
Source: Own elaboration.

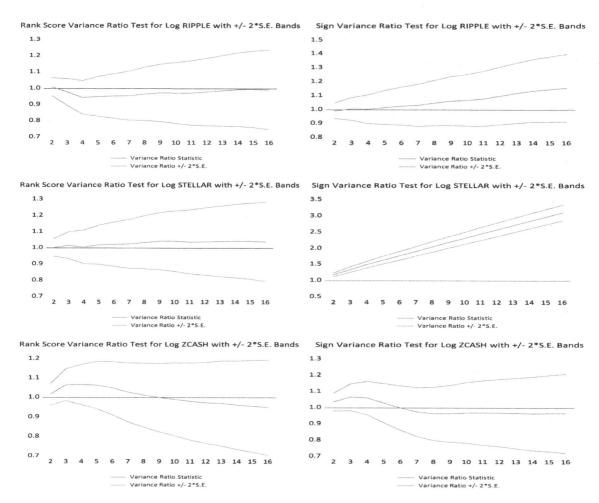

CONCLUSION

The present study aimed to examine whether the prices for different cryptocurrencies, including Bitcoin (BTC), DASH, EOS, Ethereum (ETH), LISK, Litecoin (LTC), MONERO, NEO, QUANTUM, RIPPLE, STELLAR, and ZCASH, exhibit exaggerated reactions from investors and whether this tendency contributes to the persistence in their returns. The findings primarily indicate the presence of both positive and negative autocorrelations within the cryptocurrency markets, which may result in lower volatility and comparatively restrained price fluctuations. The previously mentioned observation suggests that investors may benefit from reduced susceptibility to exaggerated market reactions when making informed investment decisions, thereby providing partial validation for the first research question. Regarding the long memories effects in cryptocurrency returns, our analysis has examined the concept of persistence. This indicates the possible existence of long-term trends or patterns in the market that could be leveraged by both individual and institutional investors. This finding partially confirms the second research question. It is essential to acknowledge that the persistence of returns does not necessarily imply market predictability or assured profitability. The volatility of cryptocurrency prices is influenced by a multitude of factors, and the dynamic nature of market conditions poses a challenge to achieving consistent profitability in trading. Given these findings, it is advisable for investors to exercise prudence and thoughtfully evaluate their risk appetite prior to making any investments in cryptocurrency markets. In summary, it is imperative to acknowledge that cryptocurrency markets exhibit a high degree of complexity and volatility, and the conduct of investors and the market as a whole can undergo swift changes. It is recommended that investors persist in monitoring market trends and adapting their investment strategies accordingly.

Table 3. Detrended fluctuation analysis (DFA).

Cryptocurrencies	DFA Exponent (Tranquil)	DFA Exponent (Stress)
BTC	$0.55^{***} \cong 0.0066$ ($R^2 = 0.99$)	$0.56^{***} \cong 0.0018$ ($R^2 = 0.99$)
DASH	$0.57^{***} \cong 0.0092$ ($R^2 = 0.99$)	$0.52^{***} \cong 0.0055$ ($R^2 = 0.99$)
EOS	$0.60^{***} \cong 0.0079$ ($R^2 = 0.98$)	$\mathbf{0.50 \cong 0.0047}$ **($R^2 = 0.98$)**
ETH	$0.62^{***} \cong 0.0171$ ($R^2 = 0.98$)	$0.54^{***} \cong 0.0087$ ($R^2 = 0.98$)
LISK	$0.56^{***} \cong 0.0081$ ($R^2 = 0.99$)	$0.53^{***} \cong 0.0031$ ($R^2 = 0.98$)
LTC	$\mathbf{0.52 \cong 0.0120}$ **($R^2 = 0.99$)**	$0.52^{**} \cong 0.0060$ ($R^2 = 0.99$)
MONERO	$0.54^{***} \cong 0.0062$ ($R^2 = 0.98$)	$0.52^{***} \cong 0.0013$ ($R^2 = 0.99$)
NEO	$0.58^{***} \cong 0.0095$ ($R^2 = 0.99$)	$0.55^{***} \cong 0.0011$ ($R^2 = 0.99$)
QUANTUM	$0.55^{***} \cong 0.0011$ ($R^2 = 0.98$)	$0.57^{***} \cong 0.0028$ ($R^2 = 0.99$)
RIPPLE	$0.58^{***} \cong 0.0080$ ($R^2 = 0.98$)	$0.56^{***} \cong 0.0085$ ($R^2 = 0.99$)
STELLAR	$0.57^{***} \cong 0.0012$ ($R^2 = 0.99$)	$0.54^{***} \cong 0.0065$ ($R^2 = 0.99$)
ZCASH	$0.56^{***} \cong 0.0017$ ($R^2 = 0.98$)	$0.53^{***} \cong 0.0064$ ($R^2 = 0.99$)

Source: Own elaboration. Note: The hypotheses are $H_0 = 0.5$ and $H_1 \neq 0.5$.

Limitations

The main constraint in the study of the exaggerated reactions of investors in cryptocurrency markets pertains to the challenge of discerning between rational and irrational behavior. The identification of the underlying causes of price fluctuations poses a challenge in ascertaining whether they stem from fundamental factors, such as changes in technology or the regulatory environment, or from irrational market behavior, characterized by exuberance or panic among investors. An additional constraint pertains to the possibility of inaccuracies or biases in the data. The nascent nature and lack of regulation in the cryptocurrency markets pose challenges in acquiring reliable and comprehensive information. Furthermore, it is possible that the data used in the research may be susceptible to selection bias, as only specific cryptocurrencies or periods may be examined. Another limitation is related to the challenge of ascertaining the fundamental drivers of sustained performance in cryptocurrency returns. Although extended trends and patterns can be discerned from the data, identifying the main causes of these trends and patterns, as well as their potential for future persistence, can prove to be a challenging task. The investigation of exaggerated reactions and persistence within cryptocurrency markets is subject to several constraints that necessitate scrutiny when interpreting findings and formulating investment strategies.

Future Research Directions

The digital era has greatly impacted financial markets, particularly in the realm of cryptocurrency exchanges. The swift and extensive availability of news, financial evaluations, and up-to-date market information distinguishes this shift. The interdependence of the cryptocurrency ecosystem on social media platforms, cryptocurrency forums, and specialized news websites has led to a convergence of conventional and digital channels for information dissemination. The use of digital connectivity empowers market participants to adapt promptly and resolutely to evolving circumstances and emerging advancements. Online platforms facilitate investors in making well-informed assessments in a prompt and effortless manner, owing to their instantaneous nature and convenient access to a wealth of information. Cryptocurrency markets operate 24/7, showing how rapidly a tweet or news article can alter prices. Cryptocurrency may be employed in academic studies to illustrate the transformative impact of technology on financial markets. Furthermore, it emphasizes the significance of ongoing academic research and empirical investigations to gain a comprehensive understanding of the complex interconnections among technology, information dissemination, and market reactions within this ever-evolving digital financial ecosystem.

In summary, future research directions may focus on comprehending the multifaceted implications of the digital era on financial markets and investor behaviour. This entails addressing the challenges of information overload, social media dynamics, inclusivity, continuous trading, risk perception, behavioural biases, and harnessing technology to enhance decision-making. These directions underscore the paramount importance of ongoing academic research and empirical investigations to gain a holistic understanding of the intricate interplay between technology, information dissemination, and market reactions within the evolving digital financial ecosystem.

ACKNOWLEDGMENT

This work would not have been possible without the support of the Instituto Politécnico de Setúbal.

REFERENCES

Achleitner, A.-K., Engel, N., & Reiner, U. (2012). The Performance of Venture Capital Investments: Do Investors Overreact? SSRN *Electronic Journal*. doi:10.2139/ssrn.2033762

Almudhaf, F. (2017). Speculative bubbles and irrational exuberance in African stock markets. *Journal of Behavioral and Experimental Finance*, *13*, 28–32. Advance online publication. doi:10.1016/j. jbef.2016.11.002

Amini, S., Gebka, B., Hudson, R., & Keasey, K. (2013). A review of the international literature on the short term predictability of stock prices conditional on large prior price changes: Microstructure, behavioral and risk related explanations. In International Review of Financial Analysis (Vol. 26). doi:10.1016/j. irfa.2012.04.002

Antweiler, W., & Frank, M. Z. (2011). Do US Stock Markets Typically Overreact to Corporate News Stories? SSRN *Electronic Journal*. doi:10.2139/ssrn.878091

Bachelier, L. (1900). Théorie de la spéculation. *Annales Scientifiques de l'Ecole Normale Supérieure*, *17*, 21–86. Advance online publication. doi:10.24033/asens.476

Borgards, O., & Czudaj, R. L. (2020). The prevalence of price overreactions in the cryptocurrency market. *Journal of International Financial Markets, Institutions and Money*, *65*, 101194. Advance online publication. doi:10.1016/j.intfin.2020.101194

Brandi, V. (2018). Short-Term Predictability of Stock Market Indexes Following Large Drawdowns and Drawups. SSRN *Electronic Journal*. doi:10.2139/ssrn.3217419

Campbell, J. Y., Lo, A. W., & MacKinlay, A. C. (1997). The Predictability of Asset Returns. In The Econometrics of Financial Markets (pp. 27–82). doi:10.1515/9781400830213-006

Chen, M. W., & Zhu, J. (2005). Do Investors in Chinese Stock Market Overreact? *Journal of Accounting and Finance Research*, *13*(3).

Chkioua, D. H. (2021). Excess Volatility in the Tunisian Stock Market: Explanation by Behavioral Finance. *South Asian Journal of Social Studies and Economics*. doi:10.9734/sajsse/2021/v12i430310

Chopra, N., Lakonishok, J., & Ritter, J. R. (1992). Measuring abnormal performance. Do stocks overreact? *Journal of Financial Economics*, *31*(2), 235–268. Advance online publication. doi:10.1016/0304-405X(92)90005-I

Cowles, A. (1933). Can Stock Market Forecasters Forecast? *Econometrica*, *1*(3), 309. Advance online publication. doi:10.2307/1907042

Cowles, A. (1944). Stock Market Forecasting. *Econometrica*, *12*(3/4), 206. Advance online publication. doi:10.2307/1905433

De Bondt, W. F. M., & Thaler, R. (1985). Does the Stock Market Overreact? *The Journal of Finance*, *40*(3), 793–805. Advance online publication. doi:10.1111/j.1540-6261.1985.tb05004.x

De Bondt, W. F. M., & Thaler, R. (1985). American Finance Association Does the Stock Market Overreact? *Source. The Journal of Finance*, *40*(3), 793–805. doi:10.1111/j.1540-6261.1985.tb05004.x

De Bondt, W. F. M., & Thaler, R. H. (2012). Do Analysts Overreact? In Heuristics and Biases. doi:10.1017/CBO9780511808098.040

Diaconaşu, D. E., Mehdian, S., & Stoica, O. (2022). An analysis of investors' behavior in Bitcoin market. *PLoS ONE, 17*(3 March). doi:10.1371/journal.pone.0264522

Dias, R., Pereira, J. M., & Carvalho, L. C. (2022). Are African Stock Markets Efficient? A Comparative Analysis Between Six African Markets, the UK, Japan and the USA in the Period of the Pandemic. *Naše Gospodarstvo/Our Economy, 68*(1), 35–51. doi:10.2478/ngoe-2022-0004

Dias, Rui, Chambino, M., & Horta, N. H. (2023). *Long-Term Dependencies in Central European Stock Markets : A Crisp-Set. 2*(February), 10–17. doi:10.58567/eal02010002

Dias, R., Pardal, P., Teixeira, N., & Horta, N. R. (2022). Tail Risk and Return Predictability for Europe' s Capital Markets. *Advances in Human Resources Management and Organizational Development*, (December), 281–298. Advance online publication. doi:10.4018/978-1-6684-5666-8.ch015

Dias, R., Teixeira, N., Machova, V., Pardal, P., Horak, J., & Vochozka, M. (2020). Random walks and market efficiency tests: Evidence on US, Chinese and European capital markets within the context of the global Covid-19 pandemic. *Oeconomia Copernicana*, *11*(4), 585–608. Advance online publication. doi:10.24136/oc.2020.024

Dias, R. T., Pardal, P., Santos, H., & Vasco, C. (2021). *Testing the Random Walk Hypothesis for Real Exchange Rates*. doi:10.4018/978-1-7998-6926-9.ch017

Dickey, D., & Fuller, W. (1981). Likelihood ratio statistics for autoregressive time series with a unit root. *Econometrica*, *49*(4), 1057–1072. doi:10.2307/1912517

Fama, E. F. (1965a). Random Walks in Stock Market Prices. *Financial Analysts Journal*, *21*(5), 55–59. Advance online publication. doi:10.2469/faj.v21.n5.55

Fama, E. F. (1965b). The Behavior of Stock-Market Prices. *The Journal of Business*, *38*(1), 34. Advance online publication. doi:10.1086/294743

Fama, E. F. (1970). Efficient Capital Markets: A Review of Theory and Empirical Work. *The Journal of Finance*, *25*(2), 383. Advance online publication. doi:10.2307/2325486

Gibson, G. R. (1889). *The Stock Markets of London*. G.P. Putnam's Sons.

Guedes, E. F., Santos, R. P. C., Figueredo, L. H. R., Da Silva, P. A., Dias, R. M. T. S., & Zebende, G. F. (2022). Efficiency and Long-Range Correlation in G-20 Stock Indexes: A Sliding Windows Approach. *Fluctuation and Noise Letters*, *21*(4), 2250033. Advance online publication. doi:10.1142/S021947752250033X

Gulec, T. C., & Aktas, H. (2019). Testing the Market Efficiency in Crypto Currency Markets Using Long-Memory and Heteroscedasticity Tests. *Osmangazi University Journal of Economics and Administrative Sciences, 14*(2).

Horta, N., Dias, R., Revez, C., & Alexandre, P. (2022). *Cryptocurrencies and G7 capital markets integrate in periods of extreme volatility*. Academic Press.

Horta, N., Dias, R., Revez, C., Heliodoro, P., & Alexandre, P. (2022). Spillover and Quantitative Link Between Cryptocurrency Shocks and Stock Returns: New Evidence From G7 Countries. *Balkans Journal of Emerging Trends in Social Sciences*, *5*(1), 1–14. doi:10.31410/Balkans.JETSS.2022.5.1.1-14

Im, K. S., Pesaran, M. H., & Shin, Y. (2003). Testing for unit roots in heterogeneous panels. *Journal of Econometrics*, *115*(1), 53–74. Advance online publication. doi:10.1016/S0304-4076(03)00092-7

Jarque, C. M., & Bera, A. K. (1980). Efficient tests for normality, homoscedasticity and serial independence of regression residuals. *Economics Letters*, *6*(3), 255–259. Advance online publication. doi:10.1016/0165-1765(80)90024-5

Karaömer, Y., & Acaravci, S. K. (2023). Adaptive Market Hypothesis: Evidence From the Cryptocurrency Market. *Iranian Journal of Management Studies*, *16*(1). Advance online publication. doi:10.22059/IJMS.2022.336833.674889

Le Tran, V., & Leirvik, T. (2020). Efficiency in the markets of crypto-currencies. *Finance Research Letters*, *35*, 101382. Advance online publication. doi:10.1016/j.frl.2019.101382

Levin, A., Lin, C. F., & Chu, C. S. J. (2002). Unit root tests in panel data: Asymptotic and finite-sample properties. *Journal of Econometrics*, *108*(1), 1–24. Advance online publication. doi:10.1016/S0304-4076(01)00098-7

Lo, A. W., & MacKinlay, A. C. (1988). Stock Market Prices Do Not Follow Random Walks: Evidence from a Simple Specification Test. *Review of Financial Studies*, *1*(1), 41–66. Advance online publication. doi:10.1093/rfs/1.1.41

Malkina, M. Y., & Ovchinnikov, V. N. (2020). Cryptocurrency market: Overreaction to news and herd instincts. *Ekonomicheskaya Politika, 2020*(3). doi:10.18288/1994-5124-2020-3-74-105

Pardal, P., Dias, R., Teixeira, N. & Horta, N. (2022). *The Effects of Russia ' s 2022 Invasion of Ukraine on Global Markets : An Analysis of Particular Capital and Foreign Exchange Markets*. doi:10.4018/978-1-6684-5666-8.ch014

Phillips, P. C. B., & Perron, P. (1988). Testing for a unit root in time series regression. *Biometrika*, *75*(2), 335–346. doi:10.1093/biomet/75.2.335

Schaub, M. (2022). Outlier Events in Major Cryptocurrency Markets: Is There Evidence of Overreaction? *The Journal of Wealth Management*, *24*(4), 142–148. Advance online publication. doi:10.3905/jwm.2021.1.155

Shiller, R. J. (2022). U.S. Stock Markets 1871-Present and CAPE Ratio. Academic Press.

Souza, O. T., & Carvalho, J. V. F. (2023). *Market efficiency assessment for multiple exchanges of cryptocurrencies*. Revista de Gestao. doi:10.1108/REGE-05-2022-0070

Teixeira, N., Dias, R., & Pardal, P. (2022). *The gold market as a safe haven when stock markets exhibit pronounced levels of risk : Evidence during the China crisis and the COVID-19 pandemic*. Academic Press.

Teixeira, N., Dias, R., Pardal, P., & Horta, N. (2022). Financial Integration and Comovements Between Capital Markets and Oil Markets. *Advances in Human Resources Management and Organizational Development*, (December), 240–261. Advance online publication. doi:10.4018/978-1-6684-5666-8.ch013

Urquhart, A. (2018). What causes the attention of Bitcoin? *Economics Letters*, *166*, 40–44. Advance online publication. doi:10.1016/j.econlet.2018.02.017

Vasco, C., Pardal, P., & Dias, R. T. (2021). Do the Stock Market Indices Follow a Random Walk? *Advances in Finance, Accounting, and Economics*, (May), 389–410. doi:10.4018/978-1-7998-6643-5.ch022

Vats, A., & Kamaiah, B. (2011). Is There a Random Walk in Indian Foreign Exchange Market? *International Journal of Economics and Finance*, *3*(6), 157–165. doi:10.5539/ijef.v3n6p157

Wen, Z., Bouri, E., Xu, Y., & Zhao, Y. (2022). Intraday return predictability in the cryptocurrency markets: Momentum, reversal, or both. *The North American Journal of Economics and Finance, 62,* 101733. Advance online publication. doi:10.1016/j.najef.2022.101733

Working, H. (1949). The investigation of economic expectations. *The American Economic Review.*

Wright, J. H. (2000). Alternative variance-ratio tests using ranks and signs. *Journal of Business & Economic Statistics, 18*(1), 1–9. Advance online publication. doi:10.1080/07350015.2000.10524842

WT Leung, R., & Li, M. (1998). Does the Hong Kong Stock Market Overreact? In *Asian Review of Accounting* (Vol. 6, Issue 2). doi:10.1108/eb060699

Yi, E., Yang, B., Jeong, M., Sohn, S., & Ahn, K. (2023). Market efficiency of cryptocurrency: Evidence from the Bitcoin market. *Scientific Reports, 13*(1), 4789. Advance online publication. doi:10.103841598-023-31618-4 PMID:36959223

Zebende, G. F., Santos Dias, R. M. T., & de Aguiar, L. C. (2022). Stock market efficiency: An intraday case of study about the G-20 group. In *Heliyon* (Vol. 8, Issue 1). doi:10.1016/j.heliyon.2022.e08808

KEY TERMS AND DEFINITIONS

Cryptocurrencies: Digital or virtual currencies that operate on a decentralized network known as blockchain and use cryptographic techniques to assure security are referred to as cryptocurrencies. Cryptocurrencies enable safe peer-to-peer exchanges and are widely used as a store of value, means of exchange, or digital asset.

Efficiency in Its Weak Form: In its weak form, efficiency implies that all previous market prices and information are already reflected in the current market price, making it challenging to achieve consistently greater returns using historical data or public information.

Long Memories: In finance or statistics, "long memories" relate to the persistence of past knowledge or events in impacting current or future results. In contrast to the concept of perfect randomness, it implies that historical facts or patterns have a long-term impact on the present.

Martingale: High-risk trading strategy in which investors double their position size following a loss in an attempt to recoup losses through subsequent profitable transactions. This strategy assumes that future gains will compensate for past losses but entails substantial risk.

Overreaction: Overreaction in cryptocurrency investors refers to the tendency of some cryptocurrency market players to overreact to new information or events, resulting in exaggerated and frequently irrational buying or selling decisions.

Price Reversal: In the realm of financial markets, mean reversal refers to the occurrence wherein the prices of assets, having strayed considerably from their historical average or mean, exhibit a tendency to revert to said mean over a time period.

Serial Autocorrelation: Serial autocorrelation, regardless of its directionality, pertains to the statistical association observed between successive data points within a given time series. Positive serial autocorrelation refers to a situation where there is a positive correlation between consecutive data points. This implies that a high value is more likely to be followed by another high value, while a low value is more likely to be followed by another low value. Negative serial autocorrelation refers to a situation where there is a negative correlation between consecutive data points. This implies that a high value is likely to be followed by a low value, and vice versa.

Short-Term Reactions: Short-term reactions among cryptocurrency investors pertain to the prompt and frequently instantaneous responses exhibited by investors in response to new information, events, or market developments within the cryptocurrency market. These reactions might result in rapid price swings or trading determinations within a short-term context.

Underreaction: Underreaction among cryptocurrency investors refers to the phenomenon in which certain cryptocurrency market players fail to immediately modify their investment strategies or asset valuations in response to new information or events, resulting in delayed or inadequate responses.

Chapter 15
ReSOLVE Framework:
When Circular Business Models Become Digital

Alexandra Costa
Instituto Politécnico de Setúbal, Portugal

Elis Ossmane
Instituto Politécnico de Setúbal, Portugal

Hortense Santos
 https://orcid.org/0000-0003-0140-1722
Instituto Politécnico de Setúbal, Portugal

Jéssica Camargo
Instituto Politécnico de Setúbal, Portugal

Luísa Carvalho
 https://orcid.org/0000-0002-9804-7813
Instituto Politécnico de Setúbal, Portugal

ABSTRACT

With the increasing focus of literature and research consolidating a positive relationship between circular business models and digital technologies, this chapter proposes a literature review on the ReSOLVE framework as a key factor to enable the development of new business models oriented towards the circular economy, in particular circular business models (CBM). For this purpose, topics such as sustainability and sustainable business models work as starting points to contextualize the urgency of rethinking alternatives to patterns of linear production and consumption in industries. In a more specific approach, the authors also seek to understand the potential of virtualization pillar under the ReSOLVE framework to implement circular economy principles in business models, as their catalysts and enablers to a sustainable industry through digitalization.

DOI: 10.4018/978-1-6684-9039-6.ch015

INTRODUCTION

Although economic growth has come to be considered the primary engine of prosperity in recent decades (WCED, 1987), it is associated with the depletion of natural resources, disturbance of ecosystems, and both direct and indirect impacts on social inequalities, especially between poor and rich countries. Furthermore, it has harmful effects on people's quality of life, both today and for future generations (WCED, 1987; Maddison, 2008; Rist, 2008; Lele, 2013). This collective consciousness began to gain public awareness in the 1980s when the Brundtland Report was published. The report defines sustainable development as "development that meets the needs of the present generation without compromising the ability of future generations to meet their own needs" (WCED, 1987, p. 43).

However, it is worth acknowledging that sustainable development is a popular yet ambiguous term. Many authors have highlighted that the term has been interpreted differently by various stakeholders due to its broad and nonspecific meaning. Different worldviews and attitudes may lead to varying goals and strategies, particularly in policymaking (Hopwood et al., 2005; Davidson, 2014). One might argue that the prevailing worldview does not promise a sustainable future, and systemic transformation is necessary (Hopwood et al., 2005). The path to sustainability necessitates a stakeholder approach in which businesses play a crucial role in innovating business models for shared value creation towards sustainability (WCED, 1987; UN, 2015; Guinot, 2020). Companies must embrace the overarching goal of avoiding negative impacts on the environment while simultaneously promoting the recovery of ecosystems and natural resources within their business strategies (Guinot, 2020). On the other hand, sustainability must also be a global priority in societal and political agendas to establish a more balanced relationship between human and natural resources (Tunn et al., cit. Toth-Peter et al., 2023).

While in the literature, Circular Economy (CE) prioritizes economic value creation (Antikainen & Valkokari, 2016) and focuses on adjacent improvements in environmental performance, implying an intentional system design (U.S. Chamber of Commerce, 2023), sustainability presents a holistic view encompassing three distinct dimensions: social, economic, and environmental (Geissdoerfer et al., 2017), along with the creation of value for a wider range of stakeholders (Antikainen & Valkokari, 2016). In this context, sustainable business models (SBMs) and circular business models (CBMs) are closely related in research and can be considered subcategories of business models (Antikainen & Valkokari, 2016), even though boundaries and synergies are still being explored in a nascent manner (Awan & Sroufe, 2022).

However, for both interlinked concepts, one might agree that information technologies (IT) serve as enablers of sustainable and circular business models in multiple ways. Digital transformation and its exponential growth leverage the implementation of digital technologies (DT) to maximize both industry and business growth, preventing the underutilization of products and their premature disposal, while rethinking their end-of-life (Rosa et al., cited in Toth-Peter et al., 2023). The increasing focus of literature and research activities establishes a positive connection between IT and CE (Chauchan et al., 2022), while mapping the strategic capacities of digitalization as a facilitator of CE principles (Seles et al., 2021) also enables exploration of new ways to create value through digital functions applied to new business models (Liu, 2022).

This chapter aims to contribute to the theoretical understanding of how digitalization operates as a starting point for the development of New Business Models oriented toward the CE, particularly CBMs. Through a literature review, the authors summarize the theoretical conceptualization of topics related to CE, SBM, CBM, and Digitalization, understanding and studying the correlation between CBMs and digitalization based on the key elements that compose the ReSOLVE framework.

To address research agendas, it also aims to identify practical applications of digitalization in CBMs, strategic orientations, potential development segments, and suggests future research agendas to advance understanding of CBM transition processes enabled by digitalization.

BACKGROUND

1. Circular Economy

Defined as a model that is 'restorative and regenerative by design and goals to maintain products, components, and materials at their highest utility and value' (MacArthur, 2015, p. 2), Circular Economy (CE) has been the focus of study in various interdisciplinary fields, representing a novel economic system that embodies paradigmatic transformations (Sucheck et al., 2021). Rooted in innovation (Roleders et al., 2022) and addressing the interconnected nature-society-material and energy flow nexus (Korhonen et al., 2018), this term extends to broader contexts, including the concept of a 'circular society' (Hofstetter et al., 2021). This concept encompasses the transition to circularity as a profound socio-ecological transformation, which in turn requires the development of appropriate legal and policy instruments.

The pressing need to swiftly decouple economic and industrial activities from their adverse environmental impacts (Barrie & Schröder, 2022) has led to the formation of large-scale international alliances and agreements, such as the New Circular Economy Action Plan (CEAP), a central component of the European Green Deal (EU, 2020). The European Green Deal is outlined as Europe's new agenda for sustainable growth. Furthermore, as a prerequisite for achieving the EU's 2050 climate neutrality target, CEAP introduces initiatives that span the entire lifecycle of products. It targets product design, promotes sustainable consumption, and aims to minimize waste while ensuring that resources are retained within the EU economy for as long as possible (EU, 2022).

The concept of Circular Economy (CE) derives from the initial definitions of sustainable development (WCED, 1987) and other constructs such as cradle-to-cradle design (Hofstetter et al., 2021), eco-effectiveness, and eco-efficiency (EMF, 2013), as well as ecological economics (Korhonen et al., 2018). It is present from various perspectives in the scientific literature and is a subject of discussion among business leaders and policymakers (Korhonen et al., 2018). From a business perspective, the top five market segments with the most published work on CE are in the areas of waste management, followed by electrical and electronic equipment, the construction industry, rubber and plastics, and agriculture, forestry, and fisheries (Mhatre et al., 2021, p. 5). The literature also predicts various gradations or options of CE, forming a hierarchy that ranges from 'refuse' to 'recover energy' (Van Buren et al., 2016).

Illustrating the multidimensional and systemic nature of CE (Uvarova et al., 2023), the development of a closed system of economy-environment interactions (Murray et al., 2017) and the principles of Rs for CE (Table 1) are points of intersection in the literature (EMF, 2013). In this context, the principles of the 3Rs - reduce, reuse, and recycle - are highlighted. 'Reduction' involves seeking eco-efficiency in the use of raw materials and in production and consumption processes. 'Reuse' entails designing products for longer service life and more sustainable consumption cycles. Finally, with 'recycling,' the goal is to recover waste materials through reprocessing for their original or other purposes (Burmaoglu et al., 2022).

Table 1. The Rs of circular economy

Refuse	Prevent the use of raw materials
Reduce	Reduce the use of raw materials
Reuse	Reuse of products (secondhand, sharing products)
Repair	Maintenance and repair
Reconditioning	Refurbishing a product
Remanufacturing	Creation of new products from (parts of) old products
Reuse	Reuse the product for another purpose
Recycle	Processing and reuse of materials
Recover energy	Incineration of waste streams

Source: Van Buren et al. (2016, p.3)

Kirchherr et al. (2023) describe several publications that attempt to review Circular Economy (CE) and provide a conceptual perspective on the topic, including various definitions (Table 2), considering its purposes and principles. To offer a perspective on different scopes of CE concepts, we analyze some of the key authors who have reflected on this topic:

Table 2. Literature reviews of scopes for CE concepts

Author(s)	Methodology	Conceptualization
Gisellini et al. (2016)	Summary of 155 EC studies	The concept of CE shows to be rooted in very diverse theoretical origins: ecological economics, environmental economics, and industrial ecology. Its inclusion in the design of products and processes allows for closing the materials and energy cycle, maximizing the use of waste, minimizing the use of virgin materials, and the release of harmful materials into the environment.
Kircherr et al. (2017)	Analysis of 114 CE definitions	Some definitions confuse CE with recycling and make a weak connection with sustainable development and social equity.
Awan et al. (2020)	Analysis of the 26 CE definitions	The CE concept is a value-oriented process. Resilience and stakeholder perspectives are, however, not explicitly included.
Friant et al. (2020)	Review of concepts and narratives of 72 CEs	By proposing a regenerative and restorative system of production and consumption, CE is seen as a promising and ideal idea to address resource scarcity, biochemical flow interruption, and climate change.
Alhawari et al. (2021)	Review of CE definitions in 91 studies	CE is the set of organizational planning processes to create and deliver products, components, and materials at their greatest utility to customers and society through the effective and efficient use of cycles.
Arruda e cols. (2021)	Review of CE Perspectives in articles published between 2015 and 2020	The concept of CE is based on a fragmented collection of ideas, which derive from semi scientific concepts such as industrial ecology, industrial ecosystems, cleaner production, eco-efficiency, and cradle-to-cradle design.

Source: Adapted from Kirchherr et. al (2023)

Additional contributions to the concept are made by Van Buren et al. (2016), who state that Circular Economy (CE) aims to create economic value concerning end products or materials, social value related to social concerns (e.g., labor conditions), as well as creating value at the environmental level (e.g., resilience of natural resources).

However, assuming that a clearer, more relevant, and more practical conceptualization of CE can help maintain the connection between CE research and practice, Kirchherr et al. (2023) present a verbal definition (Figure 1) and a coding framework that articulate the principles, objectives, and facilitators of CE identified in the review.

Figure 1. Coding and verbal definition of the CE
Source: Kirchherr et al. (2023)

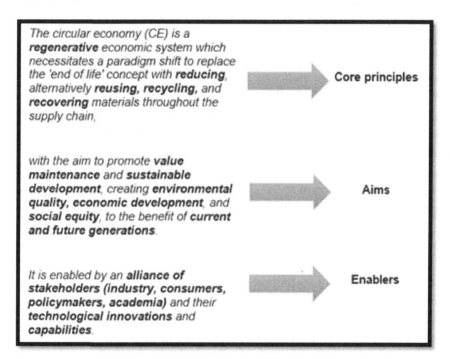

2. SUSTAINABLE AND CIRCULAR BUSINESS MODELS

2.1. Sustainable Business Models

A sustainable development path requires innovations that fundamentally transform business models, necessitating a more ambitious approach to creating social and environmental value, rather than primarily focusing on economic value (Bocken et al., 2014; Nosratabadi, 2019; Guinot, 2020). In this context, Sustainable Business Models (SBM) differ from others primarily due to their goal of generating value for multiple stakeholders, society, and the environment. This value encompasses not only economic aspects but also social and environmental considerations, while also taking into account value destruction and unrealized value as negative factors that must be minimized or avoided (Guinot, 2020; Goni et al., 2021).

Although the literature and practical applications of innovations for sustainability are extensive and fragmented, there are potential innovative approaches that can contribute to business model innovation for sustainability (Bocken et al., 2014). Boons & Lüdeke-Freund (2013, p. 44) define business model innovations for sustainability as *'innovations that create significant positive and/or significantly reduce negative impacts on the environment and/or society through changes in the way the organization and its value network create, deliver, and capture value (i.e., create economic value) or alter their value propositions."*

Recognizing the weak interconnection between the theoretical foundations of sustainable innovation and business models, particularly in the context of Sustainable Business Models (SBM), Boons and Lüdeke-Freund (2013) propose a categorization based on technological, social, and organizational aspects, which are interdependent. The authors suggest a set of fundamental regulatory requirements that must be met for the implementation of sustainable innovations. These requirements pertain to the value proposition, the supply chain, customer relationships, and the financial model. The three interdependent dimensions that appear to be most crucial in the context of SBM are as follows:

a. At the technological level, the ability to align the technological characteristics of products and services with (new) marketing approaches and the management of customer relations.
b. At the organizational level, based on alternative worldviews beyond the neoclassical paradigm, the ability to transform the way business is conducted toward sustainable development. This transformation involves affecting culture, structure, and organizational routines, which are closely tied to organizational governance.
c. At the social level, the creation of social and environmental value, acting as mechanisms that promote innovations with a social purpose.

On the other hand, Bocken et al. (2014) developed a categorization of SBM archetypes to describe mechanisms and solutions that could contribute to the development of sustainable business models. Building upon the SBM categorizations proposed by Boons and Lüdeke-Freund (2013), these archetypes aim to establish a common language for SBM in both research and practice. They seek to create new avenues for development and foster innovation, necessitating a systemic perspective to generate value.

Goni et al. (2021) explore the SBM literature and develop a distinct framework, identifying key features and elements to assist organizations in identifying opportunities and implementing sustainable business practices. Although their perspective differs, the key features they identify align with previous literature at its core, emphasizing that sustainable businesses must embed sustainability within their organizational philosophy and practices (Guinot, 2020).

Sinkovics et al. (2021) outline an integrative framework that links external and internal components influencing business models for sustainability. This framework helps recognize the systemic and complex dynamics of SBM, addressing various manifestations, such as circular, lean and green, sharing, and social models. It also considers different components of business models through which sustainable innovation can occur, including the value proposition, the type of innovation (e.g., innovations in key activities), and the organizational structure for delivering innovation (e.g., transformation). This holistic framework serves as a tool for evaluating and designing SBM that align with the environmental, social, and economic dimensions, aiming to support the achievement of the 2030 agenda.

2.2 Circular Business Models

As a manifestation of Sustainable Business Models (SBM) and a critical condition for sustainability (Geissdoerfer et al., 2017; Awan & Sroufe, 2022), Circular Economy (CE) emerges as a crucial approach compared to the linear economy (Carvalho et al., 2020) and proposes a profound transformation of production and consumption practices (Seles et al., 2021). It has been demonstrated that 91% of society still adheres to the linear economic model of 'take-make-use-dispose' (Toth-Peter et al., 2023), demanding an urgent reevaluation of production and consumption patterns. Circular Business Models (CBMs) respond to this systemic shift, aiming to mitigate the impacts of the linear economy and establish long-term resilience (Sucheck et al., 2021).

Geissdoerfer et al. (2018) emphasize that "CBMs can be defined as SBMs—business models targeting sustainable development solutions, creating both monetary and non-monetary value through proactive management of multiple stakeholders and incorporating a long-term perspective—that specifically focus on solutions for EC [i.e., closing, narrowing, slowing, intensifying, and dematerializing resource cycles] through a circular value chain and alignment of stakeholder incentives" (p. 713). These CBMs can be operationalized through four generic strategies (Table 3) for integrating circular principles into business models: circular startups, CBM acquisitions, CBM diversifications, and CBM transformations (Geissdoerfer et al., 2023).

Table 3. Types of circular business model innovation

	Internal	External
Core Business	**CBM TRANSFORMATION** There is a current business model that is changed into another business model that qualifies as a CBM.	**CIRCULAR START-UP** There is no current business model, and a new CBM is created.
Additional Business	**CBM DIVERSIFICATION** The current business model stays in place, and an additional CBM is created — this also includes joint ventures.	**CBM ACQUISITION** An existing CBM is identified, acquired, and integrated into the organization.

Adapted from Geissdoerfer et al. (2023)

In the innovation perspective illustrated by Geissdoerfer et al. (2023), financial and market-related factors often serve as the driving force behind 'Circular Start-Ups' and the 'CBM Diversification' of business models that now incorporate Circular Economy (CE) principles. In the case of 'CBM Transformations,' organizational factors become more relevant. The authors note that 'these three types are highly influenced by legal and financial barriers; however, while start-ups are more likely to encounter challenges in the value chain, established companies are more susceptible to market and organizational barriers' (Geissdoerfer et al., 2023, p. 1).

2.2.1. CE Principles in Business Models

The transition to new Circular Business Models (CBM) and the application of Circular Economy (CE) principles in business models can lead to transformative changes in six key business areas (Table 4):

Table 4. CE principles in business models

(1) **Sales model**	Service sales and product recovery after first life
(2) **Product design**	Design thinking to maximize high quality reuse of the product, its components, and materials
(3) **ICT**	Ability to track product, component, and material data
(4) **Supply circuits**	Maximization of the use of recycled materials/used components to derive additional value from product, component, and material flows
(5) **Strategic sourcing for own operations**	Development of long-term relationships with suppliers and customers, including co-creation
(6) **Human Resources**	Appropriate cultural adaptation and capacity building, reinforced by training and reward programs

Adapted from Laubscher & Marinelli (2014) cit. Lewandowski (2018)

Under the important prerogative of recognizing drivers, understanding value co-creation, maintaining a high level of coordination among different stakeholders, and assessing the economic impact of circularity principles (Kanda et al., 2021), Circular Business Models (CBMs) integrate elements from a macro to a micro perspective. They encompass global trends and drivers, relate to the ecosystem and value co-creation, and impact firms, customers, and consumers (Valkokari et al., 2014; Antikainen & Valkokari, 2016).

In this context, many authors have elucidated how circularity is embedded in business models, offering various approaches associated with circular supplies, resource recovery, Product Life Extension, sharing platforms, and products as a service (Moreno et al., 2016). Going beyond minor modifications to traditional components, these approaches also encompass material loops and adaptation factors. Lewandowski (2016) introduces the Circular Business Model Canvas (CBMC), which includes changes in the value proposition, cost structure, and revenue streams that facilitate the transition to a CBM.

Other conceptual frameworks that support the development of business models and strategies for Circular Economy (CE) may encompass the concepts of slowing loops, closing cycles, industrial symbiosis (Bocken et al., 2016), as well as the intensification of dematerialization and narrowing, and slowing down (Geissdoerfer et al., 2018). 'Slowing loops' involves extending the life of products to reduce material resource use, 'closing cycles' focuses on recycling to close the loop involving afterlife and manufacturing, and 'narrowing' entails applying fewer resources per product through design thinking and more efficient manufacturing processes (Lüdeke-Freund, 2019). Another important aspect concerns how 'Product-Service System business models,' including 'product-driven,' 'use-driven,' and 'outcome-driven' approaches, contribute to value creation and circularity (Yang et al., 2018).

Simonetto et al. (2022) introduce another important dimension of discussion related to the risks associated with adopting a Closed-Loop Supply Chain (CLSC). From the industrial perspective of closing a supply chain, especially considering the specific goals of advancing toward a more sustainable and circular industry, adopting a CLSC involves inherent risks. While a CLSC aims to 'maximize the value creation of a product throughout its entire life cycle' (Guide and Van Whassenhove as cited in Simonetto et al., 2022, p. 2), the authors identify the risks that an industry faces in the pursuit of a circular model (Table 5).

Table 5. The risks considered when adopting a CLSC

Risks related to the demand for final products	Insufficient components available for the production process. Reflects a lack of organization and external disturbances
Risks related to the demand for used products	The attitude of customers towards the use of used products and relationship between the price of remanufactured products versus new products and
Risks related to the reprocessing of returned products	It involves the predictability, quantity, and quality of returned products
Risks related to the reprocessing of returned products	It is variable in terms of costs, time, efficiency and impact on the environment, contributing to avoid disposing of products with parts and components that can still be used.
Risks related to suppliers	The wrong suppliers can compromise the entire CLSC, in terms of quantity, quality, costs, capacity and time
Risks related to manufacturing	Related to inefficient production process and productivity. Companies have to take into consideration the three aspects of CE: economic sustainability, social and environmental.
Risks related to distribution	Transportation issues can affect the entire supply chain: contributing to the unsatisfaction of costumers and inoperative activities reprocessing

Source: adapted from Simonetto et al. (2022)

3. DIGITALIZATION AND THE RESOLVE FRAMEWORK

3.1. ReSOLVE Framework

While the ReSOLVE Framework seeks economic and environmental solutions related to Circular Economy (CE) (MacArthur et al., 2015), it provides different strategies as a foundation for companies to create greater value for customers (Parida & Wincent, 2019).

Aiming to guide organizations in implementing the CE Principles, namely: (1) conserving natural capital by promoting a better balance between renewable and non-renewable resource consumption; (2) extending the useful life of resources, thereby increasing resource and energy circularity; and (3) decreasing the negative impacts of production systems, the ReSOLVE framework (MacArthur, 2015) is a reference guideline that proposes six business actions that can, in various ways, 'increase the utilization of physical assets, extend their useful life, and shift resources from finite sources to renewable sources' (MacArthur, 2015, p. 9). These actions are:

- **(Re) Regenerate:** the use of renewable and non-toxic materials and renewable energy to promote changes in energy matrices, enhance ecosystem health, and recover biological resources from the biosphere.
- **(S) Share:** maximizing product usage through reuse and sharing (peer-to-peer), extending product life cycles through maintenance, repair, and durable product/service design.
- **(O) Optimize:** increasing product efficiency by reducing waste in production and the supply chain.
- **(L) Loop:** maintaining components and materials used in a product in closed loops, focusing on recyclable and monomaterial design.
- **(V) Virtualization:** using IT to support CE by virtually delivering the utility of products.
- **(E) Exchange:** supporting new technologies, opting for new services and products, and replacing non-renewable materials with renewable ones.

Although market segments can apply the actions proposed by the ReSOLVE Framework from an individualized perspective, as described by Mhatre et al. (2021) (Table 6), it is noteworthy that each action proposed by the ReSOLVE model can facilitate the implementation of others in EC-oriented business models (MacArthur, 2015). This can substantially impact the competitiveness of sectors by reducing costs and improving performance (Bouton et al., 2016), in addition to addressing more cross-cutting issues such as climate change and biodiversity loss (Patyal et al., 2022).

Table 6. Application of ReSOLVE actions by industry segment

Regenerate	Waste management and recovery, including energy generation from waste-derived fuels, agricultural and food sector, paper and wood manufacturing, construction industry
Share	Construction industry, manufacture of electrical and electronic equipment, furniture, rubber and plastics, etc. and a range of everyday activities, related to living, working and traveling
Optimize	Manufacture of electrical and electronic equipment, machinery, furniture, waste management and construction.
Loop	Wide range of sectors – from the manufacture of electrical equipment, machinery, plastics and metals to the construction or packaging industry, agriculture, food and beverage industry
Virtualization	Information and communication technology sector, planning for construction management, modeling and product design
Exchange	Operational processes are factory. It is a dimension of less application and requires encouragement and development of policies for cleaner production processes

Adapted from Mhatre et al., (2021, pp. 10-11)

In their exploration of the potential of CE and sustainable business performance in the age of digitalization, Agrawal et al. (2022) find that digitalization can enhance the transition to a sustainable CE. CE not only supports resource conservation but also monetizes and creates value across offerings. One could argue that the 'virtualization' pillar of ReSOLVE encompasses the dimension of digitalization within Circular Business Models (CBMs). However, from various examples in the literature, it's evident that the applicability and potential impact of digitalization on CBMs, CE, and sustainability in general go well beyond virtualization or the use of IT solely for delivering the value proposition. It can also lead to significant cost reduction and enhanced performance across various industrial segments (Bouton et al., 2016).

According to Bouton et al. (2016), industry segments with high potential for cost reduction and improved performance through virtualization, as provided by the ReSOLVE Framework, include:

- Information and communication services, media, and telecommunications
- Economic activities
- Scientific R&D; other professional, scientific, and technical activities
- Education
- Human-health and social-work activities
- Administrative and support services
- Arts, entertainment, and recreation
- Financial and insurance activities
- Legal and accounting, head-office consulting, and architecture

- Distributive trades (including wholesale and retail trade)
- Manufacture of wood and paper products; printing
- Public administration and defense; compulsory social security

Mapping the impacts of Digital Transformation (DT) on vital elements in CBMs highlights IT capabilities for implementing new strategies to create and capture value for organizations (Parida et al., 2019; Ranta et al., 2021). It promotes better cost efficiency, resulting in a positive effect on the performance of involved actors and ecosystem collaborations (Parida et al., 2019).

As the review by Findik et al. (2023) concludes, Industry 4.0 applies actions of the ReSOLVE Framework in a specific way (Table 6) to transform current business models into CE business models, establishing a conceptual foundation for these models. Industry 4.0 envisions an industrialized model where humans, machines, algorithms, and products communicate with each other, both physically and cybernetically (Kagermann et al. as cited in Simonetto et al., 2022), contributing to improved sustainability performance, among other benefits.

Rusch et al. (2023) extend this perspective and assess the potential and application of digital technologies, such as artificial intelligence, big data, blockchain, and the Internet of Things, for each of the actions of the ReSOLVE Model. They conclude that the 'optimize' strategy, related to 'increasing product performance and efficiency and removing waste from production and supply chains,' is the most frequently discussed issue in the literature (Rusch et al., 2023, p. 10).

Specifically, concerning the relationship between the latest generation of IoT, a fundamental link to the ReSOLVE Framework can be established, particularly in the 'Loop' actions related to waste management and strategies for faster post-consumer collection (Ding et al., 2023), as well as in the 'Optimize' actions, which involve the transition from disposable to renewable resources (Findik et al., 2023) and resource decision-making to reduce energy consumption (Ding et al., 2023).

By connecting the ReSOLVE Model to Industry 4.0, Lopes de Sousa Jabbour et al. (2018) examine how key technologies can support each of the actions proposed by the ReSOLVE Model. Subsequently, Findik et al. (2023) elucidate how these actions of the ReSOLVE Framework establish a specific foundation for CE business models. These analyses contribute to a holistic understanding of these concepts and establish intrinsic relationships between the practices of CE, Industry 4.0, and operations management (Table 7).

3.2. The Role of Digital Technologies in the Circular Economy: State-of-the-Art Evidence

According to Chauhan et al. (2022), EC has the potential to harness and leverage emerging DT. Big data, Artificial Intelligence (AI), Blockchain, and the Internet of Things (IoT) are among the technologies identified as providing innovative digital solutions for transforming CE and business models. They reflect the flexibility and competitive potential of companies (Lopes de Sousa Jabbour et al., 2018; Agrawal et al., 2022; Nayal et al., 2022; Yusuf & Lytras, 2023). In this context, while DT is applied to change various aspects of the business model, it opens up new opportunities for revenue generation, value creation, and capture (Parida & Wincent, 2019; Gartner, 2023). Digitalization acts as an enabler of global sustainability and resilience, especially for EC, by fostering collaborative frameworks for new products, services, business models, management practices, and organizational structures (Burmaoglu et al., 2022).

Table 7. Relationships between ReSOLVE framework, Industry 4.0, and CMB

ReSOLVE Action	Key Technology	Application	CBM Background
Regenerate	Internet of things	Monitoring, and controlling factors	More efficient and renewable energy sources;
Share	Cloud manufacturing Internet of Things	Rcollection of information on consumer behaviour; Optimisation of use andvitalisation; Circular Design and logistics	Sharing Economy
Optimize		Colete data from processes and objects, such as machines; Identify faults, which can generate waste	Production processes with less waste and more efficiency
Loop:	Internet of things	Optimize design, production and logistics decisions - Product Passport	Support for technical cycles (facilitating recycling and remanufacturing) and biological cycles (facilitating waste management and fuel production)
Virtualize	Cloud manufacturing Internet of things	Interaction between organizations, suppliers and consumers	Creation of virtual and digital products Infrastructure and platform symbioses
Exchange:	Additive manufacturing	Reduction of material use; Recycling	Renewable and sustainable production

Adapted from Lopes de Sousa Jabbour et al. (2018); Findik et al. (2023)

Additionally, servitization, which focuses on creating value through services and relationships offered by companies, with a greater emphasis on services than on products (Langley, 2022), is enabling significant changes in many business models. This shift makes business models more flexible and incorporates technologies and data to understand how products are utilized.

In the view of Bressanelli et al. (2018), DT facilitates several drivers of CE, including monitoring user activities, providing advanced services like preventive maintenance or optimization during product use, digital updates, and cost estimation of products and residual components' lifespan. These advancements improve resource efficiency, extend product lifecycles, and promote closing the loop in CE (Bressanelli et al., 2018).

By examining scientific literature and identifying points of convergence between Circular Economy (CE) and Digitalization, Burmaoglu et al. (2022) present evidence regarding the evolution of this relationship in the state of the art and indicate 'progress in the convergence of these two concepts' (Burmaoglu et al., 2022, p. 2), primarily within the domains of the Sharing Economy, Additive Manufacturing, Transformation of Business Models oriented toward Digitalization, and Remanufacturing and Industrial Ecology. In addition to its capacity to support the creation and production of more intelligent products, digitalization encompasses applications related to materials and the management of reverse supply chains, thereby giving rise to novel applications that were previously absent within the linear chain. In this context, the maturity of digitalization tools in support of CE principles is principally confirmed through activities facilitating data collection, integration, and analysis (Burmaoglu et al., 2022).

- Industrial symbiosis for reuse and recycling (Agrawal et al., 2022; Voulgaridis et al., 2022).
- Networking and co-creation platforms among companies and between client-companies (Antikainen et al., 2018).
- Support for predictive and prescriptive remanufacturing and maintenance activities (Liu et al., 2022; Lopes de Sousa Jabbour et al., 2018).
- Support for design thinking activities (Santa-Maria et al., 2021; Voulgaridis et al., 2022) and marketing (Burmaoglu et al., 2022).
- Data management for the "Product Passport" and reverse logistics (Kang et al., 2016).
- Enhancing energy efficiency (Liu et al., 2022), controlling emissions levels, and managing scarce resources (Simonetto et al., 2022).
- Real-time production efficiency and inventory control, management, and supply chain collaboration (Simonetto et al., 2022).

In addition to these examples, with the increasing adoption of a product lifecycle perspective by industrial companies (Parida & Wincent, 2019), Rush et al. (2023) further emphasize that digital technology-supported enhancements during the early stages of a product's life can serve as a catalyst for circularity in subsequent phases, directly influencing the availability of product data in those subsequent lifecycle stages. In alignment with this perspective, Neligan et al. (2023) also illustrate that the ongoing digitalization in new business models can primarily contribute to enhancing circularity and efficiency in the middle of the product lifecycle, specifically in distribution, the usage phase, and customer service support.

From this perspective, for instance, the management and sharing of data – enabled by DT and applicable within both intra-organizational and inter-organizational contexts – are essential for the mid-life and end-of-life phases. Agrawal et al. (2022) further validate this insight by highlighting real-time product location tracking as an enabler for opportunities in remanufacturing, refurbishment, and recycling. According to Simonetto et al. (2022), data utilization can prevent the unnecessary disposal of still-useful components. Additionally, real-time identification and tracking of material flows contribute to more accurate assessments of returned product quality, thus mitigating risks associated with over-processing, defects, and enhancing overall quality control (Simonetto et al., 2022).

Enabled by digitization, another instance of transformation can be observed in the Sharing Economy, as discussed by De Bruyene & Verleye (2023) and Burmaoglu et al. (2022). In this context, the interaction between providers and consumers is facilitated through DT platforms. Risks associated with the search for used products can be minimized by leveraging predictive analyses, enabling the anticipation of actual demand and yielding benefits for the entire Circular Lifecycle and Supply Chain (CLSC), as noted by Simonetto et al. (2022).

As previously discussed, the convergence of digitalization, Circular Economy (CE), servitization, and other emerging trends is compelling companies to innovate and cultivate novel forms of competitive advantages (Parida & Wincent, 2019). Digital Technology's (DT) capacity to enable the Circular Economy is notably demonstrated through the transformation and creation of Circular Business Models (CBMs), particularly in the realms of resource and data management, as elaborated by Burmaoglu et al. (2022) and Yusuf & Lytras (2023). However, it necessitates circular adaptations throughout the entire value chain, as emphasized by Muller (2020) and Verleye et al. (2023). As articulated by Langley (2022, p. 13), in this emerging landscape of CBM-based value creation, companies are increasingly embracing the consumer's perspective and striving to "understand how the service adds value through remote monitoring and analysis to facilitate decision-making. decisions, control functionalities and reactivate the customer's needs".

While the state-of-the-art evidence validates the role of digitization proposed by the ReSOLVE Model in supporting Environmentally Conscious (EC) Business Models, whether they are newly conceived or pre-existing, aimed at resource optimization and lifecycle product transformation, our exploration has led to the development of a framework that diverges from the findings of these convergences and previous research conclusions. It's noteworthy, however, that we have encountered a significant challenge in attempting to establish a definitive sequence for obtaining these outcomes, as depicted in Figure 2.

Figure 2. When circular business models become digital
Source: Authors own elaboration

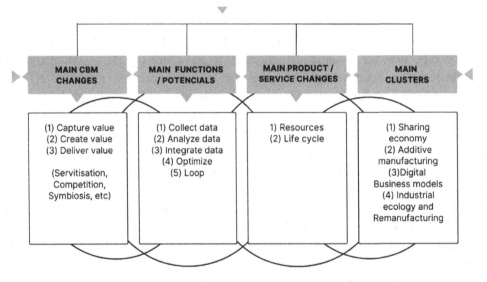

*Four different types of CBMI identified in the literature (Geissdoerfer et al., 2023)

4. RELATIONSHIPS BETWEEN CBMS AND DIGITALIZATION

While the use of DT is applied to transform various aspects of business models, create new revenue opportunities, and capture value (Parida & Wincent, 2019; Gartner, 2023), digitization serves as an enabler for sustainability and global resilience. Specifically for CE, it fosters collaborative frameworks for developing new products, services, business models, management practices, and organizational structures (Burmaoglu et al., 2022).

The power of digitalization in organizational processes is not limited to its application in various streams of sustainable business models but can also significantly impact sustainable systemic transitions across different industries and sectors (Nosratabadi, 2019). Industry 4.0 and other IT capabilities have the potential to theoretically support these transitions and enable CE processes through data-driven and smart business processes (Toth-Peter et al., 2023).

Digital transformation, particularly when powered by big data and the Internet of Things (IoT), not only makes CE concepts feasible and economically viable but also essential (Nobre & Tavares, 2020). It helps "overcome barriers to CBMs and facilitates the operationalization of circular material, components, and product flows" (Neligan et al., 2023). Although the merging of these two concepts is complex, there is a consensus that digitalization acts as an enabler for CBMs (Neligan et al., 2023).

From a broader perspective, Burmaoglu et al. (2022) argue that companies aiming for successful digital transformation need to achieve a certain level of digital readiness, acquire digital technology, and develop business models that are based on and compatible with digitalization. Bag & Rahman (2023) also assert that digital transformation and green initiatives are crucial for a company's survival in today's business landscape.

It is essential to reconsider the significance of sustainable digitalization, which provides a sustainable business environment where DT is a key factor (Yuan et al., as cited in Behera et al., 2023) and drives effective sustainable transformation for companies (Castro et al., as cited in Behera et al., 2023).

Regarding CBMs, which require outcomes based on CE principles (Ranta et al., 2020), information technologies (IT) play a crucial role in enabling sustainable industries through digitization. They lead to increased production and productivity, higher profitability, error reduction, and process optimization (Parida et al., 2019). IT mechanisms align well with circularity principles and initiatives like the ReSOLVE Framework, leading to the development and production of new technologies (Voulgaridis et al., 2022).

Furthermore, the Ecological Modernization Theory (EMT) suggests that "technology can be used to help decouple economic growth from its environmental impacts" (Hofstetter et al., 2021). Emerging technologies such as IoT, Internet of Behavior (IoB), Industry 4.0, Big Data Analytics (BDA), Artificial Intelligence (AI), Blockchain, 3D Printing, and Cloud Computing have become catalysts for innovation (Ranta et al., 2021; Liu et al., 2022; Chauhan et al., 2022; Voulgaridis et al., 2022). These technologies impact various aspects of CBMs, from key activities to resources and distribution channels, reshaping CE-oriented business models (Antikainen & Kivikytö-Reponen, 2018).

However, in the context of broader SBM transitions, business model innovation driven by digitalization necessitates changes in company ecosystems. These changes transform the ecosystem into one where value is co-created by suppliers, ecosystem partners, and customers through optimized resource utilization and effective utilization of digital technologies (Parida et al., 2019).

In summary, your study reveals the potential of DT in enhancing multiple stages of the product life cycle and facilitating CE strategies. The findings underscore the significant opportunity for broader adoption and fine-tuning of DT to accelerate the transition toward sustainability and CE (Figure 3). The examples provided illustrate that digitalization has the potential to impact all dimensions of CBMs as it integrates into various new technologies across the entire organizational value chain.

Figure 3. Digitalization enabling sustainability
Source: Authors' own elaboration

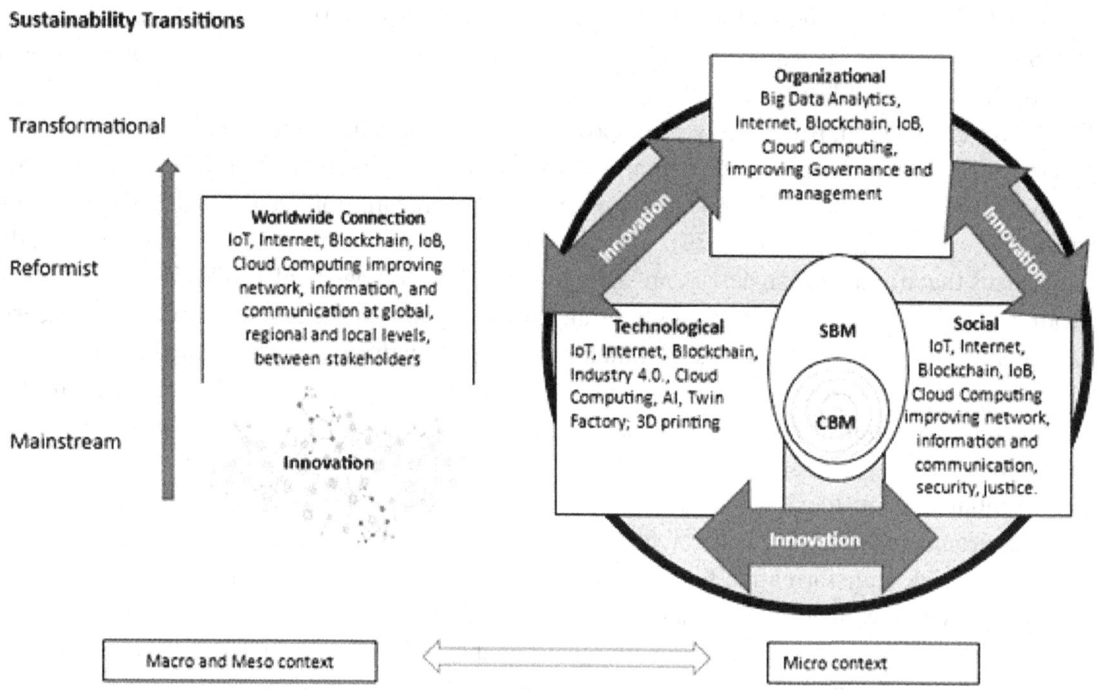

CONCLUSION

The ReSOLVE Framework offers important insights into the operationalization of Circular Business Models (CBMs). Its 'Virtualization' dimension illustrates how the digitalization of businesses intersects with circularity. However, examples from the literature show that the applicability and potential impact of digitalization on CBMs, the Circular Economy (CE), and sustainability, in general, extend well beyond virtualization or the use of IT in delivering the value proposition.

Digitalization, by facilitating the development of intelligent products and the evolution of new business models, holds immense promise for CE and sustainability on a broader scale. The integration of technologies such as the Internet of Things, big data, artificial intelligence, and blockchain can profoundly transform materials management and reverse supply chains, giving rise to applications focused on reuse, recycling, and industrial symbiosis. Additionally, DT plays a crucial role in supporting remanufacturing activities, predictive maintenance, design thinking, and energy efficiency, providing essential functions for CE strategies.

Moreover, the application of DT enhances internal resources, capabilities, activities, and functions, fostering the development of new resources. This catalyzes business model innovation, where value is co-created through the optimized utilization of resources and the efficient operation of DT by suppliers, ecosystem partners, and customers.

However, there are challenges to overcome, including issues related to predictability, psychological barriers, and information vulnerability. Furthermore, businesses must remodel their operations in alignment with their value chains and strategic initiatives to facilitate this reconfiguration.

In conclusion, digitalization stands as a pivotal enabler for transitioning toward sustainability and CE. The potential of DT in facilitating CE strategies is immense. Still, to fully harness this potential, it is essential to address these challenges, promote broader adoption and optimization of these technologies, and foster collaboration and value co-creation within the ecosystem. These steps are vital for achieving sustainability goals.

REFERENCES

Agrawal, R., Wankhede, V. A., Kumar, A., Upadhyay, A., & Garza-Reyes, J. A. (2022). Nexus of circular economy and sustainable business performance in the era of digitalization. *International Journal of Productivity and Performance Management, 71*(3), 748–774. doi:10.1108/IJPPM-12-2020-0676

Antikainen, M., Uusitalo, T., & Kivikytö-Reponen, P. (2018). Digitalisation as an enabler of circular economy. *Procedia CIRP, 73*, 45–49. doi:10.1016/j.procir.2018.04.027

Antikainen, M., & Valkokari, K. (2016). A framework for sustainable circular business model innovation. *Technology Innovation Management Review, 6*(7), 5–12. doi:10.22215/timreview/1000

Awan, U., & Sroufe, R. (2022). Sustainability in the circular economy: Insights and dynamics of designing circular business models. *Applied Sciences (Basel, Switzerland), 12*(3), 1521. doi:10.3390/app12031521

Awan, U., Sroufe, R., & Bozan, K. (2022). Designing value chains for Industry 4.0 and a circular economy: A review of the literature. *Sustainability (Basel), 14*(12), 7084. doi:10.3390u14127084

Bag, S., & Rahman, M. S. (2023). Navigating circular economy: Unleashing the potential of political and supply chain analytics skills among top supply chain executives for environmental orientation, regenerative supply chain practices, and supply chain viability. *Business Strategy and the Environment*, bse.3507. Advance online publication. doi:10.1002/bse.3507

Behera, R. K., Bala, P. K., & Rana, N. P. (2023). Creation of sustainable growth with explainable artificial intelligence: An empirical insight from consumer packaged goods retailers. *Journal of Cleaner Production, 399*, 136605. doi:10.1016/j.jclepro.2023.136605

Bocken, N. M. P., Short, S. W., Rana, P., & Evans, S. (2014). A literature and practice review to develop sustainable business model archetypes. *Journal of Cleaner Production, 65*, 42–56. doi:10.1016/j.jclepro.2013.11.039

Boons, F., & Lüdeke-Freund, F. (2013). Business models for sustainable innovation: State-of-the-art and steps towards a research agenda. *Journal of Cleaner Production, 45*, 9–19. doi:10.1016/j.jclepro.2012.07.007

Bouton, S., Bové, A.-T., Hannon, E., Magnin-Mallez, C., Rogers, M., Swartz, S., Vanthournout, H., Murphy, C., Rosenfield, J., Communications, L., Borruso, M. T., Simcock, V., Arora, R., Brown, E., Byer, H., Draper, R., Frey, T., Hanselman, H., Herbein, G., . . . Staples, M. (n.d.). *The circular economy: Moving from theory to practice is written by consultants from across sectors and geographies, with expertise in sustainability and resource productivity.* Retrieved June 23, 2023, from https://www.mckinsey.com

Bressanelli, G., Adrodegari, F., Perona, M., & Saccani, N. (2018). The role of digital technologies to overcome Circular Economy challenges in PSS Business Models: An exploratory case study. *Procedia CIRP, 73,* 216–221. doi:10.1016/j.procir.2018.03.322

Burmaoglu, S., Ozdemir Gungor, D., Kirbac, A., & Saritas, O. (2022). Future research avenues at the nexus of circular economy and digitalization. *International Journal of Productivity and Performance Management.* Advance online publication. doi:10.1108/IJPPM-01-2021-0026

Carvalho, L. C., Moreira, S. B., Dias, R., Rodrigues, S., & Costa, B. (2020). Circular economy principles and their influence on attitudes to consume green products in the fashion industry: A study about perceptions of Portuguese students. In Mapping, Managing, and Crafting Sustainable Business Strategies for the Circular Economy (pp. 248–275). IGI Global. doi:10.4018/978-1-5225-9885-5.ch012

Chauhan, C., Parida, V., & Dhir, A. (2022). Linking circular economy and digitalisation technologies: A systematic literature review of past achievements and future promises. *Technological Forecasting and Social Change, 177*(121508), 121508. doi:10.1016/j.techfore.2022.121508

Circularity vs. Sustainability. (2017, March 29). *U.S. Chamber of Commerce Foundation.* https://www.uschamberfoundation.org/circular-economy-toolbox/about-circularity/circularity-vs-sustainability

Davidson, K. (2014). A typology to categorize the ideologies of actors in the sustainable development debate: A political economy typology of sustainability. *Sustainable Development (Bradford), 22*(1), 1–14. doi:10.1002d.520

De Bruyne, M.-J., & Verleye, K. (2023). Realizing the economic and circular potential of sharing business models by engaging consumers. *Journal of Service Management, 34*(3), 493–519. doi:10.1108/JOSM-08-2021-0318

Definition of digitalization - Gartner information technology glossary. (n.d.). Gartner. Obtido 16 de agosto de 2023, de https://www.gartner.com/en/information-technology/glossary/digitalization

Ding, S., Tukker, A., & Ward, H. (2023). Opportunities and risks of internet of things (IoT) technologies for circular business models: A literature review. *Journal of Environmental Management, 336*(117662), 117662. doi:10.1016/j.jenvman.2023.117662 PMID:36913854

Ellen MacArthur Foundation. (2015). *Towards a Circular Economy: Business Rationale for an Accelerated Transition.* https://kidv.nl/media/rapportages/towards_a_circular_economy.pdf?1.2.1

Findik, D., Tirgil, A., & Özbuğday, F. C. (2023). Industry 4.0 as an enabler of circular economy practices: Evidence from European SMEs. *Journal of Cleaner Production, 410*(137281), 137281. doi:10.1016/j.jclepro.2023.137281

Geissdoerfer, M., Morioka, S. N., de Carvalho, M. M., & Evans, S. (2018). Business models and supply chains for the circular economy. *Journal of Cleaner Production, 190*, 712–721. doi:10.1016/j.jclepro.2018.04.159

Geissdoerfer, M., Pieroni, M. P., Pigosso, D. C., & Soufani, K. (2020). Circular business models: A review. *Journal of Cleaner Production, 277*, 123741. doi:10.1016/j.jclepro.2020.123741

Geissdoerfer, M., Savaget, P., Bocken, N. M. P., & Hultink, E. J. (2017). The Circular Economy – A new sustainability paradigm? *Journal of Cleaner Production, 143*, 757–768. doi:10.1016/j.jclepro.2016.12.048

Goni, F. A., Gholamzadeh Chofreh, A., Estaki Orakani, Z., Klemeš, J. J., Davoudi, M., & Mardani, A. (2021). Sustainable business model: A review and framework development. *Clean Technologies and Environmental Policy, 23*(3), 889–897. doi:10.100710098-020-01886-z

Guinot, J. (2020). Changing the economic paradigm: Towards a sustainable business model. *International Journal of Sustainable Development and Planning, 15*(5), 603–610. doi:10.18280/ijsdp.150502

Hallioui, A., Herrou, B., Santos, R. S., Katina, P. F., & Egbue, O. (2022). Systems-based approach to contemporary business management: An enabler of business sustainability in a context of industry 4.0, circular economy, competitiveness and diverse stakeholders. *Journal of Cleaner Production, 373*, 133819. doi:10.1016/j.jclepro.2022.133819

Hoessler, S., & Carbon, C. C. (2022). Digital transformation and ambidexterity: A literature review on exploration and exploitation activities in companies' digital transformation. *International Journal of Innovation Management, 26*(08), 2230003. doi:10.1142/S1363919622300033

Hofstetter, J. S., De Marchi, V., Sarkis, J., Govindan, K., Klassen, R., Ometto, A. R., Spraul, K. S., Bocken, N., Ashton, W. S., Sharma, S., Jaeger-Erben, M., Jensen, C., Dewick, P., Schröder, P., Sinkovics, N., Ibrahim, S. E., Fiske, L., Goerzen, A., & Vazquez-Brust, D. (2021). From sustainable global value chains to circular economy-different silos, different perspectives, but many opportunities to build bridges. *Circular Economy and Sustainability, 1*(1), 21–47. doi:10.100743615-021-00015-2 PMID:34888550

Hopwood, B., Mellor, M., & O'Brien, G. (2005). Sustainable development: Mapping different approaches. *Sustainable Development (Bradford), 13*(1), 38–52. doi:10.1002d.244

Kanda, W., Geissdoerfer, M., & Hjelm, O. (2021). From circular business models to circular business ecosystems. *Business Strategy and the Environment, 30*(6), 2814–2829. doi:10.1002/bse.2895

Kang, H. S., Lee, J. Y., Choi, S., Kim, H., Park, J. H., Son, J. Y., Kim, B. H., & Noh, S. D. (2016). Smart manufacturing: Past research, present findings, and future directions. *International Journal of Precision Engineering and Manufacturing-Green Technology, 3*(1), 111–128. doi:10.100740684-016-0015-5

Korhonen, J., Honkasalo, A., & Seppälä, J. (2018). Circular Economy: The Concept and its Limitations. Ecological Economics. *Ecological Economics, 143*, 37–46. doi:10.1016/j.ecolecon.2017.06.041

Langley, D. J. (2022). Digital Product-Service Systems: The role of data in the transition to Servitization business models. *Sustainability (Basel), 14*(3), 1303. doi:10.3390u14031303

Laubscher, M., & Marinelli, T. (2014a). Going Green - CARE INNOVATION. *Integration of Circular Economy in Business.*

Laubscher, M., & Marinelli, T. (2014b). *Integration of circular economy in business.* Academic Press.

Lele, S. (2013). Rethinking sustainable development. *Current History, 112*(757), 311–316.

Lewandowski, M. (2016). Designing the business models for circular economy—Towards the conceptual framework. *Sustainability (Basel), 8*(1), 43. doi:10.3390u8010043

Liu, Q., Trevisan, A. H., Yang, M., & Mascarenhas, J. (2022). A framework of digital technologies for the circular economy: Digital functions and mechanisms. *Business Strategy and the Environment, 31*(5), 2171–2192. doi:10.1002/bse.3015

Lopes de Sousa Jabbour, A. B., Jabbour, C. J. C., Godinho Filho, M., & Roubaud, D. (2018). Industry 4.0 and the circular economy: A proposed research agenda and original roadmap for sustainable operations. *Annals of Operations Research, 270*(1–2), 273–286. doi:10.100710479-018-2772-8

Lüdeke-Freund, F., Gold, S., & Bocken, N. M. P. (2019). A review and typology of circular economy business model patterns: Circular economy business models. *Journal of Industrial Ecology, 23*(1), 36–61. doi:10.1111/jiec.12763

Maddison, A. (2008). The west and the rest in the world economy: 1000-2030. *World Economy, 9*(4), 75–99.

Mhatre, P., Panchal, R., Singh, A., & Bibyan, S. (2021). A systematic literature review on the circular economy initiatives in the European Union. *Sustainable Production and Consumption, 26*, 187–202. doi:10.1016/j.spc.2020.09.008

Moreno, M., De los Rios, C., Rowe, Z., & Charnley, F. (2016). A conceptual framework for circular design. *Sustainability (Basel), 8*(9), 937. doi:10.3390u8090937

Muller, J. M. (2020). Data-based sustainable business models in the context of Industry 4.0. *International Conference on Information Systems 2020 Special Interest Group on Big Data Proceedings,* 5.

Murray, A., Skene, K., & Haynes, K. (2017). The circular economy: An interdisciplinary exploration of the concept and application in a global context. *Journal of Business Ethics, 140*(3), 369–380. doi:10.100710551-015-2693-2

Nayal, K., Kumar, S., Raut, R. D., Queiroz, M. M., Priyadarshinee, P., & Narkhede, B. E. (2022). Supply chain firm performance in circular economy and digital era to achieve sustainable development goals. *Business Strategy and the Environment, 31*(3), 1058–1073. doi:10.1002/bse.2935

Neligan, A., Baumgartner, R. J., Geissdoerfer, M., & Schöggl, J.-P. (2023). Circular disruption: Digitalisation as a driver of circular economy business models. *Business Strategy and the Environment, 32*(3), 1175–1188. doi:10.1002/bse.3100

Nosratabadi, S., Mosavi, A., Shamshirband, S., Kazimieras Zavadskas, E., Rakotonirainy, A., & Chau, K. W. (2019). Sustainable business models: A review. *Sustainability (Basel), 11*(6), 1663. doi:10.3390u11061663

Parida, V., Sjödin, D., & Reim, W. (2019). Reviewing literature on digitalization, business model innovation, and sustainable industry: Past achievements and future promises. *Sustainability (Basel), 11*(2), 391. doi:10.3390u11020391

Patyal, V. S., Sarma, P. R. S., Modgil, S., Nag, T., & Dennehy, D. (2022). Mapping the links between Industry 4.0, circular economy and sustainability: A systematic literature review. *Journal of Enterprise Information Management, 35*(1), 1–35. doi:10.1108/JEIM-05-2021-0197

Ranta, V., Aarikka-Stenroos, L., & Väisänen, J.-M. (2021). Digital technologies catalyzing business model innovation for circular economy—Multiple case study. *Resources, Conservation and Recycling, 164*(105155), 105155. doi:10.1016/j.resconrec.2020.105155

Rist, G. (2014). The environment or the New Way Nature of Development. In The History of Development: From Western Origins to Global Faith (3rd ed.). Zed Books.

Roleders, V., Oriekhova, T., & Zaharieva, G. (2022). Circular Economy as a Model of Achieving Sustainable Development. *Problemy Ekorozwoju, 17*(2).

Rusch, M., Schöggl, J.-P., & Baumgartner, R. J. (2023). Application of digital technologies for sustainable product management in a circular economy: A review. *Business Strategy and the Environment, 32*(3), 1159–1174. doi:10.1002/bse.3099

Santa-Maria, T., Vermeulen, W. J. V., & Baumgartner, R. J. (2022). The Circular Sprint: Circular business model innovation through design thinking. *Journal of Cleaner Production, 362*(132323), 132323. doi:10.1016/j.jclepro.2022.132323

Santoro, G., Vrontis, D., Thrassou, A., & Dezi, L. (2018). The Internet of Things: Building a knowledge management system for open innovation and knowledge management capacity. *Technological Forecasting and Social Change, 136*, 347–354. doi:10.1016/j.techfore.2017.02.034

Seles, B. M. R. P., Mascarenhas, J., Lopes de Sousa Jabbour, A. B., & Trevisan, A. H. (2022). Smoothing the circular economy transition: The role of resources and capabilities enablers. *Business Strategy and the Environment, 31*(4), 1814–1837. doi:10.1002/bse.2985

Simonetto, M., Sgarbossa, F., Battini, D., & Govindan, K. (2022). Closed loop supply chains 4.0: From risks to benefits through advanced technologies. A literature review and research agenda. *International Journal of Production Economics, 253*, 108582. doi:10.1016/j.ijpe.2022.108582

Sinkovics, N., Gunaratne, D., Sinkovics, R. R., & Molina-Castillo, F.-J. (2021). Sustainable business model innovation: An umbrella review. *Sustainability (Basel), 13*(13), 7266. doi:10.3390u13137266

Suchek, N., Fernandes, C. I., Kraus, S., Filser, M., & Sjögrén, H. (2021). Innovation and the circular economy: A systematic literature review. *Business Strategy and the Environment, 30*(8), 3686–3702. doi:10.1002/bse.2834

Toth-Peter, A., Torres de Oliveira, R., Mathews, S., Barner, L., & Figueira, S. (2023). Industry 4.0 as an enabler in transitioning to circular business models: A systematic literature review. *Journal of Cleaner Production, 393*(136284), 136284. doi:10.1016/j.jclepro.2023.136284

UN (2015). *Transforming our world: the 2030 agenda for sustainable development* (Vol. 16301). A/RES/70/1.

Uvarova, I., Atstaja, D., Volkova, T., Grasis, J., & Ozolina-Ozola, I. (2023). The typology of 60R circular economy principles and strategic orientation of their application in business. *Journal of Cleaner Production, 409*(137189), 137189. doi:10.1016/j.jclepro.2023.137189

van Buren, N., Demmers, M., van der Heijden, R., & Witlox, F. (2016). Towards a circular economy: The role of dutch logistics industries and governments. *Sustainability (Basel), 8*(7), 647. doi:10.3390u8070647

Verleye, K., De Keyser, A., Raassens, N., Alblas, A. A., Lit, F. C., & Huijben, J. C. C. M. (2023). Pushing forward the transition to a circular economy by adopting an actor engagement lens. *Journal of Service Research*. Advance online publication. doi:10.1177/10946705231175937

Voulgaridis, K., Lagkas, T., Angelopoulos, C. M., & Nikoletseas, S. E. (2022). IoT and digital circular economy: Principles, applications, and challenges. *Computer Networks, 219*(109456), 109456. doi:10.1016/j.comnet.2022.109456

WCED (Western Cape Education Department). (1987). *Report of the World Commission on Environment and Development: Our Common Future*. Author.

Yang, M., Smart, P., Kumar, M., Jolly, M., & Evans, S. (2018). Product-service systems business models for circular supply chains. *Production Planning and Control, 29*(6), 498–508. doi:10.1080/09537287.2018.1449247

Yusuf, N., & Lytras, M. D. (2023). Competitive sustainability of Saudi companies through digitalization and the circular carbon economy model: A bold contribution to the Vision 2030 agenda in Saudi Arabia. *Sustainability (Basel), 15*(3), 2616. doi:10.3390u15032616

Chapter 16

Stylometry–Based Authorship Identification:
An Approach from the Internet of Behaviors Perspective through Contrastive Linguistic Analysis

Duc Huu Pham

https://orcid.org/0000-0003-4564-7986

International University-Vietnam National University Ho Chi Minh City, Vietnam

ABSTRACT

The Internet has helped to collect and exchange information and data with its constant expansion and evolution for devices to be intertwined with each other. These advances provide invaluable information about people and issues related to their lives including behaviors, interests, and preferences which have brought about the Internet of Behaviors (IoB) in attempts to understand the data collected from users' online activities. From a behavioral psychology perspective, the IoB can address the question of how to understand the data, and how to apply that understanding to create things that benefit humans. The IoB is related to many fields of research including technology, data analytics, and behavior science in relationship with stylometry. The applications of stylometry within the IoB framework such as analyzing the writing style of social media posts, online reviews, journal articles, or literary works at tertiary educational organizations could provide insights into the personality or motivations of the author. Thus, stylometry could potentially be used to identify authorship.

INTRODUCTION

This chapter focuses on the stylometry-based application from the perspective of the Internet of Behaviors via measuring the style of writing of authors to identify who writers are. The chapter will depict how the Internet of Behaviors could provide critical insights that enable the identification of author writing styles from texts based on their style of writing. It can be understood that authorial identity is the sense

DOI: 10.4018/978-1-6684-9039-6.ch016

which writers have of themselves as authors and the textual identity that they construct in their writing. Stylometry can analyze the style features that can be statistically quantified, such as sentence length, vocabulary diversity, and frequencies of words, or word forms, etc.

The chapter introduces the use of comparative and contrastive methods of linguistic analysis for authorship identification. Each language has its own features compared with other languages regarding the inflectional ones (typically, English) or non-inflectional ones (typically, Chinese or Vietnamese), Therefore, this chapter aims to provide a general look with the analysis of linguistic similarities and differences in the stylometric measure through the descriptions of the vocabulary richness, the examination of the word-level features such as the word-length distribution and average word length, and the word frequency using the statistics. Since the Internet has strongly developed, which can bring both positive and negative changes for human behaviors, this chapter may help to identify the authenticity, and thus, benefit authors in their academic written contributions.

BACKGROUND

The background will discuss the definition of stylometry, including authorship identification and attribution, the historical use of stylometry for authorship identification, and the Internet of Behaviors; the relationship between stylometry and the Internet of Behavior through investigating the role of linguistics in authorship identification and the importance of contrastive linguistic analysis in stylometry.

Stylometry

Stylometry refers to the quantitative analysis of literary style through various computational methods (Holmes, 1998) and is largely used in authorship attribution as a process of ascertaining the author of a certain text or set of texts (Rybicki & Eder, 2011). The scientific study of stylometry began in the 19th century, proposing the use of word lengths and word frequency distributions as tools for authorship analysis (Mendenhall, 1887). The digital era has so far had an important impact on stylometric features when computers can analyze large numbers of texts quickly and accurately to allow for the inclusion of a variety of stylometric features (Stamatatos, 2009). The simple features such as average word length, sentence length, and the frequency of particular words are often taken into account together with more complicated ones that require the application of advanced linguistic theories, such as the use of certain syntactic constructions or the distribution of function words (Koppel et al., 2009). The field of stylometry has grown significantly with the beginning of machine learning and artificial intelligence, with larger sets of features to be considered and the creation of models that can predict authorship with high precision, even among large sets of potential authors (Kestemont et al., 2020).

Authorship Identification and Attribution

Authorship identification is the process of determining the author of a certain document or set of documents. This process involves the comparison of the features of a disputed text with those of known authorial texts, using statistical and computational methods to draw conclusions about likely authorship. It can be said that authorship identification is a task of identifying authors of anonymous texts (Zhang et al., 2014). According to Mosteller and Wallace (1964), a typical example in authorship identification is the Federalist Papers study conducted in the 1960s, using stylometric analysis to demonstrate that James Madison rather than Alexander Hamilton was the author of disputed essays.

In the modern time, new authorship identification methods often use machine learning and Natural Language Processing techniques with the use of Support Vector Machines, Naive Bayes, and Random Forests, which are popular algorithms adopted in authorship attribution (Stamatatos, 2009) though authorship identification usually indicates whether or not a particular person is the author. Meanwhile, authorship attribution typically involves multiple potential authors and is about determining the most likely among them. However, both authorship identification and authorship attribution have the same purpose of confirming the authorship. Recently, deep learning techniques have also been introduced to the field, offering promising results, with the best use of the methods based on Recurrent Neural Networks, specifically Long Short-Term Memory networks, and Convolutional Neural Networks (Kestemont et al., 2020). However, authorship identification often meets challenges, such as when it is used to identify exact authorship among potential authors, or when the text is short (Stamatatos, 2009).

The Historical Use of Stylometry for Authorship Identification

In the 19th century, Morgan proposed the use of vocabulary richness to distinguish authors, while Mendenhall suggested the analysis of word lengths as a characteristic measure for authorship analysis (Mendenhall, 1887). For instance, the authorship of Shakespeare's works has long been a subject of debate, which results in extensive stylometric investigations. In the 20th century, Fisher and Greg, who were statisticians, used stylometry to analyze linguistic features and textual patterns to support the attribution of Shakespearean works to William Shakespeare (Craig & Kinney, 2009). As for the authorship of the Federalist Papers, a collection of essays written during the formation of the United States Constitution, this was a subject of dispute. In the 1960s, Mosteller and Wallace applied stylometric methods to analyze word usage and other linguistic features to attribute disputed papers to James Madison (Mosteller & Wallace, 1964) and showcased the potential of stylometry for authorship identification.

With the advances of computational methods and machine learning, stylometry has made significant progress in authorship identification. These advancements have expanded the scope and accuracy of authorship identification using stylometry. The insights into the historical use of stylometry for authorship identification have demonstrated the application of stylometry across different periods and notable cases and indicated its evolvement from its early beginnings to become a valuable tool in the field of digital humanities and textual analysis in the age of the Internet of Things in which the Internet of Behaviors plays a crucial role in daily human life, offering valuable insights into the identification of authors based on their unique writing styles.

The Internet of Behaviors

The Internet of Behaviors (IoB) is a new concept, which focuses on the collection and the analysis of data related to an individual's behaviors, actions, preferences, and activities through various interconnected devices and systems. It leverages data from multiple sources, such as the Internet of Things devices, social media, online transactions, and more, to gain insights into human behavior patterns and enable personalized experiences, targeted advertising, and behavior modification (Kushwaha et al., 2020). The IoB aims at creating a comprehensive understanding of individual behaviors and preferences through the combination of data from various sources, with the collection, the processing, and the analysis of large volumes of behavioral data to extract meaningful insights. These insights can be used by businesses, organizations, and governments to optimize their operations, enhance customer experiences, and make data-driven decisions (Salman et al., 2020).

The IoB raises several important considerations related to privacy, ethics, and data security. As the collection and analysis of personal behavioral data increases, there is a need for robust governance frameworks to protect individual privacy rights and ensure responsible use of the data (Van Den Heuvel et al., 2019). The IoB is a relatively new concept and has the potential to have a strong impact on many domains, such as healthcare, retail, transportation, and smart cities. It can help personalize healthcare interventions, improve customer targeting and engagement, optimize transportation systems, and enhance urban planning (Chakraborty et al., 2021).

The Relationship between Stylometry and the Internet of Behavior in the Contrastive Linguistic Analysis

Though the concept of the IoB is still relatively new, and scholarly literature specifically focusing on its development and evolution may be limited, its emergence and potential impact can provide insights into development and evolution. Kshetri (2020) indicated the emergence of the IoBs as an extension of the Internet of Things (IoT) and data-driven technologies through the exploration the potential applications of the IoB in various domains, such as healthcare, retail, transportation, and governance. King (2021) provided an overview of the IoB, highlighting its potential impact on businesses, which explores how data collection and analysis can assist companies in understanding consumer behavior and suit their products and services accordingly.

According to Gantz and Reinsel (2020), the evolution of digital transformation and its impact on the IoB highlights the role of data analytics, behavioral tracking, and AI-driven technologies in shaping the IoB development. This viewpoint is also in accordance with Brody and Bednar (2021) when they highlight the evolution of the IoB. Gantz and Reinsel have discussed the transition from analyzing discrete behaviors to understanding larger processes and systems, proposing the potential implications and challenges associated with the IoB. Moreover, the ethical considerations need to be addressed when they are associated with the IoB in discussing privacy concerns, data governance, and the need for responsible data collection and usage to ensure ethical practices in the context of the IoB (Pellegrini & West, 2020). While not many research studies have been conducted on the development and evolution of the IoB, the IoB still represents a growing area of interest, and more research is expected to be conducted in the future.

Stylometry through computational methods has found new relevance in the age of the IoB with the combination of technologies such as Big Data, AI, and the IoT, to track, monitor, and influence human behavior to better understand individual behavioral patterns based on their textual interactions online. Through the analysis of writing patterns on social media platforms, IoB systems can potentially identify authorship, detect anomalies, or even predict user behaviors with a significant degree of accuracy (Castillo et al., 2019). As IoB continues to evolve, the intersection with stylometry indicates the profound ways in which digital footprints down to the choice of words can reveal the aspects of behaviors and identities.

The Role of Linguistics in Authorship Identification

As linguistics has a critical role in authorship identification, the focus is on the analysis of textual features that are unique to a particular writer. This practice, also known as stylometry, largely derives its methods from the linguistic study of an individual's idiolect, a set of linguistic features that are characteristic of a particular person (Chaski, 2005). Linguistic features used in authorship identification can range from lexical choices, grammatical structures, use of punctuation, sentence lengths, and even the frequency of function words. These patterns, often subconscious on the part of the author, form a unique stylistic signature which can be used to attribute authorship to a piece of text (Koppel et al., 2007). Advanced computational techniques, including machine learning algorithms, are often used to collect and analyze these linguistic features. Methods such as n-gram analysis, lexical frequency profiling, and bag-of-words approaches can effectively distinguish between different authors' styles (Stamatatos, 2009). However, it is necessary that successful authorship identification should require more than the computation of linguistic features. An in-depth understanding of linguistic principles and the nuances of individual language use is also important. Therefore, the role of linguistics in authorship identification is a combination of quantitative analysis and qualitative interpretation, making it an irreplaceable component in the field (Juola, 2006).

The Importance of Contrastive Linguistic Analysis in Stylometry

Contrastive linguistic analysis plays a crucial role in stylometry by providing insights into the distinctive linguistic features and patterns that characterize an author's writing style. This approach involves the comparison of the linguistic characteristics of different authors or texts to identify stylistic differences and similarities. Burrows (2002) emphasized the significance of contrastive analysis in stylometry in the Delta method, which compares the distribution of linguistic features between texts. The Delta measure enables the identification of distinctive linguistic patterns to be employed for authorship attribution. Stamatatos et al. (2000) emphasized the role of contrastive linguistic analysis in automatic text categorization, which is closely related to authorship identification. Through the comparison of the linguistic characteristics of texts from different genres and authors, the effectiveness of contrastive analysis in distinguishing between various categories and authors can be obtained.

Argamon et al. (2003) investigated different text classification methods for authorship attribution, using contrastive analysis techniques regarding the writing style of multiple authors, Argamon et al. demonstrated that contrastive linguistic analysis can significantly contribute to accurate authorship attribution. Koppel and Schler (2004) also suggested the importance of contrastive linguistic analysis in authorship verification, proposing a one-class classification approach to distinguish between authentic and impostor texts, emphasizing the significance of contrasting the linguistic features of known authors with those of unknown authors. The integration of stylometry-based authorship identification with the IoB perspective and contrastive linguistic analysis offers a powerful approach to accurately identify authorship by leveraging comprehensive behavioral data, identifying distinctive linguistic patterns, and enabling a deeper understanding of an author's unique writing style.

THE MAIN FOCUS OF THE CHAPTER

The focus of the chapter will be on the stylometry in authorship identification with case studies and examples of successful stylometric analysis through the definition and explanation of the Internet of Behaviors. This section will also identify the potential benefits and risks of the Internet of Behaviors in stylometry, and the contrastive linguistic analysis in stylometry with a typical case study for illustration to result in a new integrated approach in stylometry and the Internet of Behaviors. Finally, the section will indicate future prospects and challenges, together with implications and suggestions for future research.

Stylometry and Authorship Identification

Stylometry, the quantitative analysis of linguistic style in written texts, has become a valuable tool for authorship identification, enabling researchers to attribute authorship based on distinctive writing characteristics and patterns. Authorship identification, a field closely linked to stylometry, involves the use of computational methods and statistical analysis to determine the likely author of a text or set of texts, drawing on features such as vocabulary, syntax, word choice, and other linguistic elements. Stylometry and authorship identification have a rich historical background, with early pioneers proposing methods based on word lengths and vocabulary richness, and modern advancements incorporating machine learning algorithms and deep linguistic analysis. By comparing and contrasting linguistic features across texts, stylometry and authorship identification offer insights into an author's unique writing style, providing valuable contributions to fields such as literary studies, forensic linguistics, and digital humanities. The application of stylometry and authorship identification extends beyond traditional literature and includes domains such as historical document analysis, plagiarism detection, anonymous text attribution, and identifying pseudonymous authors. These issues give a glimpse into the broad scope and significance of stylometry and authorship identification as fields of study and research through a close look at historical development, methodologies, applications, and ongoing challenges in these areas.

The Mechanism of Stylometry in Authorship Identification

Stylometry relies on analyzing various linguistic features and patterns within texts to distinguish an author's unique writing style. Burrows (2002) introduced the concept of the "Delta" measure, which quantifies the stylistic difference between texts. The Delta measure is computed by comparing the distribution of linguistic features, such as word frequencies or sentence lengths, among texts. Significant differences in these distributions can help identify likely authorship. The effectiveness of different linguistic features for authorship identification should be based on using a combination of features, including lexical, syntactic, and semantic attributes, to achieve more accurate results (Argamon et al., 2013). Authorship attribution methods can be much more effective if they use feature-based methods, machine learning algorithms, and select and combine features to be able to achieve reliable authorship identification (Stamatatos, 2009).

According to Koppel et al. (2009), the computational methods used in authorship attribution use stylometric approaches in which appear the challenges of feature selection, feature engineering, and the potential impact of different linguistic features on the accuracy of authorship identification. With Holmes and Forsyth's (1995) study, the application of stylometry was used in analyzing the writing style of Edgar Allan Poe, through the exploration of various linguistic features, such as vocabulary richness and word length distributions, to distinguish Poe's writing style from that of other authors, showcasing the effectiveness of stylometric analysis. With a comprehensive understanding of the mechanism of stylometry in authorship identification throughout these above-mentioned studies, the importance was emphasized on analyzing diverse linguistic features, feature selection, and combining methods to achieve accurate results in determining authorship. All these empirical sources provide a foundation for understanding the underlying mechanism of stylometry in authorship identification.

Various Techniques and Approaches in Stylometry

While stylometry and authorship identification have proven successful in many cases, challenges such as the presence of ghostwriters, cross-genre variations, and the need for large and diverse training corpora continue to drive research and refinement in the field. The use of stylometry to analyze gender and genre differences in formal written texts employed various linguistic features, such as function words, character n-grams, and POS tags, to distinguish between male and female authors as well as different genres (Argamon et al. 2003). In a study by Kestemont et al. (2014), the investigation of cross-genre authorship attribution, where the goal is to attribute authorship across different literary genres, was carried out, with the use of machine learning algorithms and the exploration of the effectiveness of different feature sets, including character-level n-grams and vocabulary richness, to address the challenges of genre variation in stylometry. Eder (2017) introduced the stylometry package for the R programming language, which offers a range of techniques and tools for computational text analysis. The package includes functions for feature extraction, distance measures, and classification algorithms, which can assist researchers in working out a comprehensive toolkit for stylometric analysis.

According to Potha and Joshi (2021), the application of text mining techniques in stylometry analysis for authorship attribution can employ features such as word frequency, character n-grams, and lexical richness to identify authorship patterns and assess the effectiveness of different classification algorithms for attribution tasks. Through an extensive survey of computational methods in authorship attribution, including various stylometric approaches, Koppel et al. (2011) pointed out the strengths and limitations of different feature sets, algorithms, and evaluation methods, offering insights into the effectiveness of different techniques in authorship identification. The use of linguistic features, machine learning algorithms, and text mining techniques for authorship attribution tasks has so far showcased the versatility and effectiveness of stylometric analysis in identifying writing style patterns and distinguishing authors.

Strengths and Limitations of Stylometric Methods

Modern authorship attribution methods using stylometric approaches have the strengths of stylometric methods, such as their ability to analyze large amounts of text quickly and the potential for high accuracy in distinguishing authors, and these methods also provide limitations, such as the sensitivity of stylometric features to document length and genre variation (Stamatatos, 2013). In stylometric analysis, the strength of function words is capturing an author's writing style, as they are less influenced by topic and content. The limitations are the potential for function words to be influenced by external factors or noise in the text (Argamon & Levitan, 2005). Moreover, Juola's (2006) comprehensive overview of authorship attribution highlights the strengths of stylometric analysis in distinguishing between authors and the applicability across various text types. Juola (2006) also discussed the limitations, such as the need for careful feature selection and the challenges posed by authorship obfuscation techniques.

According to (Koppel et al., 2011), the strengths of computational methods in association with stylometric approaches in authorship attribution are the automatic analysis of large amounts of text and the potential for high accuracy in distinguishing authors; the specific limitations are potential impact of authorial obfuscation techniques and the need for carefully controlled training data. Later, Eder and Rybicki (2011) discussed the strengths and limitations of training sample selection in stylometric analysis. They highlighted the importance of selecting training samples that are representative of an author's style and the strengths of using balanced training datasets. They also discussed limitations, such as the potential for overfitting when using small or biased training samples. It can be seen that research studies have so far given an updated understanding of the strengths and limitations of stylometric methods in authorship attribution, focusing on the potential for high accuracy and the ability to analyze large amounts of text, while also addressing challenges such as feature selection, genre variation, authorial obfuscation, and training sample selection.

Case Studies and Examples of Successful Stylometric Analysis

There have been many examples showing the success of using stylometry. For instance, Mosteller and Wallace's (1964) study on the authorship of the Federalist Papers is a classic example of successful stylometric analysis. Though Mosteller and Wallace used word frequencies and other linguistic features and were able to attribute the disputed papers to James Madison, providing compelling evidence for authorship, their method needs some more investigations related to feature selection, assumption of independence, computational limitations, external validation, stylistic variability, and domain knowledge. Argamon et al. (2009) conducted a case study on detecting insider fraud using stylometric methods. They employed various stylometric features and machine learning techniques to identify linguistic patterns associated with fraudulent activities, showcasing the effectiveness of stylometry in forensic applications, but diverse writing styles and false positives/negatives should be taken into account. Koppel and Winter (2014) conducted a case study in which they successfully determined whether two documents were written by the same author. Though they had used a combination of stylometric features and machine learning algorithms, which resulted in achieving high accuracy in authorship verification, some modifications such as generalizability and variability in writing style could make the study stronger.

Eder et al. (2015) presented a case study using stylometry to attribute authorship in anonymous historical plays. They utilized a suite of stylometric tools and explored different feature sets to identify the likely authors of these plays, demonstrating the successful application of stylometry in attributing authorship to previously unknown texts. It should be noticed that domain specificity and authorship styles were the limitations of the study. Kestemont et al. (2017) conducted a case study on authorship attribution of Flemish 19th-century literature. They employed stylometric features and machine learning techniques to attribute authorship to anonymous texts, successfully identifying the likely authors and shedding light on previously unknown contributors, demonstrating the successful application of stylometric analysis in various domains. However, stylistic consistency assumption could be added to make the investigation more thorough. In conclusion, from determining authorship in historical texts to detecting fraud and verifying authorship, these studies have highlighted the effectiveness of stylometry in solving real-world problems and uncovering hidden information, especially with the involvement of the Internet of Behaviors.

Definition and Explanation of the Internet of Behaviors

Gasson (2020) presented a systematic literature review on the IoB, offering an extensive analysis of the definitions, concepts, and applications of the IoB, exploring the potential benefits, challenges, and ethical implications of the IoB, providing a detailed explanation of its scope and significance. Khormali et al. (2021) divided in groups the viewpoints regarding the definition and key technologies of the IoBs. They explained how the IoB encompasses the collection, analysis, and utilization of behavioral data to enable personalized experiences, targeted advertising, and behavior modification. They also explore the potential applications of the IoB in various sectors. Janssen and Kuk (2021) conducted a systematic literature review to explain the IoB and its impact on organizations when the IoB is considered as the combination of behavioral data, analytics, and technology to understand and influence human behavior. The study also explores the implications of the IoB on organizational practices and decision-making (as cited in Filgueiras, 2022). Kshetri (2022) provided a comprehensive definition and explanation of the IoB, highlighting its key characteristics and applications, with the discussion of the integration of behavioral data from various sources, such as IoT devices, social media, and online platforms, and the analysis of this data to gain insights into individual behaviors, preferences, and actions. Sun et al. (2023) presented a comprehensive survey on the IoB, offering an in-depth exploration of its definitions, key technologies, and challenges. Sun et al. also highlighted the integration of data from different sources, the use of AI and machine learning techniques for behavioral analysis, and the ethical considerations in the IoB ecosystem.

The Internet of Behaviors Perspectives

With Gasson's (2020) study, various aspects of the IoB, including its potential benefits, challenges, and ethical considerations were considered regarding the impact of the IoB on individual privacy, data security, and societal implications, providing a comprehensive overview of the IoB perspective. Li and Fu (2021) also provided IoB's definition, key technologies, applications, and challenges, examining the IoB perspectives in various domains, including healthcare, smart cities, transportation, and retail offered insights into its potential and limitations. Kshetri (2020) discussed the IoB, which was considered as an emerging extension of the Internet of Things (IoT), focusing on the collection and analysis of behavioral data, which are the potential applications of the IoB in different sectors, and the challenges related to privacy, security, and ethical considerations.

Baumer et al. (2020) in an analysis of the rise of the IoB and its implications for society discussed the collection and analysis of behavioral data, the potential benefits and risks associated with the IoB, and the role of ethics and governance in guiding its development. In addition, Küng and Gonçalves (2021) examined the IoB from a human-centric perspective and considered its impact on individuals and society. Therefore, the relationship between the IoB and the human value system is accelerated, with the focus on the need for ethical considerations and responsible use of behavioral data. All these works provide updated literature that delves into the IoB perspective. They cover the definition, technologies, applications, challenges, and ethical considerations associated with the IoB, offering a comprehensive understanding of its potential benefits and implications for individuals, organizations, and society.

The Influence of the Internet of Behaviors on Authorship Identification

With an overview of authorship attribution by Argamon et al. (2009), various approaches and techniques were discussed to highlight the role of linguistic features, computational methods, and statistical analysis in authorship identification, which can potentially be influenced by the IoB. Stamatatos (2009) surveyed modern authorship attribution methods, using stylometric approaches to focus on the IoB, to support the use of computational methods and feature-based approaches in authorship identification, which may be influenced by the data sources and behavioral insights offered by the IoB.

According to Holmes and Forsyth (1995), the stylometric analysis of Edgar Allan Poe's short stories to study his writing style pointed out some relationship with the IoB. The analysis showcased how linguistic analysis and stylometry can contribute to authorship identification, which can potentially be enhanced by incorporating behavioral data from the IoB. The exploration of authorship attribution using text mining techniques can utilize computational methods and textual analysis in identifying authorship patterns (Potha & Joshi, 2021). It can be said that the incorporation of IoB data could potentially enhance the accuracy and depth of authorship identification models.

The Internet of Behaviors in Gathering and Analyzing Behavioral Data

Van Laer and Escalas' (2018) overview of consumer behavior in the digital world lends weight to the use of the IoB in gathering and analyzing behavioral data. The collection of data through various sources, such as social media, wearables, and IoT devices, can contribute to understanding consumer behaviors and preferences (as cited in Kühn & Boshoff, 2023). The use of the IoB in data fusion and analysis for enhancing digital customer experience, and the integration of behavioral data from multiple sources, such as social media, mobile apps, and online platforms can gain insights into customer behaviors and deliver personalized experiences (Wang et al., 2021). An IoB framework for smart city applications, focusing on the collection and analysis of behavioral data, with the utilization of various sensors, IoT devices, and social media platforms to gather behavioral data, can enable smart city initiatives in areas such as transportation, energy management, and public safety (Arora et al., 2020).

Fuentes-Fernández et al. (2020) explore the use of the IoB in enhancing digital advertising through the utilization of IoT data. The collection of behavioral data from IoT devices, such as smartwatches and connected appliances can help understand consumer preferences and deliver targeted and personalized advertising experiences (as cited in Peyman et al., 2021). To enable technologies and meet challenges of the IoB, it is necessary that data collection techniques brought into use should be sensors, wearables, and mobile devices, and the analysis of behavioral data for applications in healthcare, smart homes, and other domains (Dwivedi at al., 2022). The use of the Internet of Behaviors (IoB) in gathering and analyzing behavioral data highlights the collection of data from various sources, such as social media, IoT devices, and sensors, and how the analysis of this data contributes to understanding consumer behaviors, enhancing digital experiences, and enabling applications in areas like smart cities and advertising.

Potential Benefits and Risks of the Internet of Behaviors in Stylometry

Potential Benefits

There may be some potential benefits of the IoB in stylometry. Firstly, for the enhancement of accuracy, the IoB can provide access to a wealth of behavioral data from various sources, enabling a more comprehensive analysis of an author's writing style. By incorporating behavioral insights, stylometric models may achieve higher accuracy in authorship attribution and identification (Hanisch et al., 2021). Secondly, for the improvement of feature extraction, the IoB can offer additional features that can enhance stylometric analysis. Behavioral data, such as writing patterns, timing of writing sessions, or preferred vocabulary, can be integrated into the feature set, potentially leading to more nuanced and reliable authorship identification (Oloo et al., 2022). Thirdly, for the enhancement of contextual understanding, considering behavioral data from the IoB, stylometric analysis can help to gain a deeper understanding of an author's socio-cultural context, writing habits, and stylistic preferences (Bories et al., 2022). This contextual understanding can provide valuable insights into authorship patterns and contribute to a more comprehensive analysis. Finally, as for the cross-domain applications, the IoB's behavioral data can facilitate cross-domain authorship identification, considering an author's behavior across various platforms, genres, or languages, stylometric models to potentially handle multi-domain authorship attribution tasks more effectively (Barlas et al., 2020). More methods for potential benefits could be enhancing data collection and using real-time analysis with behavioral insights.

Potential Risks

However, there may be some potential risks and challenges of IoB in stylometry. Firstly, for privacy concerns, the IoB relies on collecting and analyzing personal behavioral data. Stylometric analysis may access sensitive information, and the ethical collection, storage, and usage of this data must be carefully addressed to ensure privacy protection (Zhao et al., 2023). Secondly, for data quality and reliability, the accuracy, and the reliability of the IoB's behavioral data can pose challenges in stylometry. Noise, biases, or inaccuracies in the collected data can influence the effectiveness of stylometric analysis and lead to false attributions or unreliable results (Sadman et al., 2020). Thirdly, for data security, the storage and transmission of behavioral data can present security risks. For example, stylometric analysis may require access to personal data, and robust security measures must be in place to protect this data from unauthorized access, breaches, or misuse (Sarker et al., 2022). Finally, for ethical considerations, respecting individuals' privacy, obtaining informed consent, and ensuring transparency in data usage are necessary to address ethical concerns and maintain trust in the stylometric analysis process (Altman et al, 2018). Since potential disadvantages can arise from incorporating behavioral data into stylometric analysis, responsible implementation of the IoB in stylometry is important to address these considerations and ensure a balanced approach that respects privacy, data security, and ethical principles. More methods for potential risks could be related to bias, discrimination, legal and regulatory compliance.

Contrastive Linguistic Analysis in Stylometry

The analysis of contrastive linguistic analysis in stylometry needs to take into consideration many issues regarding the contrastive linguistic analysis, the role of contrastive linguistic analysis in enhancing the accuracy of stylometry and the illustration of the case study demonstrating the efficiency of contrastive linguistic analysis in stylometry.

Contrastive Linguistic Analysis in Enhancing the Accuracy of Stylometry

Contrastive linguistic analysis (CLA) in the study by Nesselhauf and Tono (2015) provides an overview of corpus-based studies in contrastive linguistics. The theoretical foundations and methodologies of CLA emphasize the comparison and analysis of linguistic features across different languages or language varieties. The use of CLA in cross-language text classification explores techniques for distinguishing similarities and differences between languages, which highlights the role of CLA in identifying linguistic features that help differentiate languages and improve classification accuracy (Zesch & Gurevych, 2009). The cross-linguistic comparison of adjective ordering restrictions using CLA. The study examined the similarities and differences in adjective order among English, Mandarin, and Japanese, illustrating the use of CLA to investigate syntactic phenomena across languages (Hung, 2018). Moreover, in CLA, typological profiling as a methodological tool is used to study linguistic diversity through comparing and contrasting linguistic features across languages to identify typological (Szmrecsanyi & Kortmann, 2009). With CLA as an approach for comparing and contrasting linguistic features across different languages or language varieties, various linguistic domains, including language classification, inter-language analysis, and cross-linguistic comparisons can be properly analyzed. According to Koppel et al. (2011), stylometric analysis in the context of 'real-world' texts results in complications that are not often considered in typical stylometric analysis. This includes elements such as multiple authors, which could potentially be analyzed with a contrastive linguistic approach. Jockers (2013) stated that digital text analysis methods in literary studies could potentially be integrated with a contrastive linguistic analysis with a contrastive dimension.

The Case Study Demonstrating the Efficiency of Contrastive Linguistic Analysis in Stylometry

According to Rybicki and Eder (2011), the application of a specific stylometric method across various genres and languages demonstrated a form of contrastive analysis. The use of the stylometry in author-ship identification is carried out in the studies by Nguyen and Dinh (2021) and Nguyen (2023) based on the model in a study by Grieve (2007), in which the comparison and the contrast of the Vietnamese and English are used. The reason for the choice of Vietnamese in this study is that Vietnamese is one of non-inflectional languages and it is Latin-based. The reason for the choice of English in this study is that English is an inflectional language and it shares the Latin-based alphabet with Vietnamese. The study uses word length, syllable length, word richness, and word frequency. The corpuses used in the study are VVC_Stylometry for Vietnamese and the Telegraph Columnist Corpus for English, as can be displayed in the following Tables 1,2,3, and 4 showing the similarities and differences between Viet-namese and English regarding the ration of word length distribution according to the letters, the ration of word length distribution according to the syllable, the richness of word, and the word frequency using the statistics, respectively.

Table 1. The ration of word length distribution according to the letters

	Numbers of Authors				Average	Impact
	10 Authors	5 Authors	3 Authors	2 Authors		
Vietnamese (VVC_ Stylometry)	39	43	55.8	65.8	50.9	fairly low
English (Telegraph Columnist Corpus)	39	54	68	79	60	fairly high

Table 1 shows that word length distribution according to the letters in authorship identification ac-counts for 50.9% of the accuracy (low) for Vietnamese (VVC_Stylometry) and 60% of the accuracy (fairly high) for English (Telegraph Columnist Corpus).

Table 2. The ration of word length distribution according to the syllable

	Numbers of Authors				Average	Impact
	10 Authors	**5 Authors**	**3 Authors**	**2 Authors**		
Vietnamese (VVC_Stylometry)	50,6	55.8	60.8	66	53.9	fairly high
English (Telegraph Columnist Corpus)	22	39	55	70	46.5	fairly low

Table 2 shows that the word length distribution according to the syllable in authorship identification accounts for 53.9% of the accuracy (fairly high) for Vietnamese (VVC_Stylometry) and 46.5% of the accuracy (fairly low) for English (Telegraph Columnist Corpus).

Table 3. The word richness

	Numbers of Authors				Average	Impact
	10 Authors	**5 Authors**	**3 Authors**	**2 Authors**		
Vietnamese (VVC_Stylometry)	32.68	44.12	49.96	56.16	45.73	fairly low
English (Telegraph Columnist Corpus)	22	37	50	68	44.15	fairly low

Table 3 shows that the word richness in authorship identification accounts for 45.73% of the accuracy (fairly low) for Vietnamese (VVC_Stylometry) and 44.15% of the accuracy for English (Telegraph Columnist Corpus) (fairly low).

Table 4. The word frequency

	Numbers of Authors				Average	Impact
	10 Authors	**5 Authors**	**3 Authors**	**2 Authors**		
Vietnamese (VVC_Stylometry)	74.95	80.2	83.65	88.1	81.73	Very high
English (Telegraph Columnist Corpus)	63	73	82	88	76.5	Fairly high

Table 4 shows that the word frequency in authorship identification accounts for 81.73% of the accuracy (very high) for Vietnamese (VVC_Stylometry) and 76.5% of the accuracy for English (Telegraph Columnist Corpus) (fairly high).

From the findings presented above, it can be said that, to improve the investigation, the case could be validated with the help of programming language R, through the use of cross-validation, feature importance analysis, domain expertise, and ethical considerations.

Stylometry and the Internet of Behaviors: An Integrated Approach

The integrated approach for the stylometry and the Internet of Behaviors needs to take into account how the Internet of Behaviors enhances stylometric techniques for authorship identification and the predictive modelling and machine learning in the integrated approach.

The Internet of Behaviors Enhancing Stylometric Techniques for Authorship Identification

According to Chen et al. (2017), data-driven human behavior modeling using the Internet of Things (IoT) is a component of the Internet of Behaviors (IoB). Moreover, in a study by Pan and Kudo (2019), which is n-gram against the machine, the feasibility of the n-gram network analysis for binary protocols could bring in positive results in stylometry using behavioral data. Moreover, the influence of contrastive linguistic analysis can affect the IoB and stylometry to some extent. Contrastive linguistic analysis aims to identify, compare, and contrast linguistic characteristics between different languages, dialects, or even individual writing styles. Stylometry applies statistical analysis to literary style, often used to determine authorship or to understand stylistic changes across texts. The IoB is a more recent concept, coined by Gartner, related to the use of technology to capture, analyze, and potentially influence human behavior. Data-driven human behavior modeling using the IoT, which could potentially be applied to stylometric techniques for authorship identification, could be enhanced with contrastive linguistic analysis (Chen et al., 2017). The methodologies used in study could more potentially be applied to stylometry through extensive data collection, cross-platform integration, validation, and evaluation.

Predictive Modelling and Machine Learning in the Integrated Approach

The application of predictive modeling and machine learning within an integrated approach for stylometry-based authorship identification combines several advanced techniques in the field of computational linguistics and data science (Eder, 2017). The rolling stylometry is considered as a machine learning approach for tracking changes in an author's style over time. It demonstrates how machine learning can be used in conjunction with traditional stylometric methods to enhance authorship identification.

Ethical and Privacy Concerns in the Integrated Approach

Dwyer, (2018) directly tackles the ethical considerations related to the application of machine learning in stylometry, proposing potential privacy issues and ethical dilemmas. Juzar et al. (2020) discusses privacy threats and countermeasures in IoT-based systems, which is related to the broader field of data privacy. The potential privacy threats in data-driven systems includes the use of stylometric techniques for authorship identification. According to Mittelstadt et al. (2016), the broader ethical implications of algorithms, including machine learning algorithms is used in stylometry. It is difficult to ensure anonymity that may lead to the violation of the rights and freedoms of an individual. There are many cases in which people erroneously assume that they remain anonymous, for example, in an anonymous social network or in a whistleblowing system.

Future Prospects and Challenges

The prosects and challenges of the contrastive linguistic analysis in stylometry look forward to the technological developments and their impact on this integrated approach, future trends in stylometry and the Internet of Behaviors, potential challenges in stylometry and the Internet of Behaviors.

Technological Developments and Their Impact on the Integrated Approach

Technological advancements have significantly influenced stylometry-based authorship identification by enabling the integration of various methods, ranging from traditional stylometric techniques to advanced machine learning models (Stamatatos, 2009). In a study by Eder et al. (2016), an example of how technology has changed stylometry, specifically through the Syuzhet package in R, uses sentiment analysis – a form of natural language processing – to analyze narrative structure. The impact of digital methods, such as text mining and machine learning, on literary analysis, can be extended to stylometric authorship identification (Jockers, 2013). The role of computers in the humanities, including their influence on authorship attribution, emphasizes the significance of technological developments on various research methods, including stylometry (Rockwell & Sinclair, 2022). Moreover, these research methods should show the strong relationship between stylometry and the Internet of Behaviors

Future Trends in Stylometry and the Internet of Behaviors

For the convergence of stylometry and the Internet of Behaviors (IoB), there are observable trends in each field separately that, when extrapolated, could provide insights about their potential intersection in the future.

1) Future Trends in Stylometry: Eder (2019) indicated that the development of new tools for stylometric analysis using the R programming language looks to a future perspective where more accessible and robust tools for stylometric analysis become available. Using stylometry will help to settle high-profile authorship disputes, given the rise of anonymous, pseudonymous, or disputed authorship on digital platforms (Akhgar et al., 2015).

2) Future Trends in the Internet of Behaviors: the IoB as an emerging trend from the use of data from the IoT to inform behavior analytics is poised to grow significantly in the coming years. The convergence of these fields – stylometry and the IoB – could lead to new capabilities like enhanced authorship identification based on behavior data or improved understanding of individual or group behavior based on stylometric analysis. However, such potential applications are currently speculative and would need to navigate significant ethical and privacy challenges (Rahaman, 2022).

Potential Challenges in Stylometry and the Internet of Behaviors

For stylometry-based authorship identification and the Internet of Behaviors, there may be some the challenges that need to be addressed.

1) Stylometry-based authorship identification: Koppel et al. (2011) indicated the challenges of applying stylometric analysis in real-world situations, where many potential authors exist, texts vary in length, and different topics may affect stylistic choices, the scarcity of corpora for certain languages or periods, the overemphasis on most common words, and the difficulties in accounting for shared influences among authors.

2) The Internet of Behaviors: Gartner (2021) identified IoB as one of the major technology trends, but also pointed out the significant ethical and privacy concerns associated with it. According to Lee and Lee (2015), there are various challenges in the broader IoT landscape, many of which are relevant to the IoB, including security concerns, interoperability issues, and the lack of comprehensive standards or regulations.

3) Overlapping challenges: Boyd and Crawford (2012) raised important questions about Big Data, many of which apply to stylometry and the IoB, such as issues of privacy, data ownership, transparency, and the potential for bias or discrimination.

The challenges may also be related to ethical considerations, legal implications, standardized ethical design in AI. Mittelstadt et al. (2016) provided a thorough overview of the ethical considerations surrounding algorithmic decision-making, a key element of many modern technologies. It touches on various topics such as transparency, accountability, and fairness, all of which will be pivotal in future technological developments. Crawford and Schultz (2014) discussed the legal implications of predictive privacy harms that may occur in the context of 'Big Data'. As technologies advance, ensuring due process and redress for such harms will be of paramount importance. Bryson and Winfield (2017) discussed the need for standardized ethical design in AI and autonomous systems. They proposed the integration of ethical considerations at the design stage itself as a potential solution. European Commission (2018) outlined the European Union's approach towards AI development, including legal and ethical considerations. It underscored the EU's focus on trustworthy AI and provides a roadmap for future development and regulation. Goodman and Flaxman (2016) examined the "right to explanation" included in the European Union's General Data Protection Regulation (GDPR), with an in-depth discussion on the potential impact of this right on the development and application of machine learning models.

Implications

The research on stylometry-based authorship identification has significant implications in multiple areas, ranging from academia and law enforcement to publishing and beyond. The main implications drawn from the discussions are that stylometry provides powerful tools for literary scholars and linguists, helping to attribute works to authors, identify plagiarism, and illuminate literary influences and trends (Juola, 2015). The implications of this research are profound and wide-reaching. It is clear that, as this field develops, it will continue to influence and intersect with a multitude of other disciplines. However, alongside its potential, it is crucial to manage the inherent challenges, such as the ethical and privacy issues involved.

Since stylometry has many practical applications, one of which typically becomes the most popular, such as the authorship attribution research in which the stylometric features are used to find the author of anonymous or disputed documents. In other words, stylometry can be used to attribute authorship to documents in many disciplines. It can be said that stylometry has legal as well as academic and literary applications, ranging from the question of the authorship of a writer's works to forensic linguistics and has methodological similarities with the analysis of text readability.

For forensics and law enforcement, forensic linguistics increasingly employs stylometry for tasks such as identifying the authors of anonymous or disputed texts. Stylometry has even been used to unmask the identities of cybercriminals or the authors of online harassment (MacLeod & Wright, 2020). For legal proceedings and dispute resolution as well, in legal scenarios, stylometry can provide critical evidence in cases involving disputed authorship or copyright issues.

For data privacy and ethical issues, stylometry-based authorship identification, especially when linked with the IoB, important concerns are raised about data privacy and the potential misuse of personal information (Boyd & Crawford, 2012). These issues necessitate stringent legal and ethical guidelines.

For advancements in machine learning and AI, the integration of machine learning and predictive modeling into stylometry boosts its accuracy and applicability (Stamatatos, 2009). These advancements, however, call for a deeper understanding of these technologies and their inherent biases or limitations.

For digital humanities, the interdisciplinary field of digital humanities stands to benefit significantly from the advancement of stylometry and computational text analysis, shedding new light on cultural and historical trends (Kestemont, 2014).

Suggestions for Future Research

The study of stylometry-based authorship identity has seen significant strides with the integration of machine learning, predictive modeling, and the Internet of Behaviors. There will be many opportunities for future research that need to be taken into consideration.

1) Improvement of current techniques: while existing stylometric techniques are effective, there is always room for improvement. Future research could focus on enhancing these methods, possibly through the integration of more advanced machine learning algorithms or by exploring novel linguistic features for analysis (Stamatatos, 2009).

2) Development of ethical frameworks: as mentioned above, stylometry-based authorship identity raises crucial ethical and privacy concerns. Future research could develop comprehensive ethical frameworks for the application of these techniques, ensuring privacy rights are respected and data is used responsibly (Boyd & Crawford, 2012).

3) Multilingual and cross-cultural stylometry: much of the work in stylometry has focused on texts in English, with considerable scope to expand research to other languages and explore cross-cultural influences on writing style (Kestemont, 2014).

4) Exploration of IoB integration: the intersection of stylometry with the IoB is an emerging field with significant potential. Future research could explore how behavioral data can enrich stylometric analyses, contributing to more accurate and nuanced authorship identification (Gartner, 2021).

5) Limitations and biases: stylometric techniques, particularly those based on machine learning, can have limitations and inherent biases. Future research should focus on identifying and mitigating these to ensure fair and unbiased results.

6) Interdisciplinary collaborations: stylometry has applications across various fields. Future research could involve collaborations between linguists, computer scientists, literary scholars, ethicists, and others, leading to more diverse and comprehensive insights. The future of stylometry-based authorship identity research holds a lot of potential, and the interdisciplinary nature of this field is likely to yield rich and interesting insights. However, it is crucial to keep in mind the associated challenges and ethical considerations that come along with them.

CONCLUSION

In conclusion, stylometry-based authorship identification is a field that leverages linguistic patterns and statistical analysis to identify authorship. The aspects discussed in the context of stylometry-based authorship identification are related to contrastive linguistic analysis, which involves the comparing and the contrasting of different languages or language styles to gain insights. When applied to stylometry, contrastive linguistic analysis can enhance accuracy and efficiency (e.g., Lucic & Milosevic, 2021). The integration with the Internet of Behaviors (IoB), an emerging field can combine data from the IoT and behavior analytics to provide critical issues. Although research on the relationship between the IoB and stylometry needs exploring, potential convergence between the IoB and stylometry could enhance stylometric techniques by integrating behavioral data (e.g., Panetta, 2017). Predictive modelling and machine learning as advanced computational techniques that have been used in stylometry for authorship identification can improve the accuracy and efficiency of traditional methods (Stamatatos, 2009). Issues such as ethical and privacy concerns are crucial in the context of stylometry and the IoB. Therefore, concerns about data privacy, consent, and the potential misuse of information must be carefully addressed (Boyd & Crawford, 2012; Gartner, 2021). Finally, emerging technologies will likely shape the future of stylometry and the IoB, potentially offering new tools and techniques. At the same time, they may also present new challenges and roadblocks (Lee & Lee, 2015; Eder, 2019). The possible directions for these fields may include the development of more sophisticated tools, enhanced integration of different data types, and a greater focus on ethical and legal considerations (Gartner, 2022, as cited in Dwivedi et al., 2023). The interplay between these aspects presents exciting opportunities for advancements in stylometry-based authorship identification. Further research should also take the issues of false positives into account regarding authorship identification and attribution.

REFERENCES

Akhgar, B., Saathoff, G. B., Arabnia, H. R., Hill, R., Staniforth, A., & Bayerl, P. S. (2015). *Application of big data for national security: a practitioner's guide to emerging technologies*. Butterworth-Heinemann.

Argamon, S. (2009). Stolen without a gun: Applying stylometric methods to the detection of surreptitious insider fraud. *Digital Investigation*, 6(3-4), 130–140.

Argamon, S., Juola, P., & Schler, J. (2003). An Evaluation of Text Classification Methods for Literary Authorship Attribution. *Literary and Linguistic Computing*, 18(4), 423–447.

Argamon, S., Juola, P., & Schler, J. (2009). Overview of authorship attribution. In J. Allan & ... (Eds.), *Handbook of natural language processing* (2nd ed., pp. 385–408). CRC Press.

Argamon, S., Juola, P., & Schler, J. (2013). The Stylistic Debates: Revenge of the Burrows. *Literary and Linguistic Computing*, 28(4), 587–598.

Argamon, S., Koppel, M., Fine, J., & Shimoni, A. R. (2003). Gender, genre, and writing style in formal written texts. *Text*, 23(3), 321–346. doi:10.1515/text.2003.014

Argamon, S., & Levitan, S. (2005). Measuring the usefulness of function words for authorship attribution. *Journal of the American Society for Information Science and Technology*, 56(3), 187–196.

Arora, A., Jain, J., Gupta, S., & Sharma, A. (2020). Identifying sustainability drivers in higher education through fuzzy AHP. *Higher Education, Skills and Work-Based Learning, 11*(4), 823-836.

Barlas, G., & Stamatatos, E. (2020). Cross-domain authorship attribution using pre-trained language models. In *Artificial Intelligence Applications and Innovations: 16th IFIP WG 12.5 International Conference, AIAI 2020, Neos Marmaras, Greece, June 5–7, 2020 Proceedings, 16*(Part I), 255–266.

Baumer, E. P. S. (2020). Charting the rise of the Internet of Behaviors. *Communications of the ACM, 63*(5), 54–61.

Bories, A. S., Fabo, P. R., & Plecháč, P. (2022). The Polite Revolution of Computational Literary Studies. *Computational Stylistics in Poetry, Prose, and Drama*, 1.

Boyd, D., & Crawford, K. (2012). Critical questions for big data: Provocations for a cultural, technological, and scholarly phenomenon. *Information Communication and Society, 15*(5), 662–679. doi:10.1080/1369118X.2012.678878

Brody, P., & Bednar, P. (2021). The Internet of Behaviors (IoB): From Discrete Behavior to Process and System. *Proceedings of the 54th Hawaii International Conference on System Sciences.*

Bryson, J., & Winfield, A. (2017). Standardizing Ethical Design for Artificial Intelligence and Autonomous Systems. *Computer, 50*(5), 116–119. doi:10.1109/MC.2017.154

Burrows, J. F. (2002). "Delta": A Measure of Stylistic Difference and a Guide to Likely Authorship. *Literary and Linguistic Computing, 17*(3), 267–287. doi:10.1093/llc/17.3.267

Castillo, E., Cervantes, O., & Vilarino, D. (2019). Authorship verification using a graph knowledge discovery approach. *Journal of Intelligent & Fuzzy Systems, 36*(6), 6075–6087. doi:10.3233/JIFS-181934

Chakraborty, A., Kung, C. Y., & Ghosh, S. K. (2021). The Internet of Behaviors (IoB): A Review on Enabling Technologies, Applications, and Challenges. *IEEE Access : Practical Innovations, Open Solutions, 9*, 68418–68433.

Chaski, C. E. (2005). Who's at the keyboard? Authorship attribution in digital evidence investigations. *International Journal of Digital Evidence, 4*(1), 1–13.

Chen, C., Zhang, D., & Guo, B. (2017). Data-Driven Human Behavior Modeling and Analysis Using Internet of Things (IoT). *IEEE Communications Magazine, 55*(9), 68–74.

Craig, H., & Kinney, A. F. (2009). *Shakespeare, computers, and the mystery of authorship*. Cambridge University Press. doi:10.1017/CBO9780511605437

Crawford, K., & Schultz, J. (2014). Big Data and Due Process: Toward a Framework to Redress Predictive Privacy Harms. *Boston College Law Review. Boston College. Law School, 55*(1), 93–128.

Dwivedi, Y. K., Hughes, L., Baabdullah, A. M., Ribeiro-Navarrete, S., Giannakis, M., Al-Debei, M. M., Dennehy, D., Metri, B., Buhalis, D., Cheung, C. M. K., Conboy, K., Doyle, R., Dubey, R., Dutot, V., Felix, R., Goyal, D. P., Gustafsson, A., Hinsch, C., Jebabli, I., ... Wamba, S. F. (2022). Metaverse beyond the hype: Multidisciplinary perspectives on emerging challenges, opportunities, and agenda for research, practice and policy. *International Journal of Information Management*, *66*, 102542. doi:10.1016/j.ijinfomgt.2022.102542

Dwivedi, Y. K., Kshetri, N., Hughes, L., Slade, E. L., Jeyaraj, A., Kar, A. K., Baabdullah, A. M., Koohang, A., Raghavan, V., Ahuja, M., Albanna, H., Albashrawi, M. A., Al-Busaidi, A. S., Balakrishnan, J., Barlette, Y., Basu, S., Bose, I., Brooks, L., Buhalis, D., ... Wright, R. (2023). "So what if ChatGPT wrote it?" Multidisciplinary perspectives on opportunities, challenges and implications of generative conversational AI for research, practice and policy. *International Journal of Information Management*, *71*, 102642. doi:10.1016/j.ijinfomgt.2023.102642

Dwyer, C. (2018). Ethical considerations in the use of machine learning in stylometry. *Proceedings of the 18th ACM Workshop on Privacy in the Electronic Society*, 148-157.

Eder, M. (2017). Rolling stylometry. *Digital Scholarship in the Humanities*, *32*(3), 457–469. doi:10.1093/llc/fqv010

Eder, M. (2017). Stylometry with R: A Package for Computational Text Analysis. *The R Journal*, *9*(1), 167–175.

Eder, M. (2015). Stylometry with R: A suite of tools. *Digital Scholarship in the Humanities*, *30*(1), 87–107.

Eder, M., & Rybicki, J. (2011). Do birds of a feather really flock together, or how to choose training samples for authorship attribution. *Digital Scholarship in the Humanities*, *26*(3), 387–401.

Eder, M., Rybicki, J., & Kestemont, M. (2016). Stylometry with R: A package for computational text analysis. *The R Journal*, *8*(1), 107. doi:10.32614/RJ-2016-007

European Commission. (2018). *Communication Artificial Intelligence for Europe*. COM (2018) 237 final.

Filgueiras, F. (2022). New Pythias of public administration: Ambiguity and choice in AI systems as challenges for governance. *AI & Society*, *37*(4), 1473–1486. doi:10.100700146-021-01201-4

Gantz, J., & Reinsel, D. (2020). *The Digitization of the World: From Edge to Core*. IDC White Paper.

Gasson, M. N. (2020). Internet of Behaviors (IoB) - The Good, the Bad and the Ugly. In *2020 International Conference on Artificial Intelligence and Information Technology (ICAIIT)* (pp. 1-6). IEEE.

Goodman, B., & Flaxman, S. (2016). EU regulations on algorithmic decision-making and a" right to explanation". ICML workshop on human interpretability in machine learning.

Grieve, J. (2007). Quantitative authorship attribution: An evaluation of techniques. *Literary and Linguistic Computing*, *22*(3), 251–270. doi:10.1093/llc/fqm020

Hanisch, S., Arias-Cabarcos, P., Parra-Arnau, J., & Strufe, T. (2021). *Privacy-Protecting Techniques for Behavioral Data: A Survey*. arXiv preprint arXiv:2109.04120.

Holmes, D. I. (1998). The Evolution of Stylometry in Humanities Scholarship. *Literary and Linguistic Computing, 13*(3), 111–117. doi:10.1093/llc/13.3.111

Holmes, D. I., & Forsyth, R. S. (1995). A Linguistic Study of Edgar Allan Poe's Tales of Terror: A Stylometric Analysis of his Short Stories. *Computers and the Humanities, 29*(4), 295–313.

Hung, J. (2018). A cross-linguistic comparison of adjective ordering restrictions in English, Mandarin, and Japanese. *Language and Linguistics (Taipei), 19*(4), 597–636.

Jockers, M. L. (2013). *Macroanalysis: Digital Methods and Literary History*. University of Illinois Press. doi:10.5406/illinois/9780252037528.001.0001

Juola, P. (2006). Authorship Attribution. *Foundations and Trends in Information Retrieval, 1*(3), 233–334. doi:10.1561/1500000005

Juola, P. (2015). The Rowling case: A proposed standard analytic protocol for authorship questions. *Digital Scholarship in the Humanities, 30*(suppl_1), i100–i113. doi:10.1093/llc/fqv040

Juzar, H., Habib, K. M., & Bhuiyan, M. (2020). A Comprehensive Study on the Privacy Threats and Countermeasures in the IoT-based Cyber-Physical System. *IEEE Access : Practical Innovations, Open Solutions, 8*, 216541–216563.

Kestemont, M., Daelemans, W., & de Gussem, J. (2014). Exploring the boundaries of cross-genre authorship attribution. *Digital Scholarship in the Humanities, 29*(1), 99–114.

Kestemont, M., Stover, J.A., Koppel, M., Karsdorp, F., & Daelemans, W. (2020). Overview of the cross-domain authorship attribution task at PAN 2020. *CLEF 2020 Labs and Workshops, Notebook Papers. CEUR Workshop Proceedings*.

Khormali, A., Park, J., Alasmary, H., Anwar, A., Saad, M., & Mohaisen, D. (2021). Domain name system security and privacy: A contemporary survey. *Computer Networks, 185*, 107699. doi:10.1016/j.comnet.2020.107699

King, D. (2021). *The Internet of Behaviors (IoB)*. What It Is and How It Can Impact Your Business. Forbes.

Koppel, M., & Schler, J. (2004). Authorship Verification as a One-Class Classification Problem. *Proceedings of the 21st International Conference on Machine Learning*, 49. 10.1145/1015330.1015448

Koppel, M., Schler, J., & Argamon, S. (2009). Computational Methods in Authorship Attribution. *Journal of the American Society for Information Science and Technology, 60*(1), 9–26. doi:10.1002/asi.20961

Koppel, M., Schler, J., & Argamon, S. (2011). Authorship Attribution in the Wild. *Language Resources and Evaluation, 45*(1), 83–94. doi:10.100710579-009-9111-2

Koppel, M., Schler, J., & Argamon, S. (2011). Computational methods in authorship attribution. *Journal of the American Society for Information Science and Technology, 62*(1), 17–49.

Koppel, M., Schler, J., & Bonchek-Dokow, E. (2007). Measuring differentiability: Unmasking pseudonymous authors. *Journal of Machine Learning Research, 8*, 1261–1276.

Koppel, M., & Winter, Y. (2014). Determining if two documents are by the same author. *Journal of the Association for Information Science and Technology, 65*(1), 178–187. doi:10.1002/asi.22954

Kshetri, N. (2020). The Internet of Behaviors (IoB). *Communications of the ACM, 63*(5), 20–23.

Kühn, S., & Boshoff, C. (2023). The role of plot in brand story construction: A neurophysiological perspective. *Journal of Strategic Marketing, 31*(2), 471–497. doi:10.1080/0965254X.2021.1968018

Küng, J., & Gonçalves, P. (2021). Internet of Behaviors (IoB) and the Human Value System: A Review. In *2021 9th IEEE International Conference on Mobile Cloud Computing, Services, and Engineering (MobileCloud)* (pp. 135-140). IEEE.

Kushwaha, D. S., Khan, S. A., & Saha, S. (2020). IoB-IoT enabled collaborative behavioral pattern analysis for smart living environments. *Journal of Ambient Intelligence and Humanized Computing, 11*, 5969–5990.

Li, Y., & Fu, X. (2021). Internet of Behaviors (IoB): A Comprehensive Review. *IEEE Access : Practical Innovations, Open Solutions, 9*, 121281–121295.

MacLeod, N., & Wright, D. (2020). *Forensic linguistics*. Academic Press.

Mendenhall, T. C. (1887). The Characteristic Curves of Composition. *Science, 9*(214), 237–246. doi:10.1126cience.ns-9.214S.237 PMID:17736020

Mittelstadt, B., Allo, P., Taddeo, M., Wachter, S., & Floridi, L. (2016). The Ethics of Algorithms: Mapping the Debate. *Big Data & Society, 3*(2). doi:10.1177/2053951716679679

Mosteller, F., & Wallace, D. L. (1964). *Inference and disputed authorship: The Federalist*. Addison-Wesley.

Nesselhauf, N., & Tono, Y. (2015). *Corpus-Based Studies in Contrastive Linguistics*. Walter de Gruyter GmbH & Co KG.

Nguyễn, T. N. (2023). *Khảo sát các yếu tố từ vựng ảnh hưởng đến phong cách viết trong văn bản tiếng Việt (đối chiếu với tiếng Anh)*. VNU Library.

Nguyen, T. N., & Dinh, D. (2021). A stylometric investigation of linguistic styles based on a Vietnamese corpus. *Open Journal of Social Sciences, 9*(12), 74–87. doi:10.4236/jss.2021.912006

Oloo, V., Wanzare, L. D., & Otieno, C. (2022). An Optimal Feature Set for Stylometry-based Style Change detection at Document and Sentence Level. *International Journal of Scientific Research in Computer Science, Engineering and Information Technology*

Pan, J., & Kudo, M. (2019). N-gram Against the Machine: On the Feasibility of the N-gram Network Analysis for Binary Protocols. In *2019 6th International Conference on Behavioral, Economic, and Socio-Cultural Computing (BESC)* (pp. 1-8). IEEE.

Pellegrini, L., Porru, S., & West, R. (2020). Ethical Issues in the Internet of Behaviors. *2020 IEEE International Workshop on Metrology for Industry 4.0 and IoT (MetroInd4.0 & IoT)*, 384-389.

Peyman, M., Copado, P. J., Tordecilla, R. D., Martins, L. D. C., Xhafa, F., & Juan, A. A. (2021). Edge computing and iot analytics for agile optimization in intelligent transportation systems. *Energies*, *14*(19), 6309. doi:10.3390/en14196309

Potha, N., & Joshi, A. (2021). Stylometry Analysis of Authorship Attribution Using Text Mining Techniques. In *Advances in Signal Processing and Intelligent Recognition Systems* (pp. 453–463). Springer.

Rahaman, T. (2022). Smart things are getting smarter: An introduction to the internet of behavior. *Medical Reference Services Quarterly*, *41*(1), 110–116. doi:10.1080/02763869.2022.2021046 PMID:35225739

Rockwell, G., & Sinclair, S. (2018). Too Much Information and the KWIC. *Fudan Journal of the Humanities and Social Sciences*, *11*(4), 443–452. doi:10.100740647-018-0230-2

Rockwell, G., & Sinclair, S. (2022). *Hermeneutica: Computer-assisted interpretation in the humanities*. MIT Press.

Rybicki, J., & Eder, M. (2011). Deeper Delta across genres and languages: Do we really need the most frequent words? *Literary and Linguistic Computing*, *26*(3), 315–321. doi:10.1093/llc/fqr031

Sadman, N., Gupta, K. D., Haque, M. A., Sen, S., & Poudyal, S. (2020). Stylometry as a reliable method for fallback authentication. In *2020 17th International Conference on Electrical Engineering/Electronics, Computer, Telecommunications and Information Technology (ECTI-CON)* (pp. 660-664). IEEE. 10.1109/ECTI-CON49241.2020.9158216

Salman, O. H., Alhalabi, B., & Hossain, M. S. (2020). Securing Internet of Behaviors (IoB) in the era of pervasive connectivity: Taxonomy, challenges, and solutions. *Future Internet*, *12*(5), 83.

Sarker, I. H., Khan, A. I., Abushark, Y. B., & Alsolami, F. (2022). Internet of things (iot) security intelligence: A comprehensive overview, machine learning solutions and research directions. *Mobile Networks and Applications*, 1–17.

Stamatatos, E. (2009). A Survey of Modern Authorship Attribution Methods. *Journal of the American Society for Information Science and Technology*, *60*(3), 538–556. doi:10.1002/asi.21001

Stamatatos, E. (2013). A survey of modern authorship attribution methods. *Journal of the American Society for Information Science and Technology*, *64*(2), 295–315.

Stamatatos, E., Fakotakis, N., & Kokkinakis, G. (2000). Automatic Text Categorization in Terms of Genre and Author. *Computational Linguistics*, *26*(4), 471–495. doi:10.1162/089120100750105920

Sun, J., Gan, W., Chao, H. C., Philip, S. Y., & Ding, W. (2023). The Internet of behaviors: A survey. *IEEE Internet of Things Journal*, *10*(13), 11117–11134. doi:10.1109/JIOT.2023.3247594

Szmrecsanyi, B., & Kortmann, B. (2009). Typological profiling: A tool for the study of linguistic diversity. *Linguistic Typology*, *13*(2), 251–257.

Van Den Heuvel, W., Aveiro, D., & Lalanda, P. (2019). The internet of behaviors: a security perspective. *Proceedings of the 34th ACM/SIGAPP Symposium on Applied Computing*, 1441-1450.

Wang, C., Teo, T. S., & Janssen, M. (2021). Public and private value creation using artificial intelligence: An empirical study of AI voice robot users in Chinese public sector. *International Journal of Information Management*, *61*, 102401. doi:10.1016/j.ijinfomgt.2021.102401

Wang, X., & Fan, L. (2020). An analysis of interlanguage features and English learning. *Journal of Higher Education Research*, *1*(1), 31–37. doi:10.32629/jher.v1i1.126

Zesch, T., & Gurevych, I. (2009). Cross-language text classification: Distinguishing similarity from language confusion. *ACM Transactions on Speech and Language Processing*, *6*(1), 1–22.

Zhang, C., Wu, X., Niu, Z., & Ding, W. (2014). Authorship identification from unstructured texts. *Knowledge-Based Systems*, *66*, 99–111. doi:10.1016/j.knosys.2014.04.025

Zhao, Q., Li, G., Cai, J., Zhou, M., & Feng, L. (2023). A Tutorial on Internet of Behaviors: Concept, Architecture, Technology, Applications, and Challenges. *IEEE Communications Surveys and Tutorials*, *25*(2), 1227–1260. doi:10.1109/COMST.2023.3246993

KEY TERMS AND DEFINITIONS

Authorship Identification: The process of determining who wrote a particular document when the authorship is uncertain or disputed through the use of statistical methods, such as stylometry, to analyze various aspects of the text to identify unique stylistic patterns that can be associated with a particular author.

Average Word Length: Referring to the average number of letters in a word within a given text. It is calculated by dividing the total number of letters by the total number of words in the text.

Contrastive Linguistics: A subfield of linguistics involving the comparing and the contrasting of two or more languages to find out the similarities and differences between two or among more than two languages in terms of the contrastive analysis of phonology, syntax, morphology semantics and pragmatics.

Internet of Behaviors (IoB): Referring to the networked connectivity of devices and information for the analysis, understanding, and prediction of human behaviors, which emerges from the Internet of Things (IoT) to connect devices and link data from these devices to human behavior.

Stylometry: The application of the study of linguistic style such as genres, usually to written language to attribute authorship to anonymous or disputed documents through statistical analysis.

Vocabulary Richness: Referring to the variety and complexity of words used in writing or speech. It is the measure of how many different words are used and how often they appear.

Word Frequency: Referring to the number of times a particular word appears in a text or a corpus (a large and structured set of texts).

Word-Length Distribution: A measure used in statistical analysis of texts that deals with the frequency of words of different lengths. It shows how many words of each length (i.e., the number of characters in a word) appear in each text.

Chapter 17
Sustainable and Autonomous Soil Irrigation:
Agro Smart Solution

Gonçalo Santos
Instituto Politécnico da Guarda, Portugal

Gonçalo Vicente
Instituto Politécnico da Guarda, Portugal

Telmo Salvado
Instituto Politécnico da Guarda, Portugal

Celestino Gonçalves
https://orcid.org/0000-0001-6144-0980
Instituto Politécnico da Guarda, Portugal

Filipe Caetano
https://orcid.org/0000-0001-6857-7971
Instituto Politécnico da Guarda, Portugal

Clara Silveira
https://orcid.org/0000-0003-2809-4208
Instituto Politécnico da Guarda, Portugal

ABSTRACT

Water scarcity is probably one of the most serious problems that humanity will have to face globally. For that reason, it will certainly be urgent to try to define practices and find solutions that, in a first phase, allow to mitigate the problem, but whose ultimate objective will be to overcome the situation. This chapter presents an irrigation system set on an internet of things platform, able to act in real time according to the atmospheric conditions. Through parameterized and automated systems, it is possible to stop the irrigation. Later, using sensors, the system may or may not be activated in case the levels of soil moisture and luminosity do not respond to the parameterized needs. It is an efficient and sustainable solution that is available for all agriculture irrigation systems. To test the proposed solution, unit tests were conducted, and a group of tests with all sensors connected was also considered. This system implements an alternative method for the data flow and its monitoring, including the fact that the system is aware of the user.

DOI: 10.4018/978-1-6684-9039-6.ch017

INTRODUCTION

The responsible and efficient use of available water resources is a key factor for the survival of human species. The overuse of water resources derived from growing per capita use (Rijsberman, 2006) and the generalization of its uncontrolled or inefficient use remains the core problem. Climate change scenarios may also accentuate some of the scarcity problems in the near future (Bates et al., 2008). Intensive agriculture, urban growth, and industrial proliferation are also responsible for the contamination of water, reducing the water availability. Fortunately, the efficient use of water has the potential to improve, as available technology, such as IoT, wireless communication, monitoring and intelligent control systems can be applied in areas like precision agriculture and smart irrigation (Bwambale et al., 2022).

In order to also contribute to the solution of the problem, we have proposed an IoT Autonomous Irrigation System - Agro Smart (Santos et al., 2022) - a system envisioned to reduce the use and waste of water resources and to autonomously monitor and activate the irrigation system, considering captured data, such as soil moisture, luminosity, temperature, among others. Consequently, it is intended that there will be irrigation only when the culture needs it. During the day, with high temperatures and luminosity, there will be a waste due to the thermal movement of molecules from the liquid to the gaseous state, so the system prefers night irrigation, only when soil moisture levels justify it. In the development of the system the dimensions of sustainability were considered (Seghezzo, 2009) and the project followed good practices for sustainable development. The sustainability of software development is a process of extreme importance. It is important to prioritize the minimization of the use of resources, including the reutilization of source code. According to (Becker et al., 2015) and based on the Karlskrona Manifest, sustainability is systemic, sustainability has multiple dimensions and transcends multiple disciplines, applies to a system as well as its contexts, requires action on multiple levels, system visibility is a necessary pre-condition for sustainability design, and requires long-term thinking. The work under study represents a different strand of data than others presented. Agro Smart represents an innovative approach compared to existing solutions due to its integration with IoT technology, efficient use of water resources, and emphasis on sustainability. The system's originality lies in its unique combination of autonomous monitoring, irrigation control, and real-time environmental data consideration, making it a highly adaptable and responsive solution.

The chapter is organized as follows. Next section discusses the state of the art, followed by a section that mentions the work methodologies, namely the agile methodology and the scrum development methodology. Then we will expose the system design, particularly the requirements analysis, the characterization of the ubiquitous system, the functional and non-functional requirements, and the sequence of activities. Next we will describe the developed system, the architecture, the LoRaWAN network, the sensorial network, the management platform, the client application, security, and hardware components. Next section discusses and analyzes the achieved results. Finally, we end the chapter with some conclusions that are drawn from the developed work and mention the work that is intended to be done in the future.

STATE OF THE ART

The implementation of technology in agriculture is not a recent topic. And areas such as precision agriculture, and especially smart irrigation, could be the way to the solution (Bwambale et al., 2022). Over the years, models have been designed and projected to increase efficiency and minimize human labor.

No system is ideal, so the study of different contributions, complementarities, and improvements of the developed work becomes essential. This section will address the study of related solutions, comparing strengths and weaknesses of the work developed by other researchers.

Related Work

A comparative analysis between the related work was performed, considering characteristics such as system purpose and objectives, autonomy, intelligence and final client application, as shown in Table 1 – Different Solutions – as well as network topology, communication protocol, communication interval, microcontroller, complexity of the sensor network, storage and actuators used – presented in Table 2 – Solutions Specifications.

Table 1. Comparative analysis: Different solutions

Solution	Solution Description	Autonomy	Intelligence	Client Application
Agro Smart (Santos et al., 2022)	Smart irrigation monitoring system	Manual and Automatic	Context-awareness	Android Mobile Application
(Saraf & Gawali, 2017)	Smart farm irrigation system	Manual and Automatic	X	Android, Web Interface
(Abba et al., 2019)	Smart irrigation system	Automatic	X	Android, Web Interface
(Somov et al., 2018)	Monitor and control greenhouse plant growth	Automatic	Reinforcement learning	Web Interface
iRain (Caetano et al., 2014)	Monitor and control irrigation	Manual and Automatic	Weather prevision	WebPortal (ASP Platform)
(Taşkin & Yazar, 2020)	Monitor and control irrigation	Automatic	Context-awareness	Software Platform
(Davcev et al., 2018)	Monitor and control irrigation	Automatic	X	Web Interface
AgriSys (Abdullah et al., 2016)	Analyze and intervene to maintain the agricultural environment	Manual and Automatic	Fuzzy controller	Web Interface
(Gaikwad et al., 2021)	Precision farming. Monitor parameters such as soil and air temperature and humidity	X	X	Android, Web Interface
IoT Backyard (Jariyayothin et al., 2018)	Monitor and control plant irrigation at home	X	X	Android
(Pornillos et al., 2020)	Monitor and control irrigation of agricultural land	Manual and Automatic	X	Web Interface
(Shadrin et al., 2018)	Predict the growth of plants and control the conditions under which they grow	Automatic	Nonlinear regression	Android, Web Interface
(Keshtgary & Deljoo, 2012)	Use of precision farming to learn data about a farm and terrain conditions	Automatic	X	X
(Ma et al., 2011)	wireless sensor network for automatic monitoring in precision agriculture	Automatic	X	Android

In the solutions under study, a variety of systems were implemented, each with its own strengths, but with the purpose of monitoring the environment for the growth of the plantation and its irrigation. The authors of (Saraf & Gawali, 2017) propose an automated irrigation system based on IoT. Intended to optimize water use for irrigation farming, Abba et al. (Abba et al., 2019) propose a low-cost autonomous monitoring and control IoT based irrigation system, from remote locations. Somov et al. (Somov et al., 2018) addresses an IoT system in a tomato greenhouse in Russia, the presented work relies on a reinforcement learning system. The system proposed in (Caetano et al., 2014), iRain, features a weather forecast to turn the irrigation system on or off. The authors of (Taşkin & Yazar, 2020) extols LoRa technology as opposed to other systems. Davcev et al. (Davcev et al., 2018) cites the cloud services architecture for a LoRaWAN network. The solution proposed in (Abdullah et al., 2016), AgriSys, features a PH sensor to measure soil basicity and provide an additional planting monitoring feature. The study presented in (Gaikwad et al., 2021) serves the irrigation of different crop types and analyzes root depth. The authors of (Jariyayothin et al., 2018) makes use of a tank for water storage for planting and uses Firebase for data storage. Pornillos et al. (Pornillos et al., 2020) uses a WiFi ESP8266 module to monitor and turn on irrigation. Shadrin et al. (Shadrin et al., 2018) proposes a solution that does plant growth monitoring with the aid of 2D/3D image processing. The study described in (Ma et al., 2011) names the advantages of applying the Internet of Things in the agricultural world, while the authors of (Keshtgary & Deljoo, 2012) name the benefits of wireless sensor networks (WSN) in the same context.

For the development of our system, there was an attempt to aggregate as many features as possible given the available material. The project developed represents an easier and alternative solution for data flow and analysis with the aid of open-source platforms and delivery of this data to the end customer, fulfilling the same purpose, irrigation condition monitoring. The developed system follows a point-to-point network topology. It is autonomous, the data management and storage is done by ThingSpeak platform (ThingSpeak, n.d.), being provided to the end user through a mobile application. The actuators present are the relay and the OLED. The defined communication time is 15 seconds. The microcontroller board used is the Arduino Due. The protocol used for communication is LoRaWan (Alliance, n.d.) and the power supply for the Arduino is 5V. In addition to the mentioned, the system is aware of the user, contrasting to the articles analyzed. That is, the system recognizes the user's movement and provides the data in place to be viewed.

WORK METHODOLOGIES

This topic discusses the methodology adopted for the development of the system. A software methodology is a procedure that plays a central role in structuring, planning, and controlling the development process of software (Jacobson et al., 2019). It is following a methodology that allows the development to be carried out in a focused manner towards the client's requirements and with a higher degree of organization and quality. To facilitate these tasks there are different types of software development methodologies and in this project, we have chosen to use the Agile Methodology.

Table 2. Comparative analysis: Solutions specifications

Solution	Network Topology	Communication Protocol	Communication Interval	Micro-Controller	Storage	Complexity of the Sensory Network (Collectors)	Actuators
AgroSmart (Santos et al., 2022)	Point-to-point	LoRaWan	15 seconds	Arduino Due	ThingSpeak Platform	Soil moisture, air temperature and humidity, carbon monoxide, motion, light	Relay, OLED display
(Saraf & Gawali, 2017)	X	ZigBee	Real time	Arduino UNO ATmega328	Cloud server	Soil moisture, temperature, humidity, water level of tank	Water pump
(Abba et al., 2019)	X	WiFi	5 min	Arduino UNO ATmega328	Cloud server	Soil moisture, temperature, pH, humidity	Water pump
(Somov et al., 2018)	Mesh	ZigBee	30 min to Libelium gateway	ATmega	MongoDB	pH, EC, temperature, humidity, CO2, PAR	High pressure sodium lamps, water heating, ventilation system
iRain (Caetano et al., 2014)	Mesh	ZigBee	15min	Atmel's	MariaDB	Humidity and temperature, wind speed, light and soil moisture	Relay
(Taşkin & Yazar, 2020)	Star	LoRaWan	N.D.	ESP32	N.D.	Temperature, soil and air humidity	Water pump using an optional relay
(Davcev et al., 2018)	N.D.	LoRaWan	N.D.	N.D.	N.D.	Temperature and Humidity, soil moisture, foilage humidity	Water pump
AgriSys (Abdullah et al., 2016)	X	N.D.	Real time	Phidget Interface Kit 8/8/8	Web Server	pH, light, ground thermocouple, soil moisture, temperature and air humidity	Double relay, fan, pump and motor
(Gaikwad et al., 2021)	X	WiFi	Real time	ESP8266, Arduino UNO	Web Server	Air temperature and humidity, soil temperature and humidity	X
IoT Backyard (Jariyayothin et al., 2018)	X	WiFi	N.D.	ESP8266, Arduino UNO	Firebase	Timestamp, soil moisture, ultrasound, temperature	2 Relays, 2 Solenoid Valves
(Pornillos et al., 2020)	Star	WiFi	Real time	Wemos D1 Mini	Web Server	Air temperature and humidity, water flow, soil moisture	Relay, Solenoid Valve
(Shadrin et al., 2018)	X	N.D	N.D	N.D	N.D	Ph, temperature, humidity, electrical conductivity	X
(Keshtgary & Deljoo, 2012)	X	WiFi	Real time	N.D	N.D	Water level, precipitation, soil moisture	X
(Ma et al., 2011)	X	WiFi	Real time	N.D	Cloud	Temperature, Air Humidity, Soil Temperature, Soil Moisture, Light	Relay

Agile Methodology

With Agile methodology, the customer is often called upon to intervene, iteration by iteration, playing a decisive role in defining new requirements. No project is totally predictable, so to be 'agile' is to be aware of this reality and accept that requirements usually change, in short, to be ready to accommodate change simply and quickly. Agile methodologies must respect the software development cycle - planning, execution, and final delivery - allowing software to be developed in stages, making it easier to identify any bugs as well as their resolution. Within the Agile methodology spectrum, we chose to use the Scrum model.

Development Methodology: Scrum

Scrum (Rubin, 2012) is characterized by development cycles or stages, defined as Sprints, and maximizing the development time of a software product. It is typically used in project management of software product development but can also be used in a business context. It is an effective model when it is not yet clear what is intended to be developed throughout the project and is used mainly when the project is complex, in which it is very difficult to fully predetermine what will happen until the final delivery.

The requirements to be considered when designing the project are kept in the product backlog. The product backlog is changeable. At the beginning of each sprint the team does a sprint planning to catalog and hierarchize the content to be worked on in the sprint. The sprint is the stage of development cycles, they are work sessions that occur until the end of the project. On a weekly basis, the team participated in a meeting with the faculty to identify the status of the work, problems that were occurring, and to plan future activities. At the end of the sprint the team identifies the functionalities, the sprint review is thus the result obtained from the sprint. Later, there is the sprint retrospective, in this period the team extrapolates the strengths and weaknesses that occurred in the sprint with the purpose of creating a plan for the next meeting to address these negative aspects and prioritize the strengths. The cycle represents a constant increment of the product until the desired result.

The Scrum methodology was employed in the development of the Agro Smart system. Scrum is particularly suitable for projects that involve evolving requirements and complexity, such as IoT-based systems. The iterative nature of Scrum, divided into Sprints, allowed the project team to adapt to changing requirements and incorporate customer feedback regularly. The product backlog served as a dynamic repository for requirements, and sprint planning sessions helped prioritize and allocate tasks. The frequent interactions between the team and the faculty ensured alignment and quick resolution of issues. The sprint review and retrospective sessions allowed continuous improvement and learning, contributing to the successful development of the Agro Smart system.

SYSTEM DESIGN

Requirements Analysis

The first phase for developing a product is the analysis of requirements, a very important aspect in project management, since it is responsible for collecting the necessary and indispensable data to define what the system should do, as well as the expectations and requirements that the customer needs to solve a problem and achieve its goals. The stakeholders involved in the system are the customer, the suppliers, and the community. The possible customers are the state (schools or colleges, public and urban gardens) and farmers who want to optimize and monitor the irrigation system and reduce water waste. The suppliers are the companies that sell material used in the project. And finally, the community, that will benefit from the green spaces. The use case diagram, Figure 1, documents what the system does from the user's point of view. In other words, it describes the main functionalities of the system and the interaction of these functionalities with the actors in the system.

The Arduino system captures data on soil and air moisture, temperature, brightness, and carbon monoxide. It also detects movement, displays the captured values, and turns the relay on or off. As for ThingSpeak, this actor averages values and amplitudes, presents the data in the form of meters, graphs, and numeric lamps and displays, and even exports data in different formats. The client (mobile app) can view the history, alerts of the relay status can create user, view the amplitudes, averages, graphs and meters.

Figure 1. Use case diagram

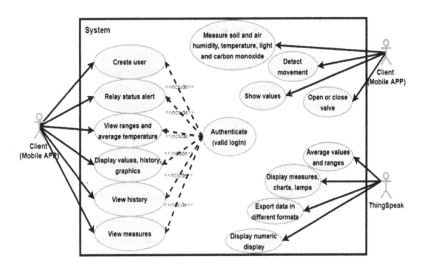

Functional Requirements

The system should be able to:

- Measure air temperature and humidity, soil moisture, carbon monoxide and brightness;
- Detect user presence and turn on the OLED to display the last captured values;
- Operate the irrigation system manually;
- Have the ability to decide to trigger the irrigation system when moisture values are low in conjunction with low light;
- Put the information accessible to be visualized in the form of graphs, dials, clocks and lamps;
- Display temperature averages and amplitudes;
- Alert the user of the irrigation system status;
- Send a daily email with the average values obtained by each sensor;

- Send the data to the mobile application with a periodicity of 1 minute;
- Have the ability to operate with a solenoid valve;
- Operate in a remote location without Wi-Fi access and at a long distance from the base station.

Non-Functional Requirements

The system should verify the following non-functional requirements:

- Performance, storage capacity of up to 3 million messages per year;
- Be supplied with an enclosure capable of preventing the ingress of dust and water (IP65);
- Security, data will be accessed after the user proves their identity;
- Interoperability of the system, sending data across platforms;
- Usability, application to be responsive;
- Usability, application to be multilingual (Portuguese and English);
- Compatibility, android SDK version to run on the largest number of devices.

Characterization of the Ubiquitous System

The characterization of the ubiquitous system gathers five fundamental properties, namely its distribution, its interaction with the user, intelligence, perception of the environment and autonomy. As for its distribution, the system uses several sensors connected to an Arduino Due, which transmits the data collected through LoraWAN technology to the Single Channel Packet Forwarder Dragino LG01-S (DRAGINO, n.d.), which in turn sends the data to The Things Network platform and then forwards the data to the ThingSpeak platform. A mobile application developed for Android is used to provide the user with a detailed visualization of the collected data with graphs for a better understanding of the evolution of the data over time. It is an implicit interaction system because it is aware of the user. The system interacts with the user through the PIR sensor so that, when it detects its presence, it turns on the OLED to facilitate the visualization of the data on site. The developed system receives the data that the sensors detect from the environment, so it is a physical system that perceives the context of the environment. The device adjusts its operation according to the data collected from the sensors, turns on the relay only when the ground is not too wet and there is not too much light, and is therefore autonomous.

The context houses the set of data collected by the sensors present in the system, with data being collected about soil moisture, air temperature and humidity, and luminosity. As for the categorization of the context the data collected by the sensors is primary. As far as secondary context information is concerned, we talk about the worked data from the primary context. That is, the data captured from the environment by the sensors are transformed into averages and amplitudes. We can catalog the system by level of interactivity. This is active context awareness, since the user does not need to intervene in the system's operation cycle, and the application works autonomously without any input from the user. The system corresponds to an intelligent environment since the system is aware of the environment and adapts to guarantee the right irrigation conditions for the environment.

Sequence of Activities

To meet the needs of the system it is important that a sequence of activities be performed to fulfill the final purpose, Figure 2. The data is collected by the sensors, sent for further analysis and monitoring, and then there is a response that translates into the activation, if needed, of the irrigation system.

Figure 2. Activity cycle

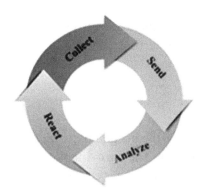

Figure 3. Flowchart of soil irrigation algorithm

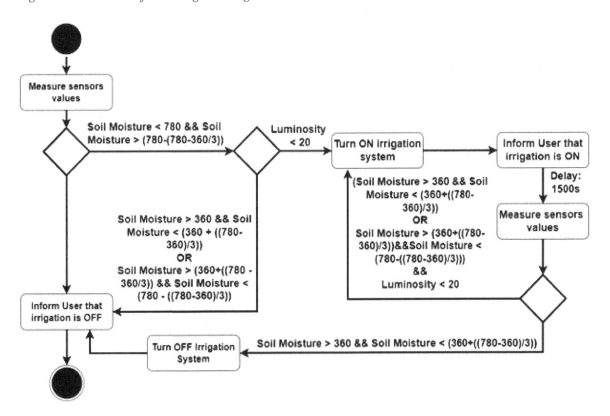

The flowchart of our irrigation algorithm is presented in Figure 3. It illustrates the logic of the algorithm and describes the steps taken to trigger the irrigation system. For the system to trigger irrigation, the humidity of the soil must verify the condition, otherwise there will be an infinite cycle until this condition is verified. Subsequently, the system gives priority to night irrigation, if the captured values also verify the condition of luminosity below 20 Lux, then the relay is activated. The system informs the user of the irrigation status. After, the system captures the data and checks whether the moisture values again meet the condition set by the system. Therefore, if the condition is met the irrigation is turned off and the user is informed. Otherwise, the system continues to collect the values until this last condition is validated.

It can be concluded that the system gives preference to nighttime irrigation, for which the soil moisture conditions must be lower than the parameterized values.

SYSTEM DEVELOPMENT

The architecture of a system defines how the integral parts are organized. Defines the components, the properties, and relationships with software. The Agro Smart system was organized into 4 subsystems, as illustrated in Figure 4. For better understanding, it is composed of a sensory network, a LoRa network, a management application and a client application. Briefly, the Arduino Due is connected to sensors that will capture data from the environment. The LoRa shield coupled to the Arduino allows the antenna to send the radio signal and data to the gateway. In turn, the gateway captures the data and will act as an intermediary to forward the data to the The Things Network (TTN) platform. Sequentially, TTN sends the data to the ThingSpeak platform, which in addition to working the data, works as our system's database. Subsequently, the processed data are requested by the Android mobile application. Authentication and registration is handled by the Firebase authentication feature implemented in the Android application.

Figure 4. Agro smart system architecture

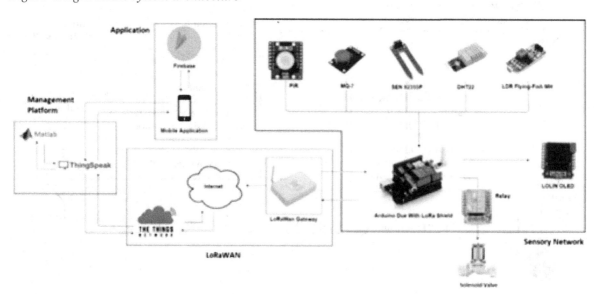

Sensor Network

The first stage of the system involves capturing data from the environment. There is a complex sensory network behind it. Collector sensors are soil moisture sensor, air temperature and humidity, carbon monoxide, motion sensor and light sensor. The actuators that will react under predetermined conditions are the OLED and the relay. The OLED to display the last captured values when it detects motion. The relay to activate the irrigation system depending on soil moisture and light values. The sensors are connected to a microcontroller. The microcontroller board used is the Arduino Due. PlatformIO (PlatformIO, n.d.) is an open source, integrated development environment to make the task of programming and uploading data to the board easier. The programming language used was C++. The development environment described was used to program the Arduino Due. Figure 5 illustrates the assembly process of the various components of the system.

Figure 5. Assembly of the system sensor network

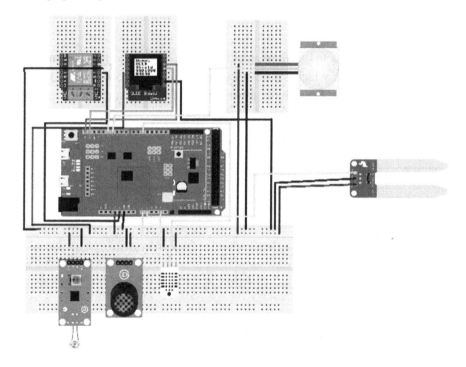

Below is a brief description of the sensors used:

- DHT22 (AM2302) – temperature and humidity sensor. It has a variation in humidity from 0 to 100% relative humidity (HR) and in temperature from -40°C to 80°C. It has a measurement accuracy at humidity of ±2% HR and temperature of <±0.5° Celsius. It has a delay of 2 seconds for each measurement.

- Wemos Pyroelectric Infrared Radial (PIR) Shield (AS312) - motion detection sensor. The sensor converts the received analog signal to digital. It has a reach of up to 500 cm and an angle of up to 100 degrees of amplitude. It has a delay of 2 seconds for each measurement.
- Flying-Fish MH LDR - light sensor.
- Wemos OLED 0.66 Shield (SSD1306). The screen has a size of 64 by 48 pixels.
- Capacitive Soil Moisture Sensor (SEN0193). The sensor measures soil moisture through soil capacitance.
- MQ-7 - carbon monoxide sensor. It has a detection range from 10 to 1000 ppm.
- Arduino Due – microcontroller board. The Arduino Due is a 32-bit Atmel SAM3X8E ARM Cortex-M3 processor-based board. It has 54 digital input or output pins of which 12 can be used as PWM, 12 analog input pins, 4 UART pins, an 84 MHz clock, a USB connection with OTG capability, 2 digital-to-analog DAC, 2 TWI, a feed entry, an SPI header, a JTAG header, a reset button, and a delete button. The Arduino Due runs at 3.3V which is the maximum input and output pins support. It has 512KB flash memory and 96KB SRAM.

LoRaWAN

Most agricultural fields are in remote locations, making a long-range wireless communication network necessary. Here resides a new topic, which is the best communication protocol ZigBee or LoRa, according to (Taşkin & Yazar, 2020). Both protocols have advantages and disadvantages, as mentioned in Table 3.

Table 3. Comparison between LoRa and ZigBee protocols

LoRa	ZigBee
Worst performance Mesh network	Best performance Mesh network
Worst for delivering large data streams	Best for delivering large data streams
Longer distance	Shorter distance
Best for delivering small data streams	Worst for delivering small data streams
Less energy consumption	More energy consumption

The choice of communication protocol is a critical aspect of IoT-based systems like Agro Smart. In the context of this project, a comparison between LoRa and ZigBee communication protocols was made. LoRa was chosen due to its longer communication range and lower energy consumption, which aligns with the remote locations of agricultural fields. This decision was based on the consideration of factors such as data delivery, distance coverage, and energy efficiency, all of which contribute to the system's successful implementation and performance.

For the system developed, the ideal will be a communication that complements a greater distance, with a lower power consumption, so the communication technology adopted for the project was LoRa.

Thus, the proposed system uses LoRaWAN technology to communicate the data collected by the sensors with the Thingspeak platform. It was programmed in Arduino Due to send data via LoRaWAN every 15 seconds. The Arduino Due device uses LoRaWAN class A, and it can send messages at any time, but it can only receive after sending a message within 2 times window. The LG01-S device will receive this message and forward it over WiFi to the The Things Network platform. The messages will be encrypted with the Advanced Encryption Standard (AES) algorithm and will pass through the TTN network server to the TTN application server and here where they are sent only the necessary data over HTTP to Thingspeak. The mobile application then allows to view the data received in Thingspeak on a mobile phone.

Management Platform

The nomenclature was attributed to the system developed on the ThingSpeak platform facing the manager. Among the IoT platforms on the market, one of the most popular and simple to use is ThingSpeak. This platform allows the sending of numerical data through different devices, enabling the reading of data in the form of graphs over time. ThingSpeak (ThingSpeak, n.d.) has a powerful iterative analysis tool, and with the MATLAB computing platform it is possible to analyze data, develop algorithms and create models. The developed system uses ThingSpeak as a database and to present the values captured by the sensors in the form of graphs over time. MATLAB analysis is used to calculate new data and build models, namely amplitudes, averages and plugins to read the data in different views. MATLAB is used to visualize and understand the data captured in histograms and correlation graphs. TimeControl to schedule actions (everyday MATLAB analysis actions occur, such as calculating the average for a defined period of time) and React to react when channel data meet certain conditions, remembering that the manager will receive alerts in case one sensor is damaged or poorly connected.

One of Agro Smart's essential features is the ability to parameterize soil moisture values according to the user's specific needs. This allows farmers and gardeners to tailor the system to the unique growing conditions of their crops. For example, a user can configure the system to activate irrigation when soil moisture drops below a customized value, ensuring their plants receive water only when needed.

Client Application

A native application for android mobile devices was developed. Android Studio was used for its development. The developed Android application uses the object-oriented programming language, Java. The application is responsive and multilingual (Portuguese and English). In the application, the user can register and authenticate. Within the application, the user can check the status of the relay, receive alerts, and view the requested ThingSpeak data. Graphics, averages, and amplitudes are some of the contents. The user can consult the history of the captured values and filter by them.

Security

As for system security, LoRaWAN specifies several security keys (Alliance, n.d.). All keys are 128bit in size and use an AES-128 symmetric encryption algorithm. The application key is used to encrypt and decrypt the payload, being only known to the device and application. The network session key is used in the interaction between Node and the network server (Security, n.d.). As for the security of mobile application authentication, authentication identifies users who request access to data as a variable that can be used in the rules (Firebase, n.d.), the auth variable. This variable contains information such as the token and uid (unique user id). Firebase authentication aggregates OAuth 2.0 protocols (OAuth, n.d.)

and OpenID Connect (OpenID, n.d.), industry standards designed for security, portability and interoperability. For private channels, ThingSpeak uses a 16-digit key that only the channel owner has access to.

RESULTS AND DISCUSSION

The objective of the tests performed was to verify whether the relay was activated under which conditions of light and soil moisture. A dehydrated soil sample was used and then a solvent (water) was gradually added, under different light conditions.

Therefore, four different types of tests were performed to verify the capabilities of the system. The first two to test system response to soils with different moisture states. Finally, two more to test the response of the system to soils with different moisture levels under different light conditions.

For the first test, the system was placed on dry soil. The dry soil makes it necessary to activate the irrigation system. As such, a calculation was then made to activate the relay when the soil was dry. For this, the soil moisture should be between 640 and 780. It was then verified on the LCD, that at 749 the relay was activated, as illustrated in Figure 6, which would turn on the irrigation system. Therefore, we can confirm that the system has passed this test and the system is able to turn on irrigation.

For the second test, and after the first test, water was added until the system turned off the relay. For this to happen, the soil moisture should be between 360 and 500. It was verified on the LCD that when the device reached 399, the relay was deactivated. Since high soil moisture was detected, the relay was turned off, which proves that the system will turn off irrigation after the ground is wet.

For the third test, the light sensor was connected. For this experiment, we want to give priority to nighttime irrigation, so the irrigation system should only be active when the luminosity is low, and the soil is dry.

Figure 6. Light signal, relay on

The system was then placed on dry soil during the day, where it did not turn on irrigation until it was nighttime. When it started to get dark, the relay was activated and so the system favors nighttime watering. We can then verify that this test was also validated, because the system only turned-on irrigation when it started to get dark.

To finish our experiment, a fourth test was made to verify if the system turned off irrigation when the soil was humid and there was already luminosity. To do this, we waited until dawn to check if it would turn off irrigation as soon as the soil was moist, and the luminosity was high. This was validated, because when dawn started, and with the soil already wet, the system turned off the relay, thus simulating the shutdown of the irrigation system.

We can say that all the tests were validated, and the system passed all of them. The tests are summarized, respectively, in Table 4.Tests were carried out in controlled spaces and the results satisfied the expected results. It was concluded that the system is working correctly.

Next, it was intended to verify the data flow from the collection of data by the sensors to their delivery to the mobile application.

Table 4. Test cases

Test Case	Description	Data Input	Requirements	Measured Values	Result
1	Measure the soil moisture and turn on the relay if the soil moisture is below 780 and above (780 − (780 − 360) / 3)	Soil Moisture	Soil must be dry	Soil Moisture: 749	Pass
2	Measure the soil moisture and turn off the relay if the soil moisture is above 360 and below (360 + (780 -360)/3)	Soil Moisture	Soil must be moist	Soil Moisture: 399	Pass
3	Measure the soil moisture and luminosity, and turn on the relay if the soil moisture is below 780 and above (780 − (780 − 360) / 3) and the luminosity below 20	Soil Moisture; Luminosity	The soil must be dry and sky must be dark	Soil Moisture: 748 Luminosity: 7	Pass
4	Measure the soil moisture and luminosity, and turn off the relay if the soil moisture is above 360 and below (360 + (780 -360)/3) and the luminosity is above 20	Soil Moisture; Luminosity	The soil must be wet and sky must be bright	Soil Moisture: 400 Luminosity: 95	Pass

In Figure 7, it is possible to visualize the VSCode's serial monitor, the data collected from the sensors and, consequently, sending it through LoRaWAN technology to the Single Channel Packet Forwarder Dragino LG01-S.

The data received in ThingSpeak from TTN and the description of the inherent fields can be seen in Figure 8.

Figure 9 shows the visualization of data retrieved from ThingSpeak through Retrofit, in list view. In the same figure, in the illustrated graphics, it is possible to view the value of soil moisture and temperature that was transmitted in that stream.

Based on the results obtained, we can conclude that the data is transmitted without any loss of information. Data is transmitted every 15 seconds.

The conducted tests confirmed the system's effectiveness in terms of efficient water use and autonomous irrigation control. This has a direct impact on water resource conservation and cost reduction compared to traditional irrigation methods (Zia, Rehman, Harris, Fatima, & Khurram, 2021). Additionally, the system's ability to prioritize nighttime irrigation under ideal soil moisture and luminosity conditions contributes to water and energy savings. Environmentally, the system aims at sustainable irrigation of agricultural areas and public gardens, while socially, the presence of more green spaces promotes a healthier lifestyle. The analysis, calculations, and notifications provided to users also enhance understanding of data values, averages, ranges, and historical data, contributing to more efficient resource utilization.

While the tests validated the system's effectiveness under various conditions, some limitations should be considered, especially when applying the system in urban and rural environments. In urban environments, limited space availability for sensor and actuator installation can affect monitoring and control capabilities. Additionally, the presence of buildings and other structures can interfere with wireless communication, such as LoRa technology. In rural environments, the distance between sensors and the network infrastructure can be a challenge, requiring additional access points.

Figure 7. Print serial monitor

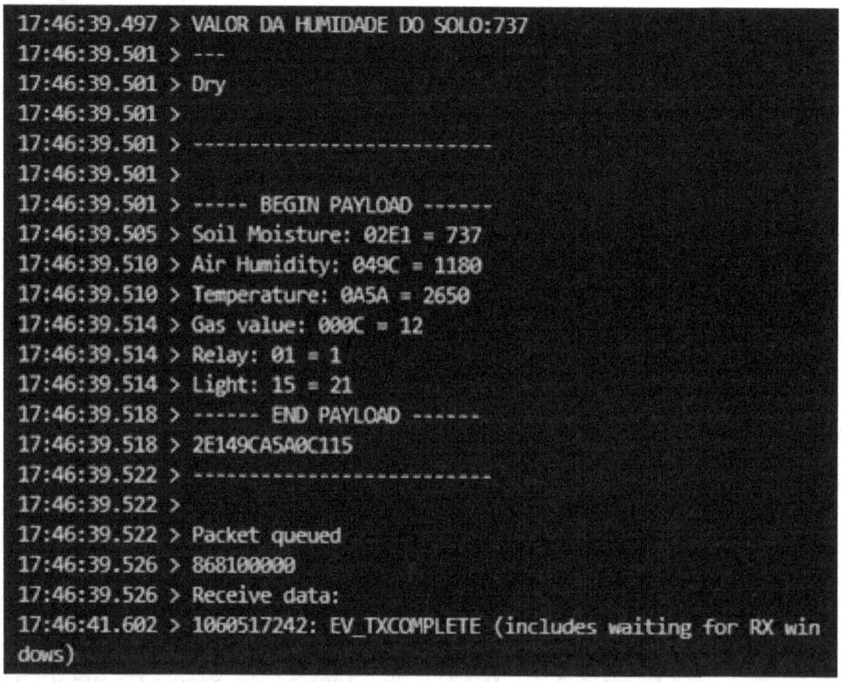

Figure 8. Description of fields and values ThingSpeak

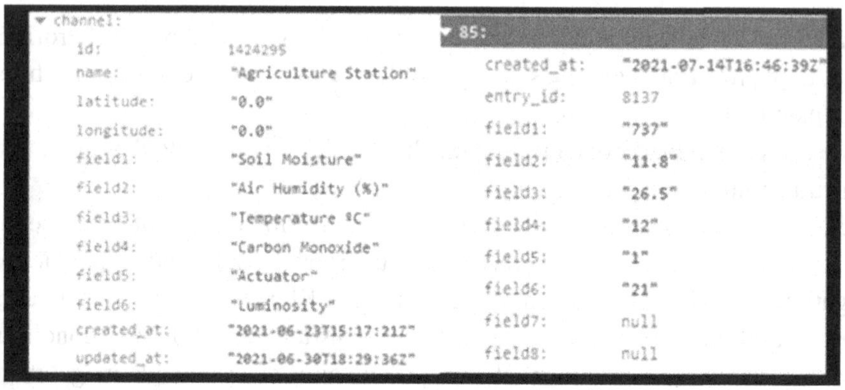

Figure 9. Mobile application

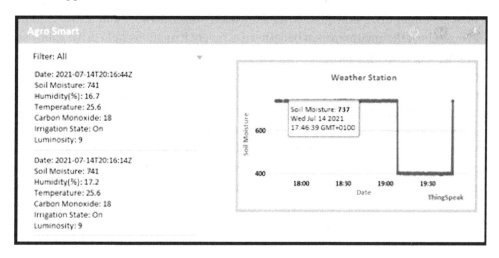

CONCLUSIONS AND FUTURE WORK

The main contribution of this study is the development of an autonomous irrigation system, capable of analyzing and controlling the favorable conditions for the sustainable crop irrigation. The system allows the analysis of the conditions of air and soil moisture humidity and temperature and measures the properties of the air such as carbon monoxide and triggers the irrigation system depending on those values. The project developed has an impact on the sustainability dimensions. At an environmental level, the system aims at the sustainable irrigation of agricultural areas and public gardens. On an economic level, we can infer that the amount of water needed results in a cost reduction by half, when compared to traditional irrigation process (Zia et al., 2021). At a social level, with more green spaces, more people will walk outdoors, contributing to a healthier society. At a technical level, users through notifications, analysis, calculations will be able to know the relationship of values, averages, ranges, and historical values.

The study elaborated represents an easy method for the flow and analysis of data with the aid of open-source platforms and the availability of this data to the final customer, fulfilling the same purpose, the monitoring of the irrigation status. In addition, this system also has a luminosity sensor in order to give preference to more favorable watering periods, such as nighttime. On the other hand, the system is also aware of the presence of the user, that is, upon detection of the user, it is prepared to make the data available in the OLED on site. These are examples of some valences that allow our system to complement the solutions of related works. The validation of the system operation allowed the confirmation of the expected response for all the considered test cases. As future work, we intend to improve our solution with more sensors, namely an anemometer, in order to calculate the wind speed with a view to further reduce water waste. We also intend a more comprehensive algorithm to trigger the irrigation system, including moisture and temperature analysis, as well as weather forecast (Caetano et al., 2014), and an artificial intelligence method (Somov et al., 2018; Bwambale et al., 2022) to learn based on inferences and contribute to better crop growth efficiency.

Looking ahead, the field of IoT-based agriculture is expected to witness continued growth. Advancements in sensor technology, communication protocols, and data analytics will further enhance the capabilities of systems like Agro Smart. Integration with weather forecasting services can enable even more accurate irrigation predictions. As the adoption of IoT in agriculture becomes more widespread, economies of scale might drive down the costs associated with hardware and setup. Additionally, increased awareness about the environmental benefits of efficient irrigation could drive policy support and incentives for adopting such systems, fostering a more sustainable agricultural landscape.

The adoption of smart irrigation solutions like Agro Smart can be challenging due to various barriers. One of the primary challenges is communication infrastructure in remote areas, where setting up communication networks can be costly. Additionally, user awareness and education about the importance of smart irrigation and efficient water use are critical factors for the success of these solutions.

The significant amount of data collected by the IoT system, such as soil moisture, luminosity, and temperature, poses both opportunities and challenges. Advanced data analytics and inference-based methods can be applied to derive valuable insights from this data. For example, machine learning algorithms can analyze historical data to predict optimal irrigation times based on weather forecasts and past patterns. These insights can lead to more efficient resource management and potentially reduce water wastage, implementation costs and ongoing maintenance requirements.

REFERENCES

Abba, S., Wadumi Namkusong, J., Lee, J. A., & Liz Crespo, M. (2019). Design and performance evaluation of a low-cost autonomous sensor interface for a smart iot-based irrigation monitoring and control system. *Sensors (Basel)*, *19*(17), 1–25. doi:10.339019173643 PMID:31438597

Abdullah, A., Al Enazi, S., & Damaj, I. (2016). AgriSys: A smart and ubiquitous controlled-environment agriculture system. *3rd MEC International Conference on Big Data and Smart City (ICBDSC)*, 1-6. 10.1109/ICBDSC.2016.7460386

Alliance, L. (n.d.). *LoRaWAN*. Retrieved 7 14, 2021, from https://lora-alliance.org/

Bates, B., Kundzewicz, Z., & Wu, S. (2008). *Climate Change and Water*. Intergovernmental Panel on Climate Change Secretariat.

Becker, C., Chitchyan, R., Duboc, L., Easterbrook, S., Penzenstadler, B., Seyff, N., & Venters, C. C. (2015). Sustainability Design and Software: The Karlskrona Manifesto. *IEEE/ACM 37th IEEE International Conference on Software Engineering, 2*, 467-476.

Bwambale, E., Abagale, F. K., & Anornu, G. K. (2022). Smart irrigation monitoring and control strategies for improving water use efficiency in precision agriculture: A review. *Agricultural Water Management*, *260*, 1–12. doi:10.1016/j.agwat.2021.107324

Caetano, F., Pitarma, R., & Reis, P. (2014). Intelligent management of urban garden irrigation. *9th Iberian Conference on Information Systems and Technologies (CISTI)*, 1-6.

Davcev, D., Mitreski, K., Trajkovic, S., Nikolovski, V., & Koteli, N. (2018). IoT agriculture system based on LoRaWAN. *14th IEEE International Workshop on Factory Communication Systems (WFCS)*, 1-4.

DRAGINO. (n.d.). *Dragino Products*. Retrieved 7 14, 2021, from https://dragino.com

Firebase. (n.d.). *Security Rules and Firebase Authentication*. Retrieved 7 11, 2021, from https://firebase. google.com/docs/rules/rules-and-auth

Gaikwad, S. V., Vibhute, A. D., Kale, K. V., & Mehrotra, S. C. (2021). An innovative IoT based system for precision farming. *Computers and Electronics in Agriculture, 187*, 1–12. doi:10.1016/j.compag.2021.106291

Jacobson, I., Lawson, H., Ng, P., McMahon, P., & Goedicke, M. (2019). *The Essentials of Modern Software Engineering: Free the Practices from the Method Prisons*. ACM Books.

Jariyayothin, P., Jeravong-aram, K., Ratanachaijaroen, N., Tantidham, T., & Intakot, P. (2018). IoT Backyard: Smart watering control system. *Seventh ICT International Student Project Conference (ICT-ISPC)*, 1-6.

Keshtgary, M., & Deljoo, A. (2012). An efficient wireless sensor network for precision agriculture. *Canadian Journal on Multimedia and Wireless Networks, 3*(1), 1–5.

Ma, J., Zhou, X., Li, S., & Li, Z. (2011). Connecting agriculture to the internet of things through sensor networks. *International Conference on Internet of Things and 4th International Conference on Cyber, Physical and Social Computing*, 184-187. 10.1109/iThings/CPSCom.2011.32

OAuth. (n.d.). *OAuth Community Site*. Retrieved 7 11, 2021, from https://oauth.net

Open, I. D. (n.d.). *OpenID Foundation website*. Retrieved 7 11, 2021, from https://openid.net

Platform, I. O. (n.d.). *Professional collaborative platform for embedded development*. Retrieved 7 14, 2021, from https://platformio.org

Pornillos, C. J., Billones, M. S., Leonidas, J. D., Reyes, E. M., Esguerra, B. J., Bolima, D. P., & Concepcion, R. (2020). Smart irrigation control system using wireless sensor network via internet-of-things. *IEEE 12th International Conference on Humanoid, Nanotechnology, Information Technology, Communication and Control, Environment, and Management (HNICEM)*, 1-6.

Rijsberman, F. R. (2006). Water scarcity: Fact or fiction? *Agricultural Water Management, 80*(1-3), 5–22. doi:10.1016/j.agwat.2005.07.001

Rubin, K. (2012). *Essential Scrum: A Practical Guide to the Most Popular Agile Process*. Addison-Wesley Professional.

Santos, G., Vicente, G., Salvado, T., Gonçalves, C., Caetano, F., & Silveira, C. (2022). Agro Smart: IoT Autonomous Irrigation System. *17th Iberian Conference on Information Systems and Technologies (CISTI)*, 1-6.

Saraf, S. B., & Gawali, D. H. (2017). IoT based smart irrigation monitoring and controlling system. *2nd IEEE International Conference on Recent Trends in Electronics, Information & Communication Technology (RTEICT)*, 815-819. 10.1109/RTEICT.2017.8256711

Security. (n.d.). *The Things Network*. Retrieved 7 11, 2021, from https://www.thethingsnetwork.org/docs/lorawan/security/

Seghezzo, L. (2009). The Five Dimensions of Sustainability. *Environmental Politics, 18*(4), 539–556. doi:10.1080/09644010903063669

Shadrin, D., Somov, A., Podladchikova, T., & Gerzer, R. (2018). Pervasive agriculture: Measuring and predicting plant growth using statistics and 2D/3D imaging. *IEEE International Instrumentation and Measurement Technology Conference (I2MTC)*, 1-6. 10.1109/I2MTC.2018.8409700

Somov, A., Shadrin, D., Fastovets, I., Nikitin, A., Matveev, S., & Hrinchuk, O. (2018). Pervasive Agriculture: IoT-Enabled Greenhouse for Plant Growth Control. *IEEE Pervasive Computing, 17*(4), 65–75. doi:10.1109/MPRV.2018.2873849

Taşkin, D., & Yazar, S. (2020). A Long-range context-aware platform design for rural monitoring with IoT In precision agriculture. *International Journal of Computers, Communications & Control, 15*(2), 1–11. doi:10.15837/ijccc.2020.2.3821

ThingSpeak. (n.d.). *IoT Analytics - ThingSpeak Internet of Things*. Retrieved 7 14, 2021, from https://thingspeak.com

Zia, H., Rehman, A., Harris, N. R., Fatima, S., & Khurram, M. (2021). An experimental comparison of iot-based and traditional irrigation scheduling on a flood-irrigated subtropical lemon farm. *Sensors (Basel), 21*(12), 1–17. doi:10.339021124175 PMID:34204584

KEY TERMS AND DEFINITIONS

Actuators: Components or devices that turn electrical signals or data into physical actions or responses, like turning irrigation systems on and off or displaying data on OLED screens.

Autonomous System: Is a system that, in a changing environment, can obtain information about the environment and make decisions, for a long period of time, without requiring human control or interaction.

Context-Awareness: The ability of a structure to understand and adjust to the specific situation or environment in which it operates, taking into account variables such as the client's area, preferences, and surrounding conditions, with the ability to adapt behaviors in conformity with the environment.

Data Analytics: The act of analyzing, cleaning, modifying and modeling data to extract conclusions, find useful patterns and trends.

Internet of Things: A concept that describes how physical objects can connect to the Internet to exchange data and communicate with each other and other devices.

LoRaWAN: A long-range, low-power communication protocol, using LoRa technology, designed for devices with low data rates and low power. It is used in IoT applications, such as wireless sensor networks.

Machine Learning: An approach to artificial intelligence (AI) that makes it possible for systems to learn and grow from data and experiences without being explicitly programmed, resulting in behavior that is more intelligent and adaptable.

Mobile Application: Software with particular features and functions that is made to run on mobile devices like smartphones and tablets.

Sensor: A device that converts physical or environmental stimuli into electrical signals or measurable data and responds to them.

Sensor Network: A set of interconnected sensors that collect and transmit environmental data to a place where it can be stored, visualized, and analyzed.

Smart Irrigation: A framework that uses sensors and algorithms to analyze and control the water system process that considers weather and soil conditions to optimize the process. This means that the system is optimized for each specific area that is being watered, which saves water and optimizes crop growth.

Sustainable System: A system that focuses on preserving natural resources while also promoting energy efficiency and minimizing environmental impact.

Ubiquitous System: Alludes to a framework that is available and coordinated into the climate consistently, offering ceaseless types of assistance and communications.

Chapter 18
Unveiling Bitcoin's Safe Haven and Hedging Properties Beyond Diversification

Rui Manuel Teixeira Santos Teixeira Dias
iD https://orcid.org/0000-0002-6138-3098
Polytechnic Institute of Setubal, Portugal

Paulo Alexandre
iD https://orcid.org/0000-0003-1781-7036
Polytechnic Institute of Setúbal, Portugal

Mariana Chambino
iD https://orcid.org/0000-0002-9444-3333
Polytechnic Institute of Setúbal, Portugal

Cristina Morais da Palma
iD https://orcid.org/0000-0002-7899-0134
Instituto Politécnico de Setúbal, Portugal

Liliana Almeida
iD https://orcid.org/0009-0002-8907-6804
Polytechnic Institute of Setúbal, Portugal

ABSTRACT

This study investigates whether Bitcoin may act as a safe haven in the capital markets, including France (CAC 40), Germany (DAX 30), the US (DJI), the UK (FTSE 100), Italy (FTSE MIB), Hong Kong (HANG SENG), Spain (IBEX 35), South Korea (KOSPI), Russia (IMOEX), and Japan (NIKKEI 225), as well as in commodities such as gold (GOLD HANDY HARMAN) and petroleum (WTI), and U.S. 10-year sovereign yields, during the 2020-2022 events. The authors analyze the financial integration and movements of markets to understand how BTC behaves during periods of global economic uncertainty. During the stress period, BTC did not integrate with the analyzed markets, suggesting that BTC exhibits properties of a hedge and a safe haven. BTC has properties of a hedge and a safe haven, and investors in these markets can benefit from investing in it as a secure asset and hedge. It is affected by CAC 40, FTSE 100, HANG SENG, and NIKKEI 225 stock indexes, and investors must carefully evaluate their investment strategies and risk tolerance when including BTC in their portfolio.

DOI: 10.4018/978-1-6684-9039-6.ch018

INTRODUCTION

Within the field of contemporary finance, the emergence of Bitcoin as a digital currency and payment mechanism, initially proposed by Nakamoto (2016), has sparked considerable academic and practical enthusiasm. Bitcoin is characterized by its decentralized nature, functioning on a complex protocol that operates without a central authority, which sets it apart from traditional fiat currencies. One noteworthy attribute of Bitcoin is its predetermined supply, a distinctive feature established by the protocol's design that distinguishes it as an exceptional financial asset (Dwyer 2015). Since its inception in 2009, Bitcoin has experienced a remarkable increase in worth, reaching an impressive valuation of $457,807,981,534 as of February 2023, as documented in the study conducted by Bouri et al. (2017). The significant increase in value of Bitcoin has generated considerable academic curiosity, leading to a growing body of research focused on exploring the economic and financial complexities associated with this cryptocurrency. Academic investigations into the multifaceted nature of Bitcoin encompass a wide range of dimensions.

In their work, Rogojanu and Badea (2014) conducted a comparative analysis to examine the position of Bitcoin within different monetary systems. Brandvold et al. (2015) and Ciaian et al. (2016) have conducted research on the topic of price discovery in Bitcoin markets, uncovering significant findings. Bouri et al. (2020) have focused their research on examining the impact of trading volume on the return and volatility of Bitcoin. In a similar vein, Balcilar et al. (2016) have developed complex models to effectively capture the persistence and existence of long-term memory effects in the behavior of Bitcoin. Yermack's (2015) provides a comprehensive analysis that categorizes Bitcoin primarily as a speculative investment rather than a legitimate currency. This classification is primarily based on the significant market capitalization of Bitcoin in relation to its practical usefulness in economic transactions. However, it is worth noting that empirical data indicates that the inclusion of Bitcoin in a diversified portfolio has proven to be a profitable strategy, despite the inherent volatility that is typically associated with this specific digital asset. This conclusion is supported by the research conducted by Brandvold et al. (2015).

The recognition of Bitcoin as a potential alternative to conventional currencies has garnered attention within academic spheres. The topic of an alternative economic system is often a subject of frequent discussion, as highlighted by Halaburda and Gandal (2014). In situations where investors witness a decrease in trust in well-established government-issued currencies or hold apprehensions regarding the overall economic landscape, Bitcoin could potentially emerge as an attractive substitute. The nickname "digital gold" has been attributed to Bitcoin, a characterization effectively expressed by Popper (2015). Furthermore, according to Dyhrberg (2016), Bitcoin possesses a coverage capacity similar to that of gold and the U.S. dollar. This implies that Bitcoin has the potential to function as a hedge for assets like the UK stock market and the U.S. dollar. Nevertheless, it is important to acknowledge that although extensive research has been conducted on Bitcoin's role as a speculative investment and its potential as an alternative to conventional currencies, there is still a significant gap in the existing body of research. This gap refers to the evaluation of Bitcoin's diverse functions as a tool for diversification, hedging, and a safe haven against price volatility across various assets, including stock indexes, bonds, oil, gold, the overall commodity index, and the US dollar index. The suitability of an asset for investment is contingent upon its correlation with other assets, as viewed from a risk perspective.

Our study adopted the research approach of Baur and Lucey (2010), Ratner and Chiu (2013), which entails distinguishing between diversifiers (assets with weak positive correlation), assets with weak coverage (lower correlation), uncorrelated or negatively correlated assets (robust coverage), and safe havens (strong negative correlation). A "diversifier" can be defined as an asset that exhibits, on average, a weak positive correlation with another asset. An asset with weak coverage exhibits a lower correlation with another asset. While not entirely uncorrelated, the correlation between this asset and others is comparatively weaker. An asset that is uncorrelated or negatively correlated with another asset is considered an advantageous feature of robust coverage. This phenomenon is characterized by a negative correlation between the two assets, such that an increase in the value of one asset is usually followed by a decrease in the value of the other asset, or at the very least, no significant change in its value. A safe haven that exhibits a weak correlation with another asset under normal market conditions but displays a higher correlation during times of market stress is referred to as a weak safe haven. On average, a strong safe haven is an asset that exhibits either no correlation or a negative correlation with another asset, even during times of greater stress. This phenomenon implies that in the event of a decline in one asset, the other asset exhibits either no movement or an upward trend, thereby serving as a robust means of diversification and risk reduction. Assets that are considered strong safe haven options include gold, bonds of high quality, and cash. Throughout financial history, there have been different assets that have exhibited robust attributes as safe havens. These assets encompass gold, high-quality bonds, and cash. The previous concepts have predominantly been linked to the precious metal known as gold, thereby reflecting the findings put forth by Baur and Lucey (2010). Furthermore, Ratner and Chiu (2013) have employed analogous principles within the realm of credit default swaps, thereby broadening the discourse to encompass modern financial instruments.

The present chapter is structured in the following manner: Section 2 provides a comprehensive overview of the existing literature, while Section 3 elucidates the methodology and data employed. Section 4 presents the findings, and Section 5 concludes the study.

LITERATURE REVIEW

Over the past few years, there has been a steady rise in both the value and volume of financial markets, resulting in a corresponding increase in the risks faced by investors. The evaluation of global financial stability is significantly influenced by the interconnection of financial markets. The phenomenon of globalization has facilitated the process of investment in global markets, leading to substantial capital inflows and enhanced financial integration between nations. Although there have been advantages associated with this phenomenon, such as the provision of financial resources to both firms and individuals, it has also amplified the likelihood of contagion, whereby issues in one market can rapidly disseminate to others. To tackle this issue, policymakers and regulators internationally have worked to enhance financial stability by bolstering the robustness of financial institutions and the financial system in its entirety. Additionally, they have sought to enhance coordination and collaboration between regulators and international organizations. Furthermore, investors have become aware of the potential risks associated with investing in interconnected markets and are implementing measures to enhance risk management and diversify their portfolios. For further insight, see the articles of Dias et al. (2020), Guedes et al. (2022), Revez et al. (2022), Dias et al. (2023), Santana et al. (2023), Dias, Horta, and Chambino (2023).

Habib and Stracca (2012), Fatum and Yamamoto (2016), Cho and Han (2021) have posited that safe port assets offer coverage advantages in times of financial market stress. The authors emphasize that exchange rates offer coverage advantages during periods of financial stability, but exhibit comparatively greater benefits during times of crisis, on average. According to Baur and Lucey's (2010) research, gold is commonly recognized as a secure investment option within financial markets due to its tangible nature.

Historically, it has been utilized as a hedge instrument to mitigate the effects of inflation. Furthermore, it is generally acknowledged that gold exhibits a low correlation with other assets, a characteristic that is deemed significant in light of the increasing interdependence of global trade. Batten et al. (2017) posit that investors may encounter practical implications when distinguishing between hedge instruments and safe port assets. Coverage instruments have the potential to serve as enduring investment vehicles that mitigate the impact of volatility and risk on anticipated returns. Conversely, safe haven assets may be deemed a feasible substitute during periods of heightened market turbulence, wherein investors experience substantial losses on their investments. The concept of "safe haven" is widely discussed in financial literature as a collection of low-risk assets, covering different kinds of currencies, sovereign bonds, and commodities. Conversely, a secure haven asset is characterized as an asset that exhibits a lack of correlation with other assets or portfolios during times of crisis.

Empirical Studies

According to the literature, a hedge instrument is characterized as an asset that exhibits a negative correlation with other assets or portfolios, resulting in a reasonable performance during financial market crises due to its low exposure to conventional risk factors. Notwithstanding the availability of said instruments, it is not a given that investors' losses will be mitigated during times of crisis, as these assets may exhibit positive correlations during periods of heightened volatility and negative correlations during periods of market stability. During times of uncertainty and pessimism in the global financial markets, financial market participants have attributed precious metals with coverage characteristics, that offer diversification benefits (Baur and Lucey, 2010; Ratner and Chiu, 2013; Christian Andreas Valstad, 2014).

The research conducted by Gilmore et al. (2008) investigates the transitions of capital between the established capital markets within the European Union (EU) and those of three Central European (EC) nations that have recently become members of the EU. The researchers employ dynamic co-integration techniques and essential elements, alongside static tests, to investigate abrupt fluctuations in both the short and long term. The findings indicate a lack of co-integration during the period spanning from July 1995 to February 2005. However, there exist alternative periods of co-integration that are intermittently disrupted by episodes characterized by short-term internal factors. The examination of the primary constituents suggests that a consistent factor accounts for a significant portion of the fluctuations in the returns. Notwithstanding the protracted process of alignment of the European Community member states with the European Union, there is an absence of empirical support for an increasing convergence of the equity markets. Furthermore, Baur and Lucey (2010) conducted a study to investigate the extent to which gold can be regarded as a safe haven in comparison to stock and bond markets. This study investigates the dynamic and static relationships between gold returns, stock returns, and bond returns in the United States, United Kingdom, and Germany. According to the authors' findings, gold can be classified as a hedge asset in capital markets and a safe haven during periods of heightened capital market volatility. Nonetheless, it is important to note that this safe haven provision is applicable in the short term.

In 2020, the study conducted by Corbet et al. (2020) examines the conduct of Chinese financial markets in the initial phases of the worldwide COVID-19 outbreak, during which they acted as a hub of contagion in both physical and financial terms. The study reveals that specific discernible features of a "flight to safety" were evident during the analyzed period. Furthermore, the volatility ratio pertaining to the major Chinese exchanges and Bitcoin has experienced noteworthy alterations in reaction to financial stress. The authors provide multiple justifications and propose that the dynamic correlations witnessed during stressful periods present a prudent rationale for incorporating Bitcoin into traditional wallet design, owing to the diversification advantages it can provide. Furthermore, Ciner et al. (2020) conducted an analysis of the interrelationships within the global metals markets spanning from 1994 to 2016, utilizing diverse econometric methods. The findings of the study indicate a significant level of return intensity and the impact of volatility in specific markets, exhibiting varying degrees of fluctuation across different time periods. This study makes a valuable contribution to the existing literature on contagion, as it demonstrates a notable rise in shocks subsequent to the financial crisis. The authors have identified aluminum as the primary catalyst for these disturbances, exerting a substantial impact on all the methodologies employed. The findings provide evidence in favor of the proposition that non-ferrous metals exhibit analogous patterns to conventional asset categories, such as equities and fixed-income securities, indicating that metals have transformed into a unique investment category. A study was conducted by Bouri et al. (2020) to compare the safe haven characteristics of Bitcoin, gold, capital markets, and commodities during the period of July 20, 2010, to February 22, 2018. The researchers employed wavelet coherence methodologies to examine the worldwide dependence among assets and capital markets across various temporal frequencies. Their findings indicate that the degree of interdependence was relatively weak, with Bitcoin exhibiting the lowest level of dependence. The researchers also examined the potential for asset diversification and observed that the level of correlation between gold and capital markets had an impact on the degree of portfolio diversification. The research findings indicate that the advantages of diversification exhibit temporal variability, wherein Bitcoin is demonstrated to be a more efficient diversification instrument relative to gold and commodities.

Subsequently, Wang et al. (2022) emphasized that commodities can serve as a viable hedge for global equity markets, particularly in times of heightened market turbulence. The study conducted by the authors demonstrates that Bitcoin, gold, and commodities are assets that exhibit limited hedging capabilities with respect to capital markets. Trichilli and Boujelbène Abbes (2022) conducted a study on the function of Bitcoin as a hedge or diversifier in the context of complementarity, both prior to and during the COVID-19 pandemic. The study conducted by the authors reveals that the returns of DJI, Bitcoin, petroleum, gold, copper, and Brent oil are being impacted by the confirmed cases of COVID-19. The study's results indicate that the incorporation of Bitcoin into portfolio optimization either prior to or during the COVID-19 era caused the Bayesian efficient border to shift towards the left, thereby enhancing the risk-to-return ratio for investors. The study conducted by Hampl et al. (2022) aimed to examine the potential of Bitcoin and Ether, which are traditional cryptocurrencies, Tether, a fiat-backed stablecoin, and Solana, a utility token, to serve as safe havens in comparison to gold, stock and commodity indexes, and foreign currencies, amidst the Russian invasion of Ukraine in 2022. The authors have highlighted that while cryptocurrencies may not possess the attributes of a safe haven for commodity markets, they do serve as effective hedge assets for foreign currencies. Furthermore, Tether and Solana exhibit characteristics of safe haven assets akin to those of gold. Despite its weaknesses, Tether serves as a relatively safe haven for the capital market. The study conducted by Lavelle et al. (2022) aimed to investigate the diversification, hedging, and safe haven properties of Bitcoin and the overall cryptocurrency market concerning various asset classes, including US stocks, US bonds, the US dollar, commodities, real estate, and gold. The authors demonstrate that Bitcoin functions primarily as a means of diversification for other assets while also serving as a substantial hedge for the overall cryptocurrency market.

More recently, Abdullah (2023) conducted an investigation into the potential safe haven properties of Bitcoin, gold, and petroleum for the U.S. Islamic stock index during the period spanning August 2014 to April 2022. The study conducted by the author reveals that there exists a low and frequently negative dynamic correlation between Bitcoin and the US Islamic stock index, particularly during significant economic and political occurrences. This finding suggests that Bitcoin functions as a safe haven and a coverage instrument, particularly in the context of the pandemic period. Our findings indicate that Bitcoin exhibits high levels of volatility, which constrains its utility as a safe haven and hedging instrument in comparison to gold. Gold is considered a stable asset that exhibits a negative correlation with the US Islamic stock index. This characteristic makes it a suitable option for diversification and hedging purposes. Furthermore, Ali et al. (2023) emphasize that Bitcoin presents a viable option for short-term diversification of sustainable and Islamic wealth, as well as energy indexes, particularly in times of low volatility and uncertainty. As a result, Bitcoin presents potential hedging opportunities akin to traditional commodities such as gold and silver in the context of political instability. In summary, the research indicates that the Economic Policy Uncertainty (EPU) holds significant importance in elucidating the mean returns of Bitcoin portfolios. This implies that the EPU can be regarded as an explanatory variable for the diversification of portfolios.

METHODOLOGY

Data

The time series used in this investigation includes distinct financial markets, such as the Bitcoin price index (BTC), and stock market indices from different nations, such as France (CAC 40), Germany (DAX 30), the USA (DJI), the UK (FTSE 100), Italy (FTSE MIB), Hong Kong (HANG SENG), Spain (IBEX 35), South Korea (KOSPI), Russia (IMOEX), and Japan (NIKKEI 225). Additionally, the time series incorporates commodities like gold (GOLD HANDY HARMAN) and oil (WTI), as well as US 10-year sovereign OTs. The data spans from February 28, 2018, to March 1, 2023. To improve the reliability of the study, the time series has been divided into two distinct subperiods. The initial subperiod, referred to as the Tranquil subperiod, covers the temporal span from February 2018 to December 2019. The second subperiod, referred to as Stress, covers the temporal range from January 2020 to March 2023.

The perception that the specified time frame represents a period of relative stability in the global financial markets supports the justification for choosing it. Furthermore, this period is notable for the occurrence of complex external events that have had significant implications for the world economy. Examples of such events include the COVID-19 pandemic, the oil price disagreement between OPEP members in 2020, and the subsequent conflict between Russia and Ukraine in 2022. The basis for selecting specific stock indices is supported by the representation of major global capital markets. The inclusion of the Russian market is justified due to two significant events: the disagreement on oil production policy with Saudi Arabia in 2020 and the invasion of Ukraine in 2022. The inclusion of the WTI index within the context of commodities is justified due to the significant decrease in demand resulting from the economic deceleration triggered by the COVID-19 pandemic. The decision to use gold as the focus of the investigation was motivated by the objective of assessing whether Bitcoin (BTC) also validates the attributes of hedging and safe haven properties typically associated with gold during periods of uncertainty and instability in the global financial markets.

In order to mitigate the potential for currency distortions, price indices are expressed in the local currency and have been obtained from the Thomson Reuters Eikon platform. Through the examination of market behaviour and commodity performance within two distinct subperiods, valuable insights can be obtained regarding the influence of significant events on these markets and their responses to instances of economic uncertainty on a global scale.

MethodsThe research will undergo multiple stages of development. Initially, we will estimate the charts in terms of levels and returns to observe the market fluctuations and their dispersion in relation to the market average. The sample characterization will be conducted utilizing descriptive statistics, the Jarque and Bera (1980) adherence test, and the q-q plots chart. In order to assess the stationarity of the time series, we will employ unit root tests from the Breitung (2000) and Hadri (2000) panels, which propose opposing stationary hypotheses. The intersection of these tests will provide robustness in determining the stationarity of the time data.

Tsay (2005) suggests that in order to examine the conduct of financial markets, it is preferable to employ a sequence of returns instead of price series, as investors are primarily concerned with determining the return on an asset or a collection of assets. Complementarity is characterized by profitability series that exhibit statistical properties that facilitate analytical treatment, specifically the property of stationarity, which is typically absent in price series. Due to the aforementioned reasons, the growth rates or series of price indexes have been adjusted by computing the differences of the Neperian logarithms between current and previous yields, which are either instantaneous or continuously compounded, expressed as follows:

$$r_t = \ln P_t - \ln P_{t-1} \tag{1}$$

where r_t is the rate of profitability on day t, and P_t and P_{t-1} are the closing prices of the series at times t and $t-1$, respectively.

The research question will be addressed by employing Gregory and Hansen's (1996) model, which incorporates the concept of regime changes. The methodology used by the authors is highly resilient during periods of financial market turbulence. This is due to the authors' extension of conventional co-integration tests, wherein they account for a change in the co-integration vector at an unspecified point in time. The researchers conducted an analysis of four distinct co-integration models. The initial model integrates a modification in level, denoted as "Level":

$$y_t = \mu_1 + \mu_2 D_t + \beta' x_t + \mu_t \quad t = 1,\ldots,T \tag{2}$$

Where x_t is a k-dimensional I(1) vector, k, μ_t is I(0), μ_1 is the independent term before change, μ_2 is the change in independent term after break, and D_t is a dummy variable.

The second model includes a time trend, denoted as "Trend":

$$y_t = \mu_1 + \mu_2 D_t + \alpha t + \beta'^{x_t} \quad t = 1,\ldots,T \tag{3}$$

In this model, μ_1 is the independent term before the structure change and μ_2 is the change in the independent word after the break. This model, compared to the previous one, introduces a change in the regime, denoted as "Regime":

$$y_t = \mu_1 + \mu_2 D_t + \alpha t + \beta^{' x_t + \beta_2' x_t D_t} + \mu_t \quad t = 1,\ldots,T \tag{4}$$

A possible change in the structure admits that the inclination vector also changes. This allows the balance ratio to move in parallel with the level. The authors call this third model the regime change model.

Finally, the fourth model is presented, which emerges to complement the previous ones, the authors add the possibility of changing structure in a model with segmented time trend, denoted as "Regime and Trend":

$$y_t = \mu_1 + \mu_2 D_t + \alpha t + \alpha_2 t D_t + \beta'_1 x_t + \beta'_2 x_t D_t + \mu_t \quad t = 1,\ldots,T \tag{5}$$

In this case, both μ_1 and μ_2 are the terms already presented in the previous models. The α_1 represents the co-integration of the inclination coefficients and the α_2 represents a change in the tilt of the coefficients.

In order to ascertain the presence of a statistical causal effect between distinct markets, the Granger causality test will be used. This test examines whether changes in a particular market consistently occur prior to changes in another market. The objective of this study is to investigate the relationships between a specific set of markets and to determine the mechanisms underlying the fluctuations observed in financial markets (Engle and Granger, 1987; Granger, 1969, 1988). The present examination employs the methodology, specifically the Granger Causality or Block Exogenety Wald Test, which uses Wald's statistics to examine the null hypothesis that the coefficients of the lagged endogenous variables of the "cause" variable are either null or lack Grangerian causality with respect to the dependent variable. It is essential to highlight that the outcome of this examination exhibits a significant susceptibility to the number of deviations considered in the model. Therefore, the primary objective is to accurately approximate this figure to attain robust evidence (Gujarati, 2004).

RESULTS

Figure 1 shows the time evolution, from February 28, 2018, to March 1, 2023, in levels of the cryptocurrency Bitcoin (BTC), the capital markets of France (CAC 40), Germany (DAX 30), USA (DJI), UK (FTSE 100), Italy (FTSE MIB), Hong Kong (HANG SENG), Spain (IBEX 35), South Korea (KOSPI), Russia (IMOEX), Japan (NIKKEI 225), commodities, gold (GOLD HANDY HARMAN) and petroleum (WTI), and U.S. sovereign yields to 10 years.

The fluctuations of BTC during the period of 2018 to 2020 were relatively minor. However, in 2021, there were significant breaks observed during the second and third quarters, as well as towards the end of the year. In 2022, a significant break was observed between the first and second quarters. In general, the examined time series of the capital markets displays notable structural breaks during the first and second quarters of 2020, which can be attributed to the declaration of the COVID-19 pandemic, and in early 2022, triggered by the commencement of the political and military conflict between Russia and Ukraine. The gold market experienced a brief decline upon the announcement of the COVID-19 pandemic crisis, but promptly rebounded and exhibited an upward trend, resulting in greater returns than those observed prior to the pandemic. Similar patterns are discernible in the 10-year U.S. government bond yields, which exhibit a slight decrease during the occurrences of 2020 and 2022. The WTI petroleum market has exhibited the most substantial decline in comparison to other markets analyzed following the declaration of the COVID-19 pandemic. The aforesaid impact can be attributed to the stalling of population and economic activities on a global scale, which was implemented as a means to curb the transmission of the virus. The temporal progression of the data series indicates that all markets experienced a breakdown during the events of 2020 and 2022. However, the pandemic crisis had a more pronounced effect on all markets except for BTC, which exhibited less volatile behavior.

Figure 1. Evolution in levels of the financial markets under study from February 28, 2018, to March 1, 2023
Source: Own Elaboration. Note: Data worked by the author (software: Eviews12).

The graphical representation depicted in Figure 2 illustrates the historical returns of different assets, including the digital currency BTC, stock indexes, commodities, and yields of U.S. sovereign debt. The observed distribution of returns exhibits a high degree of dispersion around the mean, suggesting a wide-ranging distribution of returns and indicating a deviation from the Gaussian distribution. In the initial months of 2020, a significant level of volatility in data has been witnessed, which can be attributed to the onset of the global pandemic in early 2020. The COVID-19 pandemic has resulted in significant disruptions in worldwide markets and supply chains, resulting in price volatility in different commodities, stocks, and other assets. During this period, the behavior of petroleum, specifically WTI, exhibited a high degree of volatility, which can be attributed to the prevailing uncertainty and instability in the global energy market. The behavior of BTC exhibited a high degree of volatility by the year 2022. Bitcoin (BTC) is a form of digital currency that is exchanged on decentralized networks. Its valuation is greatly influenced by fluctuations in the market's demand and supply. Throughout the year 2022, notable fluctuations in the value of BTC were observed, as evidenced by the widely dispersed distribution of returns associated with this asset. The adverse impact of the events that occurred in 2020 and 2022 on global financial markets is supported by the findings of several authors, including Pardal, P., Dias, R., Teixeira, N. and Horta (2022), Dias et al. (2022), Teixeira et al. (2022), Dias et al. (2023), Dias, Horta, and Chambino (2023), Santana et al. (2023).

Figure 2. Evolution in returns of the financial markets under study from February 28, 2018 to March 1, 2023
Source: Own Elaboration. Note: Data worked by the author (software: Eviews12).

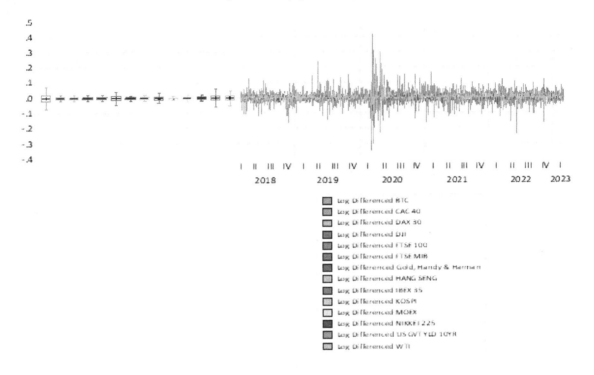

To effectively characterize the sample and provide a comprehensive description of the distribution of the data in the time series being analyzed, the statistical parameters utilized were as follows: The arithmetic average is a statistical measure that provides insight into the central tendency of a time series' deviation. The standard deviation is another statistical measure that quantifies the degree of data dispersion relative to the mean, thereby reflecting the inherent projection of future risks (volatility) associated with an investment. Additionally, the coefficients of asymmetry and kurtosis of the time series act as diagnostic instruments for assessing the normality of the data, which is an essential requirement for the application of econometric models in the financial domain (Guedes et al., 2022; Zebende et al., 2022).

Table 1 presents a summary of the descriptive statistics and the outcomes of the Jarque and Bera (1980) adherence test, which was conducted on differentfinancial markets, including Bitcoin (BTC), the capital markets of Franca (CAC 40), Germany (DAX 30), the US (DJI), the United Kingdom (FTSE 100), Italy (FTSE MIB), Hong Kong (HANG SENG), Spain (IBEX 35), South Korea (KOSPO), Russia (IMOEX), and Japan (NIKKEI 225), as well as gold (GOLD HANDY HARMAN), U.S. 10-year sovereign yields, and petroleum (WTI).

Upon analyzing Figure 3, it has been ascertained that the mean daily return of the financial markets under investigation is predominantly close to zero, although positive. However, it is noteworthy that the capital markets of Spain (IBEX 35 = -0.000449) and South Korea (KOSPI = 0.000636) are exceptions to this trend. Among the financial markets that were examined, it was observed that the petroleum market (WTI) exhibited the greatest mean daily return, with BTC and the German capital market following closely behind. (DAX 20).

Table 1. Descriptive statistics of the financial markets under study from February 28, 2018 to March 1, 2023

Market	Mean	Std. Dev.	Skewness	Kurtosis	Jarque-Bera	Obs.
BTC	0.000589	0.042637	-0.474997	7.958322	1383.756***	1303
GOLD	0.000260	0.009010	-0.364998	7.416242	1087.793***	1303
US GVT YD10YR	0.000363	0.038147	0.283247	28.35355	34916.23***	1303
WTI	0.000730	0.034243	0.626644	25.58629	27781.65***	1303
CAC 40	0.000216	0.012098	-1.245483	17.63275	11980.02***	1305
DAX 30	0.000392	0.009496	-0.706015	13.35624	5940.220***	1305
DJI	0.000234	0.013272	-0.811523	21.50085	18754.80***	1305
FTSE 100	0.000247	0.012868	-1.024620	16.85633	10668.22***	1305
FTSE MIB	4.43E-05	0.018274	-0.690860	6.711873	852.9888***	1305
HANG SENG	0.000145	0.012670	-1.135969	18.44792	13256.63***	1305
IBEX 35	-0.000449	0.015598	0.420970	8.096593	1450.949***	1305
KOSPI	-0.000636	0.006510	-0.774122	10.05792	2838.988***	1305
MOEX	7.88E-05	0.011091	-0.451367	6.327411	646.3336***	1305
NIKKEI 225	0.000347	0.011636	-1.780030	24.33614	25442.33***	1305

Source: Own Elaboration. Note: Data worked by the authors (software: Eviews12). *** represents the rejection of the null hypothesis at a significance level of 1%.

Figure 3. Means of the financial markets under study from February 28, 2018 to March 1, 2023
Source: Own Elaboration. Note: Data worked by the author (software: Eviews12).

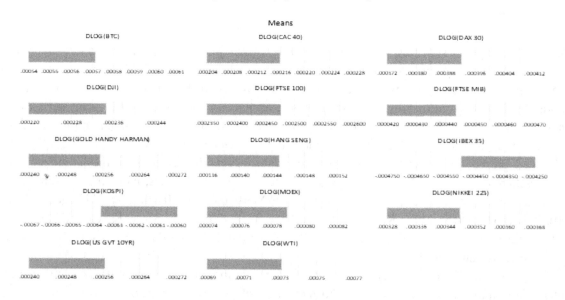

With respect to the standard deviation (market risk), it is evident from Figure 4 that BTC exhibits the highest level of standard deviation (0.042637) among the markets considered. This is followed by US 10-year yields (0.038147) and WTI (0.034243). The financial markets under scrutiny indicate that the

South Korean capital market (0.006510), the gold market (0,009010), and the German capital market (0.009496) exhibit the lowest levels of risk.

The normality of the time series was assessed by figuring the kurtosis coefficients and constructing q-q plots, as shown in Figures 5 and 6. The results indicate that all financial markets under consideration exhibit leptokurtic distributions, as evidenced by kurtosis values exceeding 3.

Figure 4. Standard Deviations of the financial markets under study from February 28, 2018 to March 1, 2023
Source: Own Elaboration. Note: Data worked by the author (software: Eviews12).

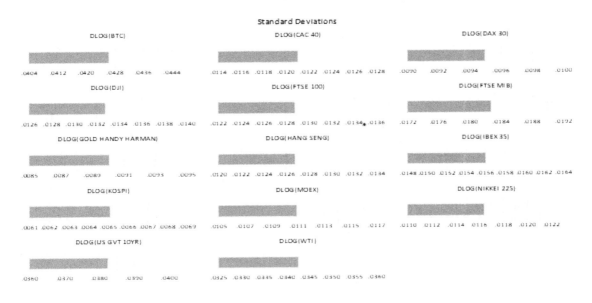

Figure 5. Kurtosis of the financial markets under study from February 28, 2018 to March 1, 2023
Source: Own Elaboration. Note: Data worked by the author (software: Eviews12).

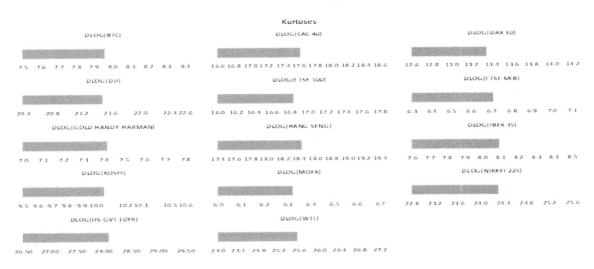

In addition, the distributions exhibit asymmetry or lack of symmetry, as the time series distribution deviates from the ideal normal distribution represented by the 45-degree line.

Figure 6. Q-Q plots, in returns, of the financial markets under study from February 28, 2018 to March 1, 2023
Source: Own Elaboration. Note: Data worked by the author (software: Eviews12).

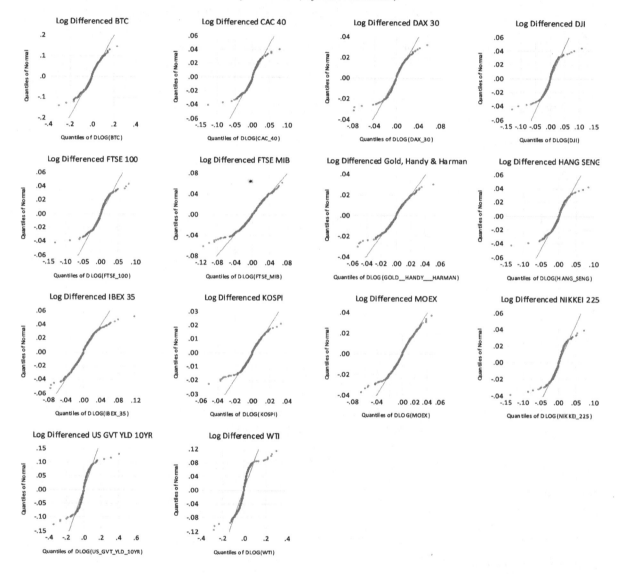

In the realm of econometric modeling, it is essential to assess the stationarity of time series data to prevent the occurrence of spurious results (Van Greunen et al., 2014; Herranz, 2017). A stationary stochastic process is characterized by variables that exhibit a consistent and constant mean and variance over time, both of which are finite in nature. In order to verify this hypothesis, two assessments known as unit root tests, which were formulated by Breitung (2000) and Hadri (2000), were employed.

The Breitung (2000) test posits a null hypothesis whereby all panels are characterized by a unit root (or non-constant variance). The proposed test by Hadri (2000) posits the null hypothesis that there are panels that exhibit trend stationarity, indicating the absence of a unit root in panel data that is common to all sections. Conversely, the alternative hypothesis suggests that at least one panel contains a unit root.

Table 2 presents the results of the Breitung (2000) test, indicating the rejection of the null hypothesis in first differences at a significance level of 1%.

Table 2. Breitung (2000) unit root test applied to the financial markets under study from February 28, 2018, to March 1, 2023

Null Hypothesis: Unit Root (Common Unit Root Process)				
Method			**Statistic**	**Prob.****
Breitung t-stat			-71.3355	0.0000
Intermediate regression results on D(UNTITLED)				
Series	S.E. of Regression	Lag	Max Lag	Obs
BTC	1596.18	0	22	1303
CAC 40	18.0011	0	22	1303
DAX 30	0.68425	2	22	1301
DJI	117.810	8	22	1295
FTSE 100	98.9822	0	22	1303
FTSE MIB	52.2664	0	22	1303
GOLD HANDY HARMAN	22.1678	0	22	1303
HANG SENG	83.6596	0	22	1303
IBEX 35	194.276	0	22	1303
KOSPI	16.8729	1	22	1302
MOEX	678.467	0	22	1303
NIKKEI 225	168.330	0	22	1303
US GVT YD 10YR	0.07568	0	22	1303
WTI	3.47850	1	22	1302
	Coefficient	t-Stat	SE Reg	Obs
Pooled	-0.51668	-71.336	0.007	18216

Source: Own Elaboration. Note: Data worked by the authors (software: Eviews12). ** Probability is assumed as asymptomatically normal.

The Hadri (2000) test was conducted, and the outcome is presented in Table 3. The test results indicate that the null hypothesis cannot be rejected at a significance level of 1%. This confirms that all-time series in the panel exhibit stationarity at first differences.

Table 3. Hadri (2000) unit root test applied to the financial markets under study from February 28, 2018 to March 1, 2023

Null Hypothesis: Stationarity		
Method	Statistic	Prob.**
Hadri Z-stat	-1.10999	0.8665
Heteroscedastic Consistent Z-stat	0.76825	0.2212

* Note: High autocorrelation leads to severe size distortion in Hadri test, leading to over-rejection of the null.

Intermediate results on D(UNTITLED)

Series	LM	Variance HAC	Bandwidth	Obs
BTC	0.1235	1466741.	11.0	1304
CAC 40	0.0525	179.7023	8.0	1304
DAX 30	0.8198	0.891815	18.0	1304
DJI	0.0449	12695.74	10.0	1304
FTSE 100	0.0712	5405.649	8.0	1304
FTSE MIB	0.0564	1786.546	12.0	1304
GOLD HANDY HARMAN	0.0988	189.7258	22.0	1304
HANG SENG	0.0575	3900.986	9.0	1304
IBEX 35	0.0452	16046.19	15.0	1304
KOSPI	0.3316	606.7164	19.0	1304
MOEX	0.1272	239567.4	5.0	1304
NIKKEI 225	0.1245	15976.92	5.0	1304
US GVT YD 10YR	0.7256	0.002708	5.0	1304
WTI	0.0831	3.249405	25.0	1304

Source: Own Elaboration. Note: Data worked by the authors (software: Eviews12). ** Probability is assumed as asymptomatically normal.

In order to assess financial integration, it is necessary to examine whether movements between market pairs tend towards equilibrium in the long-term, despite potential short-term distortions caused by shocks. To achieve this, co-integration tests with structural breaks will be used, employing the methodology of Gregory and Hansen (1996) and using panel tests such as ADF, , and . These tests are preferred due to their greater statistical power in detecting structural changes in the co-integration vector compared to other methods (Campos et al., 1996).

Table 4 displays the degree of market integration within the Tranquil subperiod, where 54 out of a possible 182 integrations were examined. The Moscow Exchange (MOEX), which represents the Russian capital market, has demonstrated complete integration with 13 of its peer markets. Bitcoin (BTC) follows closely with 12 integrations, apart from of the gold market (GOLD HANDY HARMAN), which it has not integrated with. The WTI demonstrated 5 integrations that were exclusively focused on capital markets. The US 10-year sovereign yields (US GVT YLD 10YR) exhibited a unique integration with the KOSPI. The gold market (GOLD HANDY HARMAN), does not exhibit any integration, thereby providing a safe haven for investors.

Table 4. Gregory and Hansen (1996) test applied to financial markets under study for the Tranquil subperiod

Series	Test	Test Statistic	Method	Lags	Breakpoint Date
BTC I CAC 40	Zt	-5,25**	Trend	2	15/05/2019
BTC I DAX 30	Zt	-5,1**	Trend	2	16/05/2019
BTC I DJI	Zt	-5,35**	Trend	1	15/05/2019
BTC I FTSE 100	Zt	-5,18**	Trend	2	15/05/2019
BTC I FTSE MIB	Zt	-4,92*	Trend	0	15/05/2019
BTC I HANG SENG	Zt	-5,09**	Trend	2	15/05/2019
BTC I IBEX 35	Zt	-4,95*	Trend	2	15/05/2019
BTC I KOSPI	Zt	-4,84*	Trend	2	15/05/2019
BTC I MOEX	Zt	-5,01**	Trend	0	15/05/2019
BTC I NIKKEI 225	Zt	-4,89*	Trend	2	15/05/2019
BTC I US GVT YD 10YR	Zt	-4,76*	Trend	2	15/05/2019
BTC I WTI	Zt	-5,43**	Trend	0	15/05/2019
DJI I CAC 40	Zt	-5,92***	Trend	1	10/08/2018
DJI I FTSE 100	Zt	-5,8***	Trend	1	07/08/2018
DJI I FTSE MIB	Zt	-4,88*	Trend	3	12/10/2018
DJI I HANG SENG	Zt	-5,68***	Trend	1	07/08/2018
DJI I IBEX 35	Zt	-5,18**	Trend	0	27/11/2018
DJI I KOSPI	Zt	-5,08**	Trend	3	28/11/2018
DJI I NIKKEI 225	Zt	-4,93*	Trend	3	26/11/2018
DJI I US GVT YD 10YR	Zt	-5,03**	Trend	3	15/10/2018
DJI I WTI	Zt	-5,12**	Trend	0	10/12/2018
DJI I GOLD HANDY HARMAN	Zt	-4,85*	Trend	3	15/10/2018
CAC 40 I DJI	Zt	-5,88***	Trend	1	20/08/2018
CAC 40 I FTSE MIB	Zt	-4,99*	Trend	1	08/10/2018
CAC 40 I IBEX 35	Zt	-5,16**	Trend	0	15/10/2018
FTSE 100 I DJI	Zt	-5,66***	Trend	1	07/08/2018
FTSE 100 I FTSE MIB	Zt	-4,95*	Trend	1	08/10/2018
FTSE 100 I IBEX 35	Zt	-5,21**	Trend	0	24/10/2018
FTSE 100 I WTI	Zt	-5,31**	Trend	1	26/06/2018
FTSE MIB I KOSPI	Zt	-5,07**	Trend	0	24/09/2018
HANG SENG I DJI	Zt	-5,7***	Trend	1	07/08/2018
HANG SENG I FTSE MIB	Zt	-4,86*	Trend	0	03/10/2018
HANG SENG I IBEX 35	Zt	-5,22**	Trend	1	15/10/2018
HANG SENG I KOSPI	Zt	-4,79*	Trend	1	15/10/2018
HANG SENG I WTI	Zt	-5,16**	Trend	1	24/08/2018
MOEX I BTC	Zt	-5,79***	Trend	4	31/10/2018
MOEX I DAX 30	Zt	-5,24**	Trend	1	01/11/2018

continues on following page

Table 4. Continued

Series	Test	Test Statistic	Method	Lags	Breakpoint Date
MOEX I DJI	Zt	-4,77*	Trend	1	01/11/2018
MOEX I CAC 40	Zt	-4,78*	Trend	1	01/11/2018
MOEX I FTSE 100	Zt	-4,82*	Trend	1	01/11/2018
MOEX I FTSE MIB	Zt	-5,47***	Trend	1	01/11/2018
MOEX I HANG SENG	Zt	-4,86*	Trend	1	29/06/2018
MOEX I IBEX 35	Zt	-5,26**	Trend	1	01/11/2018
MOEX I KOSPI	Zt	-5,27**	Trend	1	01/11/2018
MOEX I NIKKEI 225	Zt	-5,63***	Trend	1	01/11/2018
MOEX I US GVT YD 10YR	Zt	-5,77***	Trend	4	01/11/2018
MOEX I WTI	Zt	-4,88*	Trend	1	01/11/2018
MOEX I GOLD HANDY HARMAN	Zt	-6,01***	Trend	4	31/10/2018
US GVT YD 10YR I KOSPI	ADF	-5,34**	Regime	5	10/01/2019
WTI I DJI	Zt	-4,73*	Trend	0	08/11/2018
WTI I CAC 40	Zt	-5,27**	Trend	5	27/08/2018
WTI I FTSE 100	Zt	-5,25**	Trend	0	26/06/2018
WTI I HANG SENG	Zt	-4,79*	Trend	0	26/06/2018
WTI I IBEX 35	ADF	-4,79*	Trend	0	08/11/2018

Note: Data worked by the author (software: Stata). The critical values are found in Gregory and Hansen (1996). The critical values for the ADF and Zt parameters are: −5,45 (1%); −4,99 (5%); −4,72 (10%). For the Za parameter, the critical values are: −57,28 (1%); −47,96 (5%); −43,22 (10%). The asterisks ***, **, * indicate statistical significance at 1%, 5% and 10%, respectively.

Table 5 presents the integration outcomes for the Stress subperiod, indicating a decrease in the level of integration from 54 to 46 integrations out of a total of 182 possible integrations. During this particular subperiod, it can be observed that the South Korean capital market has achieved full integration with its counterparts, with a total of 13 integrations. The petroleum market (WTI) exhibited 6 integrations, encompassing 5 capital markets and the 10-year U.S. sovereign yields (US GVT YLD 10YR). The 10-year U.S. sovereign yields (US GVT YLD 10YR) have been integrated to 2 distinct markets, namely the petroleum market (WTI) and the German capital market (DAX 30). Furthermore, it can be observed that there appears to be a weak integration between gold and BTC during the occurrences of 2020 and 2022. The observation suggests that these two assets have the potential to serve as a viable safe haven for the purpose of diversifying one's investment portfolio. Gold is commonly regarded as a safe haven asset due to its tendency to retain its value during times of economic instability and fluctuations in the market. Likewise, Bitcoin (BTC) is commonly perceived as a safeguard against traditional financial markets, given its operation beyond the purview of traditional banking systems, thereby reducing its susceptibility to certain risks inherent in conventional financial banking systems. The apparent lack of correlation between gold and BTC amidst market instability and unpredictability implies their potential utility in portfolio diversification and risk mitigation.

Table 5. Gregory and Hansen (1996) test applied to financial markets under study for the Stress subperiod

Series	Test	Test Statistic	Method	Lags	Breakpoint Date
DJI I CAC 40	Za	-52,35**	Regime	2	10/08/2020
DJI I FTSE 100	Za	-53,25**	Trend	1	10/08/2020
DJI I HANG SENG	Za	-44,06*	Trend	2	10/08/2020
DJI I MOEX	Za	-51,17**	Trend	2	21/07/2020
CAC 40 I DJI	Za	-56,04**	Trend	2	31/07/2020
CAC 40 I FTSE MIB	Zt	-5,59***	Trend	3	24/02/2022
CAC 40 I KOSPI	Zt	-4,87*	Trend	4	24/02/2022
CAC 40 I MOEX	ADF	-5,72***	Trend	5	15/02/2022
FTSE 100 I FTSE MIB	Zt	-5,47***	Trend	3	24/02/2022
FTSE 100 I KOSPI	Zt	-5,04**	Trend	5	24/02/2022
FTSE 100 I MOEX	ADF	-5,34**	Trend	5	01/02/2022
FTSE MIB I CAC 40	Zt	-5,14**	Trend	1	24/02/2022
FTSE MIB I FTSE 100	Zt	-4,84*	Trend	3	24/02/2022
FTSE MIB I HANG SENG	Zt	-4,81*	Trend	3	24/02/2022
FTSE MIB I MOEX	ADF	-4,85*	Trend	0	14/03/2022
FTSE MIB I WTI	Za	-43,98*	Trend	2	25/07/2022
HANG SENG I CAC 40	Zt	-5,14**	Regime	2	08/03/2022
HANG SENG I FTSE MIB	Zt	-5,49***	Trend	3	24/02/2022
HANG SENG I KOSPI	Zt	-4,78*	Trend	5	24/02/2022
HANG SENG I MOEX	Zt	-5,2**	Trend	5	16/02/2022
HANG SENG I WTI	ADF	-5,66***	Regime	0	09/03/2022
IBEX 35 I BTC	Zt	-5,23**	Regime	0	28/07/2021
KOSPI I BTC	Zt	-5,03**	Regime	2	24/06/2020
KOSPI I DAX 30	Zt	-5,14**	Regime	2	02/12/2020
KOSPI I DJI	Zt	-5,3**	Regime	2	16/07/2020
KOSPI I CAC 40	Zt	-5,39**	Regime	2	24/06/2020
KOSPI I FTSE 100	Zt	-5,39**	Regime	2	24/06/2020
KOSPI I FTSE MIB	Zt	-4,88*	Regime	2	25/06/2020
KOSPI I HANG SENG	Zt	-5,36**	Regime	2	24/06/2020
KOSPI I IBEX 35	Zt	-5,11**	Regime	2	07/07/2020
KOSPI I MOEX	Zt	-5,48***	Regime	2	18/11/2020
KOSPI I NIKKEI 225	Zt	-5,36**	Regime	2	03/07/2020
KOSPI I US GVT YD 10YR	Zt	-5,77***	Regime	5	16/10/2020
KOSPI I WTI	Zt	-5,36**	Regime	2	23/06/2020
KOSPI I GOLD HANDY HARMAN	ADF	-5,02**	Regime	3	23/05/2022
MOEX I DJI	Za	-44,96*	Trend	1	20/07/2020
MOEX I HANG SENG	ADF	-4,76*	Trend	0	23/02/2022
MOEX I KOSPI	Zt	-4,73*	Trend	1	23/06/2022

continues on following page

Table 5. Continued

Series	Test	Test Statistic	Method	Lags	Breakpoint Date
US GVT YD 10YR I DAX 30	Zt	-4,88*	Regime	1	29/03/2022
US GVT YD 10YR I WTI	ADF	-5,03**	Trend	1	25/07/2022
WTI I DJI	Za	-43,77*	Trend	2	28/01/2022
WTI I FTSE 100	ADF	-5,03**	Regime	1	09/03/2022
WTI I HANG SENG	Za	-50,58**	Regime	1	08/03/2022
WTI I KOSPI	Za	-45,74*	Trend	1	25/07/2022
WTI I NIKKEI 225	Zt	-5,62***	Regime	2	29/12/2021
WTI I US GVT YD 10YR	Za	-49,08**	Regime	1	08/03/2022

Note: Data worked by the author (software: Stata). The critical values are found in Gregory and Hansen (1996). The critical values for the ADF and Zt parameters are: −5,45 (1%); −4,99 (5%); −4,72 (10%). For the Za parameter, the critical values are: −57,28 (1%); −47,96 (5%); −43,22 (10%). The asterisks ***, **, * indicate statistical significance at 1%, 5% and 10%, respectively.

According to the information provided in Table 6, the results of the integration test proposedby Gregory and Hansen (1996) indicate that BTC did not exhibit integration with the analyzed markets during the Stress period. This finding corroborates the research question that Bitcoin exhibits characteristics of a hedge and a safe haven asset. Drawing from the integration results, it can be inferred that investors who operate in these markets may reap advantages by integrating the digital currency BTC into their investment strategies as a means of hedging and as a safe haven asset. Hence, it is advisable for investors to consider incorporating BTC into their portfolio as a risk management strategy to safeguard against market deceleration. It is crucial to acknowledge that the suggestion is predicated exclusively on the information provided and must be evaluated within the context of the distinct circumstances and risk tolerance of the individual investor.

The Granger causality test was employed to ascertain the statistical significance of the predictive ability of one market's values with respect to another (Granger, 1969; Sims, 1980). In order to examine the causal relationship between the financial markets being studied, a VAR Granger Causality model or Block Exogeneity Wald Test will be used. This statistical approach employs Wald statistics to evaluate whether the independent (or exogenous) variables possess informative value in elucidating the behavior of the dependent variable. Prior to estimating the VAR, it is crucial to perform a model adjustment. Lütkepohl (1993) has noted that the VAR model's sensitivity is influenced by the number of lags. It has been emphasized that a longer lag in order-offs may result in an increase in predicting errors. Conversely, an insufficient adjustment may lead to the emergence of autocorrelated error terms, which may ultimately render the model estimators inefficient. The author elucidates a solution to the aforementioned issue by emphasizing the classical information criteria that can be employed to determine the number of lags to be incorporated in the model. These criteria include Akaike (AIC), Schwarz (SIC), and Hannan-Quinn (HQ), as well as the FPE (Final Prediction Error) and LR (Likelihood Ratio) tests. It is crucial to conduct autocorrelation testing with regards to regression model errors, as their interdependence can lead to the estimation of an unfeasible model. The importance of diagnosing correlation among error (or residues) terms has been widely acknowledged for many years as a critical factor in ensuring the robustness and suitability of the regression model.

Table 6. Summary of the Gregory and Hansen results

Series	Tranquil Subperiod	Stress Subperiod	Evolution
BTC	12 integrations	0 integrations	-
CAC 40	3 integrations	4 integrations	
DAX 30	Segmentation	0 integrations	=
DJI	10 integrations	4 integrations	-
FTSE 100	4 integrations	3 integrations	-
FTSE MIB	1 integration	5 integrations	
GOLD HANDY HARMAN	0 integrations	0 integrations	=
HANG SENG	5 integrations	5 integrations	=
IBEX 35	0 integrations	1 integration	
KOSPI	0 integrations	13 integrations	
MOEX	13 integrations	3 integrations	-
NIKKEI 225	0 integrations	0 integrations	=
US GVT YLD 10YR	1 integration	2 integrations	
WTI	5 integrations	6 integrations	
Total	54 integrations	46 integrations	-

Source: Own Elaboration.

According to the LR criterion, a model with 9 lags is recommended for the Tranquil and Stress subperiod, as shown in Tables 7 and 8. Through the application of the Lagrange Multiplier (LM) test and the consideration of the number of lags used to estimate the two models for each subperiod, the potential for autocorrelation of serial residues is eliminated by the rejection of the null hypothesis at a 1% level of significance (see Tables 9 and 10).

Table 7. VAR lag order selection criteria for the subperiod tranquil

Lag	LogL	LR	FPE	AIC	SC	HQ
0	56198.65	NA	5.11e-56	-87.58324	-87.52697*	-87.56211
1	56609.80	812.6923	3.65e-56	-87.91863	-87.07454	-87.60172*
2	56902.26	571.7070	3.14e-56	-88.06900	-86.43710	-87.45631
3	57099.59	381.4308	3.14e-56	-88.07107	-85.65136	-87.16260
4	57350.66	479.8181	2.88e-56*	-88.15691*	-84.94939	-86.95265
5	57542.58	362.5970	2.90e-56	-88.15055	-84.15521	-86.65051
6	57734.09	357.6512	2.93e-56	-88.14355	-83.36041	-86.34773
7	57889.85	287.4876	3.12e-56	-88.08083	-82.50987	-85.98922
8	58067.85	324.6489	3.22e-56	-88.05277	-81.69400	-85.66538
9	58242.79	315.2422*	3.33e-56	-88.01994	-80.87336	-85.33677
10	58367.34	221.7124	3.74e-56	-87.90855	-79.97415	-84.92960

Source: Own Elaboration. *Note: Data worked by the authors (software: Eviews12).* * Indicates lag order selected by the criterion. LR: sequential modified. LR test statistic (each test at 5% level). LR: sequential modified LR test statistic (each test at 5% level). FPE: Final prediction error. AIC: Akaike information criterion. SC: Schwarz information criterion. HQ: Hannan-Quinn information criterion.

Table 8. VAR lag order selection criteria for the subperiod stress

Lag	LogL	LR	FPE	AIC	SC	HQ
0	34256.59	NA	5.65e-55	-85.18058	-85.09892*	-85.14922*
1	34619.83	712.9190	3.73e-55	-85.59659	-84.37170	-85.12615
2	34898.91	538.0266	3.03e-55	-85.80326	-83.43513	-84.89374
3	35086.68	355.4561	3.10e-55	-85.78279	-82.27142	-84.43420
4	35304.73	405.1856	2.94e-55*	-85.83764*	-81.18304	-84.04998
5	35491.69	340.9022	3.01e-55	-85.81516	-80.01732	-83.58842
6	35673.84	325.7707	3.13e-55	-85.78068	-78.83961	-83.11487
7	35822.29	260.3417	3.55e-55	-85.66240	-77.57809	-82.55751
8	35994.51	296.0367	3.80e-55	-85.60326	-76.37571	-82.05929
9	36165.94	288.6980*	4.08e-55	-85.54213	-75.17135	-81.55909
10	36288.54	202.2071	4.97e-55	-85.35956	-73.84554	-80.93744

Source: Own Elaboration. *Note: Data worked by the authors (software: Eviews12).* * Indicates lag order selected by the criterion. LR: sequential modified. LR test statistic (each test at 5% level). LR: sequential modified LR test statistic (each test at 5% level). FPE: Final prediction error. AIC: Akaike information criterion. SC: Schwarz information criterion. HQ: Hannan-Quinn information criterion.

Table 9. VAR residual serial correlation LM tests for the tranquil subperiod

Null Hypothesis: No Serial Correlation At Lag H						
Lag	LRE* stat	df	Prob.	Rao F-stat	df	Prob.
1	241.5412	196	0.0148	1.234905	(196, 11295.4)	0.0148
2	218.1194	196	0.1333	1.114009	(196, 11295.4)	0.1333
3	277.0972	196	0.0001	1.418910	(196, 11295.4)	0.0001
4	248.6964	196	0.0064	1.271888	(196, 11295.4)	0.0064
5	245.3361	196	0.0096	1.254517	(196, 11295.4)	0.0096
6	257.9586	196	0.0020	1.319795	(196, 11295.4)	0.0020
7	263.9057	196	0.0009	1.350576	(196, 11295.4)	0.0009
8	270.1496	196	0.0004	1.382910	(196, 11295.4)	0.0004
9	246.1137	196	0.0088	1.258536	(196, 11295.4)	0.0088
10	207.4930	196	0.2732	1.059241	(196, 11295.4)	0.2733

Source: Own Elaboration. *Note: Data worked by the authors (software: Eviews12).*

Table 11 displays the shocks among different financial assets during the Tranquil subperiod, including Bitcoin (BTC), the capital markets of France (CAC 40), Germany (DAX 30), the U.S. (DJI), the UK (FTSE 100), Italy (FTSE MIB), Hong Kong (HANG SENG), Spain (IBEX 35), South Korea (KOSPI), Russia (IMOEX), and Japan (NIKKEI 225), as well as gold (GOLD HANDY HARMAN), US 10-year sovereign yields, and petroleum (WTI). During this particular subperiod, characterized by relative market stability, a total of 134 market shocks have been observed out of a possible 182 inter-market shock occurrences. The Japanese stock index and the WTI are found to have the highest impact on their peers, with a total of 13 out of 13 possible shocks. In contrast, the DJI and MOEX indexes exhibit a relatively lower level of impact, with 12 and 11 shocks, respectively. The CAC 40, FTSE, HANG SENG, KOSPI, and US GVT capital markets have been observed to induce shocks in 10 markets. The FTSE MIB, DAX 30, GOLD stock indexes, and BTC exhibit 8 and 7 co-movements, respectively, while the Spanish stock index induces 6 shocks in the analyzed markets. Furthermore, it has been confirmed that the fluctuations in BTC are solely attributed to the NIKKEI 225 stock index and WTI, indicating its potential as a safe haven in comparison to other markets.

Table 10. VAR residual serial correlation LM tests for the stress subperiod

Null Hypothesis: No Serial Correlation at Lag H						
Lag	LRE* stat	df	Prob.	Rao F-stat	df	Prob.
1	213.2898	196	0.1888	1.089729	(196, 6523.2)	0.1890
2	205.6137	196	0.3045	1.049898	(196, 6523.2)	0.3048
3	239.6810	196	0.0181	1.227022	(196, 6523.2)	0.0182
4	244.7802	196	0.0102	1.253613	(196, 6523.2)	0.0103
5	217.8495	196	0.1360	1.113411	(196, 6523.2)	0.1362
6	270.0404	196	0.0004	1.385638	(196, 6523.2)	0.0004
7	241.3512	196	0.0151	1.235730	(196, 6523.2)	0.0151
8	225.0639	196	0.0757	1.150913	(196, 6523.2)	0.0758
9	233.4836	196	0.0346	1.194733	(196, 6523.2)	0.0346
10	196.8901	196	0.4687	1.004689	(196, 6523.2)	0.4690

Source: Own Elaboration. *Note: Data worked by the authors (software: Eviews12)*

Table 12 presents the results of the Granger causality/Block Exogeneity Wald Tests for the Stress period encompassing the occurrences of 2020 and 2022. The findings indicate the existence of 135 co-movements between the analyzed markets. The NIKKEI 225 stock index has been observed to exhibit the highest frequency of market shocks among its peers, with a total of 13 out of 13 possible occurrences. In contrast, the WTI and Dow Jones indexes have experienced 12 co-movements, while the stock markets of Hong Kong, the UK, and France have caused 11 shocks on the remaining markets. The 10-year U.S. sovereign yields (US GVT YLD 10YR), as well as the IMOEX and KOSPI capital markets, exhibit 10 co-movements. In contrast, the FTSE MIB and DAX 30 show 8 shocks, while Gold and the IBEX capital market show 6 and 5 co-movements, respectively. Furthermore, our analysis reveals that BTC exhibits a significant correlation with the CAC 40, FTSE 100, HANG SENG, and NIKKEI 225 stock indexes, thereby posing challenges for achieving portfolio diversification. Consequently, it may be necessary for investors to contemplate alternative assets and investment opportunities to achieve adequate portfolio diversification.

Table 11. Granger causality/block exogeneity Wald tests, of the financial markets under analysis, in the tranquil subperiod

Series	BTC	CAC 40	DAX 30	DJI	FTSE 100	FTSE MIB	GOLD	HANG SENG	IBEX 35	KOSPI	MOEX	NIKKEI 225	US GVT YLD 10YR	WTI
BTC		1,33515	0,83447	1,35439	1,4927	0,63338	1,23434	1,62701	1,2512	0,82505	1,38157	2,45559***	0,78058	2,06981**
CAC 40	1,41506		0,91245	12,4244***	0,69817	2,34898**	1,98409***	0,87664	2,50239***	2,48196***	4,14462***	4,26002***	3,43367***	3,21714***
DAX 30	1,13208	3,48696***		6,54218***	4,09290***	1,73683*	1,24297	3,77934***	0,74993	0,57687	2,59327***	2,62176***	3,84497***	2,85001***
DJI	2,42692***	8,54677***	3,13547***		7,68464***	0,87709	3,00223***	8,29137***	0,83977	2,79791***	0,57218	3,47553***	4,93142***	2,46796***
FTSE 100	1,39531	0,77633	0,98069	13,3216***		2,24375**	2,13475**	0,63374	2,31939**	2,59839***	4,20976***	3,72164***	3,67681***	3,12504***
FTSE MIB	2,14985**	4,43511***	0,88657	9,30698***	4,33996***		1,89477**	4,43299***	2,23024**	2,25779**	8,99225***	2,25087**	1,38815	6,35189***
GOLD	1,41665	2,77229***	2,71703***	3,42111***	2,70019***	1,04344		2,64809***	1,63876*	1,72031*	2,15517**	2,79579***	8,29193***	2,57665***
HANG SENG	1,06278	0,75806	0,79368	11,5517***	0,34722	1,93371**	2,13284**		2,18738**	2,42123**	4,06236***	3,75117***	3,78486***	2,71995***
IBEX 35	2,22824**	9,31159***	1,68233*	8,56504***	9,22746***	0,93881	0,78717	9,63103***		1,33501	4,06900***	1,65067*	1,70350*	3,58109***
KOSPI	1,61255	5,92674***	2,89025***	7,03583***	5,99602***	5,89217***	1,10754	5,61068***	1,50187		3,37114***	5,18056***	1,74583*	4,77174***
MOEX	2,38387***	4,68390***	1,51432	3,84690***	4,91374***	1,16123	1,47181	5,13520***	1,35843	2,85393***		2,67556***	1,18485	2,11758**
NIKKEI 225	3,53085***	10,9688***	2,31387**	21,8681***	10,8094***	2,74244***	1,32702	11,0512***	1,98559**	3,56026***	8,51149***		6,75746***	10,2525***
US GVT YLD 10YR	2,27043***	4,58567***	4,35097***	5,92779***	4,07888***	2,40306**	3,01867***	4,36683***	1,09933	4,50999***	2,94749***	4,87399***		1,77178*
WTI	2,64193***	10,9832***	2,80970***	12,9743***	10,6839***	2,89196***	5,78262***	10,2577***	1,03925	3,04972***	4,90848***	7,87926***	4,79503***	

Source: Own Elaboration. Note: *Data worked by the author (software: Eviews 12)*. Markets in column "cause" markets in row. The asterisks ***, **, * indicate statistical significance at 1%, 5% and 10%, respectively.

Table 12. Granger causality/block exogeneity wald tests, of the financial markets under analysis, in the stress subperiod

Series	BTC	CAC 40	DAX 30	DJI	FTSE 100	FTSE MIB	GOLD H&H	HANG SENG	IBEX 35	KOSPI	MOEX	NIKKEI 225	US GVT YLD 10YR	WTI
BTC		1,68862*	0,47972	1,56689	1,84250*	0,58368	1,09469	1,88962*	1,3123	0,71458	1,12879	1,94387**	0,87806	1,4294
CAC 40	1,27112		0,99652	9,59632***	0,60413	2,19561**	1,64766*	0,83139	2,27869**	2,49548***	3,55611***	4,82906****	3,44371***	3,56251***
DAX 30	1,01642	2,82043***		6,11912***	3,45145***	2,01795**	1,34537	3,25277***	0,62361	0,84188	2,35664**	1,86721*	3,47702***	2,53904***
DJI	3,07020***	7,71381***	3,59110***		6,91985***	0,67881	2,31586**	7,36278***	0,83447	3,12725***	0,43312	3,53520***	3,85465***	2,31257**
FTSE 100	1,20161	0,69929	1,09387	10,7551***		2,14378**	1,66057*	0,89373	2,19780**	2,66686***	3,78099***	4,17168***	3,68934***	3,36617***
FTSE MIB	2,10441**	4,42952***	1,65846*	7,60934***	4,27844***		1,'72793*	4,04312***	1,81713*	2,56536***	7,12903***	2,04936**	1,34568	6,36283***
GOLD H&H	1,00795	2,55170***	2,49788***	3,20107***	2,31982**	0,79011		2,34030**	1,62916	2,17589**	1,53902	3,05551***	5,65956***	1,88504*
HANG SENG	0,84098	0,67408	0,8338	9,31054***	0,64377	1,91439**	1,61203		2,02080**	2,47695***	3,48786***	4,27694***	3,80988***	2,88277***
IBEX 35	3,39820***	6,13473***	2,02566**	5,45100***	6,00678***	0,91446	0,83398	6,36636***		0,82196	2,71197***	1,81885*	2,06698**	3,61662***
KOSPI	1,69148*	5,96670***	2,18350**	7,17692***	6,08155***	5,97939***	0,81851	5,65295***	0,83623		4,94125***	4,24991***	2,05402**	5,98942***
MOEX	2,59749***	4,63907***	0,91638	3,92705***	4,91641***	1,56028	1,0714	4,81606***	0,895	3,91850***		2,93645***	1,03629	1,73542*
NIKKEI 225	3,69467***	10,7351***	2,07275***	20,9586***	10,3445***	3,16610***	1,50564	10,4251***	2,02778**	3,82147***	8,17112***		5,85826***	10,7862***
US GVT YLD 10YR	1,96453*	4,28548***	4,17061***	4,90739***	3,84841***	1,73186*	2,43343***	3,99127***	1,29776	4,45897***	3,11634***	3,90189***		1,70931*
WTI	2,60909***	8,83412***	2,54368***	11,7226***	8,63316***	3,61772***	5,42751***	8,26730***	0,74861	3,60765***	4,71094***	6,75878***	3,89423***	

Source: Own Elaboration. Note: *Data worked by the author (software: Eviews 12).* Markets in column "cause" markets in row. The asterisks ***, **, * indicate statistical significance at 1%, 5% and 10%, respectively.

Table 13 presents a summary table of co-movements during the Tranquil and Stress subperiods. The objective of this analysis is to investigate whether the digital currency BTC is influenced by other markets during the events that occurred in 2020 and 2022. The findings indicate that the Tranquil period in BTC is caused by the stock market's NIKKEI 225 and the WTI index. Moreover, upon confirmation of the integration results that were validated in relation to co-movements, we find that BTC is caused by the stock markets CAC 40, FTSE 100, HANG SENG, and NIKKEI 225. The present study reveals that the coverage properties persisted throughout the Stress period, in which no market exhibited integrations with BTC. However, it was observed that the 4 stock markets under consideration caused shocks in the formation of BTC prices, thereby raising concerns regarding the concept of safe haven. Given the aforementioned results and the assessments of integration and co-movements, it can be posited that BTC exhibits a degree of immunity and may be regarded as a safe haven in relation to other markets. However, it should be noted that this assertion does not apply to the CAC 40, FTSE 100, HANG SENG, and NIKKEI 225 stock markets. In summary, it is noteworthy that the term "safe haven asset" may exhibit variability in its definition, however, it typically pertains to an investment vehicle that maintains or appreciates its worth during periods of financial instability or market unpredictability. Nevertheless, it remains a feasible alternative for investors who aim to achieve portfolio diversification and mitigate potential risks in other markets.

Table 13. Summary of the Granger causality results

Series	Market X "Cause in Grangerian Sense" Their Peers			Market X is "Caused in Grangerian Sense" by the Peers		
	Tranquil Subperiod	Stress Subperiod	Evolution	Tranquil Subperiod	Stress Subperiod	Evolution
BTC	7 shocks	8 shocks		2 shocks	4 shocks	
CAC 40	10 shocks	11 shocks		9 shocks	9 shocks	=
DAX 30	7 shocks	8 shocks		9 shocks	9 shocks	=
DJI	12 shocks	12 shocks	=	10 shocks	10 shocks	=
FTSE 100	10 shocks	11 shocks		9 shocks	9 shocks	=
FTSE MIB	8 shocks	8 shocks	=	11 shocks	12 shocks	
GOLD H&H	7 shocks	6 shocks	-	11 shocks	9 shocks	-
HANG SENG	10 shocks	11 shocks		9 shocks	8 shocks	-
IBEX 35	6 shocks	5 shocks	-	10 shocks	10 shocks	=
KOSPI	10 shocks	10 shocks	=	10 shocks	11 shocks	
MOEX	11 shocks	10 shocks	-	8 shocks	8 shocks	=
NIKKEI 225	13 shocks	13 shocks	=	12 shocks	12 shocks	=
US GVT YLD 10YR	10 shocks	10 shocks	=	12 shocks	12 shocks	=
WTI	13 shocks	12 shocks	-	12 shocks	12 shocks	=
Total	134 shocks	135 shocks		134 shocks	135 shocks	

Source: Own elaboration

CONCLUSION

This study aimed to investigate whether Bitcoin could act as a hedge and a safe haven in the capital markets in different countries, including France (CAC 40), Germany (DAX 30), USA (DJI), UK (FTSE 100), Italy (FTSE MIB), Hong Kong (HANG SENG), Spain (IBEX 35), South Korea (KOSPI), Russia (IMOEX), Japan (NIKKEI 225), as well as in the commodity markets of gold (GOLD HANDY HARMAN) and petroleum (WTI), and the U.S. 10-year sovereign yields during the period of events spanning from 2020 to 2022. In order to ascertain the viability of BTC as a safe haven, an examination of financial integration and fluctuations in these markets is conducted to understand the behavior of cryptocurrency during times of economic instability on a global scale.

During the Tranquil subperiod, the findings indicate that there were 54 cases of financial integration out of a total of 182 possible occurrences. The Moscow Exchange (MOEX) demonstrated complete integration with 13 peer markets, while Bitcoin (BTC) exhibited integration with 12 markets, with the exception of the gold market (GOLD HANDY HARMAN). The WTI exhibited 5 integrations that were exclusively focused on capital markets. The US 10-year sovereign yields (US GVT YLD 10YR) showed a single integration with the South Korean capital market (KOSPI). The gold market (GOLD HANDY HARMAN) lacks evidence of integration and therefore can be considered a reliable safe haven market. During the aforementioned subperiod, which encompasses the years 2020 and 2022, it has been observed that the degree of integration has declined from 54 to 46 out of a total of 182 potential integrations. During this particular subperiod, it can be observed that the South Korean capital market has achieved complete integration with its peers, as evidenced by a total of 13 integrations. The petroleum market (WTI) exhibited 6 integrations, which include 5 capital markets and the 10-year U.S. sovereign yields (US GVT YLD 10YR). The 10-year U.S. sovereign yields (US GVT YLD 10YR) have been integrated into two distinct markets, namely the petroleum market represented by WTI, and the German capital market represented by DAX 30. Furthermore, it can be observed that Bitcoin (BTC) was not integrated during the events that occurred in the years 2020 and 2022. This statement suggests that the digital currency may be perceived as a form of hedge and safe haven. To substantiate our research questioning, we additionally estimate the co-movements between the markets and analyze the first phase of apparent calmness in the financial markets. During this particular subperiod, we have confirmed the occurrence of 134 market shocks, out of a total of 182 possible. The Japanese stock index and the WTI have been observed to have the greatest influence on their peers, exhibiting shocks in all 13 possible instances. In contrast, the DJI and MOEX indexes have demonstrated co-movements in 12 and 11 instances, respectively. The CAC 40, FTSE, HANG SENG, KOSPI, and US GVT stock markets elicit shocks in 10 markets. The FTSE MIB, DAX 30, GOLD, and BTC stock indexes exhibit 8 and 7 co-movements, respectively. In contrast, the Spanish stock index induces 6 shocks across the analyzed markets. Upon examining the Stress subperiod, it was observed that there existed 135 instances of co-movements between the analyzed markets. The NIKKEI 225 stock index has been observed to cause the highest number of shocks among its peers, with an exact score of 13 out of 13. In comparison, the WTI and Dow Jones indexes have caused 12 co-movements, while the stock markets of Hong Kong, the UK, and France have caused 11 shocks among the remaining markets. The 10-year U.S. sovereign yields (US GVT YLD 10YR), as well as the IMOEX and KOSPI stock markets, exhibit 10 co-movements. In contrast, the FTSE MIB and DAX 30 demonstrate 8 shocks, while Gold and the IBEX display 6 and 5 co-movements, respectively. Furthermore, it has been observed that the behavior of BTC is impacted by the stock indexes of CAC 40, FTSE 100, HANG SENG, and NIKKEI 225. This poses a challenge in ascertaining the extent to which the digital currency possesses coverage and safe haven characteristics. Consequently, investors may need to contemplate alternative assets and investment opportunities to achieve adequate portfolio diversification.

The digital era has brought about a period characterized by unparalleled interconnectedness, where the norm is to have immediate access to news articles, financial analyses, and real-time market data. The emergence of social media platforms, forums dedicated to cryptocurrency, and specialized news websites has significantly altered the dynamics of information dissemination within the cryptocurrency ecosystem. The ability of market participants to react promptly and decisively to unfolding events and developments has been facilitated by the seamless transmission of news and data through online channels. So, the undeniable significance lies in the interplay between internet news and the behavioural dynamics exhibited by investors. The convergence of rapid information distribution, the ability of market sentiment to react quickly, and increased volatility creates a complex relationship that requires careful consideration from both market participants and regulators. The increasing impact of online news on cryptocurrency investment highlights the importance of establishing methods to improve investor education, enable well-informed decision-making, and maintain market stability in this swiftly changing financial paradigm.

Regarding recommendations for future research, a more comprehensive examination could be conducted to ascertain the fundamental factors that contribute to the changes between BTC and the aforementioned stock indexes. Subsequent investigations may delve into the correlation between BTC and other asset categories, including exchange rates, alternative digital currencies, and clean energy indexes. Such investigations could ultimately facilitate improved portfolio diversification. Through the identification of these factors, investors can potentially develop portfolios that are more efficient and diversified, leading to superior risk management and return optimization.

REFERENCES

Abdullah, A. M. (2023). *The Impact of COVID-19 and the Russia–Ukraine Conflict on the Relationship Between the US Islamic Stock Index, Bitcoin, and Commodities. Asian Economics Letters, 4.* doi:10.46557/001c.70293

Ali, M. H., Schinckus, C., Uddin, M. A., & Pahlevansharif, S. (2023). Asymmetric effects of economic policy uncertainty on Bitcoin's hedging power. *Studies in Economics and Finance, 40*(2), 213–229. Advance online publication. doi:10.1108/SEF-05-2021-0186

Balcilar, M., Bouri, E., Gupta, R., & Roubaud, D. (2016). Can Volume Predict Bitcoin Returns and Volatility? A Nonparametric Causality-in-Quantiles Approach. *Working Papers, 64*(March).

Batten, J. A., Ciner, C., Kosedag, A., & Lucey, B. M. (2017). Is the price of gold to gold mining stocks asymmetric? *Economic Modelling, 60*, 402–407. Advance online publication. doi:10.1016/j.econmod.2016.10.007

Baur, D. G., & Lucey, B. M. (2010). Is gold a hedge or a safe haven? An analysis of stocks, bonds and gold. *Financial Review, 45*(2), 217–229. Advance online publication. doi:10.1111/j.1540-6288.2010.00244.x

Bouri, E., Molnár, P., Azzi, G., Roubaud, D., & Hagfors, L. I. (2017). On the hedge and safe haven properties of Bitcoin: Is it really more than a diversifier? *Finance Research Letters*, *20*, 192–198. Advance online publication. doi:10.1016/j.frl.2016.09.025

Bouri, E., Shahzad, S. J. H., Roubaud, D., Kristoufek, L., & Lucey, B. (2020). Bitcoin, gold, and commodities as safe havens for stocks: New insight through wavelet analysis. *The Quarterly Review of Economics and Finance*, *77*, 156–164. Advance online publication. doi:10.1016/j.qref.2020.03.004

Brandvold, M., Molnár, P., Vagstad, K., & Andreas Valstad, O. C. (2015). Price discovery on Bitcoin exchanges. *Journal of International Financial Markets, Institutions and Money*, *36*, 18–35. Advance online publication. doi:10.1016/j.intfin.2015.02.010

Breitung, J. (2000). The local power of some unit root tests for panel data. *Advances in Econometrics*, *15*, 161–177. Advance online publication. doi:10.1016/S0731-9053(00)15006-6

Campos, J., Ericsson, N. R., & Hendry, D. F. (1996). Cointegration tests in the presence of structural breaks. In Journal of Econometrics (Vol. 70, Issue 1). doi:10.1016/0304-4076(94)01689-5

Cho, D., & Han, H. (2021). The tail behavior of safe haven currencies: A cross-quantilogram analysis. *Journal of International Financial Markets, Institutions and Money*, *70*, 101257. Advance online publication. doi:10.1016/j.intfin.2020.101257

Ciaian, P., Rajcaniova, M., & Kancs, A. (2016). The economics of BitCoin price formation. *Applied Economics*, *48*(19), 1799–1815. Advance online publication. doi:10.1080/00036846.2015.1109038

Ciner, C., Lucey, B., & Yarovaya, L. (2020). Spillovers, integration and causality in LME non-ferrous metal markets. *Journal of Commodity Markets*, *17*, 100079. Advance online publication. doi:10.1016/j.jcomm.2018.10.001

Corbet, S., Larkin, C., & Lucey, B. (2020). The contagion effects of the COVID-19 pandemic: Evidence from gold and cryptocurrencies. *Finance Research Letters*, *35*, 101554. Advance online publication. doi:10.1016/j.frl.2020.101554

Dias, R., Chambino, M., & Horta, N. H. (2023). *Long-Term Dependencies in Central European Stock Markets : A Crisp-Set*. *2*(February), 10–17. https://doi.org/ doi:10.58567/eal02010002

Dias, R., Horta, N., & Chambino, M. (2023). Journal of Economic Analysis. *Journal of Economic Analysis*, *9*(1), 129–151. doi:10.58567/jea02010005

Dias, R., Pardal, P., Teixeira, N., & Horta, N. (2022). Tail Risk and Return Predictability for Europe's Capital Markets. Advance online publication. doi:10.4018/978-1-6684-5666-8.ch015

Dias, R., Pardal, P., Teixeira, N., & Machová, V. (2020). Financial Market Integration of ASEAN-5 with China. *Littera Scripta*, *13*(1). Advance online publication. doi:10.36708/Littera_Scripta2020/1/4

Dwyer, G. P. (2015). The economics of Bitcoin and similar private digital currencies. *Journal of Financial Stability*, *17*, 81–91. Advance online publication. doi:10.1016/j.jfs.2014.11.006

Dyhrberg, A. H. (2016). Hedging capabilities of bitcoin. Is it the virtual gold? *Finance Research Letters*, *16*, 139–144. doi:10.1016/j.frl.2015.10.025

Engle, R. F., & Granger, C. W. J. (1987). Co-Integration and Error Correction: Representation, Estimation, and Testing. *Econometrica*, *55*(2), 251. doi:10.2307/1913236

Fatum, R., & Yamamoto, Y. (2016). Intra-safe haven currency behavior during the global financial crisis. *Journal of International Money and Finance*, *66*, 49–64. Advance online publication. doi:10.1016/j.jimonfin.2015.12.007

Gilmore, C. G., Lucey, B. M., & McManus, G. M. (2008). The dynamics of Central European equity market comovements. *The Quarterly Review of Economics and Finance*, *48*(3), 605–622. doi:10.1016/j.qref.2006.06.005

Granger, C. W. J. (1969). Investigating Causal Relations by Econometric Models and Cross-spectral Methods. *Econometrica*, *37*(3), 424. doi:10.2307/1912791

Granger, C. W. J. (1988). Some recent development in a concept of causality. *Journal of Econometrics*, *39*(1–2), 199–211. doi:10.1016/0304-4076(88)90045-0

Gregory, A. W., & Hansen, B. E. (1996a). Residual-based tests for cointegration in models with regime shifts. *Journal of Econometrics*, *70*(1), 99–126. doi:10.1016/0304-4076(69)41685-7

Gregory, A. W., & Hansen, B. E. (1996b). Tests for cointegration in models with regime and trend shifts. *Oxford Bulletin of Economics and Statistics*, *58*(2), 555–560. doi:10.1111/j.1468-0084.1996.mp58003008.x

Guedes, E. F., Santos, R. P. C., Figueredo, L. H. R., Da Silva, P. A., Dias, R. M. T. S., & Zebende, G. F. (2022). Efficiency and Long-Range Correlation in G-20 Stock Indexes: A Sliding Windows Approach. *Fluctuation and Noise Letters*, *21*(04), 2250033. Advance online publication. doi:10.1142/S021947752250033X

Gujarati, D. N. (2004). *Basic Econometrics*. https://doi.org/ doi:10.1126cience.1186874

Habib, M. M., & Stracca, L. (2012). Getting beyond carry trade: What makes a safe haven currency? *Journal of International Economics*, *87*(1), 50–64. Advance online publication. doi:10.1016/j.jinteco.2011.12.005

Hadri, K. (2000). Testing for stationarity in heterogeneous panel data. *The Econometrics Journal*, *3*(2), 148–161. Advance online publication. doi:10.1111/1368-423X.00043

Halaburda, H., & Gandal, N. (2014). Competition in the Cryptocurrency Market. SSRN *Electronic Journal*. https://doi.org/ doi:10.2139/ssrn.2506463

Hampl, F., Vágnerová Linnertová, D., & Horváth, M. (2022). *Crypto Havens During War Times? Evidence from the Russian Invasion of Ukraine*. Cryptocurrency Research Ejournal.

Herranz, E. (2017). Unit root tests. In *Wiley Interdisciplinary Reviews*. Computational Statistics. doi:10.1002/wics.1396

Jarque, C. M., & Bera, A. K. (1980). Efficient tests for normality, homoscedasticity and serial independence of regression residuals. *Economics Letters*, *6*(3), 255–259. doi:10.1016/0165-1765(80)90024-5

Lavelle, B., Yamamoto, K. N., & Kinnen, M. (2022). Cryptocurrencies, Correlations, and COVID-19: Diversifiers, Hedge, or Safe Haven? *Review of Integrative Business and Economics Research*, *11*(2).

Lütkepohl, H. (1993). Testing for Causation Between Two Variables in Higher-Dimensional VAR Models (Vol. 114, Issue 4, pp. 75–91). https://doi.org/ doi:10.1007/978-3-642-51514-9_4

Nakamoto, S. (2016). *Bitcoin: A Peer-to-Peer Electronic Cash System, Apr. 2018* [online]. Available: https://bitcoin.org/bitcoin.pdf

Pardal, P., Dias, R., Teixeira, N. & Horta, N. (2022). *The Effects of Russia's 2022 Invasion of Ukraine on Global Markets : An Analysis of Particular Capital and Foreign Exchange Markets.* https://doi.org/ doi:10.4018/978-1-6684-5666-8.ch014

Popper, N. (2015). Digital Gold: The untold story of Bitcoin. Penguin UK.

Ratner, M., & Chiu, C. C. (2013). Hedging stock sector risk with credit default swaps. *International Review of Financial Analysis, 30*, 18–25. Advance online publication. doi:10.1016/j.irfa.2013.05.001

Revez, C., Dias, R., Horta, N., Heliodoro, P., & Alexandre, P. (2022). Capital Market Efficiency in Asia: An Empirical Analysis. *6th EMAN Selected Papers (Part of EMAN Conference Collection)*, 49–57. https://doi.org/10.31410/eman.s.p.2022.49

Rogojanu, A., & Badea, L. (2014). The Issue of competing Currencies. Case Study – Bitcoin. *Theoretical and Applied Economics, 21*(1).

Santana, T., Horta, N., Revez, C., Santos Dias, R. M. T., & Zebende, G. F. (2023). *Effects of interdependence and contagion between Oil and metals by ρ DCCA : A case of study about the COVID-19.* Academic Press.

Sims, C. A. (1980). Macroeconomics and Reality. *Econometrica, 48*(1), 1. doi:10.2307/1912017

Teixeira, N., Dias, R., Pardal, P., & Horta, N. (2022). Financial Integration and Comovements Between Capital Markets and Oil Markets. *An Approach During the Russian.*, (December), 240–261. Advance online publication. doi:10.4018/978-1-6684-5666-8.ch013

Trichilli, Y., & Boujelbène Abbes, M. (2022). The impact of COVID-19 on the portfolio optimization. *EuroMed Journal of Business.* Advance online publication. doi:10.1108/EMJB-11-2021-0179

Tsay, R. S. (2002). *Analysis of Financial Time Series.* doi:10.1002/0471264105

Van Greunen, J., Heymans, A., Van Heerden, C., & Van Vuuren, G. (2014). The prominence of stationarity in time series forecasting. *Journal for Studies in Economics and Econometrics, 38*(1), 1–16. doi:1 0.1080/10800379.2014.12097260

Wang, Q., Wei, Y., Wang, Y., & Liu, Y. (2022). On the Safe-Haven Ability of Bitcoin, Gold, and Commodities for International Stock Markets: Evidence from Spillover Index Analysis. *Discrete Dynamics in Nature and Society, 2022*, 1–16. Advance online publication. doi:10.1155/2022/9520486

Yermack, D. (2015). Is Bitcoin a Real Currency? An Economic Appraisal. In *Handbook of Digital Currency.* Bitcoin, Innovation, Financial Instruments, and Big Data. doi:10.1016/B978-0-12-802117-0.00002-3

Zebende, G. F., Santos Dias, R. M. T., & de Aguiar, L. C. (2022). Stock market efficiency: An intraday case of study about the G-20 group. *Heliyon, 8*(1), e08808. doi:10.1016/j.heliyon.2022.e08808 PMID:35128100

KEY TERMS AND DEFINITIONS

Co-Movements: The principle of co-movements in financial markets pertains to the tendency of various assets to exhibit synchronized movements, either in the same direction (positive co-movements) or in opposite directions (negative co-movements). A variety of variables, including current economic conditions, market sentiment, and outside events, can affect the correlation between these movements.

Cryptocurrencies: Cryptocurrencies refer to digital or virtual currencies that employ cryptographic techniques to ensure security and function on a decentralized infrastructure known as blockchain. Cryptocurrencies facilitate secure peer-to-peer transactions and frequently function as a means of exchange, store of value, or digital asset.

Financial Integration: Financial integration covers the interdependence and alignment of financial systems, including markets, institutions, and regulations, with the aim of facilitating the flow of capital, investments, and financial services across national boundaries and inside domestic economies.

Hedging: Hedging refers to the act of assuming positions in assets or employing strategies with the purpose of mitigating prospective losses in alternative investments, hence reducing the systemic risk.

Portfolio Diversification: Portfolio diversification is a risk mitigation strategy that entails distributing investments over a range of assets or asset classes in order to mitigate the overall risk and volatility associated with a portfolio.

Safe Haven: Safe havens refer to assets that investors typically prefer during periods of market uncertainty or volatility in order to protect their capital. These assets are typically defined by low-risk profiles.

Volatility: The concept of volatility in the cryptocurrency market pertains to the tendency of digital currencies to undergo swift and substantial price swings over a short period of time. This phenomenon presents both some possible benefits and risks for individuals involved in investment activities.

Compilation of References

andMe organization. (2023). *Health + Ancestry Service.* https://www.23andme.com/dna-health-ancestry/

Abba, S., Wadumi Namkusong, J., Lee, J. A., & Liz Crespo, M. (2019). Design and performance evaluation of a low-cost autonomous sensor interface for a smart iot-based irrigation monitoring and control system. *Sensors (Basel)*, *19*(17), 1–25. doi:10.339019173643 PMID:31438597

Abdullah, A. M. (2023). *The Impact of COVID-19 and the Russia–Ukraine Conflict on the Relationship Between the US Islamic Stock Index, Bitcoin, and Commodities. Asian Economics Letters, 4.* doi:10.46557/001c.70293

Abdullah, A., Al Enazi, S., & Damaj, I. (2016). AgriSys: A smart and ubiquitous controlled-environment agriculture system. *3rd MEC International Conference on Big Data and Smart City (ICBDSC)*, 1-6. 10.1109/ICBDSC.2016.7460386

Abellera, R., & Bulusu, L. (2018). *Oracle business intelligence with machine learning.* Artificial Intelligence Techniques in OBIEE for Actionable BI. doi:10.1007/978-1-4842-3255-2

Achleitner, A.-K., Engel, N., & Reiner, U. (2012). The Performance of Venture Capital Investments: Do Investors Over-react? SSRN *Electronic Journal.* doi:10.2139/ssrn.2033762

ACM/ICPC. (n.d.). *The ICPC International Collegiate Programming Contest.* Retrieved 5 29, 2023, from https://icpc.global/

Afor, M. E., & Sahana, S. (2022, November). The internet of behaviour (IoB) and its significant impact on digital marketing. In *2022 International Conference on Computing, Communication, and Intelligent Systems (ICCCIS)* (pp. 7-12). IEEE. 10.1109/ICCCIS56430.2022.10037598

Aggar, C., Grace, S., Smith, S. (2020). Exploring healthcare professionals' understanding and experiences of artificial intelligence technology use in the delivery of healthcare: An integrative review. *Health Informatics Journal*, *26*(2), 1225-1236. doi:10.1177/1460458219874641

Agrawal, R., Wankhede, V. A., Kumar, A., Upadhyay, A., & Garza-Reyes, J. A. (2022). Nexus of circular economy and sustainable business performance in the era of digitalization. *International Journal of Productivity and Performance Management*, *71*(3), 748–774. doi:10.1108/IJPPM-12-2020-0676

Ahtiainen, A., Surakka, S., & Rahikainen, M. (2006). Plaggie: GNU-licensed Source Code Plagiarism Detection Engine for Java Exercises. *In ACM Proceedings of the 6th Baltic Sea Conference on Computing Education Research: Koli Calling*, 141-142.

Akgün, Ö., & Arslan, N. (2022). Marketing Mentality of the Modern Age. *Digital Marketing. Conference: The 5th International Academic Conference on Management and Economics.* https://www.doi.org/10.33422/5th.conferenceme.2022.07.25

Akhgar, B., Saathoff, G. B., Arabnia, H. R., Hill, R., Staniforth, A., & Bayerl, P. S. (2015). *Application of big data for national security: a practitioner's guide to emerging technologies.* Butterworth-Heinemann.

Aksoy, C. G., Barrero, J. M., Bloom, N., Davis, S. J., Dolls, M., & Zarate, P. (2022, September). *Working from home around the world.* Working Paper 2022-124. Chicago, IL: Becker Friedman Institute at the University of Chicago.

Akturk, C., Talan, T., & Cerasi, C. C. (2022, September 26-28). *Education 4.0 and University 4.0 from Society 5.0 Perspective* [Paper presentation]. *12th International Conference on Advanced Computer Information Technologies (ACIT),* Ružomberok, Slovakia. 10.1109/ACIT54803.2022.9913099

Al-Aqrabi, H., Liu, L., Hill, R., & Antonopoulos, N. (2015). Cloud BI: Future of business intelligence in the Cloud. *Journal of Computer and System Sciences, 81*(1), 85–96. doi:10.1016/j.jcss.2014.06.013

Albino, V., Berardi, U., & Dangelico, R. M. (2020). Smart cities: Definitions, dimensions, performance, and initiatives. *Journal of Urban Technology, 27*(1), 3–43. doi:10.1080/10630732.2014.942092

Albluwi, I. (2019). Plagiarism in Programming Assessments: A Systematic Review. *ACM Transactions on Computing Education, 20*(1), 1–28. doi:10.1145/3371156

Albuquerque, D. (2022, Oct. 23). A dura realidade de pessoas com deficiência em busca de emprego: de acordo com dados do IBGE, a cada dez pessoas nessas condições que buscavam emprego, sete estavam fora do mercado de trabalho. *Correio Braziliense.*

Alcabnani, S., Oubezza, M., & Elkafi, J. (2019). An approach for the implementation of semantic Big Data Analytics in the Social Business Intelligence process on distributed environments (Cloud computing*). Proceedings of the 4th International Conference on Big Data and Internet of Things,* 1-6. 10.1145/3372938.3373003

Aldianto, L., Anggadwita, G., Permatasari, A., Mirzanti, I., & Williamson, I. (2021). Toward a Business Resilience Framework for Startups. *Sustainability (Basel), 13*(6), 3132. Advance online publication. doi:10.3390u13063132

Al-Fuqaha, A., Guizani, M., Mohammadi, M., Aledhari, M., & Ayyash, M. (2015). Internet of things: A survey on enabling technologies, protocols, and applications. *IEEE Communications Surveys and Tutorials, 17*(4), 2347–2376. doi:10.1109/COMST.2015.2444095

Ali, M. H., Schinckus, C., Uddin, M. A., & Pahlevansharif, S. (2023). Asymmetric effects of economic policy uncertainty on Bitcoin's hedging power. *Studies in Economics and Finance, 40*(2), 213–229. Advance online publication. doi:10.1108/SEF-05-2021-0186

Alliance, L. (n.d.). *LoRaWAN.* Retrieved 7 14, 2021, from https://lora-alliance.org/

Allied. (n.d.). *The History of Telecommuting.* Allied. https://www.alliedtelecom.net/the-history-of-telecommuting/

Almudhaf, F. (2017). Speculative bubbles and irrational exuberance in African stock markets. *Journal of Behavioral and Experimental Finance, 13,* 28–32. Advance online publication. doi:10.1016/j.jbef.2016.11.002

Al-shammari, M. M., & Alsaqre, F. E. (2012). IT Disaster Recovery and Business Continuity for Kuwait Oil Company (KOC). *Int. Conf. Inf. Technol. Syst. Manag. (ICITSM 2012),* 25–31.

Alshater, M. (2023). Exploring the Role of Artificial Intelligence in Enhancing Academic Performance: A Case Study of ChatGPT. SSRN *Electronic Journal.* doi:10.2139/ssrn.4312358

Al-Turjman, F., & Abujubbeh, M. (2019). IoT-enabled smart grid via SM: An overview. *Future Generation Computer Systems, 96,* 579–590. doi:10.1016/j.future.2019.02.012

Amini, S., Gebka, B., Hudson, R., & Keasey, K. (2013). A review of the international literature on the short term predictability of stock prices conditional on large prior price changes: Microstructure, behavioral and risk related explanations. In International Review of Financial Analysis (Vol. 26). doi:10.1016/j.irfa.2012.04.002

Amorim, D. (2020). *8,073 milhões de pessoas estavam em trabalho remoto em setembro, diz IBGE*. Uol: https://economia.uol.com.br/noticias/estadao-conteudo/2020/10/23/8073-milhoes-de-pessoas-estavam-em-trabalho-remoto-em-setembro-diz-ibge.htm

Amorim, D. (2022). Brasil tem 20,4 mi de trabalhadores que poderiam trabalhar remotamente, diz Ipea. *CNN Brasil*. https://www.cnnbrasil.com.br/business/brasil-tem-204-mi-de-trabalhadores-que-poderiam-trabalhar-remotamente-diz-ipea/

Analytics Vidhya. (2022). *What are Smart Contracts in Blockchain?* https://www.analyticsvidhya.com/blog/2022/11/what-are-smart-contracts-in-blockchain/

Ancestry Organization. (2023). https://www.Ancestry.com

Andrade, G. (2020). *As vantagens do home office: o que dizem estudos e pesquisas*. Digilândia. https://digilandia.io/home-office/vantagens-do-home-office/#Impactos_sociais_e_ambientais

Ang, A., Chen, B., Goetzmann, W. N., & Phalippou, L. (2018). Estimating private equity returns from limited partner cash flows. *The Journal of Finance*, *73*(4), 1751–1783. doi:10.1111/jofi.12688

Antikainen, M., Uusitalo, T., & Kivikytö-Reponen, P. (2018). Digitalisation as an enabler of circular economy. *Procedia CIRP*, *73*, 45–49. doi:10.1016/j.procir.2018.04.027

Antikainen, M., & Valkokari, K. (2016). A framework for sustainable circular business model innovation. *Technology Innovation Management Review*, *6*(7), 5–12. doi:10.22215/timreview/1000

Antweiler, W., & Frank, M. Z. (2011). Do US Stock Markets Typically Overreact to Corporate News Stories? SSRN *Electronic Journal*. doi:10.2139/ssrn.878091

Arduini, F., & Morabito, V. (2010). Business continuity and the banking industry. *Communications of the ACM*, *53*(3), 121–125. doi:10.1145/1666420.1666452

Argamon, S. (2009). Stolen without a gun: Applying stylometric methods to the detection of surreptitious insider fraud. *Digital Investigation*, *6*(3-4), 130–140.

Argamon, S., Juola, P., & Schler, J. (2003). An Evaluation of Text Classification Methods for Literary Authorship Attribution. *Literary and Linguistic Computing*, *18*(4), 423–447.

Argamon, S., Juola, P., & Schler, J. (2009). Overview of authorship attribution. In J. Allan & ... (Eds.), *Handbook of natural language processing* (2nd ed., pp. 385–408). CRC Press.

Argamon, S., Juola, P., & Schler, J. (2013). The Stylistic Debates: Revenge of the Burrows. *Literary and Linguistic Computing*, *28*(4), 587–598.

Argamon, S., Koppel, M., Fine, J., & Shimoni, A. R. (2003). Gender, genre, and writing style in formal written texts. *Text*, *23*(3), 321–346. doi:10.1515/text.2003.014

Argamon, S., & Levitan, S. (2005). Measuring the usefulness of function words for authorship attribution. *Journal of the American Society for Information Science and Technology*, *56*(3), 187–196.

Aronis, S., & Stratopoulos, G. (2016). Implementing business continuity management systems and sharing best practices at a European bank. *Journal of Business Continuity & Emergency Planning*, *9*(3), 203–217. PMID:26897617

Arora, A., Jain, J., Gupta, S., & Sharma, A. (2020). Identifying sustainability drivers in higher education through fuzzy AHP. *Higher Education, Skills and Work-Based Learning, 11*(4), 823-836.

Assibi, A. (2023). Literature Review on Building Cyber Resilience Capabilities to Counter Future Cyber Threats: The Role of Enterprise Risk Management (ERM) and Business Continuity (BC). *OAlib, 10*(4), 1–15. doi:10.4236/oalib.1109882

AT. (2019, September 21). *Sobre o E-Fatura*. Retrieved from Portal das Finanças: https://info.portaldasfinancas.gov.pt/pt/faturas/pages/sobre_efatura.aspx

Attaran, M. (2022). Blockchain technology in healthcare: Challenges and opportunities. *International Journal of Healthcare Management, 15*(1), 70–83. doi:10.1080/20479700.2020.1843887

Atzori, L., Iera, A., & Morabito, G. (2010). The internet of things: A survey. *Computer Networks, 54*(15), 2787–2805. doi:10.1016/j.comnet.2010.05.010

Awan, U., & Sroufe, R. (2022). Sustainability in the circular economy: Insights and dynamics of designing circular business models. *Applied Sciences (Basel, Switzerland), 12*(3), 1521. doi:10.3390/app12031521

Awan, U., Sroufe, R., & Bozan, K. (2022). Designing value chains for Industry 4.0 and a circular economy: A review of the literature. *Sustainability (Basel), 14*(12), 7084. doi:10.3390u14127084

Azevedo, G., Tavares, M. C., Bastos, M. A., Vale, J., & Bandeira, A. M. (2023, June 20-23). *Universities in Era 5.0: the future accountant* [Paper presentation]. 18th Iberian Conference on Information Systems and Technologies (CISTI), Aveiro, Portugal. https://doi.org/ STI58278.2023.1021196310.23919/CI

Bachelier, L. (1900). Théorie de la spéculation. *Annales Scientifiques de l'Ecole Normale Supérieure, 17*, 21–86. Advance online publication. doi:10.24033/asens.476

Bag, S., & Rahman, M. S. (2023). Navigating circular economy: Unleashing the potential of political and supply chain analytics skills among top supply chain executives for environmental orientation, regenerative supply chain practices, and supply chain viability. *Business Strategy and the Environment*, bse.3507. Advance online publication. doi:10.1002/bse.3507

Bajgoric, N. (2006). Information technologies for business continuity: An implementation framework. *Information Management & Computer Security, 14*(5), 450–466. doi:10.1108/09685220610717754

Bajgoric, N., & Moon, Y. B. (2009). Enhancing systems integration by incorporating business continuity drivers. *Industrial Management & Data Systems, 109*(1), 74–97. doi:10.1108/02635570910926609

Bakari, H., Hunjra, A. L., Jaros, S., & Khoso, I. (2019). Moderating role of cynicism about Organizational change between authentic leadership and commitment to change in Pakistani publica sector hospitals. *Leadership in Health Services, 32*(3), 387–404. doi:10.1108/LHS-01-2018-0006 PMID:31298084

Balcilar, M., Bouri, E., Gupta, R., & Roubaud, D. (2016). Can Volume Predict Bitcoin Returns and Volatility? A Non-parametric Causality-in-Quantiles Approach. *Working Papers, 64*(March).

Ball, D. L., Thames, M. H., & Phelps, G. (2008). Content knowledge for teaching: What makes it special? *Journal of Teacher Education, 59*(5), 389–407. doi:10.1177/0022487108324554

Baltar, F., & Brunet, I. (2012). Social research 2.0: Virtual snowball sampling method using Facebook. *Internet Research, 22*(1), 57–74. doi:10.1108/10662241211199960

Băltescu, A. C. (2018). The green buildings: Sustainable development actions in the accommodation sector. *Annual Economic Series, 3*, 130–135.

Banerjee, S. (2022). Exaggeration in fake vs. authentic online reviews for luxury and budget hotels. *International Journal of Information Management, 62,* 102416. doi:10.1016/j.ijinfomgt.2021.102416

Bani, W., Al, I., & Ibrahim, A. (2020). Privacy, confidentiality, security, and patient safety concerns about electronic health records. *International Nursing Review, 67,* 218–230. doi:10.1111/inr.12585

Bannay, D. F., Hadi, M. J., & Amanah, A. A. (2020). The impact of inclusive leadership behaviours on innovative workplace behavoir with emphasis on the mediating role of work engagement. *Problems and Perspectives in Management, 18*(3), 479–491. doi:10.21511/ppm.18(3).2020.39

Baran, R., Rusc, T., & Fornalski, P. (2016). A smart camera for the surveillance of vehicles in intelligent transportation systems. *Multimedia Tools and Applications, 75*(17), 10471–10493. doi:10.100711042-015-3151-y

Barbosa, B., Saura, R., & Zekan, B. (2023). Defining content marketing and its influence on online user behavior: a data-driven prescriptive analytics method. *Annals of Operations Research.* doi:10.1007/s10479-023-05261-1

Bardin, L. (2015). Análise de conteúdo. Lisboa, PT: Edições 70.

Barhate, B., & Dirani, K. M. (2022). Career aspirations of generation Z: A systematic literature review. *European Journal of Training and Development, 46*(1/2), 139–157. doi:10.1108/EJTD-07-2020-0124

Barlas, G., & Stamatatos, E. (2020). Cross-domain authorship attribution using pre-trained language models. In *Artificial Intelligence Applications and Innovations: 16th IFIP WG 12.5 International Conference, AIAI 2020, Neos Marmaras, Greece, June 5–7, 2020 Proceedings, 16*(Part I), 255–266.

Barrero, J. M., Bloom, N., Davis, S. J., Meyer, B. H., & Mihaylov, E. (2022). *The shift to remote work lessens wage-growth pressures.* Working Paper 30197. Cambridge: National Bureau of Economic Research.

Bastos, S., Oliveira, H., Silva, M. M., & Azevedo, L. (2019, November 7-8). Soft Digital Skills in Higher Education Curricula: HEI's 5.0. In R. Ørngreen, M. Buhl, & B. Meyer (Eds.), *Proceedings of the 18th European Conference on e-Learning: ECEL 2019, Copenhagen* (pp. 70-77). Academic Conferences and Publishing International. https://www.academic-conferenc es.org/conferences/ecel/ecel-future-and-past/

Bates, B., Kundzewicz, Z., & Wu, S. (2008). *Climate Change and Water.* Intergovernmental Panel on Climate Change Secretariat.

Batten, J. A., Ciner, C., Kosedag, A., & Lucey, B. M. (2017). Is the price of gold to gold mining stocks asymmetric? *Economic Modelling, 60,* 402–407. Advance online publication. doi:10.1016/j.econmod.2016.10.007

Battista, M. T., & Clements, D. H. (1996). Students' understanding of three-dimensional rectangular arrays of cubes. *Journal for Research in Mathematics Education, 27*(3), 258–292. doi:10.2307/749365

Baumer, E. P. S. (2020). Charting the rise of the Internet of Behaviors. *Communications of the ACM, 63*(5), 54–61.

Bau, P., Xiao, Z., Bao, G., & Norderhaven, N. (2021). Inclusive leadership and employee work engagement: A moderated mediation model. *Baltic Journal of Management, 17*(1), 124–139. doi:10.1108/BJM-06-2021-0219

Baur, D. G., & Lucey, B. M. (2010). Is gold a hedge or a safe haven? An analysis of stocks, bonds and gold. *Financial Review, 45*(2), 217–229. Advance online publication. doi:10.1111/j.1540-6288.2010.00244.x

Beach, R., Abitbol, J. M., Allman, B. L., Esseltine, J. L., Shao, Q., & Laird, D. W. (2020). GJB2 Mutations Linked to Hearing Loss Exhibit Differential Trafficking and Functional Defects as Revealed in Cochlear-Relevant Cells. *Frontiers in Cell and Developmental Biology, 8,* 215. doi:10.3389/fcell.2020.00215 PMID:32300592

Becker, C., Chitchyan, R., Duboc, L., Easterbrook, S., Penzenstadler, B., Seyff, N., & Venters, C. C. (2015). Sustainability Design and Software: The Karlskrona Manifesto. *IEEE/ACM 37th IEEE International Conference on Software Engineering, 2*, 467-476.

Beck, L., Trombetta, W., & Share, S. (1986). Using focus group sessions before decisions are made. *North Carolina Medical Journal, 47*(2), 73–74.

Behera, R. K., Bala, P. K., & Rana, N. P. (2023). Creation of sustainable growth with explainable artificial intelligence: An empirical insight from consumer packaged goods retailers. *Journal of Cleaner Production, 399*, 136605. doi:10.1016/j.jclepro.2023.136605

Bejarano, A. M., García, L. E., & Zurek, E. E. (2015). Detection of source code similitude in academic environments. *Computer Applications in Engineering Education, 23*(1), 13–22. doi:10.1002/cae.21571

Belchior, R., Vasconcelos, A., Guerreiro, S., & Correia, M. (2021). A survey on blockchain interoperability: Past, present, and future trends. *ACM Computing Surveys, 54*(8), 1–41. doi:10.1145/3471140

Bell, J. (1997). *Como realizar um projecto de investigação*. Gradiva.

Benítez-Márquez, M. D., Sánchez-Teba, E. M., Bermudez-González, G., & Núñez-Rydman, E. S. (2022). Generation Z Within the Workforce and in the Workplace: A Bibliometric Analysis. *Frontiers in Psychology, 12*, 736820. doi:10.3389/fpsyg.2021.736820 PMID:35178005

Bennett, N., & Lemoine, G. J. (2014). What VUCA Really Means for You. *Harvard Business Review, 92*(1/2).

Bertram, L. (2020). Digital Learning Games for Mathematics and Computer Science Education: The Need for Preregistered RCTs, Standardized Methodology, and Advanced Technology. *Frontiers in Psychology, 11*, 1–10. doi:10.3389/fpsyg.2020.02127

Bhatti, F., Shah, M., Maple, C., & Islam, S. (2019). A Novel Internet of Things-Enabled Accident Detection and Reporting System for Smart City Environments. *Sensors (Basel), 19*(9), 2071. Advance online publication. doi:10.339019092071 PMID:31058879

Blanco-Moreno, S., González-Fernández, A. M., & Muñoz-Gallego, P. A. (2023). Big data in tourism marketing: past research and future opportunities. *Spanish Journal of Marketing-ESIC*. doi:10.1108/SJME-06-2022-0134

Blueprint Genetics. (2023). *Comprehensive Hearing Loss and Deafness Panel*.https://blueprintgenetics.com/tests/panels/ear-nose-throat/comprehensive-hearing-loss-and-deafness-panel/

Bocken, N. M. P., Short, S. W., Rana, P., & Evans, S. (2014). A literature and practice review to develop sustainable business model archetypes. *Journal of Cleaner Production, 65*, 42–56. doi:10.1016/j.jclepro.2013.11.039

Bogdan, R., & Biklen, S. (1994). *Investigação qualitativa em educação. Uma introdução à teoria e aos métodos*. Porto Editora.

Boldosova, V., & Luoto, S. (2020). Storytelling, business analytics and big data interpretation: Literature review and theoretical propositions. *Management Research Review, 43*(2), 204–222. doi:10.1108/MRR-03-2019-0106

Boons, F., & Lüdeke-Freund, F. (2013). Business models for sustainable innovation: State-of-the-art and steps towards a research agenda. *Journal of Cleaner Production, 45*, 9–19. doi:10.1016/j.jclepro.2012.07.007

Bordeleau, F. E., Mosconi, E., & Santa-Eulalia, L. A. (2018) Business Intelligence in Industry 4.0: State of the art and research opportunities. In *Proceedings of the 51st Hawaii International Conference on System Sciences* (pp. 3944-3953). ICISS 10.24251/HICSS.2018.495

Borgards, O., & Czudaj, R. L. (2020). The prevalence of price overreactions in the cryptocurrency market. *Journal of International Financial Markets, Institutions and Money, 65*, 101194. Advance online publication. doi:10.1016/j.intfin.2020.101194

Bories, A. S., Fabo, P. R., & Plecháč, P. (2022). The Polite Revolution of Computational Literary Studies. *Computational Stylistics in Poetry, Prose, and Drama*, 1.

Bouri, E., Molnár, P., Azzi, G., Roubaud, D., & Hagfors, L. I. (2017). On the hedge and safe haven properties of Bitcoin: Is it really more than a diversifier? *Finance Research Letters, 20*, 192–198. Advance online publication. doi:10.1016/j.frl.2016.09.025

Bouri, E., Shahzad, S. J. H., Roubaud, D., Kristoufek, L., & Lucey, B. (2020). Bitcoin, gold, and commodities as safe havens for stocks: New insight through wavelet analysis. *The Quarterly Review of Economics and Finance, 77*, 156–164. Advance online publication. doi:10.1016/j.qref.2020.03.004

Bouton, S., Bové, A.-T., Hannon, E., Magnin-Mallez, C., Rogers, M., Swartz, S., Vanthournout, H., Murphy, C., Rosenfield, J., Communications, L., Borruso, M. T., Simcock, V., Arora, R., Brown, E., Byer, H., Draper, R., Frey, T., Hanselman, H., Herbein, G., . . . Staples, M. (n.d.). *The circular economy: Moving from theory to practice is written by consultants from across sectors and geographies, with expertise in sustainability and resource productivity.* Retrieved June 23, 2023, from https://www.mckinsey.com

Boyd, D., & Crawford, K. (2012). Critical questions for big data: Provocations for a cultural, technological, and scholarly phenomenon. *Information Communication and Society, 15*(5), 662–679. doi:10.1080/1369118X.2012.678878

Brandi, V. (2018). Short-Term Predictability of Stock Market Indexes Following Large Drawdowns and Drawups. SSRN *Electronic Journal.* doi:10.2139/ssrn.3217419

Brandvold, M., Molnár, P., Vagstad, K., & Andreas Valstad, O. C. (2015). Price discovery on Bitcoin exchanges. *Journal of International Financial Markets, Institutions and Money, 36*, 18–35. Advance online publication. doi:10.1016/j.intfin.2015.02.010

Brás, J. (2018). Bootstrapping enterprise models with business continuity processes and DEMO.

Brasil. Presidência da República. (2000). *Law No 10,098, of December 19, 2000*: establishes general standards and basic criteria for promoting the accessibility of people with disabilities or reduced mobility and makes other provisions. Brasília, DF.

Brasil. Presidência da República. (2011). *Law No. 12,551, of December 15, 2011.* Alters article 6 of the Consolidation of Labor Laws (CLT), approved by Decree-Law No. 5452, of May 1, 1943, to equate the legal effects of subordination exercised by telematic and computerized means to that exercised by personal and direct means. Diário Oficial da União, Brasília, DF.

Brasil. Presidência da República. (2015). *Law No. 13,146 of July 6, 2015*: establishes the Brazilian Inclusion Law for Persons with Disabilities (Estatuto da Pessoa com Deficiência). Brasília, DF.

Brasil. Presidência da República. (2017). *Law No. 13,467, of July 13, 2017.* It changes the Consolidation of Labor Laws (CLT), in order to adapt the legislation to the new labor relations Brasília, DF.

Brasil. Presidência da República. (2020). *Provisional Measure No. 927, of March 22, 2020.* Amends the Law and disposes about labor measures to face the state of public calamity. Brasília, DF.

Brasil. Superior Labor Court. (2012). *Provisional Measure No. 1499, of February 01, 2012.* Regulates telework in the scope of the Superior Labor Court and makes other provisions. Diário da Justiça do Trabalho, Brasília, DF, no. 912, Feb. 3, 2012.

Brás, J., & Guerreiro, S. (2016). Designing Business Continuity Processes Using DEMO: An Insurance Company Case Study. In R. Pergl, M. Molhanec, E. Babkin, & S. Fosso Wamba (Eds.), *Enterprise and Organizational Modeling and Simulation. EOMAS 2016. Lecture Notes in Business Information Processing, 272.* doi:10.1007/978-3-319-49454-8_11

Breitung, J. (2000). The local power of some unit root tests for panel data. *Advances in Econometrics, 15,* 161–177. Advance online publication. doi:10.1016/S0731-9053(00)15006-6

Bressanelli, G., Adrodegari, F., Perona, M., & Saccani, N. (2018). The role of digital technologies to overcome Circular Economy challenges in PSS Business Models: An exploratory case study. *Procedia CIRP, 73,* 216–221. doi:10.1016/j.procir.2018.03.322

Brewer, M. B. (2012). Optimal distinctiveness theory: Its history and development. In P. A. M. VanLange, A. W. Kruglanski, & E. T. Higgins (Eds.), *Handbook of theories of social psychology* (pp. 81–98). Sage Publications.

Brice, S., & Almond, H. (2023). Behavior change in chronic health: Reviewing what we know, what is happening, and what is next for Hearing Loss. *International Journal of Environmental Research and Public Health, 20*(8), 5605. doi:10.3390/ijerph20085605 PMID:37107887

Brito, M., & Gonçalves, C. (2019). Codeflex: A Web-based Platform for Competitive Programming. *14th Iberian Conference on Information Systems and Technologies (CISTI),* 1-6. 10.23919/CISTI.2019.8760776

Brocardo, J., Delgado, C., Mendes, F., & Ponte, J. P. (2022). Ações do professor e desenvolvimento do raciocínio matemático durante a discussão coletiva de uma tarefa. *Educación Matemática, 34*(2), 101–133. doi:10.24844/EM3402.04

Brody, P., & Bednar, P. (2021). The Internet of Behaviors (IoB): From Discrete Behavior to Process and System. *Proceedings of the 54th Hawaii International Conference on System Sciences.*

Brooks, T. (2022). *Authentication Devices in Fog-Mobile Edge Computing Environments Through a Wireless Grid Resource Sharing Protocol.* arXiv preprint arXiv:2207.03346.

Bryson, J., & Winfield, A. (2017). Standardizing Ethical Design for Artificial Intelligence and Autonomous Systems. *Computer, 50*(5), 116–119. doi:10.1109/MC.2017.154

Budiman, K., Arini, F., & Sugiharti, E. (2020). Disaster recovery planning with distributed replicated block device in synchronized API systems. *Journal of Physics: Conference Series, 1567*(3), 032023. Advance online publication. doi:10.1088/1742-6596/1567/3/032023

Buhalis, D., Harwood, T., Bogicevic, V., Viglia, G., Beldona, S., & Hofacker, C. (2019). Technological disruptions in services: Lessons from tourism and hospitality. *Journal of Service Management, 20*(4), 484–506. doi:10.1108/JOSM-12-2018-0398

Bulchand-Gidumal, J. (2020). Impact of artificial intelligence in travel, tourism, and hospitality. In *Handbook of e-Tourism* (pp. 1–20). Springer International Publishing. doi:10.1007/978-3-030-05324-6_110-1

Burkett, I. (2016). *Using the business model canvas for social enterprise design.* Knode. https://cscuk.fcdo.gov.uk/wp-content/uploads/2016/07/BMC-for-Social-Enterprise.pdf

Burmaoglu, S., Ozdemir Gungor, D., Kirbac, A., & Saritas, O. (2022). Future research avenues at the nexus of circular economy and digitalization. *International Journal of Productivity and Performance Management.* Advance online publication. doi:10.1108/IJPPM-01-2021-0026

Burrows, J. F. (2002). "Delta": A Measure of Stylistic Difference and a Guide to Likely Authorship. *Literary and Linguistic Computing, 17*(3), 267–287. doi:10.1093/llc/17.3.267

Burtles, J. (2016). *Manager's Guide to Business Continuity Exercises: Testing Your Plan.* Rothstein Publishing eBook Collection.

Burtles, J. (2015). The hexagon hypothesis: Six disruptive scenarios. *Journal of Business Continuity & Emergency Planning, 9*(1), 60–69. PMID:26420396

Bustamante, A., Sebastia, L., & Onaindia, E. (2020). BITOUR: A Business Intelligence Platform for Tourism Analysis. *ISPRS International Journal of Geo-Information, 9*(11), 671. doi:10.3390/ijgi9110671

Bwambale, E., Abagale, F. K., & Anornu, G. K. (2022). Smart irrigation monitoring and control strategies for improving water use efficiency in precision agriculture: A review. *Agricultural Water Management, 260*, 1–12. doi:10.1016/j.agwat.2021.107324

Bzai, J., Alam, F., Dhafer, A., Bojović, M., Altowaijri, S. M., Niazi, I. K., & Mehmood, R. (2022). Machine learning-enabled internet of things (IoT): Data, applications, and industry perspective. *Electronics (Basel), 11*(17), 2676. doi:10.3390/electronics11172676

Caballero, A. (2009). Information Security Essentials for IT Managers: Protecting Mission-Critical Systems. In J. R. Vacca (Ed.), *Computer and Information Security Handbook* (pp. 225–252). Elsevier Inc. doi:10.1016/B978-0-12-374354-1.00014-5

Cabinet Office Government of Japan. (2016). *Society 5.0.* Government of Japan. https://www8.cao.go.jp/cstp/english/society5_0/index.html

Caetano, F., Pitarma, R., & Reis, P. (2014). Intelligent management of urban garden irrigation. *9th Iberian Conference on Information Systems and Technologies (CISTI)*, 1-6.

Calvaresi, D., Ibrahim, A., Calbimonte, J. P., Schegg, R., Fragniere, E., & Schumacher, M. (2021). The evolution of chatbots in tourism: A systematic literature review. *Information and Communication Technologies in Tourism, 2021*, 3–16. doi:10.1007/978-3-030-65785-7_1

Calzon, B. (2022). *13 Essential Data Visualization Techniques, Concepts & Methods To Improve Your Business – Fast.* Retrieved from: https://www.datapine.com/blog/data-visualization-techniques-concepts-and-methods/

Camp, L. J. (2001). Trust and risk in Internet Commerce. MIT Press.

Campbell, J. Y., Lo, A. W., & MacKinlay, A. C. (1997). The Predictability of Asset Returns. In The Econometrics of Financial Markets (pp. 27–82). doi:10.1515/9781400830213-006

Campos, J., Ericsson, N. R., & Hendry, D. F. (1996). Cointegration tests in the presence of structural breaks. In Journal of Econometrics (Vol. 70, Issue 1). doi:10.1016/0304-4076(94)01689-5

Cardoso, P. J., Monteiro, J., Cabrita, C., Semião, J., Cruz, D. M., Pinto, N., Ramos, C. M., Oliveira, L. M., & Rodrigues, J. M. (2021). Monitoring, Predicting, and Optimizing Energy Consumptions: A Goal Toward Global Sustainability. In *Research Anthology on Clean Energy Management and Solutions* (pp. 20–47). IGI Global. doi:10.4018/978-1-7998-9152-9.ch002

Carmeli, A., Reiter-Palmon, R., & Ziv, E. (2010). Inclusive leadership and employee involvement in creative tasks in workplace. The mediating role of psychological safety. *Creativity Research Journal, 22*(3), 250–260. doi:10.1080/10400419.2010.504654

Caroça, C., Vicente, V., Campelo, P., Chasqueira, M., Caria, M., Silva, S., Paixão, P., & Paço, P. (2017). Rubella in Sub-Saharan Africa and sensorineural hearing loss: A case control study. *BMC Public Health*, *17*(1), 146. doi:10.118612889-017-4077-2 PMID:28143602

Carreira, F., Aleixo, C., & Rebocho, S. (2021, October 14-15). *O Desenvolvimento de Competências em Auditoria: O Reconhecimento pelos Estudantes da ESCE/IPS* [Paper presentation]. XVIII Congresso Internacional de Contabilidade e Auditoria, Lisboa, Portugal. http://xviiicica.occ. pt/pt/dtrab/trabalhos/congressoxviii_cica/trabalhoscc.php

Carvalho, L. C., Moreira, S. B., Dias, R., Rodrigues, S., & Costa, B. (2020). Circular economy principles and their influence on attitudes to consume green products in the fashion industry: A study about perceptions of Portuguese students. In Mapping, Managing, and Crafting Sustainable Business Strategies for the Circular Economy (pp. 248–275). IGI Global. doi:10.4018/978-1-5225-9885-5.ch012

Casola, V., Benedictis, A. D., Rak, M., & Villano, U. (2018). Security-by-design in multi-cloud applications: An optimization approach. *Information Sciences*, *454-455*, 344–362. doi:10.1016/j.ins.2018.04.081

Castillo, E., Cervantes, O., & Vilarino, D. (2019). Authorship verification using a graph knowledge discovery approach. *Journal of Intelligent & Fuzzy Systems*, *36*(6), 6075–6087. doi:10.3233/JIFS-181934

Catho. (2022, Sept. 23). Home Office ajuda na inclusão de profissionais com deficiência. *Carreira & Sucesso (online)*. São Paulo, SP: Catho. https://www.catho.com.br/carreira-sucesso/carreira/home-office-ajuda-na-inclusao-de-profissionais-com-deficiencia/

CeGAT-Genetic Diagnosis. (2023). *Hearing Loss: Analysis of all known genes associated with hearing loss*. https://cegat.com/diagnostics/rare-diseases/hearing-loss/

Cerullo, V., & Cerullo, M. J. (2004). Business Continuity Planning: A Comprehensive Approach. *Journal Information Systems Management*, *21*, 70-78. doi:10.1201/1078/44432.21.3.20040601/82480.11

Chai, C.-S., Koh, J. H.-L., & Tsai, C.-C. (2013). A Review of Technological Pedagogical Content Knowledge. *Journal of Educational Technology & Society*, *16*(2), 31–51. https://www.jstor.org/stable/jeductechsoci.16.2.31

Chakraborty, A., Kung, C. Y., & Ghosh, S. K. (2021). The Internet of Behaviors (IoB): A Review on Enabling Technologies, Applications, and Challenges. *IEEE Access : Practical Innovations, Open Solutions*, *9*, 68418–68433.

Chang, P. C., Ma, G., & Lin, Y. Y. (2022). Inclusive leadership and employee proactive behavior: A cross-level moderated mediation model. *Psychology Research and Behavior Management*, *15*, 1797–1809. doi:10.2147/PRBM.S363434 PMID:35860206

Chan, J. (2019). Importance of Educational Technology on Learning. *Merit Research Journal of Education and Review*, *7*(6), 65–67. doi:10.5281/zenodo.3255008

Chaski, C. E. (2005). Who's at the keyboard? Authorship attribution in digital evidence investigations. *International Journal of Digital Evidence*, *4*(1), 1–13.

Chaudhary, K., & Alam, M. (Eds.). (2022). *Big Data Analytics: Digital Marketing and Decision-Making* (1st ed.). Auerbach Publications. doi:10.1201/9781003307761

Chauhan, C., Parida, V., & Dhir, A. (2022). Linking circular economy and digitalisation technologies: A systematic literature review of past achievements and future promises. *Technological Forecasting and Social Change*, *177*(121508), 121508. doi:10.1016/j.techfore.2022.121508

Chen, Y. (2023). Comparing content marketing strategies of digital brands using machine learning. *Humanities and Social Sciences Communications*, *10*(57). doi:10.1057/s41599-023-01544-x

Chen, C., Zhang, D., & Guo, B. (2017). Data-Driven Human Behavior Modeling and Analysis Using Internet of Things (IoT). *IEEE Communications Magazine*, *55*(9), 68–74.

Cheng, H., Jung, K., Parra-Lancourt, M., & Powell, R. (2020). Does the sharing economy share or concentrate? *Frontier Technology Quarterly*. https://www.un.org/development/desa/dpad/wp-content/uploads/sites/45/publication/FTQ_Feb2020.pdf

Chen, H., Chiang, R. H., & Storey, V. C. (2012). Business intelligence and analytics: From big data to big impact. *Management Information Systems Quarterly*, *36*(4), 1165–1188. doi:10.2307/41703503

Chen, M. W., & Zhu, J. (2005). Do Investors in Chinese Stock Market Overreact? *Journal of Accounting and Finance Research*, *13*(3).

Cheung, S. Y., & Ng, K. Y. (2021). Application of the Educational Game to Enhance Student Learning. *Frontiers in Education*, *6*, 1–10. doi:10.3389/feduc.2021.623793

Chkioua, D. H. (2021). Excess Volatility in the Tunisian Stock Market: Explanation by Behavioral Finance. *South Asian Journal of Social Studies and Economics*. doi:10.9734/sajsse/2021/v12i430310

Cho, D., & Han, H. (2021). The tail behavior of safe haven currencies: A cross-quantilogram analysis. *Journal of International Financial Markets, Institutions and Money*, *70*, 101257. Advance online publication. doi:10.1016/j.intfin.2020.101257

Choi, S. B., Tran, T. B. H., & Park, B. I. (2015). Inclusive leadership and work engagement: Mediating roles of affective Organizational commitment and creativity. *Social Behavior and Personality*, *43*(6), 931–943. doi:10.2224bp.2015.43.6.931

Chopra, N., Lakonishok, J., & Ritter, J. R. (1992). Measuring abnormal performance. Do stocks overreact? *Journal of Financial Economics*, *31*(2), 235–268. Advance online publication. doi:10.1016/0304-405X(92)90005-I

Chora, J., Simões-Teixeira, H., Matos, T.D., Martins, J., Alves, M., Ferreia, R., Silva, L., Ribeiro, C., Fialho, G., & Caria, H. (2012). Two Portuguese Cochlear Implanted Dizygotic Twins: A Case Report. *Case Reports in Genetics*. doi:10.1155/2012/623860

Chora, J., Matos, T., Martins, J., Alves, M., Andrade, S., Silva, L., Ribeiro, C., Antunes, M., Fialho, G., & Caria, H. (2010). DFNB1-associated deafness in Portuguese cochlear implant users: Prevalence and impact on oral outcome. *International Journal of Pediatric Otorhinolaryngology*, *74*(10), 1135–1139. doi:10.1016/j.ijporl.2010.06.014 PMID:20650534

Ciaian, P., Rajcaniova, M., & Kancs, A. (2016). The economics of BitCoin price formation. *Applied Economics*, *48*(19), 1799–1815. Advance online publication. doi:10.1080/00036846.2015.1109038

Ciner, C., Lucey, B., & Yarovaya, L. (2020). Spillovers, integration and causality in LME non-ferrous metal markets. *Journal of Commodity Markets*, *17*, 100079. Advance online publication. doi:10.1016/j.jcomm.2018.10.001

Circularity vs. Sustainability. (2017, March 29). *U.S. Chamber of Commerce Foundation*. https://www.uschamberfoundation.org/circular-economy-toolbox/about-circularity/circularity-vs-sustainability

Clark, P. (2010). Contingency Planning and Strategies. 2010 Information Security Curriculum Development Conference (pp. 131–140). Association for Computing Machinery. doi:10.1145/1940941.1940969

CMMI Institute. (2020). *Introducing CMMI V2.0.* https://cmmiinstitute.com/cmmi

CMMI Institute. (2020). *Introducing CMMI V2.0.* Retrieved abril 23, 2020, from CMMI Institute: https://cmmiinstitute.com/cmmi

CodeChef. (n.d.). *CodeChef Platform.* Retrieved 11 21, 2022, from https://www.codechef.com/

Codeforces. (n.d.). *Codeforces Platform*. Retrieved 11 21, 2022, from https://codeforces.com/

CodeSignal. (n.d.). *CodeSignal Platform*. Retrieved 11 21, 2022, from https://codesignal.com/

Codewars. (n.d.). *Codewars Platform*. Retrieved 11 21, 2022, from https://www.codewars.com/

CodinGame. (n.d.). *CodinGame Platform*. Retrieved 11 21, 2022, from https://www.codingame.com/start

Combéfis, S. (2022). Automated Code Assessment for Education: Review, Classification and Perspectives on Techniques and Tools. *Software*, *1*(1), 3–30. doi:10.3390oftware1010002

Coneglian, T. N. M. (2020). *Teletrabalho Home office: identidade, subjetividade e saúde mental dos tabalhadores*. CRV. doi:10.24824/978655578154.0

Conselho Nacional de Saúde – CNS. (2020). Recomendation No 036/2020: It recommends implementing more restrictive social distancing measures (lockdown) in municipalities with accelerated occurrence of new cases of COVID-19 and with service occupancy rates reaching critical levels. Ministry of Health, Brasília, DF.

Cook, J. (2015). A six-stage business continuity and disaster recovery planning cycle. *S.A.M. Advanced Management Journal*, *80*(3), 22–33.

Corbet, S., Larkin, C., & Lucey, B. (2020). The contagion effects of the COVID-19 pandemic: Evidence from gold and cryptocurrencies. *Finance Research Letters*, *35*, 101554. Advance online publication. doi:10.1016/j.frl.2020.101554

Cordier, R., Milbourn, B., Martin, R., Buchanan, A., Chung, D., & Speyer, R. (2017). A systematic review evaluating the psychometric properties of measure social inclusion. *PLoS One*, *12*(6), e0179109. doi:10.1371/journal.pone.0179109 PMID:28598984

Cowles, A. (1933). Can Stock Market Forecasters Forecast? *Econometrica*, *1*(3), 309. Advance online publication. doi:10.2307/1907042

Cowles, A. (1944). Stock Market Forecasting. *Econometrica*, *12*(3/4), 206. Advance online publication. doi:10.2307/1905433

Craig, H., & Kinney, A. F. (2009). *Shakespeare, computers, and the mystery of authorship*. Cambridge University Press. doi:10.1017/CBO9780511605437

Cravinho, J., Tribolet, J., Capucha, L., Silva, S., & Veiga, P. (2022). *O digital na educação*. Conselho Nacional da Educação. https://www.cnedu.pt/content/edicoes/estudos_e_relatorios/O_Digital_na_Educacao_2022.docx.pdf

Crawford, K., & Schultz, J. (2014). Big Data and Due Process: Toward a Framework to Redress Predictive Privacy Harms. *Boston College Law Review. Boston College. Law School*, *55*(1), 93–128.

Cremer, F., Sheehan, B., Fortmann, M., Kia, A. N., Mullins, M., Murphy, F., & Materne, S. (2022). Cyber risk and cybersecurity: A systematic review of data availability. *The Geneva Papers on Risk and Insurance. Issues and Practice*, *47*(3), 698–736. doi:10.105741288-022-00266-6 PMID:35194352

Creswell, J. W. (2012). *Educational research: Planning, conducting, and evaluating quantitative and qualitative research* (4th ed.). Pearson.

da Rocha, C. T. M., & Amador, F. S. (2018, March). O teletrabalho: Conceituação e questões para análise. *Cadernos EBAPE.BR*, *16*(1), 1–11. doi:10.1590/1679-395154516

da Silva, D. (2021). *Home office: vantagens e desvantagens para as empresas e colaboradores*. https://www.zendesk.com.br/blog/home-office-vantagens-e-desvantagens/

da Silva, R. R. (2009, January-June). Home-office: Um surgimento bem-sucedido da profissão pós-fordista, uma alternativa positiva para os centros urbanos. *Revista Brasileira de Gestão Urbana, Curitiba, PR, 1*(1), 1–11.

Dabbous, M., Kawtharani, A., Fahs, I., Hallal, Z., Shouman, D., Akel, M., Rahal, M., & Sakr, F. (2022). The Role of Game-Based Learning in Experiential Education: Tool Validation, Motivation Assessment, and Outcomes Evaluation among a Sample of Pharmacy Students. *Education Sciences, 12*(7), 1-13. doi:10.3390/educsci12070434

Davcev, D., Mitreski, K., Trajkovic, S., Nikolovski, V., & Koteli, N. (2018). IoT agriculture system based on LoRaWAN. *14th IEEE International Workshop on Factory Communication Systems (WFCS)*, 1-4.

Davidson, K. (2014). A typology to categorize the ideologies of actors in the sustainable development debate: A political economy typology of sustainability. *Sustainable Development (Bradford), 22*(1), 1–14. doi:10.1002d.520

De Bondt, W. F. M., & Thaler, R. H. (2012). Do Analysts Overreact? In Heuristics and Biases. doi:10.1017/CBO9780511808098.040

De Bondt, W. F. M., & Thaler, R. (1985). Does the Stock Market Overreact? *The Journal of Finance, 40*(3), 793–805. Advance online publication. doi:10.1111/j.1540-6261.1985.tb05004.x

De Bruyne, M.-J., & Verleye, K. (2023). Realizing the economic and circular potential of sharing business models by engaging consumers. *Journal of Service Management, 34*(3), 493–519. doi:10.1108/JOSM-08-2021-0318

de La Taille, Y. (2008). Ética em pesquisa com seres humanos: dignidade e liberdade. In *Ética nas pesquisas em ciências humanas e sociais na saúde*. Aderaldo & Rothschild.

de Oliveira, A., & Tchakerian, G. (2022). *Home office e teletrabalho*. Juspodivm.

Decree-Law no. 198. (2012, August 24). Decree-Law no. 198/2012, August 24th. Ministry of Finance.

Decree-Law no. 28. (2019, February 15). Decree-Law no. 28/2019, February 15th. Presidency of the Council of Ministers.

Definition of digitalization - Gartner information technology glossary. (n.d.). Gartner. Obtido 16 de agosto de 2023, de https://www.gartner.com/en/information-technology/glossary/digitalization

DeLoss, J. (2023). *Colorado State University partners in $20M AI Institute focusing on climate-smart agriculture and forestry*. Colorado State University. https://source.colostate.edu/colorado-state-university-partners-in-20m-ai-institute-focusing-on-climate-smart-agriculture-and-forestry/

Desai, S., Alhadad, R., Chilamkurti, N., & Mahmood, A. (2019). A survey of privacy preserving schemes in IoE enabled smart grid advanced metering infrastructure. *Cluster Computing, 22*(1), 43–69. doi:10.100710586-018-2820-9

Dewi, N. K., & Putra, A. S. (2021, March). Law enforcement in smart transportation systems on highways. *International Conference on Education of Suryakancana (IConnects Proceedings)*.

Diaconaşu, D. E., Mehdian, S., & Stoica, O. (2022). An analysis of investors' behavior in Bitcoin market. *PLoS ONE, 17*(3 March). doi:10.1371/journal.pone.0264522

Dias, R., Pereira, J. M., & Carvalho, L. C. (2022). Are African Stock Markets Efficient? A Comparative Analysis Between Six African Markets, the UK, Japan and the USA in the Period of the Pandemic. *Naše Gospodarstvo/Our Economy, 68*(1), 35–51. doi:10.2478/ngoe-2022-0004

Dias, Rui, Chambino, M., & Horta, N. H. (2023). *Long-Term Dependencies in Central European Stock Markets : A Crisp-Set. 2*(February), 10–17. doi:10.58567/eal02010002

Dias, R. T., Pardal, P., Santos, H., & Vasco, C. (2021). *Testing the Random Walk Hypothesis for Real Exchange Rates.* doi:10.4018/978-1-7998-6926-9.ch017

Dias, R., Horta, N., & Chambino, M. (2023). Journal of Economic Analysis. *Journal of Economic Analysis, 9*(1), 129–151. doi:10.58567/jea02010005

Dias, R., Pardal, P., Teixeira, N., & Horta, N. R. (2022). Tail Risk and Return Predictability for Europe's Capital Markets. *Advances in Human Resources Management and Organizational Development*, (December), 281–298. Advance online publication. doi:10.4018/978-1-6684-5666-8.ch015

Dias, R., Pardal, P., Teixeira, N., & Machová, V. (2020). Financial Market Integration of ASEAN-5 with China. *Littera Scripta, 13*(1). Advance online publication. doi:10.36708/Littera_Scripta2020/1/4

Dias, R., Teixeira, N., Machova, V., Pardal, P., Horak, J., & Vochozka, M. (2020). Random walks and market efficiency tests: Evidence on US, Chinese and European capital markets within the context of the global Covid-19 pandemic. *Oeconomia Copernicana, 11*(4), 585–608. Advance online publication. doi:10.24136/oc.2020.024

Dickey, D., & Fuller, W. (1981). Likelihood ratio statistics for autoregressive time series with a unit root. *Econometrica, 49*(4), 1057–1072. doi:10.2307/1912517

Dilmegani, C. (2023). *Internet of Behaviors (IoB): Its nature and importance in 2023.* AI Multiple. https://research.aimultiple.com/internet-of-behaviors/

Ding, S., Tukker, A., & Ward, H. (2023). Opportunities and risks of internet of things (IoT) technologies for circular business models: A literature review. *Journal of Environmental Management, 336*(117662), 117662. doi:10.1016/j.jenvman.2023.117662 PMID:36913854

Docker. (n.d.). *Docker: Accelerated, Containerized Application Development.* Retrieved 09 22, 2022, from https://www.docker.com/ Facebook/HackerCup

Doh, L., & Stumpf, S. (2005). *Handbook of responsible leadership and governance in global business.* Edward Elgar. doi:10.4337/9781845425562

DomiLabs. (2021). *A beginner's guide to self-sovereign identity.* https://domilabs.io/beginners-guide-ssi/

Dorado, S., Haigh, N., & Tashman, P. (2019). Advancing the understanding of social entrepreneurship: An empirical examination of the organizational processes of hybrid organizations. *Nonprofit and Voluntary Sector Quarterly, 48*(3), 591–615.

DRAGINO. (n.d.). *Dragino Products.* Retrieved 7 14, 2021, from https://dragino.com

Drake, L., Sassoon, I., Balatsoukas, P., Porat, T., Ashworth, M., Wright, E., Curcin, V., Chapman, M., Kokciyan, N., Modgil, S., Sklar, E., & Parsons, S. (2022). The relationship of socio-demographic factors and patient attitudes to connected health technologies: *A survey of stroke survivors. Health Informatics Journal, 28*(2). Advance online publication. doi:10.1177/14604582221102373

Dutt, A., Ismail, M. A., & Herawan, T. (2017). A systematic review on educational data mining. *IEEE Access : Practical Innovations, Open Solutions, 5*, 15991–16005. doi:10.1109/ACCESS.2017.2654247

Dwivedi, Y. K., Hughes, L., Baabdullah, A. M., Ribeiro-Navarrete, S., Giannakis, M., Al-Debei, M. M., Dennehy, D., Metri, B., Buhalis, D., Cheung, C. M. K., Conboy, K., Doyle, R., Dubey, R., Dutot, V., Felix, R., Goyal, D. P., Gustafsson, A., Hinsch, C., Jebabli, I., ... Wamba, S. F. (2022). Metaverse beyond the hype: Multidisciplinary perspectives on emerging challenges, opportunities, and agenda for research, practice and policy. *International Journal of Information Management, 66*, 102542. doi:10.1016/j.ijinfomgt.2022.102542

Dwivedi, Y. K., Kshetri, N., Hughes, L., Slade, E. L., Jeyaraj, A., Kar, A. K., Baabdullah, A. M., Koohang, A., Raghavan, V., Ahuja, M., Albanna, H., Albashrawi, M. A., Al-Busaidi, A. S., Balakrishnan, J., Barlette, Y., Basu, S., Bose, I., Brooks, L., Buhalis, D., ... Wright, R. (2023). "So what if ChatGPT wrote it?" Multidisciplinary perspectives on opportunities, challenges and implications of generative conversational AI for research, practice and policy. *International Journal of Information Management*, *71*, 102642. doi:10.1016/j.ijinfomgt.2023.102642

Dwyer, C. (2018). Ethical considerations in the use of machine learning in stylometry. *Proceedings of the 18th ACM Workshop on Privacy in the Electronic Society*, 148-157.

Dwyer, G. P. (2015). The economics of Bitcoin and similar private digital currencies. *Journal of Financial Stability*, *17*, 81–91. Advance online publication. doi:10.1016/j.jfs.2014.11.006

Dyhrberg, A. H. (2016). Hedging capabilities of bitcoin. Is it the virtual gold? *Finance Research Letters*, *16*, 139–144. doi:10.1016/j.frl.2015.10.025

Eder, M. (2015). Stylometry with R: A suite of tools. *Digital Scholarship in the Humanities*, *30*(1), 87–107.

Eder, M. (2017). Rolling stylometry. *Digital Scholarship in the Humanities*, *32*(3), 457–469. doi:10.1093/llc/fqv010

Eder, M. (2017). Stylometry with R: A Package for Computational Text Analysis. *The R Journal*, *9*(1), 167–175.

Eder, M., & Rybicki, J. (2011). Do birds of a feather really flock together, or how to choose training samples for authorship attribution. *Digital Scholarship in the Humanities*, *26*(3), 387–401.

Eder, M., Rybicki, J., & Kestemont, M. (2016). Stylometry with R: A package for computational text analysis. *The R Journal*, *8*(1), 107. doi:10.32614/RJ-2016-007

Elayan, H., Aloqaily, M., Karray, F., & Guizani, M. (2022). Internet of behavior (IoB) and explainable AI systems for influencing IoT behavior. *IEEE Network*, *37*(1), 62–68. doi:10.1109/MNET.009.2100500

ElayanH.AloqailyM.KarrayF.GuizaniM. (2022). *Internet of Behavior (IoB) and Explainable AI systems for influencing IoT behavior.* IEEE. arXiv:2109.07239v2 [cs.DC].

Ellen MacArthur Foundation. (2015). *Towards a Circular Economy: Business Rationale for an Accelerated Transition.* https://kidv.nl/media/rapportages/towards_a_circular_economy.pdf?1.2.1

Elvy, S.-A. (2022). *Data privacy and the Internet of Things.* Retrieved from UNESCO Inclusive Policy Lab: https://en.unesco.org/inclusivepolicylab/analytics/data-privacy-and-internet-things

Embarak, O. H. (2022). Internet of behaviour (IoB)-based AI models for personalized smart education systems. *Procedia Computer Science*, *203*, 103–110. doi:10.1016/j.procs.2022.07.015

Engle, R. F., & Granger, C. W. J. (1987). Co-Integration and Error Correction: Representation, Estimation, and Testing. *Econometrica*, *55*(2), 251. doi:10.2307/1913236

Ennis-O'Connor, M. (2018). *Dr. Google Turns 20: How Has It Changed Healthcare?* https://www.linkedin.com/pulse/dr-google-turns-20-how-has-changed-healthcare-marie-ennis-o-connor

European Commission. (2018). *Communication Artificial Intelligence for Europe.* COM (2018) 237 final.

European Commission. (2018). *Digital Education Action Plan.* European Commission. https://education.ec.europa.eu/focus-topics/digital-education/action-plan

Ewertowski, T. (2022). A Standard-Based Concept of the Integration of the Corporate Recovery Management Systems: Coping with Adversity and Uncertainty during a Pandemic. *Sustainability (Basel)*, *14*(3), 1254. Advance online publication. doi:10.3390u14031254

Fahmideh, M., Yan, J., Shen, J., Ahmad, A., Mougouei, D., & Shrestha, A. (2022). *Knowledge Management for Cloud Computing Field*. arXiv preprint arXiv:2202.07875.

Fama, E. F. (1965a). Random Walks in Stock Market Prices. *Financial Analysts Journal*, *21*(5), 55–59. Advance online publication. doi:10.2469/faj.v21.n5.55

Fama, E. F. (1965b). The Behavior of Stock-Market Prices. *The Journal of Business*, *38*(1), 34. Advance online publication. doi:10.1086/294743

Fama, E. F. (1970). Efficient Capital Markets: A Review of Theory and Empirical Work. *The Journal of Finance*, *25*(2), 383. Advance online publication. doi:10.2307/2325486

Fang, L. Y., Azmi, N. F. M., Yahya, Y., Sarkan, H., Sjarif, N. N. A., & Chuprat, S. (2018). Mobile business intelligence acceptance model for organisational decision making. *Bulletin of Electrical Engineering and Informatics*, *7*(4), 650–656. doi:10.11591/eei.v7i4.1356

Fani, S. V., & Subriadi, A. P. (2019). Business Continuity Plan: Examining of Multi-Usable Framework. *Procedia Computer Science*, *161*, 275–282. doi:10.1016/j.procs.2019.11.124

Farr, M., & Bailey, D. (2019). Uniting business continuity management and operational risk management. *Journal of Business Continuity & Emergency Planning*, *12*(4), 294–300. PMID:31200792

Fatum, R., & Yamamoto, Y. (2016). Intra-safe haven currency behavior during the global financial crisis. *Journal of International Money and Finance*, *66*, 49–64. Advance online publication. doi:10.1016/j.jimonfin.2015.12.007

Ferdman, B. M. (2014). The practice of inclusion in diverse Organizations: Toward a systemic and inclusive framewor. In B. M. Ferdman & B. Deane (Eds.), *Diversity at work: The practice of inclusion* (pp. 3–54). Jossey-Bass.

Ferdous, M. S., Chowdhury, F., & Alassafi, M. O. (2019). In search of self-sovereign identity leveraging blockchain technology. *IEEE Access : Practical Innovations, Open Solutions*, *7*, 103059–103079. doi:10.1109/ACCESS.2019.2931173

Fernandez, A. A., & Shaw, G. P. (2020). Academic Leadership in a time of crisis: The Coronavirus and Covid 19. *Journal of Leadership Studies*, *14*(18), 1–7. doi:10.1002/jls.21684

Fernández-Caramés, T. M., & Fraga-Lamas, P. (2018). A review on the use of blockchain for the internet of things. *IEEE Access : Practical Innovations, Open Solutions*, *6*, 32979–33001. doi:10.1109/ACCESS.2018.2842685

Fernando, M. S. (2017). IT disaster recovery system to ensure the business continuity of an organization. *2017 National Information Technology Conference (NITC)*, 46-48. 10.1109/NITC.2017.8285648

Figueiredo, A. D. (2017). Que competências para as novas gerações? In *O Futuro ao nosso alcance: Homenagem a Roberto Carneiro* (pp. 325–333). Universidade Católica Portuguesa.

Fiksdal, A. S., Kumbamu, A., Jadha, A. S., Cocos, C., Nelsen, L. A., Pathak, J., & McCormick, J. B. (2014). Evaluating the Process of Online Health Information Searching: A Qualitative Approach to Exploring Consumer Perspectives. *Journal of Medical Internet Research*, *16*(10), e224. doi:10.2196/jmir.3341 PMID:25348028

Filgueiras, F. (2022). New Pythias of public administration: Ambiguity and choice in AI systems as challenges for governance. *AI & Society*, *37*(4), 1473–1486. doi:10.100700146-021-01201-4

Findik, D., Tirgil, A., & Özbuğday, F. C. (2023). Industry 4.0 as an enabler of circular economy practices: Evidence from European SMEs. *Journal of Cleaner Production*, *410*(137281), 137281. doi:10.1016/j.jclepro.2023.137281

Firebase. (n.d.). *Security Rules and Firebase Authentication*. Retrieved 7 11, 2021, from https://firebase.google.com/docs/rules/rules-and-auth

Firmino, J. (2021). *Gestão no trabalho remoto: os principais desafios e as melhores práticas*. https://blog.runrun.it/gestao-no-trabalho-remoto/#:~:text=Resultados%3A%20os%20principais%20desafios%20no%20home%20office&text=Apontada%20por%2047%25%20dos%20gestores,est%C3%A3o%20sendo%20realizadas%20pelos%20colaboradores

Fisher, R., Norman, M., & Klett, M. (2017). Enhancing infrastructure resilience through business continuity planning. *Journal of Business Continuity & Emergency Planning*, *11*(2), 163–173. PMID:29256383

Foster, I., & Kesselman, C. (2022). *The history of the grid*. arXiv preprint arXiv:2204.04312.

Fourie, C. (2023). *How to identify & avoid hearing industry tricks that disempower you*. https://www.valuehearing.com.au/news/how-to-identify-and-avoid-the-hearing-industry-tricks-designed-to-disempower-you

Freire, M. (2008). Visualizing Program Similarity in the AC Plagiarism Detection System. *In ACM Proceedings of the Working Conference on Advanced Visual Interfaces*, 404-407.

Fuchs, M., Höpken, W., & Lexhagen, M. (2015). Applying business intelligence for knowledge generation in tourism destinations–A case study from Sweden. In *Tourism and leisure* (pp. 161–174). Springer Gabler. doi:10.1007/978-3-658-06660-4_11

Fukuyama, M. (2018). Society 5.0: Aiming for a new human-centered society. *Japan Spotlight*, *27*(5), 47–50.

Gaikwad, S. V., Vibhute, A. D., Kale, K. V., & Mehrotra, S. C. (2021). An innovative IoT based system for precision farming. *Computers and Electronics in Agriculture*, *187*, 1–12. doi:10.1016/j.compag.2021.106291

Gangl, C., & Krychtiuk, K. (2023). *Digital health - high tech or high touch? Wiener Medizinische Wochenschrift*. doi:10.100710354-022-00991-6

Gantz, J., & Reinsel, D. (2020). *The Digitization of the World: From Edge to Core*. IDC White Paper.

Garg, S., & Sangwan, S. (2021). Literature Review on Diversity and Inclusion at Workplace, 2012-2017. *Vision (Basel)*, *15*(1), 1–22. PMID:35076617

Gartner. (2020). *Gartner Identifies the Top Strategic Technology Trends for 2021*. https://www.gartner.com/smarterwithgartner/gartner-top-strategic-technology-trends-for-2021

Gasson, M. N. (2020). Internet of Behaviors (IoB) - The Good, the Bad and the Ugly. In *2020 International Conference on Artificial Intelligence and Information Technology (ICAIIT)* (pp. 1-6). IEEE.

Gawer, A. (2014). Bridging differing perspectives on technological platforms: Toward an integrative framework. *Research Policy*, *43*(7), 1239-1249. doi:10.1016/j.respol.2014.03.006

Gebre, E., Saroyan, A., & Aulls, M. W. (2015). Conceptions of Effective Teaching and Perceived Use of Computer Technologies in Active Learning Classrooms. *International Journal on Teaching and Learning in Higher Education*, *27*(2), 204–220.

Geisler, R. (2018). *Artificial intelligence in the travel and tourism industry adoption and impact* [Unpublished Master Thesis]. Nova School of Business and Economics.

Geissdoerfer, M., Morioka, S. N., de Carvalho, M. M., & Evans, S. (2018). Business models and supply chains for the circular economy. *Journal of Cleaner Production*, *190*, 712–721. doi:10.1016/j.jclepro.2018.04.159

Geissdoerfer, M., & Pieroni, M., Pigosso, D., & Soufani, K. (2020). Circular business models: A review. *Journal of Cleaner Production*, 277.

Geissdoerfer, M., Savaget, P., Bocken, N. M. P., & Hultink, E. J. (2017). The Circular Economy – A new sustainability paradigm? *Journal of Cleaner Production*, *143*, 757–768. doi:10.1016/j.jclepro.2016.12.048

Genomelink Organization. (2023). https://www.Genomelink.io

Gibbs, R. A. (2020). The Human Genome Project changed everything. *Nature Reviews. Genetics*, *21*(10), 575–576. doi:10.103841576-020-0275-3 PMID:32770171

Gibson, G. R. (1889). *The Stock Markets of London*. G.P. Putnam's Sons.

Gifford, S., Gripton, C., Williams, H., Lancaster, A., Bates, K. E., Williams, A. Y. Gilligan-Lee, K., Borthwick, A., & Farran, E. K. (2022). *Spatial Reasoning in early childhood*. Research Gate. https://doi.org/ doi:10.31234/osf.io/jnwpu

Gilmore, C. G., Lucey, B. M., & McManus, G. M. (2008). The dynamics of Central European equity market comovements. *The Quarterly Review of Economics and Finance*, *48*(3), 605–622. doi:10.1016/j.qref.2006.06.005

Gitchell, D., & Tran, N. (1999). Sim: A Utility For Detecting Similarity in Computer Programs. *SIGCSE Bulletin*, *31*(1), 266–270. doi:10.1145/384266.299783

Goldstein, M., & Flynn, S. (2022). Business Continuity Management Lessons Learned from COVID-19. *Journal of Business Continuity & Emergency Planning*, *15*, 360–380. PMID:35619223

Golosova, J., & Romanovs, A. (2018). The advantages and disadvantages of the blockchain technology. *2018 IEEE 6th Workshop on Advances in Information, Electronic and Electrical Engineering (AIEEE)*, 1-6. 10.1109/AIEEE.2018.8592253

Gonçalves, A. G. (2020). *Home office trouxe novos desafios para gestores*. https://cfa.org.br/home-office-trouxe-novos-desafios-para-gestores/

Goni, F. A., Gholamzadeh Chofreh, A., Estaki Orakani, Z., Klemeš, J. J., Davoudi, M., & Mardani, A. (2021). Sustainable business model: A review and framework development. *Clean Technologies and Environmental Policy*, *23*(3), 889–897. doi:10.100710098-020-01886-z

Goodman, B., & Flaxman, S. (2016). EU regulations on algorithmic decision-making and a" right to explanation". ICML workshop on human interpretability in machine learning.

Google/CodingCompetitions. (n.d.). *Google's Coding Competitions*. Retrieved 5 29, 2023, from https://codingcompetitions.withgoogle.com/

Gracey, A. (2019). Building an organisational resilience maturity framework. *Journal of Business Continuity & Emergency Planning*, *13*(4). PMID:32438952

Granger, C. W. J. (1969). Investigating Causal Relations by Econometric Models and Cross-spectral Methods. *Econometrica*, *37*(3), 424. doi:10.2307/1912791

Granger, C. W. J. (1988). Some recent development in a concept of causality. *Journal of Econometrics*, *39*(1–2), 199–211. doi:10.1016/0304-4076(88)90045-0

Gregory, A. W., & Hansen, B. E. (1996a). Residual-based tests for cointegration in models with regime shifts. *Journal of Econometrics*, *70*(1), 99–126. doi:10.1016/0304-4076(69)41685-7

Gregory, A. W., & Hansen, B. E. (1996b). Tests for cointegration in models with regime and trend shifts. *Oxford Bulletin of Economics and Statistics*, *58*(2), 555–560. doi:10.1111/j.1468-0084.1996.mp58003008.x

Grieve, J. (2007). Quantitative authorship attribution: An evaluation of techniques. *Literary and Linguistic Computing*, *22*(3), 251–270. doi:10.1093/llc/fqm020

Gros, B. (2006). Digital games in Education: The Design of Games-Based Learning Environments. *Journal of Research on Technology in Education*, *40*(1), 23–38. doi:10.1080/15391523.2007.10782494

Guedes, E. F., Santos, R. P. C., Figueredo, L. H. R., Da Silva, P. A., Dias, R. M. T. S., & Zebende, G. F. (2022). Efficiency and Long-Range Correlation in G-20 Stock Indexes: A Sliding Windows Approach. *Fluctuation and Noise Letters*, *21*(4), 2250033. Advance online publication. doi:10.1142/S021947752250033X

Guinot, J. (2020). Changing the economic paradigm: Towards a sustainable business model. *International Journal of Sustainable Development and Planning*, *15*(5), 603–610. doi:10.18280/ijsdp.150502

Gujarati, D. N. (2004). *Basic Econometrics*. https://doi.org/ doi:10.1126cience.1186874

Gulec, T. C., & Aktas, H. (2019). Testing the Market Efficiency in Crypto Currency Markets Using Long-Memory and Heteroscedasticity Tests. *Osmangazi University Journal of Economics and Administrative Sciences, 14*(2).

Guo, X., Zhang, G., & Zhang, Y. (2022). A Comprehensive Review of Blockchain Technology-Enabled Smart Manufacturing: A Framework, Challenges and Future Research Directions. *Sensors (Basel)*, *23*(1), 155. doi:10.339023010155 PMID:36616753

Gupta, R., & Shanbhag, S. (2021). A Survey of Peer-to-Peer Ride Sharing Services using blockchain. *International Journal of Engineering Research & Technology (Ahmedabad)*, *10*(8), 349–353.

Guttentag, D. A. (2010). Virtual reality: Applications and implications for tourism. *Tourism Management*, *31*(5), 637–651. doi:10.1016/j.tourman.2009.07.003

GWI. (2023). *Global Mobile Consumer Trends Report*. https://www.gwi.com/

Habib, M. M., & Stracca, L. (2012). Getting beyond carry trade: What makes a safe haven currency? *Journal of International Economics*, *87*(1), 50–64. Advance online publication. doi:10.1016/j.jinteco.2011.12.005

HackerEarth. (n.d.). *HackerEarth Platform*. Retrieved 11 21, 2022, from https://www.hackerearth.com/

HackerRank. (n.d.). *HackerRank Platform*. Retrieved 11 21, 2022, from https://www.hackerrank.com/

Hadri, K. (2000). Testing for stationarity in heterogeneous panel data. *The Econometrics Journal*, *3*(2), 148–161. Advance online publication. doi:10.1111/1368-423X.00043

Hage, J., Vermeer, B., & Verburg, G. (2013). Plagiarism Detection for Haskell with Holmes. *ACM Proceedings of the 3rd Computer Science Education Research Conference on Computer Science Education Research,* 19-30.

Haider, H. F., Flook, M., Aparício, M., Ribeiro, D., Antunes, M., Szczepek, A. J., Hoare, D. J., Fialho, G., Paço, J. C., & Caria, H. (2017). Biomarkers of Presbycusis and Tinnitus in a Portuguese Older Population. *Frontiers in Aging Neuroscience*, *1*(9), 346. doi:10.3389/fnagi.2017.00346 PMID:29163129

Hajder, P., & Rauch, Ł. (2021). Moving Multiscale Modelling to the Edge: Benchmarking and Load Optimization for Cellular Automata on Low Power Microcomputers. *Processes (Basel, Switzerland)*, *9*(12), 2225. doi:10.3390/pr9122225

Halaburda, H., & Gandal, N. (2014). Competition in the Cryptocurrency Market. SSRN *Electronic Journal*. https://doi.org/ doi:10.2139/ssrn.2506463

Hallioui, A., Herrou, B., Santos, R. S., Katina, P. F., & Egbue, O. (2022). Systems-based approach to contemporary business management: An enabler of business sustainability in a context of industry 4.0, circular economy, competitiveness and diverse stakeholders. *Journal of Cleaner Production, 373*, 133819. doi:10.1016/j.jclepro.2022.133819

Hampl, F., Vágnerová Linnertová, D., & Horváth, M. (2022). *Crypto Havens During War Times? Evidence from the Russian Invasion of Ukraine.* Cryptocurrency Research Ejournal.

Hanisch, S., Arias-Cabarcos, P., Parra-Arnau, J., & Strufe, T. (2021). *Privacy-Protecting Techniques for Behavioral Data: A Survey.* arXiv preprint arXiv:2109.04120.

Hanson, T. L., Drumheller, K., Mallard, J., McKee, C., & Schlegel, P. (2010). Cell phones, text messaging, and Facebook: Competing time demands of today's college students. *College Teaching, 59*(1), 23–30. doi:10.1080/87567555.2010.489078

HanX.HuangR. (2017). Promover o ensino da matemática e o desenvolvimento profissional do professor através do estudo de aula paralelo. *Quadrante, 26*(2), 5–18. doi:10.48489/quadrante.22953

Han, Z., Wang, Q., & Yan, X. (2019). How responsible leadership predicts Organizational citizenship behavior for the environment in China. *Leadership and Organization Development Journal, 40*(3), 305–318. doi:10.1108/LODJ-07-2018-0256

Haque, A. (2021). The COVID-19 pandemic and the role of responsible leadership in health care: Thinking beyond employee well-being and Organizational sustainability. *Leadership in Health Services, 34*(1), 52–68. doi:10.1108/LHS-09-2020-0071 PMID:33818971

Haque, A., Fernando, M., & Caputi, P. (2018). Responsible leadership, affective commitment and intention to quit: An individual level analysis. *Leadership and Organization Development Journal, 40*(1), 45–64. doi:10.1108/LODJ-12-2017-0397

Hartl, R. M. B. (2020). Implantable Hearing Aids: Where are we in 2020? *Laryngoscope Investigative Otolaryngology, 5*(6), 1184–1191. doi:10.1002/lio2.495 PMID:33364411

Hartmann, K., Heitmann, M., & Siebert, C. (2023). More than a Feeling: Accuracy and Application of Sentiment Analysis. *International Journal of Research in Marketing, 40*(1), 75-87. doi:10.1016/j.ijresmar.2022.05.005

Hassanein, K., & Head, M. (2007). Manipulating perceived social presence through the web interface and its impact on attitude towards online shopping. *International Journal of Human-Computer Studies, 65*(8), 689–708. doi:10.1016/j.ijhcs.2006.11.018

Haworth, T. J., Clarke, C. J., Rahman, W., Winter, A. J., & Facchini, S. (2018). The FRIED grid of mass-loss rates for externally irradiated protoplanetary discs. *Monthly Notices of the Royal Astronomical Society, 481*(1), 452–466. doi:10.1093/mnrasty2323

Hearing Implant Market Report. (2023). *Future Market Insights.* https://www.futuremarketinsights.com/reports/hearing-implants-market

Hecht, J. A. (2002). Business continuity management. *Communications of the Association for Information Systems, 8*, 444–450. doi:10.17705/1CAIS.00830

Heine, P. A. (2004). Anatomy of the ear. *The Veterinary Clinics of North America. Small Animal Practice, 34*(2), 379–395. doi:10.1016/j.cvsm.2003.10.003 PMID:15062614

Herbane, B. (2010). The evolution of business continuity management: A historical review of practices and drivers. *Business History, 52*(6), 978–1002. doi:10.1080/00076791.2010.511185

Herranz, E. (2017). Unit root tests. In *Wiley Interdisciplinary Reviews*. Computational Statistics. doi:10.1002/wics.1396

Hesselmann, C., Gertheiss, J., & Müller, J. P. (2021). *Ride Sharing & Data Privacy: An Analysis of the State of Practice.* arXiv preprint arXiv:2110.09188.

Hevner, A. R., March, S. T., Park, J., & Ram, S. (2004). Design Science in Information Systems Research. *Management Information Systems Quarterly*, *28*(1), 75–105. doi:10.2307/25148625

He, Z., Huang, H., Choi, H., & Bilgihan, A. (2023). Building organizational resilience with digital transformation. *Journal of Service Management*, *34*(1), 147–171. doi:10.1108/JOSM-06-2021-0216

Hilbert, M. (2011). *GoOnline! Marketing in the hearing industry.* https://www.audiologypractices.org/go-online-marketing-in-the-hearing-industry

Hiles, A. (2007). An introduction to business continuity planning. In A. Hiles (Ed.), *The Definitive Handbook of Business Continuity Planning* (2nd ed., pp. xxiii–xxvii). John Wiley & Sons, Ltd.

Hiles, A. (2011b). Developing and implementing the written plan. In A. Hiles (Ed.), *The definitive handbook of Business Continuity Management* (3rd ed.). John Wiley & Sons, Ltd.

Hlaváč, J., & Štefanovič, J. (2020). *Machine learning and business intelligence or from descriptive analytics to predictive analytics. In 2020 Cybernetics and Informatics (KandI).* IEEE.

Hočevar, B., & Jaklič, J. (2010). Assessing benefits of business intelligence systems–a case study. *Management*, *15*(1), 87–119.

Hoessler, S., & Carbon, C. C. (2022). Digital transformation and ambidexterity: A literature review on exploration and exploitation activities in companies' digital transformation. *International Journal of Innovation Management*, *26*(08), 2230003. doi:10.1142/S1363919622300033

Hoffman, L., Moreau, P., Stremersch, S., & Wedel, M. (2022). The Rise of New Technologies in Marketing: A Framework and Outlook. *Journal of Marketing*, *86*(1), 1–6. doi:10.1177/00222429211061636

Hofstetter, J. S., De Marchi, V., Sarkis, J., Govindan, K., Klassen, R., Ometto, A. R., Spraul, K. S., Bocken, N., Ashton, W. S., Sharma, S., Jaeger-Erben, M., Jensen, C., Dewick, P., Schröder, P., Sinkovics, N., Ibrahim, S. E., Fiske, L., Goerzen, A., & Vazquez-Brust, D. (2021). From sustainable global value chains to circular economy-different silos, different perspectives, but many opportunities to build bridges. *Circular Economy and Sustainability*, *1*(1), 21–47. doi:10.100743615-021-00015-2 PMID:34888550

Hollander, E., & Park, B. B. (2008). Inclusive leadership and leader-follower relations: concepts, research and applications. The Member Connector, International Leadership Association, 5, 4-7.

Hollander, E. (2012). *Inclusive leadership: The essential leader follower relationship.* Routledge. doi:10.4324/9780203809914

Holmes, D. I. (1998). The Evolution of Stylometry in Humanities Scholarship. *Literary and Linguistic Computing*, *13*(3), 111–117. doi:10.1093/llc/13.3.111

Holmes, D. I., & Forsyth, R. S. (1995). A Linguistic Study of Edgar Allan Poe's Tales of Terror: A Stylometric Analysis of his Short Stories. *Computers and the Humanities*, *29*(4), 295–313.

Hong, P., Jung, J., & Kim, H. (2019). A review of business model innovation research and trends. *Journal of Innovation Management*, *7*(3), 1–20.

Höpken, W., & Fuchs, M. (2022). Business Intelligence in Tourism. In *Handbook of e-Tourism* (pp. 497–527). Springer International Publishing. doi:10.1007/978-3-030-48652-5_3

Hopwood, B., Mellor, M., & O'Brien, G. (2005). Sustainable development: Mapping different approaches. *Sustainable Development (Bradford), 13*(1), 38–52. doi:10.1002d.244

Horakova, M., & Skalska, H. (2013). Business Intelligence and Implementation in a Small Enterprise. *Journal of Systems Integration, 4*(2), 50–61.

Horta, N., Dias, R., Revez, C., & Alexandre, P. (2022). *Cryptocurrencies and G7 capital markets integrate in periods of extreme volatility.* Academic Press.

Horta, N., Dias, R., Revez, C., Heliodoro, P., & Alexandre, P. (2022). Spillover and Quantitative Link Between Cryptocurrency Shocks and Stock Returns: New Evidence From G7 Countries. *Balkans Journal of Emerging Trends in Social Sciences, 5*(1), 1–14. doi:10.31410/Balkans.JETSS.2022.5.1.1-14

Hu, K. (2023). *ChatGPT sets record for fastest-growing user base - analyst note.* Reuters. https://www.reuters.com/technology/chatgpt-sets-record-fastest-growing-user-base-analyst-note-2023-02-01/

Huang, T., & Liao, S.-L. (2017). Creating e-shopping multisensory flow experience through augmented-reality interactive technology. *Internet Research, 27*(2), 449–475. doi:10.1108/IntR-11-2015-0321

Hung, J. (2018). A cross-linguistic comparison of adjective ordering restrictions in English, Mandarin, and Japanese. *Language and Linguistics (Taipei), 19*(4), 597–636.

Im, K. S., Pesaran, M. H., & Shin, Y. (2003). Testing for unit roots in heterogeneous panels. *Journal of Econometrics, 115*(1), 53–74. Advance online publication. doi:10.1016/S0304-4076(03)00092-7

InamdarS. R.GursoyK. (2019). *Cloud hosted business-data driven BI platforms.* doi:10.7282/t3-f5vq-4938

IoT Analytics. (2023). *IoT connections forecast.* IoT Analytics. Retrieved June 2023, from https://iot-analytics.com/number-connected-iot-devices/

Irace, A. L., Sharma, K., Reed, N. S., & Golub, J. S. (2021). Smartphone-Based Applications to Detect Hearing Loss: A Review of Current Technology. *Journal of the American Geriatrics Society, 69*(2), 307–316. doi:10.1111/jgs.16985 PMID:33341098

ISACA. (2018). *COBIT 2019 Framework - Governance and Management Objectives.* ISACA.

ISACA. (2018). *COBIT 2019 Framework - Governance and Management Objectives.* Schaumburg, IL 60173, USA: ISACA.

ISO 22300. (2021). *Security and resilience - Vocabulary.* Geneva, Suiça: ISO.

ISO 22301. (2019). *Societal security - Business continuity management systems - Requirements.* Switzerland: ISO.

ISO/IEC 27001. (2023). *ISO/IEC 27001 Information security management systems Requirements.* Retrieved from ISO: https://www.iso.org/standard/27001 ISO/IEC 27002. (2022). *Information security, cybersecurity and privacy protection - Information security controls.* Switzerland: ISO.

ISO/IEC 27031. (2011). *Information technology - Security techniques - Guidelines for information and communication technology readiness for business continuity.* ISO/IEC.

ITIL. (2019). *ITIL Foundation ITIL* (4th ed.). AXELOS.

Ivanov, S., & Webster, C. (2017). Adoption of robots, artificial intelligence and service automation by travel, tourism and hospitality companies – a cost-benefit analysis. *International Scientific Conference "Contemporary tourism – traditions and innovations".*

Jabeen, F., Al Zaidi, S., & Al Dhaheri, M. H. (2022). Automation and artificial intelligence in hospitality and tourism. *Tourism Review*, *77*(4), 1043–1061. doi:10.1108/TR-09-2019-0360

Jacobson, I., Lawson, H., Ng, P., McMahon, P., & Goedicke, M. (2019). *The Essentials of Modern Software Engineering: Free the Practices from the Method Prisons*. ACM Books.

Jacobson, I., Ng, P.-W., McMahon, P. E., Spence, I., & Lidman, S. (2012). The essence of software engineering: The SEMAT kernel. *Communications of the ACM*, *55*(12), 42–49. Advance online publication. doi:10.1145/2380656.2380670

Jagesar, R. R., Vorstman, J. A., & Kas, M. J. (2014). Requirements and Operational Guidelines for Secure and Sustainable Digital Phenotyping: Design and Development Study. *Journal of Medical Internet Research*, *23*(4), e20996. doi:10.2196/20996 PMID:33825695

Jamshidi, M., Yahya, S. I., Nouri, L., Hashemi-Dezaki, H., Rezaei, A., & Chaudhary, M. A. (2023). A Super-Efficient GSM Triplexer for 5G-Enabled IoT in Sustainable Smart Grid Edge Computing and the Metaverse. *Sensors (Basel)*, *23*(7), 3775. doi:10.339023073775 PMID:37050835

Janary, J. (2022). *Medida provisória regulamenta teletrabalho e muda regras do auxílio-alimentação*. https://www.camara.leg.br/noticias/861554-medida-provisoria-regulamenta-teletrabalho-e-muda-regras-do-auxilio-alimentacao/

Jan, B., Farman, H., Khan, M., Talha, M., & Din, I. U. (2019). Designing a smart transportation system: An internet of things and big data approach. *IEEE Wireless Communications*, *26*(4), 73–79. doi:10.1109/MWC.2019.1800512

Jankavski, A. (2021). Brasileiros querem manter home office, mas temem excesso de trabalho, diz estudo. *CNN Brasil*. https://www.cnnbrasil.com.br/business/maioria-aprova-o-home-office-mas-ha-preocupacao-com-excesso-de-trabalho/

Jariyayothin, P., Jeravong-aram, K., Ratanachaijaroen, N., Tantidham, T., & Intakot, P. (2018). IoT Backyard: Smart watering control system. *Seventh ICT International Student Project Conference (ICT-ISPC)*, 1-6.

Jarque, C. M., & Bera, A. K. (1980). Efficient tests for normality, homoscedasticity and serial independence of regression residuals. *Economics Letters*, *6*(3), 255–259. Advance online publication. doi:10.1016/0165-1765(80)90024-5

Järveläinen, J. (2013). IT incidents and business impacts: Validating a framework for continuity management in information systems. *International Journal of Information Management*, *33*(3), 583–590. doi:10.1016/j.ijinfomgt.2013.03.001

Javaid, M., Haleem, A., Singh, R. P., Khan, S., & Suman, R. (2022). An extensive study on Internet of behavior (IoB) enabled healthcare-systems: Features, facilitators, and challenges. BenchCouncil Transactions on Benchmarks. *Standards and Evaluations*, *2*(4), 100085.

Javaid, M., Haleem, A., Singh, R. P., Rab, S., & Suman, R. (2021). Internet of Behaviours (IoB) and its role in customer services. *Sensors International*, *2*, 100122. doi:10.1016/j.sintl.2021.100122

Javaid, M., Haleem, A., Singh, R., Khan, S., & Suman, R. (2022). An extensive study on Internet of Behavior (IoB) enabled healthcare systems: Features, facilitators, and challenges. *BenchCouncil Transactions on Benchmarks. Standards and Evaluations*, *2*, 1–10.

Javed, B., Abdullah, I., Zaffar, M. A., Haque, A., & Rubab, U. (2018). Inclusive leadership and innovative work behavior: The role of psychological empowerment. *Journal of Management & Organization*, *25*(4), 554–571. doi:10.1017/jmo.2018.50

Jeana, P., Tai, F., Singh-Estivalet, A., Lelli, A., Scandola, C., & Megharba, S. (2023). Single-cell transcriptomic profiling of the mouse cochlea: An atlas for targeted therapies. *Proceedings of the National Academy of Sciences of the United States of America*, *120*(26), e2221744120. doi:10.1073/pnas.2221744120 PMID:37339214

Jerónimo, H.M., Henriques, P.L., & Carvalho, S.I. (2022). Being inclusive boots impact of diversity practices on employee engagement. *Management Research: Journal of Iberoamerican Academy of Management*, *20*(29), 129-147.

Jiang, L., Wang, D., He, Y., & Shu, Y. (2023). Advances in gene therapy hold promise for treating hereditary hearing loss. *Molecular Therapy*, *31*(4), 934–950. doi:10.1016/j.ymthe.2023.02.001 PMID:36755494

Jiang, L., Yang, Z., & Jun, M. (2013). Measuring consumer perceptions of online shopping convenience. *Journal of Service Management*, *24*(2), 191–214. doi:10.1108/09564231311323962

Jiang, S., Cao, J., Wu, H., Chen, K., & Liu, X. (2023). Privacy-preserving and efficient data sharing for blockchain-based intelligent transportation systems. *Information Sciences*, *635*, 72–85. doi:10.1016/j.ins.2023.03.121

Jiffriya, M., Jahan, M. A., & Ragel, R. (2021). Plagiarism detection tools and techniques: A comprehensive survey. *Journal of Science-FAS-SEUSL*, *2*(02), 47–64.

Jira. (n.d.). *Jira Software*. Retrieved 9 15, 2022, from https://www.atlassian.com/software/jira

Jockers, M. L. (2013). *Macroanalysis: Digital Methods and Literary History*. University of Illinois Press. doi:10.5406/illinois/9780252037528.001.0001

Johnson, M., & Elbaz, F. (1984). Teacher Thinking: A Study of Practical Knowledge. *Curriculum Inquiry*, *14*(4), 465–468. doi:10.2307/3202267

Journée, R. J., & Weber, M. E. (2014). A bonded experience: "value creation as the creation of an experience, within a business relationship". *Proceedings of the 7th World Conference on Mass Customization, Personalization, and Co-Creation (MCPC 2014)*. 10.1007/978-3-319-04271-8_1

Joy, M., & Luck, M. (1999). Plagiarism in Programming Assignments. *IEEE Transactions on Education*, *42*(2), 129–133. doi:10.1109/13.762946

Juola, P. (2006). Authorship Attribution. *Foundations and Trends in Information Retrieval*, *1*(3), 233–334. doi:10.1561/1500000005

Juola, P. (2015). The Rowling case: A proposed standard analytic protocol for authorship questions. *Digital Scholarship in the Humanities*, *30*(suppl_1), i100–i113. doi:10.1093/llc/fqv040

Juzar, H., Habib, K. M., & Bhuiyan, M. (2020). A Comprehensive Study on the Privacy Threats and Countermeasures in the IoT-based Cyber-Physical System. *IEEE Access : Practical Innovations, Open Solutions*, *8*, 216541–216563.

JWT. (n.d.). *JSON Web Tokens*. Retrieved 9 15, 2022, from https://jwt.io/

Kabakuş, A. K., Özköse, H., & Ayaz, A. (2023). Society 5.0 research: performance analysis and science mapping. *Gümüşhane Üniversitesi Sosyal Bilimler Dergisi*, *14*(1), 311-328. https://derg ipark.org.tr/en/pub/gumus/issue/75752/1202690

Kahn, W. A. (1990). Psychological conditions of personal engagement and disengagement at work. *Academy of Management Journal*, *33*(4), 692–724. doi:10.2307/256287

Kanda, W., Geissdoerfer, M., & Hjelm, O. (2021). From circular business models to circular business ecosystems. *Business Strategy and the Environment*, *30*(6), 2814–2829. doi:10.1002/bse.2895

Kang, H. S., Lee, J. Y., Choi, S., Kim, H., Park, J. H., Son, J. Y., Kim, B. H., & Noh, S. D. (2016). Smart manufacturing: Past research, present findings, and future directions. *International Journal of Precision Engineering and Manufacturing-Green Technology*, *3*(1), 111–128. doi:10.100740684-016-0015-5

Kappelmann, K., Rädle, J., & Stevens, L. (2022). Engaging, Large-Scale Functional Programming Education in Physical and Virtual Space. *Electronic Proceedings in Theoretical Computer Science, 363*, 93–113. doi:10.4204/EPTCS.363.6

Karaömer, Y., & Acaravci, S. K. (2023). Adaptive Market Hypothesis: Evidence From the Cryptocurrency Market. *Iranian Journal of Management Studies, 16*(1). Advance online publication. doi:10.22059/IJMS.2022.336833.674889

Kasinathan, P., Pugazhendhi, R., Elavarasan, R., Ramachandaramurthy, V., Ramanathan, V., Subramanian, S., Kumar, S., Nandhagopal, K., Raghavan, R., Rangasamy, S., Devendiran, R., & Alsharif, M. (2022). Realization of Sustainable Development Goals with Disruptive Technologies by Integrating Industry 5.0, Society 5.0, Smart Cities and Villages. *Sustainability (Basel), 14*(22), 15285. doi:10.3390u142215258

Katsaros, K. (2022). Exploring the inclusive leadership and employee change participation relationship: The role of workplace belongingness and meaning-making. *Baltic Journal of Management, 17*(2), 158–173. doi:10.1108/BJM-03-2021-0104

Keidanren. (2018). *Healthcare in Society 5.0*. Keidranen. https://www.keidanren.or.jp/en/policy/2018/021_overview.pdf

Kellmereit, B. (2015). Focus Groups. *International Journal of Sales, Retailing & Marketing, 4*(9), 42-52. https://www.circleinternational.co.uk/journals/ijsrm/current-past-issues-ijsrm/

Kemp, S. (2023), Digital 2023 April Global Statshot Report. *Data Reportal.*

Keng, C., Ting, H., & Chen, Y. T. (2011). Effects of virtual-experience combinations on consumer- related sense of virtual community. *Internet Research, 4*(21), 408–434. doi:10.1108/10662241111158308

Keshtgary, M., & Deljoo, A. (2012). An efficient wireless sensor network for precision agriculture. *Canadian Journal on Multimedia and Wireless Networks, 3*(1), 1–5.

Kestemont, M., Stover, J.A., Koppel, M., Karsdorp, F., & Daelemans, W. (2020). Overview of the cross-domain authorship attribution task at PAN 2020. *CLEF 2020 Labs and Workshops, Notebook Papers. CEUR Workshop Proceedings.*

Kestemont, M., Daelemans, W., & de Gussem, J. (2014). Exploring the boundaries of cross-genre authorship attribution. *Digital Scholarship in the Humanities, 29*(1), 99–114.

Khanam, Z., & Tarab, S. (2022). A moderated-mediation model of the relationship between responsible leadership, citizenship behavior and patient satisfaction. *IIM Ranchi Journal of Management Studies, 2*(1), 114-134.

Khan, D., Jung, L. T., & Hashmani, M. A. (2021). Systematic literature review of challenges in blockchain scalability. *Applied Sciences (Basel, Switzerland), 11*(20), 9372. doi:10.3390/app11209372

Khormali, A., Park, J., Alasmary, H., Anwar, A., Saad, M., & Mohaisen, D. (2021). Domain name system security and privacy: A contemporary survey. *Computer Networks, 185*, 107699. doi:10.1016/j.comnet.2020.107699

King, D. (2021). *The Internet of Behaviors (IoB)*. What It Is and How It Can Impact Your Business. Forbes.

King, D. L. (2003). Moving Towards a Business Continuity Culture. *Network Security, 1*(12). https://doi.org/https://doi.org/10.1016/S1353-4858(03)00112-0

Knani, M., Echchakoui, S., & Ladhari, R. (2022). Artificial intelligence in tourism and hospitality: Bibliometric analysis and research agenda. *International Journal of Hospitality Management, 107*, 103317. doi:10.1016/j.ijhm.2022.103317

Kong, H., Wang, K., Qiu, X., Cheung, C., & Bu, N. (2023). 30 years of artificial intelligence (AI) research relating to the hospitality and tourism industry. *International Journal of Contemporary Hospitality Management, 35*(6), 2157–2177. doi:10.1108/IJCHM-03-2022-0354

Kopalle, K., Gangwar, M., Kaplan, A., Ramachandran, D., Reinartz, W., & Rindfleisch, A. (2022). Examining artificial intelligence (AI) technologies in marketing via a global lens: Current trends and future research opportunities. *International Journal of Research in Marketing*, *39*(2), 522–540. doi:10.1016/j.ijresmar.2021.11.002

Koppel, M., & Schler, J. (2004). Authorship Verification as a One-Class Classification Problem. *Proceedings of the 21st International Conference on Machine Learning*, 49. 10.1145/1015330.1015448

Koppel, M., Schler, J., & Argamon, S. (2009). Computational Methods in Authorship Attribution. *Journal of the American Society for Information Science and Technology*, *60*(1), 9–26. doi:10.1002/asi.20961

Koppel, M., Schler, J., & Argamon, S. (2011). Authorship Attribution in the Wild. *Language Resources and Evaluation*, *45*(1), 83–94. doi:10.100710579-009-9111-2

Koppel, M., Schler, J., & Argamon, S. (2011). Computational methods in authorship attribution. *Journal of the American Society for Information Science and Technology*, *62*(1), 17–49.

Koppel, M., Schler, J., & Bonchek-Dokow, E. (2007). Measuring differentiability: Unmasking pseudonymous authors. *Journal of Machine Learning Research*, *8*, 1261–1276.

Koppel, M., & Winter, Y. (2014). Determining if two documents are by the same author. *Journal of the Association for Information Science and Technology*, *65*(1), 178–187. doi:10.1002/asi.22954

Korhonen, J., Honkasalo, A., & Seppälä, J. (2018). Circular Economy: The Concept and its Limitations. Ecological Economics. *Ecological Economics*, *143*, 37–46. doi:10.1016/j.ecolecon.2017.06.041

Korkmaz, A. V., Van Engen, M. L., Knappert, L., & Schalk, R. (2022). About and beyond leading uniqueness and belongingness: A systematic review of inclusive leadership research. *Human Resource Management Review*, *32*(4), 1–20. doi:10.1016/j.hrmr.2022.100894

Korže, S.Z. (2019). From Industry 4.0 to Tourism 4.0. *Innovative Issues and Approaches in Social Sciences*, *12*(3), 29-52.

Kraus, S., Durst, S., Ferreira, S., Veiga, P., Kailer, N., & Weinmann, A. (2022). Digital transformation in business and management research: An overview of the current status quo. *International Journal of Information Management*, *63*, 1–18. doi:10.1016/j.ijinfomgt.2021.102466

Krishna, R., & Kummitha, R. (2017). *Social Entrepreneurship and Social Inclusion: Processes, practices and prospects.* Palgrave Macmillan.

Krueger, R. A., & Casey, M. A. (2009). *Focus groups: A pratical guide for applied research* (4th ed.). Sage.

Kshetri, N. (2020). The Internet of Behaviors (IoB). *Communications of the ACM*, *63*(5), 20–23.

Kühn, S., & Boshoff, C. (2023). The role of plot in brand story construction: A neurophysiological perspective. *Journal of Strategic Marketing*, *31*(2), 471–497. doi:10.1080/0965254X.2021.1968018

Kuknor, S. C., & Bhattacharya, S. (2020). Inclusive leadership: New age leadership to foster Organizational inclusion. *European Journal of Training and Development*, *46*(9), 771–797. doi:10.1108/EJTD-07-2019-0132

Küng, J., & Gonçalves, P. (2021). Internet of Behaviors (IoB) and the Human Value System: A Review. In *2021 9th IEEE International Conference on Mobile Cloud Computing, Services, and Engineering (MobileCloud)* (pp. 135-140). IEEE.

Kushlev, K., & Leitao, M. R. (2020). The effects of smartphones on well-being: Theoretical integration and research agenda. *Current Opinion in Psychology*, *36*, 77–82. doi:10.1016/j.copsyc.2020.05.001

Kushwaha, D. S., Khan, S. A., & Saha, S. (2020). IoB-IoT enabled collaborative behavioral pattern analysis for smart living environments. *Journal of Ambient Intelligence and Humanized Computing, 11*, 5969–5990.

Kwok, A. O. (2023). The next frontier of the internet of behaviors: data-driven nudging in smart tourism. *Journal of Tourism Futures*, 1-7.

Lai, W. C., & Hung, W. H. (2018). A framework of cloud and AI based intelligent hotel. *Proceedings of the International Conference on Electronic Business (ICEB)*, 36-43.

Landry, E.C., Scholte, M., Su, P.M., Hostink, Y., Mandavia, Rovers, M.M., & Schilder, A.G.M. (2022). Early Health Economic Modeling of Novel Therapeutics in Age-related Hearing Loss. *Front Neurosci., 16*, 769983. http://doi.org/.769983 doi:10.3389/fnins.2022

Langley, D. J. (2022). Digital Product-Service Systems: The role of data in the transition to Servitization business models. *Sustainability (Basel), 14*(3), 1303. doi:10.3390u14031303

Lapa, J., Bernardino, J., & Figueiredo, A. (2014). A comparative analysis of open source business intelligence platforms. *Proceedings of the International Conference on Information Systems and Design of Communication*, 86-92. 10.1145/2618168.2618182

Lappas, T., Sabnis, G., & Valkanas, G. (2016). The impact of fake reviews on online visibility: A vulnerability assessment of the hotel industry. *Information Systems Research, 27*(4), 940-961.

Lasi, H., Fettke, P., Kemper, H. G., Feld, T., & Hoffmann, M. (2014). Industry 4.0. *Business & Information Systems Engineering, 6*(4), 239–242. doi:10.100712599-014-0334-4

Laubscher, M., & Marinelli, T. (2014a). Going Green - CARE INNOVATION. *Integration of Circular Economy in Business.*

Laubscher, M., & Marinelli, T. (2014b). *Integration of circular economy in business.* Academic Press.

Lavelle, B., Yamamoto, K. N., & Kinnen, M. (2022). Cryptocurrencies, Correlations, and COVID-19: Diversifiers, Hedge, or Safe Haven? *Review of Integrative Business and Economics Research, 11*(2).

Le Tran, V., & Leirvik, T. (2020). Efficiency in the markets of crypto-currencies. *Finance Research Letters, 35*, 101382. Advance online publication. doi:10.1016/j.frl.2019.101382

Leal, J. P., & Silva, F. (2003). Mooshak: A Web-based multi-site programming contest system. *Software, Practice & Experience, 33*(6), 567–581. doi:10.1002pe.522

Lee, K., Hoti, K., Hughes, J.D., & Emmerton, L. (2017). Dr Google Is Here to Stay but Health Care Professionals Are Still Valued: An Analysis of Health Care Consumers' Internet Navigation Support Preferences. *J Med Internet Res, 19*(6), e210:1-9

Lee, J. H., Yang, G., Kim, C. H., Mahajan, R. L., Lee, S. Y., & Park, S. J. (2022). Flexible solid-state hybrid supercapacitors for the internet of everything (IoE). *Energy & Environmental Science, 15*(6), 2233–2258. doi:10.1039/D1EE03567C

LeetCode. (n.d.). *LeetCode Programming Platform.* Retrieved 11 21, 2022, from https://leetcode.com/

Lele, S. (2013). Rethinking sustainable development. *Current History, 112*(757), 311–316.

Lennerholt, C., van Laere, J., & Söderström, E. (2018). Implementation challenges of self service business intelligence: A literature review. *51st Hawaii International Conference on System Sciences*, 5055-5063. 10.24251/HICSS.2018.631

Levin, A., Lin, C. F., & Chu, C. S. J. (2002). Unit root tests in panel data: Asymptotic and finite-sample properties. *Journal of Econometrics, 108*(1), 1–24. Advance online publication. doi:10.1016/S0304-4076(01)00098-7

Lewandowski, M. (2016). Designing the business models for circular economy—Towards the conceptual framework. *Sustainability (Basel)*, *8*(1), 43. doi:10.3390u8010043

Lewnes, A. (2021). Commentary: The Future of Marketing Is Agile. *Journal of Marketing*, *85*(1), 64–67. doi:10.1177/0022242920972022

Li, Q., Wu, H., & Dong, C. (2023). A Privacy-Preserving Ride Matching Scheme for Ride Sharing Services in a Hot Spot Area. *Electronics (Basel)*, *12*(4), 915.

LibreTextsBoundless. (2023). *Interaction of Individuals, Firms, and Societies*. UCDavis Libre Texts. https://socialsci.libretexts.org/Bookshelves/Economics/Economics_(Boundless)/1%3A_Principles_of_Economics/1.3%3A_Interaction_of_Individuals_Firms_and_Societies

Ligaraba, N., Chuchu, T., & Nyagadza, B. (2023). Opt-in e-mail marketing influence on consumer behaviour: A Stimuli–Organism–Response (S–O– R) theory perspective. *Cogent Business & Management*, *10*(1), 2184244. doi:10.1080/23311975.2023.2184244

Lima Filho, J. S. F., de, & Brasil, A. L. da S. (2019, January 26). O conceito legal de teletrabalho e suas repercussões nos direitos do empregado. *Juris Unitoledo*, *1*(4), 111–126.

Lima, A. C. O., Leal, E. O. L., & Gandra, S. R. (2018). *Usabilidade e acessibilidade na concepção de novos sistemas inclusivos*. Appris.

Lim, E. P., Chen, H., & Chen, G. (2013). Business intelligence and analytics: Research directions. *ACM Transactions on Management Information Systems*, *3*(4), 1–10. doi:10.1145/2407740.2407741

Lindström, J. (2012). A model to explain a business contingency process. *Disaster Prevention and Management*, *21*(2), 269–281. doi:10.1108/09653561211220052

Ling, K. C., Chai, L. T., & Piew, T. H. (2010). The effects of shopping orientations, online trust and prior online purchase experience toward customers' online purchase intention. *International Business Research*, *3*(3), 63. doi:10.5539/ibr.v3n3p63

Li, S., Xu, L. D., & Zhao, S. (2015). The internet of things: A survey. *Information Systems Frontiers*, *17*(2), 243–259. doi:10.100710796-014-9492-7

Liu, Q., Trevisan, A. H., Yang, M., & Mascarenhas, J. (2022). A framework of digital technologies for the circular economy: Digital functions and mechanisms. *Business Strategy and the Environment*, *31*(5), 2171–2192. doi:10.1002/bse.3015

Liu, X., Ahmad, S. F., Anser, M. K., Ke, J., Irshad, M., Ul-Haq, J., & Abbas, S. (2022, October 19). Cyber security threats: A never-ending challenge for e-commerce. *Frontiers in Psychology*, *13*, 927398. Advance online publication. doi:10.3389/fpsyg.2022.927398 PMID:36337532

Liu, Y., Zhu, W., & Zhao, S. M. (2016). Research on the influence of inclusive leadership on the relations of employment relationship and employees´ active behavior. *Management Representative*, *10*(1), 1482–1489.

Li, X. (2022). Inclusive leadership and employee outcomes: A meta-analytic of multiple theories. *Proceedings - Academy of Management*, *1*(1), 1–19. doi:10.5465/AMBPP.2022.33

Li, Y., & Fu, X. (2021). Internet of Behaviors (IoB): A Comprehensive Review. *IEEE Access : Practical Innovations, Open Solutions*, *9*, 121281–121295.

Li, Y., Guo, Y., & Chen, S. (2018, September). A survey on the Development and Challenges of the Internet of Things (IoT) in China. In *2018 International Symposium in Sensing and Instrumentation in IoT Era (ISSI)* (pp. 1-5). IEEE. 10.1109/ISSI.2018.8538281

Lo, A. W., & MacKinlay, A. C. (1988). Stock Market Prices Do Not Follow Random Walks: Evidence from a Simple Specification Test. *Review of Financial Studies*, *1*(1), 41–66. Advance online publication. doi:10.1093/rfs/1.1.41

Lodygensky, O., Fedak, G., Néri, V., Cordier, A., & Cappello, F. (2003). Monte Carlo computation on a global computing platform. Proceedings of Computing in High Energy and Nuclear Physics (CHEP2003).

Longest, B. (2017). Responsible leader behavior in health sectors. *Leadership in Health Services*, *30*(1), 8–15. doi:10.1108/LHS-05-2016-0020 PMID:28128048

Lopes de Sousa Jabbour, A. B., Jabbour, C. J. C., Godinho Filho, M., & Roubaud, D. (2018). Industry 4.0 and the circular economy: A proposed research agenda and original roadmap for sustainable operations. *Annals of Operations Research*, *270*(1–2), 273–286. doi:10.100710479-018-2772-8

Lopez, C. P., Segura, M., & Santórum, M. (2019). Data analytics and BI framework based on collective intelligence and the Industry 4.0. *Proceedings of the 2019 2nd International Conference on Information Science and Systems*, 93-98. 10.1145/3322645.3322667

Lüdeke-Freund, F., Gold, S., & Bocken, N. M. P. (2019). A review and typology of circular economy business model patterns: Circular economy business models. *Journal of Industrial Ecology*, *23*(1), 36–61. doi:10.1111/jiec.12763

Lu, J. (2022). Building a smart city planning system integrating multidimensional spatiotemporal features. *Scientific Programming*, *2022*, 1–9. doi:10.1155/2022/2772665

Lütkepohl, H. (1993). Testing for Causation Between Two Variables in Higher-Dimensional VAR Models (Vol. 114, Issue 4, pp. 75–91). https://doi.org/ doi:10.1007/978-3-642-51514-9_4

Luxton-Reilly, A., Tempero, E., Arachchilage, N., Chang, A., Denny, P., Fowler, A., . . . Ye, X. (2023). Automated Assessment: Experiences From the Trenches. *ACM Proceedings of the 25th Australasian Computing Education Conference*, 1-10.

Lv, H., Shi, S., & Gursoy, D. (2022). A look back and a leap forward: A review and synthesis of big data and artificial intelligence literature in hospitality and tourism. *Journal of Hospitality Marketing & Management*, *31*(2), 145–175. doi:10.1080/19368623.2021.1937434

Maak, T. (2007). Responsible leadership, stakeholder engagement and the emergence of social capital. *Journal of Business Ethics*, *74*(4), 329–343. doi:10.100710551-007-9510-5

Maciel, Á. dos S., & Lando, G. A. (2021, April). Desafios e perspectivas do mundo do trabalho pós-pandemia no Brasil: Uma análise da flexibilização trabalhista e os paradoxos do home office/anywhere office. *Revista Espaço Acadêmico*, *20*(0), 63–74.

Mack, O., Khare, A., Krämer, A., & Burgartz, T. (2016). *Managing in a VUCA World*. Springer International Publishing AG Switzerland. doi:10.1007/978-3-319-16889-0

MacLeod, N., & Wright, D. (2020). *Forensic linguistics*. Academic Press.

Maddison, A. (2008). The west and the rest in the world economy: 1000-2030. *World Economy*, *9*(4), 75–99.

Madyatmadja, E. D., Adiba, C. N. A., Sembiring, D. J. M., Pristinella, D., & Putra, A. M. (2021). The Positive Impact of Implementation Business Intelligence and Big Data in Hospitality and Tourism Sector. *International Journal of Emerging Technology and Advanced Engineering*, *11*(6), 59–71. doi:10.46338/ijetae0621_07

Maia, A. C. B. (2020). *Questionário e entrevista na pesquisa qualitativa: elaboração, aplicação e análise de conteúdo*. Pedro e João.

Ma, J., Zhou, X., Li, S., & Li, Z. (2011). Connecting agriculture to the internet of things through sensor networks. *International Conference on Internet of Things and 4th International Conference on Cyber, Physical and Social Computing*, 184-187. 10.1109/iThings/CPSCom.2011.32

Malkina, M. Y., & Ovchinnikov, V. N. (2020). Cryptocurrency market: Overreaction to news and herd instincts. *Ekonomicheskaya Politika, 2020*(3). doi:10.18288/1994-5124-2020-3-74-105

Mansol, N. H., Mohd Alwi, N. H., & Ismail, W. (2015). Managing organizational culture requirement for Business Continuity Management (BCM) implementation Using Goal-Question-Metric (GQM) approach. *2015 IEEE Conference on Open Systems (ICOS)*, 85-90. 10.1109/ICOS.2015.7377283

Maria, J. F., & Lozano, J. M. (2010). Responsible leaders for inclusive globalization: Cases of Nicaragua and the Democratic Republic of Congo. *Journal of Business Ethics*, *93*(S1), 93–111. doi:10.100710551-010-0628-5

Márquez-Benitez, M. D., Sánchez-Teba, E. M., Bermúdez-González, G., & Nunez-Rydman, M. S. (2022). Generation Z within the Workforce and in the Workplace: A bibliometric Analysis. *Organizational Psychology*, (12), 1–12.

Martins, G. O., Gomes, C. S., Brocardo, J. L., Pedroso, J. V., Acosta Carrillo, J. L., Ucha, L. M., Encarnação, M., Horta, M. J., Calçada, M. T., Nery, R. V., & Rodrigues, S. V. (2017). *O perfil dos alunos à saída da escolaridade obrigatória*. Ministério da Educação. Direção Geral de Educação. http://dge.mec.pt/sites/default/files/Curriculo/Projeto_Autonomia_e_Flexibilidade/perfil_dos_alunos.pdf

Martins, M. E. & Ponte, J. P. (2011). *Organização e tratamento de dados*. ME – DGIDC.

Marton, F., & Carbinatto, B. (2022, Aug.). *E se trabalhássemos para sempre em regime de home office?* https://super.abril.com.br/ciencia/e-se-trabalhassemos-para-sempre-em-regime-de-home-office

Masalki, M., Grysiński, T., & Kręcicki, T. (2014, January). Biological Calibration for Web-Based Hearing Tests: Evaluation of the Methods. *Journal of Medical Internet Research*, *16*(1), e11. doi:10.2196/jmir.2798 PMID:24429353

Mathieu, J. E., Hollenbeck, J. R., van Knippenberg, D., & Ilgen, D. R. (2017). A century of work teams in the journal of applied psychology. *The Journal of Applied Psychology*, *61*(3), 349–374. doi:10.1037/apl0000128 PMID:28150984

Mattos, M. (2019). *How a circular economy narrows, slows, intensifies, and closes supply chain loops*. MIT Supply Chain. https://medium.com/mitsupplychain/how-a-circular-economy-narrows-slows-intensifies-and-closes-supply-chain-loops-d85d9bab869

Maulana, B. H., Rohman, A., & Prabowo, T. (2022). Doing qualitative research of phenomenology in accounting. *Academy of Accounting and Financial Studies Journal*, *26*(1S), 1-7. https://www.abacademies.org/articles/doing-qualitative-research-of-phenomenology-in-a ccounting-13120.html

Medline Plus organization. (2023). *Can genes be patented?* https://medlineplus.gov/genetics/understanding/testing/genepatents/

Meijer, E. (2022). *Blockchain and our planet: Why such high energy use?* PRe´. https://pre-sustainability.com/articles/blockchain-and-our-planet-why-such-high-energy-use/

Mello, Á., & Dal Colleto, A. (2019). Telework and its effects in Brazil. In J. C. Messenger (Ed.), *Telework in the 21st Century: An evolutionary perspective* (pp. 211–254). Edward Elgar Publishing. doi:10.4337/9781789903751.00012

Melumad, S., & Pham, M. T. (2020). The smartphone as a pacifying technology. *The Journal of Consumer Research*, *47*(2), 237–255. doi:10.1093/jcr/ucaa005

Mendenhall, T. C. (1887). The Characteristic Curves of Composition. *Science, 9*(214), 237–246. doi:10.1126cience. ns-9.214S.237 PMID:17736020

Mendes, F., Delgado, C., & Brocardo, J. (2021). Estudo de aula: Uma experiência na formação inicial de professores de primeiro ciclo. In *Livro de Atas do 7º Congresso nacional de práticas pedagógicas no ensino superior* (pp. 162-167). Universidade de Aveiro. 10.48528/yhzq-cp97

Mendes, F., Delgado, C., & Brocardo, J. (2022). Challenges faced by Preservice Teachers in Planning and Exploring Tasks that Promote Mathematical Reasoning. *Acta Scientiae, 24*(4), 147–182. doi:10.17648/acta.scientiae.7123

Mergel, I., Edelmann, N. & Haug, N. (2019). Defining digital transformation: Results from expert interviews. *Government Information Quarterly, 36*. doi:10.1016/j.giq.2019.06.002

Mesquita, A. (2021). *Liderança no home office: quais os desafios?* https://www.oitchau.com.br/blog/desafios-de-lideranca-no-home-office/

Messenger, J. C. (2019). *Telework in the 21st Century: an evolutionary perspective.* Edward Elgar Publishing. doi:10.4337/9781789903751

Meva, D. (2018). Issues and challenges with blockchain: A survey. *International Journal on Computer Science and Engineering, 6*(12), 488–491.

Mezair, T., Djenouri, Y., Belhadi, A., Srivastava, G., & Lin, J. C. W. (2022). Towards an advanced deep learning for the internet of behaviors: Application to connected vehicles. *ACM Transactions on Sensor Networks, 19*(2), 1–18. doi:10.1145/3526192

Mezair, T., Djenouri, Y., Bjelhadi, A., Srivastava, G., & Lin, J. (2022). Towards an advanced deep learning for the Internet of Behaviors: Application to connected vehicles. *ACM Transactions on Sensor Networks, 19*(2). *Article, 30*, 1–18.

Mhatre, P., Panchal, R., Singh, A., & Bibyan, S. (2021). A systematic literature review on the circular economy initiatives in the European Union. *Sustainable Production and Consumption, 26*, 187–202. doi:10.1016/j.spc.2020.09.008

Microsoft/ImagineCup. (n.d.). *Microsoft Imagine Cup.* Retrieved 5 29, 2023, from https://imaginecup.microsoft.com/pt-pt

Micuchova, M. (2022). Data value chain in platform business models. *Scientific Papers of the University of Pardubice, Series D, 30*(3), 16–19.

Mishra, N. (2019). Data Science and Knowledge Analytic Contexts on IoE Data for E-BI Application Case. In Edge Computing and Computational Intelligence Paradigms for the IoT (pp. 100-126). IGI Global. doi:10.4018/978-1-5225-8555-8.ch007

Mishra, L., Gupta, T., & Shree, A. (2020). Online teaching-learning in higher education during lockdown period of CO-VID-19 pandemic. *International Journal of Educational Research Open, 1*, 100012. doi:10.1016/j.ijedro.2020.100012 PMID:35059663

Mishra, N., Lin, C. C., & Chang, H. T. (2015). A cognitive adopted framework for IoT big-data management and knowledge discovery prospective. *International Journal of Distributed Sensor Networks, 11*, 718390–718391. doi:10.1155/2015/718390

Mittelstadt, B., Allo, P., Taddeo, M., Wachter, S., & Floridi, L. (2016). The ethics of algorithms: Mapping the debate. *Big Data & Society, 3*(2). Advance online publication. doi:10.1177/2053951716679679

Modiba, P., Pieterse, V., & Haskins, B. (2016). Evaluating plagiarism detection software for introductory programming assignments. *Proceedings of the Computer Science Education Research Conference*, 37-46. 10.1145/2998551.2998558

Mohammadian, H. D. (2022). Mapping the Future SMEs' HR Competencies via IoE Technologies and 7PS Model Through the Fifth Wave Theory. In *Management and Information Technology in the Digital Era* (Vol. 29, pp. 141–171). Emerald Publishing Limited. doi:10.1108/S1877-636120220000029010

Mohammed-Nasir, R., Oshikoya, K. A., & Oreagba, I. A. (2023). Digital Innovation in Healthcare Entrepreneurship. In Medical Entrepreneurship. Springer. doi:10.1007/978-981-19-6696-5_22

Mohsin, M. (2021). *7 estatísticas sobre home office para o ano de 2021*. https://www.oberlo.com.br/blog/estatisticas-home-office

Moody, G. D., Siponen, M., & Pahnila, S. (2018). Toward a Unified Model of Information Security Policy Compliance. *Management Information Systems Quarterly*, *42*(1), 285–A22. doi:10.25300/MISQ/2018/13853

MoreiraA.HenriquesS.BarrosD.GoulãoF.CaeiroD. (2020). *Educação digital em rede: princípios para o design pedagógico em tempos de pandemia*. Universidade Aberta. doi:10.34627/rfg0-ps07

Moreno, M., De los Rios, C., Rowe, Z., & Charnley, F. (2016). A conceptual framework for circular design. *Sustainability (Basel)*, *8*(9), 937. doi:10.3390u8090937

Morgan, D. L. (1996a). Focus group. *Annual Review of Sociology*, *22*(1), 129–152. doi:10.1146/annurev.soc.22.1.129

Morgan, D. L. (1997b). *Focus group as qualitative research* (2nd ed.). Sage., doi:10.4135/9781412984287

Mosteller, F., & Wallace, D. L. (1964). *Inference and disputed authorship: The Federalist*. Addison-Wesley.

Mourtzis, D., Angelopoulos, J., & Panopoulos, N. (2022). A Literature Review of the Challenges and Opportunities of the Transition from Industry 4.0 to Society 5.0. *Energies, 15*(17), 6276. https://doi-org.libauth.purdueglobal.edu/10.3390/en15176276

Mousa, M. (2019). Organizational inclusion and academics' psychological contract. Can responsible leadership mediate the relationship? *Equality, Diversity and Inclusion*, *39*(2), 126–144. doi:10.1108/EDI-01-2019-0014

Mousa, M., & Puhakka, V. (2019). Inspiring Organizational commitment Responsible leadership and Organizational inclusion in the Egyptian health care sector. *Journal of Management Development*, *38*(3), 208–224. doi:10.1108/JMD-11-2018-0338

MSI. (2022). *Research Priorities 2020-2022*. Marketing Science Institute. https://www.msi.org/wp-content/uploads/2021/07/MSI-2020-22-Research-Priorities-final.pdf-WO

Mühle, A., Grüner, A., Gayvoronskaya, T., & Meinel, C. (2018). A survey on essential components of a self-sovereign identity. *Computer Science Review*, *30*, 80–86. doi:10.1016/j.cosrev.2018.10.002

Muller, J. M. (2020). Data-based sustainable business models in the context of Industry 4.0. *International Conference on Information Systems 2020 Special Interest Group on Big Data Proceedings, 5.*

Muntean, M. (2018). Business intelligence issues for sustainability projects. *Sustainability (Basel)*, *10*(2), 335. doi:10.3390u10020335

Murray, A., Skene, K., & Haynes, K. (2017). The circular economy: An interdisciplinary exploration of the concept and application in a global context. *Journal of Business Ethics*, *140*(3), 369–380. doi:10.100710551-015-2693-2

Nagasaki, Y. (2019). *Realization of Society 5.0 by utilizing precision agriculture into smart agriculture in NARO, Japan.* FFTC Agricultural Policy Platform. https://ap.fftc.org.tw/article/1414

Nakamoto, S. (2016). *Bitcoin: A Peer-to-Peer Electronic Cash System, Apr. 2018* [online]. Available: https://bitcoin. org/bitcoin.pdf

Nakanishi, H., & Kitano, H. (2018). *Society 5.0 Co-Creating the Future. Policy Proposals Industrial Technology.* Keidanren (Japan Business Federation). https://www.keidanren.or.jp/ en/policy/2018/095_booklet.pdf

Nam, K., Baker, J., Ahmad, N., & Goo, J. (2020). Determinants of writing positive and negative electronic word-of-mouth: Empirical evidence for two types of expectation confirmation. *Decision Support Systems*, *129*, 113168. doi:10.1016/j. dss.2019.113168

Narvaez Rojas, C., Alomia Peñafiel, G. A., Loaiza Buitrago, D. F., & Tavera Romero, C. A. (2021). Society 5.0: A japanese concept for a super intelligent society. *Sustainability (Basel)*, *13*(12), 6567. doi:10.3390u13126567

Nayal, K., Kumar, S., Raut, R. D., Queiroz, M. M., Priyadarshinee, P., & Narkhede, B. E. (2022). Supply chain firm performance in circular economy and digital era to achieve sustainable development goals. *Business Strategy and the Environment*, *31*(3), 1058–1073. doi:10.1002/bse.2935

Negash, S., & Gray, P. (2008). Business intelligence. In *Handbook on decision support systems 2* (pp. 175–193). Springer. doi:10.1007/978-3-540-48716-6_9

Neligan, A., Baumgartner, R. J., Geissdoerfer, M., & Schöggl, J.-P. (2023). Circular disruption: Digitalisation as a driver of circular economy business models. *Business Strategy and the Environment*, *32*(3), 1175–1188. doi:10.1002/bse.3100

Nembhard, I. M., & Edmondson, A. C. (2006). Making it safe: The effects of leader inclusiveness and professional status on psychological safety and improvement efforts in health care teams. *Journal of Organizational Behavior*, *27*(7), 941–966. doi:10.1002/job.413

Nesselhauf, N., & Tono, Y. (2015). *Corpus-Based Studies in Contrastive Linguistics.* Walter de Gruyter GmbH & Co KG.

NFPA 1600. (2019). *NFPA 1600® Standard on Continuity, Emergency, and Crisis Management 2019 Edition.* National Fire Protection Association.

NFPA. (2020, April 28). *NFPA 1600® Standard on Continuity, Emergency, and Crisis Management.* Retrieved April 28, 2020, from National Fire Protection Association: https://www.nfpa.org/codes-and-standards/all-codes-and-standards/ list-of-codes-and-standards/detail?code=1600

Nguyễn, T. N. (2023). *Khảo sát các yếu tố từ vựng ảnh hưởng đến phong cách viết trong văn bản tiếng Việt (đối chiếu với tiếng Anh).* VNU Library.

Nguyen, T. N., & Dinh, D. (2021). A stylometric investigation of linguistic styles based on a Vietnamese corpus. *Open Journal of Social Sciences*, *9*(12), 74–87. doi:10.4236/jss.2021.912006

Nishii, L. H. (2013). The benefits of climate for inclusion for gender-diverse groups. *Academy of Management Journal*, *56*(6), 1754–1774. doi:10.5465/amj.2009.0823

NIST 800-171. (2020). *NIST Special Publication 800-171 Revision 2 - Protecting Controlled Unclassified Information in Nonfederal Systems and Organizations.* Gaithersburg, Maryland, USA: National Institute of Standards and Technology. doi:10.6028/NIST.SP.800-171r2

NIST 800-34. (2010). *NIST Special Publication 800-34 Rev. 1 - Contingency Planning Guide for Federal Information Systems.* Gaithersburg: National Institute of Standards and Technology.

Norris, M. (2020). *The Value of AI-powered Business Intelligence.* O'Reilly Media, Incorporated.

Nosratabadi, S., Mosavi, A., Shamshirband, S., Kazimieras Zavadskas, E., Rakotonirainy, A., & Chau, K. W. (2019). Sustainable business models: A review. *Sustainability (Basel)*, *11*(6), 1663. doi:10.3390u11061663

Nurgalieva, L., & Doherty, G. (2023). Privacy and security in digital therapeutics. Digital Therapeutics for Mental Health and Addiction. The State of the Science and Vision for the Future, 189-204. doi:10.1016/B978-0-323-90045-4.00002-2

Nyanga, C., Pansiri, J., & Chatibura, D. (2020). Enhancing competitiveness in the tourism industry through the use of business intelligence: A literature review. *Journal of Tourism Futures*, *6*(2), 139–151. doi:10.1108/JTF-11-2018-0069

O'Duinn, J. (2021). *Distributed teams: the art and practice of working together while physically apart*. Release Mechanix, LLC.

OAuth. (n.d.). *OAuth Community Site*. Retrieved 7 11, 2021, from https://oauth.net

Object Management Group. (2014). *Kernel and Language for Software Engineering Methods (Essence), Version 1.0*. OMG. Retrieved from https://www.omg.org/spec/Essence/1.0/

Ohlhausen, P. E., & McGarvey, D. (2018). The use of metrics to manage enterprise security risks: Understanding, evaluation and persuasion. *Journal of Business Continuity & Emergency Planning*, *12*(1), 6–16. PMID:30126523

Oloo, V., Wanzare, L. D., & Otieno, C. (2022). An Optimal Feature Set for Stylometry-based Style Change detection at Document and Sentence Level. *International Journal of Scientific Research in Computer Science, Engineering and Information Technology*

Olson, A., Maidment, D. W., & Fergunson, M. A. (2022). Consensus on connected hearing health technologies and service delivery models in the UK: A Delphi review. *International Journal of Auditing*, *61*(4), 344–351. doi:10.1080/1 4992027.2021.1936223 PMID:34182863

Open, I. D. (n.d.). *OpenID Foundation website*. Retrieved 7 11, 2021, from https://openid.net

Order no. 8632. (2014, July 03). Order no. 8632/2014, July 3rd. Ministry of Finance.

Ordinance no. 363. (2010, June 23). Ordinance no. 363, June 23th. Autoridade Tributária e Aduaneira.

Pacheco, F. L., & Deste, J. A. (2021). *O teletrabalho na legislação brasileira e sua multidisciplinaridade: aspectos teóricos e práticos*. Mizuno.

Paglialonga, A., Nielsen, A. C., Ingo, E., Barr, C., & Laplante-Levesque, A. (2018). eHealth and the hearing aid adult patient journey: A state-of-the-art review. *Biomedical Engineering Online*, *17*(1), 101. doi:10.118612938-018-0531-3 PMID:30064497

Paiva, J. C., Leal, J. P., & Figueira, Á. (2022). Automated Assessment in Computer Science Education: A State-of-the-Art Review. *ACM Transactions on Computing Education*, *22*(3), 1–40. doi:10.1145/3513140

Palermo, V., & Hernandez, Y. (2020). Group discussions on how to implement a participatory process in climate adaptation planning: A case study in Malaysia. *Ecological Economics, 177*. doi:10.1016/j.ecolecon.2020.106791

Palmer, C., Boudreault, P., Baldwin, E., Fox, M., Deignan, J., Kobayash, Y., Sininger, Y., Grody, W., & Sinsheimer, J. (2013). Deaf Genetic Testing and Psychological Well-Being in Deaf Adults. *Journal of Genetic Counseling*, *22*(4), 492–507. doi:10.100710897-013-9573-7 PMID:23430402

Palmié, M., Parida, V., Mader, A., & Wincent, J. (2023). Clarifying the scaling concept: A review, definition, and measure of scaling performance and an elaborate agenda for future research. *Journal of Business Research*, *158*. https://doi. org/ doi:10.1016/j.jbusres.2022.113630

Pan, J., & Kudo, M. (2019). N-gram Against the Machine: On the Feasibility of the N-gram Network Analysis for Binary Protocols. In *2019 6th International Conference on Behavioral, Economic, and Socio-Cultural Computing (BESC)* (pp. 1-8). IEEE.

Pan, L., Tlili, A., Li, J., Jiang, F., Shi, G., Yu, H., & Yang, J. (2021). How to Implement Game-Based Learning in a Smart Classroom? A Model Based on a Systematic Literature Review and Delphi Method. *Frontiers in Psychology, 12,* 1-13. doi:10.3389/fpsyg.2021.749837

Pan, S. Y., Gao, M., Kim, H., Shah, K. J., Pei, S. L., & Chiang, P. C. (2018). Advances and challenges in sustainable tourism toward a green economy. *The Science of the Total Environment, 635,* 452–469. doi:10.1016/j.scitotenv.2018.04.134 PMID:29677671

Pardal, P., Dias, R., Teixeira, N. & Horta, N. (2022). *The Effects of Russia ' s 2022 Invasion of Ukraine on Global Markets : An Analysis of Particular Capital and Foreign Exchange Markets.* doi:10.4018/978-1-6684-5666-8.ch014

Parida, V., Sjödin, D., & Reim, W. (2019). Reviewing literature on digitalization, business model innovation, and sustainable industry: Past achievements and future promises. *Sustainability (Basel), 11*(2), 391. doi:10.3390u11020391

Parker, C., Scott, S., & Geddes, A. (2019). Snowball Sampling. In P. Atkinson, S. Delamont, A. Cernat, J. W. Sakshaug, & R. A. Williams (Eds.), *SAGE Research Methods Foundations.*

Parker, G., & Alstyne, W. V. M. (2014). *Platform Strategy.* The Palgrave Encyclopedia of Strategic Management. doi:10.2139srn.2439323

Parmegiane, D. (2021). *Dado existencial: Análise da jornada excessiva de trabalho e o teletrabalho sob a ótica da dignidade da pessoa humana.* CRV.

Patton, M. Q. (1985). Quality in Qualitative Research: Methodological Principles and Recent Development. Invited address to Division J of the American Educational Research Association, Chicago.

Patyal, V. S., Sarma, P. R. S., Modgil, S., Nag, T., & Dennehy, D. (2022). Mapping the links between Industry 4.0, circular economy and sustainability: A systematic literature review. *Journal of Enterprise Information Management, 35*(1), 1–35. doi:10.1108/JEIM-05-2021-0197

Păunescu, C. (2017). How Prepared are Small and Medium Sized Companies for Business Continuity Management? *Quality - Access to Success, 18*(161), 43–48.

Păunescu, C., & Argatu, R. (2020). Critical functions in ensuring effective business continuity management. Evidence from Romanian companies. *Journal of Business Economics and Management, 21*(2), 497–520. Advance online publication. doi:10.3846/jbem.2020.12205

Peceny, U. S., Urbančič, J., Mokorel, S., Kuralt, V., & Ilijaš, T. (2019). Tourism 4.0: Challenges in marketing a paradigm shift. Consumer Behavior and Marketing, 39-59.

Peffers, K., Tuunanen, T., Rothenberger, M. A., & Chatterjee, S. (2007). A Design Science Research Methodology for Information Systems Research. *Journal of Management Information Systems, 24*(3), 45–77. doi:10.2753/MIS0742-1222240302

Pelled, L. H., Ledford, G. E. Jr, & Mohrman, S. A. (1999). Demographic dissimilarity and workplace inclusion. *Journal of Management Studies, 36*(7), 1013–1031. doi:10.1111/1467-6486.00168

Pellegrini, L., Porru, S., & West, R. (2020). Ethical Issues in the Internet of Behaviors. *2020 IEEE International Workshop on Metrology for Industry 4.0 and IoT (MetroInd4.0 & IoT)*, 384-389.

Pencarelli, T. (2020). The digital revolution in the travel and tourism industry. *Information Technology & Tourism, 22*(3), 455–476. doi:10.100740558-019-00160-3

Pereira, A. N. (2022). *Teletrabalho: um recorte exploratório de conceitos e de práticas normativas e jurisprudenciais celetistas e no TRT 2ª Região*. Leme: Mizuno.

Pereira, A. S., Shitsuka, D. M., Parreira, F. J., & Shitsuka, R. (2018). *Metodologia da pesquisa* científica. Santa Maria, RS: Universidade Federal de Santa Maria – UFSM; Núcleo de Tecnologia Educacional – NTE.

Pereira, A. C., & Romero, F. (2017). A review of the meanings and the implications of the Industry 4.0 concept. *Procedia Manufacturing, 13*, 1206–1214. doi:10.1016/j.promfg.2017.09.032

Peters, M. A., & Besley, T. C. (2014). Social exclusion/inclusion. Foucault's analytics of exclusion, the political ecology of social inclusion and the legitimation of inclusive education. *Open Review of Educational Research, 1*(1), 99–115. doi:10.1080/23265507.2014.972439

Petit, J., Roura, S., Carmona, J., Cortadella, J., Duch, A., Giménez, O., Mani, A., Mas, J., Rodriguez-Carbonell, E., Rubio, E., Pedro, E. S., & Venkataramani, D. (2018). Jutge.org: Characteristics and Experiences. *IEEE Transactions on Learning Technologies, 11*(3), 321–333. doi:10.1109/TLT.2017.2723389

Peyman, M., Copado, P. J., Tordecilla, R. D., Martins, L. D. C., Xhafa, F., & Juan, A. A. (2021). Edge computing and iot analytics for agile optimization in intelligent transportation systems. *Energies, 14*(19), 6309. doi:10.3390/en14196309

Phillips, R., & Tanner, B. (2019). Breaking down silos between business continuity and cyber security. *J Bus Contin Emer Plan, 12*(3), 224-232.

Phillips, P. C. B., & Perron, P. (1988). Testing for a unit root in time series regression. *Biometrika, 75*(2), 335–346. doi:10.1093/biomet/75.2.335

Pinheiro, M. M., & Santos, C. A. (2023, June 20-23). *The power of education to change society: Methodologies, academic success and well-being at Higher Education* [Paper presentation]. *18th Iberian Conference on Information Systems and Technologies (CISTI)*, Aveiro, Portugal. 10.23919/CISTI58278.2023.10211665

Platform, I. O. (n.d.). *Professional collaborative platform for embedded development*. Retrieved 7 14, 2021, from https://platformio.org

Pless, N. M. (2007). Understanding responsible leadership: Role identity and motivational drivers. *Journal of Business Ethics, 74*(4), 437–456. doi:10.100710551-007-9518-x

Pless, N. M., & Maak, T. (2012). Responsible leadership: Pathways to the future. *Journal of Business Ethics, 98*(S1), 3–13. doi:10.100710551-011-1114-4

Popper, N. (2015). Digital Gold: The untold story of Bitcoin. Penguin UK.

PORDATA. (2023). *Taxa de investimento: total e por ramo de atividade*. Retrieved from PORDATA - Estatísticas sobre Portugal e Europa: https://www.pordata.pt/portugal/taxa+de+investimento+total+e+por+ramo+de+atividade-2302

Pornillos, C. J., Billones, M. S., Leonidas, J. D., Reyes, E. M., Esguerra, B. J., Bolima, D. P., & Concepcion, R. (2020). Smart irrigation control system using wireless sensor network via internet-of-things. *IEEE 12th International Conference on Humanoid, Nanotechnology, Information Technology, Communication and Control, Environment, and Management (HNICEM)*, 1-6.

Possato, A. B., Zamoner, Z., Monteiro, P. O., & Querido de Oliveira Chamon, E. M. (2022). O uso de games: Uma prática discutida como inovadora na educação 5.0. *Interação - Revista de Ensino. Pesquisa e Extensão*, *24*(3), 23–41. doi:10.33836/interacao.v24i3.722

Potha, N., & Joshi, A. (2021). Stylometry Analysis of Authorship Attribution Using Text Mining Techniques. In *Advances in Signal Processing and Intelligent Recognition Systems* (pp. 453–463). Springer.

Powell, R., & Single, H. (1996). Focus Groups. *International Journal for Quality in Health Care*, *8*(5), 499–504. doi:10.1093/intqhc/8.5.499

Prais, J. L. de S., & Rosa, V. F. da. (2017). Nuvem de palavras e mapa conceitual: estratégias e recursos tecnológicos na prática pedagógica. *Nuances: Estudos sobre Educação*, *28*(1), 201-219.

Prakash, V. (2021). *Holistic Digital Synergies Imperative for the Internet of Behavior (IoB)*. https://dzone.com/articles/holistic-digital-synergies-imperative-for-internet

Pramudya, G., & Fajar, A. (2019). Business continuity plan using ISO 22301:2012 in IT solution company (pt. ABC). *International Journal of Mechanical Engineering and Technology*, *10*(2), 865–872.

Prasad, C. J., & Aryasri, A. R. (2009). Determinants of shopper behaviour in e-tailing: An empirical analysis. *Paradigm*, *13*(1), 73–83. doi:10.1177/0971890720090110

Precedence Research. (2021). *Internet of Behaviors (IoB) Market Size, Growth, Report 2030*. https://www.precedenceresearch.com/internet-of-behaviors-market

Prechelt, L., Malpohl, G., & Philippsen, M. (2002). Finding Plagiarisms among a Set of Programs with JPlag. *Journal of Universal Computer Science*, *8*(11), 1016–1038.

Purcell, P. L., Deep, N. L., Waltzman, S. B., Roland, J. T. Jr, Cushing, S. L., Papsin, B. C., & Gordon, K. (2021). Cochlear Implantation in Infants: Why and How. *Trends in Hearing*, *25*, 1–10. doi:10.1177/23312165211031751 PMID:34281434

Putra, E. P., & Nazief, B. A. (2018). Analysis of Main Cause Factors and Improvement Recommendation of IT Disaster Recovery Problems: A Case Study of XYZ Organization. *AIP Conference Proceedings*, 020024. doi:10.1063/1.5042880

Putzhammer, M. (2023). *Most energy efficient cryptocurrencies 2023*. Trality. https://www.trality.com/blog/most-energy-efficient-cryptocurrencies

Qi, L., Liu, B., Wei, X., & Hu, Y. (2019). Impact of inclusive leadership on employee innovative behavior: Perceived Organizational support as a mediator. *PLoS One*, *14*(2), e0212091. doi:10.1371/journal.pone.0212091 PMID:30817753

Radnan, Y. & Christin, V. (2023). The Effect of Self-Service Technology Service Quality on Customer Loyalty and Behavioral Intention. *KINERJA: Journal of Business and Economics*, *27*(1), 107-128. doi:10.24002/kinerja.v27i1.6642

Rahaman, T. (2022). Smart things are getting smarter: An introduction to the internet of behavior. *Medical Reference Services Quarterly*, *41*(1), 110–116. doi:10.1080/02763869.2022.2021046 PMID:35225739

Rajesh, T. (2017). What is Artificial Intelligence? *Learning outcomes of classroom research*, 28-36.

Ramakrishnan, R. K., & Viswanathan, S. (2011). The importance of Business Strategy in Business Continuity Planing. In A. Hiles (Ed.), *The definitive handbook of Business Continuity Management* (3rd ed.). John Wiley & Sons, Ltd.

Ramakrishnan, R. K., & Viswanathan, S. (2011). The importance of Business Strategy in Business Continuity Planingem. In A. Hiles (Ed.), *The definitive handbook of Business Continuity Management* (3rd ed.). John Wiley & Sons, Ltd.

Ramos, C. M., & Brito, I. S. (2020). The Effects of Industry 4.0 in Tourism and Hospitality and Future Trends in Portugal. In *The Emerald Handbook of ICT in Tourism and Hospitality* (pp. 367–378). Emerald Publishing Limited. doi:10.1108/978-1-83982-688-720201023

Randel, A. E., Dean, M. A., Ehrhart, K. H., Chung, B., & Shore, L. (2016). Leader inclusiveness, psychological diversity climate, and helping behaviours. *Journal of Managerial Psychology*, *31*(1), 216–234. doi:10.1108/JMP-04-2013-0123

Randel, A. E., Galvin, B. M., Shore, L. M., Ehrhart, K. H., Chung, B. G., Dean, M. A., & Kedharnath, U. (2018). Inclusive leadership: Realizing positive outcomes through belongingness and being valued for uniqueness. *Human Resource Management Review*, *28*(2), 190–203. doi:10.1016/j.hrmr.2017.07.002

Ranta, V., Aarikka-Stenroos, L., & Väisänen, J.-M. (2021). Digital technologies catalyzing business model innovation for circular economy—Multiple case study. *Resources, Conservation and Recycling*, *164*(105155), 105155. doi:10.1016/j.resconrec.2020.105155

Ratner, M., & Chiu, C. C. (2013). Hedging stock sector risk with credit default swaps. *International Review of Financial Analysis*, *30*, 18–25. Advance online publication. doi:10.1016/j.irfa.2013.05.001

República Portuguesa. (2020). *Plano de Ação para a Transição Digital de Portugal. Portugal Digital.*

Research Nester. (2023). *Internet of Behaviors (IoB) Market*. https://www.researchnester.com/reports/internet-of-behaviors-iob-market/3983

Revez, C., Dias, R., Horta, N., Heliodoro, P., & Alexandre, P. (2022). Capital Market Efficiency in Asia: An Empirical Analysis. *6th EMAN Selected Papers (Part of EMAN Conference Collection)*, 49–57. https://doi.org/10.31410/eman.s.p.2022.49

Revfine. (2021) *How Augmented Reality is Revolutionising the Travel Industry*. Retrieved from: https://www.revfine.com/augmented-reality-travel-industry/

Reyna, A., Martín, C., Chen, J., Soler, E., & Díaz, M. (2018). On blockchain and its integration with IoT. Challenges and opportunities. *Future Generation Computer Systems*, *88*, 173–190. doi:10.1016/j.future.2018.05.046

Ribeiro, P., & Guerreiro, P. (2008). Early Introduction of Competitive Programming. *Olympiads in Informatics*, *2*, 149–162.

Ribeiro, P., Simões, H., & Ferreira, M. (2009). Teaching Artificial Intelligence and Logic Programming in a Competitive Environment. *Informatics in Education*, *8*(1), 85–100. doi:10.15388/infedu.2009.06

Rijsberman, F. R. (2006). Water scarcity: Fact or fiction? *Agricultural Water Management*, *80*(1-3), 5–22. doi:10.1016/j.agwat.2005.07.001

Rimboiu, C. (2020). *Modern IT architecture to manage change, foster innovation*. Retrieved from CXOtoday Corner Office: https://www.cxotoday.com/corner-office/modern-it-architecture-to-manage-change-foster-innovation/

Rist, G. (2014). The environment or the New Way Nature of Development. In The History of Development: From Western Origins to Global Faith (3rd ed.). Zed Books.

Roberson, Q., & Perry, J. L. (2022). Inclusive Leadership in Thought and Action: A Thematic Analysis. *Group & Organization Management*, *47*(4), 755–778. doi:10.1177/10596011211013161

Roberts, L.M., & Roberts, A.J. (2019). *Toward a racially just workplace*. Academic Press.

Robin, N. (2004). Genetic testing for deafness is here, but how do we do it? *Genetics in Medicine*, *6*(6), 463–464. doi:10.1097/01.GIM.0000144186.09716.CF PMID:15545740

Rockwell, G., & Sinclair, S. (2018). Too Much Information and the KWIC. *Fudan Journal of the Humanities and Social Sciences, 11*(4), 443–452. doi:10.100740647-018-0230-2

Rockwell, G., & Sinclair, S. (2022). *Hermeneutica: Computer-assisted interpretation in the humanities.* MIT Press.

Rodríguez-Abitia, G., Sánchez-Guerrero, M. L., Martínez-Pérez, S., & Aguas-García, N. (2022). Competencies of Information Technology Professionals in Society 5.0. *IEEE Revista Iberoamericana de Tecnologias del Aprendizaje, 17*(4), 343-350. https://doi.org/. 2022.3217136 doi:10.1109/RITA

Rogojanu, A., & Badea, L. (2014). The Issue of competing Currencies. Case Study – Bitcoin. *Theoretical and Applied Economics, 21*(1).

Roitz, J., & Jackson, E. (2006). AT&T adds business continuity to the long list of telework's advantages. *Journal of Organizational Excellence, 25*(2), 3–12. doi:10.1002/joe.20085

Roleders, V., Oriekhova, T., & Zaharieva, G. (2022). Circular Economy as a Model of Achieving Sustainable Development. *Problemy Ekorozwoju, 17*(2).

Romero, C. A., Ortiz, J. H., Khalaf, O. I., & Ríos Prado, A. (2021). Business intelligence: Business evolution after industry 4.0. *Sustainability (Basel), 13*(18), 10026. doi:10.3390u131810026

Roque, H. C., & Ramos, M. (2019). Responsible leadership and expatriation: The influence of national culture. In N. Teixeira, T. Costa, I. Lisboa (Eds.), Handbook of Research on Entrepreneurship, Innovation and Internationalization (pp. 586-610). IGI Global.

Roque, H. C., & Ramos, M. (2021). Good leadership practices in contexts of unpredictability. In T. Costa, I. Lisboa, N. Teixeira (Eds), Handbook of Research on Reinvinting Economies and Organizations Following a Global Heath Crisis (pp.363-385). IGI Global. doi:10.4018/978-1-7998-6926-9.ch020

Rostami, N. A. (2014). Integration of Business Intelligence and Knowledge Management–A literature review. *Journal of Intelligence Studies in Business, 4*(2), 30–40. doi:10.37380/jisib.v4i2.95

Rouhani, S., Ashrafi, A., Ravasan, A. Z., & Afshari, S. (2016). The impact model of business intelligence on decision support and organizational benefits. *Journal of Enterprise Information Management, 29*(1), 19–50. doi:10.1108/JEIM-12-2014-0126

Rubab, S., Hassan, M. F., Mahmood, A. K., & Shah, N. M. (2015). Grid Computing in Light of Resource Management Systems. *RE:view.*

Rubin, K. (2012). *Essential Scrum: A Practical Guide to the Most Popular Agile Process.* Addison-Wesley Professional.

Rusch, M., Schöggl, J.-P., & Baumgartner, R. J. (2023). Application of digital technologies for sustainable product management in a circular economy: A review. *Business Strategy and the Environment, 32*(3), 1159–1174. doi:10.1002/bse.3099

Russo, N. (2019). *Guia de Apoio à Conceção de Plano de Continuidade de Negócio nas Organizações com Programas Informáticos de Faturação* [Master's thesis]. Instituto Politécnico de Setúbal.

Russo, N., & Reis, L. (2019a). Análise da Problemática Subjacente à Certificação de Programas Informáticos de Faturação. *CISTI'2019 - 14th Iberian Conference on Information Systems and Technologies.* 10.23919/CISTI.2019.8760638

Russo, N., & Reis, L. (2020b). Methodological Approach to Systematization of Business Continuity in Organizations. In L. C. Carvalho, L. Reis, A. Prata, & R. Pereira (Eds.), Handbook of Research on Multidisciplinary Approaches to Entrepreneurship, Innovation, and ICTs (pp. 200-223). IGI Global. doi:10.4018/978-1-7998-4099-2.ch010

Russo, N., & Reis, L. (2020c). Caracterização da Faturação Eletrónica em Portugal: sob a perspetiva da certificação de programas informáticos. *Revista Egitania Sciencia, 2*(27), 163-184. Retrieved from https://egitaniasciencia2.ipg.pt/index.php/egitania_sciencia/article/view/344

Russo, N., & Reis, L. (2020d, November 27). Updated analysis of business continuity issues underlying the certification of invoicing software, considering a pandemic scenario. *Advances in Science, Technology and Engineering Systems Journal, 5*(6), 845-852. https://doi.org/https://dx.doi.org/10.25046/aj0506101

Russo, N., Reis, L., Silveira, C., & Mamede, H. S. (2023). Towards a Comprehensive Framework for the Multidisciplinary Evaluation of Organizational Maturity on Business Continuity Program Management: A Systematic Literature Review. *Information Security Journal: A Global Perspective*. doi:10.1080/19393555.2023.2195577

Russo, N., Mamede, H. S., Reis, L., & Silveira, C. (2022). FAMMOCN - Demonstration and evaluation of a framework for the multidisciplinary assessment of organisational maturity on business continuity. *Heliyon, 8*(9), e10566. doi:10.1016/j.heliyon.2022.e10566 PMID:36148280

Russo, N., & Reis, L. (2019b). Caracterização da Faturação em Portugal: Sob a perspetiva da certificação de programas informáticos de faturação. *Revista de Ciências da Computação [Online], 14*, 67–84.

Russo, N., & Reis, L. (2020a). *Programas de Faturação Certificados - Guia Prático para a Continuidade de Negócio*. FCA - Editora de Informática.

Russo, N., & Reis, L. (2021). Certified Invoicing Software - Boosting Entrepreneurship, Innovation and Sustainability in the Post-COVID-19 era. In L. C. Carvalho, L. Reis, & C. Silveira (Eds.), *Handbook of Research on Entrepreneurship, Innovation, Sustainability, and ICTs in the Post-COVID-19 Era*. IGI Global. doi:10.4018/978-1-7998-6776-0.ch008

Rybicki, J., & Eder, M. (2011). Deeper Delta across genres and languages: Do we really need the most frequent words? *Literary and Linguistic Computing, 26*(3), 315–321. doi:10.1093/llc/fqr031

Sadman, N., Gupta, K. D., Haque, M. A., Sen, S., & Poudyal, S. (2020). Stylometry as a reliable method for fallback authentication. In *2020 17th International Conference on Electrical Engineering/Electronics, Computer, Telecommunications and Information Technology (ECTI-CON)* (pp. 660-664). IEEE. 10.1109/ECTI-CON49241.2020.9158216

Sahebjamnia, N., Torabi, S. A., & Mansouri, S. A. (2018). Building organizational resilience in the face of multiple disruptions. *International Journal of Production Economics, 197*, 63–83. doi:10.1016/j.ijpe.2017.12.009

Salkin, C., Oner, M., Ustundag, A., & Cevikcan, E. (2018). A conceptual framework for Industry 4.0. In *Industry 4.0: Managing the digital transformation* (pp. 3–23). Springer. doi:10.1007/978-3-319-57870-5_1

Salman, O. H., Alhalabi, B., & Hossain, M. S. (2020). Securing Internet of Behaviors (IoB) in the era of pervasive connectivity: Taxonomy, challenges, and solutions. *Future Internet, 12*(5), 83.

Samala, N., Katkam, B.S., Bellamkonda, R.S. & Rodriguez, R.V. (2020). Impact of AI and robotics in the tourism sector: a critical insight. *Journal of Tourism Futures, 8*(1), 73-87.

Sambo, F., & Bankole, F. O. (2016). A Normative Process Model for ICT Business Continuity Plan for Disaster Management in Small, Medium and Large Enterprises. *International Journal of Electrical & Computer Engineering*, 2425–2431.

Sandifer, A. V., Wilson, C., & Olmsted, A. (2017, December). Detection of fake online hotel reviews. In *2017 12th International Conference for Internet Technology and Secured Transactions (ICITST)* (pp. 501-502). IEEE. 10.23919/ICITST.2017.8356460

Sangaiah, K., Rezaeil S., & Javadpour, A. (2023). Explainable AI in big data intelligence of community detection for digitalization e-healthcare services. *Applied Soft Computing, 136*. doi:10.1016/j.asoc.2023.110119

Santa-Maria, T., Vermeulen, W. J. V., & Baumgartner, R. J. (2022). The Circular Sprint: Circular business model innovation through design thinking. *Journal of Cleaner Production, 362*(132323), 132323. doi:10.1016/j.jclepro.2022.132323

Santana, T., Horta, N., Revez, C., Santos Dias, R. M. T., & Zebende, G. F. (2023). *Effects of interdependence and contagion between Oil and metals by ρ DCCA : A case of study about the COVID-19.* Academic Press.

Santoro, G., Vrontis, D., Thrassou, A., & Dezi, L. (2018). The Internet of Things: Building a knowledge management system for open innovation and knowledge management capacity. *Technological Forecasting and Social Change, 136*, 347–354. doi:10.1016/j.techfore.2017.02.034

Santos, G., Vicente, G., Salvado, T., Gonçalves, C., Caetano, F., & Silveira, C. (2022). Agro Smart: IoT Autonomous Irrigation System. *17th Iberian Conference on Information Systems and Technologies (CISTI)*, 1-6.

Santos, M., Luna, M., Reyes, D. L., Traylor, A., Lacerenza, C. N., & Salas, E. (2022). How to be an inclusive leader for gender diverse teams. *Organizational Dynamics, 51*(4), 1–6. doi:10.1016/j.orgdyn.2022.100914

Saraf, S. B., & Gawali, D. H. (2017). IoT based smart irrigation monitoring and controlling system. *2nd IEEE International Conference on Recent Trends in Electronics, Information & Communication Technology (RTEICT)*, 815-819. 10.1109/RTEICT.2017.8256711

Sarkady, D., Neuburger, L., & Egger, R. (2021). Virtual reality as a travel substitution tool during COVID-19. In *Information and communication technologies in tourism 2021 (pp. 452-463).* Springer. doi:10.1007/978-3-030-65785-7_44

Sarker, I. H., Khan, A. I., Abushark, Y. B., & Alsolami, F. (2022). Internet of things (iot) security intelligence: A comprehensive overview, machine learning solutions and research directions. *Mobile Networks and Applications*, 1–17.

Sarker, I., Kayes, A., Badsha, S., Alqahtani, H., Watters, P., & Ng, A. (2020). Cybersecurity data science: An overview from machine learning perspective. *Journal of Big Data, 7*(1), 41. Advance online publication. doi:10.118640537-020-00318-5

Schaub, M. (2022). Outlier Events in Major Cryptocurrency Markets: Is There Evidence of Overreaction? *The Journal of Wealth Management, 24*(4), 142–148. Advance online publication. doi:10.3905/jwm.2021.1.155

Scherpen, F., Draghici, A., & Niemann, J. (2018). Customer experience management to leverage customer loyalty in the automotive industry. *Procedia: Social and Behavioral Sciences, 238*, 374–380. doi:10.1016/j.sbspro.2018.04.014

Scheufele, D. A., & Krause, N. M. (2019). Science audience, misinformation, and fake news. *Proceedings of the National Academy of Sciences of the United States of America, 116*(16), 7662–7669. doi:10.1073/pnas.1805871115 PMID:30642953

Schleimer, S., Wilkerson, D. S., & Aiken, A. (2003). Winnowing: Local Algorithms for Document Fingerprinting. *Proceedings of ACM SIGMOD International Conference on Management of Data*, 76-85.

Schuff, D., Corral, K., St Louis, R. D., & Schymik, G. (2018). Enabling self-service BI: A methodology and a case study for a model management warehouse. *Information Systems Frontiers, 20*(2), 275–288. doi:10.100710796-016-9722-2

Schutz, W. (1958). *Firo: A three-dimensional theory of interpersonal behavior.* Rinehart.

Secretaria de Comunicação Social – SCS. (2020). Teletrabalho: O trabalho de onde você estiver – Material Educativo. Brasília, DF: Tribunal Superior do Trabalho (Superior Labor Court) – TST.

Security. (n.d.). *The Things Network.* Retrieved 7 11, 2021, from https://www.thethingsnetwork.org/docs/lorawan/security/

Seghezzo, L. (2009). The Five Dimensions of Sustainability. *Environmental Politics, 18*(4), 539–556. doi:10.1080/09644010903063669

Seles, B. M. R. P., Mascarenhas, J., Lopes de Sousa Jabbour, A. B., & Trevisan, A. H. (2022). Smoothing the circular economy transition: The role of resources and capabilities enablers. *Business Strategy and the Environment*, *31*(4), 1814–1837. doi:10.1002/bse.2985

Sengupta, S. (2022). IoE: An Innovative Technology for Future Enhancement. In *Computer Vision and Internet of Things* (pp. 19–28). Chapman and Hall/CRC. doi:10.1201/9781003244165-3

Sera, L., & Wheeler, E. (2017). Game on: The Gamification of the Pharmacy Classroom. *Currents in Pharmacy Teaching & Learning*, *9*(1), 155–159. doi:10.1016/j.cptl.2016.08.046

Serralvo, L. L. S., & Manus, P. P. T. (2022). Teletrabalho e a responsabilidade civil do empregador: implicações para o home office. São Paulo, SP: LTr.

Serrazina, M. (2013). O Programa de Formação Contínua em Matemática para Professores do 1.º ciclo e a melhoria do ensino da Matemática. *Da Investigação às Práticas*, *3*(2), 75–97. https://ojs.eselx.ipl.pt/index.php/invep/article/view/34/34

Shadrin, D., Somov, A., Podladchikova, T., & Gerzer, R. (2018). Pervasive agriculture: Measuring and predicting plant growth using statistics and 2D/3D imaging. *IEEE International Instrumentation and Measurement Technology Conference (I2MTC)*, 1-6. 10.1109/I2MTC.2018.8409700

Shah, H. J., Ou, J. P., Attiq, S., Umer, M., & Wong, W. K. (2022). Does inclusive leadership improve the sustainability of employee relations? Test of justice theory and employee perceived insider status. *Sustainability (Basel)*, *14*(21), 1–19. doi:10.3390u142114257

Shahid, S., Islam, J., Malik, S., & Hasan, U. (2022). Examining consumer experience in using m-banking apps: A study of its antecedents and outcomes. *Journal of Retailing and Consumer Services*, *65*, 102870. Advance online publication. doi:10.1016/j.jretconser.2021.102870

Shaikh, M., Vayani, H., Akram, S., & Qamar, N. (2022). Open-source electronic health record systems: A systematic review of most recent advances. *Health Informatics Journal*, *28*(2). Advance online publication. doi:10.1177/14604582221099828

Shankar, V., Kleijnen, M., Ramanathan, S., Rizley, R., Holland, S., & Morrissey, S. (2016). Mobile shopper marketing: Key issues, current insights, and future research avenues. *Journal of Interactive Marketing*, *34*(1), 37–48. doi:10.1016/j.intmar.2016.03.002

Shanker, R., Bhanugopan, R., Van der Heijden, B. I., & Farrell, M. (2017). Organizational climate for innovation and Organizational performance: The mediating effect of innovative work behavior. *Journal of Vocational Behavior*, *100*, 67–77. doi:10.1016/j.jvb.2017.02.004

Sharma, A., Sharma, P., Manalo, J. V. I., & Anh, D. N. (2023). Customers online Reviews and Its impact on Purchase Intention in Hospitality Industry: A Quantitative Investigation. *Journal of Informatics Education and Research*, *3*(1).

Shiller, R. J. (2022). U.S. Stock Markets 1871-Present and CAPE Ratio. Academic Press.

Shiroishi, Y., Uchiyama, K., & Suzuki, N. (2018). Society 5.0: For human security and well-being. *Computer*, *51*(7), 91–95. doi:10.1109/MC.2018.3011041

Shore, L. M., Randel, A. E., Chung, B. G., Dean, M. A., Ehrhart, K. H., & Singh, G. (2011). Inclusion and diversity in work groups: A review and model for future research. *Journal of Management*, *37*(4), 1262–1289. doi:10.1177/0149206310385943

Shore, L., & Chung, B. G. (2021). Inclusive leadership: How leaders sustain or discourage work group inclusion. *Group & Organization Management*, *0*(0), 1–32.

Siddiqui, F., Zeadally, S., Alcaraz, C., & Galvao, S. (2012, July). Smart grid privacy: Issues and solutions. In *2012 21st International Conference on Computer Communications and Networks (ICCCN)* (pp. 1-5). IEEE.

Silva, I. S., Veloso, A. L., & Keating, J. B. (2014). Focus group: Considerações teóricas e metodológicas. *Revista Lusófona de Educação, 26*(26), 175–190. https://www.researchgate.net /publication/265215548_Focus_group_Consideracoes_teoricas_e_metodologicas

Silver, H. (2010). Understanding social inclusion and its meaning for Australia. *The Australian Journal of Social Issues, 45*(2), 183–211. doi:10.1002/j.1839-4655.2010.tb00174.x

Simonetto, M., Sgarbossa, F., Battini, D., & Govindan, K. (2022). Closed loop supply chains 4.0: From risks to benefits through advanced technologies. A literature review and research agenda. *International Journal of Production Economics, 253*, 108582. doi:10.1016/j.ijpe.2022.108582

Sims, C. A. (1980). Macroeconomics and Reality. *Econometrica, 48*(1), 1. doi:10.2307/1912017

Sinha, S. (2023). *State of IoT 2023: Number of connected IoT devices growing 16% to 16.7 billion globally.* IOT Analytics. Retrieved from https://iot-analytics.com/number-connected-iot-devices/

Sinkovics, N., Gunaratne, D., Sinkovics, R. R., & Molina-Castillo, F.-J. (2021). Sustainable business model innovation: An umbrella review. *Sustainability (Basel), 13*(13), 7266. doi:10.3390u13137266

Siuta-Tokarska, B., Kruk, S., Krzeminski, P., & Zmija, K. (2022). Digitalisation of enterprises in the energy sector: Drivers-business models-prospective directions of changes. *Energies, 15*(8962), 8962. Advance online publication. doi:10.3390/en15238962

Slama, S. B., Choubani, F., Benavente-Peces, C., & Abdelkarim, A. (Eds.). (2021). Innovative and Intelligent_Technology-Based Services for Smart Environments-Smart Sensing and Artificial Intelligence. In *Proceedings of the 2nd International Conference on Smart Innovation, Ergonomics and Applied Human Factors (SEAHF'20)*. CRC Press.

Sociedade Brasileira de Teletrabalho e Teleatividades – SOBRATT. (2020). *Orientação para implantação e prática do Teletrabalho e home office.*

Sommerville, I. (2011). Software Engineering. Pearson Education Inc.

Somov, A., Shadrin, D., Fastovets, I., Nikitin, A., Matveev, S., & Hrinchuk, O. (2018). Pervasive Agriculture: IoT-Enabled Greenhouse for Plant Growth Control. *IEEE Pervasive Computing, 17*(4), 65–75. doi:10.1109/MPRV.2018.2873849

Soufi, H. R., Torabi, S. A., & Sahebjamnia, N. (2019). Developing a novel quantitative framework for business continuity planning. *International Journal of Production Research, 57*(3), 779–800. doi:10.1080/00207543.2018.1483586

Souza, O. T., & Carvalho, J. V. F. (2023). *Market efficiency assessment for multiple exchanges of cryptocurrencies.* Revista de Gestao. doi:10.1108/REGE-05-2022-0070

Špaček, F., Sohlich, R., & Dulík, T. (2015). Docker as Platform for Assignments Evaluation. *Procedia Engineering, 100*, 1665–1671. doi:10.1016/j.proeng.2015.01.541

Sriram, R. (2019). *Expert Insights: when to be cautious of Dr Google's diagnosis.* https://www.healtheuropa.com/when-to-be-cautious-of-dr-googles/93725/

Srivastava, S., Pant, M., Jauhar, S., & Nagar, A. (2022, December 2). (2022). Analyzing the prospects of blockchain in healthcare industry. *Computational and Mathematical Methods in Medicine, 2022*, 1–24. Advance online publication. doi:10.1155/2022/3727389 PMID:36506597

Stahel, W. (2016). The circular economy. *Nature, 531*(7595), 435–438. doi:10.1038/531435a PMID:27008952

Stahl, G. K., & Luque, S. (2014). Antecedents of responsible leader behavior: A research synthesis, conceptual framework and agenda for future research. *The Academy of Management Perspectives*, *28*(3), 235–254. doi:10.5465/amp.2013.0126

Stamatatos, E. (2009). A Survey of Modern Authorship Attribution Methods. *Journal of the American Society for Information Science and Technology*, *60*(3), 538–556. doi:10.1002/asi.21001

Stamatatos, E. (2013). A survey of modern authorship attribution methods. *Journal of the American Society for Information Science and Technology*, *64*(2), 295–315.

Stamatatos, E., Fakotakis, N., & Kokkinakis, G. (2000). Automatic Text Categorization in Terms of Genre and Author. *Computational Linguistics*, *26*(4), 471–495. doi:10.1162/089120100750105920

Stankov, U., & Gretzel, U. (2020). Tourism 4.0 technologies and tourist experiences: A human-centered design perspective. *Information Technology & Tourism*, *22*(3), 477–488. doi:10.100740558-020-00186-y

Stary, C. (2020, December). The internet-of-behavior as organizational transformation space with choreographic intelligence. In *12th International Conference on Digital Workplace–Nucleus of Transformation,* Bremen, Germany (pp. 113-132). Springer International Publishing. 10.1007/978-3-030-64351-5_8

Sterling, S. (2011). Encouraging resilience within SMEs: The Cabinet Office's proposed approach. *Journal of Business Continuity & Emergency Planning*, *5*(2), 128–139. PMID:21835751

Strijbol, N., Van Petegem, C., Maertens, R., Sels, B., Scholliers, C., Dawyndt, P., & Mesuere, B. (2023). TESTed - An educational testing framework with language-agnostic test suites for programming exercises. *SoftwareX*, *22*, 1–6. doi:10.1016/j.softx.2023.101404

Stürmer, G., & Fincato, D. (2020). *Teletrabalho em tempos de calamidade por Covid19: impacto das medidas trabalhistas de urgência.* Jus Podvm.

Suchek, N., Fernandes, C. I., Kraus, S., Filser, M., & Sjögrén, H. (2021). Innovation and the circular economy: A systematic literature review. *Business Strategy and the Environment*, *30*(8), 3686–3702. doi:10.1002/bse.2834

Suegami, S. (2022). Smart Contracts Obfuscation from Blockchain-based One-time Program. *Cryptology ePrint Archive*.

Sujan, M., Scott, P., & Cresswell, K. (2019). Digital health and patient safety: Technology is not a magic wand. *Health Informatics Journal*, *26*(4), 2295–2299. doi:10.1177/1460458219876183

Sun, J., Gan, W., Chao, H. C., Philip, S. Y., & Ding, W. (2023). Internet of behaviors: A survey. *IEEE Internet of Things Journal*, *10*(13), 11117–11134. doi:10.1109/JIOT.2023.3247594

Sutto, G. (2022). *85% das empresas do país adotaram o trabalho remoto na pandemia, mostra pesquisa.* https://www.infomoney.com.br/minhas-financas/85-das-empresas-do-pais-adotaram-o-trabalho-remoto-na-pandemia-mostra-pesquisa/

Swanepoel, D. (2020). eHealth Technologies Enable more Accessible Hearing Care. *Seminars in Hearing*, *41*(2), 133–140. doi:10.1055-0040-1708510 PMID:32269417

Swan, M. (2015). *Blockchain: Blueprint for a new economy.* O'Reilly Media, Inc.

Swire-Thompson, B., & Laze, D. (2020). Public health and online misinformation: Challenges and recommendations. *Annual Review of Public Health*, *41*(1), 433–451. doi:10.1146/annurev-publhealth-040119-094127 PMID:31874069

Syed, A. (2004). *Business Continuity Planning Methodology.* Academic Press.

Szmrecsanyi, B., & Kortmann, B. (2009). Typological profiling: A tool for the study of linguistic diversity. *Linguistic Typology*, *13*(2), 251–257.

Tahir, W., Wagan, R. A., & Naeem, B. (2023). Smart Traffic Handling Algorithm Using Aggregated Channel Feature. In *Intelligent Sustainable Systems: Selected Papers of WorldS4 2022* (Vol. 1, pp. 635–643). Springer Nature Singapore. doi:10.1007/978-981-19-7660-5_57

Tangen, S., & Austin, D. (2020, March 13). *Business continuity - ISO 22301 when things go seriously wrong*. Retrieved from International Organization for Standardization: https://www.iso.org/news/2012/06/Ref1602.html

Tan, K. L. (2023). Responsible leadership – A brief Review of Literature. *Journal of Responsible Tourism Management*, *3*(1), 44–55.

Tariq, M. U. (2023). Healthcare Innovation & Entrepreneurship, Digital Health Entrepreneurship. In L. Raimi & I. A. Oreagba (Eds.), *Medical Entrepreneurship*. Springer. doi:10.1007/978-981-19-6696-5_16

Taskan, B., Junça-Silva, A., & Caetano, A. (2022). Clarifying the conceptual map of VUCA: A systematic review. *The International Journal of Organizational Analysis*, *30*(7), 196–217. doi:10.1108/IJOA-02-2022-3136

Taşkin, D., & Yazar, S. (2020). A Long-range context-aware platform design for rural monitoring with IoT In precision agriculture. *International Journal of Computers, Communications & Control*, *15*(2), 1–11. doi:10.15837/ijccc.2020.2.3821

Tater, U., & Jain, A. T. (2022). Artificial Intelligence must be a Revolutionary Technique of Marketing in. *Indian Journal of Business Administration*, *15*(1), 39–45.

Tavares, M. C., Azevedo, G., Vale, J., & Bandeira, A. M. (2023, June 20-23). *The Accountant in the New Era: Renewing the profession for Society 5.0* [Paper presentation]. *18th Iberian Conference on Information Systems and Technologies (CISTI)*, Aveiro, Portugal. 10.23919/CISTI58278.2023.10211382

Taylor, T. (2022). *Top 6 Cloud Computing Trends for 2022*. Retrieved from https://techgenix.com/top-6-cloud-computing-trends-for-2022/

Taylor, M., Reilly, D., & Wren, C. (2020). Internet of things support for marketing activities. *Journal of Strategic Marketing*, *28*(2), 149–160. doi:10.1080/0965254X.2018.1493523

Tecchio, M. (2021). Home office veio para ficar, mas não da forma que funciona hoje. *CNN Brasil Business*. https://www.cnnbrasil.com.br/business/home-office-veio-para-ficar-mas-nao-da-forma-que-funciona-hoje/

Teixeira, N., Dias, R., & Pardal, P. (2022). *The gold market as a safe haven when stock markets exhibit pronounced levels of risk : Evidence during the China crisis and the COVID-19 pandemic*. Academic Press.

Teixeira, N., Dias, R., Pardal, P., & Horta, N. (2022). Financial Integration and Comovements Between Capital Markets and Oil Markets. *Advances in Human Resources Management and Organizational Development*, (December), 240–261. Advance online publication. doi:10.4018/978-1-6684-5666-8.ch013

ThingSpeak. (n.d.). *IoT Analytics - ThingSpeak Internet of Things*. Retrieved 7 14, 2021, from https://thingspeak.com

Thorén, E.S., Öberg, M., Wänström, G., Andersson, G., & Lunner, T. (2013). Internet Access and Use in Adults With Hearing Loss. *J Med Internet Res.*, *15*(5), e91. : doi:10.2196/jmir.2221

Threlfall, J. (2009). Strategies and flexibility in mental calculation. *ZDM: The International Journal on Mathematics Education*, *41*(5), 541-555. https://link.springer.com/article/10.1007/s11858-009-0195-3

Tobin, A., & Reed, D. (2016). The inevitable rise of self-sovereign identity. *The Sovrin Foundation*, *29*, 18.

Topcoder. (n.d.). *Topcoder Platform*. Retrieved 11 21, 2022, from https://www.topcoder.com/

Torabi, S. A., Giahi, R., & Sahebjamnia, N. (2016). An enhanced risk assessment framework for business continuity management systems. *Safety Science*, *89*, 201–218. doi:10.1016/j.ssci.2016.06.015

Torabi, S. A., Soufi, H. R., & Sahebjamnia, N. (2014). A new framework for business impact analysis in business continuity management (with a case study). *Safety Science*, *68*, 309–323. doi:10.1016/j.ssci.2014.04.017

Toth-Peter, A., Torres de Oliveira, R., Mathews, S., Barner, L., & Figueira, S. (2023). Industry 4.0 as an enabler in transitioning to circular business models: A systematic literature review. *Journal of Cleaner Production*, *393*(136284), 136284. doi:10.1016/j.jclepro.2023.136284

Trehan, R., Machhan, R., Singh, P., & Sangwan, K. (2022). Industry 4.0 and Society 5.0: Drives and challenges. *The IUP Journal of Information Technology*, *18*(1), 40–59.

Trichilli, Y., & Boujelbène Abbes, M. (2022). The impact of COVID-19 on the portfolio optimization. *EuroMed Journal of Business*. Advance online publication. doi:10.1108/EMJB-11-2021-0179

Trueman, C. (2023). Em foco. *Computerworld*. https://www.computerworld.com.pt/2023/01/24/despedimentos-nas-tecnologicas-em-2023-uma-linha-do-tempo/

Tsay, R. S. (2002). *Analysis of Financial Time Series*. doi:10.1002/0471264105

Turktarhan, G., Gopalan, R. & Ozkul, E. (2021). *Big Data and Business Intelligence in Hospitality and Tourism*. University of South Florida M3 Center Publishing.

Tyagi, A. K., Dananjayan, S., Agarwal, D., & Thariq Ahmed, H. F. (2023). Blockchain—Internet of Things Applications: Opportunities and Challenges for Industry 4.0 and Society 5.0. *Sensors*, *23*(2), 947. https://doi-org.libauth.purdueglobal.edu/10.3390/s23020947

UN (2015). *Transforming our world: the 2030 agenda for sustainable development* (Vol. 16301). A/RES/70/1.

United Nation. (2022). *Goal 12: Ensure sustainable consumption and production patterns*. United Nation. Retrieved from: https://www.un.org/sustainabledevelopment/sustainable-consumption-production/

Urbánek, J. F., Raclavská, J. S. A., O., Š., & Vonlehmden, J. (2012). Organization Continuity Planning & Management and Societal Security Scenarios Economics and Management. University of Defence in Brno.

Urquhart, A. (2018). What causes the attention of Bitcoin? *Economics Letters*, *166*, 40–44. Advance online publication. doi:10.1016/j.econlet.2018.02.017

Uvarova, I., Atstaja, D., Volkova, T., Grasis, J., & Ozolina-Ozola, I. (2023). The typology of 60R circular economy principles and strategic orientation of their application in business. *Journal of Cleaner Production*, *409*(137189), 137189. doi:10.1016/j.jclepro.2023.137189

Vajirakachorn, T., & Chongwatpol, J. (2017). Application of business intelligence in the tourism industry: A case study of a local food festival in Thailand. *Tourism Management Perspectives*, *23*, 75–86. doi:10.1016/j.tmp.2017.05.003

Vale, H. C. P., Costa, E. M. C., & Mercado, L. P. L. (2014, June 9-13). *Aprendizagem baseada em problemas: uma estratégia de ensino aprendizagem no curso de Biblioteconomia e Pedagogia* [Paper presentation]. XV Encuentro Internacional Virtual Educa, Lima, Peru. https://recursos.educoas.org/publicaciones/aprendizagem-baseada-em-problemas-uma-estrat-g ia-de-ensino-aprendizagem-no-curso-de

Valente, J. (2020). *Menos de 1% dos sites passam em teste de acessibilidade: estudo avaliou dificuldades de acesso para pessoas com deficiência. Agência Brasil*. Empresa Brasil de Comunicação.

van Buren, N., Demmers, M., van der Heijden, R., & Witlox, F. (2016). Towards a circular economy: The role of dutch logistics industries and governments. *Sustainability (Basel)*, *8*(7), 647. doi:10.3390u8070647

Van Den Heuvel, W., Aveiro, D., & Lalanda, P. (2019). The internet of behaviors: a security perspective. *Proceedings of the 34th ACM/SIGAPP Symposium on Applied Computing*, 1441-1450.

Van Greunen, J., Heymans, A., Van Heerden, C., & Van Vuuren, G. (2014). The prominence of stationarity in time series forecasting. *Journal for Studies in Economics and Econometrics*, *38*(1), 1–16. doi:10.1080/10800379.2014.12097260

van Wier, M.F., Urry, E., Lissenberg-Witte, B.I., & Kramer, S.E. (2021). A Comparison of the Use of Smart Devices, Apps, and Social Media Between Adults With and Without Hearing Impairment: Cross-sectional Web-Based Study. *J Med Internet Res.*, *23*(12), e27599. doi:10.2196/27599

Vanbecelaere, S., & Benton, L. (2021). Technology mediated personalized learning for younger learners: Concepts, design, methods, and practice. *British Journal of Educational Technology*, *52*(5), 1793–1797. doi:10.1111/bjet.13150

Vasco, C., Pardal, P., & Dias, R. T. (2021). Do the Stock Market Indices Follow a Random Walk? *Advances in Finance, Accounting, and Economics*, (May), 389–410. doi:10.4018/978-1-7998-6643-5.ch022

Vasconcellos-Silva, P., & Araújo-Jorge, T. (2019). Análise de conteúdo por meio de nuvem de palavras de postagens em comunidades virtuais: novas perspectivas e resultados preliminares. In: *Anais 8º Congresso Ibero-Americano em Investigação Qualitativa: Investigação Qualitativa na Saúde*. Lisboa: Escola Superior de Enfermagem de Lisboa.

Vasquez, E. J., & Ortega, J. C. (2020). Design of a business contingency plan. Case study: Municipality of Cantón Suscal. *2020 International Conference on Intelligent Systems and Computer Vision (ISCV)*, 1-10. 10.1109/ISCV49265.2020.9204334

Vats, A., & Kamaiah, B. (2011). Is There a Random Walk in Indian Foreign Exchange Market? *International Journal of Economics and Finance*, *3*(6), 157–165. doi:10.5539/ijef.v3n6p157

Vazquez, E., & Landa-Silva, D. (2021). Towards Blockchain-based Ride-sharing Systems. In ICORES (pp. 446-452). Academic Press.

Veerasamy, N., Mashiane, T., & Pillay, K. (2019). Contextualising cybersecurity readiness in South Africa. *14th International Conference on Cyber Warfare and Security*, 467-475.

Velez, H. (2021). *What is a social enterprise?* The good trade. https://www.thegoodtrade.com/features/what-is-a-social-enterprise/

Verhoef, C. & Bijmolt, T. (2019). Marketing perspectives on digital business models: A framework and overview of the special issue. *International Journal of Research in Marketing*, *36*(3), 341-349. doi:10.1016/j.ijresmar.2019.08.001

Verleye, K., De Keyser, A., Raassens, N., Alblas, A. A., Lit, F. C., & Huijben, J. C. C. M. (2023). Pushing forward the transition to a circular economy by adopting an actor engagement lens. *Journal of Service Research*. Advance online publication. doi:10.1177/10946705231175937

Vial, G. (2019). Understanding digital transformation: A review and a research agenda. *The Journal of Strategic Information Systems*, *28*(2), 118–144. doi:10.1016/j.jsis.2019.01.003

Vieira, R., Monteiro, P., Azevedo, G., & Oliveira, J. (2023, June 20-23). *Society 5.0 and Education 5.0: A Critical Reflection* [Paper presentation]. 18th Iberian Conference on Information Systems and Technologies (CISTI), Aveiro, Portugal. https://doi.org/ TI58278.2023.1021138610.23919/CIS

Vilela, R. B., Ribeiro, A., & Batista, N. A. (2018). Os desafios do mestrado profissional em ensino na saúde: Uso da nuvem de palavras no apoio à pesquisa qualitativa. *CIAIQ*, *2*, 652–659.

Vilela, R. B., Ribeiro, A., & Batista, N. A. (2020). Nuvem de palavras como ferramenta de análise de conteúdo. *Millenium*, (11), 29–36.

ViscontiR.LaroccaA.MarconiM. (2017). Big data-Driven Value Chains and Digital Platforms: from Value Co-Creation to Monetization. *Big Data Analytics: Tools and Technology for Effective Planning*, 355-371. doi:10.2139/ssrn.2903799

Voegtlin, C., Frish, C., Walther, A., & Schwab, P. (2019). Theoretical Development and Empirical Examination of a Three- Roles Model of Responsible Leadership. *Journal of Business Ethics*.

Voegtlin, C., Patzer, M., & Scheer, A. G. (2012). Responsible Leadership in Global Business: A New Approach to Leadership and its Multi-level Outcomes. *Journal of Business Ethics*, *105*(1), 1–16. doi:10.100710551-011-0952-4

Voinov, A., Kolagani, N., McCall, M., Glynn, P., Kragt, M., Ostermann, F., Pierce, S., & Ramu, P. (2016). Modelling with stakeholders – Next generation. *Environmental Modelling & Software*, *77*, 196-220. doi:10.1016/j.envsoft.2015.11.016

Voulgaridis, K., Lagkas, T., Angelopoulos, C. M., & Nikoletseas, S. E. (2022). IoT and digital circular economy: Principles, applications, and challenges. *Computer Networks*, *219*(109456), 109456. doi:10.1016/j.comnet.2022.109456

Waldman, D. A., & Galvin, B. M. (2008). Alternative perspectives of responsible leadership. *Organizational Dynamics*, *37*(4), 327–341. doi:10.1016/j.orgdyn.2008.07.001

Walumbwa, F. O., Cropanzano, R., & Goldman, B. M. (2011). How leader–member exchange influences effective work behaviours: Social exchange and internal–external efficacy perspectives. *Personnel Psychology*, *64*(3), 739–770. doi:10.1111/j.1744-6570.2011.01224.x

Wang, C., Teo, T. S., & Janssen, M. (2021). Public and private value creation using artificial intelligence: An empirical study of AI voice robot users in Chinese public sector. *International Journal of Information Management*, *61*, 102401. doi:10.1016/j.ijinfomgt.2021.102401

Wang, L., Shen, X., Li, J., Shao, J., & Yang, Y. (2019). Cryptographic primitives in blockchains. *Journal of Network and Computer Applications*, *127*, 43–58. doi:10.1016/j.jnca.2018.11.003

Wang, Q., Wei, Y., Wang, Y., & Liu, Y. (2022). On the Safe-Haven Ability of Bitcoin, Gold, and Commodities for International Stock Markets: Evidence from Spillover Index Analysis. *Discrete Dynamics in Nature and Society*, *2022*, 1–16. Advance online publication. doi:10.1155/2022/9520486

Wang, X., & Fan, L. (2020). An analysis of interlanguage features and English learning. *Journal of Higher Education Research*, *1*(1), 31–37. doi:10.32629/jher.v1i1.126

Warren, M. A., & Warren, M. T. (2023). The EThIC Model of Virtue-Based Allyship Development: A New Approach to Equity and Inclusion in Organizations. *Journal of Business Ethics*, *182*(3), 783–803. doi:10.100710551-021-05002-z PMID:34840369

Wasik, S., Antczak, M., Badura, J., Laskowski, A., & Sternal, T. (2018). A Survey on Online Judge Systems and Their Applications. *ACM Computing Surveys*, *51*(1), 1–34. doi:10.1145/3143560

WCED (Western Cape Education Department). (1987). *Report of the World Commission on Environment and Development: Our Common Future*. Author.

Weber, M., & Chatzopoulos, C. (2019). Digital customer experience: The risk of ignoring the non-digital experience. *International Journal of Industrial Engineering and Management*, *10*(3), 201. doi:10.24867/IJIEM-2019-3-240

Weichbroth, P., Kowal, J., & Kalinowski, M. (2022). Toward a unified model of mobile Business Intelligence (m-BI) acceptance and use. In *Proceedings of the 55th Hawaii International Conference on System Sciences* (pp. 304-313). HICSS. 10.24251/HICSS.2022.036

Wen, Z., Bouri, E., Xu, Y., & Zhao, Y. (2022). Intraday return predictability in the cryptocurrency markets: Momentum, reversal, or both. *The North American Journal of Economics and Finance*, 62, 101733. Advance online publication. doi:10.1016/j.najef.2022.101733

Whitmore, A., Agarwal, A., & Da Xu, L. (2015). The internet of things—A survey of topics and trends. *Information Systems Frontiers*, 17(2), 261–274. doi:10.100710796-014-9489-2

WHO, World Health Organization. (2023). https://www.who.int/health-topics/hearing-loss#tab=tab_1

Wilkinson, S. (1998). Focus groups in feminist research: Power, interaction, and the co-construction of meaning. *Women's Studies International Forum*, 21(1), 111-125.

Winkler, U., Fritzsche, M., Gilani, W., & Marshall, A. (2010). A Model-Driven Framework for Process-centric Business Continuity Management. *2010 Seventh International Conference on the Quality of Information and Communications Technology*, 248-252. 10.1109/QUATIC.2010.46

Winters, M. F. (2013). From Diversity to Inclusion: An Inclusion Equation. In B.M. Ferdman & B.R. Deane (Eds.), Diversity at work: The practice of inclusion (pp. 205-228). John Wiley & Sons.

Wixom, B., & Watson, H. (2010). The BI-based organization. *International Journal of Business Intelligence Research*, 1(1), 13–28. doi:10.4018/jbir.2010071702

Working, H. (1949). The investigation of economic expectations. *The American Economic Review*.

World Green Building Council. (2022). *What is green building?* Retrieved from: https://www.worldgbc.org/what-green-building

Wright, J. H. (2000). Alternative variance-ratio tests using ranks and signs. *Journal of Business & Economic Statistics*, 18(1), 1–9. Advance online publication. doi:10.1080/07350015.2000.10524842

WT Leung, R., & Li, M. (1998). Does the Hong Kong Stock Market Overreact? In *Asian Review of Accounting* (Vol. 6, Issue 2). doi:10.1108/eb060699

Xu, C., Park, J., & Lee, J. C. (2022). The effect of shopping channel (online vs offline) on consumer decision process and firm's marketing strategy. *Internet Research*, 32(3), 971–978. doi:10.1108/INTR-11-2020-0660

Yang, L., Henthorne, T.L. & George, B. (2020). Artificial intelligence and robotics technology in the hospitality industry: Current applications and future trends. *Digital Transformation in Business and Society*, 211-228.

Yang, G., Jin, H., Li, M., Xiao, N., Li, W., Wu, Z., Wu, Y., & Tang, F. (2004). Grid computing in China. *Journal of Grid Computing*, 2(2), 193–206. doi:10.100710723-004-4201-2

Yang, M., Smart, P., Kumar, M., Jolly, M., & Evans, S. (2018). Product-service systems business models for circular supply chains. *Production Planning and Control*, 29(6), 498–508. doi:10.1080/09537287.2018.1449247

Yasin, R., Jan, G., Huseynova, A., & Atif, M. (2022). Inclusive leadership and turnover intention: The role of follower-leader goal congruence and Organizational commitment. *Management Decision*, 61(3), 589–609. doi:10.1108/MD-07-2021-0925

Yasin, R., Namoco, S. O., Jauhar, J., Abdul Rahin, N. F., & Zia, N. U. (2020). Responsible leadership an obstacle for turnover intention. *Social Responsibility Journal*, 17(8), 1175–1192. doi:10.1108/SRJ-03-2020-0092

Yermack, D. (2015). Is Bitcoin a Real Currency? An Economic Appraisal. In *Handbook of Digital Currency*. Bitcoin, Innovation, Financial Instruments, and Big Data. doi:10.1016/B978-0-12-802117-0.00002-3

Yi, E., Yang, B., Jeong, M., Sohn, S., & Ahn, K. (2023). Market efficiency of cryptocurrency: Evidence from the Bitcoin market. *Scientific Reports*, *13*(1), 4789. Advance online publication. doi:10.103841598-023-31618-4 PMID:36959223

Yin, R. K. (2017). *Case Study Research and Applications Design and Methods* (6th ed.). Sage.

Yiu, L. D., Yeung, A. C., & Cheng, T. E. (2021). The impact of business intelligence systems on profitability and risks of firms. *International Journal of Production Research*, *59*(13), 3951–3974. doi:10.1080/00207543.2020.1756506

Yonas, A., Wang, D., Javed, B., & Zaffar, M. A. (2021). Moving beyond the mechanistic structures: The role of inclusive leadership in developing change-orientation Organizational citizenship behaviour. *Canadian Journal of Administrative Sciences*, *38*(1), 42–52. doi:10.1002/cjas.1586

York, T. W., & MacAlister, D. (2015). Program Documentation and Performance Measures. In Hospital and Healthcare Security (Sixth Edition) (pp. 289-313). Elsevier. doi:10.1016/B978-0-12-420048-7.00012-X

You, J., Kim, S., Kim, K., Cho, A., & Chang, W. (2021). Conceptualizing meaningful work and its implications for HRD. *European Journal of Training and Development*, *45*(1), 36–52. doi:10.1108/EJTD-01-2020-0005

Your Genome Organization. (2023). *How did the Human Genome Project make science more accessible?* https://www.yourgenome.org/

Yousif, A., Alqhtani, S. M., Bashir, M. B., Ali, A., Hamza, R., Hassan, A., & Tawfeeg, T. M. (2022). Greedy firefly algorithm for optimizing job scheduling in iot grid computing. *Sensors, 22*(3), 850.

Yousif, A., Alqhtani, S. M., Bashir, M. B., Ali, A., Hamza, R., Hassan, A., & Tawfeeg, T. M. (2022). Greedy Firefly Algorithm for Optimizing Job Scheduling in IoT Grid Computing. *Sensors (Basel)*, *22*(3), 850. doi:10.339022030850 PMID:35161596

Yung, R., & Khoo-Lattimore, C. (2019). New realities: A systematic literature review on virtual reality and augmented reality in tourism research. *Current Issues in Tourism*, *22*(17), 2056–2081. doi:10.1080/13683500.2017.1417359

Yusuf, N., & Lytras, M. D. (2023). Competitive sustainability of Saudi companies through digitalization and the circular carbon economy model: A bold contribution to the Vision 2030 agenda in Saudi Arabia. *Sustainability (Basel)*, *15*(3), 2616. doi:10.3390u15032616

Zambon, E., Bolzoni, D., Etalle, S., & Salvato, M. (2007). A Model Supporting Business Continuity Auditing and Planning in Information Systems. *Second International Conference on Internet Monitoring and Protection (ICIMP 2007)*. 10.1109/ICIMP.2007.4

Zavanella, F., & Pinto, L. O. C. (2021). *22 Anos da SOBRATT – A Evolução do Teletrabalho: tomo I: aspectos jurídicos*. Lacier Editora.

Zebende, G. F., Santos Dias, R. M. T., & de Aguiar, L. C. (2022). Stock market efficiency: An intraday case of study about the G-20 group. In Heliyon (Vol. 8, Issue 1). doi:10.1016/j.heliyon.2022.e08808

Zeqiri, A., Dahmani, M., & Youssef, A. B. (2020). Digitalization of the tourism industry: What are the impacts of the new wave of technologies. *Balkan Economic Review*, *2*, 63–82.

Zesch, T., & Gurevych, I. (2009). Cross-language text classification: Distinguishing similarity from language confusion. *ACM Transactions on Speech and Language Processing*, *6*(1), 1–22.

Zhang, C., Wu, X., Niu, Z., & Ding, W. (2014). Authorship identification from unstructured texts. *Knowledge-Based Systems*, *66*, 99–111. doi:10.1016/j.knosys.2014.04.025

Zhang, X., Liu, J., Li, Y., Cui, Q., Tao, X., Liu, R. P., & Li, W. (2022). *Vehicle-oriented ridesharing package delivery in blockchain system*. Digital Communicatio. doi:10.1016/j.dcan.2022.12.008

Zhao, H., & Zhou, Q. (2019). Exploring the Impact of Responsible Leadership on Organizational Citizenship Behavior for the Environment: A Leadership Identity Perspective. *Sustainability (Basel)*, *11*(4), 994–1013. doi:10.3390u11040944

Zhao, Q., Li, G., Cai, J., Zhou, M., & Feng, L. (2023). A tutorial on internet of behaviors: Concept, architecture, technology, applications, and challenges. *IEEE Communications Surveys and Tutorials*, *25*(2), 1227–1260. doi:10.1109/COMST.2023.3246993

Zheng, Z., Xie, S., Dai, H. N., Chen, X., & Wang, H. (2018). Blockchain challenges and opportunities: A survey. *International Journal of Web and Grid Services*, *14*(4), 352–375. doi:10.1504/IJWGS.2018.095647

Zhou, Z., Liao, H., Gu, B., Mumtaz, S., & Rodriguez, J. (2019). Resource sharing and task offloading in IoT fog computing: A contract-learning approach. *IEEE Transactions on Emerging Topics in Computational Intelligence*, *4*(3), 227–240. doi:10.1109/TETCI.2019.2902869

Zia, H., Rehman, A., Harris, N. R., Fatima, S., & Khurram, M. (2021). An experimental comparison of iot-based and traditional irrigation scheduling on a flood-irrigated subtropical lemon farm. *Sensors (Basel)*, *21*(12), 1–17. doi:10.339021124175 PMID:34204584

Ziółkowska, M. J. (2021). Digital transformation and marketing activities in small and medium-sized enterprises. *Sustainability (Basel)*, *13*(5), 1–16. doi:10.3390u13052512

Zlatova, I. (2022). Digital marketing changes during the Russian war in Ukraine 2022. *Marketing and Digital Technologies*, *6*(3), 15–24. doi:10.15276/mdt.6.3.2022.2

Zohuri, B., & Moghaddam, M. (2020). From Business Intelligence to Artificial Intelligence. *Journal of Material Sciences & Manufacturing Research*, *1*(1), 1–10.

About the Contributors

Luisa Cagica Carvalho holds a PhD in Management in University of Évora – Portugal. Professor of Management on Department of Economics and Management, Institute Polytecnic of Setubal– Portugal. Guest professor in international universities teaches in courses of master and PhDs programs. Researcher at CEFAGE (Center for Advanced Studies in Management and Economics) University of Evora – Portugal. Author of several publications in national and international journals, books and book chapters.

Leonilde Reis is a Coordinator Professor with Aggregation at the School of Business and Administration (ESCE) of the Polytechnic Institute of Setúbal (IPS). The activities of teaching in higher education were developed since 1992 in the field of "Information Systems" and focused on undergraduate, master's and doctoral courses. Aggregation in Information Sciences, Fernando Pessoa University; PhD in Systems Information and Technologies, Minho University; Master's in management informatics, Católica University. Author of several publications in national and international journals, books and book chapters.

Nelson Russo has a Ph.D. in Web Science and Technology, University of Trás-os-Montes and Alto Douro. Collaborating with Universidade Aberta. Tax Inspector in Informatics area. Invited Lecturer between 2008 and 2019 in the Department of Systems and Informatics, Setúbal School of Technology, Polytechnic Institute of Setúbal (IPS). Specialist in Informatics in Public Administration until 2015. Author of several publications in national and international journals, books, and book chapters.

* * *

Paulo Manuel Monteiro Alexandre. Specialist Professor - Finance, Banking, and Insurance - in 2014 by the Polytechnic Institute of Setúbal, Master's Degree in Management and Industrial Strategy in 2004 by the University of Lisbon and Degree in Management in 1994 by the University of Lisbon. He is currently Adjunct Professor at the Escola Superior de Ciências Empresariais- Instituto Politécnico de Setúbal and Dean in the Degree in Accounting and Finance. Integrated member of the Centre for Research in Business Sciences (CICE-IPS). He have several scientific articles in the financial area published in Journals and conferences. More than 15 years of professional experience as a director in the banking industry (credit risk).

Mahsa Amiri has a master's degree in Management of Tourism Organizations from the University of the Algarve, and has knowledge in the area of Business Intelligence.

João Barros Neto is Coordinator of the Extension Course in Applied Leadership at the Pontifical Catholic University of São Paulo - PUC (COGEAE). Graduated in Administration with Major in Foreign Trade from Faculdade Associada de São Paulo (1991), specialization in Production Administration and Industrial Operations from Fundação Getúlio Vargas - FGV SP (1993), Master in Administration from Pontifical Catholic University of São Paulo (1998) and Doctorate in Social Sciences and Post-Doctorate from the Pontifical Catholic University of São Paulo (2002). He is currently a member of the Group of Excellence in Higher Education Institutions - GIES of the Regional Administration Council of São Paulo - CRA SP and Assistant Professor at the Pontifical Catholic University of São Paulo - PUC SP at the Faculty of Economics, Administration, Accounting and Actuarial - Department of Administration, Epistemological Area of Personnel Management. Has experience in Administration, with an emphasis on Organizational Behavior, acting on the following topics: leadership, social responsibility, people management, skills. He has 33 books published as author, co-author and organizer, in addition to several articles.

Ana Maria Boavida has a degree in Mathematics, branch of Educational Training, a master's degree in education and development and a PhD in Education, specializing in Mathematics Didactics. She is a retired professor from the School of Education of the Polytechnic Institute of Setúbal. She has developed her professional activity at the level of initial and continuous training of educators and teachers of Elementary Education and is the author of publications and articles published in specialized journals in mathematics didactics. Her research interests focus on teachers' practices, collaborative work, and Philosophy of Mathematics. She was part of the Digital Educational Resources (RED) project team.

Joana Brocardo has a degree in Mathematics, branch of Educational Training, a master's degree in education and development and a PhD in Education, specializing in Mathematics Didactics. She is a retired Coordinating Professor of the School of Education of the Polytechnic Institute of Setúbal. She has worked in initial and continuing teacher education since 1989 and is the author of books and articles published in several specialized journals. Her research interests focus on the study of Numbers and Operations from a number sense development perspective and on the introduction to Algebra. She has coordinated several research projects and recently, she coordinates the team of mathematics teachers that participated in the Digital Educational Resources (DER) project.

Mariana Chambino is a Ph.D. candidate for the Doctoral Program in Economic and Business Sciences at the University of Algarve. Master's and bachelor's degrees in accounting and finance from the School of Business Sciences at the Polytechnic Institute of Setubal She is currently the technical director at CIGIT.

Liliana da Silva Almeida is a Guest Professor of the Department of Accounting and Finance at School of Business and Administration of the Polytechnic Institute of Setubal (IPS),Portugal. Specialist Title in Accounting and Finance, School of Business Administration, Polytechnic Institute of Setúbal. Consultant in the areas of Finance, Accounting and Management Control Systems.

Anubhav De is currently working as a research scholar for the graduate program at VIT Bhopal University. He brings a wealth of knowledge to the table when it comes to putting machine learning initiatives into action.

Catarina Delgado has a degree in Mathematics, branch of Educational Training, a master's degree in education and development and a PhD in Education, specializing in Mathematics Didactics. She is a Coordinating Teacher at the School of Education of the Polytechnic Institute of Setúbal. She develops her professional activity at the level of initial and continuous training of educators and teachers of Basic Education, and she is the author of publications and articles published in specialized journals in mathematics didactics. Her interests focus on teachers' practices and digital mathematics resources. Recently, she was part of the team of the Digital Educational Resources (DER) project and currently integrates the research project Classroom Studies as a Process of Professional Development.

Rui Manuel Teixeira Santos Dias. Postdoctoral in Econophysics at the State University of Feira de Santana, PhD in Finance at the University of Évora. He is currently Guest Professor at the School of Business Sciences - Polytechnic Institute of Setúbal and Researcher (Integrated Member) at the Center for Advanced Studies in Management and Economics (CEFAGE).

Susan Ferebee earned her Ph.D. in Information Systems at Nova Southeastern University in Ft. Lauderdale, Florida. She also has an Executive Juris Doctorate from Concord Law School, and has a Masters in Educational Psychology from Purdue University Global.. She is a faculty member in the School for Business and Information Technology at Purdue University Global and has also served as a consultant with more than 25 years of experience working directly with organizations and higher education institutions. Susan has published many peer-reviewed articles. Her current research in progress includes studies on smart technology use in home schooling, personal cybersecurity behaviors, and the influence of interpretive communities on persuasion, Susan also served as a guest editor for a special issue of International Journal of Conceptual Structures and Smart Applications. Susan serves as an Editorial Review Board member for International Journal of Cognitive Informatics and Natural Intelligence. She is an active presenter at international and national conferences. Susan has received numerous teaching and outstanding contributor awards and has been awarded several research grants.

Teresa Godinho was born in Lisbon, had a degree at Lisbon Accounting School and Master's at Lisbon Business School. Lecturer since 1998, first in Beja, Alentejo, in the South of Portugal, and then in Setúbal.

Celestino Gonçalves is an adjunct professor of Informatics at School of Technology and Management of Polytechnic of Guarda in Portugal, where he has been teaching courses related to artificial intelligence, functional programming and ubiquitous computing to the Computer Science Engineering degree and to the MSc in Mobile Computing. His research interests, besides programming and programming contests, are artificial intelligence, pervasive computing and the study of deep learning algorithms for designing ambient intelligence solutions of context-aware and user-centric services.

Nicholas Lessen, Ph.D., CISSP, is a Professor at Purdue Global Online in the School of Business and Information Technology. With over 26 years of experience as an IT Consultant and the prestigious Certified Information Systems Security Professional (CISSP) certification, he has demonstrated exceptional expertise in information security. He has successfully served various distinguished clientele, including the Department of Defense and the Intelligence Community. His excellent track record of delivering high-quality solutions has earned him a reputation as a trusted advisor. Dr. Lessen earned his Master's in Information Systems Management from Strayer University, honing his skills in effectively managing complex information systems. He further expanded his knowledge by completing a Ph.D. in Information Technology from Capella University, solidifying his expertise and authority in the field. His academic achievements, his practical experience, and his CISSP certification enable him to offer students a unique perspective on the importance of information security and its applications in the business world.

Getachew Mekuria is a Research Scholar, Addis Ababa University of Science and Technology, Ethiopia.

Fátima Mendes has a degree in Mathematics, branch of Educational Training, a master's degree in education and development and a PhD in Education, specializing in Mathematics Didactics. She is a Co-ordinating Teacher at the School of Education of the Polytechnic Institute of Setúbal. She has developed her professional activity in the initial and continuous training of educators and teachers since 1988. She is the author of books, book chapters and articles published in specialized journals in mathematics and has participated in several research and development projects. Recently, she was part of the team of the Digital Educational Resources (DER) project, the ARTICULAR project - An experience of curricular articulation in the initial training of educators and teachers of the 1st cycle, and the Reason research project Mathematical Reasoning and Teacher Training.

Nilamadhab Mishra was an Assistant Professor in Post at School of Computing, Debre Berhan University, Ethiopia. He has around 15 years of rich global exposure in Academic Teaching & Research. He publishes numerous peer reviewed researches in SCIE & SCOPUS indexed journals & IEEE conference proceedings, and serves as reviewer and editorial member in peer reviewed Journals and Conferences. Dr. Mishra has received his Doctor of Philosophy (PhD) in Computer Science & Information Engineering from Graduate Institute of Electrical Engineering, College of Engineering, Chang Gung University (a World Ranking University), Taiwan. He involves in academic research by working, as an Journal Editor, as a SCIE & Scopus indexed Journals Referee, as an ISBN Book Author, and as an IEEE Conference Referee. Dr. Mishra has been pro-actively involved with several professional bodies: CSI, ORCID, IAENG, ISROSET, Senior Member of "ASR" (Hong Kong), Senior Member of "IEDRC" (Hong Kong), and Member of "IEEE ". Dr. Mishra's Research areas incorporate Network Centric Data Management, Data Science: Analytics and Applications, CIoT Big-Data System, and Cognitive Apps Design & Explorations.

Cristina Morais da Palma is a Guest Adjunct Professor at the Department of Accounting and Finance (DCF) of the School of Business Sciences (ESCE) at the Polytechnic Institute of Setúbal (IPS). PhD student in Management, Master in Accounting and Finance, and Specialist in Accounting and Taxation. Lecturer in the areas of accounting, taxation, finance, and reporting on the graduate degrees of accounting and finance, information systems management, marketing, and the professional higher technical course in management consulting. Certified accountant with experience in accounting and consulting in the areas of accounting, management, and taxation since 2002.

Elis Ossmane has worked in the environmental and occupational health field for 12 years, with technical and management tasks. Within the last 5 years, she has been Technology Transfer Officer (TTO) at a R&D, Innovation and Entrepreneurship Office of the Instituto Politécnico de Setúbal (IPS) and, for the same period, she has been Invited Assistant Professor at IPS School of Business Administration and School of Technology. Currently, she's also PhD student at Universidade Aberta, Lisbon, on Social Development and Sustainability Doctoral Programme.

Duc Huu Pham, Ph.D. (Assoc. Prof.) is a Lecturer of linguistics at the International University - Vietnam National University HCMC (IU - VNU HCMC), Vietnam; MA in TESOL from the University of Canberra, Australia in 2001; PhD in Linguistics from the University of Social Sciences and Humanities, VNU-HCMC in 2008. Visiting scholar to the Department of Applied Linguistics, UCLA in the USA from 2010-2011. Areas of teaching: applied linguistics and linguistics; Areas of research: applied linguistics with TESOL, computer assisted language learning, natural language processing, and translation. He has published several articles and book chapters in applied linguistics.

Célia M. Q. Ramos graduated in Computer Engineering from the University of Coimbra, obtained her Master in Electrical and Computers Engineering from the Higher Technical Institute, Lisbon University, and the PhD in Econometrics in the University of the Algarve (UALG), Faculty of Economics, Portugal. She is Coordinator Professor at School for Management, Hospitality and Tourism, also in the UALG, where she lectures computer science. Areas of research and special interest include conception and development of information systems, tourism information systems, big data, etourism, econometric modeling and panel-data models. Célia Ramos has published in the fields of information systems and tourism, namely, she has authored a book, six book chapters, conference papers and journal articles. At the level of applied research, she has participated in several funded projects.

Madalena Ramos graduated in Sociology. Master in Deeper Sociology and Portuguese Reality. Ph´D in Education. Professor at ISCTE-IUL, in the Department of Social Research Methods. Member of the research group of the Center for Research and Sociology Studies (CIES-IUL).

Telmo Salvado works in Software Development at COFICAB, with a degree in Computer Science Engineering from the School of Technology and Management of the Polytechnic of Guarda, Portugal.

Gonçalo Santos holds a degree in Computer Science and is currently in the process of completing his master's degree in Mobile Computing at the Polytechnic Institute of Guarda. Throughout his academic journey, he actively participated in various student associations, further expanding his expertise in this dynamic field. His active involvement demonstrated his commitment to enhancing the university experience for fellow students and showcased his fervor for advancing research in the computer sciences industry through valuable contributions to the scientific community.

Hortense Maria Carvalho dos Santos, Master in Accounting and Finance from the School of Business Sciences of the Polytechnic Institute of Setúbal, degree in Human Relations from the Polytechnic Institute of Leiria, School of Education and Social Sciences. With 15 years of experience in retail banking. He currently works at the Division for Research and International Cooperation at the Polytechnic Institute of Setúbal. PhD student in the Economics and Business at the University of Extremadura, Spain, specifically in the area of innovation in business models.

Miguel M. Soares holds a BS in Computer Engineering from the Polytechnic Institute of Guarda, Portugal. As a dedicated Software Developer, he has contributed to several projects that emphasize the importance of innovative software solutions. Known for his collaborative spirit and individual initiative, Miguel continuously seeks opportunities for growth and innovation in his field.

Carla Viana has been a higher education teacher since 2002. Currently, she is a Professor of Marketing at the School of Business Sciences at the Polytechnic Institute of Setubal, a Professor of Marketing and Management at the Polytechnic Institute of Lusophony and a Professor of Digital Marketing at Lusophone University. She has also been working as a Consultant and Certified Trainer since 2006. Since 2007, in her professional and business activity, she has held management positions in prestigious sectors and companies that are recognized in the fields of management, marketing, and branding. She is also the Vice-President of the Digital Marketing Association and serves as the Executive Director of the People Talent brand.

Gonçalo Vicente is currently studying a Bachelor's degree in Computer Science Engineering at the School of Technology and Management of the Polytechnic Institute of Guarda in Guarda, Portugal. Friendly, communicative and a helpful person. Good teamwork and social skills, always willing to learn new things.

Duarte Xara Brasil has a PhD in Management in University of Évora – Portugal. Professor of Marketing at Institute Polytecnic of Setubal– Portugal, where he teaches subjects mainly related with branding. Author of several publications in national and international journals, books and book chapters. Teaching and research activities gave been developed with a systematic international participation in academic events and courses in several countries, In Europe, Africa, Asia and America.

Index

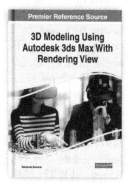
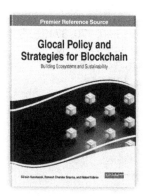
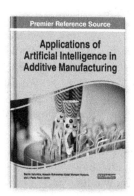
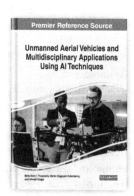

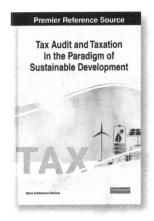

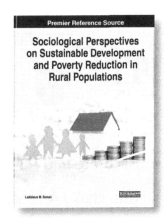

Printed in the United States
by Baker & Taylor Publisher Services